The Bábí and Bahá'í Religions, 1844–1944: Some Contemporary Western Accounts

By the same author

Dr J. E. Esslemont (Bahá'í Publishing Trust, London)

The Bábí and Bahá'í Religions 1844–1944

Some Contemporary Western Accounts

edited by

MOOJAN MOMEN M.A., M.B.

GR

GEORGE RONALD
OXFORD

GEORGE RONALD, Publisher
46 High Street, Kidlington, Oxford, OX5 2DN

ACKNOWLEDGEMENTS

Extracts are reprinted by permission of the following:
Publishers William Blackwood & Sons Ltd (A. C. Wratislaw *A Consul in the East*); Gerald Duckworth & Co. Ltd (Lady Dorothy Mills *Beyond the Bosphorus*); Faber & Faber Ltd (Sir Denison Ross *Both Ends of the Candle*); William Heinemann Ltd (C. R. Ashbee *Palestine Notebook*); Hutchinson Publishing Group Ltd (Owen Tweedy *Cairo to Persia and Back*); Librairie Plon (Gobineau *Correspondance entre le Comte de Gobineau et le Comte de Prokesch-Osten*); The North American Review and the University of Northern Iowa (Rev. James Bixby 'What is Behaism?'); Fleming H. Revell Company (Rev. H. H. Jessup *Fifty-Three Years in Syria*); Seeley, Service & Co. Ltd (Hume-Griffith *Behind the Veil in Persia and Turkish Arabia*); Yale University Press (A. D. Kalmykow *Memoirs of a Russian Diplomat*).
Institutions and Individuals Archives du Ministère des Affaires Étrangères, Bruxelles; Archives du Ministère des Affaires Étrangères, Paris; Audio-Visual Department of the Bahá'í World Centre, Haifa; British Library, London; Sir Patrick Browne (Browne Papers); Church Missionary Society Archives, London; Foreign and Commonwealth Office, India Office Records Office, London; House of Lords Records Office, London; Manuscripts and Archives Division, The New York Public Library, Astor, Lenox and Tilden Foundations; Pembroke College Library, Cambridge; Public Record Office, London; (Transcripts of Crown-copyright records in the Public Record Office appear by permission of the Controller of H. M. Stationery Office.); Royal Society of Arts; Hon. Godfrey Samuel (Samuel Papers); State Archives, Jerusalem; Syndics of Cambridge University Library.

Extracts from the following works reprinted by permission:
By Shoghi Effendi: *God Passes By*, Copyright 1944, © 1972, 1975 by the National Spiritual Assembly of the Bahá'ís of the United States. By Nabíl-i-A'ẓam: *The Dawn-Breakers*, published by the National Spiritual Assembly of the Bahá'ís of the United States. By the WORLD ORDER Editorial Board: 'Excerpts from Dispatches Written during 1848–1852 by Prince Dolgorukov, Russian Minister to Persia,' *World Order: A Bahá'í Magazine*, 1, no. 1 (Fall 1966), 17–24, Copyright © 1966 by the National Spiritual Assembly of the Bahá'ís of the United States. By Lady Blomfield: *The Chosen Highway*, published by the National Spiritual Assembly of the Bahá'ís of the United States. *The Bahá'í World, Vol. VIII, 1938–40*, Copyright 1942 by the National Spiritual Assembly of the Bahá'ís of the United States. *The Bahá'í World, Vol. XII, 1950–54*, Copyright © 1956 by the National Spiritual Assembly of the Bahá'ís of the United States.

ISBN 0–85398–102–7 (Cloth)

Printed in the United States of America

To my family
Wendi, Sedrhat, Carmel,
Gloria and Hooman

CONTENTS

SECTION D

The Ministry of 'Abdu'l-Bahá
(1892–1921)

SECTION E

The Guardianship
(1921–44)

APPENDIXES

ILLUSTRATIONS

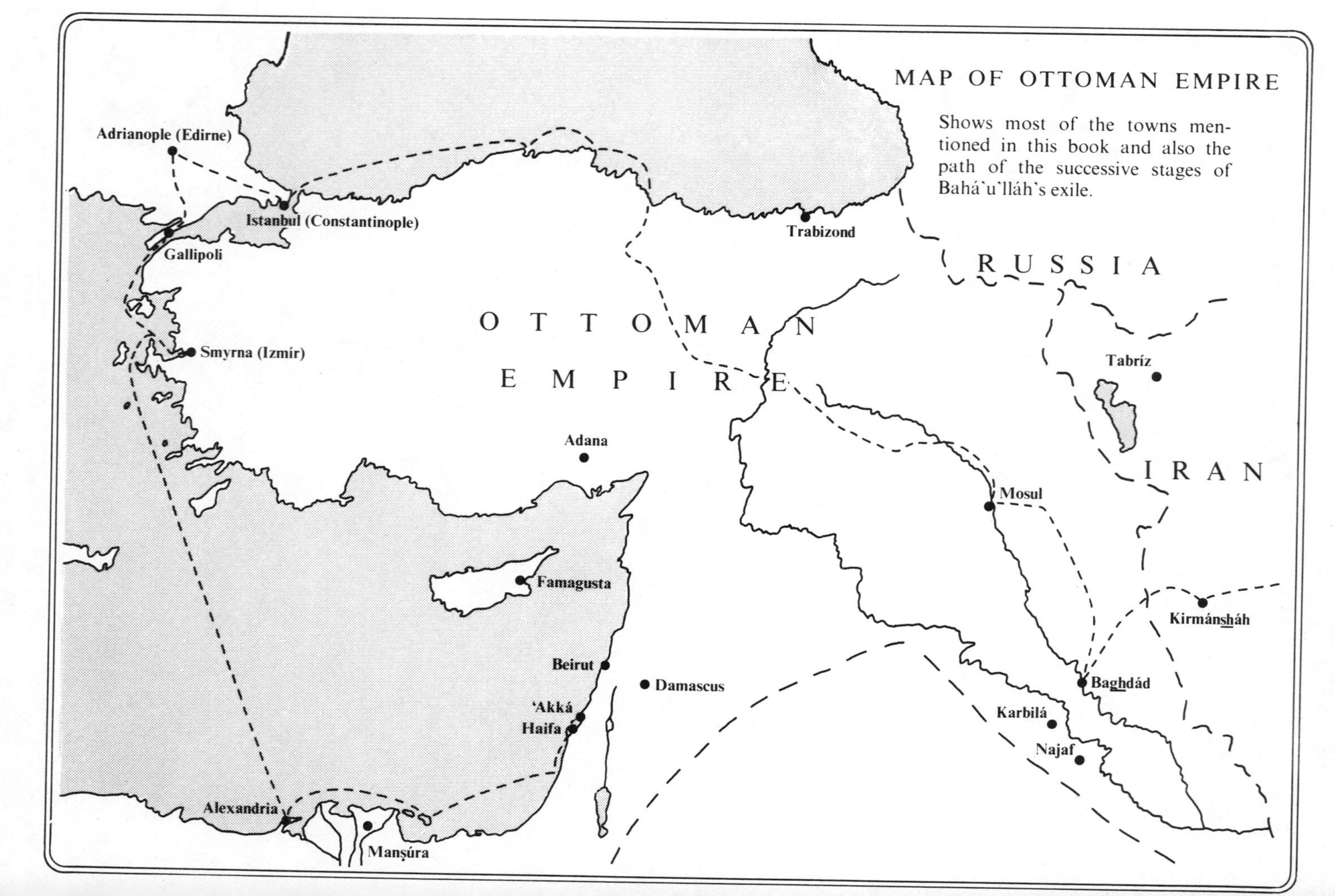
MAP OF OTTOMAN EMPIRE
Shows most of the towns mentioned in this book and also the path of the successive stages of Bahá'u'lláh's exile.
Adrianople (Edirne)
Istanbul (Constantinople)
Gallipoli
Smyrna (Izmír)
Trabizond
RUSSIA
OTTOMAN EMPIRE
Tabríz
IRAN
Adana
Mosul
Famagusta
Kirmánsháh
Beirut
Damascus
'Akká
Haifa
Baghdád
Karbilá
Najaf
Alexandria
Manṣúra

MAP OF IRAN

Shows most of the towns mentioned in this book, as well as some of the provinces of Iran. The modern international boundary has been given here although, for much of this period, the eastern and north-eastern boundaries were undefined.

Preface

It has been said of Islam that it is the first religion to grow up in the full light of History.* This statement would apply even more fittingly to the Bahá'í religion and its precursor, the religion of the Báb. Within two years of its birth in 1844, it had already been referred to in the newspapers of the West, and since that time there has been no lack of literature about its history and its doctrines. This literature, however, has for the most part, and particularly latterly, emanated either from its avowed opponents or from believers. A great deal of research was done on the subject over fifty years ago by such scholars as Prof. E. G. Browne, A.-L.-M. Nicolas and certain Russian writers, but in the last half-century scarcely half a dozen works have appeared in the academic world that may be considered to have advanced knowledge and understanding of the subject. This is all the more surprising in view of the fact that, over this same period of time, the Bahá'í religion has grown from a small religious movement in the Middle East with a few adherents in Europe and North America, into a world religion with active and organized groups of believers in almost every country of the world.

The stagnation that has overcome research on the Bahá'í religion is clearly revealed in several recently-published works wherein references to it are replete with inaccuracies perpetuated from earlier writers. In particular, in these works there has been no attempt to look beyond the writings of such authors as Browne, Gobineau and Nicolas, and utilize and assess the vast body of primary material available, both historical and doctrinal. Moreover, the works of these early scholars were only, for the most part, preliminary studies and were not regarded even by the authors themselves as definitive works. These works depended on the various manuscripts to which their authors had direct access and were consequently limited in their scope. And yet most later scholars appear neither to have fully appreciated this point nor to have bothered to make an independent approach to the primary material. They have merely extracted such parts of the works of Browne, Gobineau, etc. as suited their purposes and quoted these as authoritative statements, often conveniently forgetting material from these same authors that contradicts their point of view.

Most of the source material on the history of the Bábí and Bahá'í

* Renan in *Études d'Histoire Religieuse*, p. 220.

religions derives from the accounts of either believers or opponents. Even eminent scholars depended mainly on biased materials. Very little attention has been paid to the accounts of those persons who may be considered to have been, as far as it is possible to be, independent observers: such persons as European diplomatic and consular staff, missionaries and travellers who chanced to come into contact with the nascent faith and wrote down what they heard and saw.* It should be noted, however, that these observers were themselves often dependent for information on inaccurate or biased reports from their contacts.

The compilation of this book stems from the belief that, in the present state of knowledge, the assembling of primary source materials is of greater importance than attempts at detailed analyses. Therefore, I have endeavoured to compile in this book, from many varied sources, the accounts and opinions of those Westerners who, because they happened to be in the Middle East, were able to write what they had themselves seen or had heard from first-hand sources. It is hoped that it will be followed by the publication of the more important primary source materials in Persian. Secondarily, I have attempted to show the way in which knowledge of the new religion spread to the West in its earliest days before there were communities of Bahá'ís in those areas.

These accounts seem to me to be of interest and importance for the following reasons:

1. They are independent of (and in the case of the earlier accounts, written before the establishment of) the mutually opposed and irreconcilable positions of Bahá'í, Azalí and Muslim scholars.

2. Particularly with regard to the diplomatic records, there can be no justification for statements that the material, once received, has been tampered with or altered – an argument only too readily used about much of the primary historical material that exists. This is not to say, however, that letters could not have been forged by one party and sent to the authorities in the name of the other party. Something like this may well have occurred, for example, during the Adrianople period (see chapter 11). But we can be fairly certain that once material was received by one of the consular or diplomatic staff, it was not tampered with or altered, and has been preserved intact to the present day.

3. Since, particularly in the case of the diplomatic records, the accounts were written within a short period of the events they describe, they are invaluable for determining the dates of these events. For although the Bábí-Bahá'í religion is some 130 years old, it is unfortunately true that the Bahá'ís

* Browne does occasionally make use of accounts by European travellers and also had access to the Cyprus Government Archives. Nicolas makes occasional reference to French Government Archives.

have been lamentably neglectful in gathering materials for the history of their religion, and many of those who could have provided the most detailed knowledge of important episodes have died without recording their memoirs. Much of what was written in the way of historical accounts was recorded many years after the events took place. Thus most of *Nabíl's Narrative* is the record of what Nabíl and his informants at a relatively advanced age could remember of events that had occurred in their youth. Similarly the histories of the Bahá'í Faith in various localities in Persia that we have at present, were mostly recorded in the 1930s on the instructions of Shoghi Effendi by elderly believers recalling events that had occurred many years previously. Thus, not surprisingly, both *Nabíl's Narrative* and these other histories are often inaccurate with regard to dates (for no one can be expected to remember the exact date of an event that occurred twenty or thirty years previously).

The principal disadvantage of the Western accounts presented in this book is that these observers were for the most part ignorant of the social and religious background and framework of the Bábí and Bahá'í religions. Whatever knowledge they did have of Islam and of Persian social and cultural life tended to be prejudiced and incomplete. Thus they were often unable to understand fully the significance of the events that they recorded. Nowhere is this better borne out than in the attempts by some of the early writers to formulate the basic teaching of the Báb (see section A). What results is usually a lamentable mixture of fantasies and half-understood facts, more a reflection of the writers' own ideas and prejudices than a representation of Bábí doctrine. One of the most difficult aspects of the compilation of this book was deciding to what extent one should correct the many erroneous names and facts that are given in the sources quoted. Thus, for example, in the accounts given in chapter 12 and elsewhere, Bahá'u'lláh is frequently referred to as 'the Báb'; while when a person of the eminence of Prof. Browne persisted in calling the Bahá'ís 'Bábís' right up to his last works, it is hardly surprising that most others did also. Moreover, in giving facts such as the exact names of some of the personalities involved and the number of years since the start of the movement, the Western sources quoted in this book, and especially the earlier ones, are often inaccurate. Most of these inaccuracies are quite obvious and I have only pointed out those errors where there is possible ambiguity or where there is likely to be confusion in the reader's mind.

A further disadvantage is that many of the most important events of Bábí and Bahá'í history were not observed by outsiders and hence no report of these will be found in the present work. Thus there is no account in these pages of the Báb's declaration of his mission to Mullá Ḥusayn in 1844, the

Conference of Badas͟ht in 1848, the declaration by Bahá'u'lláh of his mission in 1863 and its open promulgation in 1866–7, etc. In an attempt particularly to remedy these defects, and to provide a framework for the subsequent accounts, a brief historical survey and an account of the teachings of the Báb, Bahá'u'lláh and 'Abdu'l-Bahá are given in the Introduction.

Section A of this book is a survey of the principal Western accounts of the Bábí and Bahá'í religions. In this survey I have concentrated on the earlier and the lesser-known accounts, touching only lightly on the more well-known accounts of such scholars as Browne and Nicolas. The following four sections contain contemporary descriptions of important events in Bábí and Bahá'í history by Europeans and Americans, including, wherever possible, official documents. At the end of the book are biographical notes (Appendix II). The abbreviation (q.v.) refers to these notes.

I have left completely untouched the whole subject of the rise of Bahá'í communities in the West during the latter part of this period, and concentrated on Western accounts of events occurring in the Middle East. A proper consideration of the former would require another volume. I have also touched only very lightly on 'Abdu'l-Bahá's journeys in the West, since these were very thoroughly documented in the newspapers of the time, and an entire book could be devoted to the subject.

One point that some may quarrel with is my division of sections B and C, i.e. the Ministry of the Báb and the Ministry of Bahá'u'lláh, at the year 1853. It is of course true that the Bábí community did not become transformed into the Bahá'í community until some time after 1867. But there was such a change following the holocaust of 1852, both in the community itself and in the nature of its relationships with the outside world (see the last part of the Introduction), that 1853 is a much more meaningful dividing point. It was, moreover, as early as the mid-1850s that Bahá'u'lláh had taken over effective leadership of the Bábí community. Thus the ministry of Bahá'u'lláh may be said to have begun many years before he openly put forward his claim to be the bearer of an independent revelation from God.

The bulk of the material presented in this book is the result of my researches in the Public Record Office, London, since 1972. To a lesser extent, my search has taken me to the British Library (formerly the British Museum Library) and the Church Missionary Society Archives, both also in London. I have made enquiries at the head-offices of various other missionary societies, but most of these have unfortunately kept only minimal archives. I have also consulted other archives and libraries as listed at the end of this Preface.

The material presented here from the French Foreign Office Archives has been found by two people, Mme Paulette Bodansen (dispatches of Ferrier and Adrianople material) and Dr Amin Mesbah (the remainder). The latter has also found a few interesting items in the Belgian Foreign Ministry Archives. I am extremely grateful to them for making the results of their research available.

During the autumn of 1974, I had the opportunity to search the Israeli State Archives for material from the records of the British Mandate in Palestine. Unfortunately, it would appear that much of what undoubtedly was there has been destroyed, but a few items are included in chapter 31.

Regrettably, it is not as yet possible to examine Russian State Archives. This source, when it eventually becomes available, should prove of great interest and to contain at least as much information as its British counterpart. We are fortunate, however, in that the Russian scholar M. S. Ivanov has published in his work *Babidskie vosstaniya v Irane (1848–1852)* much of the diplomatic correspondence of Dolgorukov related to the early Bábí period. Being unable to read Russian myself, I have used the translations into English published in *World Order* magazine ('Excerpts from Dispatches' – see Bibliography) and into Persian in Chahárdihí's *Shaykhí-garí, Bábí-garí*. I am, of course, aware of the dangers of the fact that some of the material has therefore been translated from Dolgorukov's original French into Ivanov's Russian into Chahárdihí's Persian and thence into English by myself, but as it is unlikely that we shall obtain access to the originals in the near future, this is the best available to us. One other source of Russian official documents is Nicolas's article 'Le Dossier russo-anglais de Seyyed Ali Mohammed dit le Bâb' in *Revue du Monde Musulman*. During the period that Nicolas was French Consul in Tabríz, he succeeded in persuading his Russian and English counterparts to look through their consular archives for material relating to the Báb. The results of this he published in the above article, which I have quoted in the relevant parts of this book.

Mr Sami Doktoroğlu has been searching the Turkish State Archives for material relevant to Bahá'í history and has found a number of extremely valuable documents. This book is intended primarily as a compilation of materials from Western sources but I felt that it would be a pity to lose this opportunity of making more widely known the results of Doktoroğlu's very valuable work, and have therefore included résumés of this material as addenda to the relevant chapters.

I am not going to write the customary lengthy note on transliteration; the system used will be apparent to those interested in such matters. Where uncertainties have arisen due to differences between Arabic and Persian usage, I have tended to choose the Persian usage. Transliteration of Russian words is according to the British Museum system.

During the preparation of this book and the research leading to it, I have received a great deal of help from many people. Foremost among these is

Mr Hasan Balyuzi, who has guided and encouraged me in the course of my research. Others who have helped in various ways (and I apologize to many whom I have omitted) are: Mr Mahmoud Afshar, Mr Payam Afshar, Dr Iraj Ayman, Mr Alan Coupe, Mr Ulrich Gollmer, Mr Jan Jasion, Mr Denis MacEoin, Mrs Gloria Momen, Mr Zoghollah Momen, Mr Peter Smith, Mr Rustom Sabit, and Mrs Wendy Momen, who compiled the index.

It is customary in books of a scholarly nature to render quotations in European languages in their original form. Having myself been much inconvenienced by this convention in the past, I decided that all such quotations should be translated in this book. Those wishing to consult the originals can locate these from the references given. For assistance with translations, I must thank Dr Galen Gissler (Russian); Mr Oliver Coburn, Miss Jill Hollis, Mr Timothy Armstrong (German); Miss Virginia Orbison and my brother, Dr Hooman Momen (Portuguese). Oriental names and phrases in translation have been rendered according to the system in use in the rest of the book. In some written dispatches, for the sake of clarity, the punctuation has been amended and abbreviations spelled out in full.

I must not forget to thank the staffs of the various archives and libraries where I have worked, who have without exception been helpful and patient: the Public Record Office; the Church Missionary Society Archives and Library; the British Library; Cambridge University Library; House of Lords Record Office; India Office Records; Israeli State Archives; Pembroke College Library, Cambridge; Oriental Faculty Library, Cambridge University; Wurttembergische Landesbibliothek, Stuttgart; Plymouth Central Library; Plymouth Hospital Medical Library; and Southfields Public Library, London.

I must also thank the staff of George Ronald, Publishers, and especially Mr Stratford Caldecott, for encouragement and many useful suggestions.

M. MOMEN

Cambridge, England
December 1977

NOTE: Although the manuscript of this book was completed in December 1977, various factors prevented its publication until now. In the meantime, further material has come to light, some of which has been incorporated in the present volume.

June 1980

Introduction

A Summary of the History and Teaching of the Bábí and Bahá'í Religions

The Bahá'í religion and its precursor, the religion of the Báb, arose in Iran (Persia as it then was known) in the latter half of the nineteenth century. Iran adheres to the Shí'ih sect of Islam and was, therefore, awaiting the advent of a Messianic figure, the Qá'im (the return of the hidden Imám Mahdí). This Messianic expectation was particularly strong among the followers of a movement called the Shaykhís, after their founder Shaykh Aḥmad al-Aḥsá'í (1753–1826). Thus it was first to members of this group that a young man of 25, Siyyid 'Alí-Muḥammad-i-Shírází (1819–50) by name, put forward in 1844 the claim that he was the Báb (which means Gate). Initially, many considered that this meant that he was merely the Gate to the hidden Imám whose advent they were awaiting, but at a later date it bcame clear that his claim was to be the Imám himself, and even that he had inaugurated a new prophetic Dispensation just as Muḥammad and Jesus had done in prior ages. The Báb, as he is usually called in the West, although he later took other titles such as Nuqṭiy-i-Úlá (the Primal Point), sent his disciples to all parts of Iran and nearby Iraq, and many thousands of people of all classes, including many of the 'ulamá, counted themselves among his followers. His activities, however, inevitably aroused the wrath of the majority of the 'ulamá, and the Báb spent much of his short ministry in prison or confined. The main events of the life of the Báb, as well as the clashes of his followers with the civil authority, form the chief subject-matter of section B of this book.

The present incomplete state of knowledge concerning the teachings of the Báb precludes any attempt to give an outline of his doctrines beyond what is given below. Two aspects of the teachings of the Báb must however be further considered at this point. Firstly, it would be interesting to be able to come to an understanding of the Báb's attitude towards the upheavals caused by his followers. It would seem that the Báb neither strongly advocated nor discouraged the warlike activities of his supporters.* Sec-

* A passing reference to *jihád* (religious warfare) in the sixth chapter of the seventh *váḥid* of the Persian *Bayán* indicates that the Báb was not opposed to this concept, although it was later forbidden by Bahá'u'lláh.

ondly, with regard to later developments, it should be noted that in the Báb's writings there is frequent reiteration of the announcement of the advent of yet another prophetic figure, designated as 'Him Whom God shall make manifest'. In one book alone, the Persian *Bayán*, there are over seventy important statements about this figure.

Following the upheavals of 1850 and the holocaust of 1852, the religion of the Báb was almost extirpated in Iran itself. But a group of the most prominent Bábís gathered in Baghdád in nearby Iraq, and from here emissaries were sent out who succeeded in re-establishing groups of believers throughout Iran. After the Báb had been put to death in 1850, the leadership of the community fell to a young man named Mírzá Yaḥyá (*c.* 1830–1912), who took the title Ṣubḥ-i-Azal. However, his leadership was weak and ineffective, and the community became demoralized and fragmented. During the Baghdád period, one of the Bábís, Mírzá Ḥusayn-'Alí (1817–92), who took the title Bahá'u'lláh, the half-brother of Mírzá Yaḥyá, became increasingly prominent and assumed effective leadership. Thus it was against the activities of Bahá'u'lláh and not Mírzá Yaḥyá that the Persian authorities complained to the Turkish Government. This complaint resulted in the removal in 1863 of Bahá'u'lláh and his companions to Istanbul (Constantinople) and later the same year to Edirne (Adrianople). It was at this time, at first privately in 1863, and later openly in 1866, that Bahá'u'lláh proclaimed himself to be the one announced by the Báb as 'Him Whom God shall make manifest'.* Shortly afterwards, in a series of open letters to the monarchs of the West and to the Pope, he also put forward the claim to be the Return of Christ expected by Christians.

It seemed, initially, as though the proclamation of the claim of Bahá'u'lláh to be 'Him Whom God shall make manifest' would split the Bábí community in two, since Mírzá Yaḥyá refused to accept it. Within a short time, however, the overwhelming majority of the Bábís had become followers of Bahá'u'lláh, or Bahá'ís. This was due mainly to Bahá'u'lláh's own innate authority and the influence of his writings, as well as to the clear injunctions laid down by the Báb.

In 1868, partly as a result of the discord between Bahá'u'lláh and Mírzá Yaḥyá resulting from Bahá'u'lláh's open claim, the Turkish Government decided to exile Bahá'u'lláh once more, to 'Akká on the Syrian coast (now in the State of Israel). Here, Bahá'u'lláh was kept imprisoned for over two years, and then confined to one of the houses in the town for a further period of six years. After this, he removed to a house outside 'Akká, and later took up residence in a mansion named Bahjí near 'Akká, where he passed away in 1892.

* In his writings, Bahá'u'lláh indicates that the realization of his mission came to him when he lay in chains in the dungeon of Tihrán in 1852–3 following the attempt on the life of the Sháh.

In his Will and Testament, Bahá'u'lláh left clear instructions that he was to be succeeded in the leadership of the Bahá'í community by his eldest son 'Abdu'l-Bahá. But 'Abdu'l-Bahá's station was more than just that of a figurehead, for he was authorized by Bahá'u'lláh to be the authoritative expounder and exemplar of the Bahá'í teachings. The most remarkable aspect of 'Abdu'l-Bahá's ministry was the manner in which the religion of Bahá'u'lláh spread to the West, so that by the time of 'Abdu'l-Bahá's passing, in 1921, there were Bahá'í communities throughout North America and in many European countries. The climax of 'Abdu'l-Bahá's ministry was the two tours of the West that he undertook in 1911–13. In city after city of Europe and North America, he attracted large audiences and brought the Bahá'í Faith to the attention of the West to an unprecedented extent.

In his Will and Testament, 'Abdu'l-Bahá appointed his grandson, Shoghi Effendi, as the Guardian of the Bahá'í Faith, as well as giving instructions for the establishment of those administrative institutions upon which Bahá'u'lláh's plans for the unification of the world are based. For the ensuing period of 23 years, up to the celebration of the centenary of the founding of the Bahá'í Faith in 1944 – the end of the period with which this book is concerned – the principal aim of Shoghi Effendi was to set up these administrative institutions and cause them to function. This period was also characterized by the cutting of all remaining links between the Bahá'í Faith and the Islamic community in which it had arisen. Towards the end of this period, Shoghi Effendi initiated the first of a series of plans which were aimed at taking the message of Bahá'u'lláh to every part of the world. According to a statistical booklet compiled by Shoghi Effendi himself, in 1944 the Bahá'í Faith had spread to 78 countries and territories of the world, and in 48 of them Bahá'í administrative institutions had come into being.

The writings of the Báb and Bahá'u'lláh, all of which are regarded by Bahá'ís as authoritative and canonical, may be classified thus:

1. Devotional writings: prayers, tablets of visitation, etc.
2. Polemical writings: setting out the proofs of their missions, etc.
3. Legal writings: setting out the laws and ordinances of the new religion.
4. Expositional writings: delineating the tenets and principles of the new religion.
5. Epistolary writings: letters written to kings, rulers, believers, opponents, etc.

The teachings given by the Báb and Bahá'u'lláh, and expounded by 'Abdu'l-Bahá and Shoghi Effendi, may be summarized as follows:

1. God the Creator, an infinite Being, is unknowable to man, a finite being, except in so far as His attributes are revealed to man through a series of Divine Messengers, such figures as Moses, Christ, Muḥammad, the Báb and Bahá'u'lláh.
2. The purpose of these Divine Messengers is to guide mankind towards spiritual and social advancement and evolution, their succession being likened to successive teachers of a child, and their messages to successive chapters of a book. Thus the station of such Divine Messengers as Moses, Christ, Muḥammad and others is fully recognized and the authority and sanctity of such Holy Books as the Bible and the Qur'án are acknowledged.
3. Therefore the fundamental aims and purposes of the religions of the world are one, and their principal differences are due to the different needs and requirements of the ages and areas in which they appeared.
4. The soul of man is immortal; it survives physical death. The goal of the individual during his life should be to develop those spiritual qualities and attributes which will enhance the soul in its eternal journey. Heaven is thus interpreted as the state of possessing those qualities and Hell as being bereft of them.
5. The social goal of mankind in this age is the unification of the world, summarized in Bahá'u'lláh's statement, 'The earth is but one country and mankind its citizens.' This unification is the culmination of centuries of man's social evolution on the earth, and at the same time the starting point for future progress and development. In the writings of Bahá'u'lláh, 'Abdu'l-Bahá and Shoghi Effendi may be found an outline of those institutions which would bring about this unification. The Bahá'í administrative order, which was developed by Shoghi Effendi, is the rudimentary form of some of those institutions, and thus the Bahá'í world community may be seen as the embryonic form of the future world civilization.
6. The social principles on which the unification of the world depends were expounded in the writings of 'Abdu'l-Bahá in particular. They include:

   a) The condemnation of all forms of prejudice, including racial, national, religious and sexual.

   b) The equality of rights, opportunities and privileges for men and women.

   c) Compulsory education.

   d) The elimination of extremes of poverty and wealth.

   e) The balance between religion and science as the two most powerful instruments for mankind's progress.

   f) The development of an international language and script, as well as a universal system of currency, weights and measures, etc.

g) The safeguarding of the freedom and initiative of the individual.

The Persecutions of the Bábís and Bahá'ís

Since it is the persecutions of the Bahá'ís that have attracted the attention of the West more often than any other features of its history, and these persecutions thus form the bulk of the historical accounts in this book, it would be appropriate at this stage to consider in more detail the general pattern and features of these persecutions.

The persecutions undergone by the Bábí and Bahá'í communities in the hundred years from 1844 to 1944 may be divided into three distinct phases, according to the nature of the persecutions and the attitudes and reactions of the governments, the 'ulamá, the people and the believers themselves. The dates here given are only approximate but they happen to coincide with significant dates in Bábí and Bahá'í history.

Phase I: The Bábí Upheavals (1844–53)

The first phase of opposition to the religion of the Báb was led by the 'ulamá, who regarded the doctrines of the new religion as a direct contravention of and a challenge to the tenets of Islam, and their motives were thus primarily religious. The response of the people in each place was to a certain extent determined by the attitude taken by the local 'ulamá, whose lead they were prepared to follow. The Bábís, when they found themselves opposed and threatened, in some places banded together and prepared to defend themselves. The attitude of the Government was initially to observe the debate between the Bábís and the 'ulamá without undue interference (a notable exception being Ḥusayn Khán, the Governor of Fárs, see pp. 69–70). When, however, at the beginning of Náṣiru'd-Dín Sháh's reign, the debate of words evolved into armed clashes, the Government, headed by the energetic Mírzá Taqí Khán, lost no time in backing the 'ulamá and committing the troops of the Sháh to the attack on the Bábís. Some writers have claimed that the Bábís took a much more militant attitude, but this is a matter that requires further study.

Phase II: Persecutions of the Bahá'ís (1853–1921)

The closing of the Bábí era and the beginning of the Bahá'í era was also marked by a change in the nature of the persecutions. No longer was the primary motivation purely religious, but rather there were usually grounds of personal prestige, financial gain, or political advantage. For these purposes, the Bahá'ís, and particularly the wealthier and more prominent among them, were eminently suitable pawns, belonging as they did to a minority group that was not under the protection of any of the European states (in contrast to the Christian, Zoroastrian and other minorities). The 'ulamá were again the principal instigators of these episodes of persecution, but during this period the Government was for the most part either opposed to the civil disturbances caused by the persecutions or, when it feared to oppose powerful mujtahids like Áqá Najafí, it would sit back and allow events to take their course.

As far as the people were concerned, the attitude of many had been changed by the heroic stance of the Bábís and the excesses committed in 1852, and there were many secret sympathizers and well-wishers, but, as the events in Yazd in 1903 showed, the populace was still capable of being roused by the 'ulamá to the same levels of barbarity as had been seen in 1852.

The Bahá'ís themselves, moreover, showed a marked change in their attitude. Whereas formerly the Bábís had banded together in armed defence, their successors the Bahá'ís, on the instructions of Bahá'u'lláh, ceased to proffer any resistance, thereby demonstrating their peaceful intentions and their obedience to the State.

Phase III: Attacks on Bahá'í Institutions (1921–44)

The period during and immediately after the First World War saw momentous changes in the Middle East. Apart from the more obvious political changes – the break-up of the Turkish Empire, the overthrow of the Qájár dynasty, the Bolshevik revolution in Russia – there were many social and religious changes: the abolition of the Caliphate and the secularization of the State of Turkey, the opposition of the new regime in Iran to the power of the 'ulamá, the promulgation of laws intended to abolish the traditions of Islam and inculcate the civilization of the West. These sweeping changes resulted in a fundamental alteration in the nature of the persecution of the Bahá'ís. Instead of physical violence inflicted upon individuals, persecution took the form of attacks on the organization and institutions of the Bahá'ís, their schools, houses of worship, holy places and administrative bodies. And with the decline of the power of religious leaders, the initiator of these persecutions was usually the State itself.

The attitude of the Bahá'ís also underwent a transformation. Whereas in the preceding phase they had accepted meekly whatever had been meted out to them by the fanatical 'ulamá, they now began to take a more positive (though still non-violent) defensive position. Wherever possible, action was taken through the courts of the country concerned. Otherwise appeal was made to international opinion and even, in one notable instance, to the League of Nations.

	PHASE I The Bábí Upheavals 1844–1853	PHASE II Persecutions of the Bahá'ís 1853–1921	PHASE III Attacks on Bahá'í Institutions 1921–1944
Nature of the persecutions	Mainly for religious motives. Other motives, such as political, secondary to the religious ones.	Usually motives of personal gain or political opportunism	Diverse motives; political opportunism, religious fanaticism
Attitude of the State	Supported the 'ulamá with troops	Often disapproved of the persecutions	Usually carried out the persecutions
Attitude of religious leaders	Chief instigators	Often chief instigators	Often instigated the persecutions
Attitude of the people	Supported the 'ulamá in their attacks on the Bábís	Mixed reactions. Many secret sympathizers.	Mixed reactions
Attitude of the believers	Occasionally took up armed defensive positions when attacked	Meek acceptance	Active defence through legal proceedings and appeal to international opinion and institutions

This division into three phases is to a certain extent arbitrary and many instances may be cited as exceptions; but, nevertheless, as a statement of the general pattern of events it seems to fit. The cause of the change from Phase I to II was an internal change within the religion. During the ministry of the Báb, the Bábís, without the guidance of their leader who was imprisoned, were wont to take up arms in defence of themselves, and resisted their enemies with great heroism. One of the first actions of Bahá'u'lláh as the new leader of the majority of the Bábís (later Bahá'ís) was to issue specific instructions commanding his followers that in future they were not to resist even when persecuted; 'It is better to be killed than to kill.' Henceforth, even when persecutions arose in towns where Bahá'ís formed a sizeable proportion of the population, there was no attempt by the Bahá'ís to take to armed resistance or indeed to defend themselves physically in any way.

Whereas the first dividing point arose from internal developments within the movement, the second dividing point arose principally because of external factors. The advent of strong central governments, the secularization of the State, the subsequent loss of power by the religious leaders, and the increasing pressure that international public opinion was now able to exert, all served to alter the situation in the Middle East so that the former localized outbreaks of violent persecution became infrequent and the hostility against the new religion was channelled into more subtle avenues.

Chronology of Principal Events Referred to in this Book

12 Nov. 1817	Birth of Mírzá Ḥusayn-'Alíy-i-Núrí (Bahá'u'lláh).
20 Oct. 1819	Birth of Siyyid-'Alí-Muḥammad-i-Shírází (the Báb).
27 June 1826	Death of Shaykh Aḥmad al-Aḥsá'í.
9 Sept. 1834	Accession of Muḥammad Sháh.
1841	The Báb proceeds to Najaf and Karbilá where he attends the lectures of Siyyid Káẓim-i-Rashtí, Shaykh Aḥmad's successor.
31 Dec. 1843	Death of Siyyid Káẓim-i-Rashtí.
23 May 1844	Declaration by the Báb of his mission to Mullá Ḥusayn-i-Bushrú'í at Shíráz. Birth of 'Abdu'l-Bahá.
12 Nov. 1844	The Báb sets out from Shíráz on pilgrimage to Mecca.
13 Jan. 1845	Trial of Mullá 'Alíy-i-Basṭámí at Baghdád.
15 May 1845	The Báb returns to Búshihr following pilgrimage.
June 1845	Punishment inflicted by Ḥusayn Khán on disciples of the Báb at Shíráz. The Báb arrested and escorted to Shíráz.
23 Sept. 1846	The Báb leaves Shíráz for Iṣfahán.
Mar.–July 1847	The Báb is transferred from Iṣfahán to Mákú.
10 Apr. 1848	The Báb is moved to Chihríq.
June 1848	The Conference of Badasht at which a definite break is made with the laws of the Islamic Dispensation.
July 1848	The Báb is brought to Tabríz for trial, passing through Urúmíyyih on the way. After his trial, he is returned to Chihríq.
4 Sept 1848	Death of Muḥammad Sháh. Accession of Násiru'd-Dín Sháh; Mírzá Taqí Khán, the Amír-Niẓám, becomes Prime Minister a short time later.
10 Oct. 1848	Mullá Ḥusayn and his companions enter the Shrine of Shaykh Ṭabarsí – beginning of the Mázindarán Upheaval at Shaykh Ṭabarsí.
10 May 1849	Quddús and his companions tricked into laying down their arms. End of the Mázindarán Upheaval.
19 or 20 Feb. 1850	Seven Martyrs of Ṭihrán.
Early 1850	The Yazd Episode.
c. 13 May 1850	Beginning of the Zanján Upheaval.
27 May 1850	Vaḥíd enters Nayríz. Beginning of the First Nayríz Upheaval.

21 June 1850	End of First Nayríz Upheaval.
19 June 1850	Arrival of the Báb at Tabríz.
9 July 1850	Martyrdom of the Báb.
25 Aug. 1850	Arrival of 'Azíz Khán-i-Mukrí at Zanján.
Jan. 1851	End of the Zanján Upheaval.
13 Nov. 1851	Fall of Mírzá Taqí Khán, Amír-Niẓám. Mírzá Áqá Khán-i-Núrí becomes Prime Minister shortly after.
15 Aug. 1852	The Attempt on the Life of the Sháh.
16–27 Aug. 1852	Martyrdom of Bábís in Ṭihrán.
8 Apr. 1853	Arrival of Bahá'u'lláh in Baghdád
Oct.–Dec. 1853	Second Nayríz Upheaval.
22 Apr. 1863	Bahá'u'lláh removes to the Najíbíyyih Garden (the Garden of Riḍván) where he declares himself to be 'Him Whom God shall make manifest' to a few of his disciples.
3 May 1863	Departure of Bahá'u'lláh and his companions for Istanbul.
16 Aug. 1863	Arrival of Bahá'u'lláh and his companions at Istanbul.
Dec. 1863	Departure of Bahá'u'lláh and his companions in exile to Adrianople.
May 1864	Upheaval at Najafábád.
11 Jan. 1867	Execution of 3 Bahá'ís at Tabríz followed shortly thereafter by martyrdoms in Zanján and Ṭihrán.
July 1868	Persecution of Bahá'ís in Egypt.
July 1868	Exile of Bahá'ís of Baghdád to Mosul.
12 Aug. 1868	Departure of Bahá'u'lláh and his companions in exile to 'Akká.
31 Aug. 1868	Arrival of Bahá'u'lláh and his companions at 'Akká and imprisonment in the citadel.
July 1869	Martyrdom of Badí'.
Oct. 1870	Removal of Bahá'u'lláh to a house in 'Akká.
23 Jan. 1872	Murder of 3 Azalís in 'Akká.
May 1874	Upheaval at Iṣfahán.
June 1877	Bahá'u'lláh removes to Mansion at Mazra'ih outside 'Akká.
Dec. 1877	Martyrdom of Mullá Káẓim of Ṭálkhunchih.
Mar. 1879	Martyrdom of the King and Beloved of Martyrs.
Dec. 1882	Arrest of Bahá'ís in Ṭihrán.
23 Oct. 1888	Martyrdom of Mírzá Ashraf at Iṣfahán.
July 1889	Upheaval at Najafábád.
8 Sept 1889	Martyrdom of Ḥájí Muḥammad Riḍáy-i-Iṣfahání at 'Ishqábád.
25 Feb. 1890	Sidih martyrdoms.
19 May 1891	Seven Martyrs of Yazd.
29 May 1892	Passing of Bahá'u'lláh at 'Akká.
1 May 1896	Assassination of Náṣiru'd-Dín Sháh.
May 1896	Martyrdom of Varqá and Rúḥu'lláh in Ṭihrán.
Aug. 1896	Five Martyrs of Turbat-i-Ḥaydarí.

9 Feb. 1898	Martyrdom of Ḥájí Muḥammad-i-Turk at Mas͟hhad.
10 Dec. 1898	Arrival at 'Akká of first Western pilgrims.
Apr. 1899	Upheaval at Najafábád.
12 Dec. 1902	Laying of the cornerstone of the Mas͟hriqu'l-Ad͟hkár of 'Is͟hqábád.
May 1903	Upheaval at Ras͟ht.
May–June 1903	Incident at Russian Consulate in Iṣfahán.
June–July 1903	The Yazd Upheaval.
July 1908	'Abdu'l-Bahá freed after Young Turks' Revolution.
5 Nov. 1909	Martyrdom of Ḥájí Ḥaydar at Iṣfahán.
Aug. 1910	'Abdu'l-Bahá departs for Egypt.
11 Aug.–Dec. 1911	'Abdu'l-Bahá's First Western Tour.
25 Mar. 1912–17 June 1913	'Abdu'l-Bahá's Second Western Tour.
14 Mar. 1915	Martyrdom of Shayk͟h 'Alí-Akbar-i-Qúc͟hání in Mas͟hhad.
2 May 1917	Martyrdom of Mírzá Muḥammad-i-Bulúr-Furús͟h in Yazd.
27 Apr. 1920	Knighting of 'Abdu'l-Bahá.
21 May 1920	Martyrdom of Ḥájí 'Arab at Sulṭánábád.
23 Jan. 1921	Martyrdom of Mírzá Ya'qúb-i-Muttaḥidih in Kirmáns͟háh.
28 Nov. 1921	Passing of 'Abdu'l-Bahá at Haifa.
7 Apr. 1926	The Jahrum Martyrdoms.
9 Dec. 1934	Closure of Tarbíyat Schools in Ṭihrán.
May 1944	Persecutions at Ábádih.

Section A

Survey of Western Accounts and Opinions of the Bábí and Bahá'í Religions

FROM THE VERY START of the history of the Bahá'í religion, the accounts of it written by Western travellers, diplomats and missionaries have been replete with errors.

Until the time when, in the early years of the twentieth century, Bahá'í communities arose in the West and were able to publish accurate accounts of the new religion, it was rare to find an undistorted statement of its history and teachings. This was, for the most part, because in the Persia of the latter half of the nineteenth century it was very difficult to obtain first-hand information about the religion. Severe persecutions had virtually driven the movement underground: even the words 'Bábí' and 'Bahá'í' could not be mentioned in public. Thus Westerners travelling or residing in Persia found it almost impossible to contact the Bahá'ís. Even Prof. E. G. Browne, who travelled to Persia specifically to seek out the followers of the new religion, was, despite extensive enquiries, unable to contact them until he had been in Persia for four months. The fact that the fierce persecutions of the Bábís and Bahá'ís had attracted the attention of the West, however, made it necessary for most travel books and general accounts of Persia at least to mention the new religion. Consequently, the majority of writers were forced to borrow accounts from other writers. This resulted in fabrications and inaccuracies being perpetrated and through much repetition becoming regarded as the truth.

Since, in the ensuing sections of the book, those accounts which relate to episodes in the history of the religion will be quoted extensively, this survey will deal primarily with what Western writers thought were the teachings of the Báb and Bahá'u'lláh. Details of the articles and books referred to can be found in the Bibliography.

The Earliest Accounts (1845–65)

The first notice of the religion of the Báb that is recorded by a European is the report of Major Rawlinson from Baghdád concerning the trial of Mullá 'Alíy-i-Basṭámí and the excitement in Iraq over the advent of the new religion (see chapter 2).

The first known printed reference occurred in *The Times* of London on 1 November 1845 (see p. 69). The author of the account is unfortunately not indicated. An abbreviated version of this account then appeared in a London magazine, the *Literary Gazette and Journal of Belles Lettres, Arts, Sciences etc.* on 15 November 1845.[1] For some strange reason, *The Times*, not realizing that it had originally printed this report, reproduced on 19 November 1845[2] the account in the *Literary Gazette*. This report also appeared in the *Eclectic Magazine of Foreign Literature, Science and Art* (published in New York and Philadelphia) in January 1846,[3] and the *Port Phillip Herald*[4] (published in Melbourne), thus becoming the first mention of the new religion in the North American and Australian continents also.

After this there was a hiatus until 1848 when, principally as a result of the stir caused by the spread of the teachings of the Báb and the ensuing persecutions, diplomatic personnel in Persia began to mention the Báb and Bábís in their reports. These were, of course, not made generally available, but are of great importance since they were used by later writers,* and thus influenced the opinions of various people travelling through Persia at this time, who in their turn wrote accounts of the new religion.

There were two European Legations† in Ṭihrán at this time, the British and the Russian, with Lt-Col. Sheil and Prince Dolgorukov respectively as Ministers for most of the Bábí period. As far as their reporting of the Bábí disturbances is concerned, there was not a lot of difference between the two men. Both were heavily dependent on information given to them by the Persian Government which would, of course, be biased against the Bábís. In addition, they had Consuls and native Agents throughout the country who would furnish reports of events in their areas. In this respect, Dolgorukov was better informed of events in northern Persia (e.g. the Mázindarán upheaval at Shaykh Ṭabarsí), this being Russia's principal domain of interest, while Sheil received more detailed information from the south (e.g. the Nayríz upheavals).

The third person whose reports of the Bábí upheavals will be found in section B of this book is M. Ferrier, who was the French Agent in Persia. Throughout 1850, he sent monthly reports to the French Foreign Ministry

* In particular Robert G. Watson in his *A History of Persia* makes use of British Legation documents, being himself an Attaché of the Legation. Lady Sheil's account of the Bábís is also largely based on her husband's reports.

† The Turkish Embassy is here being counted as non-European. The French had sent one Envoy, Comte de Sartiges, in 1848, but he had soon returned. The French were then without a Minister at the Qájár court until 1855 when Bourée arrived (with Gobineau as the Secretary of his Legation).

on events in Persia. Not being an officially accredited diplomat, Ferrier would have received less information direct from the Persian Government and would have been more dependent on the news 'in the bazaar'. Hence his reports of episodes are sometimes later than those of Sheil and Dolgorukov, and tend to exaggerate some facts as 'bazaar news' does. However, since Ferrier was connected with the Persian Army, his information about troop movements (to Zanján for example) is presumably accurate. Also Ferrier's reports probably reflect popular opinion more than those of his counterparts.

The opinion shared by almost all of the European colony in Ṭihrán in 1850–52 seems to have been that the Bábís were socialists, communists* and anarchists. This view must be seen in the context of contemporary European history. Europe was at this time going through a particularly turbulent period. A wave of revolution and rebellion was sweeping across the continent, promoted by socialists and anarchists. Indeed the year 1848 remains famous as the 'Year of Revolutions'. Thus it is not surprising that the Europeans in Ṭihrán should have viewed the Bábí disturbances in a similar light. The Persian Government would also have encouraged a prejudiced view of the movement.

Dominating all the earliest accounts in importance are those of the two Sheils: Justin Sheil (q.v.)† in his dispatches to the Foreign Office, and Lady Sheil in her book *Glimpses of Life and Manners in Persia*. These two accounts, virtually identical in many respects, form the basis of several subsequent accounts. Sheil's first description of the tenets of the Bábí Faith occurs in a dispatch to Lord Palmerston dated 12 February 1850:

> The tenets of this new religion seem to be spreading in Persia. Bab the founder, a native of Sheeraz, who has assumed this fictitious name, is imprisoned in Azerbijan, but in every large town he has disciples, who with the fanaticism or fortitude so often seen among the adherents of new doctrines, are ready to meet death in the assertion of their opinions, as it ensures their entrance into paradise. Bab declares himself to be Imam Mehdee, the last Imam, who disappeared from human sight but is to reappear on earth. His decrees supersede the Koran among his disciples, who not only revere him as the head of their faith, but also obey him as the temporal Sovereign of the world, to whom all other monarchs must submit. Besides this inconvenient doctrine, they have adopted other tenets pernicious to society. The votaries of this sect consider that their own supremacy has been decreed, and that to the Saints it is lawful to acquire by whatever means the wealth and goods of the Ungodly.
>
> Conversion by the sword is not yet avowed, argument and inspiration from heaven being the present means of instilling or attaining faith in the Mission of Bab. If left to their own merits the not novel doctrines of this Preacher will doubtless sink into insignificancy, it is persecution only which can save them from neglect and

* The word communist had, of course, a different connotation then to the one it has today.
† This abbreviation refers to the biographical notes in Appendix II.

contempt, and unluckily the proselytes are all of the Mahommedan faith, which is inflexible in the punishment of a relapsed Mussulman. Thus both the temporal and religious authorities have an interest in the extermination of this Sect.

It is conjectured that in Teheran this religion has acquired votaries in every class, not even excluding the artillery and regular Infantry. Their numbers in this city, it is supposed, may amount to about two thousand persons.[5]

When Lord Palmerston asked for more details, in a dispatch dated 2 May 1850, Sheil sent a lengthier report:

In conformity with Your Lordship's instructions I have the honor to enclose an account of the new Sect of Bab. The statement contained in the enclosure numbered No. 1 is taken from an account given to me by a disciple of Bab, and which I have no doubt is correct. The other is extracted from a letter from a chief Priest in Yezd, and cannot be trusted.

This is the simplest of religions. Its tenets are summed up in materialism, communism, and the absolute indifference of good and evil, and of all human actions.[6]

The first enclosure in this report is a very surprising document since it claims to be an account by a Bábí and yet is replete with inaccuracies and exaggerations. Now it is of course true that in this turbulent period the vast majority of the Bábís had but little knowledge of the writings and teachings of the Báb, and it is possible that Sheil's contact was of this category and had filled in the gaps in his knowledge by wild and fanciful statements. Another possibility, however, is that this account is in fact Sheil's own synthesis drawn from several sources including perhaps a conversation with a Bábí.* Certainly this document is not a straight translation of an account provided by a Bábí. This is proved by the tone of the account itself; a Bábí is hardly likely to write: 'The most absolute materialism *seems* to form the essence of *their* belief' (italics added). Also, the rough draft of the dispatch in Sheil's own handwriting has been preserved in the Embassy Archives, and reveals that having written a rough draft, he then went back and added in phrases and even whole sentences, again making it doubtful that this is just a translation of a Bábí account. In the following transcription of this account, square brackets have been used to indicate those phrases and sentences added to the original draft.

* Lady Sheil's book *Glimpses of Life and Manners in Persia* seems to indicate on pp.178–9 that another European knew a Bábí and had obtained some information from him. The implication is that this Bábí was a Mírzá or Oriental Secretary to one of the Legations – most probably the Russian Legation. In an article about Dolgorukov's dispatches in *World Order* magazine ('Excerpts from Dispatches' p. 17) there is also mention of a Bábí having been a secretary at the Russian Legation. At this time Bahá'u'lláh's brother-in-law, Mírzá Majíd-i-Áhí, was a secretary at the Russian Legation, and although he was not himself a Bábí he may have been regarded as such because of his relation to Bahá'u'lláh. This may be the man referred to.

The real name of Bâb is Syed Ali Mahomed. He is a native of Shiraz, where his father was a merchant. His age is 32. It is six years since he proclaimed himself to be Sahib Zeman, or Imam Mehdee, the 12th Imam or High Priest in succession to Ali the son in law of Mahomed, [who about 1,050 years ago disappeared from the earth, and whose return is expected]. Bâb signifies gate in Arabic, and he claims to be the gate of Knowledge. His disciples are supposed to be about 50,000 *men* in number,* and are distributed all over Persia, and also a few in Koordistan.

They believe in Mahomed as a Prophet and in the divine origin of the Koran; but Bab contends that until this moment only the apparent meaning of the Koran was understood, and that he has come to explain the real secret and divine essence of God's word. [But it will be seen in a subsequent part of this account that the words *Prophet* and *Divine origin* have no signification].

He declares that up to this moment all the Mussulman tenets in regard to prayer, fasting and distinctions of food were in force; but that now he has been ordained to proclaim that prayer is not obligatory, each man may pray or not according to his inclinations, but that in fact a man should always think on God [or rather on *Godness*]; the thirty days fast of the Ramazan and all other fasting, are abrogated, and all sort of food is lawful.

Charity is inculcated towards all; but among Bâbees property ought to be in common; no man ought to be richer than another.

[All men are alike; there is no distinction of pure and impure as among the Mahomedans].

The intercourse of the sexes is very nearly promiscuous. There is no form of marriage; a man and a woman live together as long as they please and no longer, and if another man desires to have possession of that woman, it rests with her, not with the man who has been her husband, if he can so be termed:- [A man may have wives without limit; a woman has a similar licence].

[It is lawful to seize the property of all who are not Bâbees. There is no distinction of rank, excepting the distinction conferred by nature from the difference of intellect].

It is a falsehood invented by the Mussulmans that the nearest relations can cohabit together – the nearest relation permitted is first cousin.

There is no hell or heaven, therefore there is no hereafter – annihilation is man's doom in fact – he with every living and vegetable thing, in short everything whatever, will be absorbed in the Divinity. Everything is God, and therefore *absorbed*, which is the phrase of the Soofees, [who consider every thing is a reflection of God].† Hell is suffered and heaven is enjoyed in this world; but there is no such thing as crime, nor of course virtue, only as they concern the relations of man and man in this world. A man's will is his Law in all things.

It is right to make converts to Babeeism, but force is not allowed, unless to Mussulmans, whom it is on all occasions lawful to slay, because they are the enemies of Bâb and his disciples, and also because the fall of the Mussulman faith has been decreed, [that is to say, is to happen], and must be executed.

Every thing being indifferent, the only reason for wishing to make converts is that through Babeeism man may advance.

The most absolute materialism seems to form the essence of their belief. God is one. Every individual substance and particle, living or not, is God, and the whole is God, and every individual thing, always was, always is, and always will be.

Bâb began to preach in Shiraz, but was soon arrested and sent to a fortress in

* In the margin, Sheil has written that '100,000 *men* are believed to be nearer the truth.'

† Draft contains: 'is not the proper term, for man and everything else is already God.' This is needed to complete the sense of this sentence.

the mountains of Koordistan where he now is. He has not much learning. His Arabic is bad in point of grammar, but he contends that he is to set aside the old rules of the grammer of that language.

Next to Bâb in renown were two disciples who had been Moojteheds or Doctors of Mahomedan Law, and who were killed fighting in Mazanderan.

In Fars Syed Yaheeya [Vaḥíd] who lately distinguished himself in Yezd against the Shah's troops, is their chief. In Zenjan, Agha Mahomed Ali, Moojtehed [Ḥujjat] is the Leader.

In Kirman another pretender has appeared, who says he is the real Bâb,* but the Bâbees abhor him.

Should Bâb be put to death it will make no difference: there will still be Bâb.

In Mazanderan 575 Babees were killed; but they destroyed three or four thousand of their opponents.

When a Babee enters a room he says Allah hoo Akbar (God is great). The others respond Allah hoo Azim (God is most glorious). [A woman says Allah hoo ajmal (God is beautiful) the others say Allah hoo abha (God is most resplendent)].[7]

The second enclosure in Sheil's dispatch is from a chief priest in Yazd. The rough draft of this account contains no additions such as the previous one and would therefore seem to be a straightforward translation of a letter sent to Kh̲án Bábá Kh̲án (q.v.), Governor of Yazd then residing in Ṭihrán, by one of the mujtahids of Yazd.

A full account of Syed Yaheeya† (a Bâbee of note in Yezd) would be tiresome. He is the son of Syed Jaffer of Darab, his mother is of the Village of Baghdadabad, near Yezd, and he was at all times a factious refractory person. At the time that Meerza Ali Mahomed gave himself the title of Bâb and styled himself the Deputy of Imam Mehdee (the twelfth high Priest in succession from Ali the son-in-law of Mahomed. Mehdee disappeared from the Earth, and is to return), this Syed Yaheeya declared himself a disciple of the wicked Bâb. By degrees he drew the people towards himself and many ignorant people attached themselves to him.

They call the wicked Bâb the Lord, and each of his principle disciples has a special title. Syed Yaheeah is called Shejreh Behâ. A Syed (descendent of Mahomed) came from Ohree and said he was the Lord Jesus, and that he had come from the skies, having come from Tehran to Yezd in forty two hours. Many of the disciples have the title of Koodoos (Holy); one is called Menzereh Oolah (support of God); another Shan Oolah (Glory of God) etc.

The following is a brief account of their belief. Marriage between the nearest relations is lawful. There are no obligations of any kind (such as prayer, fasting etc.) excepting morning prayer. A man may marry seventeen wives. It is lawful to do all that has been forbidden, and to neglect all that has been commanded by God.[8]

Lady Sheil in *Glimpses of Life and Manners in Persia* follows her husband's dispatches very closely, so that one is forced to conclude that these were the main source of her information. For example, she quotes her husband word-for-word when she writes: 'It is the simplest of religions. Its

* Presumably Ḥají Mírzá Muḥammad-Karím Kh̲án-i-Kirmání is intended. This reference is interesting in two ways. Firstly, it would seem to indicate that the Bábís were still regarded, by some at least, as a splinter group of the Sh̲ayk̲hís, even at this late date. Also it would confirm the idea that the Sh̲ayk̲hí leaders were claiming to be Bábs to the Hidden Imám.

† Siyyid Yaḥyá, Vaḥíd

tenets may be summed up in materialism, communism, and the entire indifference to good and evil and of all human actions.'[9] However, Lady Sheil's book does contain a number of important statements not found in her husband's dispatches. Her description of the Báb, for example, may be found on p. 75, and her eyewitness account of the terror caused by the attempt on the life of the Sháh on pp. 136–8. Lady Sheil was also the first to draw a comparison between the religion of the Báb and the doctrines of Ḥasan-i-Ṣabbáḥ and Mazdak. This was to become a recurring theme in subsequent accounts.*

Dolgorukov (q.v.), the Russian Minister, concurred with Sheil in his opinion of the Bábís, and in a dispatch to Nesselrode (q.v.) dated 5 February 1849, in reference to the Bábís at Shaykh Ṭabarsí he writes: 'this sect, which is promoting communism through the force of arms'.[10] He was sufficiently alarmed by the apparent insurrectionary nature of the Bábí movement to demand the removal of the Báb from near the Russian borders at Mákú (see pp. 72–3). It is clear, however, that Dolgorukov recognized the religious nature of the movement also, for in a dispatch dated 5 January 1849, he states that the Báb has declared himself to be 'the *nayib* [representative] of the twelfth Imam'.[11]

It seems that in about the middle of 1850 it came to Dolgorukov's attention that Sheil had been making close enquiries about the Bábís. Hastening to remedy this deficiency in his own reporting he wrote to N. H. Anitchkov, the Russian Consul at Tabríz, on 15 July 1850: 'The doctrine of the Báb is capturing new adherents in Persia every day. It must therefore be given our most serious attention. Consequently, I am requesting you to make every effort to gather all the information possible on the dogmas of this doctrine and the movements of its sectaries. If you would not mind communicating whatever you obtain to me, I will compare this with what I am in a position to gather in Ṭihrán.

'The presence of the Báb in Tabríz will furnish you perhaps, with the possibility of gathering the most authentic information on this matter.'[12]

On the same day, he wrote to Seniavin, the Russian Foreign Minister: 'Lord Palmerston has asked his Ambassador in Persia to send him a detailed report of the beliefs of this sect and I myself hope, in the near future, to be able to send to the Imperial Ministry a book which has been compiled by one of the famous Bábís and has been placed at my disposal.'†[13]

Later, following the attempt on the life of the Sháh in 1852, Dolgorukov

* It is interesting to note that there is a centuries-old tradition in Persia of accusing religious minorities, which threaten the majority religion, of immorality, community of wives and similar offences. These accusations were first levelled at the Mazdakites in the fifth century AD and later at the Ismá'ílís in the twelfth century. In the case of the former, it is impossible to assess the veracity of the accusations since all reports of them have come to us from their enemies. With regard to the latter they were groundless.

† Presumably through the Bábí secretary employed by the Russian Legation; see note on p. 6.

wrote: 'The Bábís, as far as I have been able to understand from talking to the Imám-Jum'ih, are opposed to the doctrines of Islam and reject them. At the same time, in the political sphere, they lay claim to the position of the King. They plan to establish a new religion and are proponents of an equal division of property. It is possible to draw a comparison between their social and political aims and objectives and those of the communists of Europe.'[14]

Ferrier (q.v.), the French Agent, gives the following account of the beliefs of the Bábís in a dispatch dated 25 June 1850 to General de LaHitte (q.v.): 'It is clear that the Persian Bábís have the same proclivities as the French socialists; the religion, for their leaders, is only a pretext, and their political views are sufficiently made clear by the work to which they put their sectaries. If they ultimately triumph, which is very problematical, Persia would not gain anything from this sudden change because it will destroy for the Persians the only instinct which replaces nationality among them: the national religion will disappear . . .'*[15]

The first person to write a paper giving an account of the Bábí religion was an American missionary, Dr Austin H. Wright (q.v.). This paper, entitled 'A Short Chapter in the History of Bâbeeism in Persia', was sent to the American Oriental Society and read at its meeting of 18–19 May 1853 but not published.[16] A translation into German by Dr Justin Perkins was published in Germany in *Zeitschrift der Deutschen Morgenländischen Gesellschaft* (1851). Dr Wright wrote:

Some eight to ten years ago, a man appeared in southern Persia in the region of Shíráz, who claimed he was the only way to attain to God, and accordingly adopted the name Báb (the Arabic word for 'Gate, Gateway'). He found some people who believed his assertion and became his followers. One of his doctrines was that all men should be his subjects, and the power exercised by the Sháh was therefore illegitimate. This continued to be disseminated, and soon reached the Monarch's ears. He was summoned to the capital, held there for a long time and then banished to Mákú, a remote district, six days' journey from Urúmíyyih on the borders of Turkey. Here he was kept in custody, but anyone who wanted to see him was admitted, and he was allowed to send letters to his friends, who had become fairly numerous in various parts of Persia. He was visited by several persons from Urúmíyyih who became his followers. He dictated to a scribe something he called his Qur'án, and the Arabic sentences flowed so fast from his mouth that many of the Persians who witnessed it believed him to be inspired. It was also related of him that he did miracles, and whole masses of people gave willing credence to this rumour, since it was known that he lived an extremely abstemious life and spent the greatest part of his time in prayer. In consequence, he was taken to 'Tschari' near Salmás, only two days' journey from Urúmíyyih; there he was completely cut off from the world; yet he continued to write to his friends letters, which they spread as the effusions of one inspired.[17]

* The view expressed in this last sentence is somewhat similar to those expressed by Prof. E. G. Browne on the Bahá'í Faith at the time of the Persian Constitutional Movement some 60 years later. (English Introduction to *Nuqṭatu'l-Káf* p. lii)

It is interesting to note, but scarcely surprising, that the dramatic events associated with Shaykh Ṭabarsí, Zanján and Nayríz went almost unrecorded in the contemporary European Press, as did the martyrdom of the Báb himself. None of these events of 1848–50 came to the notice of the European newspapers. The only references which the editor has been able to find are the following in the *Revue de l'Orient*.* In 1849, this periodical referred to the Shaykh Ṭabarsí upheaval thus: 'Persia has its Proudhons, its Blanquis, etc. etc. The *Bábís*, for it is thus they are called, profess the most advanced socialist ideas; as fanatical as one can imagine, they have already taken matters to excess against the delegates of authority in Mázindarán. Their chief is in prison in Tabríz, and they say that they have taken up arms in order to defend him, him and the dogmas which he has imposed upon them, and which they accept without a murmur.'[18]

The same periodical makes a reference to Bábí disturbances in 1850 also, but this reference is very confusing since it refers to a conspiracy of the Bábís against the Governor of Ádharbáyján, its discovery and the execution of 5 Bábís on 20 May in Tabríz;[19] all statements which find no parallel in standard histories of the Bábí movement.

Although no author is cited in these two accounts in the *Revue de l'Orient*, it is probable that it was Dr Ernest Cloquet (q.v.), the Sháh's physician, who wrote them, since he was a regular correspondent of that periodical.

The events of 1852, although no more remarkable than those of the previous years, caused a considerable stir in the newspapers of the world, involving as they did an attempt on the life of the Sháh and a large number of horrific executions in the capital city where many foreigners lived. Most of the newspapers of the period printed at least some mention of the attempted assassination, and many had more than one report. However, since at this time no European newspapers had resident correspondents in Persia, they were dependent on reports emerging from Persia by various routes. News first reached Europe of this event in early October. Over the ensuing months numerous articles were printed all over the world, but most were based on only a few reports from Persia, there being extensive 'borrowing' between newspapers:

1. A report from the Istanbul correspondent of the *Standard* (London), dated 23 September 1852 and based on a letter reaching him from Tabríz dated 28 August 1852. This report appears in the *Standard*[20] on 7 October 1852.† This article may be found on p. 129.

* When this book was in an advanced state of preparation, the editor received a copy of a short report in the *Gazzetta Uffiziale di Venezia* of 12 September 1850, based on information from Tabríz dated 31 July. This report refers to the martyrdom of the Báb and the Zanján upheaval.

† It was reproduced in the last edition of the *Morning Herald* (London) on 7 Oct. and, on 8 Oct., in the

2. On the same day, the *Sun* (London)[21] published an article based on a letter from Tabríz dated 26 August 1852, and giving somewhat different details* – see p. 128.

3. On 12 October 1852, the Austrian military journal, *Oesterreichischer Soldatenfreund*,[22] printed a letter dated 29 August from Captain von Gumoens, an Austrian working in Ṭihrán† – see p. 132.

4. On 13 October 1852, *The Times*[23] of London printed an account of the martyrdoms of Ḥájí Sulaymán Khán and Qurratu'l-'Ayn. This was in all probability taken from another newspaper which the editor has been unable to locate as yet‡ – see p. 132.

5. On 13 October 1852, the Paris newspaper *Le Constitutionnel*[24] published a letter from Constantinople which added little to the known facts.§

6. In about the third week of October 1852, copies of the Ṭihrán newspaper *Rúznámiy-i-Vaqáyi'-i-Ittifáqíyyih*, with its account of the executions of the Bábís, began to reach the West and were translated in a few newspapers‖ – see pp. 138–42.

7. Several newspapers used the report based on a letter from Tabríz of 27 September 1852, which was published in the *Journal de Constantinople*. Copies of this newspaper reached Marseilles aboard the *Télémaque* on 27 October¶ – see p. 134.

8. An article by L. Boniface in *Le Constitutionnel*[25] of Paris referred to the participation of Sulaymán Khán and Shaykh 'Alí in the events.⁑

Morning Herald (London, p. 4), the *Daily News* (London, p. 5), the *Morning Post* (London, p. 6) and the *Morning Chronicle* (London, p. 6); and on 9 Oct. in *L'Union* (Paris, p. 2) and *Le Constitutionnel* (Paris, p. 2); and on 22 Oct. in the *New York Times* (p. 6).

* This report was used on 8 Oct. 1852 in *The Times* (London, p. 6) and the *Daily News* (London, p. 5), on 13 Oct. 1852 in the *Guardian* (London, p. 674), on 16 Oct. 1852 in *Allen's Indian Mail* (London, p. 588), and on 22 Feb. 1853 in the *Southern Cross* (Auckland, New Zealand, p. 4), the last named having taken its account from the *Melbourne Argus*. Very similar articles appeared in the *Kölnische Zeitung* (8 Oct. 1852, p. 2, based on information from Tabríz of 28 Aug., relayed from Istanbul on 20 Sept. and printed in the *Hamburger Nachrichten*), and the *New York Times* (2 Nov. 1852, p. 2, based on information from Tabríz of 28 Aug. relayed from Istanbul on 25 Sept.).

† Reproduced in *Augsburger Allgemeine Zeitung* (17 Oct. 1852), *Kölnische Zeitung* (23 Oct. 1852, p. 2) and *The Times* (London, p. 8, 23 Oct. 1852).

‡ Also appeared on 16 Oct. 1852 in *Allen's Indian Mail* (London, p. 588), on 28 Oct. 1852 in the *New York Times* (p. 6), and on 22 Feb. 1853 in the *Southern Cross* (Auckland, New Zealand, p. 3).

§ Also appeared on 14 Oct. 1852 in the *Morning Herald* (London, p. 3) and on 15 Oct. 1852 in the *Daily News* (London, p. 5).

‖ For example on 18 Oct. 1852 in *L'Union* (Paris, p. 2) and on 22 Oct. 1852 in *Giornale di Roma* (p. 969).

¶ Reported on 1 Nov. 1852 in the *Morning Post* (London, p. 5), the *Morning Herald* (London, p. 3), the *Daily News* (London, p. 5), the *Standard* (London, p. 3), the *Morning Chronicle* (London, p. 7), *L'Union* (Paris, p. 2), and on 16 Nov. 1852 in the *New York Times* (p. 3), the last named quoting from the *Semaphore* of Marseilles of 26 Oct. Similar reports appeared in *Giornale di Roma* (20 Oct. pp. 961–2, based on a report in *Osservatore Trieste*) and *Kölnische Zeitung* (30 Nov., p. 2).

⁑ Reproduced on 16 Nov. 1852 in *Giornale di Roma* (p. 1049).

Thus it is clear that the newspaper reporting of this episode, of which those quoted above and in the footnotes are only a sample, was intensive and world-wide, despite the lack of newspaper correspondents in Ṭihrán itself, much of the information reaching Europe in letters written from Tabríz.*

The *New York Times* also reported the attempt on the life of the Sháh. Initially it used the reports appearing in *The Times* of London, but on 8 November 1852 it printed a letter which it stated had been received from a 'Mahommedan gentleman, resident in London.'† The text of this letter is a remarkable confusion of facts and the wildest fantasies:

A person of the name of MOOLLAH SADIQUE, dwelling at Sheeraz, made a public declaration that in the year of the Hegira, 1255, corresponding with the Christian era 1839, a prophet would make his appearance and that the name would be BAUB, which signifies that all the knowledge and sanctity of prophecy would be possessed by him; that his mission would nullify all the modes of faith set forth by the ancient prophets, and that the whole world would embrace his religion. He further announced that BAUB would receive a heavenly book, and that all the treasures of the world, both what was already discovered, and what was yet hidden in the bowels of the earth, would be put into his possession.

Shortly after this announcement, he declared himself to be the prophesied BAUB, provided a book which he called Heavenly, and obtained several followers, chiefly from amongst the ignorant and uneducated class of people . . .

On the decease, however, of the late King, and the accession of his present Majesty to the throne of Persia, the impostor returned to his old courses, declaring that, the old King being now dead, the time for his prophetic mission had arrived. He accordingly sent letters in every direction within the limits of Persia; despatched an agent to the city of Astrabad, to foment disturbances there; and having assembled round his own person a band of between three and four thousand infatuated and desperate followers, he straightway began to enforce his new doctrines by means of fire and sword. Whoever refused to embrace his religion was sentenced to be burnt in his own house, together with his family, and in this matter several thousand persons were barbarously murdered. A body of these fanatics, about the same time, made an attack upon the uncle of the present King of Persia, but he succeeded in effecting his escape – while a younger brother, who was so unfortunate as to fall into their hands, was burnt alive, according to their custom.

As this fanatic rebellion appeared to be gaining strength, a body of the royal troops were now marched from the frontiers of Mazindran and Astrabad, for the purpose of

* The reader may wonder why this news came to Europe through letters written in Tabríz, rather than in Ṭihrán where the news was occurring. The reasons for this are economic. Istanbul and Tabríz were the two poles of a trade route linking Europe and Persia. Thus the European trading houses in Istanbul had agents in Tabríz and this is, probably, how news of this episode reached Istanbul and thence Europe.

† Probably the only Persians resident in London at that time were the members of Mírzá Shafí' Khán's Diplomatic Mission to London. (Amongst the members of this Mission was Mírzá Ya'qúb Khán, the uncle of Mírzá Malkam Khán.) Thus it may be argued that this account is an attempt by the Persian Government to justify its barbaric conduct, as recorded in such accounts as von Gumoens's, which was undoubtedly occasioning adverse comments in Europe and North America.

checking it. Every effort was made, by way of exhortation, by the royal commanders to induce the rebels to return to their duty, but to no purpose. The infatuated men were resolved on enforcing their principle, and regaining power by bloodshed and rapine. A sanguinary encounter took place between them and the royal troops, in which not less than four thousand fell on both sides. Among the few of the rebels, who were made prisoners, was the vicegerent or principal agent of the impostor; but even him the King did not put to death, but sentenced him, with eleven other desperate fanatics, to be imprisoned for life . . .

Upon this a representation was made to the King of Persia on behalf of the great body of the people, showing that as the most learned Mahomedans had proved the Baub to be an impostor, and sentenced him to death, it was necessary that the sentence should be enforced, seeing that as long as he should be permitted to live, the peaceable inhabitants of the country would be in constant danger from the outbreak of his fanatical followers. On this representation, and by the advice and recommendation of the chief men of the kingdom, his Majesty ordered him to be beheaded. The freedom from seditious fanaticism that the kingdom of Persia enjoyed for upwards of two years, may be fairly cited in proof of the salutary effect of this decision.

From the private letters of friends, as well as the public intelligence from Persia, I am informed that a person named HANJEE SOOLAIMAN KHAN, who was one of the Baubs, or followers of the Baub, had formed a design to kill his Majesty the King of Persia, persuading his adherents and abetters that he was then to assume the Empire as prophet. This was the man who attempted the life of the King, and who was put to death for the crime.[26]

The writer of this account has evidently confused the Báb with a certain Mullá Ṣádiq who a few years prior to the appearance of the Báb had been preaching in the Caucasus that a new prophet was about to appear.* The rest of the wild statements in this account are inexplicable other than as indicated in the footnote on p. 13.

The first book to mention the Báb in the West was *Dawnings of Light in the East* (1854) by Rev. Henry Aaron Stern (q.v.). In April 1852 Stern was in Bárfurúsh, near the scene of the upheaval at Shaykh Ṭabarsí three years previously. Here, he met some extremist Bábís. He writes:

In returning to my lodging, I met a good number of Mahomedans, who enquired whether I had any tracts against their Prophet. Upon my asking why they wanted such pamphlets, they replied with great caution, (for I saw them gazing in all directions to see whether any of 'the faithful' were near,) 'Because we detest Mahomed,

* A certain Mullá Ṣádiq of Urdúbád on the river Aras had been preaching the Advent of the Lord of the Age in the Caucasus, and had collected several thousand followers in the area. This had caused disturbances which resulted in Mullá Ṣádiq being exiled to Warsaw by the Russian authorities. However, Mullá Ṣádiq's pupil, Siyyid 'Abdu'l-Karím-i-Urdúbádí, took up the leadership of the movement. Siyyid 'Abdu'l-Karím was in Iraq when he heard of the teaching of the Báb: and it is said that he became a Bábí, returned to the Caucasus and succeeded in converting a number of people before the Russian Government arrested him and exiled him to Smolensk. In Dec. 1860 and Jan. 1861, Siyyid 'Abdu'l-Karím wrote two letters to Kazem-Beg from his exile in Smolensk, at a time when the latter was collecting material for his book and article on the Bábís. In a footnote, Kazem-Beg states that Siyyid 'Abdu'l-Karím had been set free and was now at Astrakhan (see Kazem-Beg 'Bab et les Babis' Oct–Nov. 1866, pp. 395 and 399, and Dec. 1866, pp. 473–81; also Kazemzadeh 'Two Incidents' p. 23).

and ridicule his Koran.* During the short conversation which I had with them in the street, I learnt that they were secret followers of Baba, the renowned Persian socialist, whose community two years ago menaced both the religion and throne of Persia. The founder of this sect, and thousands of his adherents, died an ignominious death; but, notwithstanding all the rigour which has been applied in order to extirpate this heresy, there are still many thousands of the rich and learned in Mazanderan, and other provinces, who venerate Baba, and regard his violent death as a national calamity.[27]

The next book to mention the Bábís is Lady Sheil's *Glimpses of Life and Manners in Modern Persia* (1856), which has been referred to above. In 1857, there appeared a book entitled *Journal of Two Years' Travel in Persia, Ceylon etc.* by R. B. M. Binning (q.v.) of the Madras Civil Service. Unfortunately, this work reflects more the narrow and bigoted mind of its author than any features of the countries through which he was passing. Its author arrived in Persia in late 1850 and left Persia on 11 February 1852. He was in Iṣfahán when news of the termination of the Zanján upheaval reached him just before Naw-Rúz 1851. His account of the termination of the siege can be found on pp. 123–4. As to the rest of his account of Bábism, this is best summed up by Prof. Browne in the following terms: 'Of all accounts which I have read, not excluding those given by the Mussulmán historians, this is the most hostile, the most unfair – I had almost said the most libellous. The writer, not content with likening the Bábís to Mormons and Sadducees and describing their Founder as a kind of oriental Joe Smith, casts aspersions on the Báb's honesty, and almost accuses him of theft in so many words . . . In point of accuracy, too, this account leaves much to be desired.'[28]

Bernard Dorn (q.v.) was an orientalist who in 1860 travelled extensively throughout Mázindarán and Gílán and published several accounts of this journey.[29] While in Bárfurúsh (29 October – 27 November 1860), he obtained a manuscript history of the upheaval at Shaykh Ṭabarsí; concerning the acquisition of this manuscript, he wrote:

During my stay in 1860 in Mázindarán, and specifically in Bárfurúsh, where the Bábís appeared in 1849, I took the opportunity to make a closer study of them and their Qur'án. They had established themselves about 3 miles (3 *farsakhs*) from Bárfurúsh at the shrine of Shaykh Ṭabarsí, and had been overcome and forced to submit there after a battle of many months. In fact the majority of the prisoners were killed in various ways in Bárfurúsh itself. The information given me was not so satisfying as might have been expected from the eyewitnesses I questioned . . . I also collected a history of the Bábís in Bárfurúsh in both the Mázindaráni and Persian

* In general, the Báb and the Bábís venerated Muḥammad and the Qur'án. The evident animosity of this group of Bábís whom Stern met may perhaps be explained by the fierce persecution that the Bábís of this area had undergone a few years earlier at the time of the Mázindarán upheaval at Shaykh Ṭabarsí.

dialects. Attempts have been made to deny all merit to this history except that of its being composed in the Mázindarání dialect. But even those who know how one-sided such information and reports sometimes are, will scarcely be able to reject everything related by eyewitnesses, some of whom were even active in the efforts to exterminate the Bábís.[30]

In 1864, the Imperial Oriental Library obtained from N. V. Khanykov (q.v.), a number of manuscripts that the latter had obtained in Persia. Among these was a book which is named *The Qur'án of the Bábís.** Dorn presented an account of this book, and the manuscript history of Shaykh Ṭabarsí that he had obtained in Mázindarán, in two papers read to the Historico-Philological Section of the Russian Academy of Sciences on 3 January and 5 September 1865.[31] In the first of these he stated, concerning *The Qur'án of the Bábís*, that while he was in Mázindarán:

No one admitted to any knowledge of a *Qur'án of the Bábís*, in fact the very existence of such a book was challenged, even though there were supposed to be many covert Bábís actually there. This denial, however, does not appear to be well-founded, or refers only to the Bábís in Bárfurúsh, for otherwise reliable sources not only confirm the existence of such a book, but that it is to be found written down, as our manuscript shows . . . I can only add that no doubt can arise as to its authenticity, since it comes direct from the secretary† of the Báb himself, who wanted to have this Qur'án written down according to the spoken words of his Lord and Master. He had got them into European hands from his prison in Tabríz. The responsibility for the contents, therefore, rests on the secretary referred to.[32]

Three further works must be mentioned in this section. Firstly *Persien. Das Land und seine Bewohner* [Persia: The Land and Its Inhabitants] by Dr Jakob Polak (q.v.). Published in 1865, the principal importance of the book is the fact that the author was in Ṭihrán at the time of the attempted assassination of the Sháh, and indeed claims to have been present at the martyrdom of Ṭáhirih. His tribute to her courage appears on p. 144. He also, in common with most members of the Ṭihrán European community, equated the Bábís with socialists:

A great stir has been created recently by the sect of the Bábís. Its founder, a learned Siyyid . . . called himself *Bábu'd-Dín* (Gate of the Faith). He wrote a canon in Arabic, rejecting the Qur'án, introduced communism of possessions and the complete emancipation of women, and taught that anyone killed for the defence and spreading of the Faith revealed by him was immortal, and in the moment of dying would come to life again in another place . . .

Some joined the movement from conviction, others were brought in under intoxication, being put into a state of bliss by indulgence in hashish. This narcotic then was used by the Bábís to the same purpose as it was by the Assassins.[33]

* Browne sent the published portion of this '*Qur'án of the Bábís*' to Mírzá Yaḥyá who pronounced it to be the *Kitábu'l-Asmá'* (the Book of Names).

† Presumably Siyyid Ḥusayn-i-Yazdí. There is a reference to Siyyid Ḥusayn having put certain writings into European hands (see Browne *Táríkh-i-Jadíd* p. 396).

Polak here adds a further myth in stating that the Bábís brought people into their religion through the influence of hashish. Such an assertion, apart from not being supported by facts, is untenable in a society such as that of Persia where the use of hashish was commonplace.*

In 1861, Mr John Ussher and a friend travelled to Persia. The Bábí upheavals were almost a decade in the past but their memory was still vivid in the minds of the people. With regard to the doctrines of the Bábís, he reiterates the statements of Sheil and other authors: 'The principles of this Reformer, as well as can be ascertained (for the sect now proscribed keep their real belief carefully concealed) were Socialistic, for he advocated a community of property and women, alleging that if such were the case there would be no motives for most of the crimes committed by the human race.'[34]

Eastwick (q.v.), Secretary of the British Legation in Ṭihrán from May 1860 to May 1863, and Chargé d'Affaires in December 1862 during Mr Alison's leave of absence, contents himself with a brief reference of less than half a page to the Bábís in his book *Journal of a Diplomate's Three Years' Residence in Persia*, published in 1864. He follows Binning in calling the Báb 'the Joe Smith of Iran'.[35]

Gobineau

If one were to choose a single book which more than any other served to make the religion of the Báb known to the people of the West during the nineteenth century, one must turn to Gobineau's (q.v., see fig 3) *Les Religions et les Philosophies dans l'Asie Centrale* (1865). Although containing several chapters on other subjects, such as the Sufis and Persian Religious Theatre, more than half of the book is devoted to the religion of the Báb.

It is indeed ironic that the origins of the Bahá'í Faith, which in later years was to stress and promote the concept of the brotherhood of all men and the need for freedom from racial prejudice, should have been proclaimed by one who has, by some, been hailed as the father of racism. So powerful an influence did Gobineau exert on this movement that for many years it was called Gobinism after him. Gobineau's writings, however, have little in common with the horrors of the concentration camp. For, although Gobineau traces much of what he considers to be the degeneracy of his generation to the evils of racial admixture, he considers the situation to be beyond redemption; there is no hint of the 'final solution' in his writings.

Religions et Philosophies dans l'Asie Centrale was published two years

* This accusation probably springs from a desire by the S͟hí'ih 'ulamá to explain the great attraction that the Bábí Faith held for large numbers of Persians. It is similar to the fanciful story of the supernatural pomegranate syrup (see p. 111).

after Gobineau's return from Persia, where he was the French Minister. The chapters relating to the Bábí religion are as follows:

Chapter VI: Commencement of Bábism
Considers the life of the Báb and the early disciples up to the time of the death of Muḥammad Sháh. Much of this is grossly erroneous, being based on the works of the Qájár court historians.

Chapter VII: Development of Bábism
Considers the Conference of Badasht and the surrounding of the Bábís in Shaykh Ṭabarsí.

Chapter VIII: Battles and Successes of the Bábís in Mázindarán
Carries the story of the Shaykh Ṭabarsí upheaval to the martyrdom of Mullá Ḥusayn.

Chapter IX: Fall of the Fort of Shaykh Ṭabarsí . Troubles at Zanján
Completes the story of the Mázindarán upheaval and describes Mullá Muḥammad-'Alí, Ḥujjat, and his life to the commencement of the Zanján upheaval; wrongly states the Báb to have been confined to his house in Shíráz at this time.

Chapter X: Insurrection at Zanján. Captivity and Death of the Báb
Describes the Zanján upheaval; wrongly states the Báb to have been moved directly from Shíráz to Chihríq. The Báb brought to Tabríz – his trial and martyrdom.

Chapter XI: Attempt against the King
The Bábís after the martyrdom of the Báb. The attempt on the life of the Sháh and the subsequent reign of terror.

Chapter XII: The Books and Doctrine of the Bábís
Excerpts from this chapter are translated below.

Appendix: 'Ketab-è-Hukkam': The Book of Laws
This is a poor translation of most of the Arabic *Bayán*.

Gobineau's source for most of his historical material is the official Persian court history, the *Násikhu't-Taváríkh* by Mírzá Taqíy-i-Mustawfí (Lisánu'l-Mulk, Sipihr).* Gobineau also knew the other principal court

* Nicolas, who was no great admirer of Gobineau's work on the Bábís, rather overstresses its dependence on the *Násikhu't-Taváríkh* when he writes 'I well know that Gobineau is also of the opinion that Siyyid 'Alí-Muḥammad's Arabic was bad, but I must be permitted to suspect the appreciation of this point by our former Minister in Ṭihrán, who did not know a word of this language, any more than of Persian; but this did not hinder him from assuming the accolade of "Savant" – savant on the cheap because his work *Religions et Philosophies dans l'Asie Centrale*, which has been mistaken for an original work, is none other than a translation, brilliant but in places inaccurate, of the *Násikhu't-Taváríkh*, made by a Jew who knew a little French, whose name was Lálizár [Mullá Lálizár-i-Hamadání], and who was Gobineau's teacher.' (Nicolas *Seyyèd Ali Mohammed* pp. 199–200)

In Gobineau's defence it should be said that he almost certainly had a fair working knowledge of Persian. Mullá Lálizár, however, probably translated the Arabic *Bayán* which forms the appendix of

historian of the period, Riḍá-Qulí Khán, Lálih-Báshí, the author of part of *Rawḍatu'ṣ-Ṣafá*, and may well have obtained information from either him or his book, although the *Násikhu't-Taváríkh* is the only work mentioned in *Religions et Philosophies*.

Gobineau was also in contact with some Bábís in Ṭihrán. In his dissertation to Prof. Browne, Siyyid Mihdíy-i-Dihají (see p. 293n) states that Mírzá Riḍá-Qulíy-i-Tafrishí and his brother Mírzá Naṣru'lláh, who were Bábís and brothers-in-law of Mírzá Yaḥyá, Ṣubḥ-i-Azal, were in the employ of the French Legation.[36] These two persons probably provided Gobineau with much of the information that he did not obtain from the court histories. They were, most likely, responsible for the prominence given to their brother-in-law, Mírzá Yaḥyá, in Gobineau's account of the events following the martyrdom of the Báb.

Gobineau's book is also of importance in that it contains the first printed reference in a European book, albeit an inconsequential one, to Bahá'u'lláh. 'He [Mírzá Yaḥyá] had lost his mother at the moment of birth, and the wife of one of the leading Bábís, one of the members of the Unity, who carried the title of Jináb-i-Bahá (the Precious Excellency), alerted in a dream of the sad state in which the august infant found himself, took him and raised him until his fifteenth year.'[37] Through an unfortunate ambiguity in Gobineau's French, two of the articles to be discussed shortly, those of Evans and Arbuthnot, make Bahá to be the name of a woman.

Defective as Gobineau's work is from a historical point of view, it was still, at the time, the most important work on the subject. Concerning the teachings of the Báb also, Gobineau surpassed all previous authors, and his summary of the doctrines of the Báb remains to this day one of the most comprehensive, if not altogether accurate.

Concerning the nature of God, Gobineau, although he does not actually use the word 'pantheism', presents the teachings of the Báb in such a way that subsequent writers quickly came to the conclusion that they were pantheistic:

Gobineau's book and this translation, as Nicolas says, is almost incomprehensible in places. Barbier de Meynard, who was himself an orientalist and had known Gobineau personally, asserts: 'He had set about the study of Persian at the age when the memory rebels against new acquisitions, and as for the language of the Qur'án, which every innovator in the Orient takes as his example, he did not know it except through the Persian and very imperfectly: the incorrectness of the Arabic words that he cites will by itself suffice to prove that (for example *byyan*, *hukkam*, etc.) . . . I would not hesitate to say that his translation of the *Precepts*, or whatever the third *Bayán* of the Báb is called, was done at the dictation of a Persian secretary, or with the assistance of a Persian version written for his own use; in any case, it is secondhand.' (*Journal Asiatique* 8th ser., Vol. 20, 1892, p. 301) See also J. Gaulmier in *Austral. Jour. of Fr. Studies*, Vol. 1, 1964, pp. 58–70.

It is worth pointing out that the deeds of Siyyid Yaḥyáy-i-Dárábí, Vaḥíd, are completely ignored in Gobineau's book (in contrast to the *Násikhu't-Taváríkh*). Another historical inaccuracy is Gobineau's belief that Qurratu'l-'Ayn and Jináb-i-Muṭahharih (i.e. Ṭáhirih) were two distinct people.

God is single, unchangeable, eternal; He has no partner. This is the same formula that the Musulmans use; but the scope of it is different. The Musulmans of today mean to say by that that Christ is not God, and that the divine Personality, restricted to itself, does not produce any emanation, nor does it communicate itself in any manner outside strict, complete and absolute unity. The Báb intends only to establish that outside of God, there is no God; that there do not exist two divine powers, strangers to one another . . . one will see presently that, by divine unity, he means something other than an entity closed in on itself . . .

God is essentially Creator because He is Life, because He pours out life and the only way to do this is to create; otherwise, He would concentrate all of it in His own essence. In order to create, He used seven Letters – I borrow the Bábí terms. This amounts to saying that He employs the Word and the different manifestations of the Word, represented here by seven letters or words (for the Arabic expression *ḥurúf* has two meanings). These seven Letters are Force, Power, Will, Action, Condescension, Glory and Revelation; these are what we will call the Attributes. God possesses many others, an infinity of others . . . But as far as the act of creation is concerned . . . the Báb teaches that only seven of these Qualities have operated, and it is thus that the seven Qualities, in creating the actual universe, have manifested the truth of this axiom: 'God is the primordial Unity from which emanates the *supputated* [numerical, quantitative] unity.' . . . In effect, all beings, all individualities that emanated from God are *supputated*, that is to say, in the language of the Báb, that they cannot in their turn produce any act of emanation without there also being fractionation, diminution and destruction. That is the distinction between God and creatures.[38]

On the nature of the prophets of God in Bábí doctrine, Gobineau writes:

In this state of things, in this congenial current which runs from the Infinite Being to His finite portion, God proves His vitality by uninterrupted rapport with His creatures. This rapport has already found expression in one of the constituent parts of the cipher of seven: Revelation. Human nature, ignorant and forgetful, throws itself towards God in order to know ['connaître'], because knowledge is the only means it has of regenerating itself. And God, who loves man, has provided for him the measures called for by his weakness, the result of his deviation. He leads man back, He draws him towards Himself, so to speak by means of a chain, and by a series of planned jolts; the chain is the succession of prophets; the jolts are the revelations that these persons bring.

But men can no more understand the true character, the real essence of these persons who hold a mandate from God than they can understand God Himself . . . There are great kings; there are great doctors; humanity has produced, has known brilliant sages; if one were to measure the distance that separates all of these natures, however noble and lofty, from the true prophetic nature that the world has revered in a very small number of unforgettable manifestations, it is easy to convince oneself that these mandatories of God cannot be said to be, strictly speaking, men. What are they then?

They are, as is the world, and the universe itself, an emanation of the divine nature. But only these emanations [the prophets], remaining in constant communication with their point of origin, and being nearer in time, remain infinitely closer and form . . . an intermediary between God and the universe. From the human point of view, they have a personality, since their form and appearance are strictly determined and finite, just as the body of Jesus, of Muḥammad is a physical reality; but from the intellectual, prophetic point of view, they are breaths from the mouth of God, who are not actually God, but who come from Him in a more real sense, and who return to Him more rapidly, than other beings. They are His words, His letters. Thus the prophets are simultaneously both man and God himself, without being quite one or the other.[39]

Concerning the progression of the prophets in the Báb's teaching, Gobineau writes:

Gradually, however, and with shaky but uninterrupted steps, humanity advances. The law of Moses soon becomes insufficient, and the divine reality is incarnated in Jesus, bringing Christianity. That was an immense step forward. The world profited from it sufficiently so that after a lapse of time much less considerable than that which separated David, the last prophet, or if one wishes Solomon, from Jesus, Muḥammad could appear. He carried men along a little further than Jesus had taken them. However, no more than his predecessor did he manage to impart to them a uniform impulse, and many of them remained obedient to out-of-date revelations, as had happened before. Finally the Báb appeared in his turn, with his revelation, undoubtedly more complete, and . . . more progressive . . .[40]

The Báb clearly foretold the coming of a further prophet to whom, throughout his writings, the Báb refers as 'Him Whom God shall make manifest'. Writing about the *Bayán*, Gobineau states:

It is composed, in theory, of 19 unities or principal divisions, which, in their turn, are divided each into 19 paragraphs. But the Báb has only written eleven of these unities, and he has left the eight others to the true and great Revealer, to him who will complete the doctrine, and in relation to whom the Báb is no more than St John the Baptist was before Our Lord. The doctrine of the Báb is thus transitory; it prepares for what will come later; it clears the terrain; it opens the way . . . Thus, for example, the Báb has abolished the Qiblih, that is to say the Musulman and Jewish practice of turning towards a given point on the horizon when they pray . . . But he does not substitute a new Qiblih for the old abrogated ones, and declares that on this point he has nothing to ordain, and that the Great Revealer will decide this.

A great part of the *Bayán* is consecrated to announcing, to explaining, to foretelling the advent of this important facet of the truth. The Báb, who does not wish to say much about it, not being authorized to do so, calls the Great Unknown 'Him Whom God shall make manifest [Celui que Dieu manifestera]' . . .

. . . the Báb has pronounced that the appearance of 'Him Whom God shall make manifest' will coincide with the preparations for the Last Judgement, and that it will be this prophet who will, in reality, introduce the purified universe into the bosom of the Divinity who is awaiting it. By this account, 'Him Whom God shall make manifest' will be the Imám Mahdí, will be Jesus Christ, arriving on clouds to judge the earth.[41]

Gobineau mentions sundry other teachings:

. . . he [the Báb] makes alms a strict obligation. He reminds the rich that they are only repositories, that no one on earth possesses anything, it all belongs to God. Consequently, the rich must give to religion and to those who have nothing or who do not have enough. But he absolutely forbids mendicancy, he denounces it, and will not tolerate it under any pretext . . .[42]

Once married, he [the Báb] tolerates the

taking of a second wife, but he does not recommend it by any means; he severely forbids concubines, and he was so manifestly opposed to polygamy that his followers consider it bad to make use of the latitude that he has given them in allowing two wives . . . he defended divorce and abrogated the veil.[43]

Gobineau refutes the Muslim allegation of promiscuity among the Bábís:

. . . The Musulmans, however, accuse the Bábís of having secret love-feasts, where the lights are dimmed and all manner of promiscuity allowed. This is the kind of accusation made respectable by its antiquity, and one may perhaps consider it as the monument of the most ancient sectarian hatred that exists in the world. The Jews and pagans addressed the same reproach to the early Christians, and it is even doubtful that they were the inventors of it. From that time, the different sects have never ceased to preach it as a weapon of war . . . Thus generalized, this argument loses a little of its value, and after one has read the teachings of His Holiness the Supreme [i.e. the Báb], it is apparent that one must consider it as a simple insult.[44]

The success of Gobineau's book was immediate. Within a year, a second edition was necessary, an unusual occurrence in those days for a work of this nature. For several decades it continued to excite the intelligentsia of Europe with its stirring account of the Bábí heroes and their religion. Almost immediately a large number of reviews and articles appeared in some of the leading newspapers and periodicals in Europe and North America based on Gobineau's book (often together with Kazem-Beg's article which will be referred to presently). Indeed, it may be said that not until 'Abdu'l-Bahá's travels in the West did the Bábí-Bahá'í religion achieve such renown as in the years following the publication of Gobineau's book.

Ernest Renan (q.v.), one of the greatest literary and religious figures of the nineteenth century, brought out his famous book *Les Apôtres* only a few months after Gobineau's book appeared. In it he makes a reference to the Bábís: '*Bábism* in Persia was a phenomenon much more astonishing. A mild and unassuming man, in character and opinion a sort of pious and modest Spinoza, was suddenly and almost in spite of himself raised to the rank of a worker of miracles and a divine incarnation; and became the head of a numerous, ardent and fanatical sect, which came near accomplishing a revolution like that of Muḥammad. Thousands of martyrs rushed to death for him with joyful alacrity. The great butchery of his followers at Ṭihrán was a scene perhaps unparalleled in history.'[45]

Renan then goes on to quote Gobineau's account of the fierce persecution that followed the attempt on the life of the S͟háh,* to which he adds the following as a footnote: 'Another detail which I have from original sources is as follows: Several of the sectaries, to compel them to retract were tied to the mouths of cannon, with a lighted slow-match attached. The offer

* This passage from Gobineau's book may be found on p. 144.

was made to them to cut off the match if they would renounce Báb. In reply, they only stretched out their hands towards the creeping spark, and besought it to hasten and consummate their happiness.'[46]

Renan then concludes:

> Absolute devotion is to simple natures the most exquisite of enjoyments, and, in fact, a necessity. In the Bábí persecution, people who had hardly joined the sect came and denounced themselves, that they might suffer with the rest. It is so sweet to mankind to suffer for something, that the allurement of martyrdom is itself often enough to inspire faith. A disciple who shared the tortures of Báb, hanging by his side on the ramparts of Tabríz and awaiting a lingering death, had only one word to say – 'Master, are you satisfied with me?'
>
> Those who regard as either miraculous or chimerical everything in history which transcends the ordinary calculations of common sense, must find such facts as these inexplicable.[47]

With regard to the footnote quoted above, Renan writes in another footnote that he had received 'information from two individuals at Constantinople who were personally involved in the affairs of Bábism.'[48] One of these two individuals was Mírzá Malkam Khán, the wily, charming and enigmatic adventurer who, on the one hand, lent a great stimulus to the liberal reform movement in Persia through his writings, and on the other was devoted to self-aggrandizement and his own financial interests. Renan in the course of his tour of Turkey and Syria in 1860–61 met Malkam Khán in Istanbul. They remained in touch over the ensuing years chiefly through M. Brunswick in Istanbul. In a letter dated 7 June 1866 to the latter, Renan, after acknowledging the receipt of a portrait of Mírzá Malkam Khán, writes: 'Tell Malkam that there is going to appear in the *Journal Asiatique* a history of Bábism, written by Mírzá Kazem-Beg, professor at St Petersburg. I believe that he will be happy with it. But certainly, if he wants to give us his recollections, that would be much better still.'[49]

Among the most important reviews and articles based on Gobineau's book which appeared in subsequent years may be listed the following (see Bibliography for details):

1. One of the earliest reviews to appear was that of the eminent French Jewish philosopher Adolphe Franck (q.v.), in the December 1865 issue of *Journal des Savants*. This later appeared as a chapter in Franck's book *Philosophie et Religion*. Franck devotes 20 pages of this lengthy review to the Bábís. At the end of his article, Franck states: 'This system does not distinguish itself by either originality or force.'[50] This called forth the following comment from Gobineau, in a letter to Prokesch-Osten: 'Europeans are amazing. Someone whom I love among other things for his extreme candour and good faith, M. Franck of the *Institut*, has written two articles in the *Journal des Savants* on my book and he states that the doctrine of the Báb is not original! I would like to know what is meant by original.

Obviously, he [the Báb] has used existing views to give rise to his doctrines, and existing words to express it. But in present-day Asia, I found everything that he wanted to create to be very original.'[51]

2. In Germany, Gobineau's book was reviewed in *Allgemeine Zeitung* (published in Tübingen, March 1866), under the heading 'Die Babis in Persien'.

3. A review of Gobineau's book by Louis de Ronchaud (q.v.) appeared in the May 1866 issue of the French periodical *Revue Moderne* under the title 'Une Religion nouvelle dans l'Asia Centrale'. This article later appeared as a chapter in the same author's book, *Études d'Histoire Politique et Religieuse*.

4. This latter review formed the basis of an editorial article entitled 'A New Religion' in the American magazine *The Nation* (June 1866), this being the first full account of the religion of the Báb to appear in North America.*

5. The Parisian periodical *Revue Critique d'Histoire et de Littérature* published a review of the book by H. Zotenberg (q.v.) (June 1866).

6. In August 1868, a series of three papers entitled 'Le Babysme' appeared in *Le Temps* of Paris by Michel Nicolas (q.v.), Professor in the Faculty of Protestant Theology at Montauban.

7. Baron von Kremer (q.v.) in his *Geschichte der herrschenden Ideen des Islams*, published in 1868, drew on the works of both Gobineau and Kazem-Beg for a chapter entitled 'Bâb und seine Lehre'.

8. One of four important articles to appear in 1869 was a 134-page review by the French philosopher, F. Pillon (q.v.), in *L'Année Philosophique*. Although based on the works of Gobineau, Kazem-Beg and Franck, it is Gobineau who predominates.

9. In the USA, a much lengthier account than the one published in *The Nation* appeared in the January 1869 edition of *Hours at Home*, a family magazine with a large circulation, published in New York. The article was entitled 'Bab and Babism' and was by Prof. Edward P. Evans (q.v.), Professor of Modern Languages at the University of Michigan. This article is based on the writings of Gobineau, Kazem-Beg and Michel Nicolas. It begins: 'It is a singular fact, that during the last quarter of century there should have sprung up in Central Asia a new religion which already numbers its adherents by millions . . . and that, nevertheless Christendom should have remained almost as ignorant of this great event as if it had taken place in the moon or among the inhabitants of another planet . . .'†[52]

* According to W. F. Poole and W. I. Fletcher *An Index to Periodical Literature* (p. 84), this article was written by Rev. James T. Bixby (see p. 329). Although Bixby did write articles in *New World* (1897) and in *North American Review* (1912) – see Bibliography – it would seem unlikely to the editor that this much earlier article was by the same person.

† The American missionary, Rev. Edwin E. Bliss, of Constantinople, wrote an article which appeared in

The article contains the following significant statement: 'Babism, in fact, has passed through all the phases of the other great historic religions, and is entitled henceforth to a place by the side of them.'[53]

10. Britain, too, was not lacking in writers who took note of Gobineau's book. In the 17 July 1869 issue of *All the Year Round*, the famous magazine 'conducted' by Charles Dickens, an article appeared entitled 'A New Religion'.*

11. A more detailed look at the new religion was undertaken by Rev. R. K. Arbuthnot in a 41-page article in the August and October 1869 issues of *Contemporary Review*.† Once again the main source is Gobineau with a few passages taken from Kazem-Beg.

12. Dr Herman Ethé's book *Essays und Studien* (1872) contains a 61-page chapter entitled 'Ein Moderner Prophet des Morgenlandes', based principally on Gobineau (but also Kazem-Beg, Vámbéry and Wright.)

13. In the same year as Ethé's book, there appeared an article in the June issue of the *Church Missionary Intelligencer* entitled 'The Babys' and based entirely on Gobineau's book.

14. To Gobineau also must go much of the credit for having inspired the first poem composed in a Western tongue in honour of the new religion. *Gurret-ül-Eyn: Ein Bild aus Persiens Neuzeit* (1874) is an epic poem by Marie von Najmájer (q.v., see fig. 10) on Ṭáhirih.

So great was the interest which Gobineau's book aroused, and so famous did the name of the Báb become, that at a lecture delivered before the Birmingham and Midland Institute on 16 October 1871,‡ the writer and critic Matthew Arnold was able to state:

> Count Gobineau, formerly Minister of France at Teheran and at Athens, published a few years ago, an interesting book on the present state of religion and philosophy in Central Asia . . . His accomplishments and intelligence deserve all respect, and in his book on religion and philosophy in Central Asia he has the great advantage of writing about things which he has followed with his own observation and inquiry in the countries where they happened. The chief purpose of the book is to give a history of the career of Mirza Ali Mahommed, a Persian religious reformer, the original Bâb, and the founder of Bâbism, *of which most people in England have at least heard the name* . . . [italics added][54]

---

the May 1869 issue of the *Missionary Herald* (see p. 192). This was a retort to Prof. Evans's article, which had commented on the fact that no missionary magazine had mentioned the new religion.

* This article does not appear in the list of articles contributed to the magazine by Charles Dickens himself (see P. Fitzgerald *Memories of Charles Dickens*).

† In the *Wellesley Index to Victorian Periodicals (1824–1900)* (ed. W. E. Houghton) the author of this article is given as Arbuthnot, Sir Robert Keith, 2nd Baronet (1801–73), Bombay civil servant. But, since on the cover of this magazine it quite clearly states *Rev.* R. K. Arbuthnot, the editor is of the opinion that the author of this article was Rev. Robert Keith Arbuthnot (q.v.).

‡ This lecture was printed as an article in *The Cornhill Magazine* (1871) and in the third edition of Arnold's *Essays in Criticism* (1884). See Bibliography.

Nor did the influence of Gobineau's book last for just a few years after its publication. In 1885, the *Contemporary Review* published an article entitled 'The Story of the Bâb' by Mary F. Wilson, based on Gobineau's book. This article was reproduced in the American periodicals, *Littel's Living Age* and the *Eclectic Magazine*, in the same year. Towards the end of the nineteenth century, interest in Gobineau was rekindled chiefly through the efforts of Ludwig Schemann and his Gobineau Society. Schemann's interests were principally racist but in the course of this general reawakening of interest in Gobineau, a third edition of *Religions et Philosophies* was published in 1900. This edition was reviewed by Barbier de Meynard (q.v.) in *Journal Asiatique* (1899), by G. Maspéro (q.v.) in *Journal des Savants* (1900), by F. Justi (q.v.) in *Archiv für Religionswissenschaft* (1901) and by several others.

Lastly, Gobineau's book was the means whereby the interest of Edward G. Browne was aroused, and led to his extensive researches. Its effect on A.-L.-M. Nicolas was similar if for a different reason. Browne knew virtually nothing about the Bábís when he came across Gobineau's book, and its graphic and stirring account aroused his interest; Nicolas, who had spent the greater part of his life in Persia, knew about the new religion already, and Gobineau's book aroused him to put pen to paper to expose the work's many inadequacies.

Mírzá Kazem-Beg

The distinction of having been the first to have an entire book on the Bábí religion published in the West belongs to Mírzá Kazem-Beg (q.v., see fig. 1) of the University of St Petersburg. It appeared in 1865, under the title *Bab i Babidy*, and was written in Russian. The following year, he published a lengthy French version of this treatise in the *Journal Asiatique* (322 pages spread out between the April–May, June, August–September, and October–November 1866 issues).

Kazem-Beg's sources as listed by him at the beginning of the article are:
1. *Násikhu't-Taváríkh*, of which Kazem-Beg appears to have had access only to the main volume (which carries events to 1851) and not to the supplement (which describes the attempt on the life of the Sháh in 1852).
2. The manuscript history of Shaykh Ṭabarsí by Shaykhu'l-'Ajam procured by Dorn, which Kazem-Beg considers to be of no historical value.
3. Two memoranda on the Bábís, one by a pupil of his called Sevrugin, Dragoman of the Russian Legation of Ṭihrán, who had been in Persia for twenty years (this was communicated to Kazem-Beg by Khanykov), and the other by Mochenin, Dragoman of the Russian Consulate-General in Tabríz, a former pupil of the University of St Petersburg who had been

travelling in Persia during the Bábí upheavals (communicated by Mochenin himself).

An article that appears to have been inspired by Kazem-Beg's writing alone is A. de Bellecombe's * 'Une Réformatrice Contemporaine: La Belle Kourret oul Ain, ou La Lumière des Yeux' (in *L'Investigateur* 1870), one of the first of many monographs that have appeared over the years on the Bábí heroine Ṭáhirih.†

Travellers

In 1862, there arrived in Persia, as physician to an Italian diplomatic Mission, a man who was in his later years to achieve considerable eminence: Michele Lessona (q.v.). According to his own statement, Lessona met there a Persian of high lineage named Dávud Khán who spoke Italian.[55] From this man, Lessona learnt of the Bábís. Lessona also met and conversed with Gobineau, as well as visiting some of the places connected with Bábí history. Lessona returned to Italy, and in about 1870 he wrote a 66-page book entitled *I Babi*, which was printed years later in 1881 by Vincenzo Bona of Turin. Much of the book appears to be derived from Gobineau's work, but, writing from personal experience, Lessona recalls the difficulty of obtaining information about the Bábís in Persia:

> . . . In Persia it is impossible to speak of the Bábís or to learn something about their affairs. The terror which this name awakens is such that no one dares to speak, or even think, of it. The Italians whom I found in Ṭihrán, and who proved extremely kind in every way, wanted to tell me little or nothing about the Bábís, or were unable to do so; the same was true of Europeans of other nationality in Ṭihrán, Tabríz or Rasht. Nicolas,‡ with whom I made the long journey from Ṭihrán to St Petersburg, started to speak to me about them only after we passed the Persian frontier . . . Count de Gobineau, in the village of Gezer near Ṭihrán, would narrate to me episodes about this sect, making the hours of the evening pass as lightning while he wrote its history and read to me some chapters . . . Gathering material for the history of the Báb, which he was doing at the time, was fraught with danger in the heart of Persia, even for a Minister of the French Emperor . . .[56]

In 1870, a Polish traveller, Jablonowski (q.v.), met the Bahá'ís of Baghdád and wrote two articles about the new religion (see Bibliography). He was particularly impressed by the advancement in the social position of women among the Bahá'ís.

In about 1875, a Spaniard named Adolfo Rivadneyra travelled through Persia. He had, somehow, managed to have himself accredited as Spanish

* In this article, Bellecombe is described as 'Président de la 1re classe' of L'Institut Historique de France.

† Even earlier was a very short notice in the Italian periodical *Rivista Orientale* (1st year, Firenze, 1 Oct. 1867, p. 829) entitled 'Eroine persiane' and evidently drawn from another source in which Polak is cited.

‡ J. B. Nicolas (q.v.)

Consul in Persia although Spain had no formal diplomatic ties with Persia at this time. In the description of his wanderings through Persia, *Viaje al Interior de Persia*, he devotes some 10 pages to the religion of the Báb. Once again, the main authority referred to is Gobineau for, as the author states: 'In order to give an idea of the fear that, even today, the Bábís, who are to be found all over Iran, inspire in the people, it is enough to say that even I, a European, would not dare to speak aloud the name of the sect in public, for fear of thus starting an immediate conflict.

'It is, indeed, a shame that the apostles of the new Messiah did not act prudently, otherwise they would certainly have triumphed . . .'[57]

Madame Carla Serena visited Persia in 1877–8. She journeyed from Anzalí to Ṭihrán and back to Anzalí. Despite the brevity of her stay and the limited extent of her journeying, her book *Hommes et Choses en Perse* is both interesting and detailed, covering many aspects of Persian life. Seventeen pages of her book are devoted to the Bábís. In a footnote she states: 'A great deal of the details of the history of the Bábís from 1847 to 1852 were given to me by a Persian who was an eyewitness to the events that took place in Ṭihrán, when the sectaries were executed.'[58] Nevertheless, it would appear that most of her information is derived from Gobineau's book.

In 1880–81, Monsieur and Madame Dieulafoy travelled through Persia. M. Dieulafoy was an engineer who had been commissioned by the French Ministry of Education to study the ancient monuments of Persia. Mme Jane Dieulafoy (q.v., see fig. 2) wrote a lengthy account of their journey, which appeared firstly as a series of articles in the periodical *Tour du Monde* (1883–5) and later as a book *La Perse, la Chaldée et la Susiane*. While in Zanján, Mme Dieulafoy came into contact with the Bahá'ís there. In her account of this, she gives a history of the early days of the Bábí religion drawn from Gobineau. In giving the later history, she states that the head of the religion is now residing in 'Akká, but she erroneously gives his name as Mírzá Yaḥyá – no doubt under the influence of Gobineau. She makes, moreover, the following surprising statement:

> Last year, Náṣiru'd-Dín S͟háh, fearing the growing influence of the leader of the Bábís, wanted to attempt a reconciliation with [Bahá'u'lláh] and secretly sent to him one of his Imám-Jum'ihs, who was most renowned for the force of his theological arguments and the firmness of his beliefs, on a mission to return the stray sheep to the fold. I will leave you to imagine what was the surprise and indignation of the sovereign when, on his return, the venerable Imám-Jum'ih avowed to his master that the arguments of [Bahá'u'lláh] had convinced him and led him to the path of truth. Following such a success, one can easily understand why the S͟háh has not sent a second ambassador to 'Akká.[59]

Such an episode is not recorded in any Bahá'í histories, and unfortunately Mme Dieulafoy does not state from whom she heard this. While in Zanján, the Dieulafoys stayed with a Bahá'í named Muḥammad Áqá Khán, and in the book there are two drawings, entitled 'Jeune Fille Baby' and 'Jeune Fille Baby de Zendjan'.[60]

One further traveller whose writings about the Bábís are of some interest is F. C. Andreas (q.v.), who was in Persia in the late 1870s. In 1896, he published a booklet entitled *Die Babis in Persien*. This account is a useful if not always accurate summary, bringing the history of the movement to about 1880. It tends to perpetuate the idea of Siyyid Jamálu'd-Dín-i-Afghání being in some way connected with the movement. Perhaps the most interesting part of the booklet is an all-too-brief account of Bahá'í community life in Persia in the 1890s,[61] communicated to Andreas by Pastor Christian Közle, a German missionary. The book is important mainly for the wide attention that it received, for it was extensively reviewed in German magazines, and its contents were noted as far away as Finland, in an article in the periodical *Valvoja* (1897) by R. Kojanen.

E. G. Browne

It is impossible in a work of this nature to review adequately the enormous contributions made by Prof. Browne (q.v., see fig. 4) to the study of the religion of the Báb and Bahá'u'lláh. There already exists moreover such a work, Balyuzi's *Edward Granville Browne and the Bahá'í Faith*.

Edward Granville Browne first became interested in the religion of the Báb when he accidentally came across the passages in Gobineau's book dealing with this subject. He immediately became intensely interested and indeed devoted the first six years of his career as an orientalist to its study. One of the most important objectives of his journey to Persia in 1887–8 became to contact the Bábís. The story of how he was surprised to discover that the overwhelming majority of the Bábís had become followers of Bahá'u'lláh, the journey in 1890 that resulted in his meeting with both Bahá'u'lláh and Mírzá Yaḥyá, Ṣubḥ-i-Azal, his alignment with the followers of Mírzá Yaḥyá, and the disappointing nature of his later works are fully dealt with by Balyuzi.

The following is a list of Browne's works on the Bábí-Bahá'í religion:

Books entirely on the subject

1. *A Traveller's Narrative written to illustrate the Episode of the Báb* Cambridge 1891.

Vol. 1: Persian text of this book by 'Abdu'l-Bahá, in the handwriting of Zaynu'l-Muqarrabín. Vol. 2: Browne's translation of the book, preceded by a lengthy and important Introduction. After the text there are a total of 26 Notes, occupying more than half the volume and dealing with a wide variety of subjects. This second volume is the one to which the References of the present work refer as *A Traveller's Narrative.*

2. *The Táríkh-i-Jadíd or New History of Mírzá 'Alí Muḥammad the Báb* Cambridge 1893.

A translation of this history by Mírzá Ḥusayn of Hamadán. The Appendices include abridgements of the digressions omitted in the translation, a comparison with the *Nuqṭatu'l-Káf*, the text and translation of a narrative by Ṣubḥ-i-Azal, and some facsimile original documents.

3. *Kitáb-i-Nuqṭatu'l-Káf* Vol. 15 of the E. J. W. Gibb Memorial Series, Leyden 1910.

The Persian text of this work attributed by Browne to Ḥájí Mírzá Jání. There is a lengthy Introduction in English and an even lengthier one in Persian (the latter being almost certainly the work of Mírzá Muḥammad Khán-i-Qazvíní*). There is also an index of the contents of the Persian *Bayán.*

4. *Materials for the Study of the Bábí Religion* Cambridge 1918.

A conglomeration of eleven unrelated sections. Much of the book is of dubious value, but parts such as the contemporary documents and state papers, and the accounts of recent Bahá'í persecutions, are of great importance.

BOOKS WITH IMPORTANT REFERENCES TO THE SUBJECT

1. *A Year Amongst the Persians* London 1893, reprinted Cambridge 1926.

Gives an account of his journey in Persia in 1887–8 and paints a vivid description of the Bahá'í community in Persia, as well as giving certain important historical facts.

2. *The Persian Revolution of 1905–1909* Cambridge 1910.

Contains a note entitled 'Attitude of Bahá'ís towards Persian Politics' (pp. 424–9), which includes translations of three tablets of 'Abdu'l-Bahá on the subject.

3. *A Supplementary Handlist of Muḥammadan Manuscripts preserved in the libraries of the University and Colleges of Cambridge* Cambridge 1922.

Contains references to five manuscripts relating to the Bábí-Bahá'í religion (pp. 35, 239, 240).

* Balyuzi, in *Edward Granville Browne and the Bahá'í Faith*, has pointed out serious discrepancies between the English and Persian Introductions, indicating that they were written by two different people, and each without knowledge of what the other had written. Qazvíní himself admits to his own authorship of the Persian Introduction in an article written by him for the magazine *Yádgár* – see Bibliography. There exist, moreover (in private hands), three letters, dated 3 Oct. 1910, 13 and 19 Jan. 1911, from Qazvíní to Browne clearly indicating that the former was writing an Introduction for *Nuqṭatu'l-Káf.*

4. *A Literary History of Persia* Vol. 4 *Modern Times (1500–1924)* published Cambridge 1924, under the title *A History of Persian Literature in Modern Times (A.D. 1500–1924)*.

Contains a brief analysis of Bábí-Bahá'í poetry, together with the text and translation of a lengthy poem by Na'ím (pp. 194–220).

ARTICLES AND PAPERS

1. 'The Bábís of Persia'. I: Sketch of their History, and Personal Experiences amongst them. II: Their Literature and Doctrines.* *Journal of the Royal Asiatic Society* Vol. 21, London 1889, pp. 485–526 and 881–1009.

The results of Browne's researches during his journey to Persia in 1887–8. Very valuable.

2. 'Bábism'. An article contributed to *Religious Systems of the World* (2nd, 1892, and later edns) 8th edn, 1905, pp. 333–53.

Perhaps Browne's best summary of the Bábí and Bahá'í religions, although a popular work.

3. 'Some Remarks on the Bábí Texts edited by Baron Victor Rosen' *Journal of the Royal Asiatic Society* Vol. 24, London 1892, pp. 259–332.

4. 'Catalogue and description of 27 Bábí Manuscripts' *Journal of the Royal Asiatic Society* Vol. 24, London 1892, pp. 433–99 and pp. 637–710.

5. 'Personal Reminiscences of the Bábí Insurrection at Zanján in 1850' *Journal of the Royal Asiatic Society* Vol. 29, London 1897, pp. 761–827.

Some reminiscences of one of Azal's followers, Áqá 'Abdu'l-Aḥad.

6. Introduction to M. H. Phelps *Abbas Effendi: His Life and Teachings* New York 1903.

7. 'Báb, Bábís'. An article contributed to Hastings *Encyclopaedia of Religion and Ethics* Vol. 2, Edinburgh 1909, pp. 299–308.

8. 'Bábíism'. An article contributed to *Encyclopaedia Britannica* 11th edn, Vol. 3, Cambridge 1910, pp. 94–5.

OTHER MINOR REFERENCES IN ARTICLES, ETC.

1. The London newspaper *Daily News* (30 October 1891, p. 5) and the periodical *Pall Mall Gazette* (26 November 1891, p. 3) carried accounts of the episode of the Seven Martyrs of Yazd (see p. 304).

2. *The Times* on 6 May 1896 (p. 4), the *Daily News* on 12 May 1896 (p. 5) and the periodical *New Review* (Vol. 14, June 1896, pp. 651–9) published letters from Browne refuting the idea that Náṣiru'd-Dín S͟háh's assassin was a Bahá'í (see p. 360).

3. Review of Tumanski's text and translation of the *Kitábu'l-Aqdas* in

* The first paper was read before the Royal Asiatic Society on 15 Apr. 1889, the second on 17 June 1889. Following the reading of the second paper, there was a lengthy discussion which is reported in *Jour. Roy. Asiat. Soc.* Vol. 21, 1889, pp. 698–706.

Journal of the Royal Asiatic Society London 1900, pp. 354–7.
4. Two papers read before the Persia Society: *The Literature of Persia* London 1912, references on pp. 33–4, and *The Religious Influence of Persia* London 1914, references on pp. 71–2.
5. *The Press and Poetry of Modern Persia* Cambridge 1914, brief references to, for example, *Star of the West* on p. 59.
6. 'The Persian Constitutional Movement' *Proceedings of the British Academy* Vol. 8, London 1917–18, brief reference on p. 316. Also printed separately.
7. 'Sir 'Abdu'l-Baha 'Abbas' *Journal of the Royal Asiatic Society* London 1922, pp. 145–6. An obituary.

Posthumous Works

1. *A Persian Anthology* London 1927.
Edited by E. D. Ross, with an introductory memoir by J. B. Atkins. pp. 70–73.
2. *A Descriptive Catalogue of the Oriental Manuscripts belonging to the Late E. G. Browne* Cambridge 1932.
A work commenced by Browne himself and completed by R. A. Nicholson; pp. 53–87 deal with Browne's 'Shaykhí and Bábí manuscripts'.

The most striking aspect of Browne's work on the Bábí-Bahá'í movement when viewed as a whole is the way in which his initial excitement and enthusiasm as reflected in his articles for the *Journal of the Royal Asiatic Society* in 1889 and his *A Traveller's Narrative* become transformed into the more cynical, even hostile approach of his later works, most notably his introduction to *Nuqṭatu'l-Káf* and his *Materials for the Study of the Bábí Religion.* Indeed the usefulness of his later works is marred by his preoccupation with reviving a dispute which was long since over. Almost twenty years before Browne's interest in this subject was aroused, Bahá'u'lláh had put forward the claim to be 'He Whom God shall make manifest', foretold by the Báb. The vast majority of Bábís, including the survivors amongst the Báb's Letters of the Living, those of the Báb's own family who were believers, and the majority of the most eminent believers surviving, accepted this claim and rejected the feeble, uninspiring leadership of Mírzá Yaḥyá, Ṣubḥ-i-Azal. Thus at a time when the Bahá'í religion was going on from strength to strength and attaining the character of a world religion, when it was gaining adherents in Europe and North America, when its leader 'Abdu'l-Bahá was being acclaimed by leading religious, political and intellectual personalities in the West (stunning progress for an obscure movement that had been almost annihilated by the state and clergy of Persia only fifty years previously), Browne was still doggedly pursuing sterile and irrelevant arguments. Why did Browne decide to champion the cause of Mírzá Yaḥyá? Among the reasons must be:

1. The fact that Browne's first contact with the Bábí movement came through his reading of Gobineau's book, a work that he admired greatly. In this book, the history of the movement is carried up to the time when the leading Bábís were gathered in Baghdád following the attempt on the life of the Sháh. At this point, Mírzá Yaḥyá was the designated leader of the Bábís, and Gobineau's informants appear to have greatly embellished their accounts of him. Hence the surprise and even dismay expressed in his *A Year Amongst the Persians*[62] when Browne discovered that in the intervening years a revolution had occurred among the Bábís, so that there was no longer any mention of the man of whom Gobineau had written such glowing accounts.

2. Browne's growing commitment to liberal reform and the Constitutional Movement in Persia increasingly occupied his time and energies, so that everything was now judged from this point of view. Browne was particularly disappointed when 'Abdu'l-Bahá instructed the Bahá'ís not to become entangled in the politics of this era. To Browne it seemed that the very movement that had initiated and led the way towards reform in Persia was now turning its back on the process as the final struggle began.

3. In contrast to the Bahá'ís, the followers of Ṣubḥ-i-Azal were keen advocates, and even some of the most prominent leaders, of the reform movement. And so, as Browne became increasingly involved with reform, his contacts with the Azalís correspondingly multiplied and became more important to him. They, in turn, fed Browne with such works as *Hasht Bihisht*, which, from Browne's summary of its contents,[63] appears to have been written primarily to cast aspersions on and vilify Bahá'u'lláh and the Bahá'ís. Although Browne quite clearly stated that he did not have any evidence to support the statements in *Hasht Bihisht*, nor was it in keeping with what he himself had observed when with Bahá'u'lláh and among the Bahá'ís,[64] yet he still put these charges into print, and they must inevitably have prejudiced his views to an extent.

4. In April 1892, Browne chanced upon one of the manuscripts that the Bibliothèque Nationale of Paris had purchased from among the effects of Gobineau. The title of this work was *Nuqṭatu'l-Káf* but its author was not indicated. Browne sent a description of the manuscript to Mírzá Yaḥyá who speculatively identified it as the history written by Ḥájí Mírzá Jání on the rather weak grounds that 'none but he wrote (such) a history'.[65] Neither the fact that even among the Azalís no one possessed a copy of this work to which he ascribed such importance, nor the presence of much internal evidence in the manuscript to disprove the idea that its author was Ḥájí

Mírzá Jání* seems to have worried Browne. On this shaky basis, he built a monumental case seeking to discredit Bahá'u'lláh and establish Mírzá Yaḥyá's claim to leadership.

5. One of the features of the English which manifested itself *par excellence* in Browne, is their compulsion to sympathize with and support the losing side, the underdogs. It had indeed been this characteristic which had first drawn Browne into Oriental studies when he was a medical student. In *A Year Amongst the Persians* he writes:

> It was the Turkish war with Russia in 1877–8 that first attracted my attention to the East, about which, till that time I had known and cared nothing ... At first my proclivities were by no means for the Turks; but the losing side, more especially when it continues to struggle gallantly against defeat, always has a claim on our sympathy ... Ere the close of the war I would have died to save Turkey, and I mourned the fall of Plevna as though it had been a disaster inflicted on my own country. And so gradually pity turned to admiration, and admiration to enthusiasm, until the Turks became in my eyes veritable heroes, and the desire to identify myself with their cause ... possessed me heart and soul.[66]

One can discern the same course of events in Browne's 'heart and soul' with regard to the Azalís, who were very much the minority and the 'underdog'. As early as his sojourn in Persia in 1887–8, there was an episode that indicated Browne's feelings on the matter. Following a completely uncalled-for and vehement outburst against Mírzá Yaḥyá by certain Bahá'ís in Kirmán, Browne jumped to the defence of the Azalís: 'I was at first utterly taken aback and somewhat alarmed at their vehemence, but anger at the unjust and intolerant attitude towards the Ezelís which they took up presently came to my aid, and I reminded them that such violence and unfairness, so far from proving their case, could only make it appear the weaker.'[67]

6. The passage quoted above suggests that the attitude of some of the Bahá'ís themselves may have contributed to Browne's disenchantment. J. B. Atkins's memoir on Browne also points to this: 'From what he [Browne] told me I judge that the essential nobility of Babiism in its first form would have made a much deeper mark on his life if later developments

* Thus for example throughout the manuscript the author refers to himself several times as 'this wretched one', whereas in other places on at least three occasions, Ḥájí Mírzá Jání is referred to by name. Ḥájí Mírzá Jání fell a martyr during the holocaust following the attempt on the life of the S͟háh in 1852, and yet towards the end of the *Nuqṭatu'l-Káf*, its author states that the Bábí religion had numerous adherents in Istanbul, which would have been fallacious during Ḥájí Mírzá Jání's own lifetime and indeed was not true until about 1866, which is, of course, also the date of the rupture between Bahá'u'lláh and Mírzá Yaḥyá. Even more convincingly, at one point in the manuscript (p. 92 of the published text) the author gives the date current at the time that that passage was being written as being 1270/1853 – the year following Ḥájí Mírzá Jání's death. The date is given in words, moreover, rather than figures, making it less likely that there could have been any copying error.

of the faith, and the defects of some of the Babis he knew, had not disappointed him. Although he was entranced by the luxuriant imagery in the conversation of most of the Babis he met in Southern Persia, and was drugged by the subtlety of their philosophical and theological speculations, he was nevertheless conscious of a certain disgust at their vainglorious assumption of divinity – helped as it was by wine and opium-smoking.* He was at once fascinated and repelled.'[68]

7. There is no doubt that Browne came under some considerable criticism and pressure for spending so much time on what many people considered to be an unimportant subject. This may be the reason why J. B. Atkins, in his memoir on Browne, comments that Browne, although a noted conversationalist, 'would not often talk about Babiism at Pembroke except in the presence of a very few friends.'[69]

Some of the criticism was no doubt kindly, such as that of Sir Denison Ross (q.v.) who wrote: 'E.G.B. at that time was almost entirely engrossed in research into the origin and history of the Babi religion. It is a matter for regret that he should have devoted so many years to the minutest inquiries into this subject.'[70] But some of the strictures were harsh and disparaging, notably the *Oxford Magazine's* review of his book *A Traveller's Narrative*. The writer of this review (who was known to Browne) in less than one page had made the following stinging comments:

> The whole is set out with a laborious minuteness and impartiality which is worthy of a more important investigation.
>
> For speaking candidly as laymen, we must own that the history of a recent sect which has affected the least important part of the Moslem world (nor that part very deeply) and is founded on a personal claim which will not bear investigation for a moment, seems to us quite unworthy of the learning and labour which the author has brought to bear upon it. An *ex parte* statement of trivial history, a record of not very momentous experiences in easily accessible places like Famagusta and Acre, and a laborious and indiscriminate collection of very recent evidence, are hardly atoned for by a few really interesting and valuable notes on points of Shi'ite observance and doctrine. The whole presentation of the subject smacks unpleasantly of book-making; the author seems determined in his Introduction to elevate his theme to the dignity of an epoch-making religious movement, on the principle of '*omne ignotum pro magnifico*'; and to that end adopts a personal attitude almost inconceivable in a rational European, and a style unpardonable in a University teacher . . .
>
> As Mr Browne seems to have been 'struck all of a heap' whenever he met any prominent Babí whatever, he had an exceedingly emotional time in Cyprus and Syria . . .
>
> There are no signs that Mirza Ali Muhammad will leave any permanent mark on religious or political history . . . we can

* Much of this passage refers to the Azalís and some of the Bahá'ís of Kirmán. The vast majority of the Bahá'ís of Persia were obedient to the command of Bahá'u'lláh prohibiting both wine and opium, and Browne found no Bahá'ís contravening this in any town other than Kirmán. It was in Kirmán that Browne himself became addicted to opium under the influence of the Azalís there. This fact probably increased his repulsion to the whole episode in Kirmán.

only record our belief that the prominence given to the 'Báb' in this book is an absurd violation of historical perspective; and the translation of the *Traveller's Narrative* a waste of the powers and opportunities of a Persian scholar.[71]

This review stung Browne to the quick.* J. B. Atkins in his memoir on Browne writes:† 'one reviewer caused Browne considerable distress by a severe attack upon the manner of the book, especially the introduction, which he found "unbecoming" in a University teacher. Browne humorously worked off his feelings by constructing a hideous little image of cork, which he placed on his chimney-piece, calling it by the name of the reviewer and for some time pouring upon it daily execrations.'[72]

Even a decade later, as pointed out by Balyuzi,[73] Browne was still smarting from this review; in his introduction to Phelps's *Abbas Effendi: His Life and Teachings*, he commented revealingly: 'Increasing age and experience, (more's the pity!) are apt enough, even without the assistance of the *Oxford Magazine*, to modify our enthusiasms . . .'[74]

It would seem likely that such comments were at least partially responsible for Browne's decreasing interest in, and somewhat hostile attitude towards, the Bahá'ís in later years. They may also have resulted in Browne dropping certain publications in the field of Bábí and Bahá'í studies, on which he had already done some considerable work – for instance a collated text of the Persian *Bayán* on which he was working in 1892.[75]

A.-L.-M. Nicolas

No European scholar has contributed so much to our knowledge of the life and teachings of the Báb as Nicolas (q.v., see fig. 5). His study of the life of the Báb and his translations of several of the most important books of the Báb remain of unsurpassed value.

Nicolas's father, J. B. Nicolas (q.v.), was in the French Consular Service in Persia, and Nicolas himself was born at Rasht in Gílán in 1864. According to his own statement, he could speak Persian and Russian even before he learnt his native French.[76] Like his father, he joined the French Consular Service and spent most of his working life in Persia.

Nicolas, also, derived his inspiration to study the Bábís from Gobineau, but in a manner almost exactly opposite to Browne. According to a state-

* In most quarters, however, Browne's book was favourably received. Among those who praised Browne's work were Barbier de Meynard (*Journal Asiatique* 8th ser., Vol. 20, 1892, pp. 297–302), Vámbéry (*The Academy* 12 Mar. 1892, pp. 245–6), Rubens Duval (*Revue Critique* n.s., Vol. 34, 1892, pp. 77–9), Paul Horn (*Literarisches Zentralblatt* 23 July 1892, pp. 1043–4) and Ethé (*Deutsche Literaturzeitung* 13th year, 30 July 1892, pp. 1014–5). There were also favourable notices in the *Spectator* (23 April 1892, Vol. 68, pp. 560–1) and *Athenaeum* (28 May 1892, pp. 690–1).

† Atkins writes this comment in relation to *A Year Amongst the Persians*, but there is no doubt from the context that he is in fact referring to the *Oxford Magazine* review of *A Traveller's Narrative*.

ment made by Nicolas, his father had clashed with Gobineau:

> Gobineau, arriving at the Legation, imbued with diplomatic prejudices, despising his colleagues, entered into an argument with my father on the subject of a manuscript bought by the latter from a courtier.* My father made some remarks about this which turned my thoughts towards the idea of verifying for myself the background of the matter. Among his papers, he left a critique of Gobineau's book *Les Religions et Les Philosophies dans l'Asie Centrale*, which encouraged me to do some research and refute its errors, this work having been written without sufficient data with the aid of a Jew† that Gobineau had as a teacher of Persian, who could only teach his pupil the little that he knew of the sect. I collected my material largely from a native secretary,‡ Mírzá Ibráhím of Ṭihrán, who I discovered to be a Bahá'í and who put me in touch with the followers of the sect.[77]

Nicolas in the same statement goes on to describe how his interest in the subject grew:

> I was helped in my work by a young Persian, and each day we would go in the afternoon for a walk outside the town, leaving by the Shimrán gate. The purity of the air, the serenity, the mildness of the temperature, and in certain seasons, the perfume of the acacias, predisposed my soul to peace and gentleness. My reflections on the strange book [*The Seven Proofs* by the Báb] that I had translated, filled me with a kind of intoxication and I became, little by little, profoundly and uniquely a Bábí. The more I immersed myself in these reflections, the more I admired the greatness of the genius of him who, born in Shíráz, had dreamt of uplifting the Muslim world . . .[78]

In his early works, Nicolas steered clear of the barren ground over which Browne was wandering – the claims of Mírzá Yaḥyá, Ṣubḥ-i-Azal. In a letter to Browne in March 1902, he wrote concerning the documents which he had collected: 'Only those which are directly related to the Báb interest me at this time; whether they concern the history or the dogma. I consider that task sufficient for the moment, and I will concern myself later with the Imamate of Ṣubḥ-i-Azal and the second divine Manifestation in the person of Bahá.'[79]

This first phase of Nicolas's work may be considered to have been completed in 1914 by the publication of the last volume of *Le Béyan Persan*. After this there is a hiatus, and when Nicolas began writing again on this subject, in 1933, his articles were very obviously hostile and bitter towards the Bahá'ís and, although not strongly advocating the claims of Mírzá Yaḥyá in the way that Browne did, Nicolas was obviously not unfavourable to them.

The main reason for Nicolas's hostility to the Bahá'ís at this time appears

* Gobineau describes J. B. Nicolas as 'un drôle' – a rascal (letter to his sister, see Hytier *Les Dépêches Diplomatiques* p. 148n).

† Mullá Lálizár of Hamadán.

‡ Presumably at the French Legation.

to have been twofold. Firstly he seems to have acquired a profound dislike for 'Abdu'l-Bahá's historical work *A Traveller's Narrative*, and he loses no opportunity to attack this. But secondly, and much more importantly, Nicolas was deeply hurt at the disparagement and neglect that he felt the Bahá'ís showed towards the Báb. Nicolas considered that in *A Traveller's Narrative* and other Bahá'í works, the Báb's station and importance had been belittled, making him but the insignificant forerunner, the John the Baptist, of Bahá'u'lláh.

Towards the end of Nicolas's life, however, he was sent copies of two important works by Shoghi Effendi: a translation of Nabíl's Narrative of the life of the Báb, and *The Dispensation of Bahá'u'lláh*, in which the Báb's station as an independent Messenger of God equal in essence to Bahá'u'lláh is stated emphatically. Nicolas was, of course, overjoyed. To the lady who sent him these books, Miss Edith Sanderson, he wrote:

> I do not know how to thank you nor how to express the joy that floods my heart. So, it is necessary not only to admit but to love and admire the Báb. Poor great Prophet, born in the heart of Persia, without any means of instruction, and who, alone in the world, encircled by enemies, succeeds by the force of his genius in creating a universal and wise religion. That Bahá'u'lláh succeeded him eventually may be, but I want people to admire the sublimity of the Báb, who has, moreover, paid with his life, with his blood, for the reforms he preached. Cite me another similar example. At last, I can die in peace. Glory be to Shoghi Effendi who has calmed my torment and my anxieties, glory be to him who recognizes the worth of Siyyid 'Alí-Muḥammad, the Báb.
>
> I am so happy that I kiss your hands that have written my address on the envelope which carried Shoghi's message. Thank you, Mademoiselle; thank you from the depths of my heart.[80]

It is difficult to be certain that the following list represents the entirety of Nicolas's writing on the subject of the Bábí and Bahá'í religions, as he makes reference to a few works which the present author has been unable to trace and therefore assumes were never printed.*

HISTORY

Seyyèd Ali Mohammed dit le Bâb Paris 1905. 458 pp.

A history of the Bábí movement up to 1852. Nicolas gives a list of sources for this book on pp. 48–53. It is interesting to note that among his oral sources are four of the leading Bahá'ís of that period, who had been

* Nicolas apparently published an article entitled *Une Causerie sur le Bâb*, which the editor has been unable to trace. There is also reference in 'Quelque Documents relatif au Bâbisme' (see the following list) to a work that Nicolas had prepared for publication entitled 'La voie doloureuse de Seyyed Ali Mohammad, dit le Bâb', which he describes as 'crammed with numerous unedited documents', but which no editor had accepted. The article 'Quelque Documents' therefore consists of some extracts from this longer work, which presumably was never published.

designated by Bahá'u'lláh as 'Hands of the Cause': Mírzá 'Alí-Muḥammad, Ibn-i-Aṣdaq; Mullá 'Alí-Akbar-i-Shahmírzádí, Ḥájí Ákhúnd; Mírzá Muḥammad-Taqíy-i-Abharí, Ibn-i-Abhar; and Mírzá Ḥasan-i-Adíb. The other two oral sources named are Siyyid Ismu'lláh, who was presumably Siyyid Mihdíy-i-Dihají, and Mírzá Yaḥyá, Ṣubḥ-i-Azal.

TRANSLATIONS OF THE WRITINGS OF THE BÁB

1. *Le Livre des Sept Preuves* Paris 1902. 68 pp.
A translation of the Báb's *Dalá'il-i-Sab'ih.*
2. *Le Béyan Arabe* Paris 1905. 235 pp.
A translation of the Arabic *Bayán.*
3. *Le Béyan Persan* 4 vols., Paris 1911–14.
A translation of the Persian *Bayán.*

MONOGRAPHS

1. *Qui est le successeur du Bab*? Paris 1933. 16 pp.
Written to demonstrate that Mírzá Yaḥyá was the true successor of the Báb.
2. *Massacres de Babis en Perse* Paris 1936. 42 pp.
Accounts of several of the most important persecutions and martyrdoms of the Bábís and Bahá'ís. Quoted extensively in the present work.

ARTICLES

1. 'A propos de deux manuscrits "Babis" de la Bibliothèque Nationale' *Revue de l'Histoire des Religions* Vol. 47, Paris 1903, pp. 58–73.
Concerning the controversial manuscripts of *Nuqṭatu'l-Káf.*
2. 'Sur la Volonté Primitive et l'Essence Divine d'après le Bâb' *Revue de l'Histoire des Religions* Vol. 55, Paris 1907, pp. 208–12.
Abridged version of a lengthy note by Nicolas explaining some of the terms in the Bábí writings.
3. 'Le Club de la fraternité' *Revue du Monde Musulman* Vol. 13, Paris 1911, pp. 180–84.
Translation of an article by Atrpet in the Armenian periodical *Sourhandag* refuting the suggestion that the Bahá'ís played an important part in the constitutional upheavals.
4. 'Le Dossier russo-anglais de Seyyed Ali Mohammed dit le Bâb' *Revue du Monde Musulman* Vol. 14, Paris 1911, pp. 357–63.
Documents found in the British and Russian Consulates in Tabríz relating to the episode of the Báb: frequently quoted in the present work.
5. 'Abdoul-Béha et la situation' *Revue du Monde Musulman* Vol. 21, Paris 1912, pp. 261–7.
Translation of an article in the Persian periodical *Fikr* that contained an

alleged exchange of letters between 'Abdu'l-Bahá and Mírzá Ghaffár Zanúzí. Published under pseudonym 'Ghilan'.

6. 'Le Béhahis et le Bâb' *Journal Asiatique* Vol. 222, Paris 1933, pp. 257–64.

7. 'Quelque Documents relatifs au Babisme' *Journal Asiatique* Vol. 224, Paris 1934, pp. 107–42.

Some extracts from works of the Báb, as well as some Persian Government correspondence.

8. 'Le Bâb astronome' *Revue de l'Histoire des Religions* Vol. 114, Paris 1936, pp. 99–101

Other French Scholars

Apart from Nicolas, there were several other French scholars who took an active interest in the Bábí-Bahá'í religion. Hippolyte Dreyfus was himself a Bahá'í and the author of several books, articles and translations of a high scholarly standard on this subject.

Of the prominent French orientalists, Clément Huart (q.v.) wrote extensively about the new religion. According to one source, Huart studied Persian in Istanbul under Mírzá Áqá Khán-i-Kirmání, who was an Azalí and son-in-law of Mírza Yaḥyá, Ṣubḥ-i-Azal.[81] This would explain the Azalí material that Huart uses in his *La Religion de Bab*.[82] In addition to this work, Huart contributed the entries on 'Báb', 'Bábí' and 'Bahá Alláh' for the *Encyclopaedia of Islam* (1913), wrote several articles, and regularly reviewed every important book on the Bábí-Bahá'í religion that was published. The *Journal Asiatique* has three such reviews between 1909 and 1918; the *Revue de l'Histoire des Religions* has eleven such reviews between 1904 and 1924. (See Bibliography for a partial listing of Huart's writings on this subject.)

Russian Scholars

The two decades 1890–1910 saw a great deal of work being done by orientalists in several different countries on the Bábí and Bahá'í religions. In Britain and France the two principal figures were Browne and Nicolas respectively. These two writers were primarily interested in the events of the ministry of the Báb, and in so far as they dealt with further developments tended to favour Mírzá Yaḥyá. In Russia, however, the emphasis was on the writings of Bahá'u'lláh.

The first of two important Russian scholars to deal extensively with the Bahá'í religion was Baron Victor Rosen (q.v., see fig. 8). He had first dealt with the new religion in 1876–86 when cataloguing the Persian and Arabic manuscripts of the Institute of Oriental Languages of the Russian Foreign

Ministry. These consisted of 4 manuscripts, 2 Bábí and 2 Bahá'í.* Having only Kazem-Beg, Gobineau and similar works before him and having no information on subsequent developments, Rosen had great difficulty in describing Bahá'u'lláh's *Kitáb-i-Íqán* and *Súratu'l-Haykal* in these catalogues. Later, when Browne published his papers on the Bábís and Bahá'ís, Rosen was able to give a fuller account of these and other manuscripts. Rosen went on to publish several important works on this subject, the last, a collection of the tablets of Bahá'u'lláh, being published posthumously.

The second important Russian scholar was Capt. Alexander Tumanski (q.v.), who had, according to his own statements, first heard of the Bahá'ís through an account in Reclus's *Universal Geography*, which he had read while studying for the entrance examination to the officer's course in the military Oriental Languages Training Section. But it was in the winter of 1889–90, when he read an account of the martyrdom of Ḥájí Muḥammad-Riḍá in 'Is͟hqábád and the manner in which the Bahá'ís had intervened on behalf of the murderers (see p. 297), that he determined to investigate the religion more closely. The following summer, he asked special permission to proceed to Transcaspia, and there met the Bahá'ís of 'Is͟hqábád. He names three Bahá'ís as having particularly helped him in his studies of the religion: Mírzá 'Abdu'l-Karím-i-Ardibílí (Asadov), Mírzá Yúsif-i-Ras͟htí and Ustád 'Alí-Akbar.[83] In his later studies, Tumanski came into contact with the greatest of the Bahá'í scholars, Mírzá Abu'l-Faḍl-i-Gulpáygání, and was thus in a position to obtain the most detailed and accurate information regarding the new religion.

This being but a brief survey, only a list of the principal works of these scholars will be given here: (*Zapiski* here denotes the *Zapiski Vostochnago*

* Russian Consular officials seem to have been particularly zealous in collecting important manuscripts. In *Collections Scientifiques Vol. 3: Les Manuscrits Persans* (p. 50), Rosen lists the nine Bábí and Bahá'í manuscripts then in various collections in St Petersburg: four in the Institute of Oriental Languages of the Russian Foreign Office, collected by V. Bezobrazov, Con.-Gen. at Tabríz; one in the Asiatic Museum of the Academy of Sciences, collected by Bakulin, Con. at Astarábád; one in the Imperial Public Library collected by Khanykov, Con. at Tabríz (see p. 16); three belonging to Rosen himself, one of which was obtained by Ivan G. Grigorovitch, 1st Dragoman at Ṭihrán, from the library of 'Alí-Qulí Mírzá, I'taḍádu's-Salṭanih, and two by Vladimir Ignatiev, Sec.-Dragoman at the Astarábád Consulate. There was also the manuscript of the S͟hayk͟h Ṭabarsí upheaval collected by Dorn in the Imperial Public Library (see p. 15). Georgy Batyushkov, who was Russian Con.-Gen. in Beirut and travelled in Persia, wrote with the help of Grigorovitch an article entitled 'Babidy: Persidskaya Sekta'. He also collected a copy of the *Kitábu'l-Aqdas* and a manuscript of Ṭáhirih's works for the Asiatic Museum. Others who helped by supplying information to Russian scholars include A. D. Levitsky, Dragoman of the Astarábád Consulate, P. O. Orlov, Dragoman of the Political Agency at Bukhara, and Melnikov, Secretary of the Ṭihrán Mission. See also Sevrugin and Mochenin (pp. 26–7) and further information about Bakulin (p. 43). Another name that might conveniently be mentioned here is that of M. Gamazov, head of the Oriental Languages Section of the Asiatic Dept. of the Ministry for Foreign Affairs. According to Tumanski, Gamazov was the first person after Mírzá Kazem-Beg to begin to pay attention to the new religion and encourage others to study it.

Otdeleniya Imperatorskago Russkago Arkheologicheskago Obshestva edited by Rosen. Place of publication throughout is St Petersburg.)

ROSEN

1. *Collections Scientifiques de l'Institut des Langues Orientales du Ministère des Affaires Étrangères* Vol. 1 *Manuscrits Arabes* 1877, pp. 179–212; Vol. 3 *Manuscrits Persans* 1886, pp. 1–51; Vol. 6 *Manuscrits Arabes* . . . 1891, pp. 141–255.
2. *Pervuy sbornik poslanii Babida Beháullakha* [A First Collection of the Tablets of the Bábí, Bahá'u'lláh] Historico-Philological Section of the Imperial Academy of St Petersburg, 1908. 186 pp.
 A collection of the texts of 63 tablets of Bahá'u'lláh.
3. 'Novuiya Babidskiya rukopisi' [Some New Bábí Manuscripts] *Zapiski* Vol. 4, 1889, pp. 112–14.
4. 'Poslanie: "Blagiya Vesti"'. Translation of the *Lawḥ-i-Bis͟hárát*, in *Zapiski* Vol. 7, 1892, pp. 183–92.
5. 'Eschche o poslanii "Blagiya Vesti"'. More about the *Lawḥ-i-Bis͟hárát*, in *Zapiski* Vol. 7, 1892, pp. 311–16.
6. 'Babidsky antikholernuy talisman' [A Bábí Anti-Cholera Talisman] *Zapiski* Vol. 7, 1892, pp. 317–18.
7. Review of Browne *A Traveller's Narrative* and three other articles by Browne, in *Zapiski* Vol. 7, 1892, pp. 370–75.

TUMANSKI

1. *Kitabe Akdes* Zapiski Imperatorskoy Academii Nauk S. Peterburg (Mémoires de L'Académie Impériale des Sciences de St Petersbourg) 8th ser., Vol. 3, No. 6, 1899.
 Arabic text of Bahá'u'lláh's *Kitábu'l-Aqdas* (69 pp.) together with lengthy Introduction (48 pp.), Russian translation and notes on other tablets (129 pp.)
2. 'Dva poslednikh Babidskikh otkroveniya' [Two Recent Bábí Tablets] *Zapiski* Vol. 6, 1891, pp. 314–21.
3. 'Poslednee slovo Bekhá-ullui' [Bahá'u'lláh's Last Tablet] *Zapiski* Vol. 7, 1892, pp. 193–203.
 Contains the text and translation of the *Kitáb-i-'Ahd* (Book of the Covenant) as well as a poem by 'Andalíb about Bahá'u'lláh's passing.
4. 'Iz pis'ma A. G. Tumanskago' [From the Letter of A. G. Tumanski] *Zapiski* Vol. 7, 1892, pp. 310–11.
5. 'K voprosu ob avtorakh istorii babidov, izvestnoi pod imenem Tarikhe Manukchi, . . . ili Tarikhe Dzhedid . . .' [The Author of the History known

under the Name of *Táríkh-i-Manukjí* or *Táríkh-i-Jadíd*] *Zapiski* Vol. 8, 1893, pp. 33–45.

Mention must also be made of two other important articles in Russian, both by Prof. V. A. Zhukovski (q.v., see fig. 9), who journeyed in Persia in 1883–5 (for details see Bibliography):

1. 'Nedavnya kazni babidov v gorode Ezde' [Recent Executions of Bábís in Yazd]. Based on a document provided by Vladimir Ignatiev of the Astarábád Consulate.
2. 'Rossiyskii Imperatorskii Konsul F. A. Bakulin v istorii izucheniya babizma' [The Imperial Russian Consul F. A. Bakulin in the History of Bábí Studies]

This is an extremely interesting article. Feodor Abramovich Bakulin graduated from the Lazarevskaya Institute in 1865. After serving as Secretary-Dragoman at Astarábád and Tabríz, he became Consul at Astarábád where he remained until his death on 30 March 1879. In 1912, Bakulin's papers were presented to Zhukovski by his family. Among these papers was an album of drawings including one with a French inscription, 'The Remains of the Báb and His Disciple Shot at Tabríz',* together with some writings of Ṭáhirih, and some correspondence with Baumgarten who was also studying the new religion in Khurásán.

German Scholars

There was not in Germany any scholar who devoted as much attention to the Bábí-Bahá'í religion as Browne, Nicolas or Tumanski, but nevertheless a number of interesting works did emerge from that country. Foremost among these was Hermann Roemer's (q.v.) doctoral dissertation in the Higher Philosophy Faculty of the University of Tübingen, which was published in 1911 under the title *Die Bábí-Behá'í*. This is a very thorough examination of the movement and brings the history up to the date of publication, including a survey of Bahá'í activities in Europe, North America and the Far East. The German periodical *Der Islam* also published several articles (see Bibliography for details):

1. *Verhältnis des Báb zu früheren Ṣúfí Lehrern* [Relationship of the Báb to the Earlier Sufi Teaching] by I. Goldziher (q.v.).
2. Review of Browne's *Materials for the Study of the Bábí Religion* by H. Ritter. Includes a facsimile of a tablet from 'Abdu'l-Bahá, with translation.
3. *Von Babismus in Deutschland* by R. Mielk.

* 'Abdu'l-Bahá in *A Traveller's Narrative* (p. 45) and Nabíl in his *Narrative* (UK pp. 377–8, USA pp. 518–19) both relate that following the martyrdom of the Báb the Russian Consul in Tabríz instructed that a sketch be made of the remains of the Báb and his disciple. Since Bakulin had been at the Tabríz Consulate, he may well have obtained the sketch or a copy of it there.

Diplomats and Statesmen

By the last decade of the nineteenth century, the diplomatic scene at Ṭihrán appeared to have altered greatly. In 1850 there had been only three diplomatic Missions. Apart from the Turkish Ambassador and the Russian and British Ministers, there were now French, German, Austrian, American, Belgian, Dutch, and Italian Ministers. But in reality, nothing much had altered. Britain and Russia were still playing 'The Great Game', manoeuvring for influence and dominance at the Qájár court, while the rest of the Legations, as it was said, merely counted the points. Through a network of Consuls and native Agents, Britain and Russia had completely penetrated the whole of Persia. Many a conversation which took place between the Sháh and his Ministers would be reported to the British and Russian Ministers. Scarcely an important telegram would pass between the Sháh and his provincial Governors but its text would be placed on the desk of one of these two Ministers a short while later. Often they were better informed about what was going on in the provinces than the Sháh himself.

The United States' first Minister to Persia was Samuel Benjamin (q.v.), who was in Persia from 1883 to 1885. In his book *Persia and the Persians* Benjamin gives an account of the 'Bâbees'. This account, written before the investigations of Browne had revealed the evolution of the Bábís into the Bahá'ís, is replete with mistakes, but it acknowledges the growing numbers and influence of the new religion:

> But the most remarkable sect now in Persia is probably that of the Bâbees, or followers of the Bâb. Their importance is not so much due to their numbers or political influence, as to the fact that the sect is of recent origin, full of proselyting zeal, and gaining converts every day in all parts of Persia, and latterly also in Turkey. The Bâbees present one of the most important religious phenomena of the age. It must be admitted, however, that they very strongly resemble in their communistic views the doctrines enounced [*sic*] by the famous Mazdâk, who was executed by Chosroes I after bringing the empire to the verge of destruction by the spread of his anarchical tenets . . .
>
> To this doctrine was added a socialism which formulated the equality of all, sweeping away social classes and distinctions, and ordaining a community of property, and also, at first, of wives. . . .
>
> In Persia the title of the present head of the sect is Sob-e-Azêl. As his belief in the Bâb is a secret, his name is not mentioned in this connection. From all I can gather from various sources it seems safe to assume that the Bâbees of Persia now number nearly, if not quite, four hundred thousand believers. They are found among all conditions of society, and, strange to say, adherents are gained among the priesthood as well as the laity. Just now there seems to be unusual activity among the Bâbees; emissaries or missionaries are secretly pervading the country, not only seeking to make proselytes but also presenting modifications in belief. The community in wives is no longer a practised tenet of the Bâb sect, while it is proclaimed with increasing emphasis that the Bâb is none other than God himself made manifest in the flesh.[84]

If the view expressed in the above account from Benjamin were to be taken as typical of the European community in Ṭihrán in the early 1880s, it would appear that their ideas about the Bábí-Bahá'í movement had hardly progressed since the days of Sheil in the early 1850s, despite the efforts of Gobineau. The same statements about 'Mazdâk', 'community of wives' and so on pervade the account, and there seems to be only a faint awareness of the far-reaching evolution of the movement during that period.

When Sir Henry Drummond Wolff (q.v.) first came to Ṭihrán in 1888 as British Minister there, it would appear that he too was badly misinformed about the Bahá'ís. He connected them with Siyyid Jamálu'd-Dín-i-Afg͟hání, the proponent of Pan-Islamism. In forwarding a memorandum on the movement by Col. Ross (see p. 246) to the Marquess of Salisbury, he writes:

> Colonel Ross compares Babism to Nihilism and in MacGregor's Gazetteer of Persia it is described as 'a rebellion against established forms.' I have little doubt that a man named Djellaledin, an Afghan who is wandering about the Northern frontier is a member of this sect. He was a great friend of Arabi* and is now I believe closely allied with Dhuleep Singh†. He was once expelled from Constantinople for lecturing in a manner which was considered heretical and being of a restless active intriguing mind with a smattering of European knowledge he has all the qualities necessary for conducting a politico-religious conspiracy.[85]

One of the most remarkable books ever to appear on Persia is *Persia and the Persian Question* (1892), by George Nathaniel Curzon (later Lord Curzon of Kedleston, q.v.) That someone who only spent a total of two and a half months in Persia‡ and had no knowledge of the language could produce such a detailed and perceptive account of the country is evidence of that powerful intellect which was, in later years, to dominate British foreign policy.

It is not clear to what extent if any Curzon communicated with the Bahá'ís while in Persia,§ but on his return he appears to have made a thorough search of the available literature, and the seven-page account of

* 'Urábí Pás͟há, the Egyptian nationalist leader who revolted against British hegemony over Egypt.

† Maharajah Dalip Singh, the Sikh ruler deposed by the British in 1849, who was at this time trying, with Russian assistance, to organize an uprising against the British in the Punjab.

‡ Although it has been stated that Curzon was six months in Persia (see for example Denis Wright *The English among the Persians* p. 165), if one notes the dates at the head of his letters to *The Times* written on this journey, it will be seen that he was at 'Is͟hqábád on 10 Oct. 1889, at the beginning of his journey through Persia, and by 31 Dec. 1889 he was in Baṣra, having completed the journey.

§ The editor is of the opinion that there was no such communication. Curzon gives no account of the Bahá'ís in his letters to *The Times* written during the journey (except for a passing reference to the martyrdoms of the King and Beloved of martyrs). It seems probable that it was only on his return to England and his perusal of Browne's article in the *Journal of the Royal Asiatic Society* that he decided to devote some space to this subject in his book.

the new religion to be found in his book is among the most perceptive and balanced that have ever appeared.

In his opening remarks on the subject,[86] Curzon states that previous writers have made many errors about the 'Babi movement', and in two footnotes he gives a selected bibliography of the most accurate accounts of the new religion and a history of the movement up to 1852. He then traces the further development of the movement and states that nineteen-twentieths of the Bábís are now followers of Bahá'u'lláh.[87] Curzon continues with an assessment of the strength of the Bahá'í community in Persia (see p. 248) and states:

> If one conclusion more than another has been forced upon our notice by the retrospect in which I have indulged, it is that a sublime and unmurmuring devotion has been inculcated by this new faith, whatever it be. There is, I believe, but one instance of a Babi having recanted under pressure or menace of suffering, and he reverted to the faith and was executed within two years. Tales of magnificent heroism illumine the bloodstained pages of Babi history. Ignorant and unlettered as many of its votaries are, and have been, they are yet prepared to die for their religion, and fires of Smithfield did not kindle a nobler courage than has met and defied the more refined torture-mongers of Teheran. Of no small account, then, must be the tenets of a creed that can awaken in its followers so rare and beautiful a spirit of self-sacrifice.[88]

Curzon, moreover, proceeds to examine the tenets of the new religion, and in doing so brushes aside many of the misconceptions of previous writers:

> From the facts that Babism in its earliest years found itself in conflict with the civil powers, and that an attempt was made by Babis upon the life of the Shah, it has been wrongly inferred that the movement was political in origin and Nihilist in character. It does not appear from a study of the writings either of the Bab or his successors, that there is any foundation for such a suspicion. The persecution of the government very early drove the adherents of the new creed into an attitude of rebellion; and in the exasperation produced by the struggle, and by the ferocious brutality with which the rights of conquest were exercised by the victors, it was not surprising if fanatical hands were found ready to strike the sovereign down. At the present time the Babis are equally loyal with any other subjects of the Crown. Nor does there appear any greater justice in the charges of socialism, communism, and immorality, that have so freely been levelled at the youthful persuasion. Certainly no such idea as communism in the European sense, i.e., a forcible redistribution of property, or as socialism in the nineteenth century sense, i.e., the defeat of capital by labour, ever entered the brain of the Bab or his disciples. The only communism known to and recommended by him was that of the New Testament and the early Christian Church, viz., the sharing of goods in common by members of the faith, and the exercise of alms-giving, and an ample charity.The charge of immorality seems to have arisen partly from the malignant inventions of opponents, partly from the much greater freedom claimed for women by the Bab, which in the oriental mind is scarcely dissociable from profligacy of conduct . . .
>
> . . . The Bab and Beha in their writings

have enjoined the disuse of the veil, the abolition of divorce, polygamy, and concubinage, in other words, of the harem, and greater liberty of action for the female sex. They recommend a system of poor-law relief, but declare war against mendicancy . . . Broadly regarded, Babism may be defined as a creed of charity, and almost of common humanity. Brotherly love, kindness to children, courtesy combined with dignity, sociability, hospitality, freedom from bigotry, friendliness even to Christians, are included in its tenets. That every Babi recognises or observes these precepts would be a foolish assertion; but let a prophet, if his gospel be in question, be judged by his own preaching.[89]

Finally Curzon concludes: 'If Babism continues to grow at its present rate of progression, a time may conceivably come when it will oust Mohammedanism from the field in Persia . . .'[90]

Sir Thomas Gordon (q.v.), who was Military Secretary and later Attaché to the British Legation in Ṭihrán in 1889–93, returned to Persia in 1895 and wrote a book entitled *Persia Revisited.* His account of the Bahá'ís is much more accurate than most, and contains a lengthy description of the disturbances and martyrdoms in Iṣfahán and Yazd in 1890–91, during which time the author had been in Ṭihrán. However, even in this book there are some opinions expressed that are very far from the truth. Thus he states: '. . . it is believed that now sufficient education whereby to read and write is absolutely necessary for membership . . . I was told they believe in the reincarnation of the soul . . .'[91]

The Bábís and Bahá'ís in Literature

As has already been mentioned, the first to incorporate the dramatic events of Bábí and Bahá'í history into a literary work was Marie von Najmájer (see p. 25).

Eça de Queirós (q.v.) is generally acknowledged as one of the greatest of Portuguese novelists. He attempted to bring about social reform in the Portugal of the last half of the nineteenth century through his novels. *A Correspondencia de Fradique Mendes* is somewhat different from his other works. He creates an intelligent and perceptive character named Fradique Mendes, who travels to many different places and writes of them to his friends and relations – the underlying purpose being to demonstrate the evils in Portuguese society. It is said that Eça de Queirós modelled the character of Fradique Mendes upon himself, and that he reveals himself more clearly in this book than in any of his other writings.[92] Introducing the character of Fradique Mendes, he writes of their meeting in Cairo:

Upon leaving the Moujik we were wandering along, when suddenly Fradique Mendes stopped and very ceremoniously exchanged a salaam – that oriental greeting in which the fingers touch three places, the forehead, the mouth and the heart – with a pale young man of radiant eyes. It was duly returned, and I begrudged him his intimacy with 'that man with green tunic and mitred Persian head-dress'.

'He is one of the 'ulamá of Baghdád, of an ancient lineage and superior intelligence,' said Fradique, 'and one of the most elegant and captivating personalities I have met in Persia.'

Then, with a familiarity that had begun to grow between us, I asked Fradique what had detained him thus in Persia for a year and a day, just as in the fairy tales. And Fradique confessed, with all sincerity, that he had tarried so long on the banks of the Euphrates because he had by chance come into contact with a religious movement called *Bábism*, which since 1849 had been developing and had nearly triumphed in Persia. Although attracted to this new sect by a critical curiosity, and also wishing to observe how a new religion is born and established, he gradually began to take a very keen interest in Bábism – not so much because he admired its doctrine, but because of the dedication of its apostles. Bábism, he told me, as we followed a quieter lane, more favourable for the exchange of confidences, was started by Mírzá Muḥammad [Mírzá 'Alí-Muḥammad, the Báb], one of those messiahs who rise up every day or so in the ceaseless religious turmoil of the Orient, where religion is life's supreme and most preferred occupation . . .

. . . Fradique, who in Baghdád had become familiar with one of the most active and learned apostles of Bábism, 'Said-El-Souriz' (whose child he had cured of malaria by an application of fruit-salts), suggested to him one day, while they were both talking on the terrace about these matters of great spiritual interest, the idea of propagating Bábism among the agricultural peoples of the Nile valley and the nomads of Libya. Among those people of the Sunní sect, Bábism would find an easy field for conversion, and, following the traditional progress of sectarian movements in the Orient (as everywhere else), would rise from the sincere masses of the people up to the cultured classes. Perhaps this new wave of religious emotion, beginning with the fellahin and bedouin, would be able to penetrate the classrooms of some of the mosques of Cairo, especially the mosque of Al-Azhar, the great University of the Orient, where the younger 'ulamá form a group of enthusiasts always looking out for innovations and apostolic debates. Gaining there theological authority and literary refinement, Bábism could then attack with advantage the old fortresses of Muslim dogmatism. This idea had penetrated deeply into Said-El-Souriz. That pale young man with whom he [Fradique] had exchanged a salaam would soon be sent as a Bábist emissary to Madínat-Abú (ancient Thebes), to sound out Shaykh 'Alí-Ḥusayn, a man of decisive influence throughout the valley of the Nile because of his wisdom and virtue; and he, Fradique, for the moment not having any occupation in the West that attracted him, and full of curiosity about this picturesque Advent, was also to leave for Thebes, planning to meet the Bábist at the waning of the moon in Bani-Suif on the Nile. . . .

I do not remember, after so many years, whether these are the exact facts. I only know that these revelations by Fradique, thrust upon me during the festival in Cairo, impressed me unutterably. While he spoke of the Báb, and of that apostolic mission to the old Shaykh of Thebes, and of the rise of another faith within the Muslim world, with its own procession of martyrs and ecstasies, and of the possible founding of a Bábist empire – this personage [the Báb] took on grand proportions in my mind. I had never known anyone involved in such exalted matters, and I felt myself both proud and awed to be trusted with this sublime secret. I would not have been more moved if I had, on the eve of St Paul's departure for Greece to take the Word to the Gentiles, walked with him through the narrow streets of Seleucia, listening to his hopes and dreams.

As we were talking in this way, we entered

1. *Mírzá Kazem-Beg, orientalist*

2. *Madame Jane Dieulafoy, dressed as a man, the manner in which she travelled in Iran*

3. *Gobineau (on right of photograph) and Rochechouart at the French Legation in Tiḥrán (Dieulafoy* La Perse, la Chaldée et la Susiane*)*

4. Prof. E. G. Browne, English orientalist

5. A.-L.-M. Nicolas, French orientalist

The Bahai teaching brings peace and understanding.

It is like a wide embrace gathering together all those who have long searched for words of Hope.

It accepts all great prophets gone before, it destroys no other creeds and leaves all doors open.

Saddened by the continual strife amongst believers of many confessions and wearied of their intolerence towards eachother, I discovered in the Bahai teaching the real spirit of Christ so often denied and misunderstood:

Unity instead of strife, Hope instead of condemnation, Love instead of hate, and a great reassurance for all men.

Marie.

6. *Appreciation of the Bahá'í Faith in Queen Marie's handwriting*

7. *Queen Marie of Romania*

8. Baron Victor Rosen, Russian orientalist

9. Prof. Valentin Zhukovski, Russian orientalist

10. Marie von Najmájer, Austro-Hungarian poetess

11. Rev. T. K. Cheyne, eminent Biblical scholar (Cheyne The Reconciliation of Races and Religions*)*

the precincts of the mosque of Al-Azhar, where the refulgent and very strident feast of Bayrám was being celebrated. But already the surprises of that Muslim festival were failing to hold my attention – neither the mendicants dancing amid the splendour of vermilion and gold, nor the poets of the desert reciting the heroic deeds of 'Antar, nor the dervishes under their linen tents, howling in rhythm praises to Alláh. Invaded by thoughts of the Báb, I silently turned over in my mind the confused desire to undertake the adventure of this spiritual campaign! Should I leave for Thebes with Fradique? Why not? I was young, I had enthusiasm. It would be more manly and noble to start a career as an evangelist in the Orient than to return meekly to banal Lisbon, and write reams of paper under a gas light for the *Gazeta de Portugal*! Little by little this desire, like water starting to boil, changed slowly into the vapour of a vision. I saw myself become a disciple of the Báb, receiving from the 'ulamá of Baghdád, that very night, initiation into Truth. Now that I was ready to proclaim and spread the Bábist Word, where should I go? To Portugal, of course, taking this salvation to the souls most dear to me. Like St Paul, I embarked on a galley; storms assailed its apostolic prow; the image of the Báb appeared to me over the waters, and his serene glance filled my spirit with an invincible strength! One day, at last, I sighted land, and in the clear morning light the ship ploughed the limpid waters of the Tagus river, where for so many centuries no apostle of God had entered. Still at a distance, I hurled an insult at the churches of Lisbon, buildings belonging to an ancient and less pure faith. I disembarked. And, leaving behind my baggage, in an already divine indifference to worldly goods, I strode up that famous Alecrim Street to the middle of Loreto Square, at the very hour when the Director-Generals march slowly up the arcade, opened my arms wide and cried out, 'I am the Gate!'

Well, after all, I did not submerge myself in that Bábist apostolate; but it so happened that, carried away by those fantastic dreams, I lost Fradique, and could not find my way back to the Hotel Sheperd – could not even ask, as I did not know any Arabic words more useful than 'water' and 'love'![93]

A Correspondencia de Fradique Mendes appeared in 1889. At this time, there was no very great amount of material on the Bábí and Bahá'í religions available. Only Gobineau's book could have inspired such a passage. But in the above extract, Eça de Queirós shows that he knew of the spread of the new religion to Egypt and its propagation there – information not derived from Gobineau's book. It would seem possible to the editor that during his journey to Egypt from October 1869 to January 1870, Eça de Queirós may have come into contact with the Bahá'ís there, and this could have inspired him to write the above passage. It may be noted that he sets his fictional meeting with Fradique Mendes in Egypt in 1871.

Even more remarkable, in some ways, than Eça de Queirós's reference to the Bábís is the book *Un Amour au Pays des Mages* (1891), a novel set against a background of the dramatic events of Bábí history. The story revolves around a romance between a poor darvísh, 'Alí, and the daughter of a mujtahid of Qazvín, Núru'd-Dín; the events in Bábí history which form the background of the story include the Zanján upheaval, the martyrdom of the Báb and the holocaust following the attempt on the life of the Sháh. The author of this work, A. de Saint-Quentin (q.v.), was not a literary figure, indeed this is the only novel of his that the editor has been able to trace.*

During the 1890s, there was a resurgence of interest in the Bábí-Bahá'í movement in intellectual and literary circles in Europe, fired, perhaps, by the publication of Browne's works. Jules Bois (q.v.), author, poet and literary critic, writing in the American periodical *Forum* in 1925, testified to this:

> All Europe was stirred to pity and indignation. The event [the martyrdom of the Báb] occurred on the ninth of July, 1850; among the *littérateurs* of my generation, in the Paris of 1890, the martyrdom of the Bab was still as fresh a topic as had been the first news of his death. We wrote poems about him. Sarah Bernhardt entreated Catulle Mendès for a play on the theme of this historic tragedy. When he failed to supply a manuscript, I was asked to write a drama entitled *Her Highness the Pure*, dealing with the story of another illustrious martyr of the same cause, – a woman, Quarratul-Ayn, the Persian Joan of Arc and the leader of emancipation for women of the Orient.[94]

In 1911, E. S. Stevens (later Lady Drower) (q.v.) published a full-length novel *The Mountain of God* which revolved around the lives of the Bahá'í community in the Haifa–'Akká area. This novel is, indeed, only thinly disguised as fiction and most of the characters therein can be easily identified. It is based on the experiences of the writer herself when she spent six months in Haifa. 'Abdu'l-Bahá himself, although appearing only once in the book in person, pervades the whole book by the influence that he exerts on the characters.

The following year, an American writer, Gertrude Atherton (q.v.), published *Julia France and Her Times*. In this novel, the heroine, Julia France, goes to 'Akká to meet 'Abdu'l-Bahá and returns to England to try and persuade her friend Nigel, an author, to write about the Bahá'ís.

Mention must finally be made of some Russian literary works referring to the Bábís and Bahá'ís. In May 1903, Izabella Grinevskaya (q.v.) published in St Petersburg a dramatic poem in five acts entitled *The Báb*. This poem was enthusiastically received in Russia and played in one of the leading theatres of St Petersburg in January 1904.† The work, which seems to have been inspired principally by Browne's writings, is historically very inaccurate, the writer having distorted historical fact to enhance the dramatic effects.‡ As a result of this work, Mme Grinevskaya came into contact with the Bahá'ís resident in Russia, and in particular with Mírzá 'Alí-Akbar

* One other work, *Le Feu et l'eau, deux récits dramatiques* (1893), is listed in the catalogue of the Bibliothèque Nationale, Paris, while Wilson's *Bibliography of Persia* lists *Notes d'un voyage dans les montagnes de l'Elbrouz et le Mazendhéran* (1859).

† After the February Revolution it was again played in the Folk Theatre in Leningrad in April 1917.

‡ Thus a romance between the Báb and 'Houret' (Qurratu'l-'Ayn, Ṭáhirih) forms one of the themes of the story, the Báb being made a foster-child of Houret's father, and thus having grown up with her.

Nakhjaváni at Baku. But it was a Russian, Nicolas Zazuline, president of the nobility in Kishinef, who urged her to write another similar work on Bahá'u'lláh. This she did and it was published in 1912, and again received favourable reviews. Mme Grinevskaya herself travelled to Egypt and met 'Abdu'l-Bahá there in 1911. She wrote a narrative of that journey named *A Journey in the Countries of the Sun*. One who was competent to judge the worth of Grinevskaya's literary work was Gabriel de Wesselitsky (q.v.), the Russian writer and journalist. In a pamphlet entitled *A New Great Russian Poet*,* Wesselitsky, writing about Grinevskaya's *The Báb*, states: 'I . . . was at once struck by the rare combination of philosophical thought with a great power of expression, beauty of imagery and harmony of verse. I keenly felt the delight of reading a new great poem and discovering a new first-rate poet.[95]

Praise for Grinevskaya's work came from an even more eminent source, Leo Tolstoy. Wesselitsky writes: 'In the summer of that year [1903] the great Russian critic Stassoff visiting Tolstoy in Yasnaia Poliana found him deeply immersed in reading the drama, 'the Bâb', and was charged by him to give his admiring appreciation to its author.'[96]

The Western Journeys of 'Abdu'l-Bahá

In the period under consideration in this work, 1844–1944, the extent of public knowledge and awareness in the West of the Bábí and Bahá'í movements underwent two great cycles of rise and fall. Commencing in complete obscurity as a persecuted Oriental sect, it came a little into the limelight through the holocaust following the attempt on the life of the Sháh. But it was Gobineau who, through his book *Religions et Philosophies*, brought the new religion to the attention of the West in the late 1860s as a movement worthy of study and admiration. However, Gobineau's remarkable pioneer effort in this field was not followed up immediately, and thus the subject fell once more into obscurity. Browne's writings in the early 1890s caused some resurgence of interest, but this was limited principally to academic circles. During the first decade of the twentieth century there was increasing interest in the new religion, mainly through the efforts of the small band of Bahá'ís in North America and Europe, but the undoubted climax of this process was the Western journeys of 'Abdu'l-Bahá in 1911–13. Through these journeys, an unprecedented amount of publicity was given to the Bahá'í Faith in newspapers and periodicals throughout the West (see chapter 23). In consequence, the Faith seems to have become a topic of

* An address delivered before the Foreign Press Association on 15 Feb. 1907.

conversation in many circles and is referred to in literary and other writings of that period. This interest continued for a time but gradually, after the passing of 'Abdu'l-Bahá, during the 1920s it began to fall away again.

Scholars and Writers

The great interest of Europe's intellectual circles in the Bábí-Bahá'í movement had reached a peak following the publication of Gobineau's book in 1865 but was beginning to decline once more, when Browne's works started to appear. That these caused a resurgence of interest in the new religion can be seen from the following letter, dated 1 April 1893, from Oxford's foremost academic figure then living, Dr Benjamin Jowett (q.v.), Master of Balliol College. The letter was written to the Countess of Wemyss (q.v.).

> Yes, I did send you *The Episode of the Bab*,* if you will kindly accept it and perhaps read it. It seems to me the most curious passage in the history of religion which has happened in modern times. ('Bab,' or 'the Gate,' was a prophet who was martyred in our lifetime, about the year 1852.) I have often heard of him from Turguenieff,† from a Persian who was at Balliol,‡ and from General Stuart,§ who was an English secret agent in those regions, but no full account of him has been published until this one. It seems to me more like the narrative of the Gospels than anything which I have read. Read especially the narrative of the woman Koratelaim [Qurratu'l-'Ayn], who was of great beauty, and a popular Persian poetess.[97]

It should be noted that from the reference to Turgenev it may be inferred that the Bábí-Bahá'í religion was a source of interest to Russian literary circles as early as the 1870s.

Another great Oxford figure who took a deep interest in the Bahá'í movement was Prof. T. K. Cheyne (q.v., see fig. 11). His interest arose towards the end of his life when he entered into communication with several Bahá'ís and in particular Luṭfu'lláh Ḥakím and Lady Blomfield. 'Abdu'l-Bahá was Cheyne's guest at Oxford on 31 December 1912, and it was principally due to the latter's efforts that 'Abdu'l-Bahá was given such a notable reception at Oxford.

Cheyne's last major work, *The Reconciliation of Races and Religions*, is devoted to a large extent to the Bahá'í Faith, and he was even regarded by some as having become a Bahá'í. His biographer writes:

* Browne's *A Traveller's Narrative*

† Turgenev, the eminent Russian novelist who was in Oxford in 1879 to receive an honorary degree.

‡ Abu'l-Qásim K͟hán, Náṣiru'l-Mulk, later a prominent Persian statesman who rose to be Prime Minister. His grandmother had become a Bábí after conversing with Ṭáhirih in Hamadán.

§ Probably Gen. Charles Stewart, author of *Through Persia in Disguise*, is intended. This man certainly knew of the Bahá'ís and presented a report on them to the Church Missionary Society. He could with fairness have been described as a British secret agent. He was in Oxford in 1880.

His theological position became, in his later years, more and more indefinite. His last work, *The Reconciliation of Races and Religions* (1914), was not concerned with the Old Testament, but was noteworthy for its sympathy with Babism and the Bahai movement. He still spoke of himself as an anglican Christian but . . . it may be questioned whether he could be regarded as a Christian . . . but at least his heart was set on the highest things, and in a world tortured by the strife of nation and distracted by the conflict of religions he cherished the vision of unity and peace.[98]

In his *Reconciliation of Races and Religions*, Cheyne wrote of Bahá'u'lláh:

There was living quite lately a human being of such consummate excellence that many think it is both permissible and inevitable even to identify him mystically with the invisible Godhead. Let us admit, such persons say, that Jesus was the very image of God. But he lived for his own age and his own people; the Jesus of the critics has but little to say, and no redemptive virtue issues from him to us. But the 'Blessed Perfection' as Baha'ullah used to be called, lives for our age, and offers his spiritual feast to men of all peoples. His story, too, is liable to no diminution at the hands of the critics, simply because the facts of his life are certain. He has now passed from sight, but he is still in the ideal world, a true image of God and a true lover of man, and helps forward the reform of all those manifold abuses which hinder the firm establishment of the Kingdom of God . . .

If there has been any prophet in recent times, it is to Beha'-ullah that we must go . . . Character is the final judge. Beha'-ullah was a man of the highest class – that of prophets. But he was free from the last infirmity of noble minds, and would certainly not have separated himself from others. He would have understood the saying, 'Would God all the Lord's people were prophets'. What he does say, however, is just as fine, 'I do not desire lordship over others; I desire all men to be even as I am.'[99]

Concerning the Báb, Cheyne wrote:

Such a prophet was the Báb; we call him 'prophet' for want of a better name; 'yea, I say unto you, a prophet and more than a prophet.' His combination of mildness and power is so rare that we have to place him in a line with super-normal men . . . We learn that, at great points in his career, after he had been in an ecstasy, such radiance of might and majesty streamed from his countenance that none could bear to look upon the effulgence of his glory and beauty. Nor was it an uncommon occurrence for unbelievers involuntarily to bow down in lowly obeisance on beholding His Holiness . . .

The gentle spirit of the Báb is surely high up in the cycles of eternity. Who can fail, as Professor Browne says, to be attracted by him?[100]

A third Oxford theologian and scholar to speak and write of the Bahá'í movement was Prof. J. E. Carpenter (q.v.). On 31 December 1912 when 'Abdu'l-Bahá came to Oxford at Prof. Cheyne's invitation, Carpenter held a meeting for him in Manchester College and presided at the meeting, giving in Cheyne's words 'an admirable speech'. In his *Comparative Religion*, Carpenter writes:

> From that subtle race [the Persians] issues the most remarkable movement which modern Mohammedanism has produced . . . The new faith declared that there was no finality in revelation, and while recognising the Koran as a product of past revelation, claimed to embody a new manifestation of the divine Unity. Carried to Chicago in 1893 by a Bâbî merchant, it succeeded in establishing itself in the United States; and its missionaries are winning new adherents in India. It, too, claims to be a universal teaching; it has already its noble army of martyrs and its holy books; has Persia, in the midst of her miseries, given birth to a religion which will go round the world?[101]

The great French novelist Romain Rolland (q.v.), winner of the Nobel Prize for Literature, quotes from 'Abdu'l-Bahá's *Some Answered Questions* in his novel *Clerambault*. He was greatly interested in the Bahá'ís and visited the Bahá'í Centre at Geneva, as well as corresponding with such figures as Tolstoy and Forel about the Bahá'ís. In a letter written in 1918, he states:

> I first learned of Bahá'ism (evolved Bábism) at Geneva, where they hold a meeting of believers in the doctrine on the 19th of each month . . .
>
> It is or wants to be a fusion of all the religions of the East and West. It denies none, it accepts them all. It is above all a religious ethic, which does not conceive of religion without putting it into practice, and which seeks to remain in accord with science and reason, without cult or priests. The first duty is that each has a profession: work is holy, it is the divine benediction.
>
> I have noticed an analogy with Christian Science. In my spirit, I prefer Bahá'ism. I find it more flexible and subtle. And it offers the poetic imagination a rich feast. Its roots are sunk in the great metaphysical dreams of the Orient. There are some luminous pages in the discourses of St Jean d'Acre [i.e. *Some Answered Questions*] of 'Abdu'l-Bahá. Bahá'u'lláh, a prisoner, succeeded in writing and answering some 'tablets' of an admirable and moral beauty, under the name 'the Oppressed One' . . .[102]

The eminent novelist and philosopher, Leo Tolstoy, was also much interested in the Bahá'í movement. It is not clear how he first heard of the movement but he certainly was already familiar with it when in 1901 Gabriel Sacy,* a Bahá'í of Egypt, wrote to him. In his reply, Tolstoy states: 'Babism has interested me for a long time. I have read everything related to it which was accessible to me.'[103]

To a Persian statesman, Arfa'u'd-Dawlih (q.v.), Tolstoy wrote in 1901: 'I believe that everywhere, as among you in Persia with the Bábís, there are people professing the true religion and that despite persecutions, to which these people are always and everywhere exposed, their ideas are propagating themselves more and more, and will triumph in the end over the barbarity and ferocity of the Governments and, above all, over the deceit in which they try to hold their peoples.'[104]

In autumn, 1901, Tolstoy was visited by Dr Cleanthes Nicolaides, a German from Berlin who had travelled in Persia. Concerning his visit he

* Concerning this man see Browne *Materials* pp. 185–6.

wrote that he had found Tolstoy working at a new book. Of the Bahá'ís, Tolstoy had said: 'The teaching of the founder of the Bábist sect represents on the one hand an intermediary position between Islam and Christianity, and on the other aims to free man from all spiritual bondage. The main task it tries to achieve is the highest education of the individual, whereas the other religions restrict or even hinder spiritual qualities. Bábism has no hierarchy, but instead aims to educate each individual believer to become a whole person, to be a fighter for freedom and the moral advancement of humanity.'[105]

In September 1902, Mírzá 'Azízu'lláh Ja<u>dh</u><u>dh</u>áb, a prominent Bahá'í of <u>Kh</u>urásán, visited Tolstoy at Yasnaya Polyana, on 'Abdu'l-Bahá's instructions, and spoke to Tolstoy about the Bahá'í religion.

In 1903, Grinevskaya's poetic drama *The Báb* was published and found its way into Tolstoy's hands (see p. 51). In a letter to Grinevskaya, Tolstoy writes: 'I have known of the Bábís for a long time and am much interested in their teachings. It seems to me that they have a great future . . . because they have thrown away the artificial superstructures which separate [the religions] from one another and are aiming at uniting all mankind in one religion . . . And therefore, in that it educates men to brotherhood and equality and to the sacrificing of their sensual desires in God's service, I sympathize with Bábism with all my heart.'[106]

Still later in 1908, Tolstoy wrote to Fridul Khan Wadalbekov: 'The teaching of the Bábís which comes to us out of Islam has through Bahá'ism (Bahá'u'lláh's teachings) been gradually developed, and now presents us with the highest and purest form of religious doctrine.'[107]

However, Tolstoy's views on the Bahá'í religion were not entirely optimistic. In the article by Dr Nicolaides cited above, there occurs the following statement: 'And yet I have been very disappointed by this new religious formation, because it has shown that it too, without the help of external state power and means of coercion, is incapable of gaining an influence in depth on the mass of the people and carrying that people with it to great deeds.'[108]

The distinguished Swiss naturalist, sociologist and philosopher Auguste Forel (q.v.) first heard of the Bahá'í Faith in 1920, and was the recipient of a famous tablet from 'Abdu'l-Bahá. In 1927, when there was a period of persecution of the Bahá'ís in Persia, Forel wrote to the French Foreign Office bringing the matter to their attention. Prior to his death in 1931, he had prepared a spiritual testament which was read at his funeral. It included the following passage: 'In the year 1920, at Karlsruhe, I first made acquaintance with the supraconfessional world-religion of the Bahá'í, founded in the East seventy years ago by the Persian Bahá'u'lláh. It is the true religion of the welfare of human society, it has neither priests nor dogmas, and it binds together all the human beings who inhabit this little globe. I have become a Bahá'í. May this religion continue and be crowned with success; this is my most ardent wish.'[109]

Although, as has been mentioned in the Introduction, no European orientalist after Browne has done much research on the Bahá'í movement, several have made interesting references to their own experiences of the movement. Denmark's great orientalist, Professor Arthur Christensen (q.v.), refers very warmly to his experiences among the Bahá'ís of Iran when he visited that country (see his *Hinsides det Kaspiske Hav* chapter 10). He also contributed articles to the Danish *Dansk Tidsskrift* (1903) and the Swedish *Nordisk Tidskrift* (1911) on the new religion. Sir Denison Ross (q.v.), Professor of Persian at the University of London, writes in his *Both Ends of the Candle* of his meetings with Bahá'ís in Baku and Ṭihrán: 'Thanks to the writings of Edward Browne, I was deeply interested in the Babi movement which had now become the Bahá'í movement. These conclaves [of Bahá'ís in Ṭihrán] gave me the keenest intellectual pleasure; for the discussions were all on religion and philosophy . . .'[110] Ross also wrote a brief account of the new religion for the *North American Review*.[111]

In 1939, the Russian orientalist Mikhail Sergeevich Ivanov published his thesis, which was submitted to the University of Leningrad for the degree 'Candidate in Historical Science' (approximately a Ph.D.), *Babidskie vosstaniya v Irane (1848–1852)* [Bábí Uprisings in Iran 1848–1852]. The main part of the book sets out to describe the Bábí movement in terms of economic influences and Marxist-Leninist philosophy. Of more interest from the historical point of view is that the author had access to Russian Government records and has published in this book the relevant dispatches of Dolgorukov, the Russian Minister in Ṭihrán during the Bábí upheavals. These dispatches have been quoted extensively throughout section B of this work (see p. xix).

Opponents of the Bahá'í Religion

Although opposition to the Bahá'í religion had been a notable feature of the history of the movement in the East, the opposition in the West was much slower in building up. Predictably, the major opposition came from the Churches and particularly from those priests who were or had been missionaries in the East. One of these missionaries, the American James Bassett, was one of the earliest to refer in a book to the fact that Bahá'u'lláh was now the leader of the Bábís in Persia (see also p.244): in *Persia, The Land of the Imams*, he writes:

Mirza Hosein Ale, of the province of Mazandaran, and for a time a resident of Tehran, was an agent or vakiel of the Bab at the time of the death of that man in Tabriz.

He escaped from Tehran, but was arrested in Constantinople and during several years has been confined at Akka, in Syria. He professed to be the Bab, and is very generally recognised by all who now hold to the tenets of that sect in Persia. In this fortress he receives the contributions of the faithful, professes to work a miracle in proof of his divinity by writing a thousand letters in an incredible short space of time, and sends his decrees to kings and people in many places.[112]

It was moreover another American missionary, Rev. H. H. Jessup (q.v.), who was the author of a paper mentioning Bahá'u'lláh which was read at the World Parliament of Religions in Chicago on 23 September 1893: an event which is often singled out as the first step in the rise of the Bahá'í Faith in the West.

But later, as the numbers of believers in the West rose and the Faith became established, opposition arose and Christian priests and missionaries such as Wilson, Frame, Rees, Easton, Vatralsky and even Jessup wrote articles and books against the new religion.*

Other Accounts

From the 1890s onwards, and particularly with the establishment of Bahá'í communities in Europe and North America, there was a great proliferation of references to the new religion. Only a few of the more interesting accounts can be quoted within the limits of the space available.

Doctor Feuvrier (q.v.) was Náṣiru'd-Dín Sháh's personal physician for three years in the early 1890s. In his description of his sojourn in Persia, *Trois Ans à la Cour de Perse*, he refers to the Bábís and Bahá'ís when writing of Zanján:

The blood of these martyrs, I was told by the person who recounted for me these sorrowful events, has done more for the cause of Bábism than their preaching. Although the Bábís no longer make themselves known openly, there are no fewer of them in all Persia; there are even some in the Court, even in the entourage of His Majesty.

From what I have learned of the morals of Bábís, of the honourable role that it assigns to women in the family, I am obliged to conclude that it is a pity that this religion, inspired by the loftiest philosophical ideas, has not prevailed in Persia.[113]

Sir Valentine Chirol (q.v.) was one of the most respected of commentators on the Middle East and India of his generation (see also p. 222). For twelve years, he was the Foreign Editor of *The Times*. In his book *The Middle Eastern Question*, one chapter is entitled 'The Revival of Babiism'. In this chapter he writes:

That the movement which bears the apostolic name of the religious martyr who was put to death at Tabriz more than half a century ago is still a living force in Persia is

* The relations between the Bahá'í community and Christian missionaries is the subject of an essay by the editor which it is hoped will be published shortly.

almost universally recognised. But to what extent and in what shape that force is likely to make itself decisively felt opinions differ very largely . . .

. . . Regular communication is kept up between Persia and Acre, both by pilgrimages and confidential messengers; and the sacred books of Beha'ullah and Abbas Effendi are widely read by the Babi communities. That the latter are still very numerous and spread throughout the length and breadth of Persia there can be no doubt. In all the large cities, in Shiraz and Yezd, in Isfahan and Tabriz, and even in the capital, their adherents are to be found amongst all classes of the population, amongst officials and soldiers, amongst merchants and artisans, as well as amongst the humblest of the people. Amongst the rural population also, and especially in the villages around Isfahan, Kum, and Kashan, and throughout Khorasan, they have a large following. Their total strength is estimated by competent authorities at nearly one and a half millions, or about 20 per cent of the total population of Persia. But all such estimates must be largely guesswork, as the most convinced Babis cannot make any open profession of their faith; and it is difficult to distinguish between those who have fully accepted the religious teachings of Babiism and those who merely sympathise with its reforming tendencies . . . The predominant tendency at the present day is in fact to give prominence to the ethical rather than to the theological aspect of Babiism, and from the latter point of view, to dwell upon the essential truths which underlie all 'manifestations' of divine origin rather than on the outward forms which differentiate them. The new dispensation should therefore, it is claimed, be regarded chiefly as the continuation and fulfilment of the earlier Mosaic, Christian, and Muhammedan dispensations. Does not the Jew still wait for the promised Messiah, the Christian for the second advent of Christ, the Mussulman for the appearance of a Mahdi? Babiism is but the 'manifestation' they are all equally expecting, and the evolution it has undergone, even within the short period since the Bab gave his first message to the world, precludes any claim to rigid doctrinal finality. The Babis certainly profess, and within the measure of their limited opportunities, have practised tolerance and good will towards all, Christians and Jews, Sufis and Zoroastrians, and they talk with enthusiasm of the universal brotherhood of man and a millennium in which wars and civil strife shall cease.

Socially one of the most interesting features of Babiism is the raising of women to a much higher plane than she is usually admitted to in the East. The Bab himself had no more devoted a disciple than the beautiful and gifted lady, known as Kurrat-el-Ain, the 'Consolation of the Eyes,' who, having shared all the dangers of the first apostolic missions in the north, challenged and suffered death with virile fortitude, as one of the Seven Martyrs of Teheran.* No memory is more deeply venerated or kindles greater enthusiasm than hers, and the influence which she wielded in her lifetime still enures to her sex. That women, whom orthodox Islam barely credits with the possession of a soul, are freely admitted to the meetings of Babis, gives their enemies, the *Mullahs*, ample occasion to blaspheme. But they have never produced a tittle of evidence in support of the vague charges of immorality they are wont to bring against the followers of the new creed. Communism and socialism are also often imputed to them, and some of them appear to have borrowed from the West the terminology of advanced democracy.[114]

One of the most balanced analyses of the Bábí and Bahá'í religions occurs in an account by the Belgian, Auguste Bricteux, of his sojourn in Persia, *Au Pays du Lion et du Soleil* (1908). An entire chapter, 'La Religion nouvelle', is

* In fact in 1852 after the attempt on the life of the Sháh (see pp. 132ff).

devoted to the subject.[115] At the beginning of the chapter, Bricteux writes: 'What follows is only the faithful translation of an exposition of the Bábí doctrine which has been dictated to me, at my request, by one of the most eminent men of the sect. I am forced to withhold his name for reasons that the reader will understand readily enough. In any case, I can affirm that the author is one of the luminaries of the new faith, and that there is not an Arabic or Persian writing relative to Bábism and Bahá'ism that he has not studied in depth.'[116]

In Russia also many writers began to turn their attention to the Bahá'í Faith. S. I. Umanets wrote several articles about the Bábí and Bahá'í Faith, and also one booklet entitled *Sovremennyi Babizm* [Contemporary Bábism] (1904). In this he refutes the allegation of the Russian newspapers that the assassination of Náṣiru'd-Dín Sháh was carried out by a Bábí, and he speaks of the evolution of the Bábí movement, which had been little more than a sect of Islam, into the Bahá'í Faith which could be regarded as a separate religion. Another writer who is of interest is the Armenian, Sargis Mubagajian, Atrpet. Of his book *Imamat: Strana Poklonnikov Imamov* [Imanat: The Country of the Worshippers of the Imáms] (1909), the second half is devoted to a consideration of 'Bábís and Bahá'ís'. A large number of photographs and drawings accompany the text, including three of the Báb (one showing him suspended for execution), two of Qurratu'l-'Ayn and one of Ḥájí Sulaymán Khán. Unfortunately these photographs have been taken up and reproduced in other books and have gained currency despite the fact that some (and perhaps all) of them are obvious fabrications.

Queen Marie of Romania

It would not be possible to conclude a survey of Western opinion about the Bahá'í religion in the period 1844–1944 without including some mention of Queen Marie of Romania (q.v., see fig. 7). One of the most remarkable women of the twentieth century, this great Queen was beset throughout the last part of her life by a series of personal tragedies. It was just at the beginning of this period of sorrow that Queen Marie first encountered the Bahá'í Faith. Martha Root, described by Shoghi Effendi as the 'leading Ambassadress' of Bahá'u'lláh's Faith, was the source of Queen Marie's first contact with the religion. While visiting Bucharest in 1926, Martha Root sent the Queen a copy of Dr Esslemont's *Bahá'u'lláh and the New Era*. This was followed by an audience on 30 January 1926. That Queen Marie's response to Bahá'u'lláh's message was an immediate, enthusiastic and courageous acceptance can be seen from the following article published in her name in the *Toronto Daily Star* a short while later, on 4 May 1926:

A woman brought me the other day a Book. I spell it with a capital letter because it is a glorious Book of love and goodness, strength and beauty.

She gave it to me because she had learned I was in grief and sadness and wanted to help . . . She put it into my hands saying: 'You seem to live up to His teachings.' And when I opened the Book I saw it was the word of 'Abdu'l-Bahá, prophet of love and kindness, and of his father the great teacher of international goodwill and understanding – of a religion which links all creeds.

Their writings are a great cry toward peace, reaching beyond all limits of frontiers, above all dissension about rites and dogmas. It is a religion based upon the inner spirit of God, upon the great not-to-be-overcome verity that God is love, meaning just that. It teaches that all hatreds, intrigues, suspicions, evil words, all aggressive patriotism even, are outside the one essential law of God, and that special beliefs are but surface things whereas the heart that beats with divine love knows no tribe nor race.

It is a wondrous Message that Bahá'u'lláh and his son 'Abdu'l-Bahá have given us. They have not set it up aggressively, knowing that the germ of eternal truth which lies at its core cannot but take root and spread.

There is only one great verity in it: Love, the mainspring of every energy, tolerance towards each other, desire of understanding each other, knowing each other, helping each other, forgiving each other.

It is Christ's Message taken up anew, in the same words almost, but adapted to the thousand years and more difference that lies between the year one and today. No man could fail to be better because of this Book.

I commend it to you all. If ever the name of Bahá'u'lláh or 'Abdu'l-Bahá comes to your attention, do not put their writings from you. Search out their Books, and let their glorious, peace-bringing, love-creating words and lessons sink into your hearts as they have into mine.

One's busy day may seem too full for religion. Or one may have a religion that satisfies. But the teachings of these gentle, wise and kindly men are compatible with all religion, and with no religion.

Seek them, and be the happier.[117]

When Shoghi Effendi received news of this spontaneous expression of the Queen's feelings towards the Bahá'í Faith, he wrote to her expressing the 'joyous admiration and gratitude' of himself and the Bahá'ís of both the East and the West for her noble and courageous tribute to the faith. In his letter he refers to the recent martyrdoms in Jahrum (see pp. 465ff), and of the consolation that her tribute brought to those suffering for the Cause.[118] In her reply, dated 27 August 1926, Marie refers to the fact that her open pronouncement of her views had caused disapproval to be expressed in high circles:

I was deeply moved on reception of your letter.

Indeed a great light came to me with the message of Bahá'u'llah and Abdu'l Baha. It came as all great messages come at an hour of dire grief and inner conflict and distress, so the seed sank deeply.

My youngest daughter finds also great strength and comfort in the teachings of the beloved masters.

We pass on the message from mouth to mouth and all those we give it to see a light suddenly lighting before them and much that was obscure and perplexing becomes simple, luminous and full of hope as never before.

That my open letter was balm to those suffering for the cause, is indeed a great happiness to me, and I take it as a sign that God accepted my humble tribute.

The occasion given me to be able to express myself publically, was also His Work – for indeed it was a chain of circumstances of which each link led me unwittingly one step further, till suddenly all was clear before my eyes and I understood why it had been.

Thus does He lead us finally to our ultimate destiny.

Some of those of my caste wonder at and disapprove my courage to step forwarded [*sic*] pronouncing words not habitual for Crowned Heads to pronounce, but I advance by an inner urge I cannot resist.

With bowed head I recognise that I too am but an instrument in greater Hands and rejoice in the knowledge.

Little by little the veil is lifting, grief tore it in two. And grief was also a step leading me ever nearer truth, therefore do I not cry out against grief!

May you and those beneath your guidance be blessed and upheld by the sacred strength of those gone before you.

Marie[119]

Later the same year, following a journey to the United States, two further public tributes to the faith appeared in her series of articles that were syndicated to many North American newspapers. One of these stated:

At first we all conceive of God as something or somebody apart from ourselves . . . This is not so. We cannot, with our earthly faculties entirely grasp His meaning – no more than we can really understand the meaning of Eternity . . .

God is All, Everything. He is the power behind all beginnings. He is the inexhaustible source of supply, of love, of good, of progress, of achievement. God is therefore Happiness.

His is the voice within us that shows us good and evil.

But mostly we ignore or misunderstand this voice. Therefore did He choose his Elect to come down amongst us upon earth to make clear His word, His real meaning. Therefore the Prophets; therefore Christ, Muḥammad, Bahá'u'lláh, for man needs from time to time a voice upon earth to bring God to him, to sharpen the realization of the existence of the true God. Those voices sent to us had to become flesh, so that with our earthly ears we should be able to hear and understand.[120]

It is estimated that through her syndicated series, these three articles were published in over two hundred newspapers in the USA and Canada.[121]

Over the ensuing years, Martha Root kept up a correspondence with Queen Marie and also had a further seven interviews with her. Over this period the following tributes were penned by the Queen confirming her as the first crowned head of a country to embrace the Bahá'í Faith:

'The Bahai teaching brings peace to the soul and hope to the heart.

'To those in search of assurance the words of the Father are as a fountain in the desert after long wandering.'[122]

'More than ever today when the world is facing such a crisis of bewilderment and unrest, must we stand firm in Faith seeking that which binds together instead of tearing asunder.

'To those searching for light, the Bahá'í Teachings offer a star which will lead them to deeper understanding, to assurance, peace and good will with all men.'[123] (See fig. 6.)

'The Bahai teaching brings peace and understanding.

'It is like a wide embrace gathering together all those who have long searched for words of hope.

'It accepts all great prophets gone before, it destroys no other creeds and leaves all doors open.

'Saddened by the continual strife amongst believers of many confessions and wearied of their intolerance towards each other, I discovered in the Bahai teaching the real spirit of Christ so often denied and misunderstood:

'Unity instead of strife, Hope instead of condemnation, Love instead of hate, and a great reassurance for all men.'[124]

References

1. *Literary Gazette* 15 Nov. 1845, p. 757
2. *The Times* 19 Nov. 1845, p. 3, col. 6
3. *Eclectic Magazine* Jan. 1846, p. 142
4. *Port Phillip Herald* Vol. 7, No. 659, 31 Mar. 1846, p. 4, col. 3
5. Sheil to Palmerston No. 20, 12 Feb. 1850: FO 60 150
6. Sheil to Palmerston No. 72, 21 June 1850: FO 60 152
7. Enclosed in 6 *supra*
8. ibid.
9. Lady Sheil *Life and Manners in Persia* p. 179
10. Dolgorukov to Nesselrode No. 9, 24 Jan. 1849 OS (5 Feb. NS): Dossier No. 177, Ṭihrán 1849, pp. 32–3. Chahárdihí *Shaykhí-garí, Bábí-garí* p. 271 (trans. from Persian)
11. Dolgorukov to Nesselrode No. 94, 26 Dec. 1848 OS (5 Jan. 1849 NS): Dossier No. 177, Ṭihrán 1848, p. 360. 'Excerpts from Dispatches' p. 18
12. Dolgorukov to Anitchkov No. 296, 3 July 1850 OS (15 July NS): Nicolas 'Le Dossier russo-anglais' p. 359 (trans. from French)
13. Dolgorukov to Seniavin No. 53, 3 July 1850 OS (15 July OS): Dossier No. 133, Ṭihrán 1850, pp. 434–5. Chahárdihí *Shaykhí-garí, Bábí-garí* p. 279 (trans. from Persian)
14. Dolgorukov to Seniavin No. 66, 17 Sept. 1852 OS (29 Sept. NS): Dossier No. 158, Ṭihrán 1852, p. 608. Chahárdihí *Shaykhí-garí, Bábí-garí* p. 289 (trans. from Persian)
15. Ferrier to de LaHitte, 25 June 1850: MAE Sér. Corr. Polit. MD No. 24 (1833–56), p. 341 (trans. from French)
16. *Journal of the American Oriental Society* New York, Vol. 4, 1854, p. xxiv
17. Wright 'Bab und seine Secte' pp. 384–5 (trans. from German)
18. *Revue de l'Orient* 2nd ser., Vol. 5, 1849, p. 264 (trans. From French)
19. ibid. 2nd ser., Vol. 8, 1850, p. 124
20. *Standard* 7 Oct. 1852, p. 3, col. 2
21. *Sun* 7 Oct. 1852, p. 4, col. 1
22. *Oesterreichischer Soldatenfreund* 5th year, No. 123, 12 Oct. 1852, p. 513
23. *The Times* 13 Oct. 1852, p. 4, col. 4
24. *Le Constitutionnel* No. 286, 13 Oct. 1852, p. 2, col. 4
25. ibid. No. 310, 5 Nov. 1852, p. 2, col. 2
26. *New York Times* 8 Nov. 1852, p. 6, col. 4
27. Stern *Dawnings of Light in the East* pp. 261–2
28. Browne *A Traveller's Narrative* pp. 201–2

29. Dorn 'Bericht über eine wissenschaftliche Reise' and *Reise nach Masanderan im Jahre 1860*. N. Khanykov also published an account of this journey: 'Compte rendu d'un voyage'. (See Bibliography)
30. Dorn *Sammlung von Handschriften* pp. 4–5 (trans. from German). See 31 *infra*
31. The first paper was 'Die vordem Chanykov'sche', published separately as *Sammlung von Handschriften*. The second was 'Nachträge zu dem Verzeichniss', published separately as *Morgenländische Handschriften*. For full titles and details, see Bibliography.
32. Dorn *Sammlung von Handschriften* pp. 5–6 (trans. from German). See 31 *supra*
33. Polak *Persien* p. 350 (trans. from German)
34. Ussher *London to Persepolis* p. 627
35. Eastwick *Three Years' Residence in Persia* Vol. 1, p. 206
36. Balyuzi *E. G. Browne* p. 36. The relevant passage in Mírzá Mihdí's manuscript dissertation (Cambridge Univ. Library, Browne Collection, F 57) occurs on p. 284.
37. Gobineau *Religions et Philosophies* p. 248 (trans. from French)
38. ibid. pp. 281–2 (trans. from French)
39. ibid. pp. 289–90 (trans. from French)
40. ibid. p. 291 (trans. from French)
41. ibid. pp. 297–8 (trans. from French)
42. ibid. pp. 306–7 (trans. from French)
43. ibid. p. 309 (trans. from French)
44. ibid. p. 313 (trans. from French)
45. Renan *The Apostles* (English translation of *Les Apôtres*) p. 283 (transliteration altered)
46. ibid. p. 284n
47. ibid. pp. 284–5
48. ibid. p. 283n
49. Renan *Oeuvres Complètes* Vol. 10, p. 453 (trans. from French)
50. Franck *Journal des Savants* Dec. 1865, p. 786 (trans. from French)
51. C. S. Gobineau (ed.) *Correspondance* p. 289 (trans. from French)
52. Evans 'Bab and Babism' p. 210
53. ibid.
54. Arnold 'A Persian Passion Play' p. 668
55. Giachery 'An Italian Scientist Extols the Báb' p. 900
56. ibid. p. 902
57. Rivadneyra *Viaje al Interior de Persia* Vol. 1, p. 244 (trans. from Spanish)
58. Serena *Hommes et Choses en Perse* p. 36 (trans. from French)
59. Dieulafoy *La Perse, la Chaldée et la Susiane* p. 83 (trans. from French)
60. ibid. pp. 81 and 88 respectively
61. Andreas *Die Babis in Persien* pp. 67–8
62. Browne *A Year Amongst the Persians* pp. 328–9
63. Browne *A Traveller's Narrative* pp. 351–64
64. ibid. p. 364
65. Browne, English Introduction to *Nuqṭatu'l-Káf* p. xvi
66. Browne *A Year Amongst the Persians* p. 8
67. ibid. p. 578
68. Browne *A Persian Anthology* p. 39
69. ibid. p. 38
70. Ross *Both Ends of the Candle* p. 54
71. *Oxford Magazine* 1892, p. 394
72. Browne *A Persian Anthology* pp. 40–41

73. Balyuzi *E. G. Browne* p. 58
74. Phelps *Abbas Effendi* p. x
75. See Browne 'Catalogue and Description of 27 Bábí Manuscripts' p. 706, and also Browne *Nuqṭatu'l-Káf* p. lii
76. Sanderson 'An Interview with A. L. M. Nicolas' p. 885
77. ibid. (trans. from French)
78. ibid. pp. 885–6 (trans. from French)
79. Browne *Materials*, p. 275
80. *The Bahá'í World* Vol. 8, p. 625 (trans. from French)
81. Adamíyyat *Andíshih-há* p. 11
82. Huart *La Religion de Bab* pp. 40–9
83. Tumanski 'Dva poslednikh' pp. 314–16
84. Benjamin *Persia and the Persians* pp. 353–5
85. Wolff to Salisbury No. 178, 8 Sept. 1888: FO 60 493
86. Curzon *Persia and the Persian Question* Vol. 1, pp. 496–7
87. ibid. p. 449
88. ibid. p. 501
89. ibid. pp. 501–2
90. ibid. p. 503
91. Gordon *Persia Revisited* pp. 81 and 83
92. Article by Edgar Prestage in *Encyclopaedia Britannica* 11th edn (1910–11), Vol. 8, p. 845
93. Eça de Queirós *A Correspondencia de Fradique Mendes* pp. 48–54 (trans. from Portuguese)
94. Bois 'Babism and Bahaism' p. 4
95. Wesselitsky *A New Great Russian Poet* p. 1
96. ibid. p. 6
97. E. Abbott and L. Campbell *The Life and Letters of Benjamin Jowett* Vol. 2, p. 466
98. A. S. Peake in *Dictionary of National Biography* Supplement 1912–21, p. 120
99. Cheyne *The Reconciliation of Races and Religions* pp. 5 and 132–3
100. ibid. pp. 8–9 and 74
101. Carpenter *Comparative Religion* pp. 70–71
102. Letter from Rolland to Roubakine 19 Feb. 1918 (trans. from French)
103. Birukoff *Tolstoi und der Orient* p. 98 (trans. from German)
104. Letter from Tolstoy to Arfa'u'd-Dawlih 23 July 1901. Preserved in the Musée de la Paix, Monte Carlo (trans. from French)
105. Nicolaides 'Leo Tolstois Stellung zu den Religionen' pp. 566–7 (trans. from German)
106. Birukoff *Tolstoi und der Orient* pp. 99–100 (trans. from German)
107. ibid. p. 120 (trans. from German)
108. Nicolaides 'Leo Tolstois Stellung zu den Religionen' p. 567 (trans. from German)
109. Forel *Out of My Life and Work* p. 342 (transliteration altered)
110. Ross *Both Ends of the Candle* p. 85
111. Ross 'Babism' (see Bibliography)
112. Bassett *Land of the Imams* p. 300
113. Feuvrier *Trois Ans à la Cour de Perse* pp. 101–2
114. Chirol *The Middle Eastern Question* pp. 113, 122–3, 124–5
115. Bricteux *Au Pays du Lion et du Soleil* pp. 244–69
116. ibid. p. 244 (trans. from French)
117. Quoted in *The Bahá'í World* Vol. 5, pp. 322–3

118. Rabbani *The Priceless Pearl* pp. 108–10
119. Letter from Queen Marie to Shoghi Effendi 27 Aug. 1926. Photographic facsimile as frontispiece to *The Bahá'í World* Vol. 8. Original letter preserved in Haifa
120. *Evening Bulletin* Philadelphia 27 Sept. 1926 quoted in *The Bahá'í World* Vol. 5, pp. 323–4
121. Rabbani *The Priceless Pearl* p. 100
122. Open letter penned by Queen Marie in 1934. Photographic facsimile as frontispiece to *The Bahá'í World* Vol. 5. Original letter preserved in Haifa
123. Open letter penned by Queen Marie in 1936. Photographic facsimile as frontispiece to *The Bahá'í World* Vol. 6. Original letter preserved in Haifa
124. Open letter penned by Queen Marie Sept. 1936. Photographic facsimile in Rabbani *The Priceless Pearl* facing p. 280. Original letter preserved in Haifa

Section B

The Ministry of the Báb (1844–53)

ONE

Accounts of the Báb and His Martyrdom

It is a remarkable fact that within two years of the Báb's declaration of his mission to his first disciple, Mullá Ḥusayn, at a time when even most Persians were as yet unaware of his claim, the foremost newspaper of the Western world, *The Times* of London, carried a report of the advent of the new religious movement and an account of the first persecution that it encountered on Persian soil.

On 1 November 1845, under the title 'Persia', *The Times* carried the following report:

We have been favoured with the following letter, dated Bushire, August 10:-

A Persian merchant, who has lately returned from a pilgrimage to Mecca, had been for some time endeavouring here to prove that he was one of the successors of Mahomet, and therefore had a right to demand of all true Mussulmans to mention him as such in their profession of faith; he had already collected a good number of followers, who secretly aided him in forwarding his views. On the evening of the 23rd of June last, I have been informed from a creditable source, four persons being heard at Shiraz repeating their profession of faith according to the form prescribed by the new impostor were apprehended, tried, and found guilty of unpardonable blasphemy. They were sentenced to lose their beards by fire being set to them. The sentence was put into execution with all the zeal and fanaticism becoming a true believer in Mahomet. Not deeming the loss of beards a sufficient punishment for the believers in the impostor, they were further sentenced on the next day to have their faces blacked and exposed throughout the city. Each of them was led by a Mirgazah (executioner), who had made a hole in his nose and passed through it a string, which he sometimes pulled with such violence that the unfortunate fellows cried out alternately for mercy from the executioner and for vengeance from Heaven. It is the custom in Persia on such occasions for the executioners to collect money from the spectators, and particularly from the shopkeepers in the bazaar. In the evening, when the pockets of the executioners were well filled with money, they led the unfortunate fellows to the city gate, and there told them

'The world was all before them where to choose
'Their place of rest, and Providence their guide.'

After which the Mollahs at Shiraz sent men to Bushire with power to seize the impostor, and take him to Shiraz, where, on being tried, he very wisely denied the charge of apostacy laid against him, and thus escaped from punishment.[1]

This article contains clear references to the advancement of a claim by the Báb, his pilgrimage to Mecca, the fact that he had gathered followers around him, the arrest of four of his adherents in Shíráz for raising the call to prayer (*adhán*) according to a new formula, the punishment and exile of these Bábís from Shíráz by Ḥusayn Khán, Governor of Fárs,* the dispatch of men to Búshihr to arrest the Báb, and the Báb's trial in Shíráz. As to the question of whether he denied his claim, this is a point that has been the subject of controversy.†

Unfortunately, the author of this report is not indicated.‡

The Spread of the Religion of the Báb

Following this episode, the Báb remained in Shíráz for a little more than one year. After this he proceeded to Iṣfahán where the powerful Governor of that city, Manúchihr Khán, Mu'tamadu'd-Dawlih,§ became a disciple of his. With the death of Manúchihr Khán on 21 February 1847, however, the Báb was removed, on the orders of Muḥammad Sháh's Prime Minister, Ḥájí Mírzá Áqásí, to the prison-fortress of Mákú, in the remote north-western corner of Persia. From the time of the above episode in Shíráz until his arrival in Mákú, there are no further references to the Báb in contemporary Western records. His religion was, however, spreading through Persia with remarkable rapidity. Gobineau, writing in the early 1860s and familiar with Persia after a five-year residence there, wrote:

> And so, here is a religion presented and promoted by a mere youth. In a very few years, that is to say from 1847 to 1852, this religion had disseminated throughout almost the whole of Persia, and counted within its fold numerous zealous adherents. In five years, a nation of from ten to twelve million people, occupying a territory which in bygone days had supported a population of fifty millions, a nation which does not possess those means of communication considered by us as so indispensable to the spread of ideas, I mean, of course, journals and pamphlets, and which did not have a postal service, nor even a single road fit for carriages in the entire extent of its empire; this nation, I say, had in five years been, in its entirety, penetrated by the doctrine of the Bábís, and the impression produced had been such that these most serious events, which I have recounted above, resulted therefrom. And it is not at all the ignorant

* See pp. 169–71.

† For a further discussion of this point see Balyuzi *The Báb* pp. 88–9 and 94–9, and Cadwalader 'Persia: An Early Mention of the Báb'.

‡ The editor has made enquiries at *The Times* Archives Dept. and it appears that the author of this letter cannot be traced since detailed records do not go back to this date. It is almost certain that the author of the report was one of the British colony in Búshihr which consisted of a handful of merchants and the staff of the Residency. The British Resident at Búshihr, Samuel Hennell, was in receipt of regular letters from the British Agent in Shíráz, Mírzá Maḥmúd. Not all of Mírzá Maḥmúd's letters are in the Public Record Office files, and it is possible that he did report this episode in a letter that was omitted from the files.

§ See pp. 167–9.

part of the population that has been touched; it is eminent members of the clergy, the rich and learned classes, the women from the most important families; and lastly, after the Muslims, it is the philosophers, the Sufis in great numbers, and many Jews, who have been conquered by the new revelation . . .

Thus, Bábism has had a considerable effect on the mind of the Persian nation, and has even spread itself beyond the limits of that territory; it has boiled over into the pashalik of Baghdád, and also passed into India. Among the facts concerning it, one must note, as one of the most curious, that even during the lifetime of the Báb, many of the doctors of the new religion, many of its most convinced and most devout sectaries, had never even personally known their prophet, and do not appear to have attached any primary importance to receiving his instructions from his own mouth. However, they rendered to him, completely and without any reservation, the honours and veneration to which, in their way of looking at it, he was entitled. One has already seen how Her Holiness the Pure, the Consolation of the Eyes,* had never met the Báb. The Mázindaráni chief Mullá Muḥammad-'Alíy-i-Bárfurúshí† was also one; as was Mullá Muḥammad-'Alíy-i-Zanjání;‡ and also His Holiness the Eternal§ . . . It follows from this observation that the eloquence of the innovator, his personal powers of charm, two qualities which he certainly had in him to a high degree, were not the principal cause of the success of his doctrines, and that if some from among his intimate circle yielded to this mode of persuasion, the greatest number, and without doubt the most eminent, were enraptured and convinced by the depth of his teachings.[2]

Prince Dolgorukov, the Russian Minister, in a dispatch of 7 March 1849, also noted the rapid increase in the number of the Bábís. After relating the success of a rebellion in Khurásán by a Qájár prince, he writes:

However, no matter how serious this question may be, it has not preoccupied society to the same extent ever since the sectaries of the Bab have apparently had the tendency to grow in all parts of the Kingdom. The Amir [-Niẓám] confessed to me that their number can be already put at 100,000; that they have already appeared in southern provinces; that they are found in large numbers in Tihran itself; and that, finally, their presence in Adhirbayjan is beginning to worry him very much. In truth, there are rumours that in Zanjan they have appeared 800 strong, and that by their presence they threaten to disrupt the public order.[3]

Ferrier, the French Agent, also remarked on this amazing phenomenon on 25 July 1850:

The Government no longer knows how to prevent the conversion of these enthusiasts who proclaim themselves even more by the sword than by the word; they are increasing in a frightening manner from all the bottled-up discontent in Persia. The Amír had thought to strike the evil at its root in showing himself pitiless towards them; but the bloody executions that he ordered have not arrested the progress of the evil. It is in

* i.e. Ṭáhirih

† Gobineau is in error here, for Muḥammad-'Alíy-i-Barfurúshí, i.e. Quddús, met the Báb in Shíráz and accompanied him on his pilgrimage to Mecca.

‡ i.e. Ḥujjat

§ Mírzá Yaḥyá, Ṣubḥ-i-Azal

vain that the Ministers of England and Russia have pointed out that history was there for us to learn from; that religious persecution has never been of use but to the advantage of the persecuted schism. He does not wish to hear and continues his system of extermination. It is truly difficult to say that he is completely wrong, because it is impossible to govern Persians as one governs Europeans; we do not usually take sufficient account of their exceptional morals and of their profoundly ingrained prejudices. We always wish to judge them from the point of view of our civilization, with the result that occasionally we are misled in our understanding of what occurs between them in Persia; the point of view that dominates all others is that of force; that is the sovereign law – reason, humanity, right, morals will always disappear before it, and he who is inclined to use it must do so tyrannically.[4]

The Báb at Mákú and Chihríq

In July 1847, the Báb was taken on the order of the Prime Minister, Ḥájí Mírzá Áqásí, to Mákú. His presence in Mákú evidently perturbed Dolgorukov. Mákú is close to the Russian border and there had recently been religious disturbances in the adjoining Russian province of Caucasus.* The Russian Minister, therefore, fearful of a recurrence of these events, demanded the removal of the Báb from Mákú.

He refers to this in a dispatch of 16 February 1848:

> For some time now, Tihran has been subject to the influence of sinister predictions. A Siyyid, known in this country under the name of 'The Bab', who was exiled from Isfahan due to a rebellion which he caused there, and who last year, on my demand, was removed from the vicinity of our frontiers, to which he was exiled by the Persian Government, has recently circulated a small compilation in which he foretells an impending invasion by the Turkomans as a result of which the Shah would have to leave his capital.
>
> These predictions have produced a disquieting result in a people of such a volatile character as the Persian people . . .[5]

This dispatch presents two problems. Although Dolgorukov states that the removal of the Báb took place in the previous year, according to Bahá'í historians it did not occur until April 1848, after the date of this dispatch.† Also, the compilation that is referred to is somewht puzzling. There is no such work among the known writings of the Báb and its existence is not referred to in either Muslim or Bahá'í accounts of the Báb.

The next reference to the Báb in Dolgorukov's dispatches presents no such problems. It was sent on 5 January 1849. 'Several times already I have informed the Imperial Ministry of the Muslim sectary who is called the Bab. This fanatic who, due to the disorders which he tried to produce in different provinces of Persia, was removed on my demand from Russian

* See p. 14n.

† It would seem probable that Dolgorukov had submitted his demands for the removal of the Báb in the previous year, and was under the impression that this had been carried out, although it had not as yet been put into effect by the inefficient Persian administration.

borders, is now under strict surveillance in a village not far from Urumiyyih. He styles himself the *nayib* [representative] of the twelfth Imam.'[6]

The village referred to was, of course, Chihríq, where the Báb was to be kept imprisoned for over two years. It was from Chihríq that the Báb was brought to Tabríz on the orders of Ḥájí Mírzá Áqásí to be put on trial. Nabíl states that it was considered inadvisable to take the direct route to Tabríz through Khuy, so the Báb's guard took him by the much longer route via Urúmíyyih. The Báb's stay at Urúmíyyih was marked by some most remarkable scenes. Even the American missionaries, whose headquarters were situated near Urúmíyyih, did not fail to take note of these events. Dr Austin Wright (q.v.) recorded:

> He was ... then banished to Mákú, a remote district, six days' journey from Urúmíyyih, on the borders of Turkey. Here he was kept in custody, but anyone who wanted to see him was admitted, and he was allowed to send letters to his friends who had become fairly numerous in various parts of Persia. He was visited by several worthies of Urúmíyyih, who became his followers. He dictated to a scribe something he called his Qur'án [i.e. the *Bayán*], and the Arabic sentences flowed so fast from his mouth that many of the Persians who witnessed it believed him to be inspired. It was also related of him that he did miracles, and whole masses of people gave willing credence to this rumour, since it was known that he lived an extremely abstemious life and spent the greatest part of his time in prayer. In consequence of this he was taken on the government's orders to 'Tschari', near Salmás, only two days' journey from Urúmíyyih; there he was completely cut off from the world; yet he continued to write to his friends letters, which they spread further as the effusions of one inspired; I have learned nothing more about these other than that they were incomprehensible. His disciples became more and more numerous, and in some parts of the country they became involved in fierce quarrels with the so-called orthodox party ... The affair became so serious that the Government gave orders that the founder of the sect should be brought to Tabríz and given the bastinado, and that his disciples should be arrested wherever they were found and punished with fines and beatings. On the way to Tabríz, the Báb was taken to Urúmíyyih, where the Governor treated him with special consideration and many people received permission to visit him. On one occasion, a crowd were with him, and as the Governor* afterwards remarked, they were all mysteriously moved and burst into tears.[7]

The Rev. J. H. Shedd (q.v.) was another American missionary who made a special study of the Bábís (and whose name will be mentioned shortly in relation to Dr Cormick). He wrote: 'When the Bab passed through Oroomiah in 1850 on his way to his execution, the missionaries watched the excitement with great interest. The crowds of people were ready to receive him as the long-expected Imam, even the water in which he bathed was regarded as holy water.'[8]

* Malik-Qásim Mírzá (q.v.)

Finally, concerning the Báb at Urúmíyyih, the following is a passage from a book by the Rev. Dr Isaac Adams (q.v.), a Nestorian Persian who lived for many years in Urúmíyyih: 'We are told that vast numbers flocked to see him, and even the governor did not conceal his sympathy with the prisoner of such engaging manners; the crowd shed tears as they looked upon the interesting young man, and more than half believed that he might be the very "Imam Mahdi," the great desire of Moslem nations. Traditions about the town relate that when he went to the bath the people carried away the water in vessels, in which he had bathed as if it were holy.'[9]

Dr Cormick's Account

When the Báb arrived in Tabríz he was brought to trial before the Crown Prince, Náṣiru'd-Dín Mírzá (later Náṣiru'd-Dín S̲h̲áh). The trial took a somewhat ludicrous turn, and at the end of it the 'ulamá gathered to decide the sentence. It appears that the death sentence was being contemplated, and it was in connection with this that the only Westerner to have had an interview with the Báb, Dr Cormick (q.v.), met him. Dr Cormick was asked to examine the Báb in order to determine his sanity, and he wrote an account of this and of a subsequent interview with the Báb after the latter had been bastinadoed, to Rev. Benjamin Labaree, an American missionary. Rev. J. H. Shedd, a colleague of Labaree with an interest in the Bábí religion, made a copy of Cormick's account and this was forwarded to Browne by Shedd's son on his father's death. The following is Cormick's account:

You ask me for some particulars of my interview with the founder of the sect known as Bábís. Nothing of any importance transpired in this interview, as the Báb was aware of my having been sent with two other Persian doctors to see whether he was of sane mind or merely a madman, to decide the question whether to put him to death or not. With this knowledge he was loth to answer any questions put to him. To all enquiries he merely regarded us with a mild look, chanting in a low melodious voice some hymns, I suppose. Two other *Sayyids*,* his intimate friends, were also present, who subsequently were put to death with him,† besides a couple of government officials. He only once deigned to answer me, on my saying that I was not a Musulmán and was willing to know something about his religion, as I might perhaps be inclined to adopt it. He regarded me very intently on my saying this, and replied that he had no doubt of all Europeans coming over to his religion. Our report to the Sháh at that time was of a nature to spare his life. He was put to death some time after by the order of the *Amír-i-Niẓám* Mírzá Taqí Khán. On our report he merely got the bastinado, in which operation a *farrásh*, whether intentionally or not, struck him across the face with the stick

* These were, no doubt, the two brothers Sayyid Ḥasan and Sayyid Ḥusayn of Yazd, of whom the latter was especially his amanuensis. [EGB]

† This is an error. Sayyid Ḥusayn was put to death in the great persecution of 1852, two years after the Báb. [EGB]

destined for his feet, which produced a great wound and swelling of the face. On being asked whether a Persian surgeon should be brought to treat him, he expressed a desire that I should be sent for, and I accordingly treated him for a few days, but in the interviews consequent on this I could never get him to have a confidential chat with me, as some Government people were always present, he being a prisoner.

He was very thankful for my attentions to him. He was a very mild and delicate-looking man, rather small in stature and very fair for a Persian, with a melodious soft voice, which struck me much. Being a Sayyid, he was dressed in the habits of that sect, as were also his two companions. In fact his whole look and deportment went far to dispose one in his favour. Of his doctrine I heard nothing from his own lips, although the idea was that there existed in his religion a certain approach to Christianity. He was seen by some Armenian carpenters, who were sent to make some repairs in his prison, reading the Bible, and he took no pains to conceal it, but on the contrary told them of it. Most assuredly the Musulmán fanaticism does not exist in his religion, as applied to Christians, nor is there that restraint of females that now exists.[10]

Another early description of the Báb, although not this time from personal knowledge, comes from Lady Sheil:* 'Báb possessed a mild and benignant countenance, his manners were composed and dignified, his eloquence was impressive, and he wrote rapidly and well.'[11]

According to Dolgorukov, during the Mázindarán upheaval in 1849, the question of executing the Báb was brought up and indeed the order was issued, but the Governor of Ádharbáyján refused to comply. This event, which is not recorded in any other source, is related by Dolgorukov in a dispatch dated 27 March 1849:

'It is maintained that Malik Qasim Mirza (q.v.) has received a secret order to execute the leader of these fanatics [the Báb], who is incarcerated in a fortress near Urumiyyih. But the Governor of Adhirbayjan refused to do this, fearing to provoke a rebellion of the people. There is no doubt whatsoever that such a measure would have made them even more audacious and dangerous.'[12]

Mochenin, a student at St Petersburg University who was travelling in Persia during the Bábí upheavals,† appears to have passed through Chihríq shortly before the Báb's final removal from there. He records: 'In the month of June 1850, having proceeded to Chihríq in pursuit of my affairs, I saw a *bálá-khánih* [upper chamber] from the height of which the Báb was teaching his doctrine. The concourse of people was so great that the court was not large enough to contain all the audience; the majority remained in the road and listened, engrossed, to the new Qur'án. A little time later, the Báb was transferred to Tabríz in order to be condemned to death.'[13]

* Lady Sheil may well have obtained this description directly from Dr Cormick.

† Mochenin's tour may have had some connection with Russian Intelligence activities, as the British Consul, Stevens, mentions (26 July 1850) a report by Mochenin on Turkish troop dispositions along the frontier. (FO 60 153)

Transfer of the Báb to Tabríz

And so it was that Mírzá Taqí Khán, the Amír-Niẓám, witnessing his failure to contain the spread of the religion of the Báb, determined to strike at the roots of the new movement. He decided upon the execution of the Báb. Orders were therefore sent to bring the Báb to Tabríz. George Alexander Stevens (q.v.), who was in charge of the British Consulate in Tabríz in his brother's absence, records the Báb's arrival there in a dispatch to Viscount Palmerston dated 30 June 1850: 'Bâb who was a Prisoner in the Fortress of Tchehrik was brought to Tabreez yesterday, and will it is stated be put to death by being fired out of a gun tomorrow morning.'[14]

He was, of course, incorrect in his last statement. The Governor of Ádharbáyján at this time was Ḥamzih Mírzá (q.v.), but as Richard Stevens (q.v.), the British Consul in Tabríz, reports, the true power lay in other hands:

> Our Prince Governor is not a badly disposed man, at least I do not hear anything to the contrary – but his power is only nominal, the power is vested in the Vizir, Mehmed Reza Khan, and in Meerza Hasan Khan, the Vizir-i-Nizam. The former is too old, and too much addicted to the use of opium to fill such a post with advantage to the country – the latter, thinks only of accumulating wealth, caring very little about the legality of the means he employs to attain his object: both are unpopular, – one for his rough treatment of and indecent language he addresses to all who approach him in business – the other for his cruel and arbitrary character, qualities sufficiently dangerous in this country, but rendered more so when joined to his intemperate habits.[15]

The Amír-Niẓám sent an order through his brother, Mírzá Ḥasan Khán (q.v.), the Vazír-Niẓam, to the Governor of Ádharbáyján, Ḥamzih Mírzá, to effect the execution of the Báb. But Ḥamzih Mírzá refused to carry out this order, not wishing to be the instrument of the death of a descendant of the Prophet of God, particularly one who had committed no crime. The Amír-Niẓám was therefore compelled to send a second order instructing his brother, the Vazír-Niẓám, to carry out the order himself. Ferrier, the French Agent, writing on 25 July 1850, gives an account of the Báb which he concludes by referring to the fact that the Amír-Niẓám was forced to transmit his instructions a second time, although he states this to have been due to Ḥamzih Mírzá's misunderstanding of the first instructions:

> The Báb, the founder of the new sect, made his appearance four years ago. He is a mullá from Shíráz so learned that the most learned of the Shí'ih doctors have only been able to find two faults in the Qur'án which he has written for his proselytes. But these two faults seem sufficient to prove him an impostor to the Muslims; Muḥammad not having made any when he wrote his. Be that as it may, the Báb was arrested in 1847 and imprisoned in a little fortress situated on one of the islands of Lake Urúmíyyih. The Sháh

had him taken from there three weeks ago, in order to have him killed by being bayoneted in the public square of Tabríz. The order for this execution having been misunderstood by the Governor of Ádharbáyján, has still not been carried out, but a second, very urgent one has left these last few days, so that it would not be postponed an instant longer. The Báb's life should, by now, have been ended. His disciples are not aggrieved by it, believing that he will be lifted to the sky and will return to earth in the company of the Imám Mahdí.[16]

The Russian Consul in Tabríz, Anitchkov, also noted the Báb's arrival in Tabríz. On 5 July 1850, he wrote to Dolgorukov: 'The Báb, who is known to your Excellency, has been brought to Tabríz, and is, at present, detained in the arsenal. The orders of the Prime Minister as to what is to be done with him are awaited.'[17]

The Martyrdom of the Báb

The martyrdom of the Báb took place in Tabríz on 9 July 1850. Anitchkov, the Russian Consul in Tabríz, sent an account of this to the Russian Foreign Ministry on 15 July 1850. Unfortunately Anitchkov does not give full details of the event itself. One wonders whether he may not have hesitated to send a full report of the seemingly miraculous events that transpired for fear of being ridiculed by his superiors. Nevertheless, he does give a very definite indication that the affair did not pass smoothly, by alluding to the ineptitude of the soldiers and the turning of the punishment into complete 'torture'. Anitchkov's account is also important in that it bears witness to the heroism and complete self-renunciation of the Báb's companion, Mírzá Muḥammad-'Alíy-i-Zunúzí.

The Báb has been put to death in Tabríz.* One of his principal followers, named Mírzá Muḥammad-'Alí, partook of his fate.

During this punishment, no disturbances occurred, thanks to the well-considered measures taken by the local authorities. The two condemned men faced death gallantly, without asking for quarter and without complaining of their sufferings.

Muḥammad-'Alí showed a singular firmness of character. It was completely in vain that he was tempted with everything that is possible in the world, in order to save his life. In spite of all that was offered to him to abandon the Báb, rather than save his life, he begged earnestly for permission to die at the feet of his master. He had no desire to hear any talk of pardon.

Both were shot by the soldiers. But these latter, little used to proceedings of this sort, transformed the punishment into complete torture.

The bodies of the victims were then thrown outside the gates of the town, and eaten by dogs.[18]

Dolgorukov mentioned the martyrdom of the Báb in a dispatch to the Russian Foreign Ministry on 15 July. After reporting the progress of the

* 'Le Bâb a subi le dernier supplice à Tauris.'

Zanján upheaval, he wrote: 'It is reported that the founder of this sect, who is known as Báb, and has been kept under guard at a building near Urúmíyyih, has been executed by order of the Government at Tabríz.'[19]

The British Consul, Richard Stevens, was unfortunately not in Tabríz at the time of the martyrdom of the Báb.* His brother, George Alexander Stevens, was in charge of the Consulate and failed to report this event.

Sheil must therefore have obtained his information from other sources, since on 22 July 1850 he reported to Lord Palmerston, the British Foreign Secretary:

> The founder of this sect has been executed at Tabreez. He was killed by a volley of musketry, and his death was on the point of giving his religion a lustre which would have largely increased its proselytes. When the smoke and dust cleared away after the volley, Bâb was not to be seen, and the populace proclaimed that he had ascended to the skies. The balls had broken the ropes by which he was bound, but he was dragged from the recess where after some search, he was discovered, and shot.
>
> His death, according to the belief of his disciples will make no difference, as Bâb must always exist.[20]

On his return to Tabríz, Richard Stevens wrote to Sheil on 24 July 1850:

'I find my brother has omitted to report to Your Excellency officially the arrival here from Tchehrik of the Bâb and his publick execution here on the 8th Instant.† He was shot in the barracks adjoining the palace together with one of his followers, a step-son of Agha Seyed Aly, one of the Tabreez Mooshtaheds.‡

'The Vezir Nizam caused their bodies to be thrown into the Town ditch where they were devoured by dogs.'[21]

On receiving the above report, Sheil felt moved to address a note to Mírzá Taqí Khán, the Amír-Niẓám, protesting about the treatment of the body of the Báb after his execution. The note, dated 3 August 1850, reads:

> Your Excellency is aware of the warm interest taken by the British Government in all that concerns the honor respectability and credit of this Government, and it is on this account I make you acquainted with a recent occurrence in Tabreez which perhaps has not been brought to Your Excellency's knowledge. The execution of the Pretender Bab§ in that city was accompanied by a circumstance which if published in the Gazettes of Europe would throw the utmost discredit on the Persian Ministers. After that person was put to death, his body by order of the Vezeer-i-Nizam was thrown into the ditch of the town to be devoured by dogs, which actually happened. This act resembles

* He was on a tour of north-west Persia commissioned by the Persian Government.

† Although Bahá'í histories give the date of the martyrdom of the Báb as 28 Sha'bán 1266, i.e. 9 July 1850, several sources including this one and *Násikhu't-Taváríkh* give the previous day's date.

‡ Áqá Siyyid 'Alí, one of the Tabríz mujtahids.

§ By the term 'Pretender' Sheil does not necessarily intend to disparage the Báb. Britain at this time had only just emerged from the Georgian Age, the era of the 'Old Pretender' and the 'Young Pretender'. To a Victorian, the word merely meant 'one who lays claim to a title or station'.

the deeds of bye gone ages, and could not I believe now occur in any country between China and England. Feeling satisfied that it did not receive Your Excellency's sanction, and knowing what sentiments it would excite in Europe, I have thought it proper to write this friendly communication not to let you remain in ignorance of the occurrence.[22]

Sheil explained his actions in a dispatch to Palmerston dated 15 August 1850:

Although the advice and opinions of foreign agents are generally unpalatable to the Persian Minister, I nevertheless think it my duty to bring under his observation any flagrant abuse or outrage that reaches my knowledge. I persuade myself that on such occasions notwithstanding the absence of acknowledgement on the part of the Ameer-i-Nizam, he may perhaps privately take steps for applying a remedy.

I lately heard from Her Majesty's Consul in Tabreez that after the execution of the pretender Bâb, his corpse, by order of the Ameer-i-Nizam's brother, was thrown into the ditch of the town to be devoured by dogs, which actually happened. So revolting an act appeared to me to deserve reprobation, and I accordingly addressed to the Persian Minister a letter of which I have the honor to enclose a Copy.[23]

Palmerston wrote to Sheil on 8 October 1850, stating that: 'Her Majesty's Government approve of your having called the attention of the Ameer-i-Nizam . . . to the manner in which the corpse of the Pretender Bâb was treated after his execution at Tabreez.'*[24]

All of these early accounts of the martyrdom of the Báb state that the bodies of the Báb and His companion were eaten by animals outside the walls of Tabríz. It was not until the time of the investigations of Prof. Browne that it was revealed to Western readers that the body of the Báb had been rescued from this fate and hidden by the Bábís.

Wilfred Scawen Blunt (q.v.), the famous English poet and oriental traveller, met at Jeddah in 1881 an eyewitness of the martyrdom of the Báb. In his book *The Future of Islam* he writes:

Among the more respectable Shiite beliefs, however, there seems to be a general conviction in Persia that a reform of Islam is at hand, and that a new leader may be expected at any moment and from any quarter, so that enthusiasts are constantly found simulating the gifts of inspiration and affecting a divine mission. The history of

* On 9 Aug. 1850, Sheil wrote to Stevens informing him of his note to Mírzá Taqí Khán: 'I cannot tell if H.E. will convey any reprehension to [the Vazír-Niẓám].' In the same dispatch Sheil mentioned the fact that 'By the advice of H.M.'s Government, the Shah has renounced the barbarous practice of causing criminals to be executed . . . in his presence' (see p. 101), and asked Stevens 'to endeavour to effect a similar salutary change with reference to the Prince Governor of Azerbizan.' (FO 248 141.) On 4 Sept. Stevens replied that he had 'not been able to learn that any communication [regarding the body of the Báb] has been received from Tehran by the Vezir-i-Nizam or other Persian Authorities in Tabreez.' In addition he stated that he will endeavour to bring to the attention of Ḥamzih Mírzá the Sháh's changed practice with regard to the execution of criminals and 'endeavour by offering unofficial counsel to the Prince Governor, to effect a similar change in Tabreez.' (FO 248 142)

the Babites, so well described by M. de Gobineau in his *Religions of Asia*, is a case in point, and similar occurrences are by no means rare in Persia. I met at Jeddah a highly educated Persian gentleman, who informed me that he had himself been witness, when a boy, to a religious prodigy, notorious, if I remember rightly, at Tabriz. On that occasion, one of these prophets, being condemned to death by the supreme government, was bound to a cross with two of his companions, and, after remaining suspended thus for several hours, was fired at by the royal troops. It then happened that, while the companions were dispatched at the first volley, the prophet himself remained unhurt, and, incredible to relate, the cords which bound him were cut by the bullets, and he fell to the ground on his feet.[25]

There are not many other accounts of the martyrdom of the Báb that claim to be eyewitness reports. One such occurs in a book called *Cairo to Persia and Back* by Owen Tweedy. The latter together with Roy Shepheard-Walwyn travelled through Persia in the early 1930s. In Tabríz, they found an Armenian guide to show them around the city. After visiting the Blue Mosque, the group continued to the Citadel. Tweedy continues:

But my friendly Armenian was much more interesting about the citadel. Of it, too, little remains save the gaunt ruin of its immense southern wall. He escorted us to the top by the same stairways up which, in other days, criminals had walked to their doom. For until comparatively recent times the regular form of public execution had been to hurl miscreants from the summit to be dashed to pieces on to the parade ground eighty feet below. Behind us to the north there used to be another parade ground. Its metamorphosis is truly eloquent of New Persia. It is now a fair imitation of a 'Luna Park', with a grand open-air café and paths and booths and terraces and, of course, a bandstand.

Then our guide became suddenly serious. Below us was the place where some eighty years ago Mirza Ali Mohamed, the founder of the Bahai religion, had been executed for heresy and sedition. He was a native of Shiraz, and at the early age of twenty-four declared himself as the 'Bab' or Gate whereby the world might enter into the joys of the Divine Revelation which had been vouchsafed to him. His was a religion of love, and his mission was that of a John the Baptist to prepare the world to receive another and a fuller demonstration of God's mercy. He gained adherents rapidly, and as rapidly earned the hostility of the powerful orthodox oligarchy in the country, who quickly persuaded the Shah that the movement was dangerous to the dynasty and must be suppressed. The Bab was forthwith arrested, and in due course, after a farce of a trial was condemned to death.

Our guide's grandfather had been in Tabriz and had witnessed the execution. 'The Bab was to be shot with two of his disciples, but they were offered an opportunity to recant before they were pinioned. One succumbed to the temptation and was released; but the Bab and the other stood firm, and were suspended by the arms from gallows-like frames in front of the firing-squad. The order was given and the volley rang out; but when the smoke had cleared away the Bab's friend hung dead on his ropes, but the Bab himself had disappeared. The bullets had cut the ropes and he had fallen unharmed and had escaped into the crowd. Of course he was discovered almost at once, and once again he was hoisted on to the gallows. But the first firing-squad refused to act again, and it was only with the greatest difficulty that other soldiers were found to take their place.* This time there was no mistake, and the Bab died. Afterwards his body was smuggled away by his friends and buried in a secret tomb, and even to-day none save the highest leaders of the Bahai religion know where he is buried.'†

I would add that during the whole time we were in Persia we never, save on this occasion, discussed Bahaism with anyone – or perhaps it would be more accurate to say

* The following report records the fate that befell the Náṣiríyyih Regiment which carried out the execution of the Báb. In Apr. 1855, they mutinied against their commanding officer, Muḥammad Áqá. (This was not the same commanding officer that they had had on that ill-fated day in July 1850. He was to meet an untimely end during the Anglo-Persian War of 1856–7.) Keith Abbott, the British Consul in Tabríz, reported the episode in a dispatch to Mr Murray, the British Envoy in Ṭihrán, dated 28 May 1855: 'This afternoon a cruel massacre of the soldiers of the Nâsarieh Regiment took place here.

'This Regiment had whilst at Khoee revolted against its Colonel Mahomed Agha whom they accused of having deprived them of their pay. It is said that the other officers of this regiment encouraged them to revolt and then abandoned them to take part with the Colonel. However this may be, the Regiment turned out its officers and marched in an orderly way to Tabreez to demand redress. They encamped outside the walls and have remained there, I should think, for a month past without committing any outrage or giving offence to the Townspeople who seem to have been kindly disposed towards them and to have furnished them with food.

'Having found an officer formerly belonging to their Regiment they placed him in command over them though very much against his will for he feared the resentment of the Government.

'A pretended enquiry into the conduct of the officers was instituted but as it was carried on by those who were interested in maintaining the system of injustice pursued towards the soldiers generally, of course the latter were condemned. The feeble Government left here endeavoured to induce the Regiment to disperse and return quietly to their homes – but either from mistrust of the intentions of the Government towards them or hoping for redress or greater safety if they remained united, they refused to do so.

'Matters continued in this position, the presence of the Regiment was almost forgotten, but it was understood that the Kaim Mekam [Qá'im-Maqám] had directed that the matter should remain over until his arrival – no one contemplated the deliberate slaughter of these men.

'Yesterday the Kaim Mekam reached the Khalat Parshan five miles distant, and from there dispatched two Regiments under Ibrahim Agha to summon the disaffected troops to disperse. The latter appear to have refused but allowed themselves to be deprived of their arms. They demanded a Firman for their better treatment before complying with the Kaim Mekam's summons to them. In a few minutes afterwards they were fired upon, the first volley passed over their heads, a second and third were fired with more effect, a great many, I fear upwards of a hundred are killed, the wounded are probably more numerous, many fled and others were captured. The camp of this unfortunate regiment was then pillaged by their cowardly bretheren.

'The officers are, I am told, endeavouring to conceal the number of the dead. The Inhabitants of the place are heaping curses on the Government and Kaim Mekam.' (Abbott to Murray No. 54, 28 May 1855: FO 248 163)

Abbott adds, in a note appended to the above dispatch and dated the following day, 29 May 1855: 'A great many bodies have been secretly interred during the night in various spots. Poor wounded men are found in all directions and dead bodies are being brought in from the country around. The slaughter has been great, probably between 300 and 400 victims in killed and wounded. Two of the soldier's wives and two or three bye-standers were also killed.'

† It is not clear to what extent these are the recollections of their guide's grandfather, but if they are to be taken as such, they are very close to the accounts given in Bahá'í histories. The remains of the Báb were brought to Haifa and interred in a shrine on Mount Carmel on the instructions of Bahá'u'lláh. By the time of Tweedy's account, this shrine was a well-known landmark in Haifa and visited by many pilgrims.

that no one ever discussed it with us. It is still a proscribed faith in Persia, and though it has tens of thousands of adherents everywhere in the country – to say nothing of its enormous following abroad, particularly in America – it has been driven underground by official disfavour and in many ways resembles a secret society rather than a religion.[26]

References

1. *The Times* 1 Nov. 1845, p. 5, col. 3
2. Gobineau *Religions et Philosophies* pp. 276–8 (trans. from French)
3. Dolgorukov to Russian For. Min. Nesselrode No. 15, 23 Feb. 1849 OS (7 Mar. NS): Dossier No. 177, Ṭihrán 1849, pp. 80–81. 'Excerpts from Dispatches' p. 19
4. Ferrier to de LaHitte 25 July 1850: MAE Sér. Corr. Polit. MD No. 24 (1833–56), p. 348 (trans. from French)
5. Dolgorukov to Nesselrode No. 6, 4 Feb. 1848 OS (16 Feb. NS): Dossier No. 177, Ṭihrán 1848, pp. 49–50. 'Excerpts from Dispatches' p. 18 (last sentence amended)
6. Dolgorukov to Nesselrode No. 94, 24 Dec. 1848 OS (5 Jan. 1849 NS): Dossier No. 177, Ṭihrán 1848, p. 360. 'Excerpts from Dispatches' p. 18
7. Wright 'Bab und seine Secte' pp. 384–5 (trans. from German)
8. Shedd 'Babism' p. 901
9. Adams *Persia by a Persian* p. 456
10. Browne *Materials* pp. 260–62
11. Lady Sheil *Life and Manners in Persia* p. 178
12. Dolgorukov to Nesselrode No. 25, 15 Mar. 1849 OS (27 Mar. NS): Dossier No. 177, Ṭihrán 1849, pp. 136–7. 'Excerpts from Dispatches' p. 19
13. From Kazem-Beg 'Bab et les Babis' April-May 1866, p. 371 (trans. from French)
14. G. A. Stevens to Palmerston No. 24, 30 June 1850: FO 60 155
15. R. Stevens to Sheil 13 Jan. 1850: FO 248 142
16. Ferrier to de LaHitte 25 July 1850: MAE Sér. Corr. Polit. MD No. 24 (1833–56), p. 349 (trans. from French)
17. Anitchkov to Prince Dolgorukov No. 420, 23 June 1850 OS (5 July NS): Nicolas 'Le Dossier russo-anglais' p. 357 (trans. from French)
18. Anitchkov to Russian For. Ministry (Asiatic Dept.) No. 437, 3 July 1850 OS (15 July NS): Nicolas 'Le Dossier russo-anglais' p. 358 (trans. from French)
19. Dolgorukov to Russian For. Min. Seniavin No. 53, 3 July 1850 OS (15 July NS): Dossier No. 133, Ṭihrán 1850, pp. 434–5. Chahárdihí *Shaykhí-garí, Bábí-garí* p. 280 (trans. from Persian)
20. Sheil to Palmerston No. 88, 22 July 1850: FO 60 152
21. R. Stevens to Sheil No. 68, 24 July 1850: FO 248 142
22. Enclosed in 23 *infra*
23. Sheil to Palmerston No. 94, 15 Aug. 1850: FO 60 153
24. Palmerston to Sheil No. 88, 8 Oct. 1850: FO 248 140
25. Blunt *The Future of Islam* p. 38. Also quoted in Hughes *A Dictionary of Islam* p. 579
26. Tweedy *Cairo to Persia and Back* pp. 271–2

TWO

The First Persecution (1844–5)

The first person to whom the Báb declared his mission was Mullá Ḥusayn-i-Bushrú'í. This occurred on 23 May 1844. Throughout the summer of 1844, the Báb gathered his first disciples, the Letters of the Living, around him in Shíráz. No doubt he imparted to them the principal features of the mission that he was soon to make public. Then the Báb sent these disciples to various parts of Persia to prepare the people for the public proclamation of his mission. The first of these disciples to be dispatched from Shíráz was Mullá 'Alíy-i-Basṭámí. He was sent to the Turkish province of Iraq to take the message to the Shí'ih 'ulamá and to the disciples of the late Siyyid Káẓim-i-Rashtí, the Shaykhí leader who had died in Karbilá the previous year.

At Karbilá, Mullá 'Alí, who himself had been a disciple of Siyyid Káẓim, was able to speak to the Shaykhí leaders, and contacted for the first time several persons such as Ṭáhirih, Siyyid Javád-i-Karbilá'í and Shaykh Muḥammad Shibl, who were later to play important roles in the new religion.

Eventually, however, the Shí'ih 'ulamá arose against Mullá 'Alí, and he was arrested and sent to Baghdád. Here Najíb Páshá, the Governor of the province, decided to convene a court consisting of both Sunní and Shí'ih divines.

The British Consul in Baghdád was Henry Rawlinson (q.v.), who in later years achieved eminence as both an archaeologist and a statesman. On 8 January 1845 he wrote to Sir Stratford Canning (q.v.), the British Ambassador in Istanbul:

I have the honor to report for Your Excellency's information, the following circumstances which are at present causing much excitement at this place, and which threaten in their consequences to give rise to renewed misunderstanding between the Persian and Turkish Govts.

About three months ago, an inferior priest of Shiraz* appeared in Kerbela, bearing a copy of the Koran,† which he stated to have

* Mullá 'Alí was not, of course, a native of Shíráz but had travelled from there.

† Mullá 'Alí was the bearer of a copy of the Báb's first work, the *Qayyúmu'l-Asmá'*. It is probably this

been delivered to him by the forerunner of the Imam Mehdi, to be exhibited in token of his approaching advent. The book proved on examination to have been altered and interpolated in many essential passages, the object being, to prepare the Mohammedan world for the immediate manifestation of the Imam, and to identify the individual to whom the emendations of the text were declared to have been revealed, as his inspired and true precursor. It was in consequence pronounced by a part of the Sheeah divines at Nejef and Kerbela, to be a blasphemous production, and the priest of Shiraz was warned by them of the danger, which he incurred in giving currency to its contents – but a considerable section nevertheless of the Sheeas of Nejef, who under the name of *Usúlí*,* or 'Transcendentalists', have lately risen into notice as the disciples of the High Priest Sheikh Kazem, and who are in avowed expectation of the speedy advent of the Imam, adopted the proposed readings, and declared themselves ready to join the Precursor, as soon as he should appear amongst them. These parties owing to local dissensions, were shortly afterwards denounced to the Govt. by the orthodox Sheeas as heretics, and attention being thus drawn to the perverted copy of the Koran, upon which they rested their belief, the volume was seized and its bearer being brought to Bagdad, was cast into prison, as a blasphemer against Islam and a disturber of the public peace.

The affair created no great sensation at the time and from the moderate language, which Nejib Pasha held in conversing on the subject, I thought it likely that the obnoxious book would be destroyed, and that the bearer of it would merely be banished from the Turkish dominions – such indeed was the extreme punishment contemplated by the Sheeas of Nejef, in denouncing the *Usúlí* heresy to the Govt., but the matter is now beginning to wear a much more serious complexion. The Soonee Priesthood have taken up the case in a rancorous spirit of bigotry, and their inveteracy has enlisted the sympathies of the entire Sheeah sect, in favor of the imprisoned Persian; instead in fact of a mere dispute between two rival schools in the town of Nejef, the question has now become one of virulent contest, between the Soonee and Sheeah sects, or which is the same thing in this part of the Ottoman Empire, between the Turkish and Persian population. Nejib Pasha whose sectarian prejudices are peculiarly excitable, has I regret to say allowed himself to adopt to their full extent the views of the Soonee law officers, and I foresee that a determined effort will be made to obtain the condemnation and execution of the unfortunate Shirazee. This individual, who is timid, ignorant and I should say entirely harmless, pleaded on his first arrest that he was a mere messenger, irresponsible for the contents of the volume entrusted to his charge, and such a defence would probably have availed him in a Court of law; but whilst in confinement he has been unfortunately seduced in the presence of witnesses, suborned for the purpose by the Soonee Mufti, into declaring his belief in the inspiration of the perverted passages, and I am apprehensive, therefore, that according to Mohammedan law whether expounded by Sheeas or Soonees, he will be convicted of blasphemy.

Nejib Pasha at the same time, to give all due formality to his proceedings, and to divest the affair of the appearance of mere sectarian persecution, has brought in the chief Priests from Nejef and Kerbela, to hold

---

book that is being referred to here. It is a commentary on one súrih of the Qur'án, the súrih of Yúsuf. The book is written in a style similar to the Qur'án and contains many Qur'ánic phrases, hence the reference to its appearing to be a copy of the Qur'án with alterations and interpolations.

* Rawlinson is here mistaken: the followers of Siyyid Káẓim were known as S͟hayk͟hís or Kas͟hfís. The term Uṣúlí was applied to the orthodox majority of S͟hí'ihs. See Balyuzi's *The Báb* p. 62, and Browne's *Literary History of Persia* Vol. 4, pp. 374–6.

a solemn Court of Inquisition in conjunction with the heads of the Soonee religion in Bagdad, but I do not anticipate much benefit from this compulsory and most unwilling attendance of the former parties. They will probably make an effort to save the life of their unfortunate countryman, proposing the banishment of the messenger and of the heads of the *Usúlí* sect, as the simplest method of suppressing the heresy, but they will be intimidated and overruled, and I greatly fear that sentence of death will be recorded against the Shirazee by a majority of the members of the court, and against all who promulgate and adopt the readings of his spurious Koran. Nejib Pasha has however assured me that he will not attempt to carry such a sentence into execution either here or at Nejef, pending a reference to Constantinople, and Your Excellency will thus have an opportunity of interposing the pleas both of humanity and policy in favor of the condemned parties.

In the present state of irritable feeling which exists between the Govts. of Persia and Turkey, I cannot doubt, but that the capital punishment of the Shirazee or the persecution of the 'Transcendentalists' of Nejef, will be viewed with much exasperation by the Court of Tehran – for although the Persian Govt. has itself on several occasions sustained inconvenience from impostors, professing to be the forerunners of the Imam Mehdi, and although it must be thus fully cognizant of the necessity of crushing at the outset any popular movement connected with such a matter, still the Sheeah community in general will regard their coreligionist as a martyr, whilst his personal insignificance and the absence of anything like an insurrectionary spirit at Nejef, will also cause his execution to be regarded as the effect of sectarian or rather national animosity.

The Govr. of Kermanshah has already addressed a note to me upon the subject, which I have duly submitted to Nejib Pasha, and of which I have the honor to annex a translation, and it is not improbable I think that a further remonstrance will be offered by the Court of Tehran, to which the Persian Agent* has transmitted a full report of the affair – but His Excy. is not disposed to listen to any foreign mediation or interference. In reply to my own communication he has observed that Persian subjects residing in Turkey are in civil, criminal and religious matters, entirely subject to Ottoman law, and that neither the Persian Government, nor the Consuls of that power, nor the High Priests of the Sheeah sect, have any further protective privelege [*sic*], than that of seeing justice duly administered according to the forms and usages of Soonee tribunals, but that in the present case to obviate any exception being taken on this point, he has united the Sheeah and Soonee authorities, and that the interests of Islam being at stake, the law must be allowed to take its course.[1]

The enclosure in Rawlinson's dispatch was a note from the Governor of Kirmán<u>sh</u>áh, the rapacious Muḥibb-'Alí <u>Kh</u>án,† protesting about the deten-

* His name was Mullá 'Abdu'l-'Azíz. He had already demonstrated his incapacity by his behaviour at the sacking of Karbilá in 1843 (see Balyuzi *The Báb* pp. 193–201). d. Ba<u>gh</u>dád, 9 Dec. 1846.

† Muḥibb-'Alí <u>Kh</u>án was one of several persons from Ḥájí Mírzá Áqásí's home town of Mákú who were raised to high office during the latter's administration. Concerning this man, Ferrier, who passed through Kirmán<u>sh</u>áh at exactly this time (spring of 1845), wrote: 'The Emir Mohib Ali Khan, Governor of the province of Kermanshah, is the General whose ignorance and cowardice so often caused the failure of the Persian arms under the walls of Herat, in 1838; but he belongs to the family of Makoo, who are patronised by the first minister, and thus it is that in the eyes of the Shah his vices are transformed into virtues, that he has attained one of the highest military appointments, and governs one of the finest provinces of Persia. The evil would not be quite unbearable if this personage contented himself with

tion of Mullá 'Alí:

My friend – according to accounts which have reached me from Bagdad, His Excellency Nejib Pasha has arrested and imprisoned an inferior Priest of Shiraz, who is a subject of the exalted Govt. of Persia. In the first place it is improper to arrest and imprison anyone on a mere accusation, which may be true or false, – and in the second place, supposing that he (the Shirazee) were guilty; as a subject of the exalted Govt. of Persia, he ought not to be subject to arrest – if his crime were proved, his punishment should be that of banishment from the Turkish territory.

I have therefore considered it necessary to represent this matter to you my friend, and to request that, as a well wisher to the preservation of friendship between the two Governments, You will communicate with H. Excy. Nejib Pasha on the subject, and will suggest to him, that if the guilt of the Persian be fully substantiated, he may be sent to Kermanshah, in order that I may transfer him to Tehran for punishment – and if on the other hand, the accusations against him prove to be malicious and without foundation, he may be at once released and set at liberty.

Under any circumstances his continued imprisonment is unbecoming and contrary (to custom).[2]

In a dispatch to Sheil in Ṭihrán dated 16 January, Rawlinson described the outcome of the proceedings of the court that Najíb Pásh͟há had convened:

The Court of Inquisition convened for the trial of the Persian priest, was held on Monday last, H.E. Nejib Pasha presiding, and Moola Abdool Azeez being also present, to afford his countenance to the accused. The perverted copy of the Koran being produced in Court, was unanimously condemned as a blasphemous production, and parties avowing a belief in the readings which it continued [*sic*], were declared to be liable to the punishment of death. It was then argued whether or not the Shirazee had thus avowed his belief in a blasphemous production – he himself distinctly repudiated the charge,* and although witnesses were brought forward, who stated that he had in

---

taking double, or even three times the amount of taxes due from the inhabitants, but he has completely stripped them. The misery is frightful wherever his jurisdiction extends: the peasantry have hardly bread to eat, and when they complain of their grievances at Court and endeavour to obtain justice, they are treated as rebels, condemned to be bastinadoed, and Mohib Ali Khan remains their governor.

'This bad policy has produced its fruits: three-fourths of the population have emigrated; the towns-people to Azerbaiján, and the nomads to Turkey.'

H. D. Seymour MP, who edited the translation of Ferrier's book into English, added the following comment in a footnote: 'M. Ferrier's account is but too true. When I was at Kermansháh, in 1846, I witnessed the most distressing spectacle I ever beheld. The province was fearfully oppressed by this fiend in human shape, Mohib Ali Khan, who had bought its government from Hadji Mirza Agassi. He had coolly seized what every man possessed, and had driven away their flocks and herds to his own estates at Makoo near Ararat. The people were picking grass in the fields to eat and the children were naked and emaciated, except the stomach which was unnaturally swollen – a half-starved child is a horrible sight. In one street I passed through in the town, the people were lying on each side at the last gasp of death from starvation. I never shall forget one whole family, father, mother and several children, lying together in a heap, unable to move from inanition. I wrote an account of this state of things to the English Embassy at Teheran, but I believe no effort of any kind was made to check the atrocities committed.' (Ferrier *Caravan Journeys* p. 25)

* Bábí and Bahá'í histories deny that Mullá 'Alí repudiated his belief. See also Balyuzi's arguments in *The Báb* p. 65n.

their presence declared his adoption of the spurious text, of which he was the bearer, yet as there was reason to suspect the fidelity of their evidence, the Sheeah divines were disposed to give him the benefit of his present disavowal. After much discussion the Soonee law-officers adjudged the culprit to be convicted of blasphemy and passed sentence of death on him accordingly, while the Sheeahs returned a verdict, that he was only guilty of the dissemination of blasphemy, and liable in consequence to no heavier punishment than imprisonment or banishment. The criminality of other parties implicated in the affair was then argued, and the same difference of opinion was found to prevail between the Sheeah and Soonee divines – the former admitted the importance of adopting measures for the suppression of the *Usúlí* heresy, and recommended that parties openly avowing a belief in the expected immediate advent of the Imam, should be removed from Kerbela and Nejef, while the Soonees unanimously declared that all such parties were guilty of blasphemy and subject to the punishment of death. The different opinions have been duly recorded and attested, and a reference on the subject will be immediately made to Constantinople by H.E. Nejib Pasha, the Persian priest remaining in confinement, pending the receipt of instructions, as to his ultimate disposal.

I understand that considerable uneasiness is beginning to display itself at Kerbela and Nejef, in regard to the expected manifestation of the Imam, and I am apprehensive that the measures now in progress will rather increase than allay the excitement.[3]

In reporting the results of the trial to Canning on 22 January, Rawlinson wrote:

The proceedings of the Court of Inquisition are forwarded by the present post to Consple. [Constantinople], and instructions are requested by H.E. Nejib Pasha with regard to the disposal of the criminal.

Your Excellency will observe that the Sheeah divines have refused to concur in the sentence of death passed on the accused by the Soonee members of the court, and I imagine therefore that the risk is removed of giving further offence to Persia by the public execution of one of her subjects.[4]

It seems that there was a general air of expectancy that year, and Rawlinson in the dispatch just quoted goes on to comment on the unusually large number of pilgrims in Karbilá for Muḥarram: 'The concourse of Persian pilgrims at Kerbelah at the present season is immense – it is estimated that between twenty and thirty thousand of these devotees are now assembled at the shrine of Hussein.'[5]

One month later, Rawlinson reported that the excitement among the Shí'ihs was beginning to subside, particularly since 'the impostor' had failed to appear at Karbilá:

I have the honor in conclusion to acquaint Your Excellency, that the religious excitement which has been for some time prevalent amongst the Sheeahs of this quarter, is beginning gradually to subside, the impostor who personated the character of the forerunner of the Imam Mehdi, and who was expected to declare himself at Kerbela during the present month on his return from Mecca, having been deterred by a sense of personal danger from attempting any further agitation, and having accordingly joined as a private individual the Carawan [*sic*] of pilgrims which is travelling to Persia by the route of Damascus and Aleppo.*[6]

Indeed, it is also indicated in Bahá'í histories that the Báb intended to proclaim his mission in Karbilá after his return from Mecca, and had summoned his disciples to that town.[7] For reasons that are not clear, but may be related to the hostile reception accorded to Mullá 'Alí, the Báb changed his mind.

In the meantime, Sir Stratford Canning in Constantinople had taken some action on the question of Mullá 'Alí. Early 1845 was a particularly tense time for Turko-Persian relations. A short while previously, the Persian Commissioner† at Erzerum, Mírzá Taqí Khán (later Prime Minister), had been set upon and nearly killed. In a dispatch to the British Foreign Secretary, Lord Aberdeen,[8] Canning forwarded a memorandum dated 16 February that he had sent to the Russian Minister, M. Titow,‡ with suggestions for a joint approach to the Turkish Government on the subject of Turko-Persian relations. Among the points put forward in this memorandum was: '. . . to abstain from putting the Persian priest to death, inflicting on him the mildest punishment consistent with the public security . . .'[9]

In a dispatch to Rawlinson dated 26 February, Canning writes that in concert with the Russian Minister representations had been made to the Sublime Porte.[10]

At about the same time Sheil wrote to Canning from Ṭihrán:

> The condemnation to death of a Persian Mollah at Bagdad for heresy has not caused here the sensation or irritation which might be anticipated, arising chiefly I conjecture from a disbelief that the sentence will be carried into execution. I trust so extreme a penalty will not be inflicted, for with whatever indifference the Govt. may regard his fate, as this preacher belongs to the priesthood, that fanatic and influential class might be enabled to raise an inconvenient excitement among the Persian population.[11]

Meanwhile, in Baghdád, Mullá 'Alí was being held in prison pending the arrival of instructions from Constantinople. Rawlinson wrote to Canning on 5 March 1845: 'Nejib Pasha informed me that he is as yet without any instructions from the Porte . . . on the subject of . . . the condemned Persian Priest. The latter unfortunate individual is still in confinement at Baghdad . . .'[12]

* This is a somewhat surprising statement since the normal route for Persian pilgrims from Mecca via Damascus and Aleppo also passes through Baghdád. The Báb, of course, travelled by the sea route via Jiddáh.

† The Commission was itself meeting to try and sort out several disputes between Turkey and Persia including frontier questions and the matter of the massacre at Karbilá in 1843.

‡ Previously Russian Consul-General on the Danube. Recalled to St Petersburg 1852.

Then Rawlinson went on to make a remarkable statement that perhaps only demonstrates how poor his sources of information were on this matter: '. . . as the real author of the spurious Koran [i.e. the Báb] has abjured for the present his pretended mission* and the imposture is thus become patent to all, the case of the prisoner now excites no great interest or commiseration.'[13]

On 19 March, Rawlinson reported the arrival in Baghdád of a messenger who had instructions from Ḥájí Mírzá Áqásí to the Persian Consul, Mullá 'Abdu'l-'Azíz, directing the latter to demand the extradition of Mullá 'Alí to Persia. Since Mullá 'Abdu'l-'Azíz had departed to Karbilá, the Agent followed him there.[14] On 3 April, Rawlinson was able to report:

> I was informed by Moolah Abdool Azeez the Persian Agent at this place, that instructions had reached him by an express messenger from H.E. Hajee Mirza Aghassee, to demand the delivery into his own hands of the priest of Shiraz imprisoned for blasphemy, with a view to his deportation to Persia. These instructions it appears he duly communicated to H.E. Nejib Pasha, but was informed in reply that no orders had as yet reached Bagdad regarding the disposal of the criminal, and that in default of such orders, the Persian could not be released from confinement.[15]

On 15 April, Rawlinson reported that on the previous day instructions had been received from Constantinople to send Mullá 'Alí there.[16] On 30 April, Rawlinson stated that Mullá 'Alí had been sent to Constantinople with the Tartar who conveyed the previous Baghdád post.†[17]

Until recently, the ultimate fate of Mullá 'Alí had remained obscure. After his departure in custody to Istanbul nothing more was heard about him, and it was assumed by most that he had been killed either on the way or on arrival in Istanbul. Lately, however, papers have been discovered in the Ottoman State Archives which demonstrate that Mullá 'Alí did indeed arrive in Istanbul, and after a period of time in custody was condemned by the Sulṭán's own decree to work for life in the Imperial naval dockyards near Istanbul (see the addendum to this chapter). It is evident from these papers that Mullá 'Alí had neither abjured nor was he keeping quiet about his beliefs as suggested in Rawlinson's reports.

Addendum

The following documents exist in the Ottoman State Archives:

1. Report of Najíb Páshá to the Sublime Porte regarding the case of Mullá

* It may be that the Báb's failure to appear at Karbilá was taken as an abjuration. Certainly it caused great consternation among those gathered at Karbilá for him, and a few of them turned against him at this time.

† Lady Sheil in her book *Life and Manners in Persia* (p. 177) evidently confuses the Báb and Mullá 'Alí, for she states that the Báb was sentenced to death in Baghdád by the Turkish authorities and set free through the intervention of the Persian Government.

'Alíy-i-Basṭámí and the trial held in Baghdád (dated 24 Jan. 1845).
2. Letter of Najíb Páshá to the Sublime Porte suggesting that Mullá 'Alí be sent to Istanbul (dated 24 Jan. 1845).
3. Fatvá issued by the 'ulamá for Mullá 'Alíy-i-Basṭámí.
4. Letter from the Sublime Porte to the Sulṭán asking for his approval for Mullá 'Alí to be brought to Istanbul and then exiled to one of the islands (no date).
5. Letter from the Sublime Porte to the Sulṭán, after Mullá 'Alí's arrival in Istanbul, stating that if Mullá 'Alí were to be exiled to one of the islands it would be difficult to control his activities and prevent him spreading his false ideas. Therefore he should be put to hard labour imprisonment in His Majesty's naval yard (no date).

There is a note on this document by the Sulṭán signifying his approval.

References

1. Rawlinson to Canning No. 1, 8 Jan. 1845. Enclosed in 3 *infra*
2. Muḥibb-'Alí Khán to Rawlinson, no date. Enclosed in 3 *infra*
3. Rawlinson to Sheil No. 2, 16 Jan. 1845: FO 248 114
4. Rawlinson to Canning No. 6, 22 Jan. 1845: FO 195 237
5. ibid.
6. Rawlinson to Sheil 28 Feb. 1845: FO 248 114
7. *Nabíl's Narrative* UK pp. 66 and 111, USA pp. 96 and 157–8. Fáḍil, *Ẓuhúru'l-Ḥaqq* Vol. 3, p. 235
8. Canning to Aberdeen 5 Mar. 1845: FO 78 595
9. Canning to de Titow 16 Feb. 1845, enclosed in 8 *supra*
10. Referred to in dispatch detailed in 6 *supra*
11. Sheil to Canning 26 Feb. 1845: FO 195 239
12. Rawlinson to Canning 5 Mar. 1845: FO 195 237
13. ibid.
14. Rawlinson to Canning 19 Mar. 1845: FO 195 237
15. Rawlinson to Sheil No. 10, 3 Apr. 1845: FO 248 114
16. Rawlinson to Canning 15.Apr. 1845: FO 195 237
17. Rawlinson to Canning 30 Apr. 1845: FO 195 237

THREE

The Mázindarán Upheaval at Shaykh Ṭabarsí (1848–9)

The ministry of the Báb was marked by a number of great upheavals. There is need for a good deal of research into their causes. Without doubt among the factors responsible were religious ones resulting from the clash between the orthodox 'ulamá and the new religion, also the political overtones implicit in the Báb's claim to be the Mahdí* (first made formally at his trial in June 1848, and one of the matters discussed at the conference of Badasht, June–July 1848), and other factors arising from the economic and social stresses of that period.

The pattern of each of these upheavals was much the same. A band of Bábís, who were armed but for the most part unskilled in warfare, being peasants, traders and mullás, would come into conflict with the local populace incited by the 'ulamá. Troops would be called in and the Bábís besieged by the army equipped with firearms and cannons. After a prolonged and heroic defence, the defenders would be overcome through treachery and massacred.

The first and in many ways most significant of these upheavals was that of Shaykh Ṭabarsí near Bárfurúsh in Mázindarán (October 1848 – May 1849). Here the two pre-eminent disciples of the Báb, Quddús and Mullá Ḥusayn, together with over 300 adherents of the Báb,† including no less than seven other Letters of the Living, were surrounded in a building used as a shrine and place of pilgrimage – ill-suited for defensive purposes. They

* In Shí'ih Islam all political authority rests with the Imám Mahdí. During his absence (occultation), the 'ulamá hold authority in his name and as deputies for him, while the theological position of a king is even more tenuous and uncertain. For a discussion of the attitude of the Shí'ih to authority see Algar *Religion and State in Iran* pp. 1, 10, 21–5.

† All Bahá'í sources agree that there were 313 defenders at the beginning of the siege, but a number of Bábís managed to pass through the lines of the royal army and join the defenders. It was probably in order to lessen the humiliation of their losses that the Persian authorities exaggerated the number of Bábís in the ensuing reports. Captain Mackenzie (see p. 96) gives a more accurate figure.

quickly erected fortifications and defended these for some seven months. In the words of Shoghi Effendi: 'It demonstrated beyond the shadow of a doubt what the indomitable spirit of a band of three hundred and thirteen untrained, unequipped yet God-intoxicated students, mostly sedentary recluses of the college and cloister, could achieve when pitted in self-defense against a trained army, well equipped, supported by the masses of the people, blessed by the clergy, headed by a prince of the royal blood, backed by the resources of the state, acting with the enthusiastic approval of its sovereign, and animated by the unfailing counsels of a resolute and all-powerful minister.'[1]

Shaykh Ṭabarsí was situated in a rather remote spot, away from the major roads and towns (unlike the upheavals of Zanján and Nayríz which occurred in or near sizeable towns). Consequently it was but little noted by the British Chargé d'Affaires, Lt-Col. Farrant (q.v.). His only reference to it occurs in a dispatch dated 30 January 1849:

> Some disturbances have occurred in Mazanderan. About five hundred men from different parts of Persia have assembled in that Province, they are the disciples of a Fanatic, who calls himself the door, or gate of the true Mahomedan religion and pretends to be the forerunner, and agent of the lost Imam, Mehdee, who according to Mahomedan tradition, is to appear shortly before the termination of the world, and cause one religion to be established throughout the universe. This fanatic has prevailed upon numbers of the people to believe that what he preaches, is the true doctrine of Mahomedan faith, and that the Koran is neither complete or correct. The above disciples of this man endeavoured to gain followers in Mazanderan, and actually put several people to death who refused to become so,* this caused a quarrel between the Mazanderaners, and the fanatics, and some fighting took place, in which several men on both sides were killed. Abbas Koolee Khan Larajanee† has been ordered by the Government to proceed to Mazanderan, and seize the leaders of this new sect. It is supposed their true object is not in any way relative to religion, but to create a revolutionary movement against the Government.[2]

However, since Shaykh Ṭabarsí was close to Bandar Gaz where the Russians held a base and in a region dominated by Russian interests, the Russian Minister was more interested in these developments. Having referred to the Báb's removal from Mákú (see p. 72), Dolgorukov, writing on 5 January 1849, reported to Nesselrode (q.v.), the Russian Foreign Minister:

> His harmful doctrines have found many adherents; and three days ago news was received that the latter have attacked some inhabitants of Mazindaran between Sari and Barfurush and have killed about 100 men, among whom is the *sarkardih* [chief] of that

* This is incorrect but may refer to the episode of Khusraw-i-Qádí-Kalá'í, who treacherously planned to lead the Bábís into an ambush (see *Nabíl's Narrative* UK pp. 245–7, USA pp. 340–42).

† A local chief of the district of Ask in Mázindarán who was responsible for the death of Mullá Ḥusayn. This man was a friend of Sheil (see Lady Sheil *Life and Manners* pp. 261–4) and Lt-Col. Charles Stuart also stayed with him (see Stuart *Journal of a Residence* pp. 284–5).

province, named Mustafa Khan.*

After several conferences which took place between the Amir [Prime Minister] and the most influential nobles of Mazindaran, who are now in Tihran, it was decided to use military force against the furious sectaries, and Prince Mahdi-Qasim Mirza was ordered to double his vigilance towards the leader of these new disrupters of public order.[3]

This report refers to the engagement that occurred on 21 December 1848. As a result of this Náṣiru'd-Dín Sháh instructed the new Governor of Mázindarán, Mihdí-Qulí Mírzá (q.v.), to collect an army and proceed to Shaykh Ṭabarsí to crush the Bábís. Mihdí-Qúlí Mírzá's experience at the hands of the Bábís was even more disastrous, however; Dolgorukov in a dispatch on 5 February 1849 relates:

The state of Mázindarán has become serious. According to information reaching me, about two thousand persons have rebelled against the Governor of Mázindarán. And as a result of their attack, Mihdí-Qulí Mírzá, the Governor of Mázindarán, has fled and two princes, Dávud Mírzá, the son of Ẓillu's-Sulṭán, and Ḥusayn-Sulṭán Mírzá,† the son of Fatḥ-'Alí Sháh, were killed in a house set ablaze by the Bábís. Similarly, the son of Prince Malik Áqá, 'Abdu'lláh Mírzá, was killed.

The military commander, 'Abbás-Qulí Khán-i-Láríjání, who has been put in charge of the campaign against this sect, who are promoting communism through the force of arms,‡ has been unable to take effective measures and has stated that with the forces that he has under his command at present, he is not powerful enough to face the Bábís.[4]

Following this defeat, 'Abbás-Qulí Khán-i-Láríjání arrived in the vicinity of Shaykh Ṭabarsí. On 2 or 3 February his forces also suffered a crushing defeat. In this engagement, however, Mullá Ḥusayn received the wound that led to his death. Dolgorukov, on 22 February, reports:

The news from Mázindarán is even more fearful than before. The Bábís, whose numbers are day-by-day increasing in Ádharbáyján and Ṭihrán, have routed the tribes of Savád-Kúh and Hizár-Jaríb. They [the Bábís], sword in hand, and having prepared themselves to meet death, attack, and start their attack with the shout 'Yá Ṣáḥiba'z-Zamán!'§ which is the title of the twelfth Imám. This puts an extraordinary fright into the people of Mázindarán . . .

I have heard that 'Abbás-Qulí Khán-i-Láríjání has secretly sent a message to the Bábís that he would not prepare for a further attack but, since he is forced to obey the Sháh's orders, he would only appear to be engaged in combat with them. But the Láríjání commander ['Abbás-Qulí Khán] did not remain faithful to his word and when the Bábís realized that he was preparing to do battle with them, they anticipated him and killed several hundred of his men. Among these were several well-known persons and two of his nephews.[5]

* According to most accounts it was 'Abdu'lláh Khán, the brother of Muṣṭafá Khán, who was killed.

† Named probably more correctly as Sulṭán-Ḥusayn Mírzá by Gobineau. Mackenzie (see p. 97) calls him Ṣáḥib-Qirán Mírzá.

‡ Regarding this statement see p. 5.

§ 'O Lord of the Age!'

In the rest of this dispatch, Dolgorukov reports that the Amír-Niẓám had been urged to send a strong detachment of regular soldiers equipped with cannon to suppress the Bábís (the forces so far deployed were locally-recruited militia).

On 27 March Dolgorukov forwarded to the Russian Foreign Ministry a detailed report that had been written on 10 March, by the Russian Consul at Astarábád, concerning the proceedings at Shaykh Ṭabarsí. This account, which mainly relates the events already described above, will not be reproduced here in full. The section that describes Mullá Ḥusayn is however of interest:

> Having made their way into Mazindaran, they occupied several villages in the environs of Barfurush and began to lure into their sect the inhabitants of Mazindaran. Their numbers from the very start began rapidly to increase. Their chief, Mulla Husayn of Bushruih, in whom fearlessness and enterprise are joined to cunning and efficiency, managed the affairs of the sectaries so successfully that in a short time their numbers increased to 1,500 men.* Possessing considerable amounts of money, and being favoured by local inhabitants, the Babis fortified themselves in their abode, dug around their retreat a deep trench and stored food as well as everything else necessary for a siege of several months.[6]

Although Mullá Ḥusayn was already dead when this account was written, this fact was not known in the camp of the besiegers. Indeed, Bahá'í historians state that 'Abbás-Qulí Khán deliberately concealed the fact, hoping that the Bábís having been demoralized would be easily defeated, and he could claim a great victory.

In a dispatch of 9 April, Dolgorukov reported the sending of Sulaymán Khán-i-Afshár to take charge of the operations. But in a dispatch of 3 May he was compelled to write:

> In a political report I may not paint a less gloomy picture. According to the information received from Mazindaran, Sulayman Khan Afshar, who was commissioned to subdue the Babis by peaceful means, has failed in his attempts.
>
> Attacked by Sardar Abbas-Quli Khan Larijani and Sulayman Khan, who wanted to take the fortifications by force, those fanatics, in spite of numerical inferiority to the attackers, repulsed them; and the Sardar himself received a bullet wound in his shoulder.[7]

The termination of the siege is related by Dolgorukov in a dispatch of 17 May 1849. He is, of course, correct in his speculation as to the treachery used to bring the siege to a conclusion:

> According to the latest news received by the Government of the Shah, the expedition against the Babis in Mazindaran has put an end to his worries.

* A gross exaggeration of the number of defendants present: see note on p. 91. Nor, as the next sentence states, did the Bábís have any great amount of money with them.

When, according to the Prime Minister, those fanatics risked leaving the little fortress where they had fortified themselves, the troops of Abbas-Quli Khan Larijani and Sulayman Khan Afshar engaged them in combat, as a result of which 1,300 men were left on the battlefield. Others maintain, and their stories sound less suspicious to me, that the Babis were invited to leave their fortifications in order to come to a friendly agreement; and when they were coming out, they were attacked and pitilessly slaughtered by the troops of Sulayman Khan.

Perhaps you, Your Excellency, will think that the successes thus achieved are more worthy of pity than defeats, because the indignation which these successes arouse in questions where religious fanaticism is supreme, excites the spirit of a new and even more dangerous resistance.[8]

There is also a brief reference to this episode among the reports of the French Agent in Persia, Joseph Ferrier. In reporting the episode of the Seven Martyrs of Ṭihrán in a letter dated 21 February 1850, he relates the main features of the upheaval of Shaykh Ṭabarsí:

Another symptom of agitation, the origin of which goes back to the last years of the reign of Muḥammad Sháh, occurred in 1849, a development which is the cause of considerable uneasiness to the Sháh. According to the beliefs of the Shí'ihs, the twelfth Imám, of the descendants of 'Alí, is not dead but only hidden to the eyes of men, and must reappear at an indeterminate time to regenerate Islam and bring it to its final perfection. A darvísh named Báb, abusing the credulity of the people of Ádharbáyján, announced four years ago that he was the precursor of this Imám. The Government seized Báb and imprisoned him, but his doctrine, that releases Islam from all the superstitions that surround it, and truly makes of it a deism, had already numerous proselytes who were scattered throughout Gílán. On Náṣiru'd-Dín Sháh's ascension of the throne, some 1,200* of them gathered themselves into an army and came to occupy a fortified position in Mázindarán, some 4 *farsangs* to the south of Bárfurúsh. There they decreed the downfall of the Qájár dynasty and the sovereignty of the Báb, whom they had delivered from his prison.† In a little time almost the entire population of this province had adopted his new doctrine. The danger became imminent and the Persian government was obliged to send 10,000 men to overcome them. Sustained by fanaticism, the Bábís entrenched themselves and resisted for 9 months all attacks, making each day the most deadly sorties, which had soon carried off among the besiegers a good third of their total strength. But reinforcements arrived for them, the siege was renewed with fresh vigour, and, after having eaten even the leather off their shoes, they acceded to the compromise which had been proposed to them since the start of the hostilities. Prince 'Alí-Qulí Mírzá,‡ the Sháh's Commander-in-Chief in Mázindarán, allowed them their lives and liberty if they consented to leave their positions and surrender their arms and, to augment the solemnity of his pledge, he swore by the Qur'án to hold religiously to it. The Bábís surrendered, but they had scarcely laid down their arms when they were massacred with but few of them succeeding in escaping. This treacherous butchery, instead of halting the progress of Bábism, only served to stimulate it further, and in a short time it had numerous adherents in every province.[9]

* Again an exaggeration of the number of Bábís present: see note on p. 91.

† A fallacy common to several accounts of the upheaval of Shaykh Ṭabarsí is that the Báb himself was present there.

‡ Mihdi-Qulí Mírzá is intended.

In 1858, Capt. C. F. Mackenzie (q.v.) was appointed the first British Consul at Rasht. In the winter and spring of 1858–9, he undertook a journey from Rasht to Astarábád and wrote a detailed report, dated 18 July 1859, of his observations. When writing about Bárfurúsh, he comments on the profusion of Qájár princes in Persia, and the consequent hardships for the people whose toils were necessary to maintain these parasites in their life of luxury. According to an estimate by Asadu'lláh Mírzá, himself a Qájár prince, there were some 3,700 of them alive at this time.

Mackenzie writes: 'Universal disaffection, consequently, reigns, and I have it on good authority that if the "Babees" had killed the King when they attempted to assassinate him, the Kujjur rule in Persia would have ended.

'The "Babees" are not extinct, although obliged to conceal their opinions, and I have no doubt that they will seriously damage the monarchy some day or other.'[10]

Mackenzie then proceeds to give an account of the upheaval at Shaykh Ṭabarsí which is remarkably accurate in most points. Prof. Browne received a copy of this portion of Mackenzie's report from Mr H. L. Rabino, who was at one time Consul at Rasht. Browne has reproduced this report, altering the spelling of the Oriental words to his own system of transliteration:*

During this revolt the Bábís took up a fortified position 10 or 12 miles from Bárfurúsh, at the shrine of Shaykh Ṭabarsí, near the river Tálár; they were few in number, but determined and fanatic, and after putting several envoys of the authorities to death, they prepared for a siege by collecting provisions from the neighbouring country; whenever the villagers hesitated or refused to give what they required, their houses were burnt about their ears.

Their numbers gradually increased from forty or fifty to between four and five hundred, and their recruits were chiefly men from the district of Sawádkúh.† One of these latter was styled Amír-i-Ṭabardár, because his favourite weapon was the *ṭabar*, a poleaxe, from which the former name of the province Ṭabaristán was derived.

Hostilities commenced by an attack made by Áqá 'Abdu'lláh Surtej, with 200 Hazár-Jaríb *tufangchís* [rifle-men]. His camp was surprised by the Bábís the day after his arrival, and he and forty or fifty of his men were slain. The remainder fled to Sárí, and on receipt of orders from Ṭihrán, another body of troops, about 500 strong, was sent to exterminate the Bábís. Their commander was 'Abbás-qulí Khán, who in the first engagement shot Mullá Ḥusayn, the chief of the Bábís, who, before dying, bequeathed his authority to Ḥájjí Muḥammad 'Alí Bárfurúshí, and expressed a wish to be buried with his arms. After his death the

* Thus in the original report the names occurred as 'Sheikh Tubusee', 'Ameer-i-Teberdar', 'Agha Abdoollah Soortej', 'Abbas Koolie Khan', 'Hadji Mahomed Ali Barfuroshee', etc.

† In fact the numbers did not gradually increase from 40 or 50 to between 400 and 500; Mullá Ḥusayn arrived from Khurásán with over 300 men. These men were drawn from all parts of Persia. It is interesting that Mackenzie's estimate of the number of Bábís present is much more accurate than those of the European diplomats writing at the time.

Bábís made a desperate sally and put the besiegers to death.

The insurrection had now become formidable, and Prince Mahdí-qulí Mírzá was appointed to suppress it. His troops were 2000 in number and he had both field-artillery and mortars.

He took up his quarters at a place called Wáskus about two miles from Shaykh Ṭabarsí, and during the night his camp was so invaded by the Bábís that he had barely time to escape by a window and hide himself in the jungle.

The whole village was on fire; two unlucky Princes, Dáwúd Mírzá and his uncle Ṣáḥib-Qirán Mírzá, perished in the flames, and a great slaughter was made amongst the royal troops.

Mahdí-qulí Mírzá, after wandering about in fear of his life, luckily met with one of his own servants, who, although a fugitive like himself, had a horse upon which the Prince mounted and thus reached 'Alíábád.*

After collecting the scattered remnants of his army and receiving a number of *tufangchís* and other riffraff, he again set about besieging the Bábís, who, although pressed by hunger and ill furnished with ammunition, held out for two months more.

At the end of this period, the Prince, seeing that he could not take the place and that by driving the rebels to desperation he would run the risk of being defeated a second time, offered them terms.

He informed them that if they abandoned their position and went away quietly, each man to his own home, they would not be molested.

The Bábís consented to this arrangement, and came forth to the number of about 200 fighting men. They were then deprived of their arms, and the greater number, with the usual Asiatic respect for treaties, were massacred on the spot.

Some victims, amongst whom was their leader Ḥájjí Muḥammad 'Alí, were reserved for a more barbarous punishment. They were taken to Bárfurúsh and burnt alive on the Sabzi Maydán (the green plain lying between the town and the Bágh-i-Sháh). Thus ended the Bábí revolt in Mázandarán, after costing about 1500 lives.[11]

At the end of the original account, Mackenzie adds: 'For this revolt elsewhere and their prolonged and gallant defence of the town of Zingan [Zanján], I refer to appendix.'[12]

From a note at the end of his report, it appears that he was preparing a historical appendix, which he states he would forward later, since he did not want to delay sending the report. This appendix cannot unfortunately be found among his later papers and dispatches in the Public Record Office.

Prof. E. G. Browne made a special journey, 'a pilgrimage' as he calls it, to visit Shaykh Ṭabarsí on what was his last full day in Persia in 1888. The following is his account of the trip:

Next morning (Wednesday, 26th September) Ḥájí Ṣafar awoke me about 7 with the welcome intelligence that he had found a shopkeeper of Bárfurúsh, who owned two ponies, and was well acquainted with the road to Sheykh Ṭabarsí, whither, for a consideration, he was willing to guide me. While I was drinking my morning tea the aforesaid guide, an honest-looking, burly fellow, appeared in person.

'Well,' said he, 'I hear you want to visit Ṭabarsí; what for is no concern of mine, though why a Firangí [foreigner] should desire to go there baffles my understanding.

* The only major correction needed in Mackenzie's account is that 'Abbás-Qulí Khán's arrival and the death of Mullá Ḥusayn occurred after the night raid on Mihdí-Qulí Mírzá's positions at Váskus.

However, I am ready to take you, if you will give me a suitable present for my trouble. But we must start at once, for it is two good parasangs there over the worst of ground, and you must, as I understand, get to Mashhad-i-Sar this evening, so that you should be back here at least two or three hours before sunset. If you don't like fatigue and hard work you had better give up the idea. What do you say? Will you go or not?'

'Of course I will go,' I replied; 'for what else did I seek you out?'

'Well said!' replied my guide, patting me on the shoulder; 'then let us be off without delay.'

In a few minutes we were in the saddle, and moving rapidly along the high-road to Sárí on our sturdy, wiry little Mázandarání ponies. 'Whither away?' cried some of my guide's acquaintance as we clattered out of the town. 'Sheykh,' he replied laconically; whereat expressions of surprise and curiosity, which we did not stop to answer, would burst from our interrogators. Soon we left the high-road, and, striking across a broad, grassy common, entered trackless swamps and forests, in which my guide, well as he knew the country, was sometimes at fault; for the water lay deep on the rice-fields, and only the peasants whom we occasionally met could tell us whether or no a particular passage was possible. After crossing the swampy rice-fields, we came to thickets and woods, intersected by the narrowest and muddiest of paths, and overgrown with branches, through which we forced our arduous way. Thence, after fording a river with steep mud banks, we entered on pleasant open downs, and, traversing several small coppices, arrived about 10.30 a.m. at the lonely shrine of Sheykh Aḥmad ibn Abí Ṭálib-i-Ṭabarsí (so stands the name of the buried saint on a tablet inscribed with the form of words used for his 'visitation' which hangs suspended from the railings surrounding his tomb), rendered immortal by the gallantry of the Bábí insurgents, who for nine months (October 1848 to July 1849) held it against overwhelming numbers of regulars and volunteers.

Sheykh Ṭabarsí is a place of little natural strength; and of the elaborate fortifications, said by the Musulmán historians to have been constructed by the Bábís, no trace remains. It consists at present of a flat, grassy enclosure surrounded by a hedge, and containing, besides the buildings of the shrine and another building at the gateway (opposite to which, but outside the enclosure, stands the house of the *mutawallí*, or custodian of the shrine), nothing but two or three orange-trees and a few rude graves covered with flat stones, the last resting-places, perhaps, of some of the Bábí defenders. The building at the gateway is two storeys high, is traversed by the passage giving access to the enclosure, and is roofed with tiles. The buildings of the shrine, which stand at the farther end of the enclosure, are rather more elaborate. Their greatest length (about twenty paces) lies east and west; their breadth is about ten paces; and, besides the covered portico at the entrance, they contain two rooms scantily lighted by wooden gratings over the doors. The tomb of the Sheykh, from whom the place takes its name, stands surrounded by wooden railings in the centre of the inner room, to which access is obtained either by a door communicating with the outer chamber, or by a door opening externally into the enclosure.

My guide, believing, no doubt, that I was at heart a Bábí come to visit the graves of the martyrs of my religion, considerately withdrew to the *mutawallí's* house and left me to my own devices for about three-quarters of an hour. I was still engaged in making rough plans and sketches of the place, however, when he returned to remind me that we could not afford to delay much longer. So, not very willingly, yet greatly comforted at having successfully accomplished this final pilgrimage, I mounted, and we rode back by the way we had come to Bárfurúsh, where we arrived about 3 p.m. 'You are a Ḥájí now,' said my guide laughingly, as we drew near the town, 'and you ought to reward me liberally for this day's work; for I tell you that there are hundreds of Bábís who come here to visit Sheykh Ṭabarsí and can find no one to guide them thither, and these would almost give their ears to go where you have gone and see what you have seen.' So when we alighted at a caravansaray near his house I gave him a sum of money with which he appeared well content, and he, in return, set tea before me, and then came and sat with me a while, telling me, with some amusement, of the wonderings and speculations which my visit to Sheykh Ṭabarsí had provoked amongst the townsfolk. 'Some say you must be a Bábí,' he concluded, 'but most incline to the belief that you have been there to look for buried treasure, "for," say they, "who ever heard of a Firangí who cared about religion, and in any case what has a Firangí to do with the Bábís?" I, for my part, have done my best to encourage them in this belief; what took you to Ṭabarsí is no business either of theirs or of mine.'[13]

References

1. Shoghi Effendi *God Passes By* p. 38
2. Farrant to Palmerston 30 Jan. 1849: FO 60 144
3. Dolgorukov to Nesselrode No. 94, 26 Dec. 1848 OS (5 Jan. 1849 NS): Dossier No. 177, Ṭihrán 1848, p. 360. 'Excerpts from Dispatches' p. 18
4. Dolgorukov to Nesselrode No. 9, 24 Jan. 1849 OS (5 Feb. NS): Dossier No. 177, Ṭihrán 1849, pp. 32–3. Chahárdihí *Shaykhí-garí, Bábí-garí* p. 271 (trans. from Persian)
5. Dolgorukov to Nesselrode No. 13, 10 Feb. 1849 OS (22 Feb. NS): Dossier No. 177, Ṭihrán 1849, pp. 56–68. Chahárdihí *Shaykhí-garí, Bábí-garí* pp. 272–3 (trans. from Persian)
6. Report of Russian Con. at Astarábád, 26 Feb. 1849 OS (10 Mar. NS), enclosed in Dolgorukov to Nesselrode No. 25, 15 Mar. 1849 OS (27 Mar. NS): Dossier No. 177, Ṭihrán 1849, pp. 136–45. 'Excerpts from Dispatches' pp. 19–20
7. Dolgorukov to Nesselrode No. 32, 21 Apr. 1849 OS (3 May NS): Dossier No. 178, Ṭihrán 1849, pp. 53–4. 'Excerpts from Dispatches' p. 20
8. Dolgorukov to Nesselrode No. 36, 5 May 1849 OS (17 May NS): Dossier No. 178, Ṭihrán 1849, p. 93. 'Excerpts from Dispatches' pp. 20–21
9. Ferrier to de LaHitte 21 Feb. 1850: MAE Sér. Corr. Polit. MD No. 24 (1833–56), pp. 328–9 (trans. from French)
10. Mackenzie, report of a journey from Rasht to Astarábád during winter and spring of 1858/9: FO 60 245
11. Browne *Materials* pp. 241–3
12. As for 10 *supra*
13. Browne *A Year Amongst the Persians* pp. 616–19

FOUR

The Seven Martyrs of Ṭihrán (1850)

1850 was a momentous year in Bahá'í history. For it saw not only the upheavals at Nayríz and Zanján but also the martyrdom of the Báb himself. It was ushered in in a portentous manner by the execution in February of seven Bábís who have become known as the Seven Martyrs of Ṭihrán:

Ḥájí Mírzá Siyyid 'Alí, the uncle of the Báb, a merchant.
Ḥájí Mullá Ismá'íl-i-Qumí, a learned divine.
Mírzá Qurbán-'Alí, a darvísh.
Áqá Siyyid Ḥusayn-i-Turshízí, a mujtahid.
Ḥájí Muḥammad-Taqíy-i-Kirmání, a merchant.
Siyyid Murtiḍá, a merchant of Zanján.
Muḥammad-Ḥusayn-i-Marághi'í, a government official.

Very important is the point, made by the author of the *Táríkh-i-Jadíd* and reiterated by Browne, that:

> They were men representing all the more important classes in Persia – divines, dervishes, merchants, shop-keepers, and government officials; they were men who had enjoyed the respect and consideration of all; they died fearlessly, willingly, almost eagerly, declining to purchase life by that mere lip-denial, which, under the name of *ketmán* or *taḳiya*, is recognised by the Shi'ites as a perfectly justifiable subterfuge in case of peril; they were not driven to despair of mercy as were those who died at Sheykh Ṭabarsí and Zanján; and they sealed their faith with their blood in the public square of the Persian capital wherein is the abode of the foreign ambassadors accredited to the court of the Sháh.[1]

There is, moreover, an interesting story concerning the manner of execution of the Seven Martyrs. This story goes back to July of the previous year when the Russian Minister, Dolgorukov, experienced an incident that upset him greatly. He related to Lt-Col. Farrant, British Chargé d'Affaires in Sheil's absence, that he had gone to one of the royal palaces outside Ṭihrán to visit the Sháh and had been asked to wait in a tent in the garden. He had then heard

> the greatest disturbance, heavy blows with sticks mingled with cries of terror, and suddenly an immense rush of the people took place which nearly overthrew the tent

in which he was seated. Shortly after this he was conducted to the royal presence by one of the Shah's Chamberlains and the Minister for Foreign Affairs, and had advanced half way up the garden, when to his horror and dismay he and the gentlemen were thrown off the path by the executioners who were dragging along by the legs the bodies, still writhing, of eight criminals whom they had just strangled before the Shah.[2]

Executing criminals in the presence of the Sháh (or one of his Governors in the provinces) was the normal practice of this period, and it is even said that many of the Qájárs took great delight in witnessing these scenes. Public executions were almost unknown.

Dolgorukov was 'so shocked and agitated that on reaching the royal presence he could hardly speak.'[3] When he did find his voice, it was to tell the Sháh 'in very forcible language . . . that such barbarous practices did not even exist amongst the most savage nations, and that His Majesty should abolish such a revolting and degrading custom, which every European nation looked upon with horror and disgust.'[4]

Dolgorukov went also to Mírzá Taqí Khán, the Amír-Niẓám, and similarly expressed himself there. Both Dolgorukov and Farrant wrote detailed reports of the matter to their respective governments. In reply to Farrant's report, Lord Palmerston, in a dispatch dated 5 October 1849, instructed Sheil, now returned from leave of absence, to convey to the Persian Minister for Foreign Affairs 'that Her Majesty's Government fully and entirely share the sentiments expressed by Prince Dolgorouki and that they sincerely hope that the Shah will abandon the practice of having executions performed in his presence, a practice which, until the receipt of Colonel Farrant's despatch, Her Majesty's Government had imagined to be confined to the barbarous tribes of negroes in Africa.'[5] Palmerston further instructs Sheil, in the same dispatch, to 'strongly exhort the Persian Government to take care that no person is put to death, unless he shall have been convicted by fair, and open, and public trial, of some atrocious crime, which by law shall have rendered him liable to such extreme punishment.'[6]

On 15 January 1850, Sheil reported back to Lord Palmerston that the recommendation contained in His Lordship's dispatch, 'that the revolting practice of executing criminals in the Royal presence should be abandoned,' had been conveyed to the Persian Prime Minister (Mírzá Taqí Khán). Sheil further states that he 'endeavored to prove to His Excellency, how unworthy it was of a Sovereign to preside over an office which elsewhere was resigned to the lowest class of mankind.'[7] The Amír-Niẓám had replied that 'he could not make any promise as to *time*,' but 'he would endeavor to effect the gradual discontinuance of this ancient custom of the Kings of Persia.' One of the major objections that the Amír had raised, however, was that the populace might interfere in a public execution, and snatch the criminals from the hands of justice.[8]

This dispatch having arrived in London, Palmerston wrote a reply, dated 26 March 1850, stating that Her Majesty's Government approved of the manner in which, as reported in his dispatch, Sheil had attempted to impress this recommendation upon the Amír-Niẓám.[9]

Having read these various dispatches and explanations, one can now understand the various points referred to in the following dispatch of Lt-Col. Sheil's, in which he relates the episode of the Seven Martyrs of Ṭihrán. The dispatch is here quoted in its entirety.

No. 23

Tehran
February 22d 1850

My Lord

I am glad to inform Your Lordship that the exhortations of Her Majesty's Government that the Shah should abstain from executing criminals in his own presence has not been without effect. Some days ago seven persons belonging to the Babee sect suffered death for an alleged conspiracy to assasinate [*sic*] the Persian Prime Minister. The execution took place in a most public place in the presence of a considerable multitude, from whom however no interruption was experienced. I trust this convincing proof of the safety of a public execution will prevent the recurrence of such spectacles under the eyes of the Shah. In offering my congratulations to the Ameer at this step towards improvement I took the opportunity of mentioning how suitable it would be, instead of causing the Shah to sentence criminals in person, to bring them before a court of justice as is practiced in every civilized country. The Prime Minister does not seem disposed to accept of this recommendation, at least at present.

The execution of these persons has excited general sympathy, for though it cannot be denied that the infliction of death was in conformity with the precepts of Mahomedanism,* yet everyone feels that they have suffered for a mere speculation, not for an overt act or even an intended act, the alleged conspiracy not having obtained any belief among the population. They died with great firmness. Previously to decapitation life was offered to them on the condition of reciting the creed that Mahomed is the Prophet of God, but they would not consent, nor did they in the least waver from their faith. I have warned the Ameer that this is the surest mode of propagating these new doctrines, and I recommended him if he were resolved to punish these proselytes to select the penalty of banishment in the island of Karrak† or elsewhere instead of having recourse to the extreme penalty of death, which was certain to excite horror and commiseration. I am not without hopes that the Prime Minister may adopt this recommendation.

I have the honor to be with the greatest respect,

My Lord,
Your Lordship's
most obedient
humble servant
(signed) Justin Sheil[10]

Several points here are worthy of notice. Firstly, the event is reported by Sheil as being a success, by virtue of the previous correspondence on the subject of executions in the presence of the Sháh. Secondly, it must be noted that the official reason given for these seven executions – that the victims had been plotting to assassinate the Amír-Niẓám – even at that time gained

* The penalty for apostatizing from Islam is death.

† An island in the Persian Gulf.

no credence with the populace.* Thirdly, Sheil himself mentions the great firmness with which they refused to recant their faith and thus save their lives, and comments on the effect that this, together with their innocence, had upon the crowd, thus confirming the reports of other writers.[11]

On receiving the report of the execution of the Seven Martyrs, Palmerston, in a letter dated 2 May 1850, replied to Sheil that 'Her Majesty's Government have received with much satisfaction the account contained in your despatch . . . that the Shah on a recent occasion had shown that he was not inattentive to the suggestions which you were instructed to offer. . ., and if a fit opportunity for doing so should occur you will state to His Persian Majesty that you are instructed to congratulate him on his having so successfully given up the practice of attending in person such revolting exhibitions.' With regard to the executions, however, Palmerston goes on to state, 'I have to instruct you to impress upon the Persian Government that the punishment of men for religious belief, besides being unjust and cruel, is also an erroneous practice, and tends to encourage and propagate the belief which it is intended to suppress.'[12]

Unless further papers relating to this episode should be discovered, particularly Persian official documents, it cannot be stated for certain that it was Sheil and Dolgorukov's intervention that caused the execution of the Seven Martyrs of Ṭihrán to be a public one. It is nevertheless a fact that public executions in Qájár Persia were rare up to this time, criminals usually having been executed in a dark dungeon or in the presence of the S͟háh or one of his governors. Following this episode public executions became common in Ṭihrán, and two years later that city was to witness the bloodbath that followed the attempt on the life of the S͟háh. Sheil himself had no doubt that it was due to his intervention and that of Dolgorukov that this change came about.

There can be no doubt that had these and subsequent executions of Bábís occurred in the private presence of the S͟háh, or in some obscure dungeon room, the followers of the Báb could not have succeeded to the same extent in asserting their faith and devotion before multitudes of their fellow-countrymen, a demonstration that brought many conversions and much secret admiration. Nor indeed would the cause of the Báb have attracted so much attention throughout the world, for it was the public executions of 1852 that above all else brought the Bábís to the attention of the Western world through the newspapers of that period and the writings of Gobineau, Renan, etc. And it was the courage and faith of the Bábís in their martyrdom that excited the attention of all of the earliest European authors and impelled them to write on the new religion.

* See also Lady Sheil *Life and Manners in Persia* p. 180.

Dolgorukov's account of the Seven Martyrs is given in a dispatch of 24 February 1850:

Minds are in an extraordinarily excited state due to the execution [of several Babis] which has just taken place in the great square of Tihran. I have already once expressed my opinion that the method by which last year the troops of the Shah under the command of Prince Mahdi Quli Mirza exterminated the Babis will not lessen their fanaticism.

From that time on the Government has learned that Tihran is full of these dangerous sectaries who do not recognize civil statutes and preach the partitioning of the property of those who do not join their doctrine.* Becoming fearful for the social peace, the ministers of Persia decided to arrest some of these sectaries and, according to the common version, having received during an interrogation their confession of their faith, executed them. These persons, numbering seven, and arrested at random, since the Babis are counted already by thousands within the very capital, would by no means deny their faith and met death with an exultation which could only be explained as fanaticism brought to its extreme limit. The Assistant Minister of Foreign Affairs, Mirza Muhammad Ali, on the contrary affirms that those people have confessed nothing and that their silence was interpreted as a sufficient proof of their guilt.

One can only regret the blindness of the Shah's authorities who imagine that such measures could extinguish religious fanaticism, as well as the injustice which guides their actions when examples of cruelty, with which they are trying to frighten the people, are committed without distinction against the first passer-by who falls into their hands . . .[13]

Ferrier also reported this event briefly at the end of a long letter, dated 21 February 1850, describing the upheavel of Shaykh Ṭabarsí: 'Twenty of them [i.e. Bábís] have been arrested in the capital, the day before yesterday, and already seven have been publicly executed'.[14]

These accounts enable an approximate date for this event to be fixed. It would appear that these martyrdoms occurred on either 19 or 20 February 1850.†

There is one further account that would appear to be of this episode. On 5 June 1874, Sir Mountstuart E. Grant Duff (q.v.) was dining with Sir Henry Rawlinson. In his diary, he records the conversation he had with Mr Ronald Thomson (q.v.):

I sat next Mr Ronald Thompson, from Teheran, and talked to him, *inter alia*, about the extraordinary story of the Bâbis, of which Renan makes so striking a use in his *Apôtres*, and which occurred during the earlier part of Mr Thompson's residence at the Persian Court. He told me that seven Bâbis were brought before the Shah to be interrogated. The Shah said, 'We make no demand from you, except that you should pronounce the formula, "There is no god but God, and Mahomet is his prophet."

* With regard to this point, there is indeed a statement in the Persian *Bayan* (Váḥid 5, Chap. 5) permitting this. This is an example of some of the severe laws of the Báb which Bahá'u'lláh did not continue.

† *Nabíl's Narrative* (UK) p. 326, (USA) p. 445 implies a later date, after 15 Mar. 1850. This is clearly wrong.

That done, you are absolutely free and may go where you please, as you please.' They refused. The Shah then handed them over to the First Minister, telling him that before they were put to death a separate offer of life, and permission to go where they pleased, should be made to each of them. The offer was made in Mr Thompson's presence to each, and refused by all.[15]

References

1. Browne *A Traveller's Narrative* p. 216. See also *Táríkh-i-Jadíd* pp. 258–70
2. Farrant to Palmerston No. 55, 27 July 1849: FO 60 145
3. ibid.
4. ibid.
5. Palmerston to Sheil No. 19, 5 Oct. 1849: FO 248 134
6. ibid.
7. Sheil to Palmerston No. 7, 15 Jan. 1850: FO 60 150
8. ibid.
9. Palmerston to Sheil No. 19, 26 Mar. 1850: FO 248 140
10. Sheil to Palmerston No. 23, 22 Feb. 1850: FO 60 150
11. See for example Browne *A Traveller's Narrative* p. 216
12. Palmerston to Sheil 2 May 1850: FO 248 140
13. Dolgorukov to Nesselrode No. 11, 12 Feb. 1850 OS (24 Feb. NS): Dossier No. 133, Ṭihrán 1850, pp. 100–105. 'Excerpts from Dispatches' p. 21
14. Ferrier to de LaHitte 21 Feb. 1850: MAE Sér. Corr. Polit. MD No. 24 (1833–56), p. 328 (trans. from French)
15. Grant Duff *Notes from a Diary 1873–1881* Vol. 1, pp. 62–3

FIVE

Yazd and the First Nayríz Upheaval (1850)

The central figure of the Nayríz upheaval was Siyyid Yaḥyáy-i-Dárábí, surnamed by the Báb, Vaḥíd. From Bahá'u'lláh's house in Ṭihrán Vaḥíd proceeded via Qazvín, Ká<u>sh</u>án and Iṣfahán to Yazd, where he owned a house. In Yazd he was the centre of much controversy because of his open preaching of the Bábí Faith. Eventually his followers clashed with the inhabitants and a disturbance occurred, as a result of which, Vaḥíd deemed it prudent to leave Yazd. He journeyed through various towns and villages to Nayríz, where the hostile opposition of the Governor and the 'ulamá forced him and his followers to take up defensive positions in a nearby fort. There ensued an upheaval similar in many respects to that of <u>Sh</u>ay<u>kh</u> Ṭabarsí, culminating in treachery and the martyrdom of many of the defendants.

The Episode at Yazd

From the latter years of Muḥammad <u>Sh</u>áh's reign, Yazd had been in a state of turmoil and rebellion. On the accession of Náṣiru'd-Dín <u>Sh</u>áh, Ḥájí Bi<u>zh</u>án <u>Kh</u>án-i-Gurjí was sent to Yazd as Governor, but he was unable to control the situation and was withdrawn. In his place, Muḥammad-Ḥasan <u>Kh</u>án-i-Sardár, known as <u>Kh</u>án Bábá <u>Kh</u>án (q.v.), was made Governor. <u>Kh</u>án Bábá <u>Kh</u>án sent to Yazd as his deputy Áqá <u>Kh</u>án-i-Írvání. The misadventures that befell the latter are described by Keith Abbott (q.v.), the British Consul who visited Yazd from 19 November to 7 December 1849 as part of a tour of South Persia.

The Political state of the Province at the time of my visit, may be described in a few words. The City had, only a few months before, recovered from a state of rebellion and confusion subsequent to the death of Mahomed Shah, when the recently appointed Governor, Âgha Khân, a man of firmness, but a very unpopular character found himself besieged by a portion of the Inhabitants, headed by some notorious Characters, and obliged, after attempting to defend his residence to retreat into the Citadel. There he and his few attendants found themselves almost destitute of provisions, but with four pieces of Ordnance, they contrived for some days not only to hold out, but seriously to annoy the townspeople. Finally, however, driven by want to negotiate, it was agreed they should be allowed provisions and beasts of burthen, to enable them to quit the place. As soon as these were produced and admitted within the Citadel, the Governor (as he related to me himself) closed the gate, and refused to abide by the Conditions. The Camels and Asses, which had been provided, were then slaughtered, and served the Garrison for food, but they discovered that the bread they had received from the townspeople had been poisoned. Keeping up a frequent fire on the town, which the Inhabitants, being without Artillery, could not return, terms of accommodation were a second time, agreed to, and some troops arriving to the succour of the Governor, he was presently enabled to quit his Stronghold and again appear in the town. Some of the rebels were secured but it was not until after my departure that the Chief Leader, by name Mahomed Abdoollah, was taken and slain.[1]

This episode had nothing to do with the Bábís, and the Muḥammad-'Abdu'lláh referred to at the end of the above report, who appears to have been the leader of the malcontents, had gone into hiding at the time of Abbott's sojourn in Yazd, at the end of 1849. He reappeared a short while later, however, and came to Vaḥíd's assistance at a time when the latter was hard pressed by his opponents in Yazd.* Nabíl records: 'No sooner had he uttered these words than the news arrived that a certain Muḥammad-'Abdu'lláh, whom no one suspected of being still alive, had suddenly emerged with a number of his comrades, who had likewise disappeared from sight, and, raising the cry of "Yá Ṣáḥibu'z-Zamán!" had flung themselves upon their assailants and dispersed their forces.'[2]

Although advised by Vaḥíd to desist from needlessly attacking the forces of the Governor, Muḥammad-'Abdu'lláh preferred to ignore this, and the result is reported by Sheil in a dispatch from Ṭihrán dated 12 February 1850:

I have the honor to inform Your Lordship that a serious outbreak lately took place at Yezd, which however the Governor of that city with the assistance of the priesthood succeeded in quelling.

The exciters of the insurrection were the partizans of the new Sect called Babee, who assembled in such numbers as to force the Governor to take refuge in the citadel, to which they laid siege. The Moollas conscious that the progress of Babeeism is the decay of their own supremacy determined to rescue the Governor, and summoning the populace in the name of religion to attack this new Sect of infidels, the Babees were overthrown and forced to take flight to the adjoining province of Kerman. I have seen a letter from the Governor of Yezd to one of his friends in Tehran in which he earnestly calls for assistance and represents the state of disorganisation within his government in strong terms; he has since resigned his appointment, and quitted Yezd without even waiting for permission to retire.[3]

* Jahángír Mírzá (*Táríkh-i-Naw* p. 343) states that this Muḥammad-'Abdu'lláh was the custodian of a caravanserai. He had made himself the leader of a group of the town's ruffians and defied successive Governors. It is possible that he aligned himself with Vaḥíd only in an effort to re-establish his position after the episode reported above by Abbott.

Dolgorukov also briefly reports this episode in the same dispatch in which he records the episode of the Seven Martyrs of Ṭihrán, on 24 February 1850: 'A number of Bábís under the leadership of Siyyid Yaḥyá, who calls himself a disciple of the Báb, together with a crowd of the ruffians of Yazd, produced a serious disturbance in the town of Yazd. These Bábís assailed the residence of the Governor and killed 8 of the soldiers, wounding a further 26. The deputy governor has fled [the town] and sent his resignation to the Government.'*[4]

Áqá Khán-i-Írvání having tendered his resignation, Khán Bábá Khán appointed his nephew, Shaykh-'Alí Khán, to be Deputy-Governor. Shaykh-'Alí Khán proceeded to Yazd and succeeded in defeating and killing Muḥammad-'Abdu'lláh.

Ferrier also reports this episode. There is however some discrepancy between dates. Sheil's dispatch is dated 12 February 1850, Dolgorukov's was sent on 24 February, but Ferrier's report is dated 25 June 1850 and he states that the episode occurred six weeks previously. There is no reason to doubt however that Ferrier is referring to the same episode. Not being an accredited diplomatic representative, Ferrier's sources of information would be more tenuous and it may have taken longer for news of this episode to reach him.

> The Bábís of Bafk, Kirmán and Abargúh seeing that the Persian government was allowing them quietly to gather together and arm themselves without disturbing them, became emboldened and came, six weeks ago, to attack the town of Yazd. But the people of various religions that inhabit this city emerged *en masse* from the walls to repulse them, a task which their great superiority in numbers made easy. The Bábís, after having been beaten, returned to Abargúh and Bafk, where they await a more favourable occasion to resume their plans.[5]

There is a further disagreement between the dates of this upheaval as given by Sheil and Dolgorukov (January–February 1850) and that given in *Nabíl's Narrative* (April–May 1850). Indeed, according to *Nabíl's Narrative*, Vaḥíd did not leave Ṭihrán until after the arrival there of Mírzá 'Alíy-i-Sayyáḥ, the Báb's courier. Sayyáḥ's arrival could not have occurred until about the first week in February since he was at Shaykh Ṭabarsí on 23 January. Thus Nabíl places Vaḥíd in Ṭihrán at the very time that, according to Sheil and Dolgorukov, the Yazd episode, in which Vaḥíd was involved, was taking place.

There is one possible partial solution to this problem. 'Abdu'l-Bahá while

* In this same dispatch Dolgorukov relates at length a disturbance in Iṣfahán instigated by Siyyid Asadu'lláh, son of Siyyid Muḥammad-Báqir-i-Rashtí and one of the leading 'ulamá of Iṣfahán. Although Dolgorukov attributes this also to the Bábís, it had in fact nothing to do with them, and was related to disturbances caused by Aḥmad Mírzá Ṣafaví (see Algar *Religion and State in Iran* pp. 126–7).

in the USA related the episode of Sayyáḥ's meeting with Vaḥíd, of which he was himself an eyewitness.[6] In this account 'Abdu'l-Bahá states that Sayyáḥ had just come from Mákú and not Shaykh Ṭabarsí as Nabíl reports. Thus, it may be that Sayyáḥ came to Ṭihrán before proceeding to Shaykh Ṭabarsí. In that case, the meeting between Vaḥíd and Sayyáḥ in Ṭihrán could have occurred in December 1849, giving Vaḥíd sufficient time to be in Yazd by late January.*

The First Nayríz Upheaval

From Yazd, Vaḥíd travelled towards Shíráz. On the way, he stayed at Bavánát-i-Fárs, Fasá, Iṣṭahbánát, Rúníz and eventually came to Nayríz, where he owned a house. At each of these places he openly preached the religion of the Báb, until finally at Nayríz the hostile attitude of the Governor there caused Vaḥíd to take up defensive positions in a fort outside the town. Ḥájí Zaynu'l-'Ábidín Khán, the Governor of Nayríz, appealed to Shíráz for help. Fírúz Mírzá, Nuṣratu'd-Dawlih, had only just been appointed as the new Governor of Fárs and was on his way from Ṭihrán. Pending his arrival, responsibility for the government of the province lay with the Vazír, Mírzá Faḍlu'lláh, Náṣiru'l-Mulk. The British Agent in Shíráz, Mírzá Maḥmúd,† referred to the commencement of the upheaval in his report for the period 24 May to 5 June 1850: 'Syed Yahyah, a disciple of Bab, who was some time ago in Istahbanat, has it is said, assembled 1500 men, and has proceeded to Nereez where Zeynool Abedeen Khan wishes to seize him. Outside the Town he has erected a Fort, and is engaged in skirmishes. According to what is reported the Khan has had 80 men killed. When this news reached Shiraz, the Nuseer-ool Mulk ordered a Regiment of Sirbaz with two Guns to proceed to Nereez for the purpose of seizing Syed Yahyah.'[7]

* Since Mírzá 'Alíy-i-Sayyáḥ acted as courier between the Báb and the Bábí community, it may be that this meeting with Vaḥíd occurred even earlier, on another of his journeys from Mákú. But this is not the only problem with dating the whole Yazd episode. For example Nabíl states regarding Vaḥíd's journey from Yazd to Nayríz that Vaḥíd left Yazd on 10 May and arrived at Nayríz on 27 May. This only leaves 17 days for the journey, and according to most accounts Vaḥíd stayed at several towns and villages on the way, converting many people and causing a considerable stir. The *Fárs-Námih* of Ḥasan-i-Faṣá'í puts the date of the Yazd upheaval even further back than the European diplomats. Vaḥíd's departure from Yazd is stated by this source to have occurred in Nov. 1849. The *Fárs-Námih* moreover gives lengthy details of Vaḥíd's activities between Yazd and Nayríz; activities which must have taken longer than Nabíl's 17 days. Thus there are many problems associated with the dates of this episode in Yazd, and for once the European sources have only served to add to the confusion. What is needed is a reliable local history of Yazd during this period, or some dated letters or documents that could enable some of these dates to be fixed.

† Mírzá Maḥmúd was British Agent in Shíráz until Nov. 1850, when he was dismissed following irregularities over the possessions of Mr Tasker, a British subject who died in Shíráz.

In the same report, Mírzá Maḥmúd records: 'On the 3rd June Mehr Ally Khan* by order of the Nuseer-ool Mulk, with one Regiment and two Guns proceeded to Nereez to seize Syed Yahyah.'[8]

Fírúz Mírzá, the new Governor of Fárs, arrived in Shíráz on 5 June 1850. Part of Mírzá Maḥmúd's report for the period 4 to 20 June reads as follows:

I wrote to you previously that by the orders of H.R.H., a Regiment of Sirbaz and two Guns had been sent to Nereez. Information has now been received, that the followers of the Bab made a night attack upon the Sirbaz, and killed and wounded several. The next day Moostuffa Gooly Khan Sirteep† commanded the Sirbaz to attack and take the Babees and to destroy the Tower, in which was Syed Yahyah. The latter on hearing this, came out and ordered his followers to attack the Sirbaz. Accordingly an engagement ensued which continued from morning until noon, when the Babees prevailed, and the Sirbaz were defeated. Many on both sides were killed and wounded. When H.R.H. heard this news He commanded a Regiment of Sirbaz with 50 Horsemen and two Guns under Mahomed Wulee Khan to proceed and reinforce Mehr Ally Khan and Moostuffa Ally Khan. On the 19th Mahomed Salah Khan Yoozbashee with 50 Horsemen proceeded to Nereez. On the 20th Mahomed Wulee Khan Sirteep, with two Guns and the Sallakhoonee Regiment followed to the assistance of Mehr Ally Khan. The Prince sáys 50 were killed and 40 wounded of the Babees and of the Sirbaz 30 were killed and 50 wounded . . . The Prince having ordered the Heads of the slain Babees to be brought in, on the 9th [July‡] Mehr Ally Khan arrived with 12 heads. H.R.H. commanded the Sirbaz to perambulate the Streets with these Heads on the point of their Bayonets. This was accordingly done, with drums beating. It is said however in the City, that these heads did not belong to the Babees but to the Sirbaz. After they had been paraded in the streets, the heads were suspended at the Isfahan Gate . . . On the 23rd [June] H.R.H. received a letter from Mehr Ally Khan reporting that the Babees had been defeated, and that Syed Yahyah and his followers would be speedily sent to the Prince.[9]

In Mírzá Maḥmúd's report for the period 23 June to 3 July, the following events are noted:

On the 24th [June] Mehr Ally Khan having sent to Shiraz 13 Heads of the Babees, the Sirbaz placed them on their Bayonets and carried them to the Prince. H.R.H. ordered them to be paraded through the streets with drums beating, and after to be suspended at the Gate . . . On the 26th two Ghoolams arrived from Mehr Ally Khan with news of the capture of Syed Yahyah. H.R.H. gave dresses of honor to both of them. It is reported that finding he could not escape, Syed Yahyah with 4 of his men surrendered on the 17th Instant to Mehr Ally Khan. He made four requests 1st that his followers should be permitted to go free, 2nd that if doomed to die, his Captor should intercede with the Prince for a respite of three days, 3rd that if taken to the City

* Ḥájí Mihr-'Alí Khán-i-Núrí, Shujá'u'l-Mulk (q.v.).

† Muṣṭafá-Qulí Khán, I'timádu's-Salṭanih, Sartíp (Colonel) of the Qaráquzlú Regiment. He obtained promotion for his part in the Nayríz upheaval (dispatch dated 10 Feb. 1851: FO 60 158). He was sent against Shaykh 'Ubaydu'lláh in 1880, and died in 1881.

‡ Almost certainly 9 July is meant here. It is strange that Mírzá Maḥmúd should have suddenly jumped forward thus in his diary. This may have occurred during translation.

not to be escorted by the Sirbaz, 4th that in the place of the Executioner one of the Moojtehids should put him to death, after receiving his last words. All these requests were refused by Mehr Ally Khan, who said he waited orders from the Prince for his disposal. On the 25th H.R.H. sent an Executioner with two Furrashes to put him (Syed Yahyah) to death, but before their arrival he and his followers had been killed by the Sirbaz. It is reported that the Sirbaz have plundered Nereez, and taken all the women captives.[10]

Mírzá Maḥmúd, in his report for the period 1 to 16 July 1850, records:

On the 8th July Mehr Ally Khan sent to H.R.H. eleven followers of Bab, they have all been imprisoned. 10th July . . . Mehr Ally Khan and Moostufa Gooly Khan, who had been sent against Syed Yahyah, have returned to Shiraz bringing with them 25 of the Babee Sect, together with the head of Syed Yahyah and 13 others, as an offering to H.R.H.,* who ordered the Prisoners to be confined. The Prince has received these two Khans with great favor. It appears that only one Mahala† of Nereez was plundered and destroyed. The Sirbaz had with them a good quantity of the stolen property. Syed Yahyah is reported to have had four or five vessels of Pomegranete Syrup, a single drop of which was sufficient to make a man become a Babee and join him. One bottle was drunk by four Sirbaz, who instantly turned Babees, and fought against their own Commanders. They say this Syrup has been brought to the Prince.[11]

The matter of the pomegranate syrup is of course typical of the ridiculous stories circulated about the Bábís by their enemies in order to explain the success of the Bábís and their own inadequacies. There is a similar reference in Ferrier's report of this episode dated 25 July 1850:

The sect of the Bábís is increasing each day, and now counts numerous new adherents in every province. They have had more successes than reverses during the course of this month. Their position is good in Iraq, Gílán, Mázindarán, Yazd and Kirmán, but they have suffered a check in Fárs, when Siyyid Yaḥyá, one of their leaders, who had taken possession of the fortress of Nayríz situated in the west of this province, was attacked, defeated and made prisoner by the troops sent against him by Fírúz Mírzá . . . in addressing a report to Ṭihrán on this affair, the Governor of Fárs has also announced the sending of a dish containing a piece of preserve ['confiture'] found at Nayríz and considered by the Bábís as being a miraculous substance of which it was not possible to taste even the smallest amount without becoming a Bábí. Fírúz Mírzá adds that three soldiers of the Fárs division, having unfortunately eaten of it, have in fact embraced the new belief and that having beaten them to death, he was not

* Concerning this offering of the heads to the Prince Governor, Browne has noted: 'The author of the *Táríkh-i-Jadíd* in concluding this narrative takes occasion to point out how literally was fulfilled in these events the prophecy contained in a tradition referring to the signs which shall mark the appearance of the Imám Mahdí:- "In him [shall be] the perfection of Moses, the preciousness of Jesus, and the patience of Job; his saints shall be abased in his time, and their heads shall be exchanged as presents, even as the heads of the Turk and the Deylamite are exchanged as presents; they shall be slain and burned, and shall be afraid, fearful, and dismayed; the earth shall be dyed with their blood, and lamentation and wailing shall prevail amongst their women; these are my saints indeed".' (*A Traveller's Narrative* p. 259)

† *Maḥallih* means district or quarter; in this case the reference is to the quarter of Chinár-Súkhtih where most of the Bábís lived.

able to extract from them a retraction. The Sháh is awaiting this mysterious sherbet ['chorbet'] impatiently, with the intention of testing its properties on several state prisoners who are at this moment detained in Ṭihrán. The Persian can say nothing nor do anything without adding miracles to it. But what is certain is that all the sectaries who have been executed up to this day have borne their punishment with a courage and a faith worthy of the heroic times of the first martyrs.[12]

Sheil must have received information concerning the commencement of the Nayríz episode from a source other than the British Agent in Shíráz. For, on 25 June 1850, before he had received Mírzá Maḥmúd's reports from Lt-Col. Hennell (q.v.), the Búshihr Resident, he wrote to Palmerston: 'In Fars, the Bâbees who under their leader Seyed Yaheeya had fled from Yezd, have again begun to attract notice. They have approached within a short distance of Sheeraz, which they have been warned not to enter, but as yet they have abstained from any insurrectionary movement in the above province.'[13]

Later, in the same dispatch to Palmerston as the martyrdom of the Báb was reported, Sheil recorded the end of the Nayríz episode: 'His [the Báb's] followers in Fars have received a severe check. Syed Yaheeya who fled from Yezd to that province with a large force of Bâbees has been defeated and captured having however previously twice repulsed the Shah's troops.'[14]

Later that year, the following passage occurs in Mírzá Maḥmúd's reports for the period 10 to 27 August 1850: 'On the 20th His Royal Highness summoned ten Bâbees and commanded them either to curse Syed Yahiyeh or to suffer death; as they remained silent, it was concluded they were steadfast in their faith. The Prince however respited them for an hour, when they submitted to His Royal Highness' will. Some persons then interceded for them and the Prince forgave them . . . The Prince has been rather unwell for some days past, on which account, it is said, he will release all the imprisoned Bâbees.'[15]

In Mírzá Maḥmúd's report for the period 23 September to 10 October 1850, the following is reported to have occurred on 6 October:

'On the same day two Babees were delivered by Mehr Ally Khan to H.R.H. One of them was the executioner, and the other a Sirdar of Syed Yahyah. Both were beheaded.'[16]

Two further episodes described in Mírzá Maḥmúd's reports of 1850 should be noted. In the reports from 27 April to 12 May this passage occurs: 'A disciple of Mirza Ally Mahomed, the 'Bab', has been seized by the people of Sheik Aboo Toorab,* and sent by him to the Nusseer-ool Mulk. Sheik Mehdy the Moojtehid has given a Fitweh† for his execution. At present he is

* Imám-Jum'ih of Shíráz

† *Fatvá*

a Prisoner in the house of the Nuseer ool Mulk.'[17]

The editor has been unable to establish the identity of this individual. He is presumably the same individual whose fate is described in Mírzá Maḥmúd's report for 23 June 1850: 'The follower of Bab who was sent by the Imam Joomah to the Nuseer ool Mulk has been executed before H.R.H.'[18]

The editor has also been unable to establish the basis for the following statement in Mírzá Maḥmúd's reports for 23 June to 3 July 1850: 'Abbas Koolee Khan the Governor of Cazeroon has written to the Prince to the effect that several of the Babees are creating disturbances at Boronjoon. H.R.H. has sent some Horsemen to seize them.'[19]

Indeed, it is possible that this latter episode had nothing to do with the Bábís, as during this period any disturbance was automatically attributed to them.

References

1. Report prepared by K. E. Abbott on his journey through southern Persia 1849–50: FO 60 165. Abbott was given permission to proceed to Tabríz to prepare his report; he journeyed to Tabríz in Aug. 1850, and his report is dated Mar. 1851. There is also a report of his tour in *Jour. Roy. Geog. Soc.* Vol. 25, 1855, pp. 1–78, but this does not contain an account of his stay in Yazd.
2. *Nabíl's Narrative* UK p. 346, USA pp. 469–70
3. Sheil to Palmerston No. 20, 12 Feb. 1850: FO 60 150
4. Dolgorukov to Nesselrode No. 11, 12 Feb. 1850 OS (24 Feb. NS): Dossier No. 133, Ṭihrán 1850, pp. 100–105. Chahárdihí *Shaykhí-garí, Bábí-garí* pp. 276–7 (trans. from Persian)
5. Ferrier to de LaHitte, 25 June 1850: MAE Sér. Corr. Polit. MD No. 24 (1833–56), p. 341 (trans. from French)
6. Balyuzi *'Abdu'l-Bahá* pp. 284–5
7. Three reports (24 May – 5 June, 4–20 June and 23 June – 3 July 1850) were enclosed in Lt-Col. Hennell (Resident at Búshihr) to Sheil No. 274, 15 July 1850. The report from 1–16 July was in Hennell's dispatch No. 315, 14 Aug. 1850. All were translated by James Edwards, accountant at Búshihr: FO 248 138.
8. ibid.
9. ibid.
10. ibid.
11. ibid.
12. Ferrier to de LaHitte 25 July 1850: MAE Sér. Corr. Polit. MD No. 24 (1833–56), p. 348 (trans. from French)
13. Sheil to Palmerston No. 77, 25 June 1850: FO 60 152
14. Sheil to Palmerston No. 88, 22 July 1850: FO 60 152
15. Enclosed in Sheil to Palmerston 22 Oct. 1850, trans. James Edwards: FO 60 153
16. Enclosed in Hennell to Sheil 16 Oct. 1850, trans. James Edwards: FO 248 138
17. Mírzá Maḥmúd's report for 27 April – 12 May in Hennell to Sheil No. 224, 15 June 1850: FO 248 138
18. Mírzá Maḥmúd's report for 4–20 June 1850, see note 7 *supra*
19. See 7 *supra*

SIX

The Zanján Upheaval (1850–51)

The most prolonged of the upheavals which occurred during the ministry of the Báb was that of Zanján. Here, one of the most influential of the local 'ulamá, Mullá Muḥammad-'Alí, known as Ḥujjat, espoused the cause of the Báb and converted a sizeable proportion of the town. Tension grew between the Bábís and the Shí'ih 'ulamá, and after a few incidents, troops were summoned from Tabríz and Ṭihrán. It is estimated that in all some 20,000 trained soldiers together with at least 19 pieces of artillery were set against the 1,500 or 2,000 Bábí defendants, who occupied the eastern half of the town. The siege lasted 7 months.

There are contemporary Western accounts from five sources: the British Minister, Sheil, the Russian Minister, Dolgorukov, the French Agent, Ferrier (whose reports seem to be the least accurate), and the British and Russian Consuls in Tabríz, R. W. Stevens and N. H. Anitchkov respectively. There are at least 43 references to the Zanján upheaval in the dispatches of these persons and therefore, to keep this section of the book within reasonable limits, it has been necessary to summarize many of these dispatches and omit some.

The first reference to the strength of the Bábís in Zanján occurs in a dispatch of Dolgorukov's on 7 March 1849. In this report he states that 'there are rumours that in Zanjan they have appeared 800 strong, and that by their presence, they threaten to disrupt the public order.'[1]

In a letter dated 21 February 1850, Ferrier, having dealt with the Mázindarán upheaval and mentioned the Seven Martyrs of Ṭihrán, states: '. . . thirty of them [Bábís] arrived in Ṭihrán from Zanján in chains.'[2] It is difficult to correlate this statement with other accounts of the Zanján upheaval.

Shortly afterwards, Dolgorukov, in a report of 14 March 1850, mentions that: 'In Zanjan, which is situated halfway between Tihran and Tabriz, their number reaches 2,000 people, and the ideas spread by them among the people incite common discontent.'[3]

According to *Nabíl's Narrative*, the first bloodshed in the Zanján upheaval was the martyrdom of Shaykh Muḥammad-i-Túb-Chí on 16 May 1850.[4] In the ensuing days, the town was thrown into turmoil and became divided into two camps. News of these events reached Ṭihrán on 25 May 1850 and in a note written on that day and appended to his main report, Ferrier reports: 'As I was about to give my letter to the courier, I learnt that the town of Zanján, situated midway between Ṭihrán and Tabríz, has risen in rebellion, and has driven out its governor and all authorities established by the Sháh. A battery of artillery and some troops are about to leave here in order to return the town to order.

'Zanján is the principal centre of Bábism. J.P.F.'[5]

Col. Sheil writing on the same day gives the following report: 'The greater part of Persia is in a state of tolerable tranquillity. At Zenjan a city midway between Tehran and Tabreez, an attempt at insurrection was made by the Sect of the Babees, whose leader is the chief priest of the town. Five hours after the receipt of this intelligence a Battalion of Infantry 400 horse and three guns marched towards Zenjan. This is an instance unexampled in Persia of military celerity, which perhaps would not be surpassed in many countries of Europe.'[6]

In a dispatch dated 30 May 1850, Stevens reported the outbreak of a 'serious disturbance' at Zanján. The Bábís 'remained in possession of a large part of the town' and 'about one hundred lives had been lost.'[7]

Dolgorukov notified the Russian Foreign Ministry of the commencement of serious conflict with loss of life at Zanján in a dispatch of 22 June 1850.[8]

On 25 June 1850, Sheil reported the progress of the conflict:

> The insurrection at Zenjan has not yet been quelled. The Bâbees of that city continue to defend themselves with the zeal of proselytes and the contempt of life inculcated by their faith, and to maintain possession against the Shah's troops, of the portion of the town originally in their occupation. Succour is said to reach the Bâbees from the adjacent villages and districts and many lives are daily lost on both sides; but eventually of course the insurgents will have no choice but to yield to superior force. It is not a little strange that an insignificant town like Zenjan, within reach of all the military resources of Tehran and Azerbaijan, should make an attempt at revolt.[9]

On the same day as the above dispatch from Sheil, Ferrier sent a longer, more detailed but less accurate account to the French Foreign Ministry. In this account, Ferrier states that the Bábís held the Governor besieged in his palace and that when the troops from Ṭihrán arrived the insurgents said 'that they were revolting not at all on account of religion, but solely against the tyranny of their Governor, promising to lay down arms as soon as they were given another.' These statements were shown to be incorrect by later reports, as was his assertion that there were 6,000 Bábís in Zanján and triple that number in the surrounding villages. The Bábí defenders at Zanján were about 1,500 in number according to most sources. His account is of interest in stating that the troops dispatched from Ṭihrán consisted of '3,000 infantry, 1,000 cavalry and a battery of artillery' and that 'a similar body of troops set out from Tabríz for the same destination.'[10]

On 30 June 1850, George Alexander Stevens, who was in charge of the Tabríz Consulate in his brother's absence, reported to Palmerston that: 'The Bâbees have entire possession of the Town and some two hundred irregular Horse, sent against them from Tehran have been killed.'[11]

It appears that in the middle of July 1850, Mullá Muḥammad-'Alí, Ḥujjat, made a general appeal for an end to the fighting.* He wrote letters to Sheil, to Samí Effendi (the Turkish Ambassador in Ṭihrán) and to George A. Stevens who was in charge of the British Consulate in Tabríz. It is difficult to believe Sheil's statement in a dispatch dated 22 July 1850 that in Ḥujjat's letter to him, Ḥujjat states that he has 'been falsely accused of Bâbeeism'.[12] For if Ḥujjat had wanted to renounce his faith, the conflict in Zanján would have immediately come to an end. If Sheil, moreover, really believed that Ḥujjat wished to renounce Bábism why does he continue in a further ten dispatches to call Ḥujjat and his followers Bábís? Indeed, in a dispatch dated 23 November 1850, Sheil makes the equally incredible statement that 'Moolla Mahomed Ali, their chief, has the reputation of having proclaimed himself to be the true Bâb, and his predecessor to have been an impostor.'[13] Anitchkov, also in a dispatch of 22 July, repeats the allegation that Ḥujjat denied being a Bábí.[14] It would appear, therefore, that there was a deliberate attempt by the enemies of Ḥujjat to misrepresent him. *Nabíl's Narrative* states that some of Ḥujjat's letters were intercepted by the government forces and false letters substituted for them.[15] The letter to Sheil may have been one of these.

Sheil states that his letter from Ḥujjat contained as an enclosure: 'a letter of the same purport to the Ameer i Nizam. The Persian Minister replied to this person that he was willing to accept his declaration, but that in proof of his sincerity he must present himself at the Shah's Court. No notice having been taken of this condition, a further body of troops has been summoned to prosecute the siege.'[16]

It would be strange indeed if Ḥujjat, having written the original letters, then declined to accept the resulting proposals, unless the original letters did not emanate from him. An alternative explanation for this remarkable statement attributed to Ḥujjat is that in his letter Ḥujjat may have asked for the opportunity to prove publicly that he was not guilty of heresy. Ḥujjat would, by such a statement, have meant proving that the Bábí religion was not heresy, but Sheil may have misinterpreted this to be a denial of faith.

* See also Browne *Nuqṭatu'l-Káf* pp. 233–4, and *Táríkh-i-Jadíd* pp. 372–3.

Dolgorukov also reports these letters of Ḥujjat's on 26 September:

The disorders of Zanjan are not yet coming to an end. The Babis, who are engaged there in a life and death struggle against the troops of the Shah, are still resisting the attacks of Muhammad Khan, and one can only wonder at the fierceness with which they meet the danger of their situation. Their leader, Mulla Muhammad-Ali, has appealed to the Turkish Minister, Sami Effendi, and also to Colonel Sheil for their mediation. However, my English colleague is of the opinion that it would be very difficult to force the Persian Government to consent to foreign intervention in favor of the above mentioned sectaries.[17]

Anitchkov in his dispatch of 22 July states that in his letter to George Stevens, Ḥujjat asks the latter to take up his case. In this dispatch, Anitchkov also reports:

Some days ago, the besiegers dug a mine and blew up some of the houses of the Bábís. But the result was contrary to what was expected. In effect, the Bábís then made a sortie and inflicted a complete disaster on the Imperial forces. About sixty of the latter were killed and the rest put to flight . . . To the ordinary pillaging that occurs around Zanján and that I have many times reported to Your Excellency, may now be added, according to the allegations of our Ghuláms who travel along this road, the highway robbery of the soldiers sent there against the Bábís.[18]

The ensuing reports may be summarized thus:

25 July; Ferrier:

The Bábís are masters of the town and have taken shelter behind a high wall on ground protected by a dry moat three-quarters filled in. It is a shambles that 3,000 European troops would flatten in 48 hours . . . More than 900 men have perished before its walls since the siege began and almost as many have been wounded. It is again a Mullá, named Muḥammad-'Alí, who is the leader of the revolt in the town, and it is very remarkable that it is always from this class of the population and in that of the Siyyids (descendants of the Prophet) that the majority of recruits to the Bábí sect come.[19]

29 July; Anitchkov:

On the 14 June,* the Bábís at Zanján were once again attacked. The attack was repulsed with great losses on the part of the assailants who had more than 200 wounded and at least 40 dead. The Bábís have taken possession of the four main gates of the town, have constructed some fortifications, and have procured considerable ammunitions.

Their chief, Mullá Muḥammad-'Alí, has captured four notable inhabitants of the town and detained them in his camp. At present, three regiments are quartered near Zanján, of which one is from Tabríz. But the Bábís resist with splendid courage and constant success. They have, in case the enemy occupy their fortifications, assembled in one place all their goods, and have placed there inflammable materials with the intention of destroying everything by fire rather than letting it fall booty to the soldiers.[20]

31 July; R. Stevens: 'As fast as the Artillery fire shot upon the Town the

* 26 June NS

balls are picked up and returned to the Camp out of wooden Cannon bound with Iron.'[21]

On 11 August 1850, Dolgorukov reports the dispatch of Muḥammad Khán together with 2,000 men and four cannons against Zanján.[22]

On 22 August, Sheil states that, as reinforcements have been sent against the Bábís in Zanján, it cannot be long before the town is taken.[23]

On 5 September, Sheil forwards a report from the British Consul, Keith Abbott, who on his way to Tabríz had passed by Zanján.* Sheil also reports the dispatch of 'several guns . . . to Zenjan . . . a few days ago, which cannot fail to bring the matter to a speedy conclusion'.[24]

Abbott's letter:

Persian Camp before Zenjan
August 30, 1850.

My dear Sir:

I find the Begler Beggee, Mahomed Khan, still engaged before this place. The Bâbees occupy one quarter only of the Town and in two recent assaults of the troops have been driven from their hold on the Northern wall to some distance within it. They now occupy the South-eastern corner of the town, and the Begler Beggee has mounted four guns on the Boorjes (Bastions) he has lately captured and has advanced four or five other guns into the town. The resistance of the Bâbees appears to have been most determined and conducted with much skill. These people have erected Barricades and have loop-holed all the houses in their quarter, so that though their numbers are now greatly reduced by desertion and casualties and they are said not to have more than 300 fighting men left, their position is so strong that it must no doubt be a matter of considerable difficulty to dislodge them. They fight in the most obstinate and spirited manner, the women even, of whom several have been killed, engaging in the strife, and they are such excellent marksmen that up to this time a good many have fallen of the Government troops. Under these circumstances the approaches have been made with the utmost difficulty, the least exposure of the men being instantly taken advantage of by the enemy's sharpshooters. The Bâbees have also constructed a couple of guns from bars of iron bound together, but which get damaged at each discharge. A courier has just arrived from Tehran with intelligence that six heavy guns and a supply of ammunition had been dispatched hither. The Begler Beggee however intends to make another assault tomorrow at daybreak by which he expects to obtain entire possession of the place.[25]

9 September; Anitchkov: 'Muḥammad Khán has succeeded in seizing some of the towers of the fortress and has mounted some cannons on top of these. However the Bábís have managed to construct two cannons and are returning the cannon-balls fired by their enemy.'[26]

23 September; Anitchkov: About 60 Bábís surrendered and were imprisoned by Muḥammad Khán. When 'Azíz Khán arrived, 'these were released, given presents and sent back to the town to persuade their co-religionists to give themselves up, but since then, these have not returned

* From the date of his letter, it would appear that Abbott (q.v.) was at Zanján at the same time as 'Azíz Khán and may, therefore, have been accompanying him to Tabríz.

and their people continue resisting to the bitter end.'[27]

The arrival of 'Azíz Khán-i-Mukrí (q.v.) on 25 August 1850 marks an important interlude in the proceedings of the siege. According to *Nabíl's Narrative*,[28] 'Azíz Khán was at first disposed to be friendly to the Bábís but the arrest by the Amír-Niẓám's *farrásh* of Siyyid 'Alí Khán (-i-Fírúzkúhí), who was also friendly, frightened him and turned him from his initial intentions.

The history behind 'Azíz Khán's arrival in Zanján is that in October 1850, the Russian Crown Prince, Grand Duke Alexander Nicholaivich, toured the Caucasus. On 16 October, he was due to be in Íráván. The Persian Government dispatched 'Azíz Khán (who at this time held the title Ájúdán-Báshíy-i-Kull, and was in charge of all military affairs, and directly responsible to the Amír-Niẓám) with presents estimated by Sheil to be worth some 6,000 *túmáns*, to greet the Russian Prince. He was also instructed to take charge of the Zanján operations on his way to Ádharbáyján. A secretary of the Russian Embassy, accompanying 'Azíz Khán, sent a report to Dolgorukov which was forwarded to the Russian Foreign Minister on 5 October 1850:

At Qazvín, the son of the Vazír, Mírzá Músá, together with some horsemen and the Kad-khudá came out to meet us, and with all the ceremony due to his ['Azíz Khán's] rank we entered the town. It was here that a courier of the Amír's delivered to us a firmán to the effect that it was necessary for us to devise effective measures to bring the Zanján affair to a close, and that we were to remain in that area until the task was completed. When we arrived at Sulṭáníyyih we were met by senior officers from the military forces that were based in Zanján. They were full of complaints about Muḥammad Khán, the Governor* of Tabríz, and were of the opinion that were it not for him the Zanján affair would be ended.

On Friday, the thirteenth of the month† we proceeded from Sulṭáníyyih and entered Zanján. The governor of Zanján, Aṣlán Khán, and the Biglár-Bigí of Tabríz, Muḥammad Khán, and the military chiefs came out to meet us. Here, the Ájúdán-Báshí ['Azíz Khán] upbraided the commanders and asked them whether they were not ashamed, that five months had now passed that they had been besieging a mere Mullá without being able to capture him. He, himself, would capture this man the following day. The Ájúdán-Báshí wrote a letter of accusation to Mullá Muḥammad reproaching him with rebellion against the Sháh and suggesting that he return with him to Ṭihrán. This letter was delivered by Najaf-Qulí Khán of Íráván but Mullá Muḥammad-'Alí declined the suggestions of the Ájúdán-Báshí. 'Azíz Khán, for a second time, sent the same messenger to him and threatened that if he did not surrender himself, all of his property and his wives would be given over to the soldiers of the Government. But Mullá Muḥammad-'Alí replied that he, himself, was a king and that 'Azíz Khán could try to do what he liked.

On Wednesday,‡ the Ájúdán-Báshí arranged his troops around Zanján. He, once more, asked Mullá Muḥammad-'Alí to surrender himself but this action led to no

* In fact, he was the Biglár-Bigí of Tabríz.

† 13 Aug. O S, i.e. 25 Aug. 1850.

‡ 30 Aug. Note that this is also the date of Abbott's letter, see p. 118.

useful result. At length, on Sunday,* 'Azíz Khán, after exhorting the troops to deeds of valour, ordered an attack and the cannons all commenced to fire. But as soon as the soldiers approached the fortifications, ten of them were killed and the rest fled. 'Azíz Khán ordered a second attack, but because he did not anticipate a good result from the battle, he mounted his horse and, having emphasized to the soldiers that Zanján must be conquered in two days, he left the area. After his departure, the soldiers abandoned the idea of continuing the attack (out of fear). At this time, three-quarters of the town is occupied by the soldiers and only one-quarter is in the hands of Mullá Muḥammad-'Alí. The houses that are in the districts occupied by the soldiers are all in ruins, and the wooden boards have been removed from them by the soldiers for sale.

From my observations of the royal troops it is clear that from the time of their entry into Zanján until now their casualties exceed 500 dead and 200 wounded. There is not a tent in which there is not a wounded soldier. All the Bábís who were captured, were brought before the Ájúdán-Báshí and the soldiers put them to death.[29]

The reports over the next few months may be summarized thus:

25 September; Sheil: 'The disciples of Bâb have barricaded a portion of that town, from which they cannot be expelled without a greater loss of life than the assailants seem willing to encounter. A feeble attempt at an assault was lately made, of which the only result was to cause the Bâbees to retire a short distance within their position.'[30]

18 October; Dolgorukov: notes that 'The Babis have been fighting against 6,000 of the Shah's best troops for almost five months now . . . ' and that Muḥammad Khán 'is not distinguished by personal courage, and the demoralization of the troops he commands has reached extreme proportions'.[31]

25 October; Ferrier: noting 'Azíz Khán's lack of success at Zanján.[32]

25 October; Sheil: notes the continuing siege of Zanján 'contrary to all rational expectation.' Then proceeds to report: 'Notwithstanding the strong force employed in the seige [*sic*], an English subject who lately arrived in Tehran informed me that the measures of defence adopted by the besiegers were so feeble as scarcely to present the semblance of hostilities. General Sir Henry Bethune [q.v.] who visited the scene of operations, expressed a conviction that three hours with ordinary troops would finish the affair, and he stated besides that he never witnessed so humiliating a combination of ignorance, incapacity and backwardness.'[33]

7 November; Dolgorukov: 'According to reports reaching me, Sartíp [Colonel] Farrukh Khán, who had been ordered to proceed from Kirmánsháh and join the Biglár-Bigí at Zanján, fell into the hands of the Bábís. These fanatics have burnt him. The number of Bábís in Zanján, at present, is known to be about 300 persons.' Two fresh regiments under the command of the son of 'Azíz Khán had been dispatched to Zanján.[34]

* 2 Sept.

21 November; Dolgorukov: 'New military units have just been despatched against the Babis of Zanjan . . . the Governor of that city . . . Amir Aslan Khan is accused of provoking the resistance which the Babis offer . . . by his incautious behaviour.'[35]

23 November; Sheil: 'Three fresh regiments and some mortars have been despatched as reinforcements.' The rest of the report is somewhat self-contradictory as on the one hand Sheil asserts that the defenders are not Bábís and then that Mullá Muḥammad-'Alí has 'proclaimed himself to be the true Bâb, and his predecessor to have been an impostor' – both of these statements are false and probably the result of rumours circulated by the Government troops. 'A number of citizens having left the town on a safe conduct, when the party was divided they were assailed by the soldiers who ill-treated their women and pillaged their property.'[36]

29 November; Stevens: 'a large re-inforcement is now on the way to join the besieging troops . . . The Ameer-i-Nizam has authorised, if necessary, the destruction of the town and a general massacre.'[37]

In early December, Ḥujjat was wounded. On hearing of this, his companions laid down their arms and rushed to his side. The temporary lapse in the defences allowed the royal forces an opportunity to breach the fortifications. On that day, according to *Nabíl's Narrative*,[38] about one hundred of the women and children were taken captive. Their fate is described by Stevens in a dispatch dated 9 December 1850: 'I have been informed by a Persian merchant who heard it from an eyewitness, that the son of Mollah Mehmet Aly, Zenjaunee, a youth only 8 years of age, was literally cut into small pieces, by orders of Mahommed Khan, and that the wives and daughters of the Mollah's partisans were brought to the camp, and made over to the soldiers. Such cruelties need no comment.'*[39]

Sheil in reporting this to Palmerston on 16 December states: 'I brought the circumstance to the knowledge of the Persian Minister. The Ameer-i-Nizam thanked me for the information, and said he would take immediate steps for preventing such barbarous proceedings, which are entirely opposed to his sentiments and feelings.'[40]

On the 23 December, Anitchkov reports the state of affairs following the capture of the fort: 'It seems that although the fortifications of the rebels have in effect been taken, the house of their chief remains standing. In this house, a crowd of seventy men and as many women are gathered and are repelling the attacks of the entire army. A regiment has been sent from Marághih.'[41]

* It should be said that, while, no doubt, atrocities were committed, it is unlikely that the victim of the above episode was in fact a son of Ḥujjat. Such an incident could hardly have failed to come to the attention of one of the Bábí or Bahá'í historians and yet there is no mention in any such work of this fate overcoming a son of Ḥujjat.

Sheil, on 24 December, gave a similar report:

The general expectation entertained here that the reinforcements sent to Zenjan after making their first assault, would imitate the apathy of their comrades has been fulfilled. The regiment of Gerroos* soon after joining the camp, made an attack with some vigour, in which many were killed on both sides, the loss on the part of the Bâbees however being very severe. Since then the same sort of tacit truce which before existed seems to be again established. No active operation has been undertaken; both parties are on the alert, and shots are fired whenever a soldier or a Bâbee more venturesome than his companions exposes his person.

This protracted siege, if siege it can be called, is inexplicable. An English gentleman who lately passed through Zenjan informed me a few days ago that the portion of the town occupied by the Bâbees is confined to three or four houses, and that their numbers are utterly insignificant. They have adopted a mode of defence which seems to exceed the military skill of the Persian commanders. The entire [*sic*] of the space included within these houses is mined or excavated and connected by passages. Here the Bâbees live in safety from the shot and shells of the assailants, who evidently have no predilection for underground warfare.[42]

Eventually, however, following the death of Ḥujjat, the Bábí resistance crumbled. The Russian Minister gave the following notification of the end of the siege, on 7 January 1851: 'The Zanjan disturbances have ended. After a siege which lasted for almost six months the Shah's troops have destroyed the center of the rebellion. The Babis who defended themselves to the last, and whose numbers were finally reduced to twenty men, who sought refuge in a cellar, were torn to pieces. In addition to monetary expenditure, this struggle has cost Persia 1,500 in killed and disabled.'[43]

Ferrier embellishes his account (dated 24 January 1851) with various fallacies, but it is important in that it gives a date for the death of Ḥujjat which even if not the exact date, cannot be far wrong.

While the Amír was considering abandoning the siege of Zanján, and resuming it in the spring, as I mentioned in my last letter, the military operations directed against that town achieved one of those unforeseen successes by which all revolutions in Persia usually end. Mullá Muḥammad-'Alí, leader of the Bábís, was the soul and nerve of the defence. At the beginning of December he had cut the throat of his wife because she had expressed the thought of crossing to the imperial camp, a Qur'án in hand, and there imploring clemency from the besiegers.† Several advantages gained over the latter, during the course of the same month increased his presumptuousness so much

* The Colonel of this regiment was Ḥasan-'Alí Khán-i-Garrúsí (q.v.).

† This story is not correct. After the termination of the Zanján upheaval, the survivors of Ḥujjat's family were sent, on Náṣiru'd-Dín Sháh's orders, to Shíráz. Here, in later years, Mírzá Ḥabíbu'lláh Afnán met Ḥujjat's eldest daughter, Bíbí Raqíyyih, who recounted for him the details of Ḥujjat's family. According to this authoritative source, Ḥujjat had three wives: one was Bíbí Raqíyyih's mother who was sent to Shíráz with her six children after the termination of the upheaval; one wife had an infant boy and both were killed by a cannon-ball in the closing stages of the upheaval; the third had no children and was also sent to Shíráz. These details are recorded in Mírzá Ḥabíbu'lláh's narrative history of the Bahá'í Faith in Shíráz.

that he had the rashness to set himself alone, and armed with but a paltry sword, in pursuit of some retreating troops. But he was wounded by a ball in the face as he was re-entering his stronghold* and died 29 December, after some days of suffering. Deprived of their leader, the Bábís gave up the struggle and reached the countryside (by way of their underground passages) where they dispersed in all directions. The Sirbáz, astonished by 24 hours silence on the part of the besieged, were encouraged a little and attempted a new assault, but they searched everywhere without finding a single enemy and took possession of the place without a gun being fired.† Furious at finding that the Bábís had escaped him, Sardár-Panjih, Muḥammad Khán threw his horse soldiers into their pursuit. But they only succeeded in arresting thirty unfortunate inoffensive *ra'yats* [peasants] who paid for the true guilty ones, all were butchered without pity.[44]

Sheil gives what may be considered the most accurate account of the termination of the siege, dated 6 January 1851:

I have the honor to report to Your Lordship that Zenjan has been at length captured. Moolla Mahomed Ali, the leader of the insurgents, had received a wound in the arm, which terminated in his death. His followers dismayed by the loss of their chief, yielded to an assault which their relaxation in the energy of their defence encouraged the commander of the Shah's troops to make. This success was followed by a great atrocity. The pusillanimity of the troops, which the events of this siege had rendered so notorious, was equalled by their ferocity. All the captives were bayonetted by the soldiers in cold blood, to avenge, according to the Mahomedan law of retaliation, the slaughter of their comrades. Religious hatred may have conspired with the feelings excited by a blood feud, which among the tribes are very strong, to cause this ruthless act. Four hundred persons are said to have perished in this way, among whom it is believed were some women and children. Of the fact itself there can be no doubt, as it is admitted by the Government in its notification of the reduction of the city, though it may be presumed that in the number there is exaggeration.

For the present, the doctrines of Bâb have received a check. In every part of Persia his disciples have been crushed or scattered. But though there is a cessation of the open promulgation of his tenets, it is believed that in secret they are not the less cherished, especially in the provinces of Mazenderan, Yezd, Kerman and Fars.[45]

The termination of the siege of Zanján was also reported to Viscount Palmerston by Richard W. Stevens, the British Consul in Tabríz, on 25 January 1851: 'I have the honor to report to Your Lordship the final termination of the Zenjaun insurrection.

'The leading person Mollah Mehmet Aly died of his wounds which led to the surrender of his followers. The men were massacred by the troops excepting about twelve Hajees and Mollahs who were fired from the mouth of a Cannon. The Women were sent to the house of the Chief Priest.'‡[46]

Binning (q.v.), who was in Iṣfahán when news of the termination of the

* This is not the manner in which Ḥujjat was wounded, according to *Nabíl's Narrative*.

† This again is incorrect: the surviving Bábís were either taken prisoner or killed on the spot. Very few escaped, as the following accounts show.

‡ The Mujtahid, Mírzá Abu'l-Qásim.

Zanján episode reached him, relates:

The Bâbees have lately been defeated by the Shah's troops at Zenjân, and that town has been taken and dismantled. The small band of the Bâbees who garrisoned it, behaved with great determination and bravery; and for several months held out against six regiments of the royal army, till they were starved into a surrender. After the town had yielded, the troops, according to Persian custom, proceeded to wreak a savage vengeance on the conquered, as punishment for their brave and obstinate resistance. The whole Bâbee population was brought out into the plain outside of the town, and there they were all, men, women, children, and infants, deliberately bayonetted to death. The soldiery also dug up the bodies of some who had fallen in the course of the siege, and hacked them in pieces; rejoicing in all manner of savage barbarities, such as only the veriest brutes and cowards could commit. The persecution of the Bâbees is still carried on; but tempered with mercy. Every one of this sect, when arrested, is invited to recant and return within the pale of Islâm: if he complies, he is at once freely pardoned, but in case of his refusal, he is forthwith decapitated.[47]

On 24 February 1851, Ferrier recorded the return of the troops from Zanján to Ṭihrán 'with a large number of wounded. It is estimated that 4,500 soldiers have been killed during the siege of this tumbledown town.'[48]

On 14 March, Sheil reported the execution of four Bábís from Zanján. These four were Mír Riḍá (called Sardár, the Commander of Ḥujjat's forces), Mír Jalíl (the father of Siyyid Ashraf, the distinguished martyr of a later generation), Ustád Sattár-i-Kuláhdúz and one other.[49] They were martyred on 2 March in the Sabzih-Maydán in Ṭihrán.

Four Bâbees, prisoners from Zengan, were executed here a few days ago. Several other members of that sect are in confinement in Tehran, some of whom are of extreme youth. I sent a message today to the Ameer Nizam, expressing a hope that the lives of these persons might be spared. I said that abundance of blood, regarding the Bâbees simply as rebels, had been shed, and that it was not worthy of a person of his enlightenment to interfere with the merely mental speculations of any class.

The Ameer Nizam sent me an assurance that these persons should not be deprived of their lives, and that it was his intention to disperse them in various directions.

Since the subjugation of Zengan the disciples of Bâb have not ventured to disturb the public peace.[50]

Dolgorukov reports on 4 March 1851 that 'a large number' of Bábís have recently been executed in the Maydán-i-Ark (the public square of the citadel).[51]

Gobineau visited Zanján within a decade of this upheaval, in February 1858. After relating the events of one of the fiercest days of the fighting, 4 August* 1850, Gobineau states:

I have seen, in Zanján, the ruins of that fierce day; entire sections of the city have still not been rebuilt and perhaps may never be. Some of those who took part in this

* Gobineau mistakenly gives the date as 5 Ramaḍán: it was in fact 25 Ramaḍán.

tragedy have, upon the very spot, related to me the incidents that occurred. They made me picture, in my mind, the Bábís going up and down the terraces with their cannons in their arms. Often the flooring, which was of beaten earth, not very solid, would cave in; the cannon would then be lifted and remounted by the strength of their arms; the ground underneath would be shored up with beams. When the enemy approached, the crowd surrounded the cannons with enthusiasm, every arm was extended to lift them up, and when the carriers fell under the hail of enemy fire, there were a hundred competitors to dispute the honour of replacing them. Truly, their's was faith![52]

Comte Julien de Rochechouart (q.v., see fig. 3), Gobineau's successor at the French Legation in Ṭihrán, wrote a scholarly and informative book on Persia entitled *Souvenirs d'un Voyage en Perse.* After referring to the Bábí upheaval at Zanján, he states: 'This small town is still not recovered from this terrible upheaval and it is no more than a pile of ruins. Commerce and industry there are almost non-existent, and except for a few book-makers, one can find absolutely nothing there.'[53]

Colonel Charles E. Stewart visited Zanján in 1880 and reported: 'Zenjan is celebrated as the place where the Babis, a religious sect, defended themselves most bravely against the Persian army during nine months. I visited the ruins of the house of the Chief of the Babis; the Persians have never allowed the construction of a house on this site. Wonderful tales are current of the Babis having invented a machine which enabled them to dig mines with incredible speed.'[54]

Prof. E. G. Browne visited the scene of this conflict in November 1887. He gives the following account of his findings:

Our next stage brought us to the considerable town of Zanján, so celebrated for its obstinate defence by the Bábís against the royal troops in the year 1850. It lies in a plain surrounded by hills, and is situated near, but not on, the river called Zanján-áb, which is at this point surrounded by gardens. The town has never recovered from the effects of this siege, for, besides the injury which it sustained from the cannonade to which it was exposed for several months, a considerable portion was burnt by the besieged on one occasion, when they were hard pressed by the enemy, to create a diversion. We entered the town by the western gate, passing on our left an extensive cemetery, of which two blue-domed *imámzádés* constitute the most conspicuous feature . . .

We remained at Zanján during the next day, for I was anxious to examine the town and its walls, with a view to obtaining a clearer idea of the history of the siege, and the causes which had enabled the Bábí insurgents to keep the royal troops at bay so long. Sir Henry Bethune, quoted by Watson in his *History of Persia under the Kájár Dynasty*, says that in his opinion the place ought to have been subdued by a regular army in a few days, and, so far as I can judge, it possesses no natural advantages as a stronghold. It is true that it is surrounded by a wall (now destroyed in some places), but though this averages twenty or twenty-five feet in height, it is built of no stronger material than unbaked clay. The desperate resistance offered by the Bábís must therefore be attributed less to the strength of the position which they occupied than to the extraordinary valour with which they defended themselves. Even the women took part in the defence, and I subsequently heard it stated on good authority that, like the Carthaginian women of old, they cut off their long hair and bound it round the crazy guns to afford them the necessary support. The fiercest fighting was on the north and north-west sides of the town, by the cemetery and Tabríz gate. Unfortunately there was no one from whom I could obtain detailed information about the siege. This I regretted the more because I was convinced that, could I have found them, there must have been many persons resident in Zanján who had witnessed it, or even taken part in it. I had, however, at that time no clue to guide me to those who would probably have preserved the most circumstantial details about it, viz. the Bábís. There was therefore nothing to induce me to prolong my stay, and accordingly, after one day's halt, we left Zanján on 15th November for Sulṭániyyé.[55]

References

1. Dolgorukov to Nesselrode No. 15, 23 Feb. 1849 OS (7 Mar. NS): Dossier No. 177, Ṭihrán 1849, pp. 80–81. 'Excerpts from Dispatches' p. 19
2. Ferrier to de LaHitte 21 Feb. 1850: MAE Sér. Corr. Polit. MD No. 24 (1833–56), p. 329 (trans. from French)
3. Dolgorukov to Nesselrode No. 16, 2 Mar. 1850 OS (14 Mar. NS): Dossier No. 133, Ṭihrán 1850, p. 137 'Excerpts from Dispatches' p. 21
4. *Nabíl's Narrative* UK p. 395, USA p. 542
5. Ferrier to de LaHitte 25 May 1850: MAE Sér. Corr. Polit. MD No. 24 (1833–56), p. 336 (trans. from French)
6. Sheil to Palmerston No. 64, 25 May 1850: FO 60 151
7. Stevens to Palmerston No. 21, 30 May 1850: FO 60 155
8. Dolgorukov to Nesselrode No. 48, 10 June 1850 OS (22 June NS): Dossier No. 133, Ṭihrán 1850, p. 383. Chahárdihí *Shaykhí-garí, Bábí-garí* p. 278
9. Sheil to Palmerston No. 77, 25 June 1850: FO 60 152
10. Ferrier to de LaHitte 25 June 1850: MAE Sér. Corr. Polit. MD No. 24 (1833–56), p. 341 (trans. from French)
11. G. A. Stevens to Palmerston No. 24, 30 June 1850: FO 60 155
12. Sheil to Palmerston No. 88, 22 July 1850: FO 60 152
13. Sheil to Palmerston No. 148, 23 Nov. 1850: FO 60 154
14. Anitchkov to the Viceroy of the Caucasus No. 462, 10 July 1850 OS (22 July NS): Nicolas 'Le Dossier russo-anglais' p. 359. Nicolas, also, is astounded by this statement, according to his footnote.
15. *Nabíl's Narrative* UK pp. 404–5, USA pp. 554–5
16. As for 12 *supra*
17. Dolgorukov to Russian For. Min. Seniavin No. 72, 14 Sept. 1850 OS (26 Sept. NS): Dossier No. 134, Ṭihrán 1850, p. 562. 'Excerpts from Dispatches' p. 22
18. As for 14 *supra*
19. Ferrier to de LaHitte 25 July 1850. MAE Sér. Corr. Polit. MD No. 24 (1833–56), p. 348 (trans. from French)
20. Anitchkov to Prince Mikhail Semenovitch Vorontsov No. 472, 17 July 1850 OS (29 July NS): Nicolas 'Le Dossier russo-anglais' p. 360 (trans. from French)
21. Stevens to Palmerston No. 31, 31 July 1850: FO 60 155
22. Dolgorukov to Seniavin No. 59, 31 July 1850 OS (11 Aug. NS): Dossier No. 133 Ṭihrán 1850, pp. 470–71. 'Excerpts from Dispatches' p. 22
23. Sheil to Palmerston No. 97, 22 Aug. 1850: FO 60 153

24. Sheil to Palmerston No. 106, 5 Sept. 1850: FO 60 153
25. Enclosed in 24 *supra*
26. Anitchkov to the Viceroy of the Caucasus No. 574, 28 Aug. 1850 OS (9 Sept. NS): Nicolas 'Le Dossier russo-anglais' p. 361 (trans. from French)
27. Anitchkov to the Viceroy of the Caucasus No. 696, 11 Sept, 1850 OS (23 Sept. NS): Nicolas 'Le Dossier russo-anglais' p. 361 (trans. from French)
28. *Nabíl's Narrative* UK p. 406, USA pp. 556–7
29. Enclosed in Dolgorukov to Seniavin No. 76, 23 Sept. 1850 OS (5 Oct. NS): Dossier No. 134, Ṭihrán 1850, pp. 575–9. Chahárdihí *Shaykhí-garí, Bábí-garí* pp. 281–3 (trans. from Persian)
30. Sheil to Palmerston No. 109, 25 Sept. 1850: FO 60 153
31. Dolgorukov to Seniavin No. 78, 6 Oct. 1850 OS (18 Oct. NS): Dossier No. 133, Ṭihrán 1850, p. 582. 'Excerpts from Dispatches' p. 22
32. Ferrier to de LaHitte 25 Oct. 1850: MAE Sér. Corr. Polit. MD No. 24 (1833–56), p. 357 (trans. from French)
33. Sheil to Palmerston No. 134, 25 Oct. 1850: FO 60 153
34. Dolgorukov to Seniavin No. 81, 26 Oct. 1850 OS (7 Nov. NS): Dossier No. 134, Ṭihrán 1850. Chahárdihí, *Shaykhí-garí, Bábí-garí* p. 284 (trans. from Persian)
35. Dolgorukov to Seniavin No. 84, 9 Nov. 1850 OS (21 Nov. NS): Dossier No. 134, Ṭihrán 1850, p. 99. 'Excerpts from Dispatches' p. 22
36. As for 13 *supra*
37. Stevens to Palmerston No. 43, 29 Nov. 1850: FO 60 155
38. *Nabíl's Narrative* UK p. 417, USA pp. 569–70
39. Stevens to Sheil No. 117, 9 Dec. 1850: FO 248 142
40. Sheil to Palmerston No. 160, 16 Dec. 1850: FO 60 154
41. Anitchkov to the Viceroy of the Caucasus No. 741, 11 Dec. 1850 OS (23 Dec. NS): Nicolas 'Le Dossier russo-anglais' pp. 361–2 (trans. from French)
42. Sheil to Palmerston No. 171, 24 Dec. 1850: FO 60 154
43. Dolgorukov to Seniavin No. 93, 26 Dec. 1850 OS (7 Jan. 1851 NS): Dossier No. 134, Ṭihrán 1851, p. 156. 'Excerpts from Dispatches' p. 22
44. Ferrier to de LaHitte 24 Jan. 1851: MAE Sér. Corr. Polit. MD No. 24 (1833–56), p. 376 (trans. from French)
45. Sheil to Palmerston No. 3, 6 Jan. 1851: FO 60 158
46. Stevens to Palmerston No. 2, 25 Jan. 1851: FO 60 166
47. Binning *Two Years' Travel* Vol. 2, p. 164
48. Ferrier to de LaHitte 24 Feb. 1851: MAE Sér. Corr. Polit. MD No. 24 (1833–56), p. 376 (trans. from French)
49. According to Malik-Khusraví in *Táríkh-i-Shuhadáy-i-Amr* Vol 3, pp. 127–9
50. Sheil to Palmerston No. 42, 14 Mar. 1851: FO 60 159
51. Dolgorukov to Nesselrode No. 12, 20 Feb. 1851 OS (4 Mar. NS): Dossier No. 129, Ṭihrán 1851, p. 154. Chahárdihí *Shaykhí-garí, Bábí-garí* pp. 285–6 (trans. from Persian)
52. Gobineau *Religions et Philosophies* p. 220 (trans. from French)
53. Rochechouart *Souvenirs d'un Voyage en Perse* p. 5
54. Stewart *Through Persia in Disguise* p. 210
55. Browne *A Year Amongst the Persians* pp. 79–81

SEVEN

The Attempt on the Life of the Sháh (1852)

On 15 August 1852, there occurred an event that was to have far-reaching implications for the new religion. Not only did it in the short term lead to massacre of the adherents of the Báb and the exile of Bahá'u'lláh from his native land, but its dark shadow hung over the Bahá'í community for the remainder of the century, ensuring the hostility of the Sháh and the Persian Government, and providing ready ammunition for those who wished to denounce the religion as a politically-oriented, revolutionary movement. It destroyed whatever hopes there may have been for a reconciliation between the new religion and the Government following the removal of the obdurate Mírzá Taqí Khán, the Amír-Niẓám.* It confirmed in the minds of the common people the denunciations of this faith by the 'ulamá as a movement subversive of the State and of the religion of Islam. This event was the attempt on the life of the Sháh by a few Bábís, an incident in which the vast majority of Bábís were completely uninvolved.

Newspaper Reports of the Attempted Assassination

The first news to reach the West of the attempt on the life of the Sháh was through newspaper reports (see pp. 11–14). On 7 October 1852, the following paragraph appeared in the *Sun* of London:

PERSIA

Letters from Tauris [Tabríz] of the 26th August bring the news of an attempt to assassinate the Shah. While he was hunting, four men approached the monarch, under pretence of presenting a petition, which he refused to accept. Two of the fellows then seized the horse's bridle, while their companions fired two double-barrelled pistols at the Shah, who, although wounded in the thigh and mouth, was still able to quit his saddle, and keep off his assailants until his suite came up. Two of the assassins were literally hewn to pieces; the others, who were taken alive, declared that they had no accomplices, but that belonging to the Babis, they had determined to avenge the death of their chief by murdering the Shah. Dr Cloquet [q.v.] has extracted two of the bullets, but has not succeeded with a third. It is added that the Shah is not supposed to be in danger. The cholera is making terrible ravages in Persia.[1]

* See *Nabíl's Narrative* (UK) pp. 439–40, (USA) pp. 598–9.

On the same day, the *Standard* of London published an account which differed in its details. This account under the title 'Attempt to Assassinate the Shah of Persia' was from the paper's Istanbul correspondent, who had reported on 23 September:

The Erzeroom post has brought letters to the 9th inst. from that city, and to the 28th Aug. from Tabreez. On the 15th of August an attempt to assassinate the Shah of Persia had taken place at Tehran. The Shah, accompanied by his Prime Minister and by a numerous suite, had quitted that day Kasri-Millak on a hunting excursion, and had reached the skirt of a wood near Maveranda, when six ill-dressed Persians, with petitions, approached the Shah, who at once drew in the reins of his horse and took the papers held out to him. It is usual in Persia on similar excursions for the Sovereign to proceed alone, and keep his Ministers and attendants at a distance of several hundred yards, and when he stops they do likewise. The petitioners were of the sect of Babi, and, after delivering their papers, two seized the bridle of the horse, and the other four surrounded the Shah, and loudly, and with menacing gesture, demanded redress for the insult done to their religion by having put their chief to death. The Shah courageously ordered them off, but before his suite came up, two of the fanatic ruffians drew their pistols and fired at him, two balls of which took effect; the first wounded him in the mouth, and the second slightly grazed his thigh. Immediately after this attempt they took to their heels, hotly pursued by the attendants. Three contrived to escape in the wood, one was cut down by the Multezim er Rikiab, and the other two were seized and conveyed to Tehran, for the purpose of obtaining a clue to the conspiracy. The Shah's wounds were so slight that the next day he proceeded in grand pomp to the mosque, in order to offer his thanksgiving for his miraculous escape. On his return to the palace, the Ministers and the Russian and English Ambassadors, and the Charge d'Affaires of the Porte, in full costume, congratulated him. Public rejoicings also took place, and the city of Tehran was illuminated at night. On the 16th of August intelligence had been received of the seizure of the three assassins who had effected their escape, and concealed themselves in the wood. They were discovered in a well, and were drawn out and cut to pieces, according to the orders given by the Prime Minister.[2]

Le Constitutionnel of 13 October 1852 contained an article that gave yet another different account of the attempt itself. It is given here as translated in the *Morning Herald* of the following day:

A letter from Constantinople gives fresh details of the attempted assassination of the Shah of Persia. There has existed in Persia for the last few years a religious sect, called Babis, who believe in the transmigration of souls, and who neither recognise the authority of the Koran, of Mahomet, or of the Twelve Imans [*sic*].* Their only authority is that of the twelfth Imam, Saheb Zeman, of whom Bab, the chief of the sect, is the only representative. It is pretended that they profess a kind of communism, and even have a community of women. In consequence of their theory of the transmigration of souls they think themselves immortal, and consequently set no value on life. The number of these Babis are estimated at 50,000. They have been in open revolt in the provinces of Mazanderan against the authority of the Shah of Persia, and have maintained a siege

* See p. xxiv.

of several months.* Eight Babis, who had been brought to Teheran, refused the pardon which the Shah offered to them, if they would abandon their doctrines. All of them perished without making any concession. On the 15th August last three of these Babis resolved to avenge the death of their master, the famous Bab, who has already been the cause of several sanguinary actions in Persia, fell on the Shah at the moment when he was preparing to mount on horseback to go hunting. They fired two pistols at him point blank, but fortunately only wounded him very slightly. One of the assassins was immediately cut to pieces by the guards of the Shah, and the other two were thrown into prison to be tried. It is said that they have 300 accomplices, who have sworn to take the life of the Shah. This attempt has thrown the country into great consternation. Several individuals convicted as accomplices have already been executed, but all the ramifications of the plot have not yet been discovered.[3]

Sheil's Accounts and his Intervention

The British Minister, Justin Sheil, sent the following report dated 16 August 1852:

A violent attempt was yesterday made to slay the Shah. His Majesty is residing at his summer encampment a few miles from Tehran. He had just mounted his horse to proceed on a hunting excursion of a few days, when three, or as some say six men, went close up to him as if to present a petition, according to the practice of this country. One of the party placed his hand on the Shah's dress, and on being repulsed drew a pistol from his girdle, one of his confederates at the same time seizing the Shah's horse's reins. The animal finding himself checked, reared and the Minister of Finance who chanced to be close at hand, pulled the Shah from his horse. In falling, the shot took effect in the loins of the Shah, but the pistol being loaded with only partridge shot and a few slugs, the wound is merely skin deep, and I am assured by the Shah's skilful French surgeon [Dr Cloquet, q.v.] that not the least ground for alarm exists. So intent was the assassin on effecting his object that he immediately drew a formidable dagger, and in spite of several desperate wounds, persisted in assailing the Shah, ripping up the entrails of one of the attendants, nor did he cease his efforts until he was slain. Two of his confederates were captured, one being severely wounded. In the fray, two other pistols were discharged at the Shah. His Majesty is said to have displayed calmness and firmness in this trying scene.

The first intelligence of this assault was accompanied by the announcement that the Shah had been killed. The Royal Camp began to break up and the crowd rushed towards Tehran. The shops were immediately shut, and in a short time bread was not to be procured, every one struggling to lay in a stock of food for coming events. But no pillage or violence took place. Today, to reassure the minds of the people, and satisfy them of the reality of the Shah's safety, salutes of 110 guns have been fired; the large body of troops encamped near Tehran have been brought to the Royal camp to view the Shah, as well as the Clerical body, the civic authorities, and the bazars are to be illuminated for several nights.

Yesterday afternoon the Russian Minister and I waited on the Shah to offer congratulations on his escape. We found him seated as usual on such occasions, and His Majesty presented no appearance of alarm or agitation, but he repeated often with fierceness that this attempt had had instigators.

The expressions of the Shah were directed

* The Mázindarán upheaval; see ch. 3.

against the Serdar,* whose nomination to the government of Kerman I reported some days ago, and general opinion at first has pointed to this Russian subject as the leader of a plot to change the succession, and rescue himself from exile from the Court.

Although, on the rumour of the murder of the Shah, some acts open to suspicion were committed by the Serdar, I cannot believe him to be implicated in this crime. It is incredible that the assassins should devote themselves to certain death, unless through religious fanaticism, and it is asserted and believed with confidence that the attempt on the Shah's life owes its origin to Bábee† vengeance. The two survivors declare themselves to belong to this faith, that they were ready to die, and that they had come to seek death and paradise, or rather annihilation. The only symptom of conspiracy was the escape of three of the assassins, which was certainly a remarkable circumstance, as the Shah on these occasions is attended by a retinue of several hundred persons who surround him on all sides.

The Shah is said to feel deep mortification that he should be engaged in a struggle of some minutes without a simultaneous rush being made by his attendants on the assassins. I attribute this backwardness to panic and consternation, and the narrowness of the road where the attempt was made . . .

P.S. Having heard that there was an intention of inflicting torture on the two assassins who were captured, my Russian colleague and I addressed a joint note to the Minister for Foreign Affairs, of which I have the honor to enclose a copy for Your Lordship's information recommending the Government not to have recourse to this barbarous practice. Before the Government had received this note, torture had been inflicted, but since then to the present time, there has been no repetition of it.[4]

'Joint note – Lt Colonel Sheil and Prince Dolgorouki to Meerza Saeed Khan,‡ Minister for Foreign Affairs; August 17, 1852'

The Undersigned have heard with the deepest pain that an intention exists of inflicting torture, previously to execution on the wretches who were guilty of a treasonable and horrible attempt on the person of His Majesty with the design of extorting a confession of their confederates. Infamous as has been their crime, the Undersigned trust that such outrage on common sense will not be allowed to happen. If in their agonies these criminals should utter the names of certain individuals, can it be believed that they will betray their friends and companions. Is it not certain that they will accuse persons wholly innocent, and that no end will be gained excepting to fill the mind of His Majesty the Shah with suspicion against blameless persons.

His Majesty displayed the greatest courage and fortitude during the trying scene of the day before yesterday. Let the same magnanimity be maintained, and the forbearance of the sovereign will be an example to the entire Kingdom. Let the traitors suffer the punishment they deserve, but let the nations of Europe learn that the monarch of Persia has imbibed the civilization of the age, and that His Majesty Nasir:ood:deen Shah revolted from the infliction of torture even in defence of his own Royal person.[5]

On 27 October 1852, the Secretary of State for Foreign Affairs, Earl

* The Sardár was Muḥammad-Ḥasan Khán-i-Sardár, better known as Khán Bábá Khán (q.v.).

† A new sect in Persia, whose chief tenet seems to be a sort of materialism, that every atom is God, and that the Universe is God. [Note by Sheil.]

‡ Mírzá Sa'id Khán (q.v.)

Malmesbury, wrote to Sheil: 'Her Majesty's Government entirely approve of the steps taken by you in conjunction with the Russian Minister, as reported in your despatch No. 99, to dissuade the Persian Government from subjecting to torture the parties arrested on the charge of being implicated in that crime, with the view of thereby extracting from them a confession in regard to their confederates.'[6]

Newspaper Accounts of the Executions of the Bábís

Once the immediate panic over the attempted assassination was passed, the entire machinery of the Court and Government was given over to the tracking down and arresting of Bábís whether they had been implicated in the attempted assassination or not. Within a week, the executions had begun. *The Times* on 13 October 1852 mentioned the martyrdom of two of the most important Bábís: Ḥájí Sulaymán Khán and Qurratu'l-'Ayn (Ṭáhirih).

HOW THEY PUNISH TREASON IN PERSIA

We mentioned a few days since the attempt against the Shah of Persia. We now learn that Hajee Suleiman Khan, accused as the instigator of the crime, was seized, his body carefully drilled with a knife in parts which would not at the moment cause death; pieces of lighted candles were then introduced into the holes, and thus illuminated, [he was] carried in procession through the bazaar, and finally conveyed to the town gates, and there cleft in twain like a fat ram. The Kurret-il-Ain, better known as Bab's Lieutenant, or the Fair Prophetess of Kazoeen [Qazvín], who since the late religious outbreak had been kept a close prisoner at the capital, has been executed with some dozen others. His Majesty received three slug wounds in the shoulders, but all of a very slight nature.[7]

Perhaps the most dramatic of all accounts of these martyrdoms occurs in a letter from Captain Alfred von Gumoens (q.v.) which was published in *Oesterreichischer Soldatenfreund* on 12 October 1852. E. G. Browne had also been forwarded a copy of Gumoens's account by Dr Polak's (q.v.) widow. Von Gumoens's letter, dated 29 August 1852, reads as follows. (Browne's translation is given here because it is superior in literary style to that of *The Times* of 23 October – see p. 12):

Dear Friend, My last letter of the 20th inst. mentioned the attempt on the King. I will now communicate to you the result of the interrogation to which the two criminals were subjected. In spite of the terrible tortures inflicted, the examination extorted no comprehensive confession; the lips of the fanatics remained closed, even when by means of red-hot pincers and limb-rending screws they sought to discover the chief conspirator All that transpired was that they belonged to the Bábí sect. These Bábís are heretics; though they pray to the Prophet (*sic!*), yet they differ in many usages from the orthodox Musulmáns. This sect was founded about fifteen years ago by a certain *Báb*, who was shot by the King's command. The most faithful of his adherents fled to Zanján, where, two years ago, they were reduced by the Royal Troops, and, as was generally believed, were exterminated without regard for age or sex. Like all religious intolerance, this unmeasured persecution produced exactly the opposite of the effects intended. The Báb's teaching gained more and more ground, and is at the present moment diffused through the whole country. Since the government obstinately clung to the system of persecution, the schismatics found occasion to steel their resolution, and to develop qualities which, contrasted with the effeminate luxury of the State Religion, compelled respect. Very skilfully had the Prophet [*i.e.* the Báb] pointed out to the disciples of his teaching that the way to Paradise lay through the torture-chamber. If he spoke truly, then the present Sháh has deserved great merit, for he strenuously endeavours to people all the realms of the Saints with Bábís! His last edict still further enjoins on the Royal servants the annihilation of the sect. If these simply followed the Royal command and rendered harmless such of the fanatics as are arrested by inflicting on them a swift and lawful death, one must needs, from the Oriental standpoint, approve of this; but the manner of inflicting the sentence, the circumstances which precede the end, the agonies which consume the bodies of the victims until their life is extinguished in the last convulsion are so horrible that the blood curdles in my veins if I now endeavour to depict the scene for you, even in outline. Innumerable blows with sticks which fall heavily on the back and soles of the feet, brandings of different parts of the body with red-hot irons, are such usual inflictions that the victim who undergoes only such caresses is to be accounted fortunate. But follow me my friend, you who lay claim to a heart and European ethics, follow me to the unhappy ones who, with gouged-out eyes, must eat, on the scene of the deed, without any sauce, their own amputated ears; or whose teeth are torn out with inhuman violence by the hand of the executioner; or whose bare skulls are simply crushed by blows from a hammer; or where the *bázár* is illuminated with unhappy victims, because on right and left the people dig deep holes in their breasts and shoulders and insert burning wicks in the wounds. I saw some dragged in chains through the *bázár*, preceded by a military band, in whom these wicks had burned so deep that now the fat flickered convulsively in the wound like a newly-extinguished lamp.

Not seldom it happens that the unwearying ingenuity of the Orientals leads to fresh tortures. They will skin the soles of the Bábís' feet, soak the wounds in boiling oil, shoe the foot like the hoof of a horse, and compel the victim to run. No cry escaped from the victim's breast; the torment is endured in dark silence by the numbed sensation of the fanatic; now he must run; the body cannot endure what the soul has endured; he falls. Give him the *coup de grâce*! Put him out of his pain! No! The executioner swings the whip, and – I myself have had to witness it – the unhappy victim of hundred-fold tortures runs! This is the beginning of the end. As for the end itself, they hang the scorched and perforated bodies by their hands and feet to a tree head-downwards, and now every Persian may try his marksmanship to his heart's content from a fixed but not too proximate distance on the noble quarry placed at his disposal. I saw corpses torn by nearly 150 bullets. The more fortunate suffered strangulation, stoning or suffocation: they were bound before the muzzle of a mortar, cut down with swords, or killed with dagger thrusts, or blows from hammers and sticks. Not only the executioner and the common people took part in the massacre: sometimes Justice would present some of the unhappy Bábís to various dignitaries and the Persian [recipient] would be well content, deeming it an honour to imbrue his own hands in the blood of the pinioned and defenceless victim. Infantry, cavalry, artillery, the *ghulâms* or guards of the King, and the guilds of butchers, bakers, etc., all took their fair share in these bloody deeds. One Bábí was presented to the crack officers-corps of the garrison; the general in command dealt the first blow, and afterwards each one as his rank determined. The Persian troops are butchers, not soldiers. One Bábí fell to the share of the *Imam-Jum'a*, who put him to death. Islám knows nothing of charity!

When I read over again what I have written I am overcome by the thought that those who are with you in our dearly beloved Austria may doubt the full truth of the picture, and accuse me of exaggeration. Would to God that I had not lived to see it! But by the duties of my profession I was unhappily often, only too often, a witness of these abominations. At present I never leave my house, in order not to meet with fresh scenes of horror. After their death the Bábís are hacked in two and either nailed to the city gate, or cast out into the plain as food for the dogs and jackals. Thus the punishment extends even beyond the limits which bound this bitter world, for Musulmáns who are not buried have no right to enter the Prophet's Paradise.

Since my whole soul revolts against such infamy, against such abominations as recent times, according to the judgement of all, present, I will no longer maintain my connection with the scene of such crimes.[8] [Though I were to be offered honours and gold here, I long for Europe's civilization . . . I have already asked for my release, but have so far received no answer; in the East everything is delayed, only the executioner's axe moves fast.]*

The *Journal de Constantinople's* account was widely quoted by European newspapers. It is important as it gives an estimate of the total number of Bábís martyred in Ṭihrán in this episode which is markedly different from that given in the Persian Government's official report (see pp. 138–42) and quoted by Lady Sheil and others. However, if Gobineau's account (see p. 144) is to be believed, then the total must have been higher than the 26 named in the official report. The account is here given as it appeared in the *Morning Post*: 'Letters from Tauris, of 27th, bring news from Persia of some gravity. The execution at Teheran of about 400 Babis, who are said to have been accomplices of the attempt against the Shah of Persia took place in a very cruel manner. They were subjected to the greatest tortures. It is said that the Shah is much affected in consequence of the attempt made on him by the Babis . . .'[9]

Sheil's Accounts of the Executions

In a dispatch dated 22 August 1852, Sheil relates:

No doubt appears to be entertained that the late attempt on the Shah's life has been the result of a plot among the followers of Bâb. The conspiracy appears to have many ramifications. Arrests to a considerable extent have been made in Tehran, and three of the principal leaders have been apprehended. Two of these are Mollahs of high reputation in the Mahommedan faith, and the third, Suleiman Khan, is the son of the Master of the horse of the Shah's Grandfather. The latter has been put to death. Evidence was given that the Bâbees, to the number of forty, were in the constant habit

* The section in brackets was not in Browne's translation and has been translated from the original.

of assembling at his house to concert their plans, and arms in considerable quantity of every description, including a number of Butcher's cleavers, were there discovered.*

About ten persons have been executed, some with circumstances of great cruelty. Lighted candles have been stuck into the bodies of two or three, and after being allowed to linger, they have been halved with a hatchet while still alive; others have been blown from mortars; the Shah's table attendants volunteered to slay one of the criminals with their daggers, and his Steward of the household acted as the Shah's Representative in blowing out with his own hands the brains of one of the assassins in Kissáss, or Retaliation of Blood. Among those who have suffered death was a young woman, the daughter of a Teacher of the Law in Mazanderan of great celebrity who has been three years in confinement in Tehran. She was venerated as a prophetess by the Bábees, and her designation among them was 'Koorat ool aïn' – 'Pupil of the eye'.† She has been strangled by the Shah's order. The Sedr Azim has opposed some of these acts, but the Shah's anger and vindictiveness have not allowed him to pay attention to advice.

The Sedr Azim informed me that in his presence, and in that of one of the Moollahs mentioned above, evidence was given and not contradicted, that after the attack on the Shah had failed, this Moollah had assembled his followers and said to them, that the work must be completed; that when the Shah entered the town he would bare his arm, and advance with his sword on the Shah; that if they saw him lying as if dead, they were not to believe it, as it would be only a semblance; that they were to fight and that he would rise and be among them.‡

The city of Tehran is tranquil, though the minds of the people are still agitated. The uncertainty as to what extent Bábeeism may have been really propagated, and the fear of being denounced as an accomplice or as a proselyte contribute to prevent the allay of excitement. The Sedr Azim well knows that persecution is the most certain mode of proselytism, and therefore advocates lenity. I have advised him to abandon arbitrary executions and to institute a sort of court for the trial of criminals and suspected persons.[10]

Thus it would appear that the initial executions, including those of Sulaymán Khán, Ṭáhirih and about eight others, occurred within a week of the attempt on the life of the Sháh and were mainly carried out by the official public executioners. Then, as Sheil reported on 27 August 1852, there occurred to Mírzá Áqá Khán the novel idea of turning the entire Government and Royal Court into executioners:

This Court has within the last few days presented the extraordinary and disgraceful spectacle of all the Chief Officers of State being converted into Executioners. Each department of the government has had a victim among the conspirators, or supposed conspirators, against the King's life. The Minister for Foreign Affairs, the Minister of

* See Introduction, pp. xxv and xxvii.

† i.e. Ṭáhirih, who was known as Qurratu'l-'Ayn, which means 'Consolation of the Eyes'. She was the daughter of a 'Teacher of the Law' in Qazvín not Mázindarán.

‡ Shaykh 'Alíy-i-Turshízí, known as 'Azím, is probably intended by this rather fanciful account. Nabíl hints that 'Azím was, indeed, plotting some action against the State (*Nabíl's Narrative* (UK) p. 440, (USA) p. 599). The same author states that 'Aẓím's confession was one of the causes of Bahá'u'lláh's release from the Síyáh-Chál (*Nabíl's Narrative* (UK) p. 466, (USA) pp. 636–7).

Finance, the son of the Prime Minister, the Adjutant General of the Army, the Master of the Mint, each fired the first shot, or made the first cut with a sabre, at the culprit delivered over to them, who was then despatched by the subordinates. The artillery, the infantry, the cavalry, the camel artillery, each had a victim, and I believe the priesthood is also to be allotted a share in these transactions.

My remonstrances with the Sedr Azim against the disgrace which he was heaping on the reputation of the Persian Government and nation were taken in very ill part. He asked me if I wanted to place the responsibility of so many executions on him alone and bring down Bábee vengeance on himself and his family.

This device has been adopted by the Sedr Azim to divide the danger, by making as many participators as possible in a blood-feud with the Bábees. [Continuing in the same report, Sheil gives an indication of the wild rumours that were circulating and the hysteria that was being generated:] A few murders, or attempts to murder, have been committed in town. Persons who had indulged in abuse of Bábeeism have been found in the morning murdered or wounded.

Since the date of my last despatch on this subject, about twelve persons have been put to death, and I am told by the Sedr Azim that there will be no more executions. I fear that in the above number conspirators alone against the Shah's life were not comprised, and that some persons suffered death from mere speculative belief in Bábeeism. All that can be said is that this is only what the law awards as the treatment of avowed renunciation of Mahommedanism.

The Shah's alarm has prevented him from leaving his palace since the time his life was menaced.[11]

On 10 September, Sheil reports:

The Tehran Gazette having contained an account of the attack on the Shah and of the subsequent executions, I beg leave to enclose a translation of the substance of the article.*

In two or three instances the most guilty of the Criminals suffered a cruel death. I had exhorted the Persian Minister from the beginning to abstain from the infliction of torture; but so great was the terror produced by the attempt on the Shah's life, my remonstrance was not of much avail. Your Lordship may judge of the alarm that prevailed when I mention that the Shah with the entire Court, and the Russian Mission sought safety within the city walls a month before the usual season, in spite of the insalubrity of the climate. The English Mission alone has remained in the usual residence, there being no reason that I know of to fear for it any molestation from the Bábees.[12]

Lady Sheil, the wife of the British Minister, recounts the episode in her book. This account gives an impression of the horror and uncertainty caused by the attempt on the life of the Sháh and also some glimpses of the response of the Persian Government to this occurrence. Since much of her account is identical to her husband's dispatches, the following is an abbreviated extract from her book:

August, 1852 – Goolahek† felt very sultry when we returned to it from our pretty

* This article is quoted in the next section of this chapter.

† A village to the north of Ṭihrán where the English Mission camped.

encampment at the 'Sublime Well'.* My husband, however, did not wish to be long absent from the neighbourhood of the Court, so we could not prolong our stay by its cool waters. A few days after our return, when seated in the coolest chamber of a house in the village, the heat having driven us from our tents, Meerza Hoossein Koolee, the first Persian Secretary of the Mission, entered the room ghastly and gasping. 'The Shah has been killed!' faltered the Meerza, who used himself frequently to assert that he was the most timid man in Persia. 'We shall all be murdered,' I immediately exclaimed.

We were quite alone in this moment of deep anxiety, all the members of the Mission having happened to go to town that day, though in a few minutes two or three princes came to our camp, thinking it the safest place in such a crisis. We had, it is true, a guard of Persian soldiers, but on them no dependence could be placed; perhaps they would be the first to plunder us. No time was lost in despatching three messengers: one to the Shah's camp, two miles distant, to learn the state of affairs; another to Tehran, to purchase ammunition and bring out some fifty carbines and pistols from the Mission stores; and a third was despatched to an Afghan friend, a pensioner of the Indian Government, to send us some of his countrymen to resist the marauders, who would certainly soon make their appearance. In three hours thirty or forty trusty horsemen were in our camp, and we were promised one hundred and fifty before night.

I know not if I ever experienced greater relief than when a note arrived from the Prime Minister, saying that the Shah had been only slightly hurt, and that all was well . . . The two Missions, English and Russian, immediately proceeded to wait on the Shah, to offer their congratulations, which were assuredly most sincere. Notwithstanding his wound, they found his Majesty seated as usual. He was pale, but looked more angry than alarmed. The Shah said that such a thing had never been heard of as the attack he had suffered. In condoling on the event, it was easy, though scarcely appropriate, to allude to Nadir and to the founder of his own dynasty;† so his Majesty was reminded that occurrences like this were not uncommon in Petersburg, and that our own gracious Sovereign had not been free from such attempts. The Shah did not, however, seem to derive any consolation from companionship in his danger . . .

The panic at Shemeroon became general; no one thought himself safe unless within the walls of Tehran. Every bush was a Bábee, or concealed one. Shah, ministers, meerzas, soldiers, priests, merchants, all went pell-mell into Tehran, although a month of the country season still remained. The Russian Mission fled too, so that not a being was left in Shemeroon excepting ourselves, nor a tent excepting those of our camp. Colonel S[heil] declared he did not think it creditable to take flight, and that he would remain the usual time in his summer-quarters; moreover, if there were any danger, the English Mission would be the last to suffer injury . . .

A number of the conspirators had been seized, whose fate it was easy to anticipate. The Prime Minister was reminded that now was the time for a practical display of the advance Persia had made in civilisation, and that on whomsoever death was to be inflicted, it ought to be without the addition of torture. Fear has no mercy. His answer was that this was not a time for trifling; and that the punishment, however severe, of the criminals who sought to spread massacre and spoliation throughout the length and breadth of Persia, was not to be deprecated, or to be included under the designation of torture, which had been defined to be the infliction of pain to extort a confession of guilt.

About thirty persons were put to death,

* Chishmiy-i-A'lá, near Damávand.

† Both were assassinated.

and, as is customary in that sect, or, perhaps, in all new sects, they met their doom without shrinking. Suleiman Khan, the chief of the conspirators, and two others suffered torture previously to execution. The two last were either cut to pieces, or shot or blown from mortars. Holes were pierced in various parts of Suleiman Khan's body, into which lighted candles were placed, and allowed to burn down to the flesh, and, while still alive, he was divided into two parts with a hatchet. During these horrible tortures he is said to have preserved his fortitude to the last, and to have danced to the place of execution in defiance of his tormentors, and of the agony caused by the burning candles . . .

Strange was the device adopted by the Prime Minister to elude the danger personal to himself of slaying so many fanatical Bábees . . . His Excellency resolved to divide the execution of the victims among the different departments of the state; the only person he exempted was himself. . . . Even the Shah's admirable French physician, the late lamented Dr Cloquet, was invited to show his loyalty by following the example of the rest of the Court. He excused himself, and pleasantly said he killed too many men professionally to permit him to increase their number by any voluntary homicide on his part. The Sedr was reminded that these barbarous and unheard-of proceedings were not only revolting in themselves, but would produce the utmost horror and disgust in Europe. Upon this he became very much excited, and asked angrily, 'Do you wish the vengeance of all the Bábees to be concentrated upon me alone?' . . .

No people love jesting and bantering more than the Persians. In Tehran, when any one is installed in office, it is usual for his friends and those under his authority to send him sheereenee, sweetmeats, as a token of congratulation. When these executions were over, it was said that the Shah's meerghazabs [executioners] had presented sheereenee [sweetmeats] to all the ministers of state, as a mark of their admission into the brotherhood. The chief executioner at the Shah's court is a very important personage. Hateful as he is to every one, it is curious, I hear, to observe the deference with which he is treated. As the highest of the courtiers may one day fall into his fangs, and his eyes or feet be in jeopardy, they do the utmost to propitiate him beforehand by flattering civilities, something on the principle of the Indians' worship of his infernal majesty . . .*

It was said that the general impression produced on the people by all this bloodshed was not favourable. Indignation at the attempt on the Shah's life was lost in sympathy for the fate of so many sufferers. The common opinion was, that the poor misguided conspirators of mean condition, whose poverty more than any sentiment of disloyalty or irreligion had enrolled them in the ranks of Bábeeism, might have been spared. It thus appears that, even in Persia, a vague undefined feeling of liberality in religion is taking root.[13]

Official Persian Accounts

The Persian Government's account of the affair appeared in the official government gazette, the *Rúznámiy-i-Vaqáyi'-i-Ittifáqíyyih.* The following comments and translation of this article appear in the book *Queer Things about Persia* by Eustache de Lorey and Douglas Sladen.† Passages in

* Concerning the martyrdom of Ṭáhirih, Lady Sheil writes: 'This was a cruel and useless deed.'

† The French Ambassador at Istanbul, the Marquis de la Valette, reported this article to the French Foreign Office in a dispatch dated 25 Oct. 1852 and provided a translation of it by J. B. Nicolas. This

square brackets were omitted by de Lorey and Sladen.

To show the inquisitorial vengeance to which the unhappy Babis have been subjected, I cannot do better than give a translation of an article which appeared in the Official Gazette of the Persian Government, relative to the attempt by the Babis upon the Shah's life.

The account, coming from an enemy of the Babis, tries to show them at their worst, but its naïve admissions only serve to bring out the high ideals and heroism of the Babi martyrs, and the cold cruelty and bigotry of their persecutors. The article convicts its authors.

'In our last number, in giving briefly an account of the attempt upon the life of the Shah, we have promised our readers to supply them with the after results of this lamentable affair, and to let them know the result of the inquiries made to discover the motives of this vast conspiracy, directed not only against the life of our beloved sovereign, but also against the public peace, and against the property and lives of true Mussulmans. For the real aim of these malefactors was, in getting rid of the person of the King, to seize the power, and by this detestable means to secure at last the triumph of their abominable cause, in forcing, by arms and violence, the good Mussulmans to embrace their infamous religion, which differs from that sent down from Heaven, and which does not accord either with philosophy or human reason – which is, in fine, the most deplorable heresy that has ever been heard of, as may be gathered from certain of their books and pamphlets which we have been able to procure.

'The founder of this abominable sect, who began to propagate these detestable doctrines only a few years ago, and who, having fallen into the hands of the authorities, was immediately shot, was called Ali Mohammed, and had given himself the surname of Bab, wishing to give people to understand by this that the keys of Paradise were in his hands.

'After the death of the Bab, his disciples met soon under the orders of another chief, Sheikh Ali of Turshiz, who assumed the position of nayeb (vicar) of the Bab, and had imposed it on himself to live in complete solitude, showing himself to nobody, and granting audiences to his principal followers only at rare intervals. They regarded this favour as the greatest that Heaven could confer on them. He had given himself the surname of Hazret Azem, the Highest Highness.

'Among the people who were attached to him one may mention first Hadji Suleiman Khan, son of the late Yah-Yah Khan of Tabriz. It was in the house of this Suleiman Khan, in Teheran, in the quarter Sar-i-Cheshmeh, that the principal Babis used to meet to deliberate upon their hateful projects. Twelve amongst them, who appeared more zealous and determined than the others, were chosen by Hazret Azem, who had the necessary arms given to them to execute the great act that he believed to be unavoidable. Pistols, daggers, cutlasses, nothing was spared, and, armed in this way, it seemed impossible for them to miss their prey.

'They were recommended to stand in the neighbourhood of Niavaran, and to wait for a favourable opportunity.

'We may refer our readers to our last number; they will see in it how three of these madmen have taken advantage of the circumstance which presented itself on Sunday the 28th of Chavval, at the moment

dispatch and its enclosed translation are reproduced in Nicolas's book *Seyyèd Ali Mohammed*, which is undoubtedly de Lorey and Sladen's source. This same article was quoted by several European newspapers (see p. 12).

when His Majesty, having gone out of the town, directed himself, with his ordinary suite, towards the village where he was in the habit of going for his hunting parties. They will see how they flung themselves upon the King, one after the other, firing their pistols nearly point-blank at His Majesty; how one of them was immediately slain by people of well-known zeal and devotion, such as Assad Oullah-Khan, first equerry of the King, Mustofi-el-Memalek, Nizam-oul-Moulk, the Keshikchi-Bashi, and other persons who were near His Majesty; how at last the two others were seized and thrown into the prison of the town.

'An inquiry was at once made into the case, and put into the hands of . . . Hadjeb-ed-Dowleh,* the Kalentar (Minister of Police), and the Kedkhodas of the town (a sort of municipal councillors).

'Thanks to the zeal and the activity that they showed in their inquiries, they soon learned that the house of Suleiman-Khan was used as the place of meeting by these wretches. It was immediately surrounded on all sides; but whether by the neglect of the men of Hadjeb-ed-Dowleh, or by the lack of cohesion in the execution of this enterprise, they succeeded in catching only twelve, amongst them Suleiman-Khan. The others effected their escape, one does not know exactly how. But their accomplices having named several of them, the police, it may be hoped, will soon trace them.

'However, not a single day passed without the Adjutant-Bashi of the Kalentar and the *ferrashes* of the King capturing three, four, or even five Babis, whom they quickly brought before the Imperial divan or tribunal, which in such a case is held in public.

'They were interrogated at once, and condemned upon their own evidence, as well as on the denunciations of their accomplices, whom they took care to confront with them.

'These interrogatories were made in accordance with the customs and forms laid down by the law.

'We must not omit here to recall the immense service that Hadjeb-ed-Dowleh has rendered to the Faith, to the State, and to Religion, in capturing Mollah Sheikh Ali of Turchiz, in spite of all the precautions that he took not to be seen in public, and in spite of the retired and secretive life which he did not cease to lead till the moment of his arrest. By his flight from the town he had expected to find a shelter against all pursuit; he had hidden himself in a little house at Evine in the Shimran.

'He lived there, surrounded by some faithful disciples, who, like himself, had succeeded in escaping from the house of Suleiman Khan at the moment that it was surrounded.

'It is in this house that Hadjeb-ed-Dowleh, accompanied by his men, succeeded in surprising them at the moment when they expected it least. The Babis were seized, manacled, and thrown into the prisons of the town.

'His Excellency the Grand Vizier, Mirza Aga Khan, had the satisfaction of interrogating himself the chief of this hateful sect. He made him appear before him with the disciples taken at the same time as this wretch, and questioned him in their presence. Mollah Sheikh Ali of Turchiz did not attempt to excuse himself. He avowed that he had become the chief of the Babis since the death of the Bab; that he had given the order to his most devoted disciples to kill the King. He declared even that Mohammed Sadek, who had precipitated himself the first on the King, was his confidential servant, and that he had provided himself the necessary arms to execute the regicides' project. The number of these wretches who had fallen into the hands of justice does not

* Ḥájí 'Alí Khán, Ḥájibu'd-Dawlih of Marághih (q.v.)

exceed thirty-two. As for the others, the police have not been able to find them, and it is believed that they have crossed the frontiers of Persia and gone to lead a wretched life in a *foreign land.*

'We impose upon ourselves the task of pointing out to our readers the *admirable conduct* of His Excellency the Minister of Russia on this occasion.

'One of these damnable conspirators, Mirza Houssein Ali,* had taken refuge at Zerghandeh in the summer quarters of the Russian Legation. The Prince Dolgorouki, having learnt that this individual was amongst the conspirators, had him seized by his own people and sent to the Ministers of His Majesty, who, touched by an action so in conformity with the good relations that existed between Persia and Russia, evinced their profound gratitude to him. His Majesty himself had his thanks conveyed to the prince, and gave orders that the people who had been entrusted with conveying the culprit to custody should be worthily recompensed, which was done without delay.

'Amongst the Babis who have fallen into the hands of justice, there are six whose culpability *not having been well established, have been condemned to the galleys for life.*† The others have all been massacred in the following ways:-

'Mollah Sheik Ali of Turchiz, the author of this conspiracy, has been condemned to death by the Ulemas or religious judges, and put to death by them.

'Seyyed Houssein Khorassani was killed by the princes of the blood, who massacred him with pistol-shots, scimitars, and daggers.

'Mustafi-el-Memalek took charge of the execution of Mollah Zeyine-el-Abedin, Yezdi, whom he killed with pistol-shots fired point blank, after which the Mustafis of the Divan, throwing themselves upon the corpse, riddled it with pistol-shots and stabs of sword, dagger, and cutlass.

'Mollah Houssein Khorassani was killed by Mirza Kassem Nizam Oul-Moulk and by Mirza Saïd Khan, Minister of Public Affairs. Mirza Kassem was the first to approach the condemned, and shot him with his pistol point blank. Then Mirza Saïd Khan approached in his turn and fired another pistol. At last the servants of these two high functionaries threw themselves on the corpse, which they hacked to pieces with knives and daggers.

'Mirza Abdoul Wahab of Shiraz, who during his sojourn in Kazemein had rendered himself guilty in the eyes of the authorities by inciting the inhabitants to revolt, was put to death by Jaffar Kouli-Khan, brother of the Grand Vizier, by Zulfe-Khar Khan, by Moussa Khan, and by Mirza Aly Khan, all three sons of the Grand Vizier, assisted by their servants and the guards of the King and the other people present at the execution, some using pistols, others rifles, others daggers of all sorts, so that the corpse of this wretched man was reduced to mincemeat.

'Mollah Fethoulhah, son of Mollah Aly, the book-binder, the man who, shooting at the King with a pistol loaded with lead, slightly wounded His Majesty, had his body covered with holes, in which lighted candles were stuck. Then Hadjeb-ed-Dowleh received the order to kill him with a pistol-shot, which he did by shooting at the exact spot of the body where His Majesty had been wounded. He fell stone dead. Then the *ferrashes* of the King threw themselves on the body and hacked it to pieces and heaped stones upon it.

'Sheikh Abbas of Teheran has been sent to the bottom of hell by the Khans and other

* i.e. Bahá'u'lláh. Concerning this incident, see pp. 142–3.

† These six are named as: Mírzá Ḥusayn-i-Qumí, Mírzá Ḥusayn-'Alíy-i-Núrí (i.e. Bahá'u'lláh), Mírzá Sulaymán-Qulí and his nephew Mírzá Maḥmúd, Áqá 'Abdu'lláh (the son of Áqá Muḥammad-Ja'far) and Mírzá Javád-i-Khurásání. The original account merely states that they have been sentenced by the Sháh to perpetual imprisonment – 'condemned to the galleys' is a fanciful mistake by J. B. Nicolas.

dignitaries of the State, who killed him with pistols and swords.

[Muḥammad-Báqir-i-Najafábádí was killed by the royal valets and chamberlains with daggers and knives.]

'Mohammed Taghi of Shiraz had horse-shoes nailed to his feet first, like a horse, by Ased-oullah-Khan, first equerry of His Majesty, and by the employees of the Imperial stables. Then he was beaten to death with maces and with the great nails of iron which are used in the stables to fasten the horses to.

[Muḥammad of Najafábád was killed by the Ís͟hak-Áqásí-Bás͟hí and other court officials and Mírzá Muḥammad-i-Nayrízí was shot by the royal sentries and servants.]

'Mohammed Aly of Nejef-Abad was handed over to the Artillery men, who first of all tore out one of his eyes, then bound him over the muzzle of a gun and blew him to pieces.

'As to Hadji Suleiman Khan, son of Yah-Yah Khan of Tabriz, and Hadji Kassem, also of Tabriz,* they were marched through the town of Teheran with their bodies stuck with candles, accompanied by dancers and by the music of the Evening, which is composed of long horns and huge drums, and were followed by a crowd of the curious, who wished to stone them, but were prevented by the *ferrashes*.

'Suleiman Khan, when one of the candles fell, sank and picked it up, and restored it to its place. Somebody having cried, "You sing, why don't you dance?" Suleiman began to dance.†

'Once out of the town, the *ferrashes*, executing the orders which had been given them, cut them both into four pieces, which they hung over various gates of the town.

[Siyyid Ḥusayn of Yazd was put to death by the swords of the Ájúdán-Bás͟hí and by the colonels of the Imperial Army. Áqá Mihdí of Kás͟hán was delivered to the *farrás͟hes* who hacked him to death with daggers.

The body of Ṣádiq-i-Zanjání who was killed the same day, was cut to pieces and hung from the gates of the city.

Mírzá Nabí-i-Damávandí was killed by the lances and swords of the Professors of the School of Sciences [Dáru'l-Funún].

Mírzá Rafí' of Núr was killed by a company of the regular cavalry with their pistols and swords.

Mírzá Maḥmúd of Qazvín was delivered to the cross-bow archers who, after having fired many shots at him with their cross bows, hacked him with their swords.

Ḥusayn of Mílán was killed by a platoon of the infantry with their bayonets.

Mullá 'Abdu'l-Karím of Qazvín was killed by the swords of the artillery-men set to guard the King.

Luṭf-'Alí of S͟híráz fell to the footmen who stabbed him with daggers and then stoned him.]

'Nejef of Khamseh was abandoned to the fury of the mob, who beat him to pieces with their fists and stones.

'Hadji Mirza Djami,‡ merchant of Kachan, was killed by the Provost of the Merchants of Teheran, assisted by the merchants and shopkeepers.'[14]

[Ḥasan of K͟hamsih was killed by Naṣru'lláh K͟hán, the head of the arsenal, and by his employees. Muḥammad-Báqir was killed by the swords of the Qájárs.]

Other Accounts

When the attempted assassination occurred, Bahá'u'lláh was staying with Ja'far-Qulí K͟hán, a relative of the Prime Minister. He immediately set out

* In fact of Nayríz.

† This paragraph is not in the original, and has been added by de Lorey and Sladen.

‡ Ḥájí Mírzá Jání, the Báb's host in Kás͟hán and the author of a small history of the Bábí Faith.

for Níyávarán, where the headquarters of the Imperial Army was stationed. On the way he came to the village of Zarkandih, the seat of the Russian Legation, where his sister lived.[15] Prince Dolgorukov mentions Bahá'u'lláh in a dispatch of 23 August 1852:

As was to be expected, the Government, in reply to the attempt on the life of the Shah, began to arrest people accused of belonging to the sect of the Bab. Neither the massacre of Mazindaran, nor the slaughter in Zanjan would lessen the ardor of these sectaries, for recently an unwelcome discovery was made that many of them are hiding in Tihran, and that among the members of that sect there are people of all classes, not excepting even persons closest to the throne.

The Government think that they have an accurate list of the participants in the attempt of August third.* They learned that four of them were hiding in the village of Zargandih for the past month. The Director of the Ministry of Foreign Affairs wrote me a letter, asking permission to search that village. I immediately ordered the Ghulam-Bashi [Chief Servant] of the Legation to join the agents of the Persian Government to observe their search, and they found one of the persons on their list. This arrest led them to two more men who were seized by the ghulams [servants] of the Shah in a place called Ivin (Evin), located at the distance of one farsakh [about 3.5 miles] from Zargandih. The fourth person happens to be a relative of the Mirza of the Legation.† He is accused of Babism, and being a Persian subject whose name is not entered in the list of my employees must appear before the authorities.

The two accused persons arrested in Evin were transferred to Zargandih the same night and placed in the house of one of my servants. The ghulams of the Shah did not want to lead them to Niavaran at once, saying that they might be attacked on the way, but I insisted that they be transferred immediately, and gave them a guard of ten soldiers and an officer of low rank from the detachment which guards the Russian camp.

For a long time there has been imprisoned in Tihran under the surveillance of Mahmud Khan, Chief of Police, a Babi woman.‡ In spite of this she apparently found means daily to gather around herself many members of her sect. She was strangled in a garden in the presence of the Ajudan-Bashi. Four others were cut into halves. Burning candles were inserted into their flesh, and while they were thus led around the streets of the city, the poor creatures cursed the Shah and expressed joy at dying with such pomp, because such a death assured them the crown of martyrdom.

Who could dispute the right of the Government of the Shah, or rather of the Shah himself, to administer justice? However, making no distinction between real accomplices in the attempts and the thousands of persons professing Babism, he excites even more the fanaticism of these sectaries and thus exposes himself to a very serious danger.[16]

Dolgorukov reported the later executions in a dispatch of 24 August 1852:

Three days ago the Persian Government sent a messenger to St Petersburg to an-

* i.e. 15 Aug. NS

† This was Bahá'u'lláh, whose sister Nisá' Khánum, was married to Mírzá Majíd-i-Áhí, the Mírzá (or Persian secretary) of the Russian Legation.

‡ i.e. Ṭáhirih

nounce the happy outcome of the attempt on the life of the Shah.

The repulsive spectacles which we have been witnessing since that fatal event have forced me to visit Mirza Agha Khan and personally let him understand, in the interests of the Persian Monarch, the necessity of putting an end to this, or at least making a distinction between the real accomplices to the crime and persons who merely profess the doctrines of the Bab. I did not at all hide from him the danger to which the Shah is exposing himself by failing to limit to some extent the public executions, and that he must not kill just because he is free to put to death whomsoever he pleases.

The Sadr-Aazam [Prime Minister] entirely shares my opinion, but at the same time he confessed to me that he is having difficulties fighting against the irritation of the Shah and the provocations of those who imbue the Shah with the desire for vengeance, namely, his mother* and his Farrash-Bashi†. . . . The number of the above mentioned persons has already reached nine; and it is planned to distribute among the chief personages of the court, the army and the clergy, several Babis, whom they would kill with their own hands.

Here they talk about all of this with a joyful air, trying to make people think that all this slaughter is a most common and natural thing.[17]

Dr Polak's (q.v.) account of the holocaust of 1852 is particularly interesting in that not only was he present in Ṭihrán during this period, but he states that he was even present at the martyrdom of Ṭáhirih: 'I was an eyewitness of the execution of Qurratu'l-'Ayn [Ṭáhirih], the Minister for War and his adjutant performed it. That beautiful lady suffered her slow death with superhuman fortitude.'[18]

Gobineau's account of those days is very dramatic, and is here given as translated by de Lorey and Sladen:

One saw that day in the streets and bazaars of Teheran a spectacle that the population will never forget. One saw, walking between staffs of executioners, children and women, with the flesh gaping all over their bodies, with lighted wicks soaked in oil stuck in the wounds. The victims were dragged by cords and driven with whips. The children and women walked singing a verse, which says, 'In truth we come from God, and we return to Him.' Their voices rose piercingly in the middle of the profound silence of the mob; for the population of Teheran is neither bad-hearted nor much devoted to Islam. When one of the tortured people fell, he was forced to rise with blows from whips and prods from bayonets. If the loss of blood which ensued from the wounds all over the body left him strength enough, he began to dance and shout with fervour, 'We belong to God, and we return to Him.' Some of the children expired *en route*. The executioners threw their bodies under the feet of their father and sister, who walked fiercely upon them, without looking.

When they arrived at the place of execution near the new gate, life was again offered to the victims if they would abjure their faith, and, though it seemed difficult, means were sought to intimidate them. The executioner hit upon the device of signing to a father that if he did not abjure he would cut the throat of his two sons upon his chest. These were two small boys, the eldest being fourteen, who, red with their own blood and

* Malik-Jáhán Khánum, Mahd-i-'Ulyá (q.v.)

† Ḥájí 'Alí Khán, Ḥájibu'd-Dawlih

with flesh scorched by the candles, listened unmoved. The father answered by lying down on the earth that he was ready, and the eldest of the boys, claiming his right of birth, begged to have his throat cut first. It is not impossible that the executioner refused him this last satisfaction. At last everything was ended, and the night fell upon a heap of mangled human remains. The heads were strung in bundles to the Posts of Justice, and all the dogs of the suburbs made their way to that side of the town.

This day gave to the Bab more secret partisans than many preachings could have done.[19]

Mílán

At Mílán, a village near Tabríz, a large number of the inhabitants had been converted to the religion of the Báb through the efforts of Mullá Yúsif-i-Ardibílí, one of the Letters of the Living, and through the personal presence of the Báb himself for one night on his way to Tabríz under guard. Following the attempt on the life of the Sháh, a group of government servants and soldiers came from Tabríz and fell upon the hapless Bábís of the village and sacked their houses. A number suffered martyrdom immediately while a further group were taken to Tabríz.

Stevens (q.v.) reports the arrival of the Bábís in Tabríz in a dispatch to Sheil dated 7 September 1852:

A number of ryots [ra'yats] said to be 15, belonging to the neighbouring village of Milan, have been seized and thrown into prison on a charge of being Baubees. Understanding that they positively deny the fact, I called upon the Prince Governor yesterday and expressed a hope that these men would not be unfairly treated. I said that in a matter of religion their denial ought to receive consideration. The Prince replied that a list of their names had been submitted to him by the Imam-i-Jooma, and their seizure therefore was unavoidable, but that if the Akhond Mollah Mehmed, the chief of a religious party opposed to the Imam-i-Jooma, should, after examining them, declare them not Baubees they will be immediately released.

While on this subject I may mention that the recent religious persecution and executions at Tehran have created very general disgust here. People seem to think that the King's anger had carried him far beyond what was necessary to produse [*sic*] a good effect, and that the contrary may be the case.

I shall continue to watch the case of the people of Milan, or any others which may occur, and I trust that in my humble endeavours to prevent, as far as it lays in my power, the infliction of unmerited punishment, or the repetition in Tabreez of the horrible scenes recently enacted in Tehran, I may reckon on receiving Your Excellency's powerful support.[20]

Núr

The repercussions from the attempted assassination of the Sháh were felt with particular severity in the home village of Bahá'u'lláh, Tákur in Núr. At the time when the attempted assassination of the Sháh was being contemplated, Mírzá Yaḥyá, Ṣubḥ-i-Azal, had gone to Tákur in order to stir up a rising there to coincide with the attempt. When news of this reached Ṭihrán, troops were dispatched from the capital under Mírzá Abú-Ṭálib Khán, a relative of both the Prime Minister and Bahá'u'lláh. These arriving at Tákur and finding no insurrection, fell upon the village and looted it, killing a number of innocent people.

Sheil refers to this episode in a dispatch to the Earl of Malmesbury dated 2 October 1852:

> Although the utmost tranquillity prevails in Tehran, it appears that in Mazanderan, which has always been the stronghold of Bábeeism, the disciples of that creed have assumed an insurrectionary attitude, probably in self defence. A party of about one hundred Bábees has taken up a position of considerable strength, and some troops have been sent from hence to reduce them to obedience. The followers of the new faith have invariably fought with unflinching resolution, and it may therefore be anticipated that the dislodgment and capture of the above body will not be accomplished without trouble and loss.
>
> The Persian Ministers have been often reminded that interference and persecution are the most efficacious mode of propagating new doctrines.[21]

References

1. *Sun* 7 Oct. 1852 (4th edn), p. 4, col. 3
2. *Standard* 7 Oct. 1852, p. 3, col. 2
3. *Morning Herald* 14 Oct. 1852, pp. 3–4
4. Sheil to Malmesbury No. 99, 16 Aug. 1852: FO 60 171
5. Enclosed in 4 *supra*, translated into Persian by Ronald F. Thomson for delivery
6. Malmesbury to Sheil No. 56, 27 Oct. 1852: FO 248 147
7. *The Times* 13 Oct. 1852, p. 4, col. 4
8. Browne *Materials* pp. 268–71
9. *Morning Post* 1 Nov. 1852, p. 5
10. Sheil to Malmesbury No. 110, 22 Aug. 1852: FO 60 171
11. Sheil to Malmesbury No. 111, 27 Aug, 1852: FO 60 171
12. Sheil to Malmesbury No. 124, 10 Sept. 1852: FO 60 172
13. Lady Sheil *Life and Manners in Persia* pp. 273–82
14. Lorey and Sladen *Queer Things about Persia* pp. 307–15
15. *Nabíl's Narrative* UK p. 442, USA p. 603
16. Dolgorukov to Seniavin 11 Aug. 1852 OS (23 Aug. NS): Dossier No. 158, Ṭihrán 1852, pp. 501–3. 'Excerpts from Dispatches' p. 23
17. Dolgorukov to Seniavin No. 56, 12 Aug, 1852, OS (24 Aug. NS): Dossier No. 59, Ṭihrán 1852, pp. 508–9. 'Excerpts from Dispatches' pp. 23–4
18. Polak *Persien* Vol. 1, p. 353
19. Gobineau *Religions et Philosophies* pp. 267–70: trans. in Lorey and Sladen *Queer Things about Persia* pp. 315–16
20. Stevens to Sheil No. 73, 7 Sept. 1852: FO 248 149
21. Sheil to Malmesbury No. 143, 2 Oct. 1852: FO 60 173

EIGHT

The Second Upheaval of Nayríz (1853)

Following the bloody termination of the Nayríz episode and the martyrdom of Vaḥíd* in 1850, the Bábí community in Nayríz, as in other parts of Persia, drifted in a confused and leaderless state. The Governor of Nayríz, Ḥájí Zaynu'l-'Ábidín Khán, continued to persecute the community until eventually a group of five persons, driven to extreme measures, attacked the Governor in the public baths and killed him on 26 March 1853.

As in the case of the attempt on the life of the Sháh the preceding year, this action brought the community no relief and, indeed, led to a further upheaval.†

Mírzá Na'ím-i-Núrí (q.v.), a cousin and brother-in-law of the Prime Minister, was sent to Nayríz as Governor with specific instructions to subdue the Bábís. On Mírzá Na'ím's approach to Nayríz, Mírzá 'Alíy-i-Sardár and several of the leading Bábís came out of the town to meet him, hoping for a reconciliation and endeavouring to avert bloodshed. Within a short time of his arrival, however, Mírzá Na'ím demonstrated his true intentions when he seized some 130 of the Bábís including Mírzá 'Alíy-i-Sardár.

Mírzá Faḍlu'lláh,‡ the British Agent at Shíráz, in his October report for 1853 states:

> Merza Naeem having falsely accused the people of Neireez of being Babees, obtained an order from the Government to seize one hundred and seventeen of the inhabitants, put them in chains and sent [*sic*] them to Tehran to be punished. Thus empowered he proceeded to Neireez with a number of people and there he pillaged and plundered the houses of the people and committed every kind of excess. The Neireezees fled, some to the mountains and others to various places, and a large body of them took sanctuary a few days ago in a Shrine outside the city. Meerza Naeem then bribed the worthless characters who frequent the city to assist his people in seizing the Neireezees

* See ch. 5.

† According to *Nabíl's Narrative* UK p. 471, USA p. 643, it was Ḥájí Zaynu'l-'Ábidín Khán's widow who urged Mírzá Na'ím to take action against the Bábís.

‡ Mírzá Faḍlu'lláh-i-Qazvíní, British Agent in Shíráz from June 1852 to Mar. 1854 when he was dismissed after W. Taylour Thomson had observed a report from him on the state of Fárs, in the Persian Prime Minister's girdle.

and dragging them from their place of sanctuary, and at night he sent his people thus aided to effect this. A dreadful uproar ensued and in the confusion one young lad was seized and conveyed to Meerza Naeem's house, where he was beaten with the bastinado until he died. Hajee Kavam,* the Vezeer of Shiraz on learning this, sent people to prevent the seizure of the rest of the Neireezees. In truth should Meerza Naeem be permitted to remain here he will drive the people into rebellion, for they are quite annoyed at the conduct of the Government in acting in this manner at the instigation of a man like this.

Alee Beg who had been sent to Sheeraz to take charge of the above people accused of Babeeism having arrived at Neireez where he committed every kind of outrage, the people returned and having withdrawn their families from the place, again fled to the mountains where they have conveyed provisions, enough to maintain them for three or four months.

Meerza Naeem has demanded and received from the new Governor, who knows nothing of the matter, a force amounting to four hundred soldiers, two guns with artillerymen and ammunition, and he has started for the purpose of seizing these poor people and sending them to the Capital. The Governor has also given him orders to receive aid from the different Districts in the vicinity. But the Neireez people have fixed upon a very strong place in the mountains for their quarters and there is only one road to it, so it is believed that the troops will not be able to seize them. They made a descent upon Neireez and killed those who had remained there and were hostile to them.[1]

In a further report dated 14 November, Mírzá Faḍlu'lláh states:

On the 1st Mohurrum† news reached Sheeraz concerning the conflict of the People of Neereez in the mountains.

I wrote you word last month that Meerza Naeem had proceeded with Sirbaz and Guns, and a body of villagers to exterminate the Neereezees. On reaching the foot of the mountains, where the enemy lay, Meerza Naeem incited and urged the Sirbaz, villagers, and artillery to ascend the single pass that leads into the heart of the mountain, (along which the Neereezees had erected a few towers, and in each one planted a number of men armed with firelocks), and having reached the interior, to cut all the people to pieces. Yielding to the pressing importunities of Meerza Naeem, the army ascended, and, as luck would have it, they reached the first tower about Sunset – the garrison (located therein) were perfectly quiet – not a Sound was heard – so still did they remain that one would have thought the tower deserted and empty:- the troops gaining confidence pressed onwards to number two tower, where they found the same stillness prevailing, and having passed them all they entered the mountain itself. (No sooner had they done so than) the Neereezees, who were in the van of the Troops, backed up by those who were in the rear in the Towers, fell upon and commenced slaughtering the men of the unfortunate and ill-starred army:- there being no mode of escape, and the disaster having come upon them thro' the ill-management of their commander, the Neereez women clambered up the rocks, and, beating their mouths with their hands, vented forth cries of exultation. Night was succeeded by darkness – the troops were scattered over the mountains, and one of their guns fell into the hands of the Enemy.

Being desirous that so severe a calamity should be kept secret, a story was put in circulation that two of the Gulpaeeganee Sirbaz had been killed in the fray, and some

* Ḥájí Mírzá 'Alí-Akbar, Qavámu'l-Mulk (q.v.)
† 4 Oct. 1853

few had gone astray in the mountains, who would shortly return.

From the villagers, who accompanied the forces, however, it became known that many were killed, that the Neereezees had carried off the horses, and everything pertaining to the army; in short that Meerza Naeem and his army had been shamefully dis-comfited. The new Ruler proposes sending a fresh commander with fresh troops. Report has it that Meerza Naeem had been in two or three engagements prior to this one, and in one and all was he defeated.

Neereez has to pay of Revenue 5,500 Tomans:- the Governors and Revenue Collectors were wont in former days to levy 10,000 Tomans at the very least, but so completely has Meerza Naeem ruined the Country, and that too out of pure selfish motives, that expectation of payment of Revenue hereafter must be out of the question altogether. Hosts of the inhabitants have been slain and many yet will follow . . .

On the 15th Mohurrum* 600 of the Kashkaee† Sirbaz, 200 Shiraz Sirbaz and Two Guns, with complement of Gunners and ammunition, the whole under command of Lutf Alee Khan Sirteep,‡ were in orders to proceed to the assistance of Meerza Naeem in Neereez.[2]

On 18 November, Capt. Arnold Burrowes Kemball (q.v.), the British Resident at Bú<u>sh</u>ihr, in forwarding the two above reports of the <u>Sh</u>íráz agent to W. Taylour Thomson (q.v.), the British Chargé d'Affaires, sent his own assessment of the situation:

The enclosed Extracts from the monthly Report of the British Agent at Shiraz, received on the 14th Instant, communicate the discomfiture of a small body of the King's troops sent against Neereez, a district in the neighbourhood, whose inhabitants would appear to have been driven into rebellion by the oppressive and extortionate conduct of Meerza Naeem Nooree, a relation of the Sadr-i-Azim:§ Accused by this individual of being Bābees, orders had been issued by the Persian Ministers for the translation of a number of their principal men to Tehran, the execution of which they now determined to resist by force of arms. That some few followers of the sect are present in that part of the Country seems to be very generally believed; but the measures taken to suppress them have been certainly unfortunate, and may give rise to more serious complications.

Tahmasb Meerza,‖ the new Governor of Fars, is mentioned by our Agent as devoid of the talent and energy requisite to conduct his charge, and to keep in subordination the several factions into which the notables of the Province are divided. He is accompanied too by a large number of relatives and needy retainers for whom employment and emolument could only be provided at the expence of influential persons whose loss of place must render them inimical to his administration.[3]

* 18 Oct. 1853

† Qa<u>sh</u>qá'í, a tribe of Fárs.

‡ Luṭf-'Alí <u>Kh</u>án, Sartíp of the Qa<u>sh</u>qá'í Regiment. Mírzá Faḍlu'lláh in his report of the termination of this episode states, 'On the 6th Suffur [8 Nov. 1853] H.R.H. wrote word to Lutf Alee Khan nephew of the Eel Khanee "Now the affairs of the Neereezees have come to such a pass, you must by no means return to Shiraz, but proceed to Laristan and the Sabaijat, and there await my arrival."'

§ Ṣadr-i-A'ẓam, Prime Minister.

‖ Ṭahmásb Mírzá, son of Muḥammad-'Alí Mírzá, the son of Fatḥ-'Alí <u>Sh</u>áh. Governor of Fárs 1853–8 and 1860–62. Ussher describes thus an interview with him in 1860: 'We remained in the room for some minutes before any one appeared, conversing in a low tone with the secretary, when at last a door

As with the Nayríz upheaval of 1850 and indeed the upheaval at Shaykh Ṭabarsí, the government forces, despairing of success, resorted to treachery. Kemball, in transmitting the reports of the Shíráz agent, makes the following statement in a dispatch dated 15 December 1853: 'The details of the massacre at Nereez are confirmed by a letter from another party. The inhabitants – for the most part not Babis – having given all the proofs required that they did not belong to the obnoxious Sect, were induced by the most solemn protestations of safety to surrender themselves when 100 of the men were ruthlessly butchered and the women handed over to the soldiery.'[4]

Mírzá Faḍlu'lláh's report gave more details of the circumstances of the termination of the episode:

On the 5th Suffur* the Prince Governor despatched Abdul Hassan Beg to the Capital with letters detailing the proceedings at Neereez. Report hath it that Lutf Alee Khan and Meerza Naeem – both Officers of the Army sent against Neereez – contrived by means of promises and oaths to conciliate the Neereezees and to induce them to cease fighting. No sooner however had they become passive than the Army (treacherously) fell upon them, cut off the heads of about 100 men, youths, and children, and took 300 male prisoners. The Sirbaz and Artillerymen have likewise made 300 women and maidens captives, and violently compelled them to become their wives – whatever goods and property came to hand was also plundered and carried off . . .

Masoon Khan Ainaloo,† one of those who proceeded against Neereez, stated on the 9th instant as follows:

The Neereezees came forth from their defences on the day of the 28th Mohurrum,‡ and cried aloud 'We are no Babees – a curse upon Bab and everything belonging to Bab§ – seeing that Meerza Naeem has

---

opened, and a tall, stout, middle-aged man, wearing the usual high conical cap of black lambskin, entered the room at the end furthest from us, and taking his seat on the gilt chair, while the secretary and various others of his household stood by the walls, motioned us at the same time to be seated. We sat down on the chairs placed for us, the whole length of the room thus intervening between us and the prince. The conversation commenced with the usual inquiries after our health, which, being duly responded to, were followed by a topic on which the Shahzadeh showed great curiosity, viz., geography. Numerous and highly entertaining were the questions he asked us about the countries of Europe, the ways of travelling, the extent and power of the different kingdoms. He made several inquiries about the Americans, but it was evidently beyond his power to comprehend a republic. How a man in command of an army should not avail himself of his authority to seize the supreme power for himself, was an enigma which he could not solve.' (Ussher *Journey from London to Persepolis* p. 522.) In one of the dispatches reporting the second Nayríz upheaval, Mírzá Faḍlu'lláh also states: 'On the 15th Ultimo [i.e. 18th Oct. 1853] our new Governor sent his own Peesh Khidmut, Nasr-oollah Beg, with letters post to the capital; He wrote word to the King and his ministers that "the administration of the Province of Fars rested with 4 people – the Eel Khanee, the Hajee Kuwaum, the Nazim-ool Mulk, and the Nooree Tribe – should matters continue thus, he (the Prince) would scarcely be able to rule the Country; he begged therefore that they would either make him supreme, or recall him altogether."'

* 7 Nov. 1853

† Ma'ṣúm-'Alíy-i-Aynálú commanded the forces raised from the Aynálú tribe who resided around Dáráb and Fasá.

‡ 31 Oct. 1853

§ This statement that the beseiged Nayrízís denied their faith is not corroborated by any other source.

robbed us of all we possessed and, not satisfied with our property, has sent in false accusations against us to the King. Moreover Alee Beg Furash has come to bind us with chains, and carry us away captives, hence, fearing for our lives and afraid of the Tyrant Meerza Naeem, we have betaken ourselves to these mountains – were we assured that our lives were not in jeopardy we would not fight or resist – let therefore one of Lutf Alee Khan's people come and promise us safety, we will cease contending.' Messengers of Peace were sent by either party, and after many oaths and promises (of safety) the Neereezees became relieved of all fear. No sooner however had they been conciliated by the above promises than the Army fell upon them, cut off the heads of about one hundred, and made some 300 women and maidens prisoners.

Meerza Naeem arrived in Shiraz on the 22nd Suffur* bringing with him the Neereez prisoners. 4 of the number, said to have killed many Sirbaz, were bayonetted by order of the Prince. The rest of the male captives they shut up in store houses. Of the 300 women and maidens, all such as seemed fitting were taken by the Sirbaz and Government Servants. The rest being set at liberty are scattered about the city of Sheeraz, and seek their bread by begging. The heads of one hundred slain in action have also been kept for transmission to the Capital.[5]

From Shíráz, the heads of the Bábís together with some 60 prisoners were dispatched to the capital. When the party arrived at Ábádih, orders were received to bury the heads. Those that survived the harsh journey to Ṭihrán in the middle of winter were thrown into prison. Some were executed, some died in prison, and some, after a lengthy period, were released.

Nayríz was visited by Major B. Lovett (q.v.) of the Royal Engineers some two decades after these twin upheavals. He describes the town thus:

This town, which is situated about 12 miles east of the shores of the 'Deria Numuk,'† is of considerable commercial importance. Its exports are chiefly almonds and figs, which are shipped in great quantities *viâ* Bunder Abbas for Bombay. The population is said to be about 3500, and the revenue paid to the Government of Fars amounts to 12,000 tomans. It is a large town with many orchards, vineyards, and gardens interspersed between houses built of sun-dried bricks. It is divided into three parishes or 'mahalehs'; that to the south, termed the 'Mahaleh Bala', is well known to be peopled almost entirely by Bâbis, who, though they do not openly profess their faith in the teachings of Syud Ali Mahomed, the Bab, still practise the principles of communism he inculcated. It is certain, moreover, that the tolerance which was one of the chief precepts inculcated by the Bab is here observed, for not only was I invited to make use of the public humam [bath], if I required it, but quarters also were assigned to me in a 'Madresseh'.[6]

* 24 Nov. 1853

† Daryáy-i-Namak, Salt Sea. A large lake which is often also named Lake Nayríz.

References

1. Enclosed in W. Taylour Thomson to Earl of Clarendon No. 166, 18 Dec. 1853: FO 60 183
2. Enclosed in Capt. A. B. Kemball (Resident at Búshihr) to W. T. Thomson No. 350, 18 Nov. 1853. The report itself is dated 14 Nov. 1853, and is translated by H. F. Disbrowe, Asst to the Resident: FO 248 150
3. Kemball to Thomson No. 350, 18 Nov. 1853: FO 248 150
4. Kemball to Thomson No. 383, 15 Dec. 1853: FO 248 150
5. Enclosed in 4 *supra*, translated by H. F. Disbrowe
6. Maj. B. Lovett 'Surveys on the Road from Shiraz to Bam' p. 203

NINE

Some Principal Characters and Their Fates

In the following pages will be found sketches by Western observers of some of the principal participants in the dramatic events of the episode of the Báb. These are not meant to be objective historical assessments of these persons. They are merely the descriptions and opinions of those who came into contact with them.

Muḥammad S͟háh

It was during the reign of Muḥammad S͟háh (see fig. 17), the third of the Qájár dynasty, that the ministry of the Báb commenced in 1844. Muḥammad S͟háh ascended the throne in 1834, and one of his early acts as S͟háh was to order the death of his talented Prime Minister, Mírzá Abu'l-Qásim, the Qá'im-Maqám. Bahá'u'lláh was later to reproach Muḥammad S͟háh for this action as well as for his failure to bring the Báb to Ṭihrán and meet him.

Lieutenant-Colonel Charles Stuart, who came as part of Sir Henry Ellis's Mission to Persia in 1835, met the S͟háh on 23 November 1835 just outside the walls of Ṭihrán:

> We met the Shah near the walls; he graciously beckoned to Ellis to approach him, and as we rode close behind, I had a good opportunity of observing his Majesty. He is short and fat; apparently about twenty-eight years of age; his face is pale, his nose aquiline, and his countenance agreeable, though scarcely to be called handsome. He is passionately fond of soldiering, of which he has seen something practical, both in the last Russian war and in Khorasan, and is never in such good humour as when with his troops. To-day he wore the usual riding costume of a Persian gentleman. It consists of a black lambskin cap, pinched into a conical shape, which is worn alike by prince and peasant.[1]

For the last decade of his life Muḥammad S͟háh became increasingly incapacitated by gout, so that in his last year he was completely crippled. Complications set in, and on 4 September 1848, Farrant (q.v.), who was Chargé d'Affaires, reported: 'His Majesty the Shah is labouring under a severe illness . . . His malady, I understand, arose in the first instance by indigestion followed by Erysipelas in the left arm, great excitement of the stomach, constant vomiting and purging, total loss of appetite and great prostration of strength.'[2]

Dr Dickson (q.v.), the physician to the British Mission, was called to the royal palace by the Sháh's physician, Dr Cloquet (q.v.), and he reported on the same day: 'The King is still extremely weak . . . his tongue is a little better and he has less fever, but the state of debility is very great indeed.'[3]

That same evening at 9.00 p.m. Muḥammad Sháh died.

Ḥájí Mírzá Áqásí

Ḥájí Mírzá Áqásí's (see fig. 12) functioning as Prime Minister of Persia under Muḥammad Sháh was a remarkable affair. So complete was the ascendancy that this former tutor of the Sháh had gained over his master, that the latter was willing to leave all the affairs of state in his hands. Suspicious and avaricious, this eccentric and obscurantist character concentrated all the workings of the state in himself and the condition of the country gradually deteriorated.

From the very beginning of the mission of the Báb, Ḥájí Mírzá Áqásí, fearing the threat that it might pose to his own position, was its implacable foe. From one of the letters written by the Báb to Muḥammad Sháh it would appear that in the very first year of his ministry, he had sent a messenger (probably Mullá Ḥusayn) to the Sháh with a book. However, the book was not delivered and it was almost certainly Ḥájí Mírzá Áqásí who prevented this.* Later, while the Báb was enjoying the friendship of the Governor of Iṣfahán, Manúchihr Khán, Ḥájí Mírzá Áqásí incited the clergy of that town to act against him. Very much more significant was the scheming whereby the Prime Minister managed to forestall the Sháh's intention of receiving the Báb in Ṭihrán, and had the latter consigned to the remote border fortress of Mákú.† It was Ḥájí Mírzá Áqásí, also, who arranged for the trial of the Báb in Tabríz that resulted in the infliction of the bastinado upon the Báb. Thus, the Báb refers to him as 'Satan'[4] and Shoghi Effendi stigmatizes him as 'the Antichrist of the Bábí Revelation'.[5]

Lt-Col. Stuart, who met Ḥájí Mírzá Áqásí on 23 November 1835, wrote: 'From the Shah we proceeded to his Prime Minister – as, I suppose, Hajee Meerza Aghassee may now be called. He is a quizzical old gentleman, with a long nose; and his countenance, though not stupid, betokens the oddity and self-sufficiency of his character. He says he is a lion in battle!'[6]

* Further evidence that Mullá Ḥusayn was indeed the bearer of a book to Muḥammad Sháh is a statement to this effect in *Násikhu't-Taváríkh*, although this work seems to imply that the book was delivered.

† Although belonging to a family of Íraván, Ḥájí Mírzá Áqásí was born in Mákú and brought up there. Throughout his administration, he was wont to favour the citizens of this town and gave them many important posts. The fact that he consigned the Báb to this town is an indication of how seriously he regarded the threat that the Báb posed.

Eugène Flandin, the distinguished archaeologist, met Ḥájí Mírzá Áqásí when the latter was accompanying the Sháh to Iṣfahán in 1841. He describes well the antics of the Prime Minister:

The visit to the Prime Minister of Muḥammad Sháh was to follow immediately upon the royal audience. Leaving the throne-room, we proceeded to the quarters of the vazír, Ḥájí Mírzá Áqásí, who had a residence within the walls of the palace. He received us without any pomp and with a simplicity which had shocked the ambassador . . .

Imagine a nose, very long and curved, over an edentulous mouth and surmounted by badly-dyed hair, bloodshot, but lively and spirited eyes, a brusque gesture, a subtle or rather sly appearance, and one has the exact portrait of this singular personage. This little old man, still vigorous, was like all Persians, vain to excess . . .

Our visit to Ḥájí Mírzá Áqásí was short; his conversation was scarcely of a nature to destroy the prejudices, little favourable to his person, which had been in our minds before this presentation. The ignorance of the Mulla betrayed itself each time that he diverged from the commonplaces of politeness and touched on matter a little more serious. We could scarcely maintain our gravity [of demeanour] in seeing this little man complementing his words by grotesque gestures, and, frequently, hitting his hat with a blow of his fist, thus setting it awry in one way or other. This singular pantomime signified anger or admiration according to the desire of this personage.[7]

Lt-Col. Farrant, reporting on the disastrous state of Persia after some 13 years of misrule by Ḥájí Mírzá Áqásí, wrote:

The infatuation of the Shah is incredible, blinded by the wiliness of his Minister he appears contented, but is ignorant of the real state of his Kingdom.His Excellency [Ḥájí Mírzá Áqásí] has persuaded His Majesty that by his foresight alone Persia has remained quiet (treating the disturbances in Khorassan as insignificant) whilst the whole of Europe has been convulsed by revolutions and outbreaks, and that His Majesty must rely on him for the safety of his crown and the peace and welfare of the Kingdom, he has filled the royal mind with suspicion and distrust for those who are permitted to approach the Royal Person – and the dread of His Excellency's displeasure, of being accused of treason and of being sent into exile, pervades the higher classes, for they all feel that the Shah has not the courage to support them against his Minister.

It is wonderful, My Lord, to witness the extraordinary power the Prime Minister exercises over the Shah. It could be imagined that the folly of his proceedings, the wildness of his language, and the absurdity of his reasoning would be sufficient to develop his true character to His Majesty; but the authority of His Excellency is paramount, and the Shah rules only in name.

Most of the evils which overwhelm this country may be attributed to the Prime Minister's grasping cupidity and love of power . . . it will be a task of great difficulty to raise it [the country] from the miserable state into which it has been plunged by so many years of His Excellency's misrule.[8]

Sir Henry Layard (q.v.) who, as a young man, met Ḥájí Mírzá Áqásí in 1842, wrote:

'The Haji' – the name by which he was familiarly known – was, by all accounts, a statesman of craft and cunning, but of limited abilities. He was cruel and treacherous, proud and overbearing, although he affected the humility of a pious Mulla . . .

The religious character which he assumed made him intolerant and bigoted . . . His misgovernment, and the corruption and general oppression which everywhere existed, had brought Persia to the verge of ruin. Distress, misery and discontent prevailed to an extent previously unknown. He was universally execrated as the cause of the misfortunes and misery from which the people and the state were suffering.

. . . He was a man of small stature, with sharp and somewhat mean and forbidding features and a loud shrill voice. His dress was simple – almost shabby – as became a Mulla and a man devoted to a religious life.[9]

Ḥájí Mírzá Áqásí came to an ignominious end. On the death of Muḥammad S͟háh a large body of the notables of Ṭihrán took refuge in the British Legation, declaring that while they remained loyal to the new S͟háh they would not tolerate Ḥájí Mírzá Áqásí any longer. The latter, terror-stricken, took sanctuary in the shrine of S͟háh 'Abdu'l-'Aẓím near Ṭihrán, while the populace expressed their delight at being relieved of his tyranny by looting all of his property as well as that of his principal followers and retainers. Shorn of the ill-gotten gains of the rapacity and avarice that marked his years as Prime Minister, he was expelled from Persia and died, forgotten, in Karbilá* the following year (1 August 1849).

Náṣiru'd-Dín S͟háh

Upon the death of Muḥammad S͟háh, his son ascended the throne as Náṣiru'd-Dín S͟háh (see fig. 16). It appears that as a child, Náṣiru'd-Dín S͟háh had been extremely beautiful. Lt-Col. Stuart, who saw him in October 1835, writes: 'The Walee Ahud† was, like his uncle, seated at an open window. I never saw so beautiful a child; the expression of his countenance is mournful, and the poor thing was evidently shy. We were given sherbet, sugar-candy and tea, presented by servants who knelt. The ablutions of the Walee Ahud were carefully performed after he had drunk his tea. He wiped his little chin, where, "Inshallah," his beard will be, with most dignified gravity.'[10]

However handsome his external appearance may have been, his tutor Mírzá Ibráhím, who had formerly taught Persian at Haileybury College in England, despaired of his intellectual achievements. Sheil, writing in March 1846, says: 'Meerza Ibraheem, the Prince Royal's tutor, represents the Prince's understanding and acquirements to be equally deficient. He is even imperfectly acquainted with reading and writing in his own language, and Meerza Ibraheem is so hopeless of his instruction being of any service, from

* Charles Burgess wrote, on 31 Mar. 1849, concerning Ḥájí Mírzá Áqásí: 'The former Prime Minister now an exile at Kerbelai, has got into some theological disputes with the Mollahs of that place, and has been pelted by the people. His enormous wealth has been confiscated by the crown, at least all that was not plundered by the people in the disturbances which succeeded the late king's death.' (Burgess *Letters from Persia* p. 106)

† Valí-'Ahd, Crown Prince

the natural want of intellect and capacity in the Prince, that it is only by my recommendation that he has consented to retain his appointment of Tutor to His Royal Highness.'[11]

In January 1848, Náṣiru'd-Dín Mírzá was appointed Governor of Ádharbáyján, where he remained until his father's death later that year. It was during this period that he acted as president of the court at the trial of the Báb, although he played no active part in the proceedings.

On the death of Muḥammad Sháh, Náṣiru'd-Dín proceeded from Tabríz to Ṭihrán. The first four years of his reign are marked by the fiercest and bloodiest of the persecutions of the religion of the Báb and Bahá'u'lláh. Indeed, during the whole of Náṣiru'd-Dín Sháh's reign there were sporadic persecutions and, in at least some cases, he himself was directly responsible for the death of the martyrs.

Binning, who met the Sháh in early 1851, wrote: 'The Shah is now in his twenty-second year, but looks older. His complexion is very sallow, and his countenance, though not disagreeable, cannot be pronounced handsome: he wears moustaches, with but the rudiments of a beard. He was plainly dressed in a frockcoat in European style, over which was a joobba [*jubbih*, cloak or gown] of dark shawl stuff trimmed with sables, and on his head the ordinary black lambskin cap.'[12]

Ussher, who visited Persia in 1861 and met the Sháh, described him thus:

> On entering the saloon, a small and simply decorated apartment, we found the Shah standing alone before a chair painted green and decorated with a few emeralds, placed in front of a throne on a small platform. The Shah was dressed in a mixture of European and Asiatic costume. He wore white trousers, and a pink silk frock coat buttoned across with large diamond buttons, each of a single stone. A swordbelt, the buckle of which was set with the famous Deriah Noor, or 'Sea of Light' diamond, encircled his waist, and from it was suspended a diamond-hilted dagger, similar to those in use among the Circassians. Over the coat was a pink cloth of gold dressing gown lined with ermine, and on his head the usual Astrachan fur cap worn by all classes. He wore a large moustache, but his beard was clipped, not shaven, as closely as possible, a custom peculiar to the Kajar tribe, who never use a razor, and which is followed by the present king. The scissors being but an imperfect substitute for the razor, he had an unshaven look, his beard appearing dirty and stubbly, by no means improving his naturally bad expression of countenance. He was of middle height, and rather dark; his features were good, but marred by a furtive look, in which meanness and cowardice seemed struggling for the mastery.[13]

As Náṣiru'd-Dín Sháh's reign progressed, however, opinions about him expressed by Europeans gradually improved. Typical of the later opinions is that of Curzon (1889):*

* It should be pointed out that this account of Náṣiru'd-Dín Sháh has been considerably toned down from Curzon's original statement. In Nov. 1891, just as the book was ready for press, Curzon was appointed Under-Secretary of State for India. With Curzon now a member of the Government, Lord Salisbury, the Prime Minister, felt obliged to vet the contents of the book and he found Curzon's

Though sixty years of age, the Shah is erect, active, and robust, making the most of a middle stature, and walking with a slow step and a peculiar jaunty movement of the hips, which has a certain air of distinction . . .

He is believed to be naturally shy, which may account for a somewhat abrupt and fidgety manner, and for an utterance rapped out in short, incisive periods . . .

Called to the throne at the early age of seventeen, and surrounded therefore from youth upwards by the sycophants and flatterers who buzz round an Oriental crown, it is surprising that Nasr-ed-Din Shah has turned out so well. This happy development he owes to abilities considerably above the average, and to decided strength of character.[14]

The year 1896 marked the 50th anniversary of Náṣiru'd-Dín Sháh's accession to the throne.* Inspired no doubt by the great Jubilee celebrations of Queen Victoria in 1887, Náṣiru'd-Dín Sháh spared no expense in planning a great festival at the beginning of May. It was to be a great public holiday. All businesses and schools were to be closed for a week, the buildings were decorated, Governors and notables were summoned from every part of Persia to attend the celebrations and troops also converged upon the capital to take part in the parades. A general amnesty was to be declared and prisoners released. The town was to be illuminated and the poor fed. It was even said that the Sháh intended to renounce his despotic powers and proclaim himself 'a kind father' to all his people, while the great mujtahids would, for a time, suspend the persecutions of 'the babis and other infidels'. The climax of the festivities, on 6 May, was to be a day the like of which Persia had never witnessed. One of the preliminary events leading up to 6 May was a visit by the Sháh to the shrine of Sháh 'Abdu'l-'Aẓím, a few miles outside Ṭihrán. It was here on 1 May 1896 that a crowd of thousands, brought from every part of Persia to participate in the celebrations, witnessed instead the termination of Náṣiru'd-Dín Sháh's reign by assassination. The French Minister, de Balloy (q.v.), records the events of that day in a dispatch dated 2 May 1896:

I am making use of a Russian courier who is leaving today in order to send you the details that I received this evening about the assassination of the Sháh, the sad news of which I have already sent you by my Telegram No. 5.

His Majesty, before going to make his Friday devotions at the Mosque of Sháh 'Abdu'l-'Aẓím, which is, as your Excellency knows, about a dozen kilometres from the town, had the previous day given leave, for that day, to Dr Schneider, who took advantage of this to go and visit his encampment at Shimrán. In this last interview with our physician, the King heard for more than half an hour about the socialist movement of Paris and, remarkably enough, about the assassination of President Carnot . . .

---

statements regarding the Sháh to be 'more severe than I expected' and considered that 'no doubt it would give the deepest offence'. Curzon was compelled to submit to bowdlerization of his text. (Ronaldshay *The Life of Lord Curzon* Vol. 1, pp. 154–5)

* by lunar reckoning

. . . it was about 4 o'clock, [we] received a word from one of the secretaries, M. de Sermontow, saying that an attempt had been made against the Sháh at Sháh 'Abdu'l-'Aẓím, that His Majesty had been wounded in the leg . . . I sent some riders to look for Dr Schneider. I had already put in cipher for Your Excellency the news as I have related above, when our physician arrived very excited. The horsemen of the Sháh had met him before mine, and he was already returning from the Palace where he had found the Sháh to be dead. This is what had happened. His Majesty was about to leave the Mosque of Sháh 'Abdu'l-'Aẓím, where he was surrounded by almost 3,000 persons, when an individual approached him with an open petition in his hand. The King was about to take it when a shot rang out. That wretched man had had a revolver hidden beneath the sheet of paper and fired it point-blank. The bullet went through the heart by the fifth left intercostal space. The King took a further 3 paces and fell stone-dead. The Ṣadr-i-A'ẓam* was at his side, as well as a Persian physician, Shaykh Muḥammad, who realized immediately that death had occurred. The Sháh was taken to his carriage, which was waiting at the gate, and saying that he had only been wounded, they returned to the town at full speed. His body was placed in one of the reception rooms to avoid the disorder that would have inevitably occurred had he been taken back to the anderún.† The Ṣadr-i-A'ẓam and the Russian Chargé d'Affaires, who was immediately summoned to the Palace, took the important steps with great composure and presence of mind. They ordered the gates to be closed and summoned every possible soldier and armed person. M. Steheglow had, at the first news, summoned the Russian Colonel who commands the Persian Cossack Brigade, and ordered him to put the brigade onto armed patrols. The Valí-'Ahd‡ was advised by telegraph to leave Tabríz immediately and to arrive in Ṭihrán as quickly as possible. In order to gain time, the order was given to spread everywhere the story that His Majesty had only been wounded in the leg, that he was very weak and that he would soon be restored to health. Náyibu's-Salṭanih§ was asked to leave the Palace and return to his home.

The murderer, who was arrested immediately, will be a Siyyid or a Bábí, it is still not known exactly. It is asserted that he had already been put in prison on several occasions and had only recently been released [from prison] by the Sháh at the request of the mujtahids of Ṭihrán . . .

The contrast between the celebrations of the Jubilee, which had been prepared for 6 May and this tragic death is . . . striking . . .

10 o'clock

The murderer of the Sháh is neither a Siyyid nor a Bábí as was at first believed. He is a revolutionary named Mírzá Muḥammad-Riḍá Kirmání, an associate of Siyyid Jamálu'd-Dín and of Malkam Khán, former Minister of Persia in London, the editors of the journal *Qánún*, of which I have spoken on different occasions. It was at the special request of Mírzá Ḥasan-i-Ashtíyání, the same mujtahid who had been the originator of an attack directed against the Palace of the Sháh in the month of January 1892, that the murderer had been set at liberty, as I indicated above . . .

3 o'clock

I am returning from offering my condolences to Amínu's-Sulṭán. His Highness confirmed all the details that I have given above and added some new facts. It was he who succeeded in shielding the assassin from the fury of the crowd and in having him imprisoned without having been much maltreated. He had, however, had an ear torn off in the crowd. Anticipating the fate that

* Prime Minister, Mírzá 'Alí-Aṣghar Khán, Amínu's-Sulṭán (q.v.)
† Women's quarters
‡ Heir to the throne, Muẓaffaru'd-Dín Sháh.
§ Kámrán Mírzá (q.v.), 3rd son of Náṣiru'd-Dín Sháh

awaited him, he had fired a second revolver shot at himself, but in the mêlée which followed the first, the shot misfired into the air. Amínu's-Sulṭán had telegraphed this morning to Constantinople to lodge a complaint against Siyyid Jamálu'd-Dín who is there, it appears, in prison.[15]

Mírzá Taqí Khán

Mírzá Taqí Khán (see fig. 13) was the first Prime Minister of Náṣiru'd-Dín Sháh. It was during his ministry and partly as a result of his orders that there occurred the bloodshed and upheavals that marked the years 1848 to 1850 – principally the upheavals at Shaykh Ṭabarsí and Zanján, the first Nayríz upheaval and the episode of the Seven Martyrs of Ṭihrán. The culmination of his hostility to the new religion was his order for the execution of the Báb.*

Mírzá Taqí Khán is now regarded by most historians as having been a great reformer and one of the founders of modern Iran. However, in the first years of his ministry those Europeans who were in Ṭihrán were not so enthusiastic about him. Ferrier, the French Agent, in an article that he wrote about the state of Persia in 1851, is particularly severe on Mírzá Taqí Khán, 'whose mad vanity and ambition have further increased the disorder and anarchy in which this country has struggled for many years.'[16] He accuses Mírzá Taqí Khán of many personal vices as well as of having brought the country to the verge of ruin.

British accounts of Mírzá Taqí Khán are equally unfavourable in these early years, although this is probably partly due to the fact that the British considered him to be under Russian influence. Lt-Col. Farrant, who was Chargé d'Affaires in Sheil's absence, reported to Palmerston after six months of the Amír's administration:

> I regret to say the Ameer gains no popularity, his haughty deportment and his assumption of all the executive power, added to which his financial reforms are the chief causes of the dislike of all classes towards His Excellency. His suspicious character prevents him adding stability to the Shah's throne, he trusts to no one, not even to those who render the best services to the State. The Shah is completely in his hands, over whom he exercises more influence if possible than the Hajee did over his late Father.
>
> It is evident that the presence of the two Missions of England and Russia have up to this time alone upheld the authority of the Shah, but discontent will encrease [*sic*] above all control, the finances are exhausted, and should affairs in Khorassan become more complicated (and rumours are rife that the Salar's cause in that province has gained fresh vigour) I am not without fears that disorder will gain ground in every part of the Kingdom, and the province of Azerbijan will be the first to declare itself independent . . .[17]

* Despite this, 'Abdu'l-Bahá spoke thus of Mírzá Taqí Khán: 'Despite the fact that he oppressed this Cause in such wise as no one else has, Mírzá Taqí Khán, the Prime Minister, in matters of state and politics, laid what were truly the firmest of foundations, and this although he had never attended a

12. Ḥájí Mírzá Áqásí, Grand Vizier in the reign of Muḥammad Sháh

13. Mírzá Taqí Khán, the Amír Niẓám. This portrait is said to have been drawn by Náṣiru'd-Dín Sháh himself, shortly after the execution of Mírzá Taqí Khán.

14. Mírzá Áqá Khán, second Grand Vizier of Náṣiru'd-Dín Sháh

15. Muḥammad-Báqir-i-Há'í, Bahá'í of Najafábád

16. Muḥammad Sh͟áh

17. Náṣiru'd-Dín Sh͟áh

18. Manúchihr Khán, Mu'tamadu'd-Dawlih, Governor of Iṣfahán (by permission of the British Library)

19. Arnold Burrowes Kemball, British Consul at Baghdád, a cartoon by 'Ape' in Vanity Fair *(Bodleian Library, Oxford, PER. 2288b. 46 opp. p. 347)*

20. Group of Bahá'ís in Adrianople. Standing (L. to R.): Áqá Muḥammad-'Alíy-i-Nahrí, Mírzá Naṣru'lláh-i-Tafrishí, Mullá Muḥammad-i-Zarandí (Nabíl-i-A'ẓam), Mírzá Áqá Ján-i-Káshání (Khádimu'lláh), Áqá Ḥusayn-i-Iṣfahání (Mishkín-Qalam), Mírzá 'Alíy-i-Sayyáḥ, Áqá Ḥusayn-i-Áshchí, and Áqá 'Abdu'l-Ghaffár-i-Maḥallátí. Seated (L. to R.): Mírzá Muḥammad-Javád-i-Qazvíní, Mírzá Mihdí (son of Bahá'u'lláh), 'Abdu'l-Bahá, Mírzá Muḥammad-Qulí (half-brother of Bahá'u'lláh, with, presumably, one of his children), and Siyyid Mihdíy-i-Dihají. Seated on the ground (L. to R.): Majdu'd-Dín (nephew of Bahá'u'lláh) and Mírzá Muḥammad-'Alí (half-brother of 'Abdu'l-Bahá).

Sheil returned to Ṭihrán in November 1849. In mid-December, he addressed a lengthy dispatch to Viscount Palmerston informing the latter of the state in which he found Persia on his return.

It seems desirable I should attempt to convey to your Lordship some conception of the condition of this Government and country, which my own previous knowledge and my intercourse since my return with a number of persons of every class, justify me in considering that I am able to form a correct estimate of.

The King may be passed over as a cipher in the administration. He is twenty years of age, and though perhaps not altogether destitute of intelligence, his education has been wholly neglected, and he seems to have no desire to take a share in the Government of his Kingdom. The Prime Minister apparently encourages this disposition as a means of rendering the Shah dependent on himself, and of perpetuating the power he now engrosses. The King has the merit of endeavouring to remedy his defective education by acquiring a conversational knowledge of history and geography.

The Prime Minister appears to me to be a man of some talent, though scarcely equal to the difficulties he has to surmount, and full of prejudice and suspicion. He has a character for obstinacy, which is said not always to be under the control of good sense. Avarice which is the national passion does not seem to exercise an engrossing influence over him, and he is one of the few Persians of my acquaintance who appear to be actuated by some desire for the good of their Country. His feelings at present are adverse to Russia, yet he can scarcely be said to be favorably disposed towards England, or to believe fully in the good wishes of the British Government towards Persia . . .

He scarcely possesses a single friend or supporter; by pride and overbearing and most ungracious manners, and perhaps by a somewhat precipitate reduction of all salaries and pensions, he has excited against himself personally the strong dislike and discontent of all classes in Tehran, and the state of the provinces shows that these feelings are not confined to this city . . .

I do not exaggerate when I assert that discontent, if not disaffection, pervades all classes. My short residence here has already given me opportunities of hearing the complaints of every rank of society. In the upper ranks this discontent is mainly selfish, proceeding from anxiety to obtain place and opportunities of corruption; but among the priesthood and the commercial classes the same discontent prevails, and the lower grades of the population naturally imitate the example of their superiors. On every side one hears the reasonable enquiry, of what benefit has been the administration of the Ameer during the year and a half that he has guided the Government; and it is contended with too much truth, that not only is there no amelioration, but that Persia is in a much worse condition than when the Ameer assumed the Government.

This sketch of the Prime Minister comprehends very nearly a sketch of the entire Government, for like Hajee Meerza Aghassee he has concentrated all power in his own hands. The only apology that can be offered for adopting his predecessor's example is his not unreasonable fear that if he surrounds himself with men of talent, the efforts of each individual will be directed to the overthrow of his supremacy in the hope of succeeding to the post of Prime Minister. The Minister of Finance and the former Minister for the Army, with one or two subordinate functionaries, are almost the only persons of capacity on whose co-operation the Ameer can count . . .

The conclusion I have come to is this; that

European school. Indeed, true education promotes the state of the individual so that he attains wisdom, awareness and divine confirmations.' (Zarqání *Badá'i'u'l-Á<u>th</u>ár*, Vol. 2, p. 144)

though the Ameer is not a man of much capacity, or very enlightened understanding, and in all likelihood will be unable to effect reforms of much value, and though he is a man of great obstinacy of temper, determined not to listen to good advice from the British Government or from the British Minister, still his apparent determination to resist the progress of Russia, covers many faults, and entitles him under present circumstances to a trial to such support as I can give him; one of his great errors is, in my opinion, the monopoly in his own person, of all power and place, instead of dividing the labours of the Government, and reserving for himself the supervision and control of affairs, to which the dignity of Grand Vizeer justly entitles him.[18]

Binning's description of the Amír-Niẓám reflects much the same opinion:

The Ameer, Mírzá Takee, is of low origin: his father was a cook, and I have heard that he himself was, in his youth, a *pehlavân*, or public wrestler;* a report in no way belied by his large athletic frame. He is unquestionably an able and clever man; but has many faults common to any half-educated, ill-formed [*sic*] Persian. Ignorant of the world at large, and knowing but little of the condition and powers of other nations, such a minister must necessarily be too often short-sighted and erring in his policy. He is said to be occasionally harsh and cruel; and by no means free from the most prominent vices of his countrymen. His brother, who is *vazeeri nezâm*† or minister of war, is a savage and inhuman brute, universally and deservedly detested. Mirza Takee is married to a sister of the Shah, and this alliance will probably maintain and strengthen him in the, always precarious, position of counsellor to a capricious self-willed despot. With all his defects, it might be no easy matter to find any one of his countrymen better qualified to fill the situation.[19]

Binning, however, was impressed by the Amír-Niẓám's personal manner:

Leaving the palace, we proceeded to the tent of the prime minister, Mirza Takee, surnamed the Ameer Atâbek, who inhabited a small garden, a few hundred yards distant from the Kasri Kajar. He received us with much politeness; chairs were brought for the whole party, and kaleons and tea handed round. The Ameer is a large, portly, good-looking man, with an open intelligent countenance: he sat and talked with us for nearly half an hour; and though his conversation was principally directed to the British Minister, he addressed some part of it to every separate individual present: the true way, according to Theodore Hook, of making one's self agreeable. He is said to be jealous of Europeans generally; and has persuaded the Shah to discard several from his service: he is also particularly anxious to exclude all foreign manufactured goods from Persia, by way of encouraging native industry – a short-sighted policy, in no way tending to the advancement of commerce or of civilization. Our visit being ended, I took my departure along with the suite, leaving the Minister in private conference with the Ameer.[20]

British opinion of Mírzá Taqí K͟hán's administration improved with time, however. Typical of later views is the following from Robert G. Watson (q.v.), who was attaché to the British Legation in Ṭihrán from 1857 to 1859:

* This is not true, as far as the editor is aware.

† Mírzá Ḥasan K͟hán, the Vazír-Niẓám (q.v.), Mírzá Taqí K͟hán's brother, was made personally responsible by his brother for carrying out the martyrdom of the Báb (see p. 76).

> Meerza Teki Khan . . . owed his elevation entirely to his talents and his services. He was a man altogether of a different nature from that of his countrymen in general. Belisarius did not tower over the degenerate Romans of his day more than did the Ameer-i-Nizam over his contemporaries . . . The race of modern Persians cannot be said to be altogether effete, since so recently it has been able to produce a man such as was the Ameer-i-Nizam. Feraghan, near Sultanabad in Irak, had the honour to give birth to him who perhaps alone of all the Oriental statesmen and governors whose names appear in the history of modern Persia, would have satisfied the scrutiny of a Diogenes, and was fully entitled to be considered that 'noblest work of God,' an honest man.[21]

And having given an account of Mírzá Taqí Khán's death, Watson writes: 'Thus perished . . . the man who had done so much to regenerate Persia: the only man who possessed at the same time the ability, the patriotism, the energy and the integrity required to enable a Persian Minister to conduct the vessel of State in safety past the shoals and rocks which lay in her course.'[22]

The Amír-Niẓám's two bitterest enemies were the Sháh's mother and Mírzá Áqá Khán. These two intrigued to raise suspicions in the Sháh's mind; whispering that the Amír-Niẓám was concentrating too much power in his own person and that perhaps he was planning to overthrow the Monarchy. Eventually, on the night of 13 November 1851, Náṣiru'd-Dín Sháh was pushed into acting determinedly and decisively. Having summoned some 500 of his bodyguard to his presence, the Sháh sent word to the Amír-Niẓám that he was henceforth to be in charge of the army only.

Initially, the Sháh only intended to reduce Mírzá Taqí Khán's powers and establish his own authority more firmly. Thus he wrote the following letters to Mírzá Taqí Khán which the latter communicated confidentially to the British Legation:

> The Shah of Persia to the late Meerza Tekkee Khan (November 15th 1851).
>
> Your Excellency the Ameer Nizam.
>
> I swear by God, I swear by God, and I now write to you with the utmost truth, that I love you passionately, and may the Almighty deprive me of life if I attempt to desert you as long as I live, or if I should wish to lessen your dignity by a hairsbreadth.
>
> I will treat you and behave to you in a way that not a single soul shall know what has been the matter; it will look as if you were wearied with the multiplicity of affairs, and had thrown two or three of the departments on my shoulders. All the orders and fermans, both military and civil, which formerly had to be sealed and signed by you must still continue to be sealed by you in the same manner; the only difference will be that people will now see for a short time that I myself transact the business not connected with the army. I shall not interfere in any way with the affairs of the army, but will do whatever you deem proper . . .[23]

> Autograph note from the Shah to the Ameer-i-Nizam (written the 15th or 16th November 1851)
>
> Your Excellency the Ameer-i-Nizam:
>
> I swear it by God I was ashamed to see you today. What am I to do, would to God I had never been Shah, and that it had not been in my power also to commit such an act. I swear it by God that while I write this I

weep. By the Lord, by the Lord, my heart yearns for you. I love you. If you believe me not you are unjust.

The Mayor came and I gathered from what he said that you were afraid how this would end. Who is the whoreson who could for an instant speak before me in disparagement of you. I swear it by God also, if any one should speak a disrespectful word of you either before me, or before others, I am a bastard if I don't blow him from the cannon's mouth. By the Lord, I have no other intention than that you and I should be one, and both of us manage affairs. By my own head, by my own head, if you should be grieved, by the Lord, I cannot bear to see you grieved. While you live and I live I shall never forsake you . . .[24]

Eventually, however, the S͟háh was persuaded to strip Mírzá Taqí K͟hán of all power and exile him to Káș͟hán.

The Amír-Niẓám's exile in Káș͟hán did not last long. Mírzá Áqá K͟hán could not allow such a potent adversary to remain in a position where a change of the S͟háh's mind could precipitate a reversal of events. Further intrigue ensued, and eventually the S͟háh consented to the Amír's execution. Sheil reports the execution thus, in a dispatch to Viscount Palmerston dated 16 January 1852:

I lament to inform your Lordship that the late unfortunate Prime Minister, Meerza Tekkee Khan, has by order of the Shah been murdered at Kashan, where for the last two months he has been confined. This crime has been aggravated by the cruel means chosen to accomplish it.

The murder was perpetrated in the following manner. It happened on the 9th Instant, but for a fortnight previously the Ameer's guards adopted the practice of summoning him out of his room under the pretence of ascertaining that he had not fled. On these occasions he was accompanied by the Princess his wife, the Shah's sister, as a protection. After some days, this ceremony appearing to be a mere form, she ceased to accompany him. This was what was aimed at. The Shah's Ferrash Bashee,* a sort of Steward of the Household, was despatched to superintend the execution. When he arrived, the Ameer was summoned and appeared alone as was anticipated. He was seized, gagged and dragged to an adjoining house, where he was cast on the floor, stripped and tied. The veins in both arms and legs were opened. He lingered in this mortal agony three or four hours. He is said to have borne his fate with resignation, and to have given directions relative to his interment . . .

The principal instigators were the Shah's mother, the most guilty of all; her brother; the Ferrash Bashee; and the Serdar,† who is a Russian subject, married to a sister of the late Shah.

I fear I cannot exonerate the Sedr Azim from connivance in the tragedy. He had promised to give me timely notice of danger, yet he did not do so until some hours after the departure of the Ferrash Bashee, the same day that my letter was delivered to the Shah, and even then he did not reveal the above conclusive fact . . .

The Shah is not equally condemned. His youth and the pernicious influence of his mother, are considered an extenuation of his unworthy treatment of a man who had conferred so many benefits on him . . .

I ought not to conclude this despatch without an allusion to the admirable conduct of the Ameer's wife. In spite of the

* Ḥájí 'Alí K͟hán, Ḥájibu'd-Dawlih (q.v.)

† Muḥammad-Ḥasan K͟hán, K͟hán Bábá K͟hán (q.v.)

remonstrances and entreaties of her mother, this Princess, who is seventeen years of age, insisted on accompanying the Ameer, to protect his life, and to live with him in solitude. To secure him from poison, she invariably partook first of all his food and displayed throughout a firmness and decision of character, unheard of perhaps in a Persian woman, least of all in the dissolute tribe to which she belongs.[25]

Mírzá Áqá Khán

Mírzá Naṣru'lláh-Khán-i-Núrí, known as Mírzá Áqá Khán (see fig. 14), I'timádu'd-Dawlih, was Náṣiru'd-Dín Sháh's second Prime Minister. A man of unbounded ambition and much disposed to intrigue, his foremost desire was to become Prime Minister. During Muḥammad Sháh's reign, he quarrelled with Ḥájí Mírzá Áqásí and was exiled to Káshán, where he came into contact with the Bábís. His expressions of sympathy for the Bábí cause were in all probability feigned to ensure himself against the possibility of the Bábís coming to power. On the death of Muḥammad Sháh, he hurried to Ṭihrán hoping to present himself as a candidate for Prime Minister. His precipitate actions, however, endangered his life, and Farrant, who was Chargé d'Affaires at the British Legation, found it necessary to intercede for him with the new Sháh's mother, who was in charge of the Government pending the arrival of Náṣiru'd-Dín Sháh from Tabríz. Later, fearing for his safety at the hands of Mírzá Taqí Khán, Mírzá Áqá Khán was placed under formal British protection. There is no doubt that Mírzá Áqá Khán plotted to bring about the downfall of Mírzá Taqí Khán and in this he received powerful support from the Sháh's mother. On the fall of Mírzá Taqí Khán in November 1851, he was appointed Prime Minister.

His time as Prime Minister was marked by the gradual reversal of the reforms initiated by Mírzá Taqí Khán and the disastrous Anglo-Persian War of 1856–7. With regard to the religion of the Báb, he directed the persecutions that followed the attempt on the life of the Sháh.

In August 1858, he was dismissed from his position, much of his wealth was confiscated and he and his family exiled to Sulṭánábád. For almost seven years, he wandered from city to city, a broken man, begging to be allowed to return to Ṭihrán. Gradually various diseases afflicted him, leading to tightness in the chest, pain in the eyes and inflammation of his legs. Eventually he died at Qum in March 1865. He was buried at Karbilá but later a road was constructed over his grave which is now, therefore, lost.

On 22 October 1850, Sheil wrote to Palmerston: 'There is no doubt of Meerza Agha Khan being a person of venality, and much disposed towards intrigue.'[26]

It was during the ministry of Mírzá Áqá Khán that the Anglo-Persian War (1856–7) occurred. Indeed, the war itself may be said to have been caused by the intrigue of Mírzá Áqá Khán and the stubbornness and maladroitness of the British Minister, Charles Murray. Thus the following memorandum by Murray should be read with the great antagonism between these two in mind:

The Sadrazem Mirza Aga Khan was at this time between forty-five and fifty years of age; but his long face, with a long Persian cap above it and a long flowing beard below it, gave him the appearance of being older than he really was. He was an admirable specimen of the modern Persian of the upper class: grave and dignified in appearance when in company, yet his manner and conversation were both easy and agreeable in *tête-à-tête*. He had a great deal of drollery and wit, though the latter tended towards obscenity when not checked by the presence of some one before whom he was obliged to act his part. I know not which was most constantly between his lips, falsehood or his *kaliän*, for he smoked from early morning till late at night without ceasing. He was an adept in every form and species of lie – the figurative, the implied, the circumstantial, and the direct: all these he told with a readiness, fluency, and *bonhomie* that were really charming, and he took care that this talent should not rust for want of practice. Let one illustration of this suffice, selected out of a hundred I might record. Not many weeks after my arrival, I had gone to pay him a visit and to talk over with him some affair of little moment. While smoking our *kaliäns tête-à-tête*, he took occasion to offer me some friendly counsel and warning in the following language: 'As you have not been very long in our country, let me give you this friendly information – that all Persians are naturally and habitually liars.' 'You must not believe a word of what they may tell you. Whilst you remain here, if ever you want accurate information on any subject whatever, always come to me; I will never tell you anything but what is strictly true.' And as I expressed myself duly grateful for his kindness, he added an asseveration the weight and solemnity of which no man who has not been in the East can appreciate. Passing his hand caressingly down his flowing jet-black beard, he said, 'Remember that for every falsehood that I tell you while you reside in Persia, I will give you leave to pluck a hair out of this beard.'. . .

[One day, about a year later,] I said to him –

'Does your Highness remember telling me soon after my arrival that I might always rely upon your truthfulness, and that you would permit me to pluck out from your beard one hair for every falsehood that you might tell me during my stay in Persia?'

'Yes, I remember it well,' said he; 'and what then?'

'Only,' I replied, 'that if I had availed myself of your permission, your Highness would not now have one hair left in your beard!'[27]

Concerning the administration of Mírzá Áqá Khán, Sheil wrote on 22 February 1852:

Excepting the continuance of tranquillity throughout the Kingdom generally, there is little to report in favor of the Sedr Azim's administration. The machinery of Government set in motion by the late Prime Minister still works, but no one allows himself to believe in its endurance. The Sedr Azim appears to be unable to obtain any control over the Shah, or even to exert a proper degree of influence over his colleagues and the other officers of the Court. According to his own confidential statements, he is entirely devoid of power; his recommendations to the Shah are constantly thwarted by His Majesty's maternal relations, or even by the obscure officers of his household, and the Shah may be said to rule his Kingdom directly, in his own person. This offers a gloomy prospect for the future. Though there is no question of the intelligence of the Sedr Azim, he has not displayed the ability which was anticipated, and there is a general conviction that valuable as he was, as second in authority to the late Ameer Nizam, yet, that he does not possess capacity sufficient to undertake the charge and responsibility of First Minister. Nevertheless, no one is able to point out his successor. He has complained to me confidentially of his fears of severe financial embarrassments, and of the revenue not being equal to meet the expenditure. This he attributes to the Shah's personal extravagance, and to his propensity for wantonly augmenting the salaries of the persons who have access to his presence.

Some slight symptoms of disorganization have appeared in Tehran. Burglaries, from which even Her Majesty's Mission has not been exempt, are nightly perpetrated, and it is apprehended that these disorders will gradually extend to the highroads and remoter districts. It will serve to convey to your Lordship an idea of the unsettled state of men's minds, to mention that I lately received a formal letter from a Prince governing one of the Chief provinces of Persia, the whole purport of which was, that he had ceased to consider himself a subject of the Shah, and had transferred his allegiance and loyalty to England.[28]

Manúchihr Khán

Manúchihr Khán, Mu'tamadu'd-Dawlih (see fig. 18), was one of the most remarkable men of nineteenth-century Persia. Brought by Ághá Muḥammad Khán-i-Qájár from Tiflis to Iran, he was made a eunuch, converted to Islam and commenced work in the royal harem. His ability and intelligence were recognized, and he was given a succession of important and responsible positions. So great was the trust in which he was held that in 1828, when following the disastrous Russian campaigns, the Treaty of Turkumancháy was signed giving Russia an indemnity of 5 million túmáns, Manúchihr Khán was dispatched from Ṭihrán with the greater part of this money. In the same year he was given the title Mu'tamadu'd-Dawlih (The Trusted of the Government). On the death of Fatḥ-'Alí Sháh in 1834, while many wavered to see how matters would resolve themselves, Manúchihr Khán came immediately to the assistance of Muḥammad Sháh with money and troops. He proceeded to Ṭihrán with the Sháh and was sent against the southern rebels, Shujá'u's-Salṭanih and the Farmán-Farmá. In reward for his service he was made Governor of Kirmánsháh in 1836 and Governor of the important central province of Iṣfahán in 1838. He pacified this turbulent province and for the next nine years he maintained a severe but just rule over the area until his death on 21 February 1847. At his death he was one of the richest men in Persia.

In September 1846 the Báb left Shíráz after a period under house-arrest on the orders of Ḥusayn Khán, the Governor. At Iṣfahán, his reception was markedly different from the opposition shown by Ḥusayn Khán. Manúchihr Khán asked the Imám-Jum'ih, Siyyid Muḥammad (see p. 271n), to receive the Báb into his house. With an open-mindedness and fairness, characteristic of the Mu'tamadu'd-Dawlih but so uncommon among the leaders of nineteenth-century Persia, he listened to the Báb and was soon to be numbered as the most prominent of his adherents. The death of Manúchihr Khán marked the end of a period of tranquillity for the Báb and the commencement of imprisonment and opposition that was to lead to his martyrdom.

Sir Henry Layard met Manúchihr Khán in 1842 in Iṣfahán. Layard had reason to be inimical to the Governor of Isfahán, who had imprisoned his friend, the rebel Bakhtíyárí leader, Muḥammad-Taqí Khán. Layard describes Manúchihr Khán thus:

> . . . he was employed when young in the public service, and had by his remarkable abilities risen to the highest posts. He had for many years enjoyed the confidence and favour of the Shah. Considered the best administrator in the kingdom, he had been sent to govern the great province of Ispahan, which included in its limits the wild and lawless tribes of the Lurs and Bakhtiyari, generally in rebellion, and the semi-independent Arab population of the plains between the Luristan Mountains and the Euphrates. He was hated and feared for his cruelty, but it was generally admitted that he ruled justly, that he protected the weak from oppression by the strong, and that where he was able to enforce his authority life and property were secure. He was known for the ingenuity with which he had invented new forms of punishment and torture to strike terror into evildoers.[29]

As to the physical appearance of the Mu'tamadu'd-Dawlih, Layard wrote:

> The Matamet had the usual characteristics of the eunuch. He was beardless, had a smooth colourless face, with hanging cheeks and a weak, shrill, feminine voice. He was short, stout, and flabby, and his limbs were ungainly and slow of movement. His features, which were of the Georgian type, had a wearied and listless appearance, and were without expression or animation. He was dressed in the usual Persian costume – his tunic being of the finest cashmere – and he carried a jewel-handled curved dagger in the shawl folded round his waist. He received us courteously, said a few civil things about the English nation, . . .[30]

Two persons who benefited from and greatly praised the fairness of Manúchihr Khán were the missionaries Henry Stern (q.v.) and P. H. Sternschuss, who visited Iṣfahán in March 1846:

> *March 6* – Called upon Mohammed I. Dowlah,* the governor. His Excellency received us very kindly. Tea, coffee, fruit, and a great variety of sherbets were served up. We remained some time with his Excellency, and while partaking of his hospitality he asked us a variety of questions, such as the following:- he asked us whether Mohammed was foretold by Moses and the Prophets? Who was referred to in Deuteronomy xviii.15? The meaning of 'Eli, Eli, lama sabacthani?' and many other questions, which we explained and answered. He considered Deut. xviii.15,

* Mu'tamadu'd-Dawlih

more applicable to Mohammed than to Christ; and to support his opinion, he made use of two arguments. First, it says, 'From thy brethren,' which he thought must mean Ishmael, the brother of Isaac and the progenitor of Mohammed; and secondly, because it says, 'like unto me,' whereas Jesus was greater than Moses. But 'from the midst of thee,' as it is given in the text, would not allow of the first interpretation; and the loftier seat in heaven which Mohammed is supposed to occupy than that of Christ, would be detrimental to his second argument. He said he should be happy to converse with us on these subjects, when we could speak more fluently in Persian. We asked him, if the Jews would be subject to persecution, if they were to embrace Christianity? He replied, that no one would dare to molest them on that account. He told us that he intended to assemble the Jewish mullahs, that we might argue with them in his presence.[31]

These two missionaries wrote letters to their headquarters (Church's Ministry among the Jews, London) warmly praising the qualities of Manúchihr Khán and suggesting that the headquarters of their mission be transferred to Iṣfahán on this account. This was agreed to by their central committee, but their return to Iṣfahán the following year was not such a happy episode. They arrived a few days before the death of Manúchihr Khán and were witnesses to the upheaval that ensued once the firm rule of the Mu'tamadu'd-Dawlih had been removed:

It is our painful duty to inform you of the loss we have sustained in the death of Mehommed-i-Dowleh, Governor of Ispahan; he had been very kind to us on our first visit to this place, and we have sufficient cause to regret him as our friend and patron, although he was a Moslem. His death was occasioned by a severe cold. On Sunday last, the 21st instant, in the evening, he expired. He was Governor for nine years, during which time Ispahan enjoyed a tranquillity the like of which the present generation do not remember. Both Jews and Christians have reason to lament his death. The principal part of the population of this place, consist of a notoriously bad set of people; but, by his wise and energetic administration of justice, he subdued their ferocity. They have now taken up arms, and the honest part of the population, even Moslems, have just cause to be full of apprehension. The Christians have lost a great friend in the death of the excellent Governor; they had not enjoyed such a peace for several years, as they did under him.

We are not able at present to move out of our house, and we cannot even send a servant to town to procure the necessary articles of food. Armenians, whose business obliges them to go to town, return plundered and beaten. At night the inhabitants of Julfa are in constant expectation of an attack; some houses have been broken open and plundered, and we cannot tell to what extent these bad men will succeed in their outrages. Few Governors have been able to keep Ispahan in good order; and even, should a good Governor be appointed, it will take some time till peace is restored in this lawless country.[32]

Ḥusayn Khán

Ḥusayn Khán, the Ájúdán-Báshí, Niẓámu'd-Dawlih, was the first to arise in opposition to the Báb. As Governor of Shíráz, he caused the cruel punishment of a group of the Báb's followers that was reported in *The Times* (see

p. 69). Furthermore, he caused the Báb to be brought from Búshihr under arrest, and being displeased with one of the Báb's replies ordered him to be struck on the face by one of the attendants.

Layard relates the following about Ḥusayn Khán:

> I afterward found that Hussein Khan bore a very bad character. He was accused of having appropriated to his own use the pay allowances of several French Officers whom he had induced when at Paris, where he was also sent as ambassador, to enter the Shah's services for the purpose of instructing the Shah's troops . . . He charged the Government for the travelling expenses at a high rate, although he had compelled the inhabitants of the towns and villages through which he had passed to supply them gratuitously with both provisions and carriage. Finding himself greatly in debt on his return from his mission, through his extravagance during his journey in Europe and his residence in Paris and in London, and the superintendent of his estates not being able to furnish him with the money he required, he accused him of having embezzled it. He placed the unfortunate man in confinement and inflicted the most cruel tortures upon him, even compelling the son of the victim, a boy of only 6-years-old, to burn his father with hot irons, and giving his wife over to the 'Farrashes' or common servants. He died under the treatment to which he was subjected.[33]

When Muḥammad Sháh died in September 1848, Ḥusayn Khán, in his eagerness to curry favour with the new regime, put himself into debt in order to be one of the first to forward revenue to the capital. But it availed him nothing. For when at the instigation of Ḥáji Mírzá 'Alí-Akbar, Qavámu'l-Mulk (q.v.), and Muḥammad-Qulí Khán (Ílbágí of the Qashqá'ís), the people of Shíráz arose against him and besieged him in his palace, he received little support from the capital. Indeed, Mírzá Taqí Khán seems to have completely ignored Ḥusayn Khán's plight and merely appointed a new Governor instead. When the new Governor, Bahrám Mírzá,* arrived, the province was pacified, but this did not end Ḥusayn Khán's problems – as the following dispatch dated 30 January 1849 from Farrant shows:

> The Prince Governor Bahram Meerza accompanied by the Eelkhanee of Fars, had arrived in Shiraz, which at once had put at end [*sic*] to those scenes of anarchy and disorder which for some time past have reigned in that city. The late Governor Hoossein Khan (who throughout the difficulties in which he has been placed) appears to have behaved with much fortitude, had been well treated by the Prince, but the troops had made him their prisoner demanding their arrears of pay. His liabilities are enormous and unless the Government will assist him in realizing the revenues for the past year due to him, for which he has already accounted to the Government, his utter ruin must follow, in which that of many others will be involved. The Government is in justice bound to assist the Khan, for the greater portion of the monies due to him, was advanced to the late Prime Minister for the payment of the Troops, and other Government expenses, and which he borrowed at an enormous rate of interest.

* Uncle of Náṣiru'd-Dín Sháh.

But from some conversation I had with the Ameer it appeared to me, the Government intended to throw on Hoossein Khan all the unpaid Government bills which have been made payable on Fars, and to collect and appropriate the revenues due to him.[34]

Complete ruin followed for Ḥusayn Khán, and he spent the ensuing years penniless and friendless wandering about Persia trying to regain favour. Thus, when in 1851 Sheil attempted to intercede with the Persian Government on behalf of a British Indian subject* who was owed a great deal of money by Ḥusayn Khán, the British Consul in Tabríz reported that it was impossible to obtain the money from Ḥusayn Khán, who was completely bankrupt and extremely ill, while the Persian Government declined to accept liability for either the debts that he had incurred while Governor of Fárs or the promissory notes that he held from Ḥájí Mírzá Áqásí.[35]

Maḥmúd Khán, the Kalántar of Ṭihrán

Maḥmúd Khán was the Kalántar of Ṭihrán in the fateful year of 1852 when the attempt on the life of the Sháh was made. He played a prominent part in the arrest and execution of many innocent Bábís and is chiefly remembered for his association with the captivity and martyrdom of Ṭáhirih.

In 1860–61 a great famine gripped Ṭihrán. Eastwick describes in the following way the events leading to the death of the Kalántar:

The distress in Tehran was now culminating, and, the roads being almost impassable, supplies of corn could not reach the city. The bakers' shops were besieged by mobs clamouring for bread. As soon as a European showed himself in the streets he was surrounded by famishing women, supplicating assistance, who were not to be kept back by any scruples of their own, or remonstrances of the men. Matters were evidently growing very serious, and on the 1st of March, as Mr Alison and myself were sitting at Mr Dickson's examining the Nauroz presents for the servants, the chief Persian secretary came in, pale and trembling, and said there was an émeute, and that the Kalántar, or mayor of the city, had just been put to death, and that they were dragging his body stark naked through the bazars. Presently we heard a great tumult, and on going to the windows saw the streets filled with thousands of people, in a very excited state, surrounding the corpse, which was being dragged to the place of execution, where it was hung up by the heels, naked, for three days.

On inquiry we learned that on the 28th of February,† the Shah, on coming in from hunting, was surrounded by a mob of several thousand women, yelling for bread, who gutted the bakers' shops of their contents, under the very eyes of the king, and were so violent, that as soon as the Shah had entered the palace, he ordered the gates of the citadel to be shut.

Next day, the 1st of March, the disturbances were renewed, and, in spite of the gates being closed, thousands of women made their way into the citadel, and began to assail the guards with large stones, being urged on

* This was Ḥájí 'Abdu'l-Karím; full details of this case may be found in A. K. S. Lambton 'The Case of Ḥájjí 'Abd al-Karím', pp. 331–60.

† 1861

by their male relatives, who under cover of this attack, were looking out for an opportunity to effect a more serious rise. Meantime, the Shah had ascended the tower, from which Hajji Baba's Zainab was thrown, and was watching the rioters with a telescope. The Kalántar, who had been seen just before entering the palace, splendidly dressed, with a long retinue of servants, went up the tower and stood by the Shah, who reproached him for suffering such a tumult to have arisen. On this the Kalántar declared he would soon put down the riot, and going amongst the women with his servants, he himself struck several of them furiously with a large stick. One of the women so assailed ran as far as the English Mission, and came in calling out for help and showing her clothes covered with blood. On the women vociferously calling for justice, and showing their wounds, the Shah summoned the Kalántar, and said, 'If thou art thus cruel to my subjects before my eyes, what must be thy secret misdeeds!' Then turning to his attendants, the king said, – 'Bastinado him, and cut off his beard.' And again, while this sentence was being executed, the Shah uttered that terrible word, *Tanáb*! 'Strangle him.' In a moment the executioner had placed the cord round the unhappy man's neck, and in an instant more their feet were on his chest, trampling out the last signs of life. At the same time the Kadkhudas, or magistrates of all the quarters of Tehran were subjected to the bastinado, and at sight of these punishments, the frenzy of the populace was for that day appeased, and Tehran was saved by a hair's breadth from a revolution.[36]

Gobineau also relates the fate of the Kalántar in relation to the martyrdom of Ṭáhirih. This episode occurred about a year prior to Gobineau's second period of residence in Persia. After the news that she would be taken to Níyávarán on the following day had been delivered to Ṭáhirih, she predicted that this would in fact be the day of her martyrdom. Gobineau then writes:

'Do not hope', cried the Consolation of the Eyes* [addressing the Kalántar] in a more serious tone, 'that I will deny my faith, even to outward seeming, even for a moment and for a goal so foolish as that of preserving for a few days more a transitory form that has no value. No! if I am interrogated on this matter, and if it comes to it, I would gladly give my life for God. And you, Maḥmúd Khán, listen now to what I am going to say to you, and tomorrow my death will be a sign to you that I am not deceiving you. The master that you serve will not reward you for your zeal; on the contrary, you will perish cruelly by his orders. Strive then, before your death, to have elevated your soul to the knowledge of the truth.'

I have heard this prophecy recounted many times, and by Muslims as well as Bábís. No one has any doubt that she made it; and this is what did in fact happen later: four years ago, a terrible famine ravaged Ṭihrán. People were dying of hunger in the streets. The population, pushed to the limit by suffering, arose and came in a crowd to the citadel to obtain justice from the King . . . The King ordered the gates to be shut; then having learnt that the people were accusing, among others, the Kalántar, he summoned the latter to appear before him. It was absolutely necessary to find someone to blame. It is not that the official accused had committed any of the crimes for which he was denounced; he had only a few instances of misappropriation of public funds with which to reproach himself, so

* Qurratu'l-'Ayn, i.e. Ṭáhirih

that he hardly reproached himself at all, holding himself to be perfectly innocent, because he had, on this count, many fewer deeds on his conscience than did others greater than him. Nevertheless the King was angry, the tumult of people would take no more; the women were hammering on the gates of the citadel; their furious shouts could be heard. The King put on his red cloak, which is called *the cloak of anger*, and which he wears when he is going to order a punishment.

Maḥmúd Khán was led trembling before the Monarch. Instead of replying, he lost his head and stuttered. The King ordered his beard to be shaved off; the executioners threw themselves upon him; he struggled and gave a dreadful cry. The King, aroused, said 'strike him with sticks!' They hit him, and the King, aroused even more, said 'strangle him!' And they strangled him. Thus was fulfilled the prediction of Qurratu'l-'Ayn.[37]

References

1. Stuart *Journal of a Residence* p. 185
2. Farrant to Palmerston 4 Sept. 1848: FO 60 138
3. Enclosed in 2 *supra*
4. Báb, *Selections* p. 25
5. Shoghi Effendi *God Passes By* p. 164
6. Stuart *Journal of a Residence* p. 214
7. Flandin 'Souvenirs de Voyage: II' p. 989 (trans. from French)
8. Farrant to Palmerston, 31 Aug. 1848: FO 60 138
9. Layard *Early Adventures* Vol. 1, p. 257
10. Stuart *Journal of a Residence* p. 136
11. Sheil to Aberdeen 17 Mar. 1846: FO 248 124
12. Binning *Two Years' Travel* Vol. 2, p. 236
13. Ussher *London to Persepolis* p. 632
14. Curzon *Persia and the Persian Question* Vol. 1, pp. 394–5 and 397
15. Balloy to Hanotaux No. 18: MAE Sér. Corr. Polit. 2 May 1896 (trans. from French)
16. Ferrier 'Situation de la Perse' p. 141 (trans. from French)
17. Farrant to Palmerston 29 May 1849: FO 60 145
18. Sheil to Palmerston No. 14, 15 Dec. 1849: FO 60 146
19. Binning *Two Years' Travel* Vol. 2, p. 285
20. ibid. pp. 236–7
21. Watson, *History of Persia*, p. 364
22. ibid. p. 404
23. Enclosed in 25 *infra*
24. ibid.
25. Sheil to Palmerston 16 Jan. 1852: FO 60 169
26. Sheil to Palmerston 22 Oct. 1850: FO 60 153
27. Maxwell *The Honourable Sir Charles Murray* pp. 278–83
28. Sheil to Granville No. 20, 22 Feb. 1852: FO 60 169
29. Layard *Early Adventures* Vol. 1, p. 311
30. ibid.
31. *Jewish Intelligence* Aug. 1846, p. 299
32. Letter from Mr Sternschuss 24 Feb. 1847: *Jewish Intelligence* Aug. 1847, p. 294
33. Layard *Early Adventures* Vol. 1, p. 264

34. Farrant to Palmerston No. 6, 30 Jan. 1849: FO 60 144
35. Stevens to Sheil 10 July 1851: FO 248 145
36. Eastwick *Three Years' Residence in Persia* Vol. 1, pp. 287–90
37. Gobineau *Religions et Philosophies* pp. 263–4 (trans. from French)

Section C

The Ministry of Bahá'u'lláh

(1853–92)

TEN

Bahá'u'lláh in Baghdád (1853–63)

Bahá'u'lláh's involvement in the events following the attempt on the life of the Sháh in 1852 has already been noted. Imprisoned in the Síyáh-Chál in Ṭihrán for four months, he was then exiled and chose to go to Baghdád, where he arrived on 8 April 1853.

The Rev. H. A. Stern (q.v.), who lived in Baghdád from 1844 to 1850, describes the city from the European point of view:

From the plain, the town, surrounded by a strong kiln-burnt brick wall, fortified by several bastions, gives an imposing appearance; but, like every Eastern city, the delusion vanishes as you approach. When I looked upon Bagdad from our encampment, and saw the extensive date-tree groves, intersected by ranges of houses and blue glazed tapering minarets, it had a grand and imposing aspect; but, as the poet says, 'distance lends enchantment to the view;' for no sooner did I enter its narrow filthy streets, than the illusion vanished. In threading my way through its labyrinth of lanes and alleys, my eye met everywhere the disgusting and repugnant sight of naked, squalid children, and lazy, idle men; the former gambling and rolling in the dust of the unpaved streets, and the latter indolently smoking or sleeping, under a thatched shed which constitutes the coffee shops. The external appearance of the houses is not calculated to convey any favourable idea of internal comfort; a brick wall, intersticed with two or three apertures, covered with lattice work to admit light, is the uniform aspect of the dwellings, both of rich and poor. Only a few houses have windows projecting over the path, where one generally sees four or five Turks lounging on easy cushions, and whiffing their chibouks; or, should the master be away from home, the caged inmates of his harem may be seen timidly favouring the busy street with a propitious glance of their gleaming dark eyes.

The Bazaars are the most attractive and fascinating spots in all Eastern towns, but particularly so in Bagdad, where one sees people of all shades and grades, – from the walls of China to the shores of the Mediterranean, the haughty Turk, sedate Arab, rapacious Bedouin, ferocious Kurd, cheerful Persian, unhappy Jew, demure Christian, grave Hindoo, and grinning African . . .

According to the latest census, it counts within its wall, 40,000 Mahomedans, 1500 Christians, and 16,000 Jews. The latter, as a striking illustration of the decay of Moslem power, wealth, and industry, are the governing element of the place. They have their stored booths in every bazaar, occupy all the principal caravanseries with their merchandize, and entirely control the business of bankerage and monopolies. They are all strictly rabbinical Jews, superstitious, bigoted, and intolerant.[1]

John Ussher visited Baghdád in December 1860, at a time when Bahá'u'lláh was there. He describes the city thus:

> The desert comes up to the very walls of Baghdad. The town is entered by three gates; one of which, that on the eastern side, or side furthest from the river, is bricked up, in consequence of its being that by which Sultan Murad entered the city after he had captured it from the Persians. This custom of walling up a gate through which a great personage has passed on a memorable occasion, is very widespread in the East . . . The jackals come in troops to the foot of the walls at night, and feed on the garbage and filth that is thrown over, retreating to their holes and hiding-places during the day.
>
> On the bank of the river, a few hundred yards from the water, are melon and cucumber-gardens, well irrigated and cultivated; but the desert extends all around the back of the town. The other gates are shut from sunset to sunrise, and are always guarded by a small party of regular troops. In the present deplorable state of the government, the Bedoween plunder and foray, almost unchecked, up to the very walls of the town, and revenge upon the unhappy inhabitants the oppressions and exactions which they undergo at the hands of their Turkish rulers . . .
>
> The winters at Baghdad are sometimes very severe, and, although snow does not fall, there is often a smart frost, and the winds sweeping over the surface of the desert are bitterly cold. Captain Selby, the commander of the 'Comet', told us that he had seen the ice an inch thick on the paddle-boxes of his vessel, during the course of one winter rather more severe than usual. In summer the heat is intense, often rising to 140° Fahrenheit in the shade. When this is the case, the inhabitants sleep in the open air, upon the housetops, which are surrounded with walls of some feet in height for the sake of privacy.
>
> We had, from the top of a minaret which we ascended for the purpose, a fine view of both the modern and ancient towns, built respectively on the east and west banks of the river, and connected by the rotten bridge of boats. The older town existed before the time of Haroun al Raschid, who built the more recent city on the east or the left bank of the Tigris. It was also surrounded by high embattled walls and towers, beyond which suburbs seemed to extend for some distance. Graveyards occupied a large space within the walls, and there was also a large portion of ground lying waste and covered with heaps of rubbish and ruins . . .
>
> A number of date-trees grew within the walls of the city on both sides of the river, and gave a peculiar aspect to the scene, the delicate green of the palms contrasting with the snowy whiteness of the house-tops which they overshadowed. There were also many small gardens in which fig-trees, vines, and pomegranates were carefully cultivated, but, the season being so advanced, they looked bare and waste. The gilded cupolas of the great mosque of Kathimain, the burial-place of the two Imams of the Sheah sect of Moslems, Tukah and Moussa Kathim,* from the latter of whom it appears to take its name, glittered in the sunbeams, towering high over the surrounding date groves. The domes of some other mosques, none of which were of any great size or celebrity, were to be seen scattered through the town. The desert stretched away on all sides into the far distance, the sight losing itself in the boundless waste.[2]

When Ussher visited Baghdád in December 1860, the Governor was Muṣṭafá Núrí Páshá:

* Káẓimayn, the burial-place of Músá al-Káẓim and Muḥammad at-Taqí, the 7th and 9th Imáms respectively.

The dignitary who lived in this rather plain manner, divested of the state which is so dear to the mind of an Oriental, was a man of some fifty-five or sixty years, with an exceedingly sharp and cunning expression of countenance. He was surrounded by a few of his secretaries and employés, who seemed also to have all their wits about them. Yet this was a personage whose pashalic extended, in former days, from that of Diarbekir to the Persian Gulf, thus comprehending the ancient Assyria and Babylonia, and whose authority yet reached from the Zab to Bassora, and from the Persian frontier to the desert, as far as the Bedoween tribes find it convenient or beneficial for the moment to acknowledge it. The salary and allowances of this frugal individual equalled those of the Governor-General of India, not to mention the enormous sums which by the most oppressive means he wrung from the Arabs and villagers of the great province over which he ruled.

. . . This Pasha had most likely ere now returned to Constantinople with the spoils of his short tenure of office, which, if a portion only of the stories we afterwards heard of his exactions be correct, must have been enormous. His name is indifferent. Individual dignitaries of this description are remembered only by those who have suffered some act of spoliation more than usually severe. Pashas, as Captain Marryat remarks, are ephemeral beings, and, without particularizing any individual, it is in general enough to say with him of any member of a class so fleeting and evanescent, 'There was a Pasha.'[3]

Only two months after Ussher's departure, Muṣṭafá Núrí was dismissed from his post and, in May 1861, was put on trial for bribery and corruption. But it later came to light that these accusations had been the plottings of his enemies, and he was restored to favour. He left for Istanbul in September 1861.

During Bahá'u'lláh's sojourn in Baghdád, there were several people who intrigued against him. One of the most notable of these was Mírzá Buzurg Khán, the Persian Consul-General from July 1860 to February 1863. Shoghi Effendi described him as 'a man of mean intelligence, insincere, without foresight or honor, and a confirmed drunkard'.[4] Nor is Shoghi Effendi the only one to have a low opinion of him. When in July 1865 there was talk of re-appointing Mírzá Buzurg Khán as Persian Consul in Baghdád, Sir Henry Bulwer (q.v.), the British Minister at Istanbul, wrote to his colleague at Ṭihrán, Charles Alison (q.v.): 'He has already given us much trouble, and it would be in the interest of peace if you could obtain that some other person should be appointed in his place.'[5] And in another dispatch: 'I believe him to be a rogue, and . . . I know him to be a quarrelsome fellow.'[6]

Námiq Páshá (q.v.) was Governor of Baghdád at the end of Bahá'u'lláh's sojourn there. Shoghi Effendi states:

Námiq-Páshá, impressed by the many signs of esteem and veneration in which He [Bahá'u'lláh] was held, called upon Him to pay his personal tribute to One Who had already achieved so conspicuous a victory over the hearts and souls of those who had met Him. So profound was the respect the governor entertained for Him, Whom he regarded as one of the Lights of the Age, that it was not until the end of three months, during which he had received five successive commands from 'Álí Páshá, that he could bring himself to inform Bahá'u'lláh that it was the wish of the Turkish government that He should proceed to the capital.[7]

F. C. Webb, who visited Baghdád in March 1865, describes Námiq Páshá:

> One day we paid our respects to His Excellency Namik Pasha, the Governor of the Pashalic of Bagdad, who received us with great courtesy. On our taking our seats on divans which extended all round a very simply decorated room, His Excellency, plainly attired in a black closely-buttoned up coat with brass military buttons, soon joined us, and after shaking hands, took a seat on a divan near us, conversing in French in the most unostentatious manner . . .
>
> Namik Pasha appears, from all accounts, to be well liked by his subjects.[8]

There are not many contemporary references to the presence of Bahá'u'lláh and the Bábí community in Baghdád.* This was a turbulent and unsettled period in the history of the Bábí community. With a lack of effective leadership from its nominal leader, Mírzá Yaḥyá, the morals of the community declined and its unity was fragmented. Some of its more unruly members gave vent to the anger they felt towards the Shí'ih Persians who had persecuted the community so ruthlessly. Nor was Bahá'u'lláh, who had become the most influential member of the community, although not yet its formal head, always able to control these fractious elements, despite his stern disapproval of their actions.

Some of the incidents resulting from this unsettled state of the Bábí community were reported by the British Consul, Capt. Arnold Burrowes Kemball (q.v., see fig. 19). On 9 June 1858 he wrote:

> His Highness† had scarcely quitted Hilleh on his return to Baghdad when Yacoob Effendi, the Govr. of Kerbelah, presented himself in Camp to report that a conspiracy had been discovered there, which though ostensibly aiming at his own life alone, threatened a general revolution in the town for the subversion of Turkish Authority. The conspirators he said were 18 in number who had taken the most solemn oath of secrecy and cooperation, and so resolute had they proved themselves that the seizure of four of the ringleaders, (the rest having effected their escape to the Country) had cost the lives of three of the Govt. employés. The origin of this movement was not declared nor are its particulars yet sufficiently authenticated to entitle them to credit. By Omer Pasha, the agents are supposed to be persons of the sect called Babee, whose numbers in this Quarter and boldness are certainly on the increase, but the influence of these enthusiasts must be still too limited for an organized revolt and the comparatively large number of troops dispatched to Kerbelah would seem to

* Prof. H. Petermann was in Baghdád in 1854–5. In his book *Reisen in Orient* (Vol. 2, p. 282), he states that his native guide, Mullá Ṣádiq, had affirmed that there were 5,000 Bábís among the Muslims of Baghdád, [a greatly exaggerated number], who had fled there from Persia. Then, after referring to Ṭáhirih's activities in Baghdád, he writes: 'According to the Mullá's statement, . . . they have a few holy writings, and he himself has seen one such with them; they do not betray one another, do not tell lies, and teach that all their property should be held jointly in every respect.'

† The Governor of Baghdád, 'Umar Páshá.

indicate rather a general disaffection of the inhabitants occasioned by the Conscription than a mere outburst of fanaticism as the contingency to be guarded against.

Having had occasion to allude to the Babees I may mention that at Baghdad they are said to number from two to three thousand men,* and that their Chief is a certain Meerza Hassan Ali [Mírzá Ḥusayn-'Alí, i.e. Bahá'u'lláh], a relative of the Prime Minister of Persia.† A murder committed in broad day and in a crowded thoroughfare by some of these sectarians being Persians, upon the persons of two Dervishes also Persians, who had given umbrage to their Chief, was permitted to pass unpunished, owing to the unwillingness of the Pn. [Persian] Consul to prosecute and more than one instance is related of their threatening death to individuals who should denounce or thwart them.

The circumstances thus casually noticed have perhaps rather reference to a prospective than a present evil, though bearing in mind the proceedings of the Babees in Zenjan and at Teheran not many years ago, I have thought it right to prepare you for the embarrassments, which if unchecked, this sect may also sooner or later occasion to the Turkish Authorities in this Quarter.[9]

The murder referred to in the above dispatch is probably the murder of two renegade Bábís, Mírzá 'Alíy-i-Nayrízí and Mírzá Riḍáy-i-Iṣfahání who had deserted their companions and were acting in concert with the enemies of the Bábís.‡

A similar episode is reported by Kemball on 28 September 1859. This dispatch is of great interest because it confirms the reports by many of the early Bábís that Mírzá Yaḥyá kept himself strictly secluded, and that access to him was almost impossible even for the believers. It also highlights the great prestige and influence of Bahá'u'lláh, at a time when he had not yet claimed for himself any special station.

An incident has occurred at Baghdad which illustrates the growing power and influence of the sect of Bâb, a sect whose tenets though still not openly avowed have of late made great strides and are secretly professed by a considerable and not insignificant portion of the population of every large town in Persia.

A mulla of no note having publicly reviled Bâb in the Musjid was cautioned by the Chief of the Sect not to repeat the offence. This warning he thoughtlessly disregarded and on the second occasion his death was determined. The person selected to execute the decree also a Persian, a confectioner by trade, in broad day in the public bazaar attacked the mulla with a dagger and was only prevented from despatching him by the bystanders.§ Both parties were immediately taken before the local Authorities who transferred them to the custody of their national Representative, and to him the Bâbi so far from denying or extenuating his crime avowed his motives expressed his regret that he should have failed in his purpose and boldly declared his intention to effect it whenever the opportunity should offer.

For the second time under similar circumstances the Persian Consul hesitated to

* Bahá'í accounts state that there were about 50 Bábís in Baghdád at this time. See Balyuzi *Bahá'u'lláh, The King of Glory*, p. 143.

† Bahá'u'lláh was distantly related to Mírzá Aqá Khán-i-Núrí, the Persian Prime Minister at that time.

‡ See Balyuzi *Bahá'u'lláh, The King of Glory*, p. 128.

§ This may refer to the action of Mullá Báqir, a young Bábí who had attacked a companion of his, a young Shaykhí, when that person refused to desist from abusing the Báb and the Bábís. However, Mullá Báqir was not a confectioner as far as is known.

punish the murderer but sent him to Meerza Hassan Ali [Bahá'u'lláh] the Chief of the Babees, who of course declining to commit himself by openly acknowledging the man returned him to the Persian Consul to be dealt with as the latter might think proper. He was simply released as soon as the precaution had been taken to deport his intended victim to Persia and thither he has since followed him.

Meerza Hassan Ali though the ostensible agent is not the real representative of Bâb, his brother Meerza Yahya who lies perdu and the secret of whose whereabouts is mysteriously preserved being recognized by the Babis as the second incarnation of the looked for Imaum* of whom the first was represented by the person of the original founder of the sect killed at Tabriz, yet this individual [i.e. Bahá'u'lláh] enjoys a consideration which partakes of absolute devotion and reverence on the part of his followers numbering it seems in Turkish Arabia from 4,000 to 5,000 souls. He receives from Persia large contributions in money, which however he in his turn liberally dispenses and he is recognized as the Director and Guide of the Babees of that country with whom he maintains a constant correspondence. Your Excellency may remember that some years ago the life of the King of Persia was attempted by the Babees. My observations lead me to believe that the subversion of the Kajjar Dynasty is still the main object of their ambition, and that that attempt will sooner or later be repeated.[10]

Shoghi Effendi states that the Bábís while in Ba<u>gh</u>dád were forced by circumstances to change their citizenship.[11] Indirect evidence of this may be found in the files of the Public Record Office. Shortly after Bahá'u'lláh's departure from Ba<u>gh</u>dád, the Persian Consul-General, Muḥammad-Zamán <u>Kh</u>án, addressed a complaint to Námiq Pá<u>sh</u>á. Kemball relates this matter in a dispatch dated 15 July 1863:

The Persian Consul General having solicited my intervention against the practice adopted by Namik Pasha, of granting Turkish Tezkerehs, a sort of letters of naturalization, to Persian subjects settled or resident in this Province, without previous reference to himself, I have considered that the issues contingent thereon are too complicated to warrant my taking, of my own authority, any official action in the matter.

The facts are these – Mahomed Zeman Khan adduces a Vizirial letter dated 10th Zilkaadeh 1279, which instructs His Excellency Namik Pasha, whenever a Persian subject, who for the purposes of this discussion may be regarded as an immigrant, shall desire to transfer his allegiance to the Sultan, to suspend compliance with his application, until it shall have been ascertained from the Persian Consulate whether any claim exists against the applicant, or whether the applicant be under the ban of a criminal or civil judgment of the Persian Consul; and he complains that His Excellency reverses the prescribed order of procedure by first granting a Tezkereh to the Persian subject, and afterwards, when announcing the fact to the Persian Consul, inviting him to declare any claim or complaint that he may have to make against the applicant.

The terms of the Vizirial Instruction are as usual ill defined. Their interpretation of the same is justified by the Persians on the ground that none but Babis, criminals and fraudulent debtors would seek to divest themselves of their nationality, whence the necessity of obtaining the previous sanction

* This is an exaggeration of Mírzá Yaḥyá's position in the Bábí community. At most, he was regarded as a figurehead pending the advent of 'Him Whom God shall make manifest'. Even then, his authority was contested by a number of Bábís who set forth claims of their own.

of their Consular Authority; and by the Turks, that the real motive of Persian subjects in seeking Turkish protection, being to escape Consular extortion and oppression, often attended with corporal punishment and even torture, it would obviously defeat their object to impose the condition of Consular sanction before that protection had been secured.

My own experience prompts me to ascribe the greater weight to the Turkish argument, though instances may not be wanting to illustrate the Persian view.[12]

In a note written in the margin of this dispatch, Kemball added: 'Apart from the unscrupulousness of the Persian Authorities in inventing charges against intending applicants for Turkish protection, in order to justify their punishment or deportation, the Pasha refers also to the obligations of the Porte towards political refugees such as Babees. His Excy. also lays much stress upon the analogy afforded by Tartar Emigrants from the Crimea; but in their case at least, the consent of the Russian Govt. must be assumed.'[13]

Bahá'u'lláh's departure from Baghdád was noted by Kemball in a dispatch dated 6 May 1863:

The only other matter worthy of report to Your Excellency on this occasion is the departure of Meerza Hassan-Ali, the ostensible head of the Babee sect to Constantinople. His presence at Baghdad had long given umbrage to the Persian Government, and his removal has at length, Namik Pasha informs me, been conceded by the Porte to the demands of the Shah. The Babees however are said to be still numerous in Persia and even at Teheran, and their brethren here affect to believe that this act of the Shah will provoke their revenge in the form of another attempt upon the life of His Majesty.[14]*

According to several Bahá'í sources, Arnold Burrowes Kemball called on Bahá'u'lláh and offered him British citizenship and protection.[15] It may seem surprising at first that there is no reference to this in Kemball's official reports; however it is quite clear from reading Kemball's private letters to Sir Austen Layard,[16] who was at this time Parliamentary Under-Secretary of State for Foreign Affairs and later British Ambassador at Istanbul, that Kemball conducted a great deal of his official business through private letters rather than official dispatches, and reference to his contact with Bahá'u'lláh may well have been in such a letter addressed to Bulwer.

References

1. Stern *Dawnings of Light in the East* pp. 35–6 and 46–7
2. Ussher *London to Persepolis* pp. 449–51
3. ibid. p. 443
4. Shoghi Effendi *God Passes By* p. 142

* The basis of this statement is probably the fact that, during the Baghdád period, Mírzá Yaḥya was still concocting plans for the assassination of Náṣiri'd-Dín Sháh, and went as far as to send one of the Bábís to Írán for this purpose. (See Shoghi Effendi *God Passes By* p. 124.)

5. Bulwer to Alison 6 July 1865: FO 248 229
6. Bulwer to Alison 26 Aug. 1865: FO 248 229
7. Shoghi Effendi *God Passes By* p. 131
8. Webb *Up the Tigris to Bagdad* pp. 36 and 38
9. Kemball to Bulwer No. 28, 9 June 1858: FO 195 577
10. Kemball to Bulwer No. 51, 28 Sept 1859: FO 195 624
11. Shoghi Effendi *God Passes By* p. 146
12. Kemball to Bulwer No. 24, 15 July 1863: FO 195 752
13. ibid.
14. Kemball to Bulwer, 6 May 1863: FO 195 752
15. Shoghi Effendi *God Passes By* p. 131. Browne *Materials* p. 11
16. British Museum, Layard Papers, Add. 38994–5, Add. 39013–21, Add. 39105–13

ELEVEN

Bahá'u'lláh in Adrianople (1863–8)

From Baghdád, Bahá'u'lláh and his companions proceeded overland to Sámsún where they boarded a steamer bound for Istanbul. Bahá'u'lláh was in Istanbul for almost four months, and at the end of that time Sulṭán 'Abdu'l-'Azíz, in concert with his Prime Minister, 'Álí Páshá (q.v.), and his Foreign Minister, Fu'ád Páshá (q.v.), decreed that he be exiled to Adrianople (Edirne).

A nineteenth-century description of Adrianople is as follows:

> Near the northern extremity of this unattractive plain, at the confluence of Maritza and Tunja, lies the city of Adrianople, enveloped in trees, whose sight delights the eye of the weary traveller. Adrianople, in reality, consists of a number of villages, separated from each other by orchards, poplars, and cypresses, above which peep out the minarets of some hundred and fifty mosques. The sparkling waters of the Maritza and Tunja, of rivulets and of aqueducts, lend animation to the picture, and render Adrianople one of the most delightful places. But it is more than this. It is the great centre of population in the interior of Turkey [in Europe], and its favourable geographical position has always secured to the city a certain amount of importance. The ancient city of Urestis, the capital of the Kings of Thracea, stood on this site, and was succeeded by the Hadrianopolis of the Romans, which the Turks changed into Edirneh, and made their capital until Constantinople fell into their power . . . But here, likewise, the Osmanli [Ottomans] are in a minority. The Greeks are their equals in numbers whilst the Bulgarians, too, muster strongly, and, as in other towns of the East, we meet with a strange mixture of races, from Persian merchants down to gipsy musicians. The Jews are proportionately more numerous in Adrianople than in any other town of Turkey.[1]

Bahá'u'lláh's sojourn in Adrianople was marked by a number of very important events. These include the open proclamation by Bahá'u'lláh of his mission, the acceptance by the majority of the Bábís of his claim, the open rupture between him and Mírzá Yaḥyá, Ṣubḥ-i-Azal, and the writing of some of his letters to the kings. But it was not until towards the end of this period that Bahá'u'lláh and his companions came into contact with Europeans.

Gobineau and Prokesch-Osten

Some particularly interesting references to Bahá'u'lláh occur in the correspondence between Gobineau (q.v., see fig. 3) and Count von Prokesch-Osten (q.v., see fig. 21), the Austrian Ambassador at Constantinople. Gobineau and Prokesch had first met at Frankfurt when the former was First Secretary of the French Legation at Frankfurt and the latter was there as the Austrian delegate and President of the Assembly of German States. They formed a close association and their correspondence continued over almost 20 years. When Gobineau published his *Religions et Philosophies dans l'Asie Centrale*, he sent a copy of it to Prokesch. On 29 December 1865, Prokesch wrote that he was now at chapter 7 of the book and reading about Bábism, of which he had not heard before.[2] In his next letter, dated 5 January 1866, Prokesch states:

> I am at page 336 of your book in the middle of the doctrine of the Bábís and on the point of becoming a Bábí myself. Everything is fascinating in the story of this historical and humanitarian phenomenon, even to the fact of Europe's ignorance on a matter of such colossal importance. And I myself, the dignified representative of Europe, in this respect, do not know the first thing about it. It is from you that I have learnt of it.
>
> Since there does not exist a human intelligence which can tell us something about God, and the difference between the various theodicies* consists only in greater or lesser absurdities, one must agree that the Bábí theory has a particular charm, something endearing and noble which is pleasing to the soul and invites belief in its self-sufficiency. The creation of the world by the emanation of God is an Indian idea, but the explanation of evil, by the sole fact of the remoteness of the emanated being from its source, is completely new and seems to me more dignified, more exalted than what has been said by any of the founders of religion or philosophy. It follows logically that on the return of the emanation to its source, the evil ceases of itself and becomes nothing, without any necessity for its annihilation or for preserving it through monstrous, unfair and disgusting punishments in a hell or kingdom of the devil. The co-existence of Ormuzd and Ahriman, of good and evil as equal principles, so incompatible with the idea of God, is turned by Bábism in a manner both new and successful. Also, the doctrine regarding the prophets pleases me infinitely, because it is conciliatory and completely excludes all fanaticism. It is at the same time very bold and no more absurd than any other. I expect more discord as soon as Bábism seeks to apply itself to the political world, to the organization of society and of its own hierarchy. It will plunge itself into the mire, I suppose, like all other doctrines. I will find out more this evening, reading before I go to bed.[3]

Prokesch's next letter, dated 10 January 1866, is the first to mention the presence of Bahá'u'lláh at Adrianople:

> I was mistaken in expecting that the Báb would entertain us with a hierarchy *ad usum delphini*,† and attempt to apply his doctrine to political society. I was charmed to have

* Theodicy – the vindication of divine providence in view of the existence of evil.

† For the use of the Dauphin, i.e. expurgated.

found nothing of that, but rather humane and paternal counsels that do it honour . . .

'Álí Pás͟há has spoken to me with great veneration of the Báb, interned at Adrianople, who he says is a man of great distinction, exemplary conduct, great moderation, and a most dignified figure. He has spoken to me of Bábism as a doctrine which is worthy of high esteem, and which destroys certain anomalies that Islam has taken from Jewish and Christian doctrines, for example this conflict between a God who is omnipotent and yet powerless against the principle of evil; eternal punishments, etc. etc. But politically he considers Bábism unacceptable as much in Persia as in Turkey, because it only allows legal sovereignty in the Imamate, while the Osmanlis [Ottomans] for example, he claims, separate temporal from spiritual power. The Báb, at Adrianople, is defrayed of all expenses by the order of and to the charge of the Persian government.[4]

In his next letter, Prokesch discusses a few theological points that arose from his reading of the poor translation of the Arabic *Bayán* that forms the appendix to Gobineau's book, but then discussion of this subject ceases in their published correspondence for over two years, until the time of Bahá'u'lláh's exile from Adrianople to 'Akká. (see pp. 207–9).

Rev. Rosenberg's Intervention

It was not until the time when the Imperial decree for Bahá'u'lláh's removal from Adrianople was published that the various Europeans in that town began to take a more marked interest in Bahá'u'lláh.

At this point, however, there are very serious historical difficulties and discrepancies which the editor has not been able to explain. Shoghi Effendi, in *God Passes By*, writes an account of this period based on the narratives of Áqá Ḥusayn-i-Ás͟hc͟hí and Áqá Riḍáy-i-S͟hírází, who were eyewitnesses to these events, as well as statements by Bahá'u'lláh himself. Concerning the intervention of the foreign consuls in Adrianople he writes: 'Some of the consuls of foreign powers called on Bahá'u'lláh, and expressed their readiness to intervene with their respective governments on His behalf – suggestions for which He expressed appreciation, but which He firmly declined. "*The consuls of that city* (Adrianople) *gathered in the presence of this Youth at the hour of His departure*," He Himself has written, "*and expressed their desire to aid Him. They, verily, evinced towards Us manifest affection*".'[5]

The accounts preserved in the Public Record Office of the United Kingdom and other places, whether through misunderstandings or for other reasons, give a somewhat different picture. On 5 August 1868, Rev. L. Rosenberg (q.v., see fig. 22), a Protestant missionary in Adrianople, wrote a letter to Mr J. E. Blunt (q.v.), the British Consul there, giving an account of an interview that he had had that morning:

This morning, as I told you in company with Boghos Agha, two of our protestant native christians called upon me bringing a message from the chief of the Babee sect that

I should call on him,* and accordingly I went along with the Head of the protestant community of this town and other two parties.

Our visit to him took us more than four hours!

Schiech Merza Hosain Ali Effendi [i.e. Bahá'u'lláh] aged forty seven years, a native of Teheran in Persia, and chief of the Babee sect, unfolded to us the whole of his history during the last twenty five years; and all the misfortunes which happened to him and to a great number of his sect.

The name Babee has two meanings with this people: first, it is the name of the founder of their sect; and secondly it means a door towards the truth, and on the latter account they call themselves Babees, and number one third of the moslems in Persia.

It is their principle not to interfere in politics; and strictly speaking with the Gospel truth in their mouth, they say that every authority derived its power from God, and therefore a man should render unto Caesar what belongs to Caesar, and to God what is due to God.

The foundation of their religion is the word of God as contained in the old and new Testaments as essential to salvation; and they also admit certain portions of the Koran on the ground that they are taken from the word of God. They object to call themselves Christians for the reasons: First because the most of them are not learned; secondly the impression they got of Eastern Christianity is enough to check them from professing the truth of real christianity,† they therefore prefer to have no name until the whole nation be converted in fact to protestantism. On account of this principle they suffered persecution seven years in Persia; and with the consent of the Persian Authorities Schiech Merza gave up his rights as a Persian subject; and settled down at Bagdad as an Ottoman subject, and was recognized as such by the Sublime Porte with a monthly allowance of 5000 piasters.‡ After 12 years residence in Bagdad by order of the Sublime Porte he was removed to Constantinople and after four years§ residence in Constantinople he was exiled to Adrianople where he has lived now six years. As a peaceful subject of the Ottoman Authorities he feels grieved that three of his men have been imprisoned in Constantinople‖ and he himself and forty others await exile in two days to some unknown place in the interior.¶ All this he suspects is caused by the Persian Authorities and it is purely a religious persecution, as he is not conscious of the least political offence with the liberty of conscience granted by the late Sultan to all his subjects taken into consideration.

For the sake of truth and humanity and the friendly relations which exist between Her Majesty's Government and the Sublime Porte he begged me to appeal to you as Her Majesty's Vice Consul to exert your influence in his behalf in order to put a stop

* According to the account which Rosenberg gave to the Evangelical Alliance (see p. 194), it was his two fellow Christians who asked him to call on Bahá'u'lláh.

† See the different account of this conversation given to the Evangelical Alliance (p. 195).

‡ This figure represents the sum of the monthly allowances payable to each member of Bahá'u'lláh's family and those exiled with him.

§ Rosenberg is mistaken here; the period was four months in Istanbul.

‖ The three men who are referred to may be Mírzá 'Alíy-i-Marághi'í (known as Sayyáḥ), the famous Mishkín-Qalam and Áqá Jamshíd-i-Gurjí who were then residing in Istanbul and were arrested; or three others, Darvísh Ṣidq-'Alí, Áqá Muḥammad-Báqir-i-Maḥallátí and Ustád Muḥammad-'Alíy-i-Salmání who had set out from Adrianople to sell some horses for Bahá'u'lláh and were arrested upon their arrival in Istanbul. Áqá 'Abdu'l-Ghaffár was also arrested. Of Mírzá Yaḥyá's supporters, Siyyid Muḥammad-i-Iṣfahání and Áqá Ján Big were arrested. Some of the Turkish government documents relating to these arrests and the subsequent interrogations are detailed in an addendum to this chapter.

¶ It had not at this time been decided where the exiles were to be sent.

to any further exile and that he may be allowed to remain and exercise the liberty of conscience granted by the Sultan; and I beg you to represent the case to Her Britannic Majesty's Ambassador who I hope through the Blessing of the Almighty will succeed in obtaining the liberty of these our fellow men.[6]

Blunt forwarded Rosenberg's letter to Mr H. Elliot (q.v.), the British Ambassador at Istanbul, with the following dispatch dated 6 August 1868:

I have the Honor to transmit herewith inclosed to Your Excellency the copy of a letter which the Reverend Mr Rosenberg Protestant missionary at this place has addressed to me respecting a certain Shek [Shaykh] Mirza Hussein Ali Effendi, chief of a Persian sect called 'Babee' who with a party of 40 of his adherents has been undergoing exile at Adrianople during the last six years, and is about to be deported to Gallipoli and thence to the interior of Africa – I believe.

Yesterday before this letter was addressed to me the Reverend Mr Rosenberg and Boghos Agha, chief of the native protestant community called on me and requested me to endeavour to persuade the local Ottoman Authorities not to deport from here this Shek and his adherents, but as they also told me that the measure complained of by the Shek has not originated with these Authorities but that it is the result of an imperative order addressed to them by the Sublime Porte, I respectfully declined to comply with their request.

Mr Rosenberg then said that he should address to me the letter I have inclosed; and expressed the hope that I would report the subject to Your Excellency.

I do not know what the tenets of this 'Babee' sect are. The Reverend Mr Rosenberg and Boghos Agha believe that they are adopted from the Holy Scripture; and this belief has naturally excited their sympathy and zeal on behalf of the Shek.

All I can say is that the Shek in question has led a most exemplary life in this city; that he is regarded with sympathy, mingled with respect and esteem, by the native Mahomedans and has received good treatment at the hands of the Ottoman Authorities; and that the general impression here is that the persecution he is now made the object originates with the Persian Government and its Legation at Constantinople.[7]

On 10 August 1868, Blunt telegrammed to Elliot, and in a dispatch of the same date he relates the circumstances that led to the dispatch of this telegram:

With reference to my dispatch No. 54 of the 6th Instant relative to the case of Shek Hussein Ali Effendi chief of the Persian Sect called "Babee" I have the Honor to further report to Your Excellency that I received this morning from the Shek in question the inclosed paper written in Turkish in which he appeals for protection to this Consulate. A similar appeal has been addressed by the Shek to my colleagues in this City.

Shortly after the appeal in question was put in my hands my Austrian Colleague called on me and asked me what I proposed doing in the matter. I replied that in my humble opinion it was not a case in which I could in any way officially interfere on the spot without instructions from the Embassy; and that I had already reported the subject to Your Excellency. Monsieur de Camerloher appeared to be entirely of the same opinion and told me that he had also submitted the case to Baron Prokech.

But as Monsieur de Camerloher has strong reasons to think that the Shek and his party are about to be delivered by the Ottoman Government into the power of the

Persian Authorities; and that by so doing the Ottoman Government will be guilty of a breach of faith towards this unfortunate people, dangerous to their lives and at the same time hurtful to its credit, we agreed to address to our respective Embassies the Telegram we dispatched this morning and of which the following is a copy:

'Hussein Ali Effendi with Seventy others will be sent today to Gallipoli there to be made over to an Agent of the Shah. He has addressed a written appeal for protection to Foreign Consular Corps. Undersigned decided to solicit instructions from their respective Embassies before acting. My colleague begs present may be communicated to Baron Prokech'.

I beg leave also to add that my Austrian Colleague told me that Baron Prokech is personally acquainted with the Shek and wrote to the Austrian Consulate here very strongly on his behalf.

I regret that the early departure of todays mail leaves me no time to prepare a translation of the paper I have inclosed herein.[8]

This letter indicates that Baron Prokesch-Osten had been taking a deep interest in the Bábís since reading Gobineau's book (see above). Unfortunately, the enclosure referred to in this dispatch, the one allegedly from Bahá'u'lláh, is missing from the files of the Public Record Office. As Blunt states, however, that a similar message was sent to other foreign consuls in Adrianople, a search was made in the French Foreign Office Archives and the following dispatch was found from F. Ronzevalle (q.v.), Acting French Vice-Consul in Adrianople, to Monsieur Bourée (q.v.), the French Ambassador in Istanbul, dated 14 August 1868:

I have the honour to transmit to your Excellency the enclosed note with its translation, sent by one named Ḥusayn-'Alí, originally from Persia. This man has been here for about four years with fifty of his fellow-countrymen living on the fruits of their labour, when suddenly, a fortnight ago, the local authorities had their belongings sold at public auctions and notified them of orders to leave the country. It is from Constantinople that our Governor-General has received the instructions which have made him impose these measures, and he himself does not know the reason [for them].

It is claimed that Ḥusayn-'Alí and his people are sectaries of a doctrine contrary to the Muslim religion, and this is why they had been exiled six years ago by the government of the Sháh of Persia. They were resident some time in Baghdád, and without ever having disturbed public order, at the request of Persia, they were removed from the Turko-Persian frontier and sent to Adrianople. Ḥusayn-'Alí and his disciples left here on the 11th of this month for Gallipoli, escorted by several *zaptís*,* and without knowing their destination. It is believed that they will be interned in the countries of Africa.

The foreign agents resident in Adrianople have received copies of this petition, with the exception of the Russian Consul who is charged with the protection of Persian subjects. These strong measures by the local authorities have caused a bad impression in the town, and particularly among those persons who come seeking refuge in Turkey.[9]

The accompanying letter, allegedly from Bahá'u'lláh, has survived in the French Archives, unlike its counterpart in the British Archives. But it

* policemen (*ḍábiṭí*)

presents some serious problems of identification, for neither the handwriting nor the signature 'Ḥusayn-'Alí' is in the handwriting of Bahá'u'lláh or one of his amanuenses.* Because of this and the previously-noted Bahá'í accounts of this period, there must be considerable doubt as to whether this document is indeed from Bahá'u'lláh.†

The Enquiries of European Ambassadors in Istanbul

Thus there were at least three ambassadors in Istanbul making enquiries of the Ottoman Government concerning Bahá'u'lláh: the British, Austrian and French Ambassadors. They all met with the same answer, a refusal by the Ottoman authorities to reconsider their decision.

When Blunt's dispatch of 10 August 1868 was received in Istanbul, Elliot sent Étienne Pisani (q.v.), First Dragoman of the Embassy, to the Grand Vazír, 'Álí Pá<u>sh</u>á, to make enquiries. Pisani reported back on 12 August:

> Aali Pasha told me that the Babees who have been apprehended in the Vilayat of Adrianople are to be exiled, some to Cyprus and the remainder to St Jean d'Acre.
>
> These people, observed His Highness, are disturbing public peace by trying to spread their religious doctrines all over the world. Their religion is a new one and unknown. Each Babee considers himself as a Prophet, nay more, as God.
>
> Although their apparent object is to subvert the principles and dogma of the Mussulman faith, yet there are indications which make one believe that some political views are involved in their scheme. Under these circumstances, said the Grand Vizir, the Porte cannot tolerate their presence in the Sultan's dominions, and without treating them with rigour as they do in Persia, they are merely banished to some remote place.[10]

On 13 August, Elliot telegrammed to Blunt, 'Your telegram received yesterday – you must not interefere.'[11] On the same day, Elliot wrote to Blunt in the following terms:

> I entirely approve of your having declined to take any step with regard to them without referring to H.M. Embassy.
>
> It appears that these people have endeavoured to excite the sympathy of the Christians by causing it to be believed that their new doctrines are a step towards Christianity, for which there is not, as far as I am aware, the slightest foundation.
>
> However repugnant anything resembling religious persecution must always be, this does not seem a case in which I can properly interfere, as I am assured that the efforts of the Babees to make proselytes is exciting an ill feeling among the Mussulman population which might lead to inconvenience if allowed to go on.
>
> The Babees, having inaugurated their

* This opinion has been confirmed by the Research Department at the Bahá'í World Centre, Haifa (letter dated 17 Feb. 1975). See also Preface, xvi, pt. 2.

† Similarly there exist in the collection of the papers of Gobineau held at the University of Strasburg, five or more letters purporting to be from Bahá'u'lláh. Once again, the handwriting is not that of Bahá'u'lláh or any of his amanuenses, and the style and content of the letters are not compatible with the alleged authorship.

secession from Mahometanism with an attempt to assassinate the Shah of Persia, are looked upon with much jealousy in that Country, but I have no reason to believe the present measure with regard to those of Adrianople to have been adopted at the suggestion of the Persian Government.[12]

Ronzevalle received much the same reply from Bourée: 'The measures taken towards those individuals being purely an internal affair and furthermore, touching on religious matters, I would stipulate complete abstention [from interference].'[13]

While in a dispatch dated 15 August, Blunt recorded the efforts that Baron Prokesch-Osten had been making:

I also beg leave to inform Your Excellency that my Austrian Colleague has read to me a Dispatch dated the 12th Instant which he received yesterday morning from Baron Prokech in which His Excellency states that on representing to Fuad Pasha the intolerant acts of the Ottoman Government towards the Babee Sect, he was informed by His Highness that the Porte had ordered Mirza Hussein Ali and his adherents to be deported to Tripoli in Africa on account of their having tried to propagate religious dissensions in the Mahomedan Element in Roumelia; that the Porte was entirely responsible for this measure, the Persian Legation having taken no part in it; and that the subvention of 5000 piasters per month which was allowed to the Mirza by the Authorities at Adrianople would not be discontinued at Tripoli.

Baron Prokech also informs my Colleague that he has acted in concert with Your Excellency in this matter.[14]

Documents from the Ottoman State Archives appear to indicate that the principal cause of Bahá'u'lláh's further exile was the actions of some of his followers at Istanbul, and the accusations and counter-accusations between the Bahá'í and Azalí factions. These resulted in the arrest of several Bahá'ís and Azalís in Istanbul and the convening of a Commission of Inquiry. It was this Commission which recommended Bahá'u'lláh's further exile. An account of these Turkish documents will be found as an addendum to this chapter.*

Rev. Edwin E. Bliss (q.v.), an American missionary of the American Board of Commissioners for Foreign Missions, resident in Istanbul, wrote an account in the *Missionary Herald* of May 1869, in which he seems to imply that the main initiative in asking for the intervention of foreign ambassadors came from the Christians of Adrianople:

The Adrianople colony, increased by subsequent arrivals, after being allowed to remain there in peace for six years, was last summer suddenly broken up by the Turkish Government (again evidently at Persian instigation); the poor men were compelled to sell all their property at great loss, were put under arrest, and sent off to Acre, on the

* It should be noted that Bahá'u'lláh himself attributes some of the responsibility for his further exile to 'Akká to the activities of Mírzá Ḥusayn K͟hán, Mus͟híru'd-Dawlih (q.v.). (See p. 196 of the present work and Bahá'u'lláh, *Epistle to the Son of the Wolf*, p. 69.)

Syrian coast, where, it is said, many of them are now in prison, and otherwise subjected to very cruel treatment.

The very quiet and honest conduct of these people at Adrianople, their apparent acquaintance with the doctrines of the Bible, and their professed acceptance of these doctrines, made a very favourable impression on their Christian acquaintances there; so that when it was known that they were to be sent into another exile, an effort was made to prevent, through the intervention of the foreign ambassadors here, what seemed a great outrage upon an unoffending people. But the reputation that Babism had acquired of being a secret political movement prevented that effort from being pushed as it might otherwise have been, and nothing was accomplished.[15]

Bahá'u'lláh's Departure

On 13 August, Blunt reported to Elliot:

I beg leave to report that I have acted in this business in conformity with Your Excellency's order.

Before I received this order Mirza Hussein Ali who I am told is a relative of the Shah of Persia,* requested me through the Revd. Mr Rosenburg to call on him, but I respectfully declined doing so, as he was confined to his house and vigilantly watched by the police . . .

The Mirza and his adherents were sent from here to Gallipoli on Monday Evening last; and it now transpires that they will not be delivered to the Persian Authorities, but are to be confined in a fortress in the Island of Cyprus.[16]

In the dispatch of Blunt dated 15 August referred to above, there is also the following statement regarding the Bahá'ís:

The Babees during their residence at Adrianople have done nothing that I know of to warrant the suspicion, much less the conviction, of the Porte that they were occupied in fomenting religious dissensions in Roumelia. They may have been indirectly engaged in the propagation of their tenets in *Persia*, but during the Six years they remained in this City they led a very retired life; mixed up very little with the Mahomedan element; and appear to have studiously avoided doing anything which might create the suspicion that they abused the hospitality accorded to them by the Porte.

With reference to their alleged illtreatment by the authorities of Adrianople, I have every reason to believe that the Governor General and most of the members of the local administration regarded their Chief Mirza Hussein Ali with respect and consideration; and that till the order to deport them reached this place they were not subjected to persecution.

The Defterdar who is acting as Governor General during the absence of Hourschid Pasha, and who received the above order, displayed, from all I am told, unnecessary haste and much harshness and severity in carrying it out, to a degree which excited the sympathy and compassion of all classes of the population.[17]

This was not however the end of Rev. Rosenberg's efforts. On 15 August 1868 he addressed a letter to Blunt, enclosing a petition that he had addressed to the Evangelical Alliance in London. This society specialized in

* This is probably a confusion caused by the fact that Bahá'u'lláh was a relation of Mírzá Áqá Khán-i-Núrí, the former Prime Minister.

combating persecution of Christians in every part of the world. Rosenberg hoped to obtain their assistance on behalf of Bahá'u'lláh. In this petition he writes of Bahá'u'lláh as 'a God fearing man and one who has sacrificed everything already, and is ready even to lay down his life for the honour of God and for the truth.'[18] He goes on:

The circumstances which led me to make his acquaintance are most singular, also most painful and providential, proving that God is indeed always a present help to his people though there be none to help, but the whole world against them.

Several days ago the Authorities apprehended all the Persians here and obliged them to sell their businesses and their furniture at great losses, some they imprisoned, and the houses of others were guarded on all sides by police until they were ready for deportation.

Their exemplary and godly lives during six years residence in this town and the inhuman treatment they received roused the sympathies of all Christians.

Two of our bretheren who had sold them many copies of the Scriptures asked me to visit their chief, and during the visit I found out that he is the Apostle of the Babee sect.

The word Babee means etymologically a *Door*.* The founders of this sect, and their followers took this appellation because they found '*the door to the truth*'.

The names of the founders of this Sect are Mirza Hussein Ali Ishan and Mohammed Ali.† The former is a descendant of the Royal family of Persia and therefore he bears the title of Ishan. In 1849 his father was grand Vizier in Persia, and if I be not mistaken he is related to the present Shah.‡

I asked the Ishan whether he knew who I was as he manifested a spirit of reserve on account of spies. His son§ said 'yes, more than two years ago I was sitting with a number of Beys in one of their houses when a Jew came telling us that a protestant missionary had come to convert the Jews to protestantism. He further told us that he had been seeing the missionary and told him that if he would give him money he would turn a protestant. All the Turks burst into laughter. I told the Jew your faith is in money which is very wrong why did not you ask him to prove to you from your own scriptures that Jesus is the Messiah? It is very wrong for a man to put faith in money. Upon the Jew answering that there is no proof in scripture I asked him "why then does the prophet Isaiah say 'a Virgin shall conceive and bear a son and his name shall be called Immanuel'?"

'He replied that he would ask the Rabbi about this and bring me an answer.'

The means which God employed to lead the Chiefs of the Babee sect to find the truth were the inconsistencies of the doctrines of the molas in reference to the contents of the Koran, the inconsistencies of the Koran itself, and the direct testimony which the false prophet gave to the old and new testaments of their being the word of God, and hence they betook themselves to the study of the Scriptures.

Having received the word of God as the rule of faith and practice, and as a test of all other religious books and religions as far back as 25 years, Mirza Hussein Ali Ishan and Mohammed Ali began to preach in Iran before the Shah of Persia to all the moslems, and during seven years they bore the 'cross of the gospel' under heavy persecutions till at last Mohammed Ali was apprehended, tied to a tree and 750 soldiers discharged their guns at him; thus he fell a martyr

* Of course 'Báb' means 'door' and 'Bábí' means 'follower of the Báb'.

† Siyyid 'Alí-Muḥammad, the Báb.

‡ See note on p. 193n.

§ Almost certainly 'Abdu'l-Bahá, since Bahá'u'lláh's other sons were mere children at this time.

to the truth by the order of the Persian Government.

Mirza Hussein Ali Ishan on the other hand was allowed to take up his residence at Bagdad as a Persian subject.

About three millions of moslems have been converted through the instrumentality of the preaching of these two men, of the doctrines of 'repentance towards God, faith in the Lord Jesus, and the new birth by the Holy spirit', and through God's help, the Ishan told me, he has been the means of breaking down the middle wall that separated the Moslems from the professors of other religions (the former having looked upon the Christians and others as unclean, neither touching their hands nor anything from their hands) by inculcating the principle of love towards one another as a duty which humanity requires, and which the Gospel so much insists upon.

As to the Babee sect, he said ' my people are taught to follow the injunction of the Saviour "if any one strike you on one cheek turn to him the other also" hence you find among them many widows, orphans and widowers, their husbands, parents and wives having fallen martyrs for the truth without the least retaliation, the more the persecution continued the more their faith was strengthened.' In one instance he said, when a wife lost her husband, she went preaching among the people and became the instrument of converting forty individuals.

For some time the Babee sect were not separated, but now they have in every town and village their own place of worship with their teachers though in many other respects they mix with their moslem bretheren. They even go to their mosques if allowed to preach and to do them spiritual good.

After visiting the chief four successive days, along with two protestant bretheren, each visit occupying at least four hours, and having gained each other's confidence and Christian fellowship I asked whether as believers in Christ they observe the sacraments of baptism and the Lord's supper. He said 'No, we have to do with an ignorant set and fanatical people, if we were to do this they would think we wish to introduce the Christianity of the East, which they consider as idolatrous and thus we would put a stop to the progress of the truth among our people. The Lord Jesus says that "no man can enter the kingdom of heaven, except he be born again of the spirit", and "he that believeth not is condemned." To be born again and to believe and lead a holy life are most essential to salvation, and these we inculcate upon our converts, and upon all. When we educate one we give him a copy of the Scriptures to read for himself, and leave all other injunctions till the nation be converted for them to settle.'

I also found out that since that [*sic*] their persecutions they, to a great extent, have adopted the practice of the primitive Christians of having part of their goods in common in order to help one another especially the needy.

He further communicated to me the following facts.

In Bagdad he lived for twelve years as a Persian subject, but through the invitation of the Sublime Porte promising protection and liberty with a monthly allowance of 5000 piasters he and many of his co-religionists became Ottoman subjects as he had full confidence that what was promised to him would be fulfilled. Three months had scarcely passed after his having become an Ottoman subject, when the Authorities at Constantinople exiled him with forty others to Constantinople – there they were kept four months and again exiled to Adrianople where they have resided for the last six years. The Ishan thought this would be the last place and the end of his deportation, but six months ago he received information that a number of his followers in Egypt had been deprived of their properties and exiled to somewhere in Abyssinia in a most merciless manner.* In Bagdad one of them had been

* See p. 257.

stabbed by a Persian,* and his own property there to the value of nearly £50.000 had been confiscated, his stepmother and others of his family left to be a disgrace, and about thirty of his flock banished somewhere among the blacks in Africa. His letters and money sent to him from Bagdad were intercepted by the authority of the Sublime Porte. He sent, some time ago seven men with horses to be sold in Constantinople, the horses were taken from the men, and they imprisoned, and last of all his deportation from here to an unknown place, some say somewhere in Africa, others say to be handed over to the Persian Authorities to be executed has been signalized to him.

The Authorities here obliged them to sell their furniture for almost nothing, forty of them were put under arrest, and the Ishan's house was watched by soldiers in all directions that no one might run away.

In short the treatment they received here was such as to induce some of them to ask the Authorities here to kill them at once, which would be preferable. One of these poor people actually cut his throat with a razor† when he was asked why he did such a deed he replied he could not see the disgrace which befell his Ishan.

The Ishan says that he could not account for anything on his part to cause this persecution.

He has a certificate from the Persian Government, and one from the Governor of Bagdad that he had nothing to do with politics, and that he lived at peace with all men, and as to his conduct during his six years residence here, not one single charge has been brought against him before the Authorities. He accounts for it as a political and religious persecution. The Persian Government instigated by Russia, look for an occasion to go to war with Turkey; and have made him and his people the cause of offence. The Turkish Authorities wishing to avoid words, and to please the Persian Government have subjected them to inhuman treatment. As to his opinion of a religious persecution he received information from his men at Constantinople that they were brought before the Shek-ul-islam and were asked whether the Ishan had gained the favor of half of the moslem people in Adrianople, after this came the order that he and Seventy others to be found here should be exiled.

The chief of our protestant Community and myself reported their case to J. E. Blunt Esq. Her Majesty's Vice Consul. He took a statement of their case from me, with a very kind letter from himself and sent them to His Excellency the Ambassador at Constantinople. We also reported their case to Mr Camerloher, Austrian Consul, who also telegraphed to his Ambassador to take permission from the Turkish Authorities to stop their departure for a few days. The same Evening he went to converse with the Ishan, and the following day he dispatched by post a very affecting account of their unjust deportation, and asking His Excellency to use his influence in their behalf.

The following day the Ishan presented a protest against the unjust treatment to the British, Austrian, French, American, Prussian and Hellenic Consuls to be transmitted to their respective Authorities.

On Monday the 10th Instant Messrs Blunt and Camerloher had a consultation, as it was reported that a Persian Agent was waiting at Gallipoli to receive the exiles. They again telegraphed to their respective Embassies desiring to do their best.

Our Consul told me that if they would declare themselves Protestants he would detain their departure. I reported that to the Ishan, but he said that he would not do it on any account as it hinders the progress of the Gospel among his people in Persia. If it be God's will that he should suffer death for the truth's sake he is both willing and ready by suffering in the body to glorify God.

* See ch. 16.

† Ḥájí Ja'far, see pp. 198 and 205.

Our Consuls did their best, and deserve thanks for their trouble and the efforts they made in behalf of these poor Exiles.

On the 10th Instant at one o'clock about twenty waggons carried off seventy of them. All of them before leaving shook hands with us and said 'We hope to meet you in Heaven should it please God that we do not meet again on Earth.'

The protestant Community and I myself am of opinion that this is [not?] a political, but especially a religious persecution. If political why are all the Babees everywhere, in Persia and in Turkey persecuted, and suffer exile both in Turkey and Egypt?

What reason has the Shek-ul-islam to inquire as to how many of the moslems in this town have become friends of the Ishan. Most of our moslem inhabitants already say that the Authorities have exiled these people because they abjured their faith in the Koran for that of protestantism. This case alone strikes terror into the heart of every inquiring moslem into the claims of Christianity and doubtless it will check the work of Evangelizing the Turks.

When a Christian is converted the Turkish Authorities manifest a spirit of indifference but when a moslem shews a desire of embracing the truth then we see how they persecute, and even exile the inquirers as at the time of Sir Henry Bulwer, so now in the case of the poor Babees.

We cannot believe that this is a political persecution on the ground that the Turkish Authorities fully protected the Hungarian and Polish refugees, when the Austrian Government insisted that they should be delivered up to their respective Governments.

My Lords, and Gentlemen; In unity with the Revd J. N. Ball,* American missionary and all the protestants in this town, I submit to your earnest consideration the case of the exiled Babees and the case of those in Persia, praying for the sake of the cause of the Gospel and humanity, that God may make you the honoured instruments in his hand of working out salvation for these people and may bless your efforts and persons.

I am, my Lords and Gentlemen,
Your Most Obedient Servant,
Signed – L. Rosenberg.

P.S. The Ishan very much requested that great caution should be observed in making use of these statements as it might hinder the progress of true religion among his Persian bretheren.

Revd L. Rosenberg.
British Missionary at Adrianople.[19]

There are not, unfortunately, sufficient records kept by the Evangelical Alliance to enable one to ascertain what action if any was taken upon this petition.

There is one further report of the Bahá'is at Adrianople. This account appeared in the Parisian periodical *Revue des Deux Mondes* in 1871, and is by Albert Dumont (q.v.), a French scholar, who chanced to be in Adrianople a few weeks after the departure of Bahá'u'lláh and his companions. From the townspeople and from Ḥájí Ja'far, who had cut his throat and was left behind until it healed, he learned something of the new religion:

Persians are not rare in Adrianople; they have the reputation of being very clever merchants; the Turks, who do not like them, and from whom they differ much in their vivacity of character and high spirits, accuse them of lack of good faith. The town had until the month of August 1868 a colony [of them] who had come from Ṭihrán. These

* Missionary of the American Board of Commissioners for Foreign Missions.

were the *Bábís*, followers of the *Báb*, an innovator who tried to found some years ago in the Empire of the Sháh a religion in which both Europe and the Orient would be equally engrossed. After a long and bloody persecution in which the sectaries of the Báb showed no weakness, but, by the courage with which they sought and accepted martyrdom, renewed scenes which we believed to have disappeared from history, the authorities, who had put a great number of them to death, and among these their chief, took the decision to exile the others. Turkey, which is never on friendly terms with the Court of Persia, willingly gave asylum to this persecuted people; it assigned to them for their residence Adrianople and some of the villages of Rumelia; the brother of the *Báb* was interned in the capital of the Vilâyat [i.e. Adrianople]. The life of the exiles was a perpetual subject of edification. Scarcely were they installed than each of them took up an occupation – it is a principle of their faith that each man must work – and they appeared to live as the other Muslims, with this single difference that they never ceased to give an example of charity and gentleness. They attended regularly the public prayers in the mosques. However, they did not renounce their beliefs, each one of them was a prophet and an apostle. When a Turk would come to buy tobacco at the shop of a Bábí, the shopkeeper would speak to him of salvation, of the reform of souls, and of virtue; he would do it in a familiar tone and with that facility characteristic of his race, not without mixing into his discourse metaphors and parables. If the listener was interested in the conversation, the Bábí would touch on some of the points particular to the new doctrine. This apostolate which is both for the people and completely personal, and is carried out in the bazaars, while mending shoes or weaving mats, is essentially Oriental. It is interesting to rediscover in our day the actions and habits which we can scarcely understand when we see them in ancient records, in particular in the *Acts of the Apostles*. The Bábís made converts; this was enough to frighten the Porte; the Válí knew nothing of this religion, he cared even less; the Legate of Caesar was hardly any more interested in the religious ideas that could be found at the bottom of the quarrels of the Jews in Jerusalem, [but] neither the Roman Governor nor the Turkish Governor like such disturbances; the Válí cut short the propaganda. The Bábís received orders to make preparations to leave, without their even being told where they were going to be taken; the brother of the Báb gathered them together and spoke to them of these fresh ordeals: 'His small flock', he said, 'does not need to be troubled, since it has remained united during these early days of exile; everyone can with justice be said to have been good, charitable and worthy of the holy memory of that martyred leader whom they venerate. Only one will remain in Adrianople, and not partake of the journey that has been imposed upon them; he is not to blame, but by marrying a Turkish woman he has lost the confidence of his brothers.' This unfortunate man, who helped in [composing] this discourse, returned home in despair and cut his own throat:* a surprising fact, if one remembers that suicide is almost unknown among Orientals. In 1868 the Bábís were transported, I was told, to Cyprus; perhaps they must soon leave that island as they left Adrianople.[20]

Addendum

The following documents are to be found in File No. 1475 among miscellaneous files in the Ottoman State Archives. (Some details of these documents were given by Muḥammad-'Alí Muvaḥḥid – see Bibliography.) The

* This must refer to Ḥájí Ja'far-i-Tabrízí, who cut his own throat because he believed he had been left out of the party accompanying Bahá'u'lláh. He rejoined them when his wounds had healed (see p. 205).

papers are given as numbered in the file – they are not, as will be observed, in chronological order:

No. 4: The Sublime Porte, having received the letter of the Válí of Edirne (No. 9), and its enclosures, refers the letter and the whole file to the Police (Security) Department. Dated 20 Dhi'l-Ḥijjih 1284 (14 April 1868). There is a note appended to this document stating that although the Válí of Edirne reports that he has found no cause to complain about the conduct of the exiles, the enclosures indicate that both Mírzá Ḥusayn-'Alí (Bahá'u'lláh) and Mírzá Yaḥyá are claiming a station for themselves, and this may become the cause of disorder among the people of Islam. The signature to this note is unreadable. Dated 5 Muḥarram 1285 (28 April 1868).

No. 6: The report of the Commission investigating the Edirne Exiles. An account is given of their interrogation of various persons and their conclusions are that Mírzá Ḥusayn-'Alí is claiming that he is the Mahdí and that he reveals verses by Divine Inspiration, and that Mírzá Yaḥyá claims prophethood. These claims are liable to foment disorder among Muslim peoples and therefore, according to article 28 of the Criminal Law, they are liable to perpetual banishment and imprisonment. There are four seals appended to the report that are unreadable. Dated 26 Ṣafar 1285 (18 June 1868).

No. 9: Letter of Válí of Edirne forwarding Bahá'u'lláh's letter and explaining that Siyyid Muḥammad-i-Iṣfahání was a partisan of Mírzá Yaḥyá, and that Bahá'u'lláh had good reason to complain of the activities of these two.

No. 10: Having received the report of the Investigating Commission (No. 6), the Sublime Porte refers the matter to Sulṭán 'Abdu'l-'Azíz with the recommendation that Bahá'u'lláh be exiled to 'Akká and imprisoned there, and Mírzá Yaḥyá to Famagusta in Cyprus. Any of their followers whether in Baghdád or Edirne should, if they refuse to recant, be similarly exiled. Date difficult to read but probably 19 Rabí'u'l-Avval 1285 (11 July 1868). Appended is a note giving the Sulṭán's approval for these measures. Date difficult to read but probably 20 Rabí'u'l-Avval (12 July).

No. 11: Interrogation of Mírzá 'Alíy-i-Sayyáḥ. Dated 6 Dhi'l-Ḥijjih 1284 (31 March 1868).

No. 12: Letter of Bahá'u'lláh to Válí of Edirne.

No. 13: List of 10 followers of Mírzá Yaḥyá (Ṣubḥ-i-Azal).

No. 19: Interrogation of Áqá Ján Big. Dated 7 Dhi'l-Ḥijjih 1284 (l April 1868).

No. 20: Interrogation of Mírzá Muḥammad-Báqir. 13 Dhi'l-Ḥijjih 1284 (7 April 1868).

No. 24: Interrogation of Darvísh 'Alí. 13 Dhi'l-Ḥijjih 1284 (7 April 1868).

No. 26: Some writings of Ṣubḥ-i-Azal, some of them in the form of a circle, stating that great events would occur and the promised one be manifested in the year A.H. 1285.

No. 28: Interrogation of Mírzá Muḥammad-'Alíy-i-Iṣfahání. Dated 13 Dhi'l-Ḥijjih 1284 (7 April 1868).

No. 30: Interrogation of Mírzá Muḥammad-Báqir for the second time. Dated 13 Dhi'l-Ḥijjih 1284 (7 April 1868).

Also in this file are the following papers:

A statement bearing the seal Ḥusayn-'Alí [Bahá'u'lláh] giving the numbers of persons who accompanied him from Baghdád. These are stated to be 54 persons: Bahá'u'lláh's two brothers, 12 ladies, 11 children (one of whom died leaving 10), 20 servants and 10 muleteers.

A large bundle of letters and other writings of Bahá'u'lláh taken when Bahá'u'lláh's followers were arrested at Istanbul.

A list of writings sent to the Investigating Commission, consisting of 54 items. These were sent to Fatúḥí Amín Effendi (Shaykhu'l-Islám?) on 9 Ṣafar 1285 (1 June 1868), read and returned the same day.

References

1. Reclus *The Universal Geography* Vol. 1, p. 106
2. C. S. de Gobineau *Correspondance* pp. 284–5
3. ibid. pp. 286–7 (trans. from French)
4. ibid. pp. 288–9 (trans. from French)
5. Shoghi Effendi *God Passes By* p. 180
6. Rosenberg to Blunt 5 Aug. 1868. Enclosed in 7 *infra*
7. Blunt to Elliot No. 54, 6 Aug. 1868: FO 195 901
8. Blunt to Elliot. No. 55, 10 Aug. 1868: FO 195 901
9. Ronzevalle to Bourée No. 52, 14 Aug. 1868: MAE Corr. Polit., Consulat d'Adrinople (trans. from French)
10. Pisani to Elliot No. 172, 12 Aug. 1868: FO 195 913
11. Quoted in 16 *infra*
12. Elliot to Blunt No. 8, 13 Aug. 1868: FO 195 914
13. Bourée to Ronzevalle No. 76, 20 Aug. 1868: MAE Corr. Polit., Consulat d'Adrinople (trans. from French)
14. Blunt to Elliot No. 59, 15 Aug. 1868: FO 195 901
15. Bliss 'Bab and Babism' p. 147
16. Blunt to Elliot No. 56, 13 Aug. 1868: FO 195 901
17. As for 14 *supra*
18. Petition from Rosenberg to Committee of the Evangelical Alliance 13 Aug. 1868. Enclosed in 14 *supra*
19. ibid.
20. Dumont 'Souvenirs de la Roumélie. II' pp. 834–5 (trans. from French)

TWELVE

Bahá'u'lláh in 'Akká (1868–92)

As a result of Sulṭán 'Abdu'l-'Azíz's decree, Bahá'u'lláh reached the Bay of Haifa by ship on 31 August 1868. He and his family and companions disembarked at Haifa and were carried across the bay to 'Akká in a boat. Thus began the last stage of Bahá'u'lláh's exile. He was to live in the vicinity of 'Akká for almost twenty-four years until his passing in 1892.

The City of 'Akká[1]

The city of 'Akká to which Bahá'u'lláh came was a city in decline. It had been, in the Middle Ages, the celebrated capital of one of the Crusader Kingdoms, and it was the last Crusader stronghold in Palestine to fall to the Mameluke armies (1291). From that time, 'Akká was in a state of decline until the mid-eighteenth century when an Arab bedouin Shaykh, Ẓáhiru'l-'Umár, captured 'Akká and made it the capital of a small province that he had carved out for himself in northern Palestine. Ẓáhir pacified the province, and rebuilt and refortified the city. Ẓáhir's downfall came about as a result of allying himself with an Egyptian rebel, 'Alí Bey. A combined Syrian-Lebanese force with Ottoman naval assistance besieged 'Akká, which eventually fell through betrayal in 1775.

Ẓáhir's successor was Aḥmad al-Jazzár, a Bosnian and a former slave who had been one of the commanders in the besieging forces. Although made Governor of Sidon, al-Jazzár preferred to establish himself at 'Akká. He is chiefly remembered for his severity and cruelty, but he was also a very capable Governor, bringing peace and prosperity to the whole of the area he controlled. This area was gradually increased until by the 1780s he was effectively ruler over almost all of the Eastern Mediterranean littoral. Syria, Lebanon and Palestine had all effectively come under his control, and the affairs of such cities as Damascus, Beirut and Jerusalem were being directed from 'Akká. With his increasing power and wealth, al-Jazzár sought to make 'Akká a worthy capital for his empire. He strengthened the fortifications of the city and built or enlarged many of the mosques, public baths and caravanserais that survive to the present day. Water was brought to the city by an aqueduct from the al-Kabrí springs.

'Akká came to the attention of the world when in 1799 it was besieged by Napoleon Bonaparte. Napoleon was unable to take the town and this, together with the diseases that ravaged his army, put an end to his plan for emulating the feat of Alexander the Great and marching to India. Al-Jazzár died in 1804 and under his successor, Sulaymán Pás͟há, 'Akká continued to prosper, particularly through the efforts of Sulaymán's able minister, a Jew named Ḥa'ím Fárk͟hí. Sulaymán Pás͟há died in 1818 and was succeeded by 'Abdu'lláh Pás͟há.* During the first part of the latter's governorship there was a continuation of the peace and prosperity that had characterized his predecessor's period of government. Soon, however, trouble loomed from the south. Muḥammad-'Alí Pás͟há of Egypt was determined to carve out an empire for himself, and on a trumped-up pretext he sent an army under his son Ibráhím Pás͟há to besiege 'Akká. After a prolonged siege, and having received almost no help at all from the Ottoman Government, 'Akká fell on 27 May 1832 and Ibráhím Pás͟há swept on, taking Damascus without a fight and defeating the Sulṭán's army at Hums. Ibráhím Pás͟há inflicted a further crushing defeat on the Sulṭán when he routed an army superior in numbers and equipment sent against him in 1839. But Britain was reluctant to sit idly by and watch the dismemberment of the Ottoman Empire. With Austria, she came to Turkey's aid. The critical engagement of the campaign was once again at 'Akká. The British fleet bombarded the city on 3 November 1840. At four o'clock the citadel's powder magazine blew up, killing, it is said, 2,000 people. The Egyptians retired that night and the besiegers took the city the next day. This defeat sealed the fate of Ibráhím Pás͟há's army. He retreated to Egypt and Muḥammad-'Alí Pás͟há gave up his dreams of an Arab empire.

The British bombardment in 1840 marked the end of a golden age for 'Akká. Thereafter, the city declined in importance both politically and commercially. From being the capital of a large province, the seat of a Válí, it fell to being but a satellite town to Damascus and Beirut, the centre of a Sanjak, the seat of a Mutaṣarrif.† Its population fell from 40,000 at its peak under Al-Jazzár to 9,800 in 1886 and 6,420 in 1922. As a further sign of its decline, the various foreign powers that had maintained Consuls at 'Akká

* Two of the buildings constructed by this Pás͟há were intimately connected with the history of the Bahá'í Faith. His country mansion at Mazra'ih, four miles north of 'Akká, was Bahá'u'lláh's first residence outside 'Akká, where he remained for two years. 'Abdu'lláh Pás͟há's palace in 'Akká was rented by 'Abdu'l-Bahá shortly after the passing of Bahá'u'lláh, and Shoghi Effendi was born there.

† The Turkish Empire was divided into a number of provinces, Viláyats (Pás͟háliks), each in the charge of a Válí. These Viláyats were further subdivided into Sanjaks, each in the charge of a Mutaṣarrif. The Sanjaks were divided into Qaḍás, each in charge of a Qá'im-Maqám. The smallest subdivision was that of a Náḥiya, which usually consisted of a cluster of villages in the charge of a Mudír. This system was not uniformly applied throughout the Empire.

now withdrew them one by one until by the time of Bahá'u'lláh's arrival not one remained, and the foreign powers were represented by native Consular Agents*. Most of 'Akká's trade, moreover, was taken over by the growing town of Haifa.

By the time of Bahá'u'lláh's arrival, 'Akká had sunk into decay and insignificance. Conditions within the town had deteriorated as its importance had declined.† When it was suggested that a missionary of the Church Missionary Society should take up residence in 'Akká in 1876, Rev. J. Huber (q.v.), while not exactly refusing to go, demonstrated in his letters his marked distaste for the town. 'On the whole,' he wrote, 'it is well known that the people of Acca are a very bad set of people and all the sins and vices of a sea-town are practised in the same; for there are many Greeks and Europeans who teach the natives all the bad things which are done in their countries.'[2]

At this time, 'Akká's principal function was to act as prison for criminals and political prisoners from every part of the Ottoman Empire.‡ Charles Hamilton, who visited 'Akká in 1873, wrote 'Acre abuts, as it were, into the sea; and crossing a portcullis we went through a very heavy gateway guarded by troops, for be it remembered that the worst criminals are sent here from all parts of Syria.'[3] It was as one of these prisoners that Bahá'u'lláh arrived in 1868 and was locked up in the citadel. Prisoners who came to 'Akká were usually committed there for life, but that was not expected to be for very long in the appalling conditions there. This fact is strikingly demonstrated by the fate of 86 Bulgarian political prisoners who arrived in 'Akká in January 1878. Since Turkish atrocities in Bulgaria in the years 1876–7 had aroused considerable sympathy and concern in England, the British Consul in Beirut was asked to extend every possible help to these prisoners, and the British Consular Agent in 'Akká, Mr Finzi,§ was similarly instructed. As a result of these interventions, temporary medical and hospital facilities were made available to these prisoners at the Greek convent – a privilege which the other prisoners certainly did not enjoy. And

* A report by Eldridge, the British Consul at Beirut in 1867, stated that the old English merchant houses that used to trade through 'Akká and the other Syrian coastal ports had all ceased trading – hence the abolition of the various consular establishments (FO 78 1990).

† Ida Pfeiffer, who visited 'Akká in 1842, described the streets and interiors of the houses as being 'choked up with rubbish' (*Visit to the Holy Land* p. 162).

‡ Rev. J. Neil, whose account of 'Abdu'l-Bahá may be found on p. 213, wrote: 'Acca is used as the place of incarceration for all Turkish political prisoners through the East.' (*Jewish Intelligence* Dec. 1872, p. 299)

§ Mr Moses d'Abraham Finzi, an Italian Jew, had been British Consular Agent in 'Akká since May 1837, when the British Vice-Consulate in 'Akká had been closed. He was now an old man and was replaced the following year by Dr Schmidt of the German Templar Colony in Haifa (see p. 224n).

yet, despite this and the fact that there was no particular epidemic raging at the time, less than a month after their arrival in 'Akká the British Consul in Beirut, Eldridge (q.v.), reported, on 4 February 1878: 'Notwithstanding the care and attention shown towards the Bulgarian prisoners at Acre, six more of them have died in the temporary hospital at the Greek convent, so that out of the original 76 only 51 now remain, showing a mortality of one third of their number within a month.'[4]

Haifa began the nineteenth century as a small insignificant town. Ẓáhiru'l-'Umár had strengthened its fortifications and improved its harbour facilities, and this marked the turning point in its fortunes. From that time on the city flourished, and as 'Akká was slowly declining, across the bay Haifa was expanding and enlarging. This process was accelerated by the arrival of the Templar Colonists, a German Adventist sect, in the same year as Bahá'u'lláh's arrival, 1868. Soon the plain to the west of the walled town of Haifa, where the Templars had built their houses, was flourishing as a result of their labours.

When Col. Trotter, the British Consul in Beirut, toured Syria in May 1891, he submitted the following report on Haifa and 'Akká:

Haifa. We arrived at Haifa in Her Majesty's Ship 'Melita' on the 13th May. The Kaimakam Ahmed Shukri Effendi sent officials on board to welcome us and was afterwards civil to us on shore.

The most striking object at Haifa is the German Colony which lies to the South of the town, stretching along the plain between the base of Carmel and the sea. The township which consists of about 60 houses and 400 inhabitants is regularly laid out in two long parallel streets – each house having its garden and outbuildings and in traversing it one imagines oneself to be in the heart of Germany. German signboards, waggons, drivers, costumes, everything thoroughly national. To the South of the township is a large fertile plain about two miles in length and one in width every part of which is well cultivated and the whole presenting a most flourishing appearance, highly creditable to the hard working colony which is composed entirely of the sect of the Temple, emigrants from Wurtemberg. There are three other similar colonies in Palestine, viz: at Jaffa, Savona [Sarona] and Jerusalem (Refai [Rephaim]) numbering in all about 2000 souls.

Although the Haifa colony has been established in Syria more than twenty years they keep entirely to themselves – and do not mix or intermarry with their Syrian neighbours. The fact that a German man-of-war (the 'Loreley' from Constantinople) was at Haifa during our visit with the object of registering the adults of the colony for military service – and that German sailors were parading the streets – almost completed the illusion that one was in a small flourishing German sea-port.

St Jean d'Acre. From Haifa we went across the bay to St Jean d'Acre (Akka) where we landed and exchanged visits with the Governor Sadik Pasha, a brother of the Grand Vizier. His Excellency kindly sent an officer to accompany me around the extensive but ancient fortifications which, although I believe Akka is considered a first class fortress, is practically in the state it was left in after the bombardment by the British Fleet in 1840 – many traces of which are still visible. Old smooth bore guns still lie dismounted on the massive ramparts, and the only modern guns it possesses are eight 9 centimetres Breach Loading Krupp Guns quite recently received from Constantinople. Its present garrison consists of about 300 Artillery men.

As the fiction of its being a strong fortress is still kept up, no one is allowed to build outside the ramparts and the place looks melancholy and deserted offering a strong contrast to the flourishing, prosperous and rapidly increasing town of Haifa on the opposite side of the Bay.

At both places great interest was naturally taken in the projected line of Railway to Damascus – the concession for which was recently given to Mr Pilling an Englishman.

The projected line is from St Jean d'Acre to Damascus (about 120 miles) with a branch from Mejdel to Haifa (10 miles) and other branch lines . . .[5]

Bahá'u'lláh's Arrival in 'Akká

Bahá'u'lláh's arrival in 'Akká on 31 August 1868 marked the beginning of a period when Bahá'u'lláh himself was to withdraw from contact with the outside world to a large extent – a fact commented on, usually unfavourably, by several of the accounts to be referred to in the ensuing pages. Although this was to a certain extent Bahá'u'lláh's own decision and wish, it was also what the Imperial decree banishing Bahá'u'lláh to 'Akká had ordained – that he was not to be allowed to have contact with the populace. From this time on, he tended to meet only the Bahá'ís who were resident in 'Akká or had made the arduous journey from Persia. One of the results of this virtual isolation of Bahá'u'lláh was the spread of fanciful and exaggerated rumours in the town of 'Akká about their mysterious and important prisoner.

Ḥájí Ja'far-i-Tabrízí, who had cut his own throat in Adrianople on hearing that he was not to be among the companions of Bahá'u'lláh in the next stage of his exile, remained at Adrianople with his brother until his wound was healed. Then the two brothers joined the exiles in 'Akká. They brought with them a letter from Rev. Rosenberg.* 'Abdu'l-Bahá replied to this letter and gave an account of what had happened to the exiles since they left Adrianople. Unfortunately the original letter of 'Abdu'l-Bahá does not exist any longer, and a transcript of it that Rosenberg sent to Blunt (q.v.) is almost unintelligible in places and has obviously been very poorly copied. The following translation must therefore be regarded as only an approximation to 'Abdu'l-Bahá's account:

Let me now describe what happened to us after we left Adrianople. When we arrived at Gallipoli from Adrianople, I wrote you a letter, and I gave it to the agent of the glorious state of England in order that he should forward it. I do not know whether you have received it or not. Then at Gallipoli they put us on board a ship and made us pay most of the passage money. And they took us to 'Akká under guard and without rations. But four men they set apart from us and sent to Cyprus. One of the four tried hard to be sent to 'Akká with us, but they would not let him. Eventually after His

* See previous chapter, pp. 187–97.

Holiness the Master had left the boat, he threw himself into the sea.* We did not know how this came to pass. We then arrived in 'Akká and saw that there were 30 policemen [*Ḍábiṭíyyih*] there who took us to an empty barracks. The policemen stood guard at the barracks gate. That night everyone, including the children, remained without food. They did not allow us to go outside the barracks gate. To be brief, there was an order from Istanbul that we should be kept imprisoned forever in the prison of 'Akká. They did not allow us to communicate with anyone, not even the policemen. We have now been imprisoned in the barracks of 'Akká for one month. They want to take us to the 'Akká prison in a few days time. In the first four days they gave three loaves of bitter bread to each person, and after the first four days they even stopped giving those three loaves. As for 'Akká, it is roughly half as large as the fortress of Adrianople. And half of this too is made up of the prison and the port. Its climate is infernal. Most of the prisoners are troubled and sick. Most of us too have fallen ill, because the air and water here are most evil, particularly in the port and in the prisons. They send here those whom they wish to destroy, in order that they should die here. However, our hope is that the grace of the Holy Spirit will encompass us all. His Holiness the Master, our father, sends you his greetings and also to Artin Effendi and Boghos Effendi and all our friends. 'Abbás.[6]

Rosenberg sent this letter of 'Abdu'l-Bahá to Blunt with the following note, dated 24 November 1868:

I inclose in this a letter which I received from the chief of the Babbies who is now at Acre in Syria.

I take the liberty of requesting you to submit this letter to his Excellency the honourable Elliot H.B.M's Ambassador in Constantinople whose powerful influence I humbly solicit in the name of humanity on behalf of this unfortunate Schaik and his people with a view to induce the Ottoman Government to alleviate the harsh and even cruel treatment they are now submitted to by the authorities at Acre; and I shall ever feel most grateful to his Excellency, and pray to the Almighty to bless him and his efforts.

I regret very much that ill health prevented me from handing over to you the copies of these letters immediately upon receipt, besides, through the mistake of the representative of our Protestant Community, the originals were handed over to the Austrian Vice-Consul instead of copies. Mr Camerloher having no time to copy them so as to be in time for the next post sent them to his Excellency the Austrian Ambassador in Constantinople, and they were only on Friday on 12th inst. returned to him.[7]

Blunt forwarded these letters to the British Embassy at Istanbul, with an accompanying note that betrayed a certain amount of exasperation at Rosenberg's efforts on behalf of Bahá'u'lláh and his companions.

I hope Your Excellency will pardon me if I take the liberty to again trouble you with the case of the Persian Babees who were recently removed from Adrianople, by submitting to Your Excellency herewith Inclosed a note with its two Inclosures which the Reverend Mr Rosenberg, protestant missionary at this place has addressed to me on their behalf. One of the two papers inclosed in Mr Rosenberg's note is the original letter he has received from the son of the Chief of the Babees, in which a description is given of the alleged harsh treatment this Chief and his followers suffer at the hands of the Ottoman

* This was Áqá 'Abdu'l-Ghaffár.

Authorities at Acre.

Mr Rosenberg having asked me if I would allow him to forward through my office his letters to the Shek [Shaykh] of the Babees, I declined doing so.

The Reverend Gentleman also requested me to furnish him with an authentic copy of the Dispatch No. 9 which Your Excellency did me the honor to address to me on the 13 of August last relative to the removal from this City of certain members of the sect in question, but I told him that I could not give such publicity to the dispatches which I receive from Her Majesty's Embassy, without a special order from the latter to do so.

From what Mr Rosenberg told me I gather that he has again invited the attention of the Evangelical Alliance in London to the case of these Babees; and that he hopes that this Alliance will take the matter up strongly.[8]

In his reply of 3 December, Elliot (q.v.) seems to reflect Blunt's mood of annoyance and exasperation:

I have made enquiry into the treatment of the Persian Babees at Acre, in favour of whom, at the request of Mr Rosenberg, you have requested my intervention . . . and am assured that they are not treated with harshness, though they are not allowed to spread their doctrines beyond the bounds of the fortress.

The efforts of this sect to proselytise from among the mussulman population and the large admixture of political element in their constitution, indisposes me to exert in their behalf the efforts I would gladly make if they could fairly be regarded as being persecuted on account of their religious convictions.

Their adoption of some cant phrases, and of some scraps of Christian morality, form, as far as I can learn, their only claim to the approach to Protestantism which there seems to be a disposition to advance in their behalf.

You judged quite properly in not giving Mr Rosenberg a copy of my despatch.[9]

Gobineau and Prokesch-Osten

The correspondence between Gobineau and Prokesch-Osten has already been quoted in the previous chapter, and Prokesch-Osten's intervention on behalf of Bahá'u'lláh at the time of his exile from Adrianople may be inferred from the statements of the Austrian Consul in Adrianople (see p. 192). Discussion of the Bábí religion ceased in the published correspondence between these two for a period of two years. Then Gobineau read in the *Courier d'Orient* an article describing Bahá'u'lláh's exile. He wrote immediately to Prokesch-Osten, on 25 August 1868:

But I wish to speak with you of another matter. Here is an article from the *Courier d'Orient* which will put you in the picture.

It does not appear to me wise on the part of the Turkish Government to persecute a people who are seeking its support and who have even made themselves its citizens. There are 300,000 Persians in the Pásháliks of Van and Baghdád, many are Bábís; if it [the Turkish Government] torments them, and above all if it causes them grief, and renders itself odious in their eyes by a severe course of action against their spiritual leader, it will lose the marked goodwill which they hold towards it. What is more, it will lose the favour of their co-religionists in Persia and by that, a great force against the very aggressive tendencies of the Qájár dynasty. And finally, as the Bábís have need of support, they will find it close at hand with the Russians, and when the Ottoman Government finds on its hands in the extreme south a people provided with Russian passports and acting accordingly, I cannot think what they will gain by it. It is even probable that Mírzá Ḥusayn Khán* or his Chargé d'Affaires is involved in this matter. But I believe that Fu'ád Páshá is not, perhaps, sufficiently informed about it, and, in supplicating you on behalf of these poor Bábís, for whom I ask your protection, I believe that I am also doing something of benefit to the Porte.[10]

At some time, Prokesch must have written to Gobineau of the measures that he had taken in favour of Bahá'u'lláh, since in his next letter dated 31 August 1868, Gobineau continues:

I appreciate everything that you have recently done for the Bábís. I was delighted to learn that there was exaggeration in the reports, but, however, I believe that Fu'ád does not know everything.

It is evident that the situation of the Báb and his followers is critical, and they are not at all Muslims. Their doctrine has made and is making immense progress among the two or three hundred thousand Persians scattered throughout the Empire, particularly in the Páshálíks of Baghdád and Van, and it is very true that this would give umbrage to the Mullás.

As to the missionaries, they are imbeciles if they imagine they can encroach upon the youthful enthusiasm of the new Faith.† I will tell you confidentially that the Báb addressed himself to me some months ago, in order to give me an account of the persecutions perpetrated against the Bábís at Manṣúra in Egypt,‡ at the request and with the participation of the Persian Consul. I am persuaded, as I have already told you, that the Dívan§ has a very serious interest to protect there, and that it does not realize that it must act cautiously.

I am writing to the Báb to inform him of what you have tried to do for him, and I am sending you my letter with the translation and ask that you be good enough to have it delivered. It will perhaps calm 'Alí-Ḥusayn [Mírzá Ḥusayn-'Alí, i.e. Bahá'u'lláh] a little and will give him hope that he will not be ill-treated . . .[11]

As a postscript, Gobineau added: 'Do you know that the Russians have at Kazán‖ some Bábís whom they are protecting and seeking to indoctrinate for the occasion? It is unfortunate that the Russians, being Orientals themselves, understand by instinct, and not even through ability, things that are to their profit and which our ignorance never perceives, or is not able to judge when it does see.'[12]

Gobineau adjoined to this letter a translation of his letter to Bahá'u'lláh, whom he addresses as Ḥájí Mírzá Ḥusayn-'Alí:

Your Excellency has not replied to the letter that I wrote to him through the intermediary of the Greek Consul,¶ and the news of what has happened has reached me

* Persian Ambassador at Constantinople. See p. 192n.

† Prokesch-Osten must have written of the intervention of Rev. Rosenberg.

‡ See p. 257.

§ The Turkish Council of State.

‖ This may be a reference to Siyyid 'Abdu'l-Karím-i-Urdúbádí, who was living in Astrakhan (see p. 14n).

¶ Gobineau, being the French Ambassador at Athens at this time, presumably asked the Greek

through the journals.

I have addressed myself to His Excellency the Ambassador of Austria for the protection of your adherents, and His Excellency has immediately displayed the most benevolent and humane disposition, and has informed me that he has been very insistent with Fu'ád Páshá and the members of the Ottoman Government about this affair. I am persuaded that every effort that can be made, he will make, and if you judge it appropriate, write to him. As for myself, I will act similarly in Paris, with respect to the Government of the Emperor.

If you wish to communicate with me, do so through the medium of the French Consul at the address given herewith. It is useless to trouble you further now, greetings.[13]

In the last letter in the published series to make reference to Bahá'u'lláh, Gobineau speaks of having received a further communication from Bahá'u'lláh. Gobineau's letter is dated 18 November 1868 and is sent from France where Gobineau was living prior to his next diplomatic mission as French Minister to Brazil:

I received a long letter from the Báb. He is at St Jean d'Acre, a prisoner in some ruinous barracks with a party of his people, men, women and children, lacking water and watching his world die of misery. The guards that have been set over him have completely pillaged and plundered them. A party of the faithful have been sent to Cyprus where their chances are not worth much.

I want to believe, as Fu'ád Páshá told you, that the money and intrigues of the Persian Legation had nothing to do with this affair, but then what remains is a Turkish brutality, which they had not the least pretext for committing. As to the suspicion that the Bábís wish to become Christians, that is also too ridiculous.

When one believes oneself a God and companion of a God, and one leaves one's country and is subjected to every persecution in the world for it, one is not going to be converted to another cult.

I am trying to do what I can to extricate these unfortunate people from their dreadful situation. But you know what chance I have of being understood. It is thus you above all, Excellency, that I continue to ask for help. The Báb wrote to me to tell you how much he, as well as his people, are moved by the evidences of your interest. You will do well if you manage to obtain for them their liberty and give them something to compensate for the losses to which they have been subject, and lastly, to let those who are in Cyprus rejoin their leader and their friends. If it is thought necessary to keep them under surveillance, let them be placed in a town where European Consulates can see to it that they are not tormented. I cannot commend this matter to you too much, Excellency, because I am afraid that my book, in drawing attention to Mírzá 'Alí-Ḥusayn [Mírzá Ḥusayn-'Alí, i.e. Bahá'u'lláh] and his partisans, has been a factor in their persecution, and my conscience is troubled.[14]

Dr Chaplin

Bahá'u'lláh remained in the citadel of 'Akká for over two years, until eventually, at a time when the citadel was required for barracking troops, he was moved into confinement in a house in the western quarter of the city called the house of Malik. After three months, he was moved to the house of

Government to forward his letter through diplomatic channels.

Khavvám and after a few more months to the house of Rábi'ih. It was while Bahá'u'lláh and his family were in one of the latter two houses that they were visited by Dr Chaplin (q.v., see fig. 24), an English physician who was attached to the Jerusalem Hospital of the London Society for Promoting Christianity among the Jews, usually called the London Jews' Society.*

In mid-April 1871, Dr Chaplin together with Rev. Frederick Smith (q.v.) and two native Agents undertook a tour of Tiberias and Nazareth. In addition they visited 'Akká. In May of that year, Dr Chaplin left Jerusalem with his family for a short holiday in London. While in London, he submitted the following letter to the editor of *The Times* which was printed on 5 October 1871. Apart from an inconsequential reference in Gobineau's book and associated articles, this is the first substantial printed reference to Bahá'u'lláh in the West.† From the letter it appears that Chaplin did not meet Bahá'u'lláh himself, but had a long interview with 'Abdu'l-Bahá. He wrote:

THE BABS OF PERSIA

To the Editor of the Times

Sir, – Notices of the rise of a new *quasi* Christian sect in Persia have, I believe, appeared from time to time in English newspapers. Little, however, appears to be known upon the subject in this country, and the following information may therefore be acceptable to many of your readers.

Of all the followers of Mahomet the Metawely‡ of Persia are among the most bigoted and fanatical. Not only will they not eat or drink with Christians, but they dash to pieces any vessel belonging to them out of which a Christian has drunk, gather their garments round them as they pass a Christian in the street lest they should be contaminated by contact with him, and should any Christian book be in their way they remove it with tongs rather than defile themselves by touching it. About 30 years ago some intelligent and thoughtful members of the sect, of good position and education, were led by this very excess of bigotry to inquire into the reason of it, and, having procured from some Christians copies of the New Testament in the Arabic language, devoted themselves to its careful study. The result of their investigation was that they became convinced of its truth, accepted it as the Word of God, and embraced its doctrines. They did not, however, abandon their faith in Mahomet as a prophet of God, and the Koran as a divinely inspired book, but believed themselves able to reconcile the hitherto antagonistic creeds of Islam and Christianity. Their doctrine, which received the name of Bab el Huk (door of truth), spread rapidly, and in the course of a few years was professed by 200,000 persons. A persecution now arose, during which 20,000 adherents of the new doctrine were slain, and its founder, known as Beheyah Allah, took refuge with a small band of friends at Bagdad. Here he continued to hold communication with his followers in Persia, and exercised so much influence that the Government of that country requested the Sultan of Turkey to remove him from such dangerous proximity to some place where he could less easily be communicated with. He was accordingly sent to Edernay,§ and subsequently to another fortress where he now is.

* Now known as the Church's Ministry among the Jews.

† But see Addendum to this chapter. Bliss (see p. 192) in his article refers to 'the present head of the sect'.

‡ i.e. Shí'ih

§ Edirne or Adrianople

In the spring of the present year I had an opportunity of visiting the Babs in their place of confinement. Beheyah Allah himself does not readily concede an interview to strangers, and receives only such as are desirous of obtaining from him instruction in religious truth. We were received by his son, who is apparently about 30 years of age, and has a fine intellectual countenance, with black hair and beard, and that sallow, melancholic look which distinguishes nearly all Persians of the intelligent and religious class. He was dressed in a robe of white flannel, with cap of the same material, and a small white turban. Over his shoulders was thrown a brown cloth abbái. He appeared pleased to see us, but objected to answer questions respecting the origin and history of the sect. 'Let us speak of things spiritual,' he said, 'what you are now asking me is of no importance.' But on our telling him that people in England would naturally be curious to know in what way so remarkable a religious movement had arisen, and who were the originators of it, he gave us the information here detailed. He had a remarkably earnest, almost solemn manner, spoke excellent Arabic fluently, and showed a minute and accurate knowledge of the Old and New Testaments, as well as an acquaintance with the history of religious thought in Europe. Our interview lasted two hours, during the whole of which time an animated conversation was maintained. Like a true Oriental, he seldom gave a direct answer to a question upon any point of doctrine, but replied by another question, or by an illustration, his object throughout apparently being to convince his questioners of what he considered to be truth. He seemed to speak as one conscious of possessing superior light – as a great teacher might speak to his disciples. 'Why,' he inquired, 'did not the Jews, who at the time of our Lord's advent were in expectation of their Messiah, believe on him?' And, assenting to our reply that it was because they misunderstood the Scriptures, he asked whether it might not be the case that Christians in like manner now misunderstood the Scripture – the inference (not expressed) being that his father was sent by God to teach the true doctrine. We did not obtain from him a clear statement of the views of the sect with reference to his father's character and office, but a very intelligent convert subsequently informed us that he was (at least by some) believed to be the angel spoken of in the first verse of the 18th chapter of Revelation. The fundamental doctrines of the sect we ascertained to be – 1. That Christ is the Son of God and the Saviour of the world. 2. That he died and rose again. 3. That justification is by faith in him. 4. That the new birth is necessary to salvation and good works as an evidence of it. 5. That the Holy Spirit operating upon the heart produces this new birth. They have no priests and no baptism. Circumcision is practised among them, but is not essential. They have several works written by Beheyah and other members of the sect, but it does not appear that these are regarded as authoritative. They believe that Christ will return, but spiritually.

Beheyah Allah is said to have arrived at the truth solely by study of the Word of God. It is believed that he has at present 70,000 or 80,000 followers in Persia, but not openly professed. When persecuted they do not fight or resist, but are ready to die for their opinions. Between 70 and 80 share the exile and imprisonment of their leader. They are allowed considerable liberty within the walls of the city, Beheyah alone being confined to his house. They are allowed about 5d. a day per man by the Turkish Government. It is 15 years since they left their native country and between two and three since they were brought to their present place of confinement.

This remarkable movement and its history are suggestive of many reflections. In its religious, social, and political aspects it is full of interest, and it seems surprising that public attention has not been earlier drawn to it. Some may be disposed to ask whether England, Bible-loving and freedom-loving as it is her boast to be, has no voice to raise in behalf of men whom she, by her Bibles, has, probably, been the unconscious means of enlightening, and whose enlightenment appears to be their only crime. From all that I could learn, these people lead pure and harmless lives, and hold no political opinions which could render them dangerous.

But the subject has a wider interest than that involved in the fate of these individuals. A question as great as any that have ever agitated the world is beginning to press for settlement – namely, whether the progress of enlightenment, and, in particular, of Christian enlightenment among Mahomedan races is to be stopped by the rude hand of persecution and massacre. It is not in Persia alone that this question is presenting itself.

Your obedient servant,
THOMAS CHAPLIN, M.D.

16 Lincoln's-inn-fields.*[15]

The next house that Bahá'u'lláh moved to was the house of 'Údí Khammár, and it was while Bahá'u'lláh was here that an event occurred that was to have dire repercussions and to besmirch the good name and reputation of the Bahá'ís.

The Interrogation of Bahá'u'lláh

The most serious crisis that Bahá'u'lláh faced while in 'Akká was caused not by the actions of either the Government or the religious leaders, but by the impetuous and deplorable act of a handful of his followers. When the decree for the exile from Adrianople had been enforced, four of Bahá'u'lláh's followers had been sent with Mírzá Yaḥyá, Ṣubḥ-i-Azal, to Cyprus (see p. 306), while several of the followers of Azal were sent to 'Akká with Bahá'u'lláh. These Azalís had been causing great difficulties for Bahá'u'lláh and his companions by continuously feeding false information to the 'Akká town authorities and preventing the Bahá'í pilgrims from entering the city. Eventually a group of the Bahá'ís, without Bahá'u'lláh's knowledge, decided to rid themselves of the Azalís, and fell upon them one day in their house and killed them. This event occurred on 22 January 1872.

'My captivity cannot harm Me,' wrote Bahá'u'lláh in connection with this event. 'That which can harm Me is the conduct of those who love Me, who claim to be related to Me, and yet perpetrate what causeth My heart and My pen to groan.'[16] The populace of 'Akká had already good reason to hate and distrust the Bahá'ís because of the harsh wording of the Imperial decree for the exile of the captives, which had been published in 'Akká and which spoke in very severe terms of the exiles. The immediate consequence of these killings was an intensification of the fear and hatred that the population of 'Akká felt towards Bahá'u'lláh and his companions.

It was shortly after this episode that there arrived in 'Akká a further group of missionaries of the London Jews' Society. The leader of this group

* Address of the headquarters of the London Jews' Society.

was Rev. James Neil, who had only joined the Society as a missionary in April 1871, but was already in charge of the Jerusalem Mission. He was conducting a tour of Northern Palestine with Mr Bernstein, Mr Iliewitz (the surgeon of the Jerusalem Hospital) and Mr Wiseman, all of the same society. When they arrived in 'Akká, they decided to follow up Dr Chaplin's visit of the previous year and call on the Bahá'ís. Rev. Neil's account of the journey provides a graphic description of the attitude of the populace of 'Akká towards the Bahá'ís at this time, as a consequence of the murder of the three Azalís.

On the following day, being Sunday, we held our simple morning service in one of the gardens, near the town, which fringe the north shore of the bay. A wealthy Mohammedan, who is a convert to the new sect of the Babs of Persia, had invited us there, and requested, together with a Mohammedan friend, to be allowed to join with us. Beneath the palm-tree grove we sung and knelt in prayer, and preached Christ to those two followers of the false prophet. We found almost all the members of this new and interesting sect of Babyum in prison, where they had been thrown just before our coming in consequence of a fracas in which two of their number had perished. Very contradictory accounts were abroad of this sad affair, the townspeople alleging that the members of the sect had murdered those who had died on account of their secession from the body, and they themselves declaring that these two young men, who had long separated from them, instigated by the orthodox Mohammedans, had continued ever since the most insulting conduct towards their former brethren, which was on the occasion in question at last resented by certain rash young men, and led to fatal consequences. So great was the dislike or dread felt towards these apparently harmless and peaceful people that we could not induce any one to accompany us when we visited them in prison.

We had a long interview with the son of their prophet.* It was indeed strange to find an Eastern in Syria so well educated, and to hear him speak so tolerantly and intelligibly of Christ and Christianity. His views, drawn from him in a series of questions from which he seemed very apt to break away into abstruse philosophical disquisitions, left us under the impression that he was, with regard to the Saviour, an earnest Socinian.† He admitted the divinity of Christ, it is true, but then qualified his remark with such sophistries as to make it plain that all mankind might by nature partake of the same divinity.‡ He acknowledged an atonement, but shrunk from the plain scriptural teaching that it is the blood of the Lamb of God. He insisted on the mission of Mahomet. 'I agree with you,' said he, 'that salvation is by faith – faith in all the Word of God.' 'And what Scriptures,' we asked, 'are we to understand by the Word of God?' He replied, 'The Old and New Testament, and the Koran.' We pointed out the great difference between the style and matter of this latter book and the Bible, and pressed the question of how we could receive Mahomet, of whom no mention is made in Scripture, or believe that any merely human agent could possibly be required to add to and complete the work of the Son of God? His acquaintance with the New Testament and Church history is certainly most re-

* i.e. 'Abdu'l-Bahá

† Followers of Laelius and Faustus Socinus, sixteenth-century Italian Protestant thinkers who were opposed to the concept of the Trinity.

‡ See p. xxiv.

markable. We could not but deeply sympathise with this persecuted sect. It is sad to see, amidst the toleration and liberty of conscience springing up the wide world over, the Persian government still retaining the impress of that terrible tyranny which marked it in the days of Daniel and Mordecai. It is still sadder to see that, in its weakness and decline, it can find an instrument in the Sultan of Turkey to wreak its vengeance on its innocent Mohammedan subjects. Oh, when will Europe wake up to her duty, and effectually protest in the name of religion and liberty against these cruel efforts to extinguish light and knowledge amongst the thoughtful and intelligent subjects of the Shah![17]

One of the consequences of the murder of the Azalís was that Bahá'u'lláh was arrested and kept in custody while 'Abdu'l-Bahá was put in chains and thrown into a dungeon. Shoghi Effendi states that Bahá'u'lláh was brought before the Governor of 'Akká and interrogated about the episode. When questioned about his name, he said, 'My name is Bahá'u'lláh (Light of God), and My country is Núr (Light). Be ye apprized of it.' Then having spoken certain other words to which none could make reply he left the Court, and was informed by the Governor that his attendance at the Court was no longer required and that he was at liberty to return to his home, it being clear that he was free of any blame in the crime.[18]

Laurence Oliphant (q.v.), the traveller, writer and mystic was not in 'Akká at this time, indeed he did not come to live in Haifa until 1882; but at that distance in time, he heard something of the proceedings of this interrogation before the Governor, which he recorded thus:

Not long ago . . . one of his [Bahá'u'lláh's] Persian followers stabbed another for having been unworthy of some religious trust, and the great man himself was summoned as a witness.

'Will you tell the court who and what you are?' was the first question put.

'I will begin,' he replied, 'by telling you who I am not. I am not a camel driver' – this was an allusion to the Prophet Mohammed – 'nor am I the son of a carpenter' – this in allusion to Christ. 'This is as much as I can tell you today. If you will let me retire, I will tell you tomorrow who I am.'

Upon this promise he was let go; but the morrow never came. With an enormous bribe he had in the interval purchased an exemption from all further attendance at court.*[19]

In the winter of 1887–8, Oliphant lent his house in Haifa to Sir Mountstuart Grant Duff (q.v.), the former Governor of Madras. The latter, having read Oliphant's account, was interested to find out more about this episode. He succeeded in finding a certain Mr Cardahi who had been present at the interrogation years previously and asked him to recount what he had heard:

* In a footnote in his book *Abbas Effendi: His Life and Teachings* (pp. 75–6), Phelps records that when this account of Oliphant was put to 'Abdu'l-Bahá, the latter emphatically denied the truth of these last two paragraphs and gave reasons why it could not possibly have occurred in this way.

Oliphant, in his book on Haïfa, has given an account of the appearance of the father of Abbas Effendi, mentioned on an earlier page, in a Court of Justice at Acre. Some time ago Mr Schumacher [q.v.] described to me the same transaction, and last night he brought Mr Cardahi, who was present in Court.

According to the latter, the first question put to the Bâb was:-

'What is your name?'

To that he replied:- 'It is unnecessary to state my name; you know it well; it is known in all the world.'

It was then explained to the witness that it was absolutely necessary that he should state his name.

To that he replied:- 'My name is the Light of God.'

He was next asked:-

'What is your occupation?'

He answered:- 'I will tell you what I am not: I am not a carpenter, I am not a camel driver; but you need not ask me any further questions, for I will answer none.'

In Mr Schumacher's version, a second and highly probable question was interposed between the two I have quoted.

'Who was your father?'

To that the Bâb is said to have replied:- 'If you ask my followers they will tell you – that I had no beginning, and shall have no end.'

I suspect that Mr Cardahi was the fountain-head alike of the Oliphant and of the Schumacher version, but the event occurred in 1871, and exactitude is not the strong point of people in this country.

Thanks to one of those mysterious transactions familiar to the justice of Turkey, the Bâb did not again appear before the tribunal.[20]

There is also a curious report of Azalís being sent to 'Akká and there murdered. It occurs in the account of William Eleroy Curtis in *Today in Syria and Palestine*: 'In 1884 Mirza [Yaḥyá] obtained permission from the authorities to send ambassadors to Acre to effect a reconciliation between the two factions, but his envoys were murdered by agents of Beha, and since then very little has been heard from the Cyprus branch.'[21] There is no such episode recorded in any Bahá'í, Azalí or any other history. The only Azalí who is known to have come to 'Akká in later years was Mírzá Áqá Khán-i-Kirmání, and he was certainly not murdered there.

The German Templars

It is interesting that both the Templars, who came to Palestine fired by the desire to witness the imminent return of Christ, and Bahá'u'lláh, who claimed to be that return, arrived in the Haifa-'Akká area within a few months of each other.

The Templars were formed in Germany by Christoph Hoffmann (q.v.) of Württemberg, South Germany. He had observed the decline of the influence of the Church and attributed this to the failure of its members to live the life inculcated by Christ in the Gospels. Through his study of the Scriptures, he became convinced that the second coming of Christ was imminent, and, seeing the state of the Church, he determined to set up a colony where people would abide by the ethical teachings of the Bible and thus be fit to be accepted by Christ on his return. His views inevitably led to a clash with the Lutheran Church from which he and his followers were eventually expelled. His teachings, however, gained acceptance throughout Europe and in North America. Believing the second coming of Christ to be so near, Hoffmann and the other leaders of the movement decided to move their colony to Palestine where the Advent was expected to occur. Hoffmann with his principal lieutenant Georg David Hardegg (q.v., see fig. 23) landed in Haifa on 30 October 1868. Hardegg remained in Haifa as the head of the colony, while Hoffmann moved on to found the colony at Jaffa. The Haifa colony became the largest and most important of the Templar colonies in Palestine. In 1873 it numbered 170 adults and 84 children; by the end of the century it had grown to about 1,000 persons.

All the evidence seems to indicate that from the very beginning there were close relations between the Bahá'ís and the German Templars, and later Bahá'u'lláh is known to have lived in the colony among the Templars for a short time. On 8 July 1872, Rev. John Zeller (q.v., see fig. 25), a German who was also from Württemberg and who was a missionary in Nazareth of the English Church Missionary Society, forwarded to his society the following translation of a letter which is said to have been addressed by Bahá'u'lláh to the leader of the Templar Colony, Hardegg:

> In the name of God the most high! Exalted teacher!
>
> Your sealed letter to the oppressed arrived, and we recognized from the same your uprightness towards the allmighty all-preserving God. We ask God, that He may reveal to you the hidden knowledge written upon a tablet and let you hear the rustling of the leaves from the tree of knowledge and the murmuring of the waters flowing from the essence of the creator ruling over all with wisdom and intelligence.
>
> It is your first duty to contemplate the word of God whose excellence and sweetness fills the worlds. He who believes in the Spirit receives him, he will be clothed with the word of righteousness and through the same he will receive and believe, though he may be cut off from all that is in the hands of men. This is necessary even for the great fishes in the greatest sea. Oh you learned experienced and clearsighted teacher, know, that indulgence prevented most mortals from approaching to God who rules the heavens. He however, who wants to see, perceives the light, which testifies, so that he may exclaim: Praise be to the Lord, the most high! The righteousness of the Lord is made known to land and sea, he has promised the restorer of all errors! He builds the temple, and blessed are those who can comprehend it. When the appointed time has come, Carmel will break out in joy as if moved by the gentle breathing of the Lord, blessed are those who hear it! He who walks with open ears receives an answer from the rock. He shouts with a loud voice and bears witness to the eternal God. Blessed is he who finds the knowledge with assurance; who enters the Kingdom and is free of all doubts! If that appears, which is written in the books, men will see and not comprehend. My dear friend! Contemplate the mystery of assimilation [*tankís*]* the type of the leader [*ar-*

* *Tankís*, which is written in Arabic characters in the original, means reversal or inversion. The sentence probably read, 'Contemplate the mystery of the reversal of the station of leadership whereby the exalted is debased and the debased is exalted.'

rayyis] whereby the exalted is debased and the debased is exalted. Consider also, that when Jesus appeared he was denied by the learned, the wise and the educated, and fishers received the Kingdom. Thus was fulfilled what had been indicated in obscure words by types and signs.

The matter is great and important; for Peter the Apostle according to his excellence and supremacy pronounced the word, when he was asked.

When you consider past events in the light of the Lord you will see his light appear before your face and before your eyes. Truth is too clear to be covered by veils and the road too open to be hidden by obstructions and faith by obscure meanings. Those who have erred, have followed their lusts and are now among the slumbering and sleeping; they awake, run, and are not to be found. Blessed is he who finds knowledge, and being uneasy penetrates as others of the redeemed servants of God . . .

Oh thou bird in the heights of science; he who knows how water crystalizes, he who knows the silent happiness, the secret assurance, the covered rise of the sun, he draws in the rays of light in such a manner that he flies with the wings of desire in the atmosphere, approaching the completion of holiness.

What you, learned Sir, have mentioned with regard to the darkness of ignorance is confirmed by us, for the same encircles the sleeping. Blessed is he, who sees in the horizon the rays of the morning with the mercy of the most Holy Lord. Darkness is the illusion of the sleeping, who thereby are prevented from the pilgrimage towards the Kingdom which the Almighty Ruler revealed by His express order. We fully agree to your words with regard to the spirit and see that there is no difference between us.

The spirit is too pure to be attained by differences, neither can it be comprehended by outward signs, for he is the appearance of the light of unity among creatures and the symbol of progress between nations. He who receives him, receives him who has sent him and he who opposes him, opposes him from whom he proceedeth. He is what he is and remains what he has been, but his rays differ according to the purity of the mirrors and according to the difference of forms and colours. – Oh friend, when the symbol is revealed to those who may be convinced, then the hearts of those will tremble, who have robbed what they possess and thrown away what belongs to the Lord. – Honoured Sir! when you consider what we told you, then will come to pass through you that which formerly happened. Oh friend! the bird is in the claws of oppression and wickedness and findeth no nest where he may rest nor space where to flee to. In this condition the creature supplicates for life everlasting. Blessed is the ear that hears and the eye that sees! We ask God that He may unite us in the same place and give unto us that which is wellpleasing in His sight.

[Signed] The imprisoned
The oppressed[22]

In the accompanying letter, Zeller shows that he understood the claims that Bahá'u'lláh was making:

Enclosed I beg to transmit to you . . . the copy translation of a letter from the leader of the Babys, Beheya Allah, who is at present imprisoned in Acca. I read with much interest the article in the Missy [Missionary] Intelligencer of June about this sect and believe the enclosed letter will be interesting to the editor of the Intelligencer. The original is written in Arabic with frequent use of rhymes, which somewhat obscure the meaning and could not be imitated in a *literal* translation. I would not wish a public use to be made of this letter as I do not know whether the owner would like it. – Though Beheya Allah knows very well how to use scriptural language and references and spiritual ideas, which formerly deceived Dr Chaplin and Mr Smith, it is yet quite clear from this letter that he claims divine authority only for himself. This appears also from frequent conversations which I had during the last years with some of his followers who passed through Nazareth.* The extreme fanaticism of the Babys and the true spirit of Beheya Allah is shown by the fact, that last winter three of his adherents who shared his exile were secretly murdered *by his order* and some time afterwards three other Babys were publicly and partly under the eyes of the Pasha of Acca killed at Beheya's command.†[23]

Rev. James Huber (q.v., see fig. 26), who like Zeller was a German born in Württemberg and a missionary of the Church Missionary Society stationed at Nazareth, was also in close communication with the German Templars. In his Annual Letter dated 28 November 1872, Huber records a visit that he paid to the Bahá'ís in 'Akká in the company of Hardegg.

One cannot say, that the Mohammedans are unwilling to listen to religious conversations, and especially Europeans are treated with civility. They also know now the difference between evangelical Christianity, and that of the Eastern Churches which they cannot esteem very highly.

About a month ago, I had occasion to see some of the Persian 'Baabys' at Akka. As the Germans have a colony at Caiffa, which being about nine miles distant, some of the Persians came several times to Mr Hardegg, the head man of the colony, and he thought that they are anxious to learn something about Christianity, but he could never exactly ascertain their real desire, and as they invited him, and promised him an interview with their Prophet, 'Behau Allah' (Lustre of God) Mr Hardegg wrote to me, inviting me to join him. I informed Mr Zeller about it, and he thought it also interesting and told me to go. From Caiffa we went early in the morning and arrived at Akka at 8 o'clock. We went on a carriage kept by the German Colonists which being a great improvement and a pleasure to every one who wishes for the spiritual and temporal welfare of this country.

After we had rested a little we went to the house where 'Behau Allah', and his son, Abbas Effendi are living and watched by some Turkish police-men. After some conversation we found out that it is not their wish to bring us near their Prophet, and all possible excuses were made why we could not see him and converse with him. We then began to speak to Abbas Effendi about the miserable state of fallen mankind; the necessity of a Redeemer; and how it was our duty to do something for our own salvation, and for that of our fellow men; especially those who were considered heads of a religious sect ought to employ their time in that way, etc. Abbas Effendi, like the Druses, agreed to all we said, and seemed very well informed; but he thought it necessary to learn some of the European languages well, in order to be able to converse with Europeans in their own language. We told him, that there was more important work to do for spiritual men. The wisdom of this world seems to be to them more than the simple faith in Christ and his word, as they are too wise in their own imagination. I think they are seeking for the protection of a European Power and for nothing else. It may be, that, if there was a missionary at Akka, who could see them often some of them might be led to the truth and knowledge of Christ.[24]

* Several of the followers of Bahá'u'lláh are known to have passed through or even stayed in Nazareth. Among these are Áqá Muḥammad-'Alíy-i-Qá'iní, Nabíl-i-A'ẓam and Ḥájí Jásim of Baghdád, who was sent by Bahá'u'lláh as a messenger to the exiled Bahá'ís in Kharṭúm.

† See p. 212.

The CMS Missionaries

Over the next few years, Huber and Zeller, the CMS missionaries operating from Nazareth, continued to have occasional contacts with the Bahá'ís in 'Akká. In his Annual Letter dated December 1872, Zeller writes: 'Occasionally we had opportunities to enter into conversations with Persians and Babys and our native brethren had once a very interesting discussion at Acca with a learned Moulla from Constantinople.'[25]

In his report for the quarter ending 31 March 1874, Huber reports that he visited 'Akká on 12 January of that year: 'I made also the acquaintance of a young Turk, Ahmad Effendi, who, on account of his liberal views, was banished to Akka, which town he is not allowed to leave. I was only sorry to see him in the company of Abbas Effendi, the son of the chief of the "Babees", Behau Allah, who is doubting every existing religion and putting the wisdom of man far above its proper place.'[26]

Zeller finally met 'Abdu'l-Bahá in 1874, and in a letter dated 7 September 1874 records his impressions of him. He, however, wrongly identifies 'Abdu'l-Bahá as 'the chief of the imprisoned Babíes': 'I also saw Abbas Effendi the chief of the imprisoned Babíes; he is a highly-gifted fascinating young man.'[27]

In his report for the quarter ending 31 March 1875, Huber states:

> The 'Babees' of Persia, who are living as exiles at Akka, are rather prospering and increasing in number. Some of them have fine shops and do a good business, whilst others are artisans.
>
> 'Behau Allah' their Prophet does not show his person in public, and he only goes sometimes to his neighbour (a Christian) from his terrace door of the third story.* His people pay him great deference and hardly dare to look at him in his presence.
>
> The Babees do not deny the Word of God, but on the contrary they defend the genuineness of the same in order to support their system; and that being the reason why the Mohammedans at Akka search the scriptures. They also believe in the divinity and incarnation of our Lord Jesus Christ.[28]

Further Accounts

Over the ensuing years, there were sporadic visits to the Bahá'í community in 'Akká from various Europeans and an American. Although a few of these mention having met Bahá'u'lláh himself, there must be some doubt whether they did in fact do so. By this time, 'Abdu'l-Bahá was managing all of the external affairs of the community in 'Akká and would undoubtedly have dealt with any Europeans who came to 'Akká wanting to meet the Bahá'ís. The immense knowledge and personal magnetism of 'Abdu'l-Bahá to which the preceding accounts by Dr Chaplin and the missionaries have

* What is now known as the house of 'Abbúd was then in two halves: the back half (away from the sea) being the house of 'Údí Khammár was occupied by Bahá'u'lláh, the front half by 'Abbúd, the Christian referred to here. Later Bahá'u'lláh occupied the whole of the house.

borne witness, may have misled the travellers to think that they were meeting the 'Prophet' of the new religion.

In 1880, Rev. Henry R. Coleman*, an American Freemason, travelled through the Holy Land and came to Akká. In his book, *Light from the East*, he appears to describe an interview with Bahá'u'lláh which he prefaces with the following remark: 'I have received the notice of a sect among the Mohammedans of Persia, which will interest the reader.'[29] In fact, this passage is a translation of Hardegg's account of his interview with 'Abdu'l-Bahá (see Addendum to this chapter).

Laurence Oliphant (see fig. 27), who has already been mentioned in connection with the interrogation of Bahá'u'lláh, arrived in Haifa in December 1882, and settled in a house in the German Colony. Later he also acquired a house at Dálíyatu'l-Karmil, a Druze village ten miles south of Haifa where he spent the summer months.

Only a year after his arrival in Haifa, Oliphant penned for the *New York Sun*, to which he was a regular contributor, an account of the Bahá'í community in 'Akká. His letter was published on 10 December 1883 and later appeared, along with a number of Oliphant's other contributions to that paper, in his book called *Haifa, or Life in Modern Palestine*. The chapter is entitled 'The Babs and Their Prophet'.

HAIFA, NOV. 7 [1883] - The Nahr N'aman, called by the ancients the river Belus, rises in a large marsh at the base of a mound in the plain of Acre called the Tell Kurdany, and, after a short course of four miles, fed by the swampy ground through which it passes, it attains considerable dimensions. Before falling into the sea it winds through an extensive date-grove, and then, twisting its way between banks of fine sand, falls into the ocean scarcely two miles from the walls of Acre. Pliny tells us that glass was first made by the ancients from the sands of this river, and the numerous specimens of old glass which I found in grubbing bear testimony to the extensive usage of this material in the neighbourhood. The beach at its mouth was also celebrated as a locality where the shells which yielded the Tyrian purple were to be found in great abundance, and I have succeeded in extracting the dye from some of those I have collected here. It was also renowned for a colossal statue of Memnon, which, according to Pliny, was upon its banks, but the site of this has not been accurately identified. The only point of attraction now upon its waters is a garden† belonging to an eminent Persian, whose residence at Acre is invested with such peculiar interest that I made an expedition to his pleasure-ground on the chance of discovering something more in regard to him than it was possible to do at Haifa.

Turning sharply to the right before reaching Acre, and passing beneath the mound upon which Napoleon planted his batteries in 1799, we enter a grove of date-trees by a road bordered with high cactus hedges, and finally reach a causeway which traverses a small lake formed by the waters of the Belus, and which, crossing one arm of the river, lands us upon an island which it

* Coleman, Rev. Henry Roush (b. 1834). Evidently he was a resident of Louisville, Kentucky, since five editions of his book were published privately there.
† The garden of Riḍván near 'Akká.

encircles. This island, which is about two hundred yards long by scarcely a hundred wide, is all laid out in flower-beds and planted with ornamental shrubs and with fruit-trees. Coming upon it suddenly it is like a scene in fairy land. In the centre is a plashing fountain from which the water is conveyed to all parts of the garden. The flower-beds are all bordered with neat edges of stone-work, and are sunk below the irrigating channels. Over a marble bed the waters from the fountain come rippling down in a broad stream to a bower of bliss, where two immense and venerable mulberry-trees cast an impenetrable shade over a platform with seats along the entire length of one side, protected by a balustrade projecting over the waters of the Belus, which here runs in a clear stream, fourteen or fifteen feet wide and two or three deep, over a pebbly bottom, where fish of considerable size, and evidently preserved, are darting fearlessly about, or coming up to the steps to be fed. The stream is fringed with weeping willows, and the spot, with its wealth of water, its thick shade, and air fragrant with jasmine and orange blossoms, forms an ideal retreat from the heats of summer. The sights and sounds are all suggestive of langour and *dolce far niente*, of that peculiar condition known to Orientals as *kief*, when the senses are lulled by the sounds of murmuring water, the odours of fragrant plants, the flickering shadows of foliage, or the gorgeous tints of flowers and the fumes of the narghileh.

The gardener, a sedate Persian in a tall cap, who kept the place in scrupulous order, gave us a dignified welcome. His master, he said, would not come till the afternoon, and if we disappeared before his arrival we were welcome to spread our luncheon on his table under the mulberry-trees, and sit round it on his chairs; nay, further, he even extended his hospitality to providing us with hot water.

Thus it was that we took possession of Abbas Effendi's garden before I had the honour of making that gentleman's acquaintance, an act of no little audacity, when I inform you that he claims to be the eldest son of the last incarnation of the Deity. As his father is alive and resident at Acre – if one may venture to talk of such a being as resident anywhere – my anxiety to see the son was only exceeded by my curiosity to investigate the father. But this, as I shall presently explain, seems a hope that is not likely to be realized. Meantime I shall proceed to give you, so far as I have been able to learn, an account of who Abbas Effendi's father is, and all that I know about him, premising always that I only do so subject to any modification which further investigation may suggest . . . [Oliphant then gives an account of the ministry of the Báb.]

The Bab before his execution gave it to be understood that though he was apparently about to die, he, or rather the divine incarnation of which he was the subject, would shortly reappear in the person of his successor, whom, I believe, he named secretly. I do not exactly know when the present claimant first made known his pretensions to be that successor, but, at all events, he was universally acknowledged by the Bab sect, now numbering some hundreds of thousands, and became so formidable a personage, being a man of high lineage – indeed, it is whispered that he is a relative of the Shah himself – that he was made prisoner by the government and sent into exile. The Sultan of Turkey kindly undertook to provide for his incarceration, and for some years he was a state prisoner at Adrianople. Finally he was transported from that place to Acre, on giving his parole to remain quietly there and not return to Persia, and here he has been living ever since, an object of adoration to his countrymen, who flock hither to visit him, who load him with gifts, and over two hundred of whom remain here as a sort of permanent bodyguard.

He is visible only to women or men of the poorest class, and obstinately refuses to let his face be seen by any man above the rank of a fellah or peasant. Indeed, his own disciples who visit him are only allowed a glimpse of his august back, and in retiring from that they have to back out with their faces towards it. I have seen a lady who has been honoured with an interview, during which he said nothing beyond giving her his blessing, and after about three minutes motioned to her to retire. She describes him as a man of probably about seventy years of age, but much younger-looking, as he dyes both his hair and his beard black, but of a very mild and benevolent cast of countenance. He lives at a villa in the plain, about two miles beyond Acre, which he has rented from a Syrian gentleman of my acquaintance, who tells me that once or twice he has seen him walking in his garden, but that he always turns away so that his face shall not be seen. Indeed, the most profound secrecy is maintained in regard to him and the religious tenets of his sect.[30]

With regard to Oliphant's account, Browne wrote:

'Several erroneous statements are made, especially one to the effect that Behá "is visible only to women or men of the poorest class," and that "his own disciples who visit him are only allowed a glimpse of his august back." I myself, during the week which I spent at Acre (April 13th–20th, 1890), was admitted to the august presence four times, each interview lasting about 20 minutes; besides which on one occasion I saw Behá walking in his garden of Janayn surrounded by a dozen or so of his chief disciples. Not a day passes but numerous Bábís of all classes are permitted to wait upon him.'[31]

This account by Oliphant was written as has been mentioned only a year after Oliphant's arrival in Haifa and it seems likely that over the ensuing years, Oliphant developed close relations with the Bahá'ís in 'Akká. Certainly the following statement written by Valentine Chirol (q.v.) in his *The Middle Eastern Question* in 1903 tends to confirm this point of view. It must be noted that the phrase 'enjoyed the favour of Beha'ullah's hospitality' may indicate that Oliphant and Chirol did not meet Bahá'u'lláh himself and certainly the 'party of Americans' referred to did not play a part in establishing the religion of Bahá'u'lláh in America.*

Beha'ullah not only became the recognised head of Babiism, but he composed voluminous scriptures, which gradually superseded the writings of the Bab himself, and he claimed even more emphatically than the Bab to be revered as a divine incarnation. Pilgrims from Persia flocked at one time to the modest court he held in Acre, and he used occasionally to receive a few privileged European visitors, such as Professor Browne, of Oxford, the chief English authority on Babiism, and the late Laurence Oliphant, who, from his latter-day retreat on Mount Carmel, used to keep up friendly relations with the leaders of a movement in which, as in all religious speculations, he was deeply interested. It was as Oliphant's guest that in 1885 I enjoyed the favour of Beha'ullah's hospitality, and under the same auspices were entertained by him a party of Americans in search of new spiritual truths, from whose visit, and more directly from the preachings of a Babi missionary, Ibrahim Khairullah, who lectured in America, there

* This may be a reference to the arrival in 'Akká of the first party of American Bahá'í pilgrims, but that did not happen until 1898, six years after Bahá'u'lláh's passing. Their visit was in no way connected, as is suggested by Chirol, with Laurence Oliphant, who had in any case died in 1888.

has sprung up an American branch of the Babi Church, which counts, it is said, some 4,000 adherents, chiefly in Chicago.[32]

In 1893, there appeared an article in the German magazine *Aus Allen Weltteilen*. It is, of course, written in German and the author is not indicated. The title of the article is 'The Persian God in 'Akká'. From the contents and tone of the article it would appear that the author must have lived in the vicinity of 'Akká over a number of years and was not particularly friendly towards the Bahá'ís. It is probable that the author was one of the German Templar colonists. In the early part of the article, much of the material dealing with Shaykh Aḥmad and the Báb was probably derived from a study of Browne's writings. The section here translated, for what it is worth, is the part of the article dealing with 'Akká and demonstrates the sort of rumours and fantasies current among the people of Haifa and 'Akká about the Bahá'í colony:

They did not have to stay in Baghdád for long, for they were too near Persia. They were now banished to Adrianople. Yaḥyá* became bored in his solitude and emerged from hiding. The sect was thus split into two parts, who were opposed to each other. The one adhered to the Mírzá,† the other to Yaḥyá. The Government was compelled to intervene, and banished Yaḥyá to Cyprus and Mírzá to 'Akká. The latter now has a following of 200 adherents in 'Akká and about 80,000 followers in Persia. He lives like a Prince but lets no one see him. He possesses two palaces, one in the town‡ and one outside,§ as well as a large garden.‖

His followers offer him the best that they have, and consider it as the greatest good fortune to be allowed to live near him. One paid 6,000 francs to obtain the post of a caretaker, another 40,000 francs for the position of a gardener. This Persian god leads a very soft life in his harem.¶ He only goes out at night, always wrapped up and with a great following; he receives visitors from behind a wall. One of his sons, who is appointed to be his successor, must also lead a retired life. In the year 1886, there was once some jewellry stolen, worth 600 francs, and the robbed man, as is customary when the thief cannot be discovered, went for help to sorcery. During the spell there appeared to the sorcerer a host of spirits, and from them he heard the following words: 'Could you not have found another time to trouble us? Do you not see that we are fully occupied in preparing a feast for the dying Persian goddess?' In this manner was it learned that a wife of the Persian god was dying, and a few days later this wife died.⁑[33]

* i.e. Mírzá Yaḥyá, Ṣubḥ-i-Azal

† i.e. Mírzá Ḥusayn-'Alí, Bahá'u'lláh

‡ i.e. the house of 'Abbúd

§ i.e. the mansion of Bahjí

‖ i.e. the garden of Riḍván

¶ The statement that his followers paid Bahá'u'lláh to obtain employment is false. And although some accounts seem to indicate that Bahá'u'lláh was living in the greatest luxury, those who actually entered the mansion of Bahjí, and were in a position to report – persons such as Browne – do not speak of an excessive display of luxurious living.

⁑ Ásíyih Khánum, the wife of Bahá'u'lláh and mother of 'Abdu'l-Bahá, did indeed die in 1886.

Sir Mountstuart Grant Duff whose visit to Haifa in 1887 has been referred to above,* records in his diary for 1 December 1887 a meeting with 'Abdu'l-Bahá: 'After I had paid my official visit I went with my companions – the English Vice-Consul at Haïfa,† and Mr Haskett Smith,‡ a friend of Oliphant's, now looking after his affairs in this part of the world – to call on Abbas Effendi, son of a man who claims to be the head of the very remarkable Persian sect known as the Bâbis. He promised some day to come to see me at Haïfa and to give me an account of their history, which is most imperfectly known in Europe. "Inshallah",§ said he, and so say I!'[34]

One further account of Bahá'u'lláh deserves mention at this point. Although derived from an Oriental and as such outside the scope of this book, nevertheless it was published in 1896 in one of the best-known French periodicals, the *Revue Bleue – Revue Politique et Littéraire*, and for this reason has been included here. The author, Amír Amín Arslan (q.v.), was a noted Druze writer of a princely family. He writes:

> I have had the honour of catching a glimpse of him who is the incarnation of 'the Word of God' in the eyes of the Persians. It was in 1891, during a journey that I made to St Jean d'Acre ['Akká]. As soon as I arrived, I was eager to pay a visit to 'Abbás Effendi, the eldest son of 'the Word' who was in charge of the external relations of the community. I had known him at Beirut, in Syria, and there had quickly been established between us the bonds of a true friendship.
>
> 'Abbás Effendi received me in the sumptuous palace where he lives with his father, 'the Word' . . . Naturally, I solicited from him the honour of an audience with his holy father. He explained to me, in a very kindly manner, that it was not the custom of him who represented the Divinity to admit to his presence unbelieving mortals. Since I insisted, he promised to make every possible effort to bring about the realization of my wish.
>
> Eventually, after three days, I received word that this signal favour had been accorded to me . . . I thought then that I was going to be able to converse with him who was the reflection on earth of the rays of Divinity, but my illusions were quickly dispersed. I had to content myself with catching a glimpse of the illustrious Bahá'u'lláh at the moment when he came out to take his daily walk in the immense park surrounding his residence. In fact, 'the Word' never left the inside of his house except to take a walk in his park in the evening, a time when he could better elude the prying attentions of outsiders.
>
> But 'Abbás Effendi had carefully positioned me behind a part of the wall, along his path, in such a manner that I could easily contemplate him for a short while. I even

* See p. 214.

† This was Dr Schmidt, the Medical Officer of the Templar Colony. He was descended from the German Mennonites who colonized South Russia, and thus held a Russian passport. This created difficulties when he was first appointed English Vice-Consul in 1879 to replace Mr Finzi. He remained Vice-Consul until 1898. He had studied medicine in Germany and Vienna.

‡ A clergyman in England who, under Oliphant's influence, came to Haifa as a sort of missionary to the Druzes and as Oliphant's right-hand man. Certain scandals with the girls in the village of Dálíya forced him to leave Palestine (see Henderson *The Life of Laurence Oliphant* pp. 251–2).

§ 'God willing!'

believe that 'the Word of God' had realized the presence of a stranger and had understood that it was a question of granting a favour to a friend. His appearance struck my imagination in such a way that I cannot better represent it than by evoking the image of God the Father, commanding, in his majesty, the elements of nature, in the middle of clouds.*

Bahá'u'lláh died three years ago at the age of eighty-six years.† The Persians prepared for him a funeral that was of a magnificence without precedent, and each drop of the water with which they washed his body was contended for and bought at the price of gold.

He is buried in his property at St Jean d'Acre.[35]

Arslan concludes with the following tribute to 'Abdu'l-Bahá:

He is a man of rare intelligence, and although Persian, he has a deep knowledge of our Arabic language, and I possess some Arabic letters from him which are masterpieces ['chefs-d'oeuvre'] in style and thought and above all in oriental calligraphy.[36]

E. G. Browne's Visit

Of all these accounts of Bahá'u'lláh, Browne's journey to 'Akká and his audience with Bahá'u'lláh in 1890 must remain the most interesting, not only because of Browne's vivid description of it, but also because here for the first and only time was a European who had studied the Bábí and Bahá'í movement and was fully aware of the station of the person that he met. Furthermore, the various steps that Browne took as he approached 'Akká are of interest in that these are the very steps that a Bahá'í pilgrim from Persia would also have taken. Hence the following rather lengthy extract from Browne's description of his visit to 'Akká:

As I had now but two weeks at my disposal ere I must again turn my face homewards I was naturally anxious to proceed as soon as possible to Acre, especially as I learned that should I fail to find a steamer bound directly for that port, three days at least would be consumed by the journey thither. It was, however, necessary for me first to obtain permission from the Bábí head-quarters; for though I could without doubt proceed to Acre if I so pleased without consulting any one's inclination save my own, it was certain that unless my journey had previously received the sanction of Behá it would in all probability result in naught but failure and disappointment. Now there reside at Beyrout, Port Said, and Alexandria (by one of which places all desirous of proceeding to Acre by sea must of necessity pass) Bábís of consequence to whom all desirous of visiting Behá must in the first instance apply. Should such application prove successful, the applicant is informed that he may proceed on his journey, and receives such instruction, advice and assistance as may be necessary. To the Bábí agent at Beyrout (whose name I do not feel myself at liberty to mention)‡ I had a letter of recommendation from one of his relatives§ with whom I had become ac-

* 'Dieu le Père, commandant dans sa majesté, au milieu des nuées, aux éléments de la nature.'

† This should in fact be seventy-four years or seventy-six lunar years.

‡ Siyyid 'Alíy-i-Afnán, the son-in-law of Bahá'u'lláh.

§ Mírzá 'Alí Áqá, whom Browne met in Persia.

quainted in Persia. The first thing which I did on my arrival was to send a messenger to discover his abode. The messenger shortly returned, saying that he had indeed succeeded in finding the place indicated, but that the agent was absent from Beyrout. This was a most serious blow to my hopes, for time was against me, and every day was of vital importance. There was nothing for it, however, but to make the best of the matter, and I therefore went in person to the abode of the absent agent and presented myself to his deputy, who opened and attentively perused my letter of recommendation, and then informed me that his master was at Acre and was not expected back for ten days or a fortnight. In reply to my anxious enquiries as to how I had best proceed, he advised me to write a letter to his master explaining the state of the case, which letter, together with the letter of recommendation, he undertook to forward at once, as the post fortunately chanced to be leaving for Acre that very evening. I at once wrote as he directed, and then returned to my lodging with the depressing consciousness that at least five or six days must elapse ere I could receive an answer to my letter or start for Acre . . .

Fortunately matters turned out much better than I expected. In the first place I made the acquaintance of Mr Eyres [q.v.], the British Vice-Consul, whose kindness and hospitality did much to render my stay at Beyrout pleasant, and who, on learning that I wished to proceed to Acre, told me that he himself intended to start for Acre and Ḥaifa on the following Friday (April 11th), and that I might if I pleased accompany him. In the second place it occurred to me that I might save two or three days' delay by telegraphing to Acre so soon as my letter must, in the natural course of things, have reached its destination, and requesting a telegram in reply to inform me whether I might proceed thither. On Wednesday, April 9th, therefore, I sent a telegram to this effect. On Thursday evening, returning after sunset to my hotel from a ride in the hills, I was met with the welcome news that a Persian had called twice to see me during the afternoon stating that he had important business which would not brook delay, and that he had left a note for me which I should find upstairs. From this note, hurriedly scribbled in pencil on a scrap of paper, I learned that permission had been granted, and that I was free to start as soon as I pleased.

On receiving this intelligence my first action was to verify it beyond all doubt by calling at once on the deputy of the absent agent, whom I fortunately found at home. He congratulated me warmly on the happy issue of my affairs, and handed over to me the original telegram. It was laconic in the extreme, containing, besides the address, two words only:- '*Yatawajjahu'l-musáfir*' ('Let the traveller approach'). He then informed me that as no steamer was starting for Acre I must of necessity proceed thither by land, and that the reason why he had been so anxious to communicate with me earlier was that the post left that day at sundown and I might have accompanied it. I then told him of Mr Eyres' kind offer; which, as we agreed, was a most exceptional piece of good-fortune for me, inasmuch as he proposed to start on the following morning, and expected to reach Acre on April 13th. . . .

We entered Acre towards sun-down on April 13th, and, wending our way through the fine bazaars, on the smooth stone pavement of which our horses' hoofs slipped as on ice, alighted at the house of a Christian merchant named Ibrahím Khúrí, who accorded to us the usual hospitable reception. That same evening I sent a note to the Bábí agent, which was brought back by the messenger unopened, with the disagreeable news that my mysterious correspondent had gone to Ḥaifá with Behá's eldest son 'Abbás Efendí. This was most unwelcome information; for as Mr Eyres was leaving the next day for Ḥaifá, and I did not wish to trespass further on the hospitality of Ibrahím Khúrí, it was absolutely essential that I should obtain help from the Bábís in finding other quarters. Evidently there was nothing for it but to wait for the morrow and what it might bring forth.

Next morning I enquired if there was any representative of the absent agent who might be cognizant of his movement, and was conducted to a shop in the bazaar, where I found a tall handsome youth clothed entirely in white save for his red fez,* from beneath which a mass of glossy black hair swept back behind his ears, at the lower level of which it terminated. This youth, accosting me in Turkish, enquired first somewhat haughtily what might be my business. I answered him in Persian, whereat he appeared surprised; and, after hearing what I had to say, bade me follow him. He led me to a house situated near the seashore, at the door of which we were met by an old Persian with long grizzled hair and beard,† whose scrutinizing gaze was rendered more rather than less formidable by an enormous pair of spectacles. This man, after conversing for a few moments with my guide in an under tone, led me into a large room devoid of all furniture save a sort of bench or divan which ran round its four sides. I had scarcely seated myself when another Persian,‡ evidently superior in authority to the other two, entered and saluted me. He was a man of middle height and middle age, with a keen and not unpleasing countenance, whereof the lower part was concealed by a short crisp beard. After bidding me reseat myself (for I had of course risen on his entrance) and ordering his servant (for such, I discovered, was the old man who had met me at the door) to give me a cup of coffee, he proceeded to subject me to a most minute cross-examination as to my nationality, my occupation, my travels in Persia, the objects of my present journey, and the like. My answers appeared to satisfy him; and when he had finished his questioning he asked me what I proposed to do. I told him that I would be guided entirely by his advice. He then asked me whether I would proceed to Ḥaifá, where I was certain to find the agent whom I sought with Behá's son 'Abbás Efendí. To this I replied that as I had but a few days at my disposal, and as Acre and not Ḥaifá was the goal of my journey, I would rather remain than depart. 'In that case,' said he, 'I myself will go to Ḥaifá this afternoon and bring back word tomorrow what you must do.' . . .

Towards evening I received another visitor, whose mien and bearing alike marked him as a person of consequence.§ He was a man of perhaps thirty or thirty-five years of age, with a face which called to one's mind the finest types of Iranian physiognomy preserved to us in the bas-reliefs of Persepolis, yet with something in it beyond this, which involuntarily called forth in my mind the thought, 'What would not an artist desirous of painting a saint or an apostle give for such a model!' My visitor (who, as I afterwards discovered, was a son of Behá's deceased brother Músá) was clothed, save for the tall red fez which crowned his head, entirely in pure white; and everything about him, from his short well-trimmed beard and the masses of jet-black hair swept boldly back behind his ears, to the hem of his spotless garment, was characterized by the same scrupulous neatness. He saluted me very graciously, and remained conversing with me all the evening. Shortly after supper he bade me good-night, saying that I must doubtless be fatigued with my journey. I was then conducted by my host's son and the old servant to the room where I had spent the afternoon, where, to my astonishment, I

* Áqá Mírzá 'Abdu'r-Rasúl, the son of Áqá Muḥammad-Ibráhím, Khalíl-i-Káshání.

† Áqá Muḥammad

‡ Áqá Mírzá Asadu'lláh of Iṣfahán, brother-in-law of 'Abdu'l-Bahá's wife.

§ This was Mírzá Majdu'd-Dín, who was in later years to become 'Abdu'l-Bahá's most implacable enemy.

found that a bed provided with the most efficient mosquito-curtains and furnished with fair white sheets and soft mattress had been prepared for me . . .

I arose next morning (Tuesday, April 14th) after a most refreshing sleep, and was served with tea by the old man with the spectacles. Soon after this a sudden stir without announced the arrival of fresh visitors, and a moment after my companion of the previous evening entered the room accompanied by two other persons, one of whom proved to be the Bábí agent from Beyrout, while the other, as I guessed from the first by the extraordinary deference shewn to him by all present, was none other than Behá's eldest son 'Abbás Efendí. Seldom have I seen one whose appearance impressed me more. A tall strongly-built man holding himself straight as an arrow, with white turban and raiment, long black locks reaching almost to the shoulder, broad powerful forehead indicating a strong intellect combined with an unswerving will, eyes keen as a hawk's, and strongly-marked but pleasing features – such was my first impression of 'Abbás Efendí, 'The master' (*Áḳá*) as he *par excellence* is called by the Bábís. Subsequent conversation with him served only to heighten the respect with which his appearance had from the first inspired me. One more eloquent of speech, more ready of argument, more apt of illustration, more intimately acquainted with the sacred books of the Jews, the Christians, and the Muhammadans, could, I should think, scarcely be found even amongst the eloquent, ready, and subtle race to which he belongs. These qualities, combined with a bearing at once majestic and genial, made me cease to wonder at the influence and esteem which he enjoyed even beyond the circle of his father's followers. About the greatness of this man and his power no one who had seen him could entertain a doubt.

In this illustrious company did I partake of the mid-day meal. Soon after its conclusion 'Abbás Efendí and the others arose with a prefatory '*Bismi'lláh*,' and signified to me that I should accompany them, which I did, without having any idea whither we were going. I observed, however, that the saddle-bags containing my effects were carried after us by one of those present; from which I concluded that I was not intended to remain in my present quarters. We left the house, traversed the bazaars, and quitted the town by its solitary gate. Outside this gate near the sea is a large shed which serves as a coffee-house, and here we seated ourselves, my companions evidently awaiting the arrival of something or somebody from a large mansion half-hidden in a grove of trees situated about a mile or a mile and a half inland, towards which they continually directed their glances. While we were waiting thus, a weird-looking old man, who proved to be none other than the famous *Mushkín-Ḳalam*, came and seated himself beside us. He told me that he had heard all about me from a relation of his at Isfahán (that same *dallál* who had been the means of my first introduction to the Bábí community), and that he had been expecting to see me at Acre ever since that time.

Presently we discerned advancing towards us along the road from the mansion above mentioned three animals, one of which was ridden by a man. Thereupon we arose and went to meet them; and I soon found myself mounted on one of those fine white asses which, in my opinion, are of all quadrupeds the most comfortable to ride. A quarter of an hour later we alighted in front of the large mansion aforesaid, whereof the name, *Behjé* (Joy), is said to be a corruption (though, as the Bábís do not fail to point out, a very happy corruption) of *Bághcha* (which signifies a garden). I was almost immediately conducted into a large room on the ground-floor, where I was most cordially received by several persons whom I had not hitherto seen. Amongst these were two of Behá's younger sons, of whom one was apparently about twenty-five and the other about twenty-one years of age. Both were handsome and distinguished enough in appearance, and the expression of the younger was singularly sweet and winning. Besides these a very old man with light blue eyes and white beard, whose green turban proclaimed him a descendant of the Prophet, advanced to welcome me, saying, 'We know not how we should greet thee, whether we should salute thee with "*as-selámu 'aleykum*" or with "*Alláhu abhá*.*"' When I discovered that this venerable old man† was not only one of the original companions of the Báb but his relative and comrade from earliest childhood, it may well be imagined with what eagerness I gazed upon him and listened to his every utterance.

So here at *Behjé* was I installed as a guest, in the very midst of all that Bábíism accounts most noble and most holy; and here did I spend five most memorable days, during which I enjoyed unparalleled and unhoped-for opportunities of holding intercourse with those who are the very fountain-heads of that mighty and wondrous spirit which works with invisible but ever-increasing force for the transformation and quickening of a people who slumber in a sleep like unto death. It was in truth a strange and moving experience, but one whereof I despair of conveying any save the feeblest impression. I might, indeed, strive to describe in greater detail the faces and forms which surrounded me, the conversations to which I was privileged to listen, the solemn melodious reading of the sacred books, the general sense of harmony and content which pervaded the place, and the fragrant shady gardens whither in the afternoon we sometimes repaired; but all this was as nought in comparison with the spiritual atmosphere with which I was encompassed. Persian Muslims will tell you often that the Bábís bewitch or drug their guests so that these, impelled by a fascination which they cannot resist, become similarly affected with what the aforesaid Muslims regard as a strange and incomprehensible madness. Idle and absurd as this belief is, it yet rests on a basis of fact stronger than that which supports the greater part of what they allege concerning this people. The spirit which pervades the Bábís is such that it can hardly fail to affect most powerfully all subjected to its influence. It may appal or attract: it cannot be ignored or disregarded. Let those who have not seen disbelieve me if they will; but, should that spirit once reveal itself to them, they will experience an emotion which they are not likely to forget.

Of the culminating event of this my journey some few words at least must be said. During the morning of the day after my installation at *Behjé* one of Behá's younger sons entered the room where I was sitting and beckoned to me to follow him. I did so, and was conducted through passages and rooms at which I scarcely had time to glance to a spacious hall, paved, so far as I remember (for my mind was occupied with other thoughts) with a mosaic of marble. Before a curtain suspended from the wall of this great ante-chamber my conductor paused for a moment while I removed my shoes. Then, with a quick movement of the hand, he withdrew, and, as I passed, replaced the curtain; and I found myself in a large apartment, along the upper end of which ran a low divan, while on the side opposite to the door were placed two or three chairs. Though I dimly suspected whither I was going and whom I was to behold (for no distinct intimation had been given to me), a second or two elapsed ere, with a throb of wonder and awe, I became definitely conscious that the room was not untenanted. In the corner where the divan met the wall sat a wondrous and venerable figure, crowned with a felt head-dress of the kind called *táj* by dervishes (but of unusual height and make), round the base of which was wound a small white turban. The face of him on whom I gazed I can never forget, though I cannot describe it. Those piercing

* i.e. with the salutation ordinarily used by Muḥammadans, or with that peculiar to the Bábís. [EGB]
† Ḥájí Mírzá Siyyid Ḥasan, Afnán-i-Kabír

eyes seemed to read one's very soul; power and authority sat on that ample brow; while the deep lines on the forehead and face implied an age which the jet-black hair and beard flowing down in indistinguishable luxuriance almost to the waist seemed to belie. No need to ask in whose presence I stood, as I bowed myself before one who is the object of a devotion and love which kings might envy and emperors sigh for in vain!

A mild dignified voice bade me be seated, and then continued:- 'Praise be to God that thou hast attained! . . . Thou hast come to see a prisoner and an exile. . . . We desire but the good of the world and the happiness of the nations; yet they deem us a stirrer up of strife and sedition worthy of bondage and banishment. . . . That all nations should become one in faith and all men as brothers; that the bonds of affection and unity between the sons of men should be strengthened; that diversity of religion should cease, and differences of race be annulled – what harm is there in this? . . . Yet so it shall be; these fruitless strifes, these ruinous wars shall pass away, and the "Most Great Peace" shall come. . . . Do not you in Europe need this also? Is not this that which Christ foretold? . . . Yet do we see your kings and rulers lavishing their treasures more freely on means for the destruction of the human race than on that which would conduce to the happiness of mankind . . . These strifes and this bloodshed and discord must cease, and all men be as one kindred and one family. . . . Let not a man glory in this, that he loves his country; let him rather glory in this, that he loves his kind. . . .'

Such, so far as I can recall them, were the words which, besides many others, I heard from Behá. Let those who read them consider well with themselves whether such doctrines merit death and bonds, and whether the world is more likely to gain or lose by their diffusion.

My interview lasted altogether about twenty minutes, and during the latter part of it Behá read a portion of that epistle (*lawḥ*) whereof the translation occupies the last paragraph on p. 70 and the greater part of p. 71 of this book.

During the five days spent at *Behjé* (Tuesday, April 15th to Sunday, April 20th), I was admitted to Behá's presence four times. These interviews always took place an hour or two before noon, and lasted from twenty minutes to half-an-hour. One of Behá's sons always accompanied me, and once Áḳá Mírzá Áḳá Ján (*Jenáb-i-Khádimu'lláh*) the amanuensis (*kátib-i-áyát*) was also present. In their general features these interviews resembled the first, of which I have attempted to give a description. Besides this, one afternoon I saw Behá walking in one of the gardens which belong to him. He was surrounded by a little group of his chief followers. How the journey to and from the garden was accomplished I know not: probably under cover of the darkness of night.

At length the last day to which my departure could possibly be deferred if I were to reach Cambridge ere the expiration of my leave arrived. Loath as I was to go, there was no help for it; and reluctantly enough I declined the pressing invitations to prolong my stay which the kindness of my friends prompted them to utter. Finding that I was bent on departure, and that I could not remain longer without running a great risk of breaking my promise, they ceased to try to dissuade me from going, and, with most considerate kindness, strove to make such arrangements for my return journey as might most conduce to my comfort. In spite of all my assurances that I could easily return by myself, it was settled that the Bábí agent of Beyrout should accompany me thither. I was very unwilling to put him to such inconvenience, but was finally compelled to accede to this arrangement, which, of course, made the return journey far pleasanter than it would otherwise have been . . .

At length the moment of departure came, and, after taking an affectionate farewell of my kind friends, I once more turned my face towards Beyrout. I was accompanied by the Bábí agent; and a servant, who, left fatherless in childhood by one of the Bábí persecutions in Persia, had since remained in the household of Behá, went with us as far as Tyre. I have seldom seen one whose countenance and conversation revealed a more complete contentment with his lot. That night we slept in a caravansaray at Tyre. Next day the servant bade us farewell and turned back toward Acre, while we continued on our way, and shortly after sunset passed through the beautiful gardens which surround Sidon, that fairest and most fragrant of Syria's cities. Here we alighted at the house of a Bábí of Yezd,* whose kindly hospitality formed a pleasant contrast to our somewhat dreary lodgings of the previous night.

On the evening of the following day (Tuesday, April 22nd) we entered Beyrout, and halted for a while to rest and refresh ourselves with tea at the house of a Bábí of Baghdad† which was situated in the outskirts of the town. This man had as a child gone with his father to Persia in the hope of seeing the Báb. This he was unable to do, the Báb being at that time confined in the fortress of Chihríḳ, but at Teherán he had seen Mullá Ḥuseyn of Bushraweyh. I asked him what manner of man Mullá Ḥuseyn was. 'Lean and fragile to look at,' he answered, 'but keen and bright as the sword which never left his side. For the rest, he was not more than thirty or thirty-five years old, and his raiment was white.'[37]

Browne's notebook of his journey to Cyprus and 'Akká exists. Unfortunately the notes that he kept of the last part of the journey are somewhat scanty. For his famous interview with Bahá'u'lláh from which he quotes in the above passage, the following occurs:

Wednesday April 15th: In morning admitted to audience with Behá. It was wonderful – only one of his sons besides myself was present. He motioned me to a seat, and began to talk – Marvellous fire and vigour – He kept beating the ground with his foot (slippered) and now and then looking out of the window. He began by saying *'Al-ḥamdu'lilláh kih fá'iz shudihíd* [Praise be to God that you have attained].' Then he said You have come to see a prisoner.' He went on to speak of his sufferings and the letters he had written to the Kings, asking me if I had read them. He then read part of a *Lawḥ* [tablet] beginning . . .[38]

There are also notes of another interview:

Friday April 17th, 1890: Admitted to audience with Behá in morning for some 20 min. or ½ an hour . . . He again insisted very strongly on the necessity of unity and concord amongst the nations, and spoke of the *Sulḥ-i-Akbar* [translated by Shoghi Effendi as Lesser Peace to distinguish it from *Sulḥ-i-A'zam*] which will come soon . . . There must be one language and one writing. The former may be either one of those now existing, or one invented for the purpose by a conference of *savants* of all countries. All nations must bind themselves to combine and put down any nation which attempts to disturb the general peace.

Behá also spoke of the *Bayt al-'Adl* [House of Justice] which, he said, is to settle all disputes. The members of this will be '*inspired*' (*mulham*). *Jihád* [holy war] is entirely forbidden in this *Zuhúr* [manifestation].[39]

* Áqá Muḥammad-'Alí, Sabbágh-i-Yazdí

† Mírzá Musṭafáy-i-Baghdádí; his father was Shaykh Muḥammad Shibl (see *Nabil's Narrative* UK pp. 193–5, USA pp. 271–3.

Browne also records going to the garden of Junayna on Thursday April 16th and seeing there 'BEHA himself, who was walking round the garden surrounded by a perfect court of Bábís. I only just saw him that time.'[40]

The Missionaries Again

The initial interest shown by the CMS missionaries in the Bahá'ís at 'Akká had waned somewhat over the years and particularly with the removal of both Zeller and Huber from the Nazareth Mission. In any case there is no further mention of the Bahá'ís in their reports until the last year of Bahá'u'lláh's life. In May 1890, it had been decided to make 'Akká a permanent missionary station, and Miss Elizabeth Wardlaw-Ramsay (q.v.) had offered to go there. On 1 January 1891, she was joined by Miss S. Louie Barker (q.v.). It was the latter who, in her Annual Letter dated December 1891, wrote of a visit she had made to the mansion of Bahjí in October 1891:

> The end of October we were taken by a Native lady to visit the hareem of the leader of a strange sect of Persians, who, fifty years ago, separated from the Moslems and were exiled from their own country, and allowed to live in Acca. The ladies were most warm in their reception. Judging from their delight and their naive remarks, I should say we were the first European ladies they had seen! The news soon spread in the little community that the English ladies had come, and many came to see us. I have been once since to take Miss Coote (q.v.), and then the son of the old gentleman came in and gave us a kind welcome; he is very learned, and is supposed to succeed to his father's honours. He offered us horses if we preferred riding back. This is indeed an open door, and I hope that, now we have a Biblewoman, they will be often visited.[41]

Miss Barker wrote a much more condescending account of this visit for *The Children's World*, the children's magazine of the CMS:

> Would you like to hear about a visit we paid the other day to some Persian ladies? Some fifty years ago there was a sect in Persia who separated from the Moslems. The leader of this sect calls himself 'a god.' He and his numerous followers were banished from their own country and exiled to Acca, where they have been many years. The greater part of the old 'god's' family live in a large building about half an hour's walk from Acca, with his sons' families, and some of the followers. To this place we paid a visit with a native lady. The lower part of the building is for the women only, and to this part we went. It is called the 'Hareem.' We were shown into a large bright room where about fifteen women were sitting, most of them on the well-carpeted floor, but some on divans. There were two of the old gentleman's wives, and they did most of the talking in very imperfect Arabic. They asked heaps of questions, and were greatly surprised at my not being married. One of the wives said how she would like me for her son, which was a great honour! These people are very rich; they get very handsome presents from their followers. Every member of the family is treated with the greatest respect. Some ladies who came in, hearing the English ladies were there, kissed the hem of the dresses of the two wives, and also the sons' wives, and afterwards saluted us.
>
> Lemonade was brought in, with a white silk towel to wipe the mouth, then a large brass urn called a 'Lemarir' on a brass tray was put on the floor, with a tray of very

small glasses and silver teaspoons; then a tray full of tea, from which the youngest girl present took a handful and put in a teapot, which she filled with boiling water from the 'Lemarir' and shook, then poured away all the water; this she did three times, after which she filled the glasses, putting a quantity of sugar in each; these glasses were then handed round by a servant. They never put milk in their tea. By the side of the girl was a basin and towel, and as the visitors finished their tea she washed the glasses and refilled them; thus tea was handed round two or three times. One of the ladies told me they drank tea nearly the whole day long!

We were, of course, objects of great curiosity. One of the sons' wives, I was told by our native friend, came and stood behind me while I was busy talking to see if she was not nearly as tall. They showed us the house, etc. and even took us on the verandah. They so seldom go out – they are shut up more than the Moslems – that one told me it was years since she has been even on this verandah.

Our visit lasted about two hours, as it was too hot to return until towards evening; but though it would seem a very long visit in England, it is not considered too long here. Every one begged us to come again, and one lady said to me, 'Do come every day; it is a nice walk for you.'[42]

The contacts between the missionaries and the Bahá'ís continued and in February 1892, when Dr Bruce's Persian translation of the Gospel had been printed, there was a request from the Palestine Mission for twenty copies to be sent to Miss Wardlaw-Ramsay for the use of 'a half-Moslem, half-Christian sect of Persian immigrants,' who had settled in 'Akká.[43]

The Passing of Bahá'u'lláh

Bahá'u'lláh passed away on 29 May 1892. His passing was but little noticed in the West. The CMS missionaries made brief references to it. John Zeller, who had in former times been in Nazareth, was now the Acting Secretary of the Palestine Mission at Jerusalem. On 12 July 1892, he reported to his society: 'Lately the prophet of the Babis, Beha-eddin, died at his country house in Acca. He was towards 80 years old. There is a large community of Persians, Baabis, in Acca, some of whom have much influence.'[44]

At the beginning of 1892, Rev. C. H. V. Gollmer (q.v.) moved from Nazareth to take up the 'Akká station of the CMS. In his Annual Letter dated 5 May 1893, he wrote: 'One important event happened during the past year, viz: the death of their [the Persians'] leader, who professed to be *the Father Incarnate*. He resided in a large rented house, half an hour from Acre. He was rarely seen by his followers, but every time he was pleased to manifest himself to them for a short time as he quickly passed before them, they would bow down and not behold his face.* One of his sons is very intelligent and knows our Bible well.'[45]

Browne learned of the passing of Bahá'u'lláh directly from 'Akká. He appended this news to the end of his paper, 'Catalogue and Description of

* See Browne's comments on this, p. 222.

27 Bábí Manuscripts', which appeared shortly thereafter in the *Journal of the Royal Asiatic Society.** According to a footnote in this paper, a short paragraph announcing Bahá'u'lláh's demise appeared in a Russian newspaper called *Le Caucase*, published at Tiflis.[46]

Baron Victor Rosen (q.v.) announced the passing of Bahá'u'lláh at a meeting of the Oriental Section of the Imperial Russian Archaeological Society on 29 September 1892. At this same meeting, Rosen read Tumanski's paper which deals with this and gives the text of Bahá'u'lláh's Book of the Covenant. The paper also contains a poem by 'Andalíb† lamenting this event.[47]

Europeans who met Bahá'u'lláh

The only two Europeans who are known to have seen the Báb were, as has been mentioned in a previous chapter, Dr Cormick (see pp. 74–5) and M. Mochenin (see p. 75).

It is more difficult to draw up a list of those who met Bahá'u'lláh since there are various uncertainties involved (see p. 219). The following is a provisional list classified as far as possible to indicate the source of information and the degree of reliability.

According to the testimony of Bahá'u'lláh himself or of 'Abdu'l-Bahá:

1. Lt-Col. Arnold Burrowes Kemball, British Consul in Baghdád.[48]
2. Dr Shíshmán, who attended Bahá'u'lláh in Adrianople, following Mírzá Yaḥyá's attempt to poison him, is recorded as having been a foreigner and a Christian.[49] The name itself is Bulgarian and as in Adrianople there was a large colony of Bulgarians, it seems almost certain that he was Bulgarian.
3. Some of the Foreign Consuls resident in Adrianople[50] among whom must be numbered Camerloher, the Austrian Consul, but not Blunt, his British counterpart.[51]
4. Some of the members of the German Templar Colony in Haifa, since Bahá'u'lláh on several occasions visited Haifa and stayed in the houses of the Colony.[52]
5. An unnamed European General.[53]
6. E. G. Browne.[54]
7. Arthur Cuthbert, one of the early British Bahá'ís, evidently saw Bahá'u'lláh from a distance as confirmed by 'Abdu'l-Bahá in an unpublished tablet addressed to him. In a letter to Browne dated 21 April 1911, Cuthbert writes:

   'You have been so familiar to me by name ever since the day that you

* Barbier de Meynard, reviewing *A Traveller's Narrative* in the *Journal Asiatique* (8th ser., Vol. 20, Sept.–Oct. 1892, p. 302), refers to this article and the news of the passing of Bahá'u'lláh.

† Bahá'í poet whom Browne met in Yazd.

arrived in Akka overland from Beyrouth, and Mr Ayres [Eyres], British Vice-Consul, came on to us in Haifa where I was with Laurence Oliphant, that I feel I ought to have made your acquaintance long ago . . .

'So far as I know, you and myself are the only two living Englishmen who have seen Baha'u'llah; but unfortunately when I saw him it was only as a stranger in the street and I could not at the actual time be sure it was he, though I have since found out it was and can remember seeing him at three different times.'[55]

Since it is known that at the time of Browne's arrival at 'Akká, Bahá'u'lláh was staying in the German colony at Haifa, it would appear that Cuthbert had seen Bahá'u'lláh walking in the streets in the German colony at Haifa, where indeed the Oliphant house was situated. Oliphant himself had died by this time.

Evidence from other sources, of variable reliability:

1. Prince Dolgorukov, the Russian Minister in Ṭihrán, and his daughter.[56]
2. Rev. Rosenberg in Adrianople (see pp. 187–8).
3. Europeans in Adrianople. Adrianople was a very cosmopolitan town, over half its population being Greeks, Bulgarians and other Europeans (see p. 185). Since at this time Bahá'u'lláh had not entered the seclusion which characterized his period in 'Akká, it seems probable that many of the townspeople must at least have seen him and some met him.
4. Carmelite monks in the monastery on Mount Carmel. Bahá'u'lláh is known to have pitched his tent near this monastery.[57] These monks were principally French.
5. Laurence Oliphant (see p. 222).
6. Valentine Chirol (see p. 222).
7. Henry Edward Plantagenet, Count Cottrell, together with his wife and daughter (later Mrs Spruit). Just before the outbreak of the Second World War, Mr Ḍíyá'u'lláh (Ziaullah) Aṣgharzádih, who was then living in London, came into contact, through a set of fortuitous circumstances, with Cottrell. The latter had been in 'Akká in connection with the construction of the 'Akká – Damascus railway (work on this was started in the last year or two of Bahá'u'lláh's life). It appears that Cottrell, his wife and daughter had enjoyed Bahá'u'lláh's hospitality while in 'Akká, and prior to their departure had been accorded an interview with Bahá'u'lláh. He had also been given a copy of the *Kitábu'l-Aqdas* in the handwriting of Mírzá Áqá Ján.* When his

* The following interesting notice, also by Cottrell, appeared in *The Academy*:

'BABISM – I have personal and intimate knowledge of the present leaders of the Babist movement in

daughter, Mrs Spruit, was questioned about this visit several years later, she stated that all she could remember was that, in fun, Bahá'u'lláh's wife wished to keep her in 'Akká, but her mother would not let her stay![58]

8. Monsieur Richards, from Alsace, France, whom Browne refers to in his *A Year Amongst the Persians* as M.R., who 'had been for some while among the Bábís in Syria', and 'had received from their chiefs letters of introduction and recommendation.'[59] In his diary of that journey, Browne writes that M. Richards 'had been to 'Akká and was furnished with letters of recommendation from Behá.'[60]
9. An unnamed Greek physician who tended Bahá'u'lláh towards the end of his life.[61]

Addendum

When this book was at an advanced stage of preparation, Dr Alex Carmel drew the editor's attention to a number of articles about the Bahá'ís which appeared in the German Templar's Magazine *Süddeutsche Warte*. The first mention was in a letter from Schumacher (q.v.) and was published in the number for 29 June 1871 (p. 101).

I can give notice of yet another spiritual phenomenon which can strengthen our belief. This concerns 70 Persians, who have been banished to 'Akká on account of their beliefs. Mr Hardegg has already spent considerable time and effort trying to discover the actual basis of their belief, and had dealings with them through an interpreter just yesterday. He has found that these people base themselves on the Holy Scriptures and, like us, are awaiting the hour of Redemption in God's Kingdom. The home of this movement is the Persian border-country near Baghdád. The greater part of these Persian friends of the Bible are still to be found in their homeland. Since the Sháh was unable to suppress the movement, he has taken captive the leaders and sent them into exile ever further from their homeland until they finally arrived in 'Akká, where they now live imprisoned. These people have endured the ordeals and agonies of the first Christians, have no connections with any European missionary society and

---

Persia, the four sons of the late Mirza Hussein, who are political prisoners in Akka, though the Shah within the last twelve months has repealed the penal laws against the sect, and is now very friendly.

'These princes have a large library of books written by their father on the peculiar doctrines of the sect, which aim at nothing less than the reconciliation of Buddhism, Christianity, and Mahomedanism. The father in his will directed his sons to transmit to all the sovereigns of Europe copies of certain of his works, accompanied by an autograph letter.

'The late Czar of Russia, since Mirza Hussein's decease, sent to the sons and obtained copies of several of the principal works and had them translated into Russian.

'The princes are very anxious to carry out the wish of their late father, and to have copies of the works presented to Her Majesty the Queen; and also to obtain, unofficially, the countenance of the British Foreign Office to enable them to reach the other sovereigns with a similar object. They have furnished me with summaries of the principal works in Arabic and Persian, with the object of having them translated and published in Britain and the United States of America. H. COTTRELL'

live their simple Bible beliefs untouched by European influence. . . . Could the signs of the times be clearer? What more could happen to show us what times we are living in? Let us on the other hand consider recent events in Paris and then no one will fail to realize that God's plan is rapidly nearing its completion.

A few numbers later, on 20 July 1871, the *Süddeutsche Warte* (pp. 113–14) published an article dated 15 June 1871 from Hardegg himself. It shows that Hardegg had met 'Abdu'l-Bahá long before the interview at which Huber was present (see above). The publication of this account also of course precedes that of Dr Chaplin to which I have above given the honour of being the first substantial printed account of Bahá'u'lláh. Hardegg's article was as follows (in translation):

A BRIEF SKETCH OF THE STORY OF A SECT AMONG THE MUḤAMMADANS IN PERSIA

In the town of Haifa by Carmel live a few Persians, who earn their living as metal and wood-workers. They stand out on account of their sensible and friendly faces and their Persian dress. They are members of a Persian sect, the leader and members of which, together with wives, children and servants, to the number of about 80 souls, are confined by the Ottoman Government to 'Akká, three hours from here. An acquaintance sprang up between myself and these Persians in Haifa and, in the course of our exchanges, I received the impression that these people, despite all the obscurity of their knowledge, were seeking the truth.

In order to be more accurately informed, I sought an interview with the leader, Bahá'u'lláh, which may be translated as 'the Light or Illuminer of God'; his family name is Núrí, formerly large landowners in Persia. The interview took place on 2 June in 'Akká with the son of Bahá'u'lláh, 'Abbás Effendi, a man of twenty-seven years, one of the educated inhabitants of 'Akká acting as interpreter.

I opened by saying to 'Abbás Effendi that if my communication with him would bring about difficulties with the authorities, I would leave it to his discretion to discontinue. To this he replied: in Persian there is a saying: beyond black, there is no other colour, i.e. after so much suffering it could hardly become worse.

This then is his story:

About 23 years ago there appeared in Persia a simple merchant Ḥaḍratu'l-Báb who through the reading of the Holy Scripture of the New and Old Testaments had suddenly shown forth higher enlightenment and gifts, in a most noticeable way, and was waiting for the coming of the Messiah. He acquired followers.

The King of Persia, to whose notice this came, summoned him. He answered him: the King should organize a debate between his wise men and Ḥaḍrat. This took place and the wise men could not refute him. Meanwhile the king had to go to war and gave the order that Ḥaḍrat should be locked in prison.

After the war the king came home and died and his son ascended the throne.

Meanwhile the sect in Persia had grown stronger and the new king, in order to stop it spreading, had Ḥaḍrat put to death. It is said that he prophesied his fate three days before his death in the presence of some of his disciples. One of these desired to die with him, which was what happened to him. Yet in spite of this the sect continued to spread. The king then ordered a general persecution and extermination in which, in the course of time, 18,000 persons were killed, amongst whom some were tortured to death, for example, the skin was dissolved from their heads, on to which inflammable material was poured and ignited, or a hole was bored in their chest with a bayonet, into which a candle was thrust and set light to. Yet all this did nothing to quench the movement.

Ḥaḍratu'l-Báb had designated Bahá'u'-lláh to continue his work.

It happened then that someone attempted to kill the king with a pistol shot. Since the pistols were loaded only with light shot, the king was not harmed, but he succeeded in convincing himself that Bahá had hired the murderer. When summoned he explained to the king that this was not the case and that if he or his people had wished to kill the king they would have found a better way than birdshot. The European ambassadors, namely the Russian, intervened in the case too; Bahá was released, but the ambassadors advised him to make his way under the protection of the Sublime Porte to Baghdád.

This he did; but now the new light began to spread through Baghdád too. That day Pilate and Herod became friends; the Persian and Turkish Governments began to co-operate in persecuting the sect. Bahá's possessions in Baghdád were confiscated too, and he was sent to Constantinople, together with his followers; there it was thought best to confine him to Adrianople, since Rumelia or the European part of Turkey offered more certainty against the spreading of the contagion. But because of their conduct they found friends there too. Now it was decided to send Bahá and his followers to 'Akká. The European Consuls in Adrianople offered to prevent this but Bahá explained to them that if they thought it good to take steps on his behalf, they should do this without his petition and independently from him, but that he was decided to follow the decree of God. Thus he came to 'Akká.

In Persia the sect is at present left in peace. When I came to Haifa in Nov. 1868, I found the Persians here already.

I hope and expect that the German Kaiser as the successor of Charlemagne and Frederick the Great of Prussia will cause his influence in the East to spread and make itself felt in favour of justice and freedom of conscience; the Sublime Porte will, I think, come to realize, if it is of such persuasion, that the new Empire and its subjects are not hostile to it.

A third article appeared in this magazine on 30 November 1871 (pp. 191–2) but this was a translation of Dr Chaplin's letter to *The Times* (see pp. 210–12).

Then in 1872 (p. 46) this paragraph appears with relation to the Azalís: 'The Persian sect in nearby 'Akká have murdered three of their companions in secret behind closed doors, as a result, it appears, of a religious controversy. The murdered men had separated themselves from the leader of the group and had caused every imaginable harm to the rest of the company. The result is that the sect is even more closely guarded and locked up by the Government.'

On the passing of Bahá'u'lláh, the Templar magazine, now called *Warte des Tempels* (4 August 1892, p. 243), printed a letter from Haifa dated 5 July 1892:

Here [in 'Akka], at first, he [Bahá'u'lláh] was kept as a prisoner. The imprisonment was, however, made gradually lighter and finally was completely annulled. It did not last long, for Bahá'u'lláh ('Beheijah Allah') gained prestige, particularly with the Government officials, and his protection became much sought after. Bahá'u'lláh himself claimed to be a holy man, a Manifestation of God ('Offenbarung

Gottes'), therefore he never appeared before strangers, but remained to them an inaccessible sacred figure. Whoever wanted to have something received or known from him, had to use his son 'Abbás Effendi as an intermediary. According to 'Abbás Effendi's earlier statements, he wanted this Sect to act as a mediator in the conflict between the Christian and Mohammadan religions. It would appear however that as time goes by, it has been steered further and further back into the path of Mohammadanism. Perhaps to this fact may be ascribed the great influence that they exert on their surroundings. They take advantage, it is true, of every opportunity which the Government is pleased to present them. Thus, for example, they erected several tents in the square for the opening of the Kishon bridge, in order to provide temporary quarters for the Páshá. In the tents they entertained the officials and all those who would be received by them, with tea and sweet pastries. They must after all have followers, or at least people who are much inclined to them, in the highest Government circles. It is now a month ago that Bahá'u'lláh, who was, for this Sect, the representative of God, has died. It is as yet to be ascertained what effect this death will have on the Sect, who are said to be very numerous in Persia.

References

1. Historical information obtained from several sources including Hitti *Lebanon in History* and *History of Syria*, al-Kurdí *'Akká*, Dichter *Maps of Acre* and Ma'oz *Ottoman Reform*
2. Letter dated 30 Mar. 1876, CM/O 34/1852–80: CMS Archives
3. Hamilton *Oriental Zigzag* p. 104
4. Eldridge to Layard No. 14, 4 Feb. 1878: FO 195 1201
5. Trotter to White 12 May 1891: FO 195 1723
6. 'Abdu'l-Bahá to Rev. Rosenberg, no date given, enclosed in Rosenberg's letter to Blunt, 24 Nov. 1868. This in turn was enclosed in Blunt to Elliot No. 87, 26 Nov. 1868: FO 195 901 (trans. from Turkish)
7. Rosenberg to Blunt, see 6 *supra*
8. Blunt to Elliot, see 6 *supra*
9. Elliot to Blunt No. 15, 3 Dec. 1868: FO 195 914
10. C. S. de Gobineau *Correspondance* pp. 332–3 (trans. from French)
11. ibid. pp. 333–4
12. ibid. p. 334
13. ibid. pp. 334–5
14. ibid. pp. 336–7
15. *The Times* 5 Oct. 1871, p. 8, col. 3
16. Shoghi Effendi *God Passes By* p. 190
17. *Jewish Intelligence* Dec. 1872, pp. 300–301
18. Shoghi Effendi *God Passes By* p. 190
19. Oliphant *Life in Modern Palestine* p. 107
20. Grant Duff *Notes from a Diary 1886–88* Vol. 2, pp. 20–21
21. Curtis *Today in Syria and Palestine*, p. 221
22. CM/O 72 (a): CMS Archives
23. ibid.
24. CM/O 34: CMS Archives
25. As for 22 *supra*
26. As for 24 *supra*
27. As for 22 *supra*

28. As for 24 *supra*
29. Coleman *Light from the East* pp. 347–9
30. Oliphant *Life in Modern Palestine* pp. 103–7
31. Browne *A Traveller's Narrative* pp. 209–10
32. Chirol *The Middle Eastern Question* p. 122
33. 'Persische Gott in Akka' pp. 165–6 (trans. from German)
34. Grant Duff *Notes from a Diary 1886–88* Vol. 1, p. 251
35. Arslan 'Une Visite au Chef du Babisme' pp. 314–16 (trans. from French)
36. ibid. p. 316
37. Browne *A Traveller's Narrative* pp. xxvii–xliii
38. Supp. 21, Browne Manuscripts, Cambridge University Library
39. ibid.
40. ibid.
41. *Annual Letters* 1891–2 CMS Library. Also printed as an article: Barker 'A North Palestine Station'
42. Barker 'Afternoon Calls in Palestine' pp. 40–42
43. Letter from Charles Gibbern of Eastbourne, G2/PE O/1892/16: CMS Archives
44. G3/O/1892/282: CMS Archives
45. *Annual Letters* 1893, CMS Library
46. *Jour. Roy. Asiat. Soc.* 1892, pp. 706–10
47. Tumanski 'Poslednee slovo Bekhá-ullui'
48. Shoghi Effendi *God Passes By* p. 131
49. ibid. p. 166. The fact that Dr Shíshmán was a Christian is recorded by Áqá Riḍá in his narrative (see Balyuzi *Bahá'u'lláh, The King of Glory* p. 225n).
50. Shoghi Effendi *God Passes By* p. 180
51. See pp. 193 and 196 supra
52. Shoghi Effendi *God Passes By* p. 194
53. ibid. p. 192
54. ibid. p. 194
55. Supp. 22, Browne Manuscripts, Cambridge University Library
56. *Nabíl's Narrative* UK pp. 442–3, USA pp. 603–4
57. Shoghi Effendi *God Passes By* p. 194
58. From an unpublished account by Z. Aṣgharzádih
59. Browne *A Year Amongst the Persians* p. 321
60. Browne's diary of his journey in Persia, Vol. 2, p. 318: Pembroke Coll. Library, Cambridge
61. Aḥmad Sohrab's Diary quoting 'Abdu'l-Bahá: *Star of the West* Vol. VIII, No. 13, 4 Nov. 1917, p. 178 (reprinted in *Star of the West* Vol. 5, Oxford 1978). The editor is grateful to Denis MacEoin for pointing this information out to him.

THIRTEEN

The Progress of the Faith of Bahá'u'lláh

Following the holocaust of 1852, the religion of the Báb appeared to be on the verge of extinction. It retreated to an underground existence, and although writers such as Gobineau kept alive the memory of the pre-1852 days, there was a period of some twenty or thirty years when there was almost no reference to the contemporary activities of the Bábís by European writers. It was not until the latter half of the 1860s, when most of the Bábís had become Bahá'ís, that there was a renewal of activity amongst them. And it was not until more than a decade later that this re-emergence began to attract the attention of Europeans.

The Situation in Persia

During this period when there was a hiatus in the activities of the new religion, Persia was experiencing a series of calamities which exceeded anything in living memory.

Concerning just the first half of 1853, Sheil wrote to Lord Clarendon on 21 June 1853:

> The present has been a year of unusual calamity for Persia. In addition to the almost total destruction of the town of Sheeraz by an earthquake,* many districts of the Province of Fars have been ravaged by flights of locusts. In other provinces the crops have been seriously damaged by mildew caused by the unusual quantity of rain which has fallen during the last three months. Great loss has also been sustained in various districts by showers of hail stones of great weight; the crop of opium, which is the staple produce of Yezd, was destroyed by a violent wind from the desert; and the cholera still commits fearful ravages in the central districts of Persia as well as in the provinces of Mazanderan and Asterabad. The Prime Minister told me the mortality

* Concerning this earthquake that devastated the Báb's native city, Kemball reported from Búshihr on 31 May 1853: 'I take this opportunity to convey to you translation of the account I have received from the British Agent at Shiraz of the severe Earthquake which occurred in that City on the morning of the 4th inst. The destruction of life and property on this occasion is described as far exceeding the effects of a similar visitation in 1824. Half the town has been either laid in ruins or rendered uninhabitable and allowing for native exaggeration the mortality cannot be estimated at less than 5000 souls.' (FO 248 150)

The British Agent in Shíráz, Mírzá Faḍlu'lláh Khán-i-Qazvíní, is somewhat more dramatic in his

had been so great in many of his villages in Mazanderan, that the peasantry, although the harvest had commenced, had left the crops standing and fled in a body, some of the villages remaining without a single inhabitant. Its course is now directed both to the East and South; in the former it has reached the town of Shahrood, half way to Meshed, and, in the latter, Cashan, if it has not already appeared in Ispahan. In the town of Tehran it still exists, but, although a great diminution has taken place in the number of deaths, the average number now being about twenty-five daily instead of about one hundred and thirty when at the highest range, the disease is said to have acquired extraordinary virulence. Hardly a single patient attacked has of late recovered, and the cases generally terminate in from two to six hours from the moment of seizure.*[1]

Nor does this complete the catalogue of woes that afflicted Persia. Over the ensuing years, famine and disease ravaged the country. The famine that

---

description of the events:

'On Wednesday the 24th of Rujub [Rajab], about an hour and a half before dawn of day, a violent shock occurred, which in 10 or 12 minutes laid desolate and overthrew the whole city – multitudes perished, and it is computed that at the very least 10,000 lives were lost, some people say that the numbers of deaths exceeded that amount, but 10,000 may, I think, be considered a fair and unexaggerated statement. The property of all the inhabitants is buried in ruins . . .

'The day of resurrection and judgment has arrived. The atmosphere is close, and the air tainted with the smell from the dead bodies. I am in trouble, and perplexed how to act – the city is uninhabitable, I know not whether to leave it or what to do. On the same day (Wednesday 24th Rujub) shortly after noon a second shock occurred, which destroyed a number of people. The earth is continually shaking, and never seems at rest.

'Hadee Khan, son in law of the Sedr Azim, his wife and family, one and all perished and most families have shared a similar fate: Every one is for himself and it is impossible to extricate the dead from the ruins. The day of judgment is upon us. If indeed either a wall or a roof be left standing, yet so full of cracks, and tottering are they, that it is necessary to hire workmen to pull them down, lest they should fall on the passers by. A house in ruins is preferred to one not in ruins. Some of the buildings of the late Kureem Khan are standing, but they too are cracked.' (FO 248 150)

There is also the report, dated 14 May, of a Swedish doctor, M. Fagergren, who was in Shíráz:

'You will have heard that the town of Shíráz no longer exists, that it was completely destroyed following an earthquake. So far, the tremors have not ceased completely, and God knows when we will be delivered from our anxiety. It is impossible for me to describe all the horrors of that first tremor, which lasted five minutes. All the inhabitants were deep in slumber from which they were awakened by a sound louder than thunder and by a mass of stones which fell into their rooms.

'Of the several thousand victims, only a very small number could be saved. These scenes have continued to repeat themselves for five days, during which 12,000 bodies were counted. On the fourth day, bands of brigands appeared inside and outside the town, who pillaged the unfortunate inhabitants . . .

'This disaster is not the only one to afflict Persia this year, for locusts have ravaged the districts of Fárs and Faraydún, and the province of Iṣfahán. Also, at Iṣfahán the river is completely dried up; in one place, hailstones have devastated all; in another, the seeds have all been ruined by worms; in the province of Yazd, flooding has destroyed the plantations of tobacco and opium.' (From the magazine *Caucase*, quoted in *Revue de l'Orient* 1853. Trans. from French. See Bibliography under Fagergren.)

* On 26 December 1852, George Stevens, in charge of the Tabríz Consulate, reported to Sheil: 'I have the honor to announce for your Excellency's information that the cholera in Tabreez has entirely ceased. The deaths in the town and its suburbs from the 19th October to the 19th instant are variously estimated between 9 and 12,000.'* (FO 248 149)

gripped Ṭihrán at about the time of Mírzá Maḥmúd the Kalántar's death has already been alluded to (see p. 171). A decade later, a similar affliction held most of Persia in its grip. A British magazine gave, in September 1873, a description of the famine of 1871–2 by a missionary, Rev. George Gordon:

> No traveller can pass through Persia at this time without being painfully impressed with the awful ascendency of starvation and famine. To a mind not wholly callous to the claims of suffering humanity, it is a terrible thing to witness daily evidence of distress which it cannot relieve, – to see men, women, and children lying down to die in the snow and frost, with hardly a garment to cover them, or a crust to support them; or to see a mother mourning over her dead child, which she is unable to bury, or a son over his father, while the haggard expression and bony limbs show that it is only a question of days or hours how soon that mother or son will lay down the burden of life, and become the prey of the raven and the jackal. And yet this is no fiction, but what I have daily witnessed. In the streets and bazaars of Teheran, within sight of the bakers' shops and the merchants' stalls, at the doors of the wealthy, and in the pathway of the proud rulers of the land, the helpless victims of starvation and mismanagement are perishing like dogs, and being flung into a nameless grave. It was stated officially by the governor's secretary, that in one night alone in that city, which is but four miles round, there were three hundred deaths, from cold and want.[2]

It is not improbable that these visitations and the consequent demonstration of both gross inefficiency and corruption in the Government, as well as the hypocrisy and worldliness of the Shí'ih divines,* were catalytic factors that created a general feeling of unrest in the country and contributed to the rapid spread of the Bahá'í religion on the one hand, and prepared the minds of the people for political agitation towards liberal reform on the other.

In addition to these natural disasters, there were other factors that increased the restlessness and dissatisfaction of the people and may have created circumstances favourable to the growth of the new religion. On the political front, since the beginning of the nineteenth century, Persia had become increasingly under the political domination of Britain and Russia. Europeans rode through town and country humiliating Persians by their imperious and condescending attitudes and even the least of them considered himself the equal of any Persian prince or governor. Economically also the country was in a parlous state. The cheap goods of Europe, backed by an aggressive mercantilism, had stifled traditional Persian handicrafts and were draining the country of its gold and silver, since Persia was producing little that was desired in Europe. There was a gradual debasement of the coinage and a subsequent inflation in prices that affected the

* In several cities, for example, the 'ulamá hoarded grain during the famine and sold it at great profit. The wealth of Shaykh Muḥammad-Báqir, the 'Wolf' (q.v.), was created in this manner.

lower class in particular. The switch-over from subsistence farming to cash crops benefited the upper classes at the expense of the peasants. All this was particularly hard to bear for a nation as proud and independent as the Persians. In a society where religion is the central theme of life, and in Persian Shí'ism in particular, where the messianic motif is especially strong, it is understandable that the social tensions described above might foster a vigorous, socially-oriented religious movement.

The Spread of the Bahá'í Religion

Although the resurgence of the Bahá'í Faith in Persia dated from Bahá'u'lláh's open proclamation of his claim in 1866–7 and its acceptance by the majority of the Bábís, it was not until the 1870s that Europeans began to note the rapid spread of the religion.

The first European to note that the Bábí community in Persia was rapidly turning into the Bahá'í community was Rev. Dr Bruce (q.v.), the missionary of the Church Missionary Society at Iṣfahán. In a letter to the Society dated 19 November 1874, he wrote:

> As the Baabi persecution* has blown over I think things are getting much smoother here.
>
> I am just now reading the latest *Bible* of the Baabis. The sect of Baabis which is now increasing in Persia is that called Bahâ'i – their chief is now in prison in Acca; he calls himself *The Father* and says Bâb bore to him the same relation as John the Baptist did '*The Son*.' His book is a collection of Divine revelations (?) addressed to 'The Pope', '*The Queen* of London', 'The King of Paris' and other crowned heads. In all his letters to Christians he never alludes to Mahomed but freely quotes the N.T. and says His appearance is the fulfilment of the promise of the Son that he would return.[3]

Arthur Arnold (q.v.), who travelled through Persia with his wife in 1875–6, passed through Iṣfahán and it was doubtless also from Rev. Dr Bruce that he obtained the statement that he makes in his book, *Through Persia by Caravan*:

> Yet the Bábis remain the terror and trouble of the Government of Ispahan, where the sect is reputed to number more followers than anywhere else in Persia. But many of them have, in the present day, transferred their allegiance from Báb to Behar, a man who was lately, and may be at present, imprisoned at Acca, in Arabia, by the Turkish Government. Behar represents himself as God the Father in human form, and declares that Báb occupies the same position, in regard to himself, that John the Baptist held to Jesus Christ. We were assured that there are respectable families in Ispahan who worship this imprisoned fanatic, who endanger their property and their lives by a secret devotion, which if known, would bring them to destitution, and probably to a cruel death.[4]

One of the first Europeans to attempt to assess the renewed vigour within the Bábí-Bahá'í movement was J. D. Rees (q.v.), an Indian civil servant who travelled through Persia in 1885. He wrote an article 'The Bab and Babism'

* See pp. 269–73.

for the periodical *Nineteenth Century* in 1896. This article is based on Gobineau's work but also embodies the results of Rees's own enquiries. Thus, he writes:

So died the Bab at the age of twenty-seven;* but his place was at once taken, if not filled, by Baha, a youth of sixteen years, who, for reasons not very clearly established, was considered by the leaders of the faith to be destined to succeed. Pursued by the emissaries of the prime minister, this youth established himself at Baghdad, where . . . he continued to preach the doctrines of his predecessor and to show the way to the gate of heaven. By some in Persia I was told that . . . he never shows his face, though he interviews all comers. I must confess that to my annoyance and disappointment I could learn nothing of himself in Baghdad. Some said the Sultan kept him in prison to please the Shah . . .†[5]

Referring to the holocaust following the attempt on the life of the S͟háh, Rees writes:

These terrible reprisals . . . produced outwardly at any rate, the desired effect. No man dared name Bab or Babee without a curse as deep as that deserved by Omar. The very subject became a dangerous one to speak of, and it still continues to be so. An official at Teheran, who was I know conversant with the whole subject, denied all knowledge. Officials all declared not one of the sons of burnt fathers remained. Princes, who are plentiful in Persia, considered a reference to the matter in bad taste and would change the subject. Traders, sitting cross-legged amidst their grain and wares, would suggest that if you wanted to buy nothing you had better move on. The result is that even those Europeans who have been long resident in the country really know extremely little about the tenets of the Babees, or their present position, numbers and prospects. The writings of Bab and Baha are hard to get, and when got still harder to read with understanding.[6]

In conclusion Rees writes:

To come to any conclusions as to the extent to which Babees now exist in Persia is most difficult. At Kazneen [Qazvín] a Georgian who had been many years in the country, and was at that time in the service of a high official there, told me that he thought that amongst the rich and educated perhaps one-third were followers of Bab. This is probably an over-estimate, but that among the classes named there is a large proportion which is dissatisfied with the Islam of the priests is well known. Among the nomads of the Hills, the Turki tribes and others, there are no Babees . . . Near Kermanshah one day I met a Seyyad, or a descendant of the Prophet, . . . and he said there was not a Babee left in all Persia . . . In Hamadan – one of the largest towns in Persia – I have reason to believe, from inquiries made on the spot, that there are very large numbers who in secret hold to the faith of the young and martyred prophet. At Abadeh there certainly are many such, though gruesome pits full of Babees' skulls exist within the walls of the town.

In Khorassan and the western [*sic*] provinces of Persia I have not travelled, but my inquiries went to show that in the holy city of Mashad, around the shrine of the Imam Reza itself, Babees abound . . .[7]

* The Báb was in fact thirty years old at the time of his martyrdom.

† It is evident that Rees has here confused Mírzá Yaḥyá, who was 16 at the death of the Báb and 'never shows his face', with Bahá'u'lláh, to whom the majority of the Bábís had given their allegiance.

At the conclusion of another article on Persia, Rees states:

It is not, as is said, true that the followers of Bab are no more. They increase and multiply in secret after the fashion of persecuted religions. They are not Nihilists or Communists or Atheists, as all men say of them. They reject the doctrine of circumcision, plurality of wives, and facile divorce. They allow one wife, and divorce her on much the same terms as we do . . . In every city of Persia, among the rich and educated, Babees abound who will one day make their voices heard. Their Christianlike tenets and patient endurance are as admirable as the follies of Sufeeism are the reverse, and their gentleness contrasts with the fierceness of the Wahabee reformers.[8]

Mary F. Wilson, writing in *Contemporary Review* in 1885, states:

They write many books, which are secretly circulated and eagerly read; and while converts are made among all classes, their views have taken the deepest hold among the educated and intelligent. Meanwhile, the rulers, taught by experience, continue their policy of toleration. They make no enquiry, lest they should hear too much; they are determinedly blind to indications of indifference to the true faith; for when it is believed that many, even among the moullas, and the highest officers of state, and those nearest the person of the king, belong to the dreaded and mysterious community, it is felt to be the wisest and safest course not to know.

Dr Bruce, writing lately from Persia, gives the present number of Bâbys as 100,000; but while their policy is what has been indicated, how can they be anything like accurately numbered?[9]

Among the diplomatic corps in Ṭihrán, the resurgence of the Bábí-Bahá'í movement did not go unnoticed, although their information was sadly deficient. On 8 September 1888, Sir Henry Drummond Wolff forwarded to the Marquess of Salisbury a dispatch from the British Consul in Bú<u>sh</u>ihr, Colonel E. C. Ross (q.v.). In this dispatch, Ross gives an account of the progress of the Bahá'í religion. Although wrong in many details, this account, nevertheless, emphasizes the growing importance of the movement.

A respectable and usually well-informed correspondent of mine in Shiraz has written me some curious statements regarding the alleged great increase and wide-spread existence of the 'Babi' sect in Persia, Turkey etc. I have from time to time heard from other sources of the extensive spread of this secret society, which is considered perhaps justly as somewhat analogous to 'nihilism'. The statements, I now refer to, are somewhat startling and I must guard myself from vouching for their truth and accuracy.

What I know to be fact is that a good deal of stir [was] made in Shiraz about 'Babi-ism' by a fanatical priest* and a few days ago it was openly stated three persons *in Bushire* have embraced Babi-ism.

At first, the followers of the 'Bab' scorned to deny their faith preferring torture and death. Now it appears the spiritual head of the sect has given a dispensation and Babis now practice ('Takiyeh') concealment with mental reservation or denial, even to the extent of reviling openly the 'Bab' and all his works. This sect has an intense fascination for the subtle and versatile Persian mind.

* This priest was named Siyyid 'Alí-Akbar. Concerning these troubles in <u>Sh</u>íráz and Bú<u>sh</u>ihr, see the letter from Mírzá 'Alí Áqá to Browne quoted in *A Traveller's Narrative* pp. 410–11.

May it not also hold the germs of political revolution? May not a sorely crushed ill-treated people cherish hopes of liberation through its means? Certain it is that it is a force to be reckoned with, an element well worthy of attention. From private statements of members of the sect one is to believe that it numbers five million souls in Persia, Turkey, India etc, the spread and increase being in the direct ratio of the opposition and danger, greatest of course in Persia. A still more startling assertion is that the sect is favoured by some of the most influential men in Persia, next to the Royal family, who are not suspected of playing with the heresy. The Zil-es-Sultan is well-known to be freethinking on religious subjects, but he was found as an active opponent of Babi-ism. It is hinted that the secret influence of the society contributed to his fall. To understand the scope of this idea it must be explained that the allegations referred to, go so far as to claim the Amin-es-Sultan for a Babi at heart,* and to place Babis at the head of the chief departments Customs Governments etc.

My correspondent writes 'I omitted to write that Saad-ul-Mulk owes his promotion to the post of Governor of Bushire simply to his being a Babi. His brother, Saad (Nizam) es-Sultaneh, owes his advancement to his present high position, to the same cause'.†

I am inclined to think some persons have been imposing on the credulity of my informant who apologizes for 'opinions too freely expressed' and information of a serious 'character'. I am sure he writes in good faith however.[10]

In a letter to E. G. Browne, dated 12 December 1889, Sidney Churchill (q.v.), who was then Oriental Second Secretary at the British Legation in Ṭihrán, wrote:

The Babi sect are multiplying in numbers daily, and their increasing multitudes are giving cause for anxiety as to the attitude which the authorities will have to adopt towards them in the immediate future. The extraordinary development of this faith is not quite in itself a source of surprise. The Persian as a rule is ready to adopt any new crede [*sic*] no matter what it is; but when he finds in it as one of its fundamental principles the liberty of thought and the expression thereof with the ultimate possibility as a result that he may shake off the oppression he suffers at the hands of the local authorities who are beyond the sphere of the Shah's immediate supervision and control, he readily affiliates himself with those holding such doctrines with the object of combating existing evils.

The spread of Babism of late in Persia, particularly its development during the Shah's absence has caused much surprise and is likely to give us trouble. But the question is what are the real ideas of most of those professing Babism. Do they look upon themselves as followers of a new religion or as the members of a society for political and social reform?[11]

The Hon. George Curzon (later Lord Curzon of Kedleston, the distinguished British Foreign Secretary) visited Persia in 1889–90. In his brilliant work *Persia and the Persian Question* he gives what is, in many ways, the most penetrating analysis of the religion of Bahá'u'lláh penned in the nineteenth century (see pp. 45–7). After describing the developments within the religion since the time of the Báb, Curzon goes on to consider the situation as he found it when he was in Persia.

* This was not, of course, true; but Amínu's-Sulṭán was well informed about the religion; see p. 358.
† These two brothers were Bahá'ís.

It will thus be seen that, in its external organisation, Babism has undergone great and radical changes since it first appeared as a proselytising force half a century ago. These changes, however, have in no wise impaired, but appear, on the contrary, to have stimulated its propaganda, which has advanced with a rapidity inexplicable to those who can only see therein a crude form of political or even of metaphysical fermentation. The lowest estimate places the present number of Babis in Persia at half a million. I am disposed to think, from conversations with persons well qualified to judge, that the total is nearer one million. They are to be found in every walk of life, from the ministers and nobles of the Court to the scavenger or the groom, not the least arena of their activity being the Mussulman priesthood itself. It will have been noticed that the movement was initiated by *Seyids*, *hajis*, and *mullahs* - i.e. persons who, either by descent, from pious inclination, or by profession, were intimately concerned with the Mohammedan creed; and it is among even the professed votaries of the faith that they continue to make their converts. Many Babis are well known to be such, but, as long as they walk circumspectly, are free from intrusion or persecution. In the poorer walks of life the fact is, as a rule, concealed for fear of giving an excuse for the superstitious rancour of superiors . . .

If Babism continues to grow at its present rate of progression, a time may conceivably come when it will oust Mohammedanism from the field in Persia.[12]

One facet of the rapid progress of the Bahá'í religion during this period was the conversion of a large number of Jews in towns such as Hamadán* and Káshán, and Zoroastrians in Yazd;† communities which for over a thousand years had faced and rejected Islam now through conversion to the religion of Bahá'u'lláh also accepted Muḥammad. Sidney Churchill submitted a memorandum dated 30 January 1890, on the subject of the conversion of Jews to the new religion. This was forwarded by Sir Henry Drummond Wolff to the Marquess of Salisbury.

According to the Jews of Tehran a remarkable movement has developed itself amongst their coreligionists all over the country in the spontaneous adoption of Babism by them.

Babism, apparently, first broke out amongst the Jews of Hamadan and the followers of the new creed gave themselves out as Protestant converts. Now, however, that their numbers have considerably increased they have thrown off the mask they had assumed and openly profess Babism. Some of the original converts have visited Mirza Husain Ali, the present head of the Babis, residing in banishment at Acre; and since their return to Persia have even been honoured by the receipt of Luhs [*Lawh*, or tablet]; missives from the Bab which they look on as holy writings.

At Kermanshah and at Hamadan together there are about 200 Jewish Babis and spread over the rest of Persia, in Iraq, Kashan, Tehran, Isfahan and other places about another hundred. This total is gradually swelling.[13]

* Hamadán has been an important centre of Judaism since the time of the Babylonian exile. The tombs of Esther and Mordecai are said to be sited there.

† When missionaries of the Church Missionary Society first began to work in Yazd and Kirmán in the early 1890s they found that many of the Zoroastrians had become Bahá'ís. Thus Rev. Stileman wrote from Kirmán in February 1899: 'I was much surprised to learn that many of the Parsees, both of Yazd and Kirmân, have adopted the Behâî Faith, thus following the example of many Jews in other parts of Persia.' (CMS Archives, G2/PE/0/1899)

Curzon, too, reports this trend, in his *Persia and the Persian Question*: 'Quite recently the Babis have had great success in the camp of another enemy, having secured many proselytes among the Jewish populations of the Persian towns. I hear that during the past year they are reported to have made 150 Jewish converts in Teheran, 100 in Hamadan, 50 in Kashan, and 75 per cent of the Jews at Gulpaigan.'[14]

Sir Henry Drummond Wolff's Intervention

Sir Henry Drummond Wolff (q.v., see fig. 28) was the British Minister in Ṭihrán for less than three years (April 1888 to November 1890), and yet in this short time he made more of a mark than many Ministers who stayed much longer. During his period of time in Ṭihrán, he greatly raised British prestige at the court of the Sháh. His warm humanitarian influence is demonstrated by a decree promulgated in 1888 by the Sháh, under Wolff's influence, guaranteeing security of life and property to the subjects of the Sháh. The fact that the decree was never enforced does not detract from the credit that is Wolff's for attempting to establish the concepts contained within it.

When the existence of the Bahá'í community first came to his attention through Ross's dispatch in 1888 (see above), Wolff was for some reason badly misinformed about the Bahá'ís, imagining them to be political revolutionaries led by Siyyid Jamálu'd-Dín-i-Afghání (see p. 45). Sidney Churchill, who was then Second Secretary at the Legation and in touch with E. G. Browne, doubtless provided him with more accurate information (Browne sent Churchill a copy of his paper 'The Bábís of Persia' in 1889). In any event when the upheavals in Sidih and Najafábád erupted (see chapter 17), Wolff spared no effort to put a stop to the persecutions and to obtain justice for the victims of oppression.

It was illness that eventually terminated Wolff's period of office in Ṭihrán. For much of 1890, he was dangerously ill. Towards the end of that year, he had recovered sufficiently to make it feasible for him to be moved to London. Although Wolff himself very much wanted to return, his state of health made this impossible and he was transferred to the Madrid Legation.

One of Wolff's last acts before leaving Persia in November 1890 was to attempt to persuade the Sháh to issue a proclamation establishing religious liberty and toleration in Persia for all religions and sects. He failed in this attempt, but he pressed for it right up to his last days in Ṭihrán. At his farewell interview with Amínu's-Sulṭán, on 8 November 1890, Wolff made one last effort to push through this measure. In his final dispatch as British Minister in Ṭihrán, Wolff gave the Marquess of Salisbury the following account of his audience:

I expressed to His Highness my earnest desire for the publication of the proclamation establishing religious liberty in Persia, for all sects and denominations. His Highness replied that the principles of such a proclamation were already in force and would be carried out but that it was thought premature to embody these principles in a proclamation on account of the opposition of the mollahs; it would, however, be done on the first occasion.

I asked His Highness whether this piece of intelligence might be made generally known in England: to this he replied that there was no objection.

I especially enquired whether it would apply to dissidents of the Mussulman faith, intending, without mentioning the name, to allude to the Babis. His Highness replied that it would apply equally to all sects.[15]

References

1. Sheil to Clarendon No. 50, 21 June 1853: FO 60 180
2. Account by Rev. George Gordon quoted in Maj.-Gen. Lake's article in the magazine *Sunday at Home* Sept. 1873. This article is quoted in Piggot *Persia – Ancient and Modern* pp. 174–5
3. File CI 1/o 61, No. 12: CMS Archives
4. A. Arnold *Through Persia by Caravan* Vol. 2, pp. 34–5
5. Rees 'The Bab and Babism' pp. 59–60
6. ibid. p. 61
7. ibid. pp. 65–6
8. Rees 'Persia' p. 453
9. Wilson 'The Story of the Bâb' p. 829
10. Ross to Wolff 25 Aug. 1888, enclosed in Wolff to Salisbury No. 178, 8 Sept. 1888: FO 60 493
11. Browne *Materials* p. 293. Original letter in Cambridge Univ. Library (Browne Papers, Folder 2, No. 17)
12. Curzon *Persia and the Persian Question* Vol. 1, pp. 499–500, 503
13. Churchill's memo 30 Jan. 1890, enclosed in Wolff to Salisbury No. 33, 4 Feb. 1890: FO 60 510
14. Curzon *Persia and the Persian Question* Vol. 1, p. 500
15. Wolff to Salisbury No. 310, 10 Nov. 1890: FO 60 512

FOURTEEN

Martyrdoms in Persia (1867–74)

The Tabríz Episode, 1866–7

The period immediately after Bahá'u'lláh had openly put forward his claim to be 'Him Whom God shall make Manifest', in Adrianople in 1866, was one of intense turmoil, as communities of Bábís, brought together again with great difficulty after the persecutions of 1850–52, dealt with the implications of Bahá'u'lláh's momentous declaration. In many places, the entire community accepted Bahá'u'lláh's claim, while in others the believers were split: altercation ensued and even violence. Tabríz appears to have been an example of the latter phenomenon. It is difficult to be certain from the various accounts exactly what transpired, but it would appear that in the middle of a heated religious argument, violence broke out that resulted in the death of the old and feeble Áqá Siyyid 'Alíy-i-'Arab.* This death was seized upon as an excuse to make arrests of numerous Bahá'ís throughout Tabríz. Most of these had nothing whatsoever to do with the incident, but the great revival of spirit among the Bahá'ís was evidently worrying the authorities, as the following accounts indicate. A short while later, three of those arrested were executed: Shaykh Aḥmad-i-Khurásání, who is accused of the actual murder in the dispatch of the Russian Consul; Mírzá Muṣṭafáy-i-Naráqí, who had been in the presence of Bahá'u'lláh at Constantinople; and Mírzá 'Alí-Naqí; the remainder were forced to pay a considerable amount of money to effect their release.

* There are several conflicting Bahá'í and Azalí accounts of this episode in addition to the European sources quoted here. Of the Azalí accounts, the author of the *Hasht Bihisht* claims that the murder of Siyyid 'Alí was a part of a deliberate and premeditated plan to assassinate the leading Azalís (Browne *A Traveller's Narrative* p. 363), while the Azalí source quoted by Nicolas makes it clear that the death occurred in the middle of a religious argument (Nicolas 'Le Dossier russo-anglais' p. 362n). Bahá'í sources (such as 'Abdu'l-Bahá in *Memorials of the Faithful* p. 149, and Mírzá Javád in Browne's *Materials* p. 35) concentrate on the martyrdom of the three followers of Bahá'u'lláh; however, the manuscript history of the Bahá'í Faith in Ádharbáyján by Mírzá Ḥaydar-'Alíy-i-Uskú'í (with notes by Áqá Muḥammad-Ḥusayn-i-Mílání) gives details of the death of Siyyid 'Alíy-i-'Arab and states that the quarrel had broken out when Siyyid 'Alí began to abuse Bahá'u'lláh.

The Russian Consul reported these proceedings to the Chargé d'Affaires at the Russian Legation in Ṭihrán in a dispatch of 23 December 1866:

I respectfully take the liberty of bringing to your attention that latterly, in Tabríz, there has appeared a great movement towards conversion to Bábism. The Government has effected numerous arrests in the town.

These are the facts as they appear:

A Siyyid of Tabríz, an old man, whose name I do not know, was killed by a Khurásání, Shaykh Aḥmad. The latter was immediately seized and taken to the house of the Mushír-Lashkar, Mírzá Qahramán.* There in the presence of the Mujtahid Ḥájí Mírzá Báqir, Shaykh Aḥmad was subjected to an interrogation on the causes of his crime. Shaykh Aḥmad replied that the Siyyid deserved his fate because he did not carry out the laws of the Sharí'at. Further, he confessed to being one of the leaders of the new sect.

Among the papers found in the lodgings of Shaykh Aḥmad, 90 letters addressed to different persons, either in Persia or Turkey, were seized. He himself had been the courier, charged with ensuring the delivery of these letters to their addresses. There were also found numerous examples of the Bábí Qur'án.

Everyone whose name was found on the letters and who lived in Tabríz was arrested. Now one of these letters was addressed to Ḥájí Ja'farof, a merchant in manufactured goods in Ṭihrán. This was telegraphed to Sardár Qulí,† who took the necessary measures to arrest this merchant and who telegraphed to Mushír-Lashkar to search out carefully and arrest all suspected persons. The number of persons thrown into prison has reached, it is said, 100 men. It is not known what fate awaits them, but this will soon, I think, be announced.[1]

A few days later, on 31 December, the Russian Consul appended the following to his previous report:

In completing my report dated 11 December,‡ No. 992, I take the liberty of presenting you with a copy of the instructions, which I have secretly acquired, given by the Murshid of the Bábís§ to Shaykh Aḥmad, an adherent of the aforementioned sect, arrested at Tabríz.

In this town the arrests under the charge of Bábism continue.[2]

A further two weeks passed before, finally, the Russian Consul announced the execution of the three Bahá'ís, in a dispatch of 15 January 1867:

* Nicolas adds a note to the effect that this is evidently a lapse, as Mírzá Qahramán had the military title Amín-Lashkar. But Abbott also mentions Mushír-Lashkar. It is probable that Mírzá Qahramán was at this time called Mushír-Lashkar and was later given the title Amín-Lashkar. This man was acting as deputy to 'Azíz Khán-i-Mukrí, Sardár-i-Kull (q.v.), who was Minister to the province of Ádharbáyján. The Governor of the province was Muẓaffaru'd-Dín Mírzá (later Sháh). A few years later, Mírzá Qahramán was arrested on charges of embezzling army funds.

† Presumably Sardár-i-Kull, i.e. 'Azíz Khán-i-Mukrí.

‡ OS, i.e. 23 Dec. NS

§ Presumably Bahá'u'lláh. Nicolas did not obtain a copy of these 'instructions' but Tumanski appears to have come across the same set of correspondence and obtained the 'instructions' which he published in the introduction to his translation of the *Kitábu'l-Aqdas*. This is a very strangely-worded letter of instructions, not at all similar to Bahá'u'lláh's style.

Through my reports dated 11 and 19 December* of last year, I have had the honour of bringing to your attention that a great number of Bábís have been arrested in Tabríz.

Four days ago telegraphic orders were received from Sardár Qulí† to execute the arrested sectaries. The same day, three of them, notably Shaykh Aḥmad, Mírzá Muṣṭafá and a darvísh whose name escapes me, were executed. The bodies remained abandoned at the place of execution‡ for three days and were left exposed to the malevolence of the passers-by and to injury from wandering animals. They were, in effect, devoured by the dogs and their remains were interred on the fourth day.[3]

The British Consul at Tabríz, Keith Abbott (q.v.), also reported these executions in a dispatch dated 16 January 1867, to Mr Charles Alison (q.v.), the British Minister at Ṭihrán:

The murder of a Bâbee Seyed took place here lately under very atrocious circumstances, the perpetrators of the act being associates of his own who appear to have adopted some new style of Bâbism and to have fallen out with him in consequence. They put him to a most cruel death. They were arrested and two of them have since been executed – but a third man, one Mirza Mustafa, Nerâkee, suffered with them though he does not appear to have had anything more serious laid to his charge than that of being a Bâbee. This man had obtained Turkish protection at Baghdad – some interference on his behalf was made by the Turkish Consul here and a promise was made the latter that he should not be punished beyond imprisonment without due notice to him. He was however put to death without any such formality.

Several other men are now confined in the dungeon here on a charge of the above heresy and orders were given from Tehran, I understand, for their execution but this has been deferred in consequence of the Mushir e Lashker having pleaded for them. It is however to be feared that with the well known feelings of the Shah towards this sect, little mercy will be shown them.§[4]

Martyrdoms in Zanján and Ṭihrán, 1867

Shortly after these martyrdoms at Tabríz, there occurred several other martyrdoms in Persia. At Zanján, Mírzá Muḥammad-'Alí, a physician, was seized and beheaded. His name is mentioned in the letter of instructions to Shaykh Aḥmad forwarded by the Russian Consul in Tabríz in his dispatch of 31 December (19 December OS) 1866 (see above), and published by Tumanski.[5] It was probably this captured letter that sealed Mírzá Muḥammad-'Alí's fate.‖

* OS, i.e. 23 and 31 Dec. NS

† See note p. 252n.

‡ The Haft-Kachal Square, according to a note by Nicolas. This is confirmed in Mírzá Javád's account (Browne *Materials* p. 35).

§ They were in fact later released on payment of a fine.

‖ The manuscript history by Mírzá Ḥaydar-'Alíy-i-Uskú'í, mentioned in a note on p. 251, states that the cause of Mírzá Muḥammad-'Alí's fate was a petition which he had addressed to Bahá'u'lláh, found among Shaykh Aḥmad's papers.

In Ṭihrán, at about this time, Áqá Najaf-'Alí of Zanján, who had been one of the disciples of Ḥujjat and had but recently returned from Adrianople, was arrested, and after a term in prison, during which he was tortured to make him reveal the names of his fellow-believers, he was executed.

These two martyrdoms in Zanján and Ṭihrán, following closely upon those in Tabríz, were reported by Alison, the British Minister at Ṭihrán, to Lord Stanley, the British Foreign Minister, on 9 March 1867:

> A disturbance occurred lately in the town of Zenjan after the execution of a Babee. It appears to have been got up by an idle rabble in the hope of obtaining plunder, instigated probably by some intriguers inimical to the local Authorities. It was soon quelled, however, and the Shah has sent orders for the punishment of the ringleaders. About the same time a few other men of the sect of Báb were executed at Tehran and Tabreez.
>
> These events have somewhat alarmed the Shah, who was no doubt reminded by them of the attempt made in 1852 upon His life, and His Majesty has consequently shown of late an increased eagerness to conciliate the Priesthood.[6]

The Martyrdom of Badí'

During the last years in Adrianople and the first few years at 'Akká, Bahá'u'lláh addressed a number of letters to various monarchs. The letter to Náṣiru'd-Dín Sháh required a special bearer, since whoever delivered it risked almost certain death. Although many asked for the privilege of taking the letter, Bahá'u'lláh waited until there arrived in 'Akká a young man from Khurásán, Áqá Buzurg, whom Bahá'u'lláh renamed Badí' (Wonderful).

Badí' set off alone for Persia and guided by Bahá'u'lláh's instructions* communicated with no one on the way. Eventually he arrived in Ṭihrán and was successful in fulfilling his mission. M. de Bonnières,† the French Minister, described, in a dispatch dated 10 July 1869, the delivery of Bahá'u'lláh's letter to the Sháh and the fate of its bearer:

> The King left the palace of Níyávarán‡ a fortnight ago in order to proceed, as he does every year, to Mázindarán where the wild forests afford him a temperature more bearable than that of our surroundings, and more abundant chase.
>
> Some days ago, His Majesty was returning to his camp when a man wearing a strange costume appeared on his path. The *Farráshes* who always accompany the King drove him away with blows of their sticks as is customary when someone dares to show himself on the path of the King. The King gave orders to arrest this man and to ask him what he wanted. He declared that he was instructed to present a petition ['une requête'] to the Sháh. An envelope was found on him which contained a long letter

* These may be found in Browne *A Traveller's Narrative* pp. 390–92.

† E. de Bonnières de Wierre, French Minister in Ṭihrán 23 March 1867 – 17 July 1871.

‡ See fig. 29.

in Persian on parchment. This petition was drafted in a remarkable manner as much with respect to its style as to its writing, similar to what would come from a high-born personage. It contained many Arabic words and the particular phraseology of the Bábís. It emanated, according to the word of the person who bore it, from the Báb or chief of the Bábís, who is in prison at this moment in St Jean d'Acre. In this letter, the Báb addresses the King in terms that are respectful but do not lack audacity. He calls himself the leader of the new and only true religion and asks to come to Persia in order to demonstrate publicly in a gathering composed of the theologians of Islam, the superiority and the truth of the belief of which he is the incarnation.

As soon as the King had been apprised of this petition, he gave orders to submit the sectary to torture. They wanted to extract from him some curse against the Báb. He refused consistently. They wanted to obtain information about the people with whom he had had contact during his journey to Ṭihrán. He did not give it to them, and he showed under torture great courage and an invincible will.

Doctor Tholozan [q.v., see fig. 30] who is accompanying the King, advised him to be clement: he argued that torture was a barbaric custom and that it had not been applied among civilized nations for a long time, and that it was, in any case, always an ineffective method when used against persons who were under the influence of religious exaltation, and finally he emphasized the point that the sectary was not armed.

This advice was not listened to and the unfortunate man was beheaded the next day.*

It is evident that this event is connected with the secret designs of the sect of the Bábís, which the King believed had been exterminated in the bloody and barbarous executions of 1854, following an attempt committed by a Bábí against his person in the streets of Ṭihrán; it indicates in any case a considerable strength of spirit in the leader of this sect and in these sectarians.

The discredit of the Qájár dynasty and the Persian Government has reached the point where the most serious events can be expected, particularly in the presence of a frightening increase in the impoverishment of the people, and a lack of all produce from the countryside, that can only be attributed to the present bad administration.

The Bábís are not ignorant of this unfortunate situation, and it is not surprising that they cherish any means that will cause to disappear whatever puts an obstacle in their path. They have, supporting them, a large part of the population and functionaries of all ranks, for one is assured that even in the entourage of the King and among the Ministers there are Bábís.[7]

Upheaval in Káshán

The French Minister, M. Mellinot, reported at the close of 1874, an upheaval in Káshán. His dispatch, which is dated 30 December 1874, is addressed to the French Foreign Minister, Duc Decazes (q.v.), and in the first part, he deals with the Sháh's plan to seize Baghdád and Karbilá should hostilities commence between Russia and Turkey:

. . . in any case, I have believed it necessary to urge Mírzá Ḥusayn Khán [q.v.] to deter his master from all hazardous ventures of this sort. Advice which is all the more justified since the discontent of the people against His Majesty can one day

* According to an eyewitness account, the head of Badí' was crushed. (See Balyuzi *Bahá'u'lláh, The King of Glory* pp. 306–7.)

create for him the most serious difficulties in the interior, as can be demonstrated by the arrest of a dozen Bábís in Káshán, a town situated 35 leagues south of Ṭihrán. These people have been led to the capital and put in chains and imprisoned. Their first interrogation has demonstrated the vitality of this sect and the ardour of their convictions. According to the declarations of the captives the numbers of their co-religionists has risen to 500,000, among which may be counted a certain number of mullás.

The Sháh, very excited, as occurs every time that the existence of the Bábís reveals itself, has convoked in this case an extraordinary Council in which one of the foremost doctors in the Sharí'at has been consulted on the punishment to be inflicted on these prisoners. Must one apply the death penalty or simply guard them in prison, when they have haughtily declared that their lives could be taken but they will have avengers?* After long deliberation, the Council had been of the opinion that His Majesty must not manifest any fear of their menaces, but should instead give them their liberty. The Sháh adopting this solution has added that his life was in the hands of God and that if his destiny was to perish at the hands of the Bábís, he would not know how to avoid it. The prisoners, whose only definitive crime was to belong to the religion preached by the former Báb, which has been vouched for by the blood of his martyrs, have, therefore, been set free.[8]

References

1. Russian Con. at Tabríz to Chargé d'Affaires at Ṭihrán No. 992, 11 Dec. 1886 OS (23 Dec. NS): Nicolas 'Le Dossier russo-anglais' pp. 362–3 (trans. from French). In this article, the date of this dispatch is in fact given as being 21 Dec. OS (i.e. 2 Jan.); but this is obviously an error, as the next dispatch quoted shows.
2. Russian Con. to Chargé d'Affaires No. 1021, 19 Dec. 1866 OS (31 Dec. NS): Nicolas 'Le Dossier russo-anglais' p. 363 (trans. from French)
3. Russian Con. to Chargé d'Affaires No. 4, 3 Jan. 1867 OS (15 Jan. NS): Nicolas 'Le Dossier russo-anglais' p. 363 (trans. from French)
4. Abbott to Alison No. 4, 16 Jan. 1867: FO 248 239
5. Tumanski, *Kitabe Akdes* p. xviii
6. Alison to Stanley No. 14, 9 Mar. 1867: FO 60 304
7. De Bonnières to de La Valette No. 40, 10 July 1869: MAE Sér. Corr. Polit., Perse 34, pp. 69–72 (trans. from French)
8. Mellinot to Duc Decazes No. 16, 30 Dec. 1874: MAE Sér. Corr. Polit., Perse 37, pp. 294–6 (trans. from French)

* The idea that the Bábís were bent on vengeance seems to have been current and was probably a legacy from the attempt on the life of the Sháh. (See p. 128.)

21. Baron von Prokesch-Osten, Austrian Ambassador at Istanbul

22. Rev. L. Rosenberg, missionary in Adrianople

23. Georg David Hardegg, leader of the German Templar colony in Haifa

24. Dr Thomas Chaplin, British medical missionary

25. Rev. John Zeller, German missionary at Nazareth (Church Missionary Society)

26. Rev. James Huber, German missionary at Nazareth (Church Missionary Society)

27. Laurence Oliphant

28. Sir Henry Drummond Wolff, British diplomat, a cartoon by 'Ape' in Vanity Fair

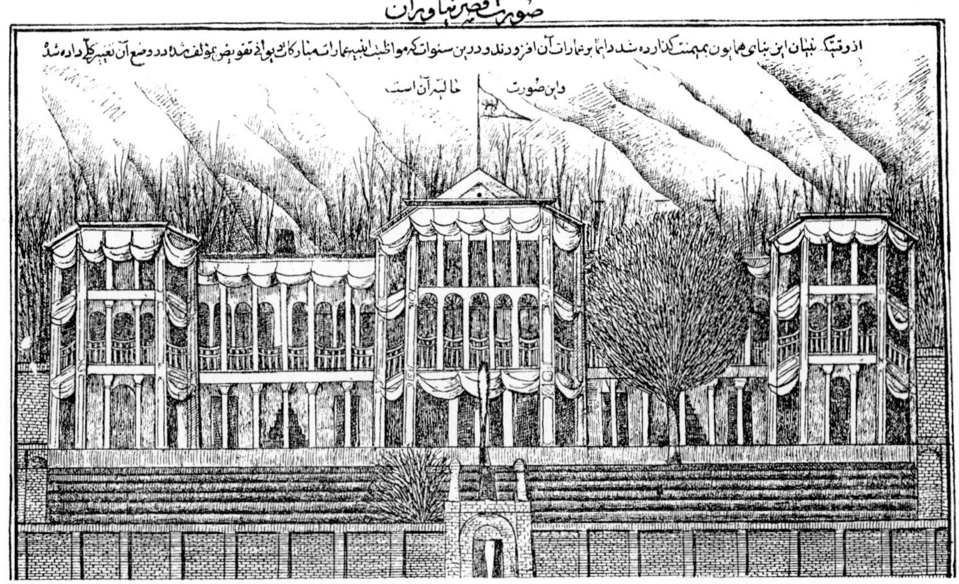

29. *Palace of Níyávarán, outside which Badí' was arrested*

30. *Dr Tholozan, French personal physician to the Sháh (Dieulafoy* La Perse, la Chaldée et la Susiane*)*

31. *Rev. Robert Bruce, British missionary at Iṣfahán (Church Missionary Society)*

32. Shaykh Muḥammad Báqir, mujtahid of Iṣfahán, stigmatized by Bahá'u'lláh as 'The Wolf'

33. Sulṭán-Mas'úd, the Ẓillu's-Sulṭán, Governor of Iṣfahán

34. Siyyid Muḥammad-Ḥasan, the King of Martyrs

35. Siyyid Muḥammad-Ḥusayn, the Beloved of Martyrs

FIFTEEN

Events in Egypt (1867–9)

During the time that Bahá'u'lláh was at Adrianople, there grew up a small community of Persian Bahá'ís in Egypt. They were mostly merchants who settled at Manṣúra, near Cairo, and were carrying on a trade between Persia, India and Egypt. The most prominent of these was Ḥájí Mírzá Ḥaydar-'Alí of Iṣfahán.

Although they had done nothing contrary to the law, nor were they engaged in any subversive activity, seven Bahá'ís were arrested by the Persian Consul at Cairo, Mírzá Ḥasan K͟hán-i-Giránmáyih, who had asserted his power over them, as Consul, and obtained the co-operation of the Egyptian authorities. After a period of time in prison, these unfortunate people were exiled, under severe circumstances, to K͟hartúm in the Sudan.

A few months later, Mírzá Ḥasan K͟hán moved against the elderly Mírzá Abu'l-Qásim and accused him of being a Bahá'í. Threatening him with similar exile to K͟hartúm, he succeeded in mulcting him of a considerable sum of money.

Mírzá Ḥasan K͟hán, urged on by the Persian Ambassador at Istanbul, Mírzá Ḥusayn K͟hán (q.v.), who was sharing the spoils, now decided to turn his attention to a group of seven wealthy merchants who were of Persian origin but had come under British protection by virtue of having been born or lived for a long time in India. He accused them of being Bahá'ís and there ensued a lengthy process of investigations, claims and counter-claims which are recorded in the files of the British Foreign Office.

In one of these letters, dated 28 July 1868, Mr Frederick Ayrton, a respected British resident of Cairo, refers to the previous persecutions of the Bahá'ís. With regard to the arrest of the Bahá'ís at Manṣúra, he writes: 'Several Persians, who were quietly located and carrying on their industry at Mansura were, on a similar charge seized last winter, and those of them, who could not pay, were actually, I am informed, deported to the Upper Nile – The Local Government, not seeing the distinction between lending its aid for a religious and corrupt persecution, and for purposes of established law and justice.'[1]

And concerning the extortion of money from Mírzá Abu'l-Qásim,* Ayrton in the same letter, writes:

Only last week, the Persian Consul here forbore to have an industrious quiet man, advanced in age, by name Abu-l-Kasino,† who had accumulated about *£1,500*, deported to the Upper Nile on a charge of belonging to a heretical sect, known as the Bâbî sect, on his paying *£1,000*, which the unfortunate sufferer has consented to pay; and to facilitate its realization, a Persian Consular Kavas, has been sent round with him to remind Persian debtors of their obligations. This was no simple threat, the order was from Hussein Khan.[2]

In order to be able to move against this group of seven British-protected merchants, it was necessary to persuade the British Government to withdraw their protection from these people. Mírzá Ḥusayn Khán, therefore, asked Ḥájí Muḥsin Khán (q.v.), the Persian Chargé d'Affaires in London to address the British Foreign Office on this point.

In his letter to Lord Stanley (q.v.), Ḥájí Muḥsin Khán complains that these persons are 'Bábís', and asks that British protection be withdrawn from them so that their activities could be checked. In fact, as the subsequent correspondence indicates, only one of these seven was a Bahá'í, Siyyid Ḥusayn-i-Káshání, and the real purpose of this manoeuvre was to put Mírzá Ḥasan Khán in a position to be able to extort money from them. Ḥájí Muḥsin Khán's letter is dated 15 July 1868:

My Lord

I have the honour to reveal to you, from information supplied by the Consulate-General of Persia in Egypt, that some Persian subjects have obtained, from the Consul-General of Her Britannic Majesty, passports and letters of naturalization as English subjects. They have only sought this status because of the position in which they find themselves *vis-à-vis* our authorities. It is scarcely necessary for me to add that some of them are Bábís, and have directly attempted the life of my sovereign or are mixed up in such an attempt.

I am convinced that Your Excellency will assess these facts with the profound impartiality that distinguishes him and, in view of the treaties and the amicable relations that exist between England and Persia, will wish to give instructions to the Consul-General of Her Majesty the Queen in Egypt so that the passports and letters of naturalization accorded to the said Persian subjects may be withdrawn and we may no longer fear the repetition of such events.

I have the honour to communicate to you herewith the list of the Persian subjects to whom have been accorded the abovementioned passports.[3]

The list mentioned in this dispatch was as follows:

1. Ḥájí Mírzá Javád‡ of Shíráz, merchant.

* Mírzá Abu'l-Qásim of Shíráz had settled in Egypt for many years as a merchant. He was converted by the Bahá'ís resident at Manṣúra, shortly after their arrival in about 1866. He then proceeded to Adrianople to visit Bahá'u'lláh, and it was shortly after his return that he was arrested.

† The poor wretch would be repersecuted if his name escaped you. [Note by Ayrton]

‡ Also called Ḥájí Mírzá 'Abdu'l-Javád in the subsequent correspondence.

2. Ḥájí Áqá of Shíráz, merchant.
3. Mírzá 'Alí-Akbar of Shíráz, merchant.
4. Ḥájí 'Abbás-'Alíy-i-Namází of Shíráz, merchant.
5. Ḥájí Mírzá Rafí' of Iṣfahán, merchant.
6. Siyyid Ḥusayn of Káshán, merchant.
7. Ḥájí Maḥmúd of Kirmánsháh, merchant.[4]

On receiving this note from Ḥájí Muḥsin Khán, Lord Stanley wrote to Col. Stanton (q.v.), the British Consul-General at Alexandria, instructing him to furnish him with a report on the matter.[5]

Stanton instituted his investigations by writing to Raphael Borg (q.v.), Acting Consul at Cairo, asking him to make enquiries. Based on Borg's reply, Stanton wrote to Lord Stanley on 29 July, 1868:

... I have the honour to report that immediately on the receipt of Your Lordship's despatch I called upon Her Majesty's Acting Consul at Cairo to inform me by what authority British protection had been accorded to the persons mentioned by the Persian Chargé d'Affaires and have received from Mr Borg a statement to the following effect, viz: Hadji Mirza Abdul Gewadh (Djevad) is registered as a British subject on the strength of Foreign Office Passport No. 81967 of the 12th of August 1864.

Hadji Aqa upon a Foreign Office Passport No. 165 of the 22nd of November 1865.

Mirza Aly Akbar in virtue of a Certificate of Naturalization, issued by the Bombay Government, a Memorandum from the Under Secretary to Government Bombay and a Passport, dated respectively 13th, 27th and 28th of March 1867.

Hadji Abbas Aly being the son of a naturalized British subject in India.

Hadji Mirza Rufeed (Rufy) in virtue of a Certificate of Naturalization issued by the Bombay Government and the Certificate of the senior Police Magistrate dated respectively 28th November and 1st December 1865.

Seid Hussein in virtue of a Certificate of Naturalization and a Passport granted by the Bombay Government and bearing date respectively 18th and 27th December 1866, and Hadji Mohamed de Kirmanchar in virtue of Certificate of Naturalization and Passport issued by the Bombay Government bearing date respectively 17th April and 14th May last.

These statements will I imagine be sufficient to prove to Your Lordship how unfounded is the assertion made by the Persian Chargé d'Affaires and I trust it is hardly necessary for me to add the assurance that no letters of naturalization have been issued from this agency and Consulate General since I have had the honour of holding that post and my conviction that no Passport has been improperly issued by any of Her Majesty's Consular Offices in this Country.

In order, however, to prove to Your Lordship the serious view taken of this matter by the persons, whose right to British protection is questioned, I beg to forward herewith copies of a confidential despatch that has been addressed to me on this subject by the Acting Consul at Cairo and of a letter I have received from Mr Frederick Ayrton who has been a resident in this Country for many years.

These letters will probably throw a fresh light on the reasons that have induced the demand of the Persian Authorities and will, I trust, convince Your Lordship that the British protection that has been accorded to the persons in question should not be withdrawn from them.[6]

The first enclosure in Stanton's dispatch was a letter from Borg dated 27 July 1868, which indicated the unease felt by those persons who were being thus threatened:

I think it my duty to bring to your notice, in a confidential form, a quasi demonstration which took place to-day on the part of the persons named in my despatch No. 14 of this day's date.

On producing their papers, they stated they received a short time since an indirect intimation that the Persian Consul General was preparing to moot the question of their right to British protection and finding by my enquiry for those documents that such is the case, they felt bound to add that, in the event of the British Authorities declining to continue their protection to them they were not prepared to submit to that officer's authority and would rather present a memorial to H.H. the Vice-Roy demanding his protection for a time that might enable them to terminate their affairs and leave the Country. They then proceeded to inform me that they had come to this determination owing to the disgraceful proceeding of the Persian Consul General whose subjects have been, and are, repeatedly called upon to pay to him large sums of money which they are obliged to do, to avoid the imprisonment, bastinadoes and vexations, insulting or otherwise degrading processes to which the recusants are, by his order, often subjected. They went further to say that several applications for redress made to the Ambassador at Constantinople had been disregarded, that officer conniving at these proceedings and sharing in the plunder.

I may here say that the above statement corresponds with a similar information given by Mr Gregoire d'Ellia, Chancellier to the Russian Vice Consulate, to Mr Consul Reade a few days before his departure for Europe.[7]

The second enclosure was a lengthy letter from Mr Frederick Ayrton dated 28 July 1868, part of which has already been quoted.

I think you know Hussein Khan; but I do not know whether you are aware of all the iniquities of the Persian Consular system, before which, in the way of corruption and injustice, every other pales.

The object of the present move is to draw within the power of Persian exaction, a few respectable men who have been long connected with India and made money, by turning to account in trade with and in Egypt, their Indian connection, which still subsists; and it is to India they would most probably return, if their operations here ceased.

Ayrton's letter then digresses to discuss several points of international law regarding nationality, before returning to the subject of the corruption within the Persian Consular Service:*

* In describing the corruption of the Persian Consulate in Egypt in this same letter, Ayrton cites an episode involving Mírzá Malkam Khán. Since the episode is not recorded elsewhere (but see Algar's *Mírzá Malkum Khán* p. 63 and n.), and since it sheds an interesting light on the more unsavoury aspects of the latter's life as well as on the rapacity of Persian officials in general whether in Persia or elsewhere, it is quoted here in full: 'The case also of the Suez Customs is well known. The Persian merchants claimed to pay the same duties as Europeans, on goods arriving by sea at Suez. A representation was made on the subject to the late Said Pasha, who allowed the differences to remain unpaid, reserving a right to them, should their remission be ultimately decided to be inadmissible. Ismaïl succeeded to the Government, and one Malkom Khan, a most clever and cunning little Persian Armenian, was sent by Hussein Khan, to take charge of the Persian Consulate at Cairo. At that time the arrears of differences at Suez had amounted to about £1500. Malkom Khan insisted upon these arrears being deposited by the merchants who were liable for them in the Consulate, which done he applied to Ismaïl Pasha to remit

The Persian Consulates in the Turkish and Egyptian towns, I am informed from several good sources, independent of the persons whose position is now questioned, are systematically sold by Hussein Khân; the terms being $\frac{2}{3}$ of what the Consul can squeeze out of his administrés to be remitted to Constantinople. These squeezes are sometimes on a great scale . . .

The estates of persons under Persian jurisdiction dying here, are simply swallowed up, as it were, in a gulph [*sic*] of the Persian Consulate . . .

I know Hussein Khan sufficiently. He was formerly Persian Consul in Bombay. He is of pleasing address, plausible in speech, versed in French, besides Turkish, Arabic and Hindustani and of prepossessing manners, but very subtle, and I should be very sorry to rely upon his word, if it was his interest to mislead. I am afraid also he is somewhat heartless, as well as corrupt. He has become a rich man out of his subjects' pockets. He has just now been called to Teheran where he will probably find that his gains have not been carelessly appraised.

I hope that the people in whose interest I write may receive all due consideration and not be handed over for pillage and spoliation, or be disturbed in a way to do them injury.[8]

On 15 August 1868, Mr Hammond (q.v.), in Lord Stanley's absence, sent a reply to Ḥájí Muḥsin Khán: 'With reference to my Note of the 17th ultimo, I have the honour to inform you that it appears by a report which I have received from Col. Stanton that the several parties now residing in Egypt to whom you refer in your Note of the 15th ultimo as being Persian subjects and therefore wrongfully protected by H.M.'s Consulate General, are Naturalized British Subjects; and that they are accordingly entitled in any other country but Persia to British Protection.'[9]

This was not, however, the end of the story, for on 26 September 1868, Ḥájí Muḥsin Khán retorted with some documents, representing these to be evidence that three of these merchants, Ḥájí Mírzá Javád-i-Shírází, Siyyid Ḥusayn-i-Káshání and Ḥájí Maḥmúd-i-Kirmánsháhí,* had obtained their British protection under false circumstances. In order not to prolong this chapter unnecessarily, only the case against Siyyid Ḥusayn will be considered further since he was the only Bahá'í in this group. Ḥájí Muḥsin Khán's letter states:

I must submit to Your Excellency, in view of your reply, some observations which do not allow me to regard it as decisive, and keeping within the facts of the matter, will clarify for you the value of these letters of naturalization.

Two of these individuals are Persian subjects, residing in Egypt for several years, and have never left this country. It is only latterly that they have obtained, by correspondence with a friend in London, some ordinary passports, and it is on presenting these passports that they have become British subjects without having ever set foot

---

them on the ground of justice to Persian traders; to which, the Pasha consenting, he appropriated the money deposited in the Consulate, entering it in the Consular books as a voluntary offering to himself from the Persian Merchants in Cairo, and returned forthwith to Constantinople. This was not all, he borrowed money on his note of hand from persons, among them £*100* from our Mirza Abd al Guwâd, who has never been repaid one farthing. The little man in question is one of the confidants of Hussein Khan.

* As a result of these enquiries, British protection was in fact withdrawn from Ḥájí Maḥmúd-i-Kirmánsháhí, since it was found that he had obtained it under false pretences.

in England or in any English territory . . .

Three others of these individuals, have, it is true, left Egypt for some months, but the only aim of their journey was to proceed to Bombay and there, by false testimony, obtain the object of their manoeuvres.

With regard to the aforementioned Siyyid Ḥusayn of Káshán in particular, who has been hunted at times as a Bábist and has for a long time taken refuge in Cairo, I enclose in my letter the documents establishing that if he has left Egypt, it is only for a short time. A Persian businessman, living in Cairo, Ḥájí Abu'l-Qásim, sent him at his expense to Shíráz, from where he has instructed him to bring back his family. It was on his way from Shíráz to Egypt that he proceeded to Bombay and brought back from there, by means already indicated, a certificate of naturalization. The document which establishes these facts is signed not only by the above-mentioned Ḥájí Abu'l-Qásim, but also by several notable merchants living in the same town.[10]

Once more Lord Stanley wrote to Stanton, forwarding the documents supplied by the Persian Chargé d'Affaires, and asking him to institute a full inquiry into the matter.[11] Stanton passed the papers on to Raphael Borg at Cairo for further investigation.

Borg's report, dated 31 October 1868, is lengthy; the section dealing with Siyyid Ḥusayn is as follows:

With regard to the inclosure, marked No. 2, in your same despatch, purporting to be the evidence of various persons against the right of Saïd Hossein to British protection, I have to observe, firstly: that on a careful scrutiny, by the Interpreter of this Consulate, of the signatures to this document he is of opinion that six are in the same, and four in another, handwriting, which militates against those signatures being genuine; nor is it usual for persons of the East to use signatures, but rather seals, as in the case of the document, No. 1. Secondly: Several of the persons signing document No. 2, are said to be native Egyptians who could know little connected with the nationality of a Foreigner. The statement to which their names appear, goes no further than saying that he was absent at some epoch, for some time, from Mansourah which is a town of the Delta on the Damietta branch of the Nile, about 90 miles below Cairo. I may mention that there is evidence in this Consulate that one of the signatories to No. 2, by name Hadj Abu-el-Kassim, at the time of his signing it, must have been in prison in the Persian Consulate in Cairo, and it is well known that this man has been a sad victim – on the plea of his being a Baabee – to Persian Consular Authority, having been completely stripped of the little fortune (said to have been from £1,500 to £2,000) that he had made. Saïd Hossein enjoys British protection in Egypt by virtue of Letters of Naturalization granted to him by the Government of Bombay on the 18th of December 1866. His business seems to consist in dealing in Egypt with Indian wares.[12]

Stanton forwarded Borg's report to Lord Stanley on 12 November 1868, together with his own assessment of the evidence: 'Under these circumstances and considering the fact that should British protection be withdrawn from these persons they will undoubtedly be subjected to a persecution by the Persian Consulate I trust Your Lordship will confirm their naturalization and not deprive them of the protection they have found under the British Flag.'[13]

Lord Stanley wrote to Ḥájí Muḥsin <u>Kh</u>án on 25 November 1868, stating that:

> With reference to my letter of the 1st of Oct. last, and to your letter of the 16th inst. respecting the withdrawal of British protection from one of the Parties referred to in your letter of the 26th of Sept. I have the honour to acquaint you that after a careful enquiry by H.M.'s Agent and Consul General in Egypt into all the circumstances connected with the grant of British protection to the other Parties referred to in your letter, it appears that Hadji Mirza Djevad and Said Hussein are clearly entitled to such protection which cannot therefore be withheld from them.[14]

In a memorandum dated 28 November 1868, Lord Stanley notes:

'The Persian minister called, and complained, but in very fair and moderate terms, of our decision in the cases of claimants for British protection . . .

'I told him if he had any reason to think the consul's decision unjust, he had better put it in writing, and the matter should be considered.'[15]

The Persian authorities were not prepared to allow the matter to rest there, however. On 4 January 1869, Ḥájí Muḥsin <u>Kh</u>án raised the matter once more with Lord Stanley's successor at the Foreign Office, Lord Clarendon (q.v.).

In this letter, he reviews the Persian case against Ḥájí Mírzá 'Abdu'l-Javád and Siyyid Ḥusayn-i-Ká<u>sh</u>ání and then goes on to claim that the British Government in protecting these two persons was contravening Article 12 of the Anglo-Persian Treaty of Paris.*[16]

Lord Clarendon, in a firm reply to Ḥájí Muḥsin <u>Kh</u>án dated 9 January 1869, stated:

> . . . I have the honour to acquaint you that I see no reason to differ from the decision of my Predecessor as conveyed to you in his letter of the 25th of November last. The 12th Article of the Treaty of Paris to which you refer, applies only to the question of the protection of Persian subjects by H.M.'s Representatives in Persia, and in no way relates to the case of the Persons in question, one of whom Hadji Mirza Djeward appears from a declaration made before the Acting British Consul at Cairo in October last, to have been born in Bombay and to have never been under Persian protection, having in the year 1854, when Persian subjects were called upon to register themselves, claimed exemption on the ground of being a British subject. As regards the other, Said Hossein, who enjoys British protection in Egypt by virtue of letters of naturalization granted to him by the the Govt. of Bombay, there does not appear to be any proof that those letters were improperly obtained or that he has since that time been under Persian protection in Egypt.[17]

On 11 February 1869, Ḥájí Muḥsin <u>Kh</u>án wrote yet again to Lord Clarendon. On this occasion, his contention with regard to Siyyid Ḥusayn was that this individual had not fulfilled the conditions necessary to obtain a certificate of naturalization: 'As to Siyyid Ḥusayn Ká<u>sh</u>ání, I must vig-

* Signed in Paris in March 1857 after the Anglo-Persian War.

orously protest about the value of his letters of naturalization. There is no proof, I am told, that they have been obtained irregularly. Is this apparent absence of illegality sufficient for good justice? I affirm that he has made false statements, that Siyyid Ḥusayn has never fulfilled the conditions of birth required to become an English subject.'[18]

Yet again, Col. Stanton was asked to investigate the matter and to refer it to the Government of Bombay if necessary.[19] Stanton's reply, dated 1 April 1869, deals at length with Mírzá 'Abdu'l-Javád's case, but concerning Siyyid Ḥusayn he wrote: 'I regret it is not in my power to offer any further remarks on the case of Said Hussein, as this person is not at present forthcoming and serious doubts are felt whether he has not been the victim of some foul play. The cause of his disappearance is being investigated through Her Majesty's Consulate at Cairo, and should any light be thrown on the matter I shall not fail to report to Your Lordship on the subject without delay.'[20]

It is probable that Siyyid Ḥusayn had decided to absent himself for a while to allow the matter to blow over. There are no further reports on this matter from Stanton, and it appears that Siyyid Ḥusayn turned up again in Egypt a short while later.

References

1. Ayrton to Stanton 28 July 1868. Enclosed in Stanton's dispatch detailed in 6 *infra*
2. ibid.
3. Muḥsin Khán to Lord Stanley 15 July 1868: FO 60 316 (trans. from French)
4. ibid.
5. Stanley to Stanton No. 39, 15 July 1868: FO 78 2037
6. Stanton to Stanley No. 88, 29 July 1868: FO 78 2039
7. Borg to Stanton 27 July 1868, enclosed in 6 *supra*
8. As for 1 *supra*
9. E. Hammond, Under-Sec. of State of For. Off. in charge of Eastern Dept. (for Lord Stanley), to Muḥsin Khán 15 Aug. 1868: FO 60 316
10. Muḥsin Khán to Stanley 26 Sept. 1868: FO 60 316 (trans. from French)
11. Stanley to Stanton No. 55, 1 Oct. 1868: FO 78 2037
12. Borg to Stanton No. 29, 31 Oct. 1868, enclosed in 13 *infra*
13. Stanton to Stanley No. 147, 12 Nov. 1868: FO 78 2039
14. Stanley to Muḥsin Khán 25 Nov. 1868: FO 60 316
15. Memo by Lord Stanley 28 Nov. 1868: FO 78 2039
16. Muḥsin Khán to Lord Clarendon 4 Jan. 1869: FO 60 323 (trans. from French)
17. Clarendon to Muḥsin Khán 9 Jan. 1869: FO 60 323
18. Muḥsin Khán to Clarendon 11 Feb. 1869: FO 60 323 (trans. from French)
19. Clarendon to Stanton No. 12, 16 Feb. 1869: FO 78 2091
20. Stanton to Clarendon No. 39, 1 Apr. 1869: FO 78 2092

SIXTEEN

Events in Baghdád (1867–70)

When Bahá'u'lláh left Baghdád on the second stage of his exile, he left behind a considerable number of his followers. These included such important figures as Mírzá Zaynu'l-'Ábidín-i-Najafábádí, named by Bahá'u'lláh, Zaynu'l-Muqarrabín (Ornament of the Near Ones), and Mírzá Muḥammad-i-Vakíl, the custodian of the House of Bahá'u'lláh.

In 1867, while Bahá'u'lláh was at Adrianople, the Baghdád community appears to have addressed an appeal to the Congress of the United States of America through the American Consul in Beirut. The Rev. Henry Jessup (q.v.), who was an American missionary in Beirut, records:

An extraordinary document reached Beirut April 3d, addressed to the United States consul, from fifty-three Persians in Bagdad, petitioning the United States Congress for the release of their leader, Beha Allah, the Babite Persian reformer, who appeared in 1843,* and was followed by thousands, 30,000 of whom were killed by the Shah of Persia. He was arrested in Bagdad by the Turkish government, and is now (1867) in prison in Adrianople, European Turkey. His particular doctrine is 'the universal brotherhood of man.' The petitioners claim that they number 40,000. A German traveller writes from Bagdad enclosing the petition and speaks admiringly of the reformer, and asks for his release on the ground of religious liberty which is now granted by the Sultan to all his subjects. One of the documents appended to the petition is signed with a Free Masonic Seal.[1]

In 1868, the principal Bahá'ís in Baghdád, including Zaynu'l-Muqarrabín, were arrested by the Turkish authorities and exiled to Mosul. Kemball, in a dispatch to Henry Elliot, the British Ambassador in Constantinople, dated 15 July 1868, records the circumstances of this action:

Sir,

Some excitement has been occasioned here by the apprehension and imprisonment of the principal followers of Bab to the number of 30 or 35 persons almost exclusively Persian subjects who had renounced their allegiance to the Shah and had accepted Turkish tezkerehs (corresponding to letters of naturalization). These sectarians, though long resident at Baghdad, had not hitherto openly professed the new creed, but during the last Mohurrem they

* Evidently Bahá'u'lláh is being confused with the Báb here.

attracted the ill-will of true Shiahs by ridiculing the ceremonies usual with the latter at that season,* and three or four of their number have since lost their lives in encounters with the Persians.†

Up to the present time the Turkish Authorities had attached no importance to the spread of Babiism amongst Natives or Foreign subjects in this Quarter, but rather encouraged the transfer of allegiance which invariably followed on the conversion of a Persian. Shiahs only, it was believed, had come under the influence of the Babee Doctrines and as yet Sunnis had been exempt from proselytism, but a few days ago Ameen Effendi Yuz-Bashi (Captain) of Cavalry the son of an 'Alim,‡ Ensuff Effendi Naib-i-Kazee,§ openly avowed himself a Babi, and though imprisoned, heavily ironed and subjected to every indignity he refuses to recant. The case of Ameen Effendi has furnished the ostensible cause of the seizure of other professing Babis, but this measure I am told, which has been ordered by the Porte, has been prompted also by the doings of Meerza Hassan Ali [Mírzá Ḥusayn-'Alí, Bahá'u'lláh] the present leader of the Sect, who on his deportation from Baghdad in May 1863 was exiled to Adrianople and is said to have effected there numerous conversions.

The followers of Bab in this province are estimated at 1,000 to 1,500 souls. Their leaders now in confinement are to be deported in parties to Kerkook, Mosul and Jezireh.[2]

Elliot, in a dispatch to the British Foreign Secretary, Lord Stanley, dated 14 August 1868, writes:

I have the honour to enclose the copy of a Despatch from Sir A. Kemball upon the expulsion from Bagdad of some members of the Persian Sect of Babees.

A similar measure having been adopted at Adrianople and at other places, I made enquiry into the cause of a step which had the appearance at least of religious persecution, and I received an explanation very similar to that given to Sir A. Kemball.

It was apprehended that the efforts of the Babees to make proselytes from among the Mussulman populations was likely to lead to bad blood and dissensions.

Since the attempt of the Babees to assassinate the Shah of Persia, the Sect is looked upon with jealousy by that Government, but I have no reason to believe that the present measure has been instigated by it, or that there is any intention of putting them into its power.[3]

Hadjoute de Pellissier (q.v.), the French Consul at Baghdád, also noted these arrests, in a dispatch to the French Ambassador at Constantinople, Nicolas Bourée (q.v.), dated 4 August 1868: 'Our Valí has recently put under arrest about forty individuals belonging to the religious sect of the Bábís, whose great Shaykh, Ḥusayn-'Alí, was exiled several years ago to Adirnih [Adrianople]. These sectaries, who did not want to recant, have been exiled to Jazirih. Three or four persons, suspected of being Bábís, were

* Bahá'ís were frequently accused of ridiculing or 'scoffing' at Islam because their joyful celebrations of the birth of the Báb and Bahá'u'lláh (1st and 2nd of Muḥarram) coincided with the Shí'ih period of mourning for the Imám Ḥusayn.

† Áqá 'Abdu'r-Rasúl-i-Qumí, water-bearer for the house of Bahá'u'lláh, was martyred at this time. His place was taken for a time by Badí'. (See p. 254).

‡ 'Álim, a learned person

§ Ná'ib-i-Qáḍí, Deputy Judge

at the same time put into the custody of the Persian Consulate, which released them upon their declaring that they were not Bábís, and making, it is said, a payment in consequence.'[4]

Náṣiru'd-Dín Sháh decided in 1870 to perform a pilgrimage to the sacred shrines in Iraq. In preparation for this, Mírzá Sa'íd Khán, the Persian Foreign Minister, asked for the removal of all of the Bahá'ís from Baghdád. Charles Herbert (q.v.), the acting British Consul in Baghdád, in a dispatch to Henry Elliot dated 17 August 1870, relates:

Reverting to Colonel Sir A. B. Kemball's letter No. 24 dated 15th July 1868 I have the honor to report that on the 5th Instant a rumour reached me that a fresh order had been issued for the imprisonment of the Babis in Baghdad.

I immediately took measures to ascertain the ground of this rumour and learnt that, in consequence of the expected visit of the Shah of Persia, His Excellency Midhut Pasha,* with the view of preventing the occurrence of any acts on their part that might endanger the safety of His Majesty or give cause of umbrage, had called upon the Babis to retire for a time from this city and had even offered assistance to those who might be without the means of travelling.

Having an opportunity of conversing with His Excellency a few days later I mentioned the subject when he unreservedly confirmed this account stating that the Persian Minister of Foreign Affairs having caused the presence of the Babis, and the dangers to the Shah that might arise therefrom, to be brought to the notice of the Porte, he had received orders to provide against any such contingency.

He had accordingly summoned the principal known members of that sect, and had requested them to leave Baghdad offering, as above stated, pecuniary assistance to such as might need it.

His Excellency stated that he is, as he has shewn himself, above all religious persecution, that provided persons were good subjects of the state he had no concern with their religious opinions, but, that in regard to the feelings and safety of the distinguished guest who is expected here in the course of two months, it is absolutely necessary to adopt the most efficacious measures in his power.

Of this there can be no doubt and the people of Baghdad have every reason to feel assured that His Excellency would not adopt unnecessary measures of harshness on this occasion.[5]

References

1. Jessup *Fifty-Three Years in Syria* Vol. 1, p. 329
2. Kemball to Elliot No. 24, 15 July 1868: FO 195 803A
3. Elliot to Stanley No. 310, 14 Aug. 1868: FO 78 2022
4. Pellissier to Bourée No. 80, 4 Aug. 1868: MAE Corr. Polit. du Consulat de Bagdad (1868) (trans. from French)
5. Herbert to Elliot No. 15, 17 Aug. 1870: FO 195 949

* Midḥat Páshá (q.v.)

SEVENTEEN

Events in the Iṣfahán Area (1864–91)

Since the inception of the Bábí-Bahá'í Faith, Iṣfahán has been a city in which the Bábí and, later, Bahá'í community has been very strong. Many of the towns and villages around Iṣfahán, such as Najafábád, have large Bahá'í populations. With regard to persecution of the Bahá'í community, moreover, Iṣfahán has a persistent record of violent outbursts.

The Najafábád Upheaval of 1864

The first major upheaval occurred in Najafábád in 1864. The instigator of this episode was Shaykh Muḥammad-Báqir (q.v., see fig. 32), who throughout two decades was to terrorize the Bahá'í inhabitants of Iṣfahán and the surrounding areas to such an extent that he earned himself designation as 'The Wolf' from Bahá'u'lláh. On this occasion, he collected the names of all the Bábís* of Najafábád and had them arrested and brought to Iṣfahán, intending to put them all, several hundred persons, to death. He was prevented from carrying out his designs by the other 'ulamá of Iṣfahán, and eventually it was decided to send 18 of the more important Bábís to Ṭihrán under arrest.

The French Chargé d'Affaires, M. le Comte de Rochechouart (q.v., see fig. 3), evidently heard something of this episode and wrote to the French Foreign Minister, Drouyn de Lhuys (q.v.), on 5 May 1864:

> One last event that has occurred to add to the concern in our minds: it appears that some Bábís, about a dozen, have been taken in the town of Iṣfahán and have been brought here to be submitted to all sorts of tortures; I am still hoping that this news will be refuted because the people, more advanced than their Government, view with disgust and repulsion these massacres which are completely unnecessary: the Bábís are an inoffensive sect – they preach, it is true, against the vices of the members of the Government and above all against corruption; they are very well disposed towards Europeans in general and us in particular.
>
> If, contrary to my expectations, these facts are true, I will make every effort to prevent a massacre, for which there is not even the excuse of anger provoked by a first move [on the part of the Bábís]. I shall make the

* It was some three or four years after this that the majority of Bábís became Bahá'ís.

observation that it [the Persian Government] is exposing itself to terrible reprisals and will be breaking completely with the civilized world by committing such infamies.[1]

Shaykh Muḥammad-Báqir had the satisfaction of having one Bábí, Mírzá Ḥabíbu'lláh, executed; and another of them, Ustád Ḥusayn-'Alíy-i-Khayyáṭ, was also executed before the prisoners left for Ṭihrán. The remaining Najafábádís were sent back to their town where each received a severe beating on arrival.

When the prisoners arrived in Ṭihrán they were put in a dungeon, but after about three months the Sháh decided to release them. On 1 June 1864, Rochechouart wrote: 'The Bábís, whose arrest I have reported to your Excellency, have not been executed. The King secretly blames the Governor of Iṣfahán* for his zeal, and has recommended him to arrange some way in which they could be allowed to escape from the prison where they have been detained. This is the wisest course to have taken because this sect, although peaceful at present, would have been disgusted by this attack, and the number of these sectaries is so great as to make the Government stop to think.'[2]

When the Ṭihrán prisoners were set free, several of them returned to Iṣfahán. Of these, two, the learned Ḥájí Mullá Ḥasan and Ḥájí Muḥammad-Ṣádiq, were again apprehended by Shaykh Muḥammad-Báqir, despite their having been given their freedom by the Sháh himself. On Shaykh Muḥammad-Báqir's orders they were beaten, then executed in the Maydán-i-Sháh. Although there is some room for doubt,† it is probably these two persons who are referred to in a dispatch from the British Agent in Iṣfahán, Stephen Aganoor (q.v.), to Mr Charles Alison (q.v.) in Ṭihrán, dated 13 September 1864: 'A few days ago three men were beheaded, two of whom were Baubies and the one was a murderer.'[3]

The Iṣfahán Upheaval of 1874

On 8 May 1874, the eldest son of Náṣiru'd-Dín Sháh, Sulṭán-Mas'úd Mírzá, Ẓillu's-Sulṭán (q.v., see fig. 33), arrived in Iṣfahán as Governor at the age of twenty-five. He was to remain at this post for thirty-two years during which he either instigated or did nothing to prevent numerous persecutions and martyrdoms of the Bahá'ís. Indeed, his Governorship was inaugurated

* Qavámu'd-Dawlih

† According to Avárih *Al-Kavákibu'd-Durríyyi* (Vol. 1, pp. 401–2), after being released from prison in Ṭihrán, the prisoners returned to Iṣfahán, and their executions did not occur until 1868. This would, of course, mean that these could not be the persons referred to in the dispatch. However, the date of Aganoor's dispatch being 13 September leaves ample time for the Najafábádís to have spent 3 months in prison in Ṭihrán and then returned to Iṣfahán.

by a general persecution of the Bahá'ís within a few days of his arrival. The origin of this outburst can be traced once again to Shaykh Muḥammad-Báqir. Robert Bruce (q.v., see fig. 31) of the Church Missionary Society, who was in Iṣfahán, sent a full report to both his society and to the British Minister, William Taylour Thomson (q.v.). The latter report, dated 22 May 1874, is here produced:

I had the honor to send your Excellency through Major Smith two telegrams about the persecution of Baabys and others in Ispahan, begun by Shaik Mahomed Bakir.

As I have been requested by General Lake [q.v.], to send information on everything relating to religious liberty in Persia, for Lord Lawrence [q.v.]* and H.M. Minister for Foreigh Affairs at home, I think it right to send Your Excellency a copy of the information which I am forwarding to London.

The Persecution was first commenced about a month ago by Shaik Mahomed Bakir, while H.R.H. The Hissam us Sultaneh† was governor of Ispahan. The Shaik imprisoned one of the sect called Shaiky's, followers of Haji Abdul Kereem Khan of Kerman.‡ This sect has no connection with Baabyism. H.R.H. The Hissam us Sultaneh at once ordered the Shaik to release the Shaiky and reproved him for trying to cause a rebellion among the Shah's subjects.

No sooner had H.R.H. been removed from this to the Province of Fars than the Shaik at once arrested the same Shaiky a second time and banished him from Ispahan to a village of Charmahal called Chamasman.

Seeing he was not opposed in this he had the names of considerably more than one hundred (some say 400) persons taken down who were accused of being Baabys.

About twenty or more were arrested in one or two days. But the greater number having had timely information of the Shaik's designs fled from their homes, and either concealed themselves in Ispahan or fled to other parts, leaving their families in a state of alarm and giving up their shops and professions.

Numbers of men and women flocked to Julfa and tried to take refuge in the Telegraph Office and houses of the Europeans.

As is always the case advantage was taken of this state of things, by malicious persons to accuse their enemies of being Baabys and also by the Ferashes, darogas§ etc. to extort money from unoffending and innocent citizens, by threatening them with being taken before the Shaik.

I was informed by several persons not Baabys that the Shaik preached publicly in the great Mosque that the blood of all those arrested and proscribed was *hallal*‖ for him to shed, and that their wives daughters and property were at the mercy of the Mahomedans to do what they liked to them.

* Lawrence was particularly interested in procuring freedom for Christian missionaries to work among Muslims in Persia. To this end he had asked that any instances of religious intolerance be brought to his notice in order that these cases could be used to bring pressure to bear on the Persian authorities. When Bruce's letter concerning this upheaval reached him, however, he replied that he felt it better to let the matter rest for the present: 'our authorities are not very zealous in the way of interference and it would be inadvisable to strain any influence we may have with them but rather keep it for very special cases.' (CMS Archives, CI 1/o 61, No. 177)

† Sulṭán-Murád Mírzá, Ḥisámu's-Salṭanih (q.v.)

‡ Ḥájí Muḥammad-Karím Khán-i-Kirmání is intended here.

§ policemen

‖ Lawful – in the religious sense.

Things would have been much worse had not the Saham ud Doulat* used all his influence to obtain the release of some of those arrested, and also to dissuade the Shaik from proceeding further with the Persecution.

A few days after the telegrams were sent to Your Excellency from Julfa things became much quieter – the greater number of those imprisoned were set at liberty and no more arrests were made. It is presumed that this was owing to the kind intervention of Your Excellency and the action of the Persian Government in Teheran.

Many of those proscribed were certainly not Baabies.

A Syad who studies English in my school was arrested but though set at liberty by the kind intervention of the Saham ud Doulat has not been able since to continue his studies.

My own Mirza – certainly not a Baaby was in such a state of alarm – relations of his having been arrested – and himself threatened that for several days he could do no work for me.

A family of persons a father and two sons who are in the habit of working for the Telegraph staff in Julfa were proscribed. They have been taking refuge in my school house and the R.C. Church. They certainly are not Baabys and are in every way quiet well-behaved industrious men.

A poor weaver who makes cloth for English and Armenians was in the same position – and several others whom I know myself.

Notwithstanding all that has been done there are still some five or six prisoners in custody and these mentioned above, and many others are still kept out of employment and afraid to leave their hiding places.

Shaik Mahomed Bakir was till lately the third in rank of the High Priests here. The Imam Juma† and Syad Ussad Ullah‡ were always opposed to his persecuting propen-

* Muḥammad-Ibráhím Khán-i-Núrí, the Sahámu'd-Dawlih, was put in command of three regiments in Iṣfahán in 1856. He received the title Sahámu'd-Dawlih in 1874. He was later Governor of Mázindarán, Kurdistán, and Commander of the Túpkhánih [Artillery] of Ṭihrán.

† Mír Siyyid Muḥammad, the Imám-Jum'ih. This is the same man in whose house the Báb resided during part of his stay in Iṣfahán. Although at first expressing his admiration for the Báb, particularly after the latter had written the *Commentary on the Súrih of Va'l-'Aṣr* at his request, the Imám-Jum'ih, later, did not oppose the machinations of the enemies of the Báb, and even endorsed the death warrant that they drew up for the Báb. Ussher met the Imám-Jum'ih in 1861, and records thus his impressions:

'We went up a narrow filthy staircase to the roof, under an archway, on which we found four chairs had been placed, three for us, and one for the Imam Jumah. We were surrounded by a crowd of servants, who we were told were never paid anything, being maintained by the voluntary contributions and presents made by those who had business to transact with, or favour to solicit from, the great dignitary. To these we were objects of intense curiosity, and as infidels rejecting the faith which they cherished, they seemingly found it hard to believe that so holy a man as their master could hold any intercourse with us. A few minutes after we sat down there was a movement in the crowd. A tall, stout man of about forty appeared in the doorway leading from the interior of the house to the roof, and followed by a young-looking individual, who, from the kalemdun or writing-case which he wore in his belt, appeared to be his secretary, came towards us with much stateliness and dignity. He had taken but a few steps, when there was a commotion among the bystanders. A black sheep which had been kept in the background was dragged forward by the horns, and with many pious ejaculations, led twice round the religious dignitary, after which it was taken away and given to some wretched and poverty-stricken people in the court below, who were eagerly waiting for the prize. [*Continued on next page.*]

‡ Siyyid Asadu'lláh-i-Rashtí was the son of the renowned Siyyid Muḥammad-Báqir-i-Rashtí (Shaftí). He had refused to associate himself with the enemies of the Báb when the latter was in Iṣfahán. He was Shaykhu'l-Islám of Iṣfahán and had died in Feb. 1874.

sities. The two former never persecuted any sect. Syad Ussad Ullah lately died and the Imam is very feeble and ill.

I saw the Imam this morning and he expressed the strongest disapproval of the whole transaction, in public before a great number of Persians. Unfortunately he is too unwell to take active measures about anything or else it never could have happened. The Shaik is the only one who oppresses any class of people here.[4]

The report that Bruce sent to the Church Missionary Society on this episode differs from the above only in that it praises the role played by the Sahámu'd-Dawlih: 'Things would have been much worse had not the Brigadier-General – the Saham ud Dowlah – used his influence to obtain the release of several of the prisoners and also to dissuade the Shaik from going too far.'[5]

Bruce also mentions that: 'Sayad Momin the brother and successor of Haji Sayad Ussad Ullah preached yesterday to the same effect [as the Imám Jum'ih – i.e. strongly disapproving of Shaykh Muḥammad-Báqir's conduct.]'[6]

The British Agent in Iṣfahán, Aganoor, also reported this episode but more briefly. On 14 May 1874 he sent a telegram announcing the arrests, and followed this with a short report dated 23 May 1874:

'Since that I have heard that orders have been sent from Tehran to the Authorities here not to allow innocent and harmless people to be molested – but Sheik Mahomed Bakher is still in search of Bobbies and Sheikies to arrest and punish them.

'The Imam jooma of Isfahan appears to be against this act of the Vezeer and Sheik Mahomed Bakher, and he does not wish these poor people to be ill-treated.'[7]

In planning this outburst against the Bahá'ís, Shaykh Muḥammad-Báqir and the Ẓillu's-Sulṭán sought to prevent any means whereby the Bahá'ís could appeal to Ṭihrán against the persecution. Thus the Telegraph Office and the Postmaster were instructed to refuse any petitions from the Bahá'ís,

'The object of this strange ceremony, we afterwards learnt, was, that a disease under which the holy man had for some time laboured, should pass from his body into that of the sheep, which had been presented by one of his most faithful followers, with the design of thus relieving his spiritual director from his ailments. We were not told whether the flesh of the animal thus transformed into a scapegoat would convey, in the opinion of the devotees around, the malady into the bodies of those who consumed the meat. On the conclusion of this ceremony the Imam came forward, bowed stiffly, and seating himself in the chair opposite us, asked us a few insignificant questions about our journey, evidently not believing us when we told him we were travelling for pleasure . . .

'Our entertainer was gifted with one of the very worst countenances it was possible to witness. Every low passion seemed plainly written on it, and with truth, if the stories told us of his conduct and general behaviour were to be relied on.' (*London to Persepolis* pp. 591–3.)

Mír Siyyid Muḥammad died in 1874 and was succeeded by his brother Mír Muḥammad-Ḥusayn (see p. 274n).

while a special watch was kept at the city gates. The Bahá'ís, however, managed to smuggle a messenger* out of the city who rode in haste to Ká<u>sh</u>án. Here he mobilized the Bahá'ís of the town to march to the Telegraph Office, and thus succeeded in getting a message to the central Government. Eventually orders arrived from Ṭihrán that the persecution must cease.

The Martyrdom of Mullá Káẓim of Ṭál<u>kh</u>un<u>ch</u>ih (1878)

One of those arrested in the 1874 episode recounted above was a certain Mullá Káẓim of Ṭál<u>kh</u>un<u>ch</u>ih. This man had been one of the 'ulamá of Iṣfahán, and had returned to the village of Ṭál<u>kh</u>un<u>ch</u>ih as its leading religious figure. He was converted to the Bahá'í Faith† by Siyyid 'Abdu'r-Raḥím, and this led to his expulsion from Ṭál<u>kh</u>un<u>ch</u>ih and his return to Iṣfahán. After the upheaval of 1874, Mullá Káẓim was forced to leave Iṣfahán and lived for a time in <u>Sh</u>íráz and Ṭihrán. Eventually he returned to Iṣfahán.

On one occasion when he went to Ṭál<u>kh</u>un<u>ch</u>ih, Siyyid Ḥusayn who was mujtahid there caused him to be arrested and sent back to Iṣfahán. Nicolas, who was in Iṣfahán a few years later and was able to question eyewitnesses and investigate this episode fully, wrote:

> In the month of <u>Dh</u>i'l-Ḥijjih 1294,‡ he [Mullá Káẓim] went to Ṭál<u>kh</u>un<u>ch</u>ih. There he entered into discussions with the Mullá of the place and was once again arrested with Siyyid Áqá Ján.
>
> He was taken back to Iṣfahán, where they began to pillage [the houses of the Bahá'ís] again. Some others, among them Ḥájí Há<u>sh</u>im-i-Rízí, who lived in the village of Ríz and was Kad-<u>Kh</u>udá of it, were arrested.
>
> Mullá Káẓim, with the others, was taken to Iṣfahán and led to the house of Ḥájí <u>Sh</u>ay<u>kh</u> Báqir. There he reaffirmed his religion and, on the orders of Mírzá Báqir,§ was taken to the Square of the <u>Sh</u>áh [Maydán-i-<u>Sh</u>áh] in Iṣfahán: Mullá Káẓim with his own hands removed his clothing and asked the executioner to carry out his work quickly. In the presence of a large crowd, his head was cut off at the Pá Qápúq,‖ a Ṣafavid construction.
>
> 'After he had been killed,' Siyyid Zaynu'l-'Ábidín recounted, 'I arrived at the Maydán-i-<u>Sh</u>áh and I saw the people with sticks and

* This man is named as Ḥájí 'Abdu'lláh by Nicolas (*Massacres de Babis en Perse* p.16) and in a manuscript history of the Bahá'í Faith in Iṣfahán (author not indicated). There is, however, another account which seems to be of this same episode although some details differ. This account, by Áqá Ḥusayn-'Alíy-i-Núr names the messenger as Ma<u>sh</u>hadí Ḥusayn.

† Browne in *A Traveller's Narrative* (p. 400) makes the statement that Mírzá Yaḥyá, Ṣubḥ-i-Azal, claimed that Mullá Káẓim was an Azalí. This fact is refuted not only by Bahá'í historians but also in the following account by Nicolas, who was in Iṣfahán a few years after Mullá Káẓim's martyrdom. Nicolas's account concludes with a tablet revealed by Bahá'u'lláh in honour of Mullá Káẓim.

‡ Dec. 1877

§ <u>Sh</u>ay<u>kh</u> Muḥammad-Báqir, 'The Wolf'.

‖ In the centre of the Maydán-i-<u>Sh</u>áh in former times was an execution pole from which during the Ṣafavid dynasty the victim would be hung by the heels and then dashed to the ground or else have his throat cut.

stones, gathering around the body of Mullá Káẓim and beating it. Even though it is said in Islam that it is forbidden to burn bodies and to kill or beat even animals with sticks and stones.'*

After the execution of Mullá Káẓim, Siyyid Áqá Ján was tied to a post at the Kaysaríyyih† which is near the Maydán-i-Sh※áh, and there he was beaten from morning until midday. Then his ears were cut off and he was led through the bazaars.[8]

The 'King of Martyrs' and the 'Beloved of Martyrs'

Ḥájí Siyyid Muḥammad-Ḥasan (see fig. 34) and his brother, Ḥájí Siyyid Muḥammad-Ḥusayn (see fig. 35), were two rich and respected merchants of Iṣfahán. Although well known as Bahá'ís, they were nevertheless entrusted by the Imám-Jum'ih of Iṣfahán, Mír Muḥammad-Ḥusayn,‡ with the care of all his business affairs. In the course of managing the Imám-Jum'ih's affairs the brothers would settle any debt that had occurred, and over the course of several years the Imám-Jum'ih came to owe them a considerable sum of money. It was principally to avoid paying this debt that the Imám-Jum'ih devised a plan to encompass the death of these two brothers, whom Bahá'u'lláh subsequently designated as the 'King of Martyrs' and the 'Beloved of Martyrs'.

Dr C. J. Wills (q.v.), who was medical officer attached to the Indo-European Telegraph Office in Iṣfahán and a personal friend of the two brothers, described their cruel fate thus:

> I made the acquaintance of three brothers who were Syuds, or holy men, but who had the reputation of being freethinkers; these men called on me and insisted on my breakfasting with them in the town: they were wealthy landed proprietors and merchants. I found their house beautifully furnished and their hospitality was great; they discoursed much on the subject of religion, and were very eloquent on the injustices perpetrated in Persia. They were nearly related to the Imám-i-Juma, or high priest, a very great personage indeed, who ruled the town of Ispahan by his personal influence. It was said that any one who incurred his displeasure always, somehow or

* 'Rev. James Bassett in *Persia: Eastern Mission* (p. 51) gives another account of this martyrdom:

'Several persons charged with being Baubs were arrested in a village about 9 farsaks from Ispahan. The accused were brought before the shaik ul Islam. The investigation opened with a discussion. One of the accused, Kazim, asked the Shaik if he believed the New Testament, and on the shaik replying that he did, Kazim replied "Then you must find testimony to Mohammed in the New Testament, for that book was written before Mohammed." Whereupon the shaik cried out, "Kafir, infidel!" and ordered that Kazim be slain. The man was led away to the place of execution and beheaded.'

† the main bazaar

‡ Mír Siyyid Muḥammad, the Imám-Jum'ih who had opposed the persecutions in 1874 (see p. 271n), had died and his place was taken by his brother Mír Muḥammad-Ḥusayn, designated by Bahá'u'lláh as 'Raqshá' (She-serpent). It is reported that when the other conspirators were hesitating to put the brothers to death, the Imám-Jum'ih had said that if there was any wrong in their action let it be on his neck. Shortly afterwards, he contracted a disease (some say scrofula and some say cancer of the neck) that caused an abcess on his neck and emitted a foul odour (see Browne 'The Bábís of Persia' p. 491). Having caused riots and disorder, he was banished to Mashhad. He died 21 June 1881.

other, lost his life.

Under the shadow of such a relation, the Syuds Hassan and Houssein and their brother openly held their very liberal opinions. They were, in fact, sectaries of the Baab . . .

A few days [later], my friends the three brothers were arrested, their valuables looted by the king's son the Zil-es-Sultan, the then Governor of Ispahan, and by the Imám-i-Juma, the successor of their former protector, in the office of high priest of Ispahan. Their women, beaten and insulted, fled to the anderún (harems) of friends and relations, but were repulsed by them for fear of being compromised. They then came to the telegraph-office in Julfa and sat in an outer room without money or food. After a few days the relatives, rather than let the (to them) scandal continue of the women being in the quarters of Europeans, gave them shelter.

The real cause of the arrest of these men was not their religion; the Imám-i-Juma owed them eighteen thousand tomans (seven thousand two hundred pounds); they were sent for and told that if they did not forgive the debt they would be denounced and inevitably slain. But habit had made them bold; they declined to even remit a portion of the sum owing; they were politely dismissed from the high priest's presence, and a proposition made to the prince that the whole of their property should be confiscated by him, and that they should be accused of Baabiism and executed. This was agreed to. They were sent for and taken from the prince's presence protesting their innocence, the youngest brother cursing Baab as proof of his orthodoxy.

The next day all were savagely beaten in prison, and it was generally given out that they would be executed; but being men of wealth and influence, no one believed in this.

The English missionary in Julfa,* the assistant superintendent of the telegraph,† and a few Armenians, addressed a letter to the prince which, while apparently pleading their cause, really, I fear, accelerated their fate (if it had any effect). The prince was furious, and vouchsafed no reply.

I happened to see him professionally, and he asked me why I had not signed this letter. I replied that I had not been asked to in the first place; and that I should hesitate to mix myself up in the politics of the country, being a foreign official. He appreciated my motives, and asked if I knew the three men.

I replied that all three were my intimate friends, and I trusted that their lives were not really in danger.

I never have been able to ascertain if his reply was merely given to quiet me or not; it was this:-

'The matter is really out of my hands – it has been referred to the king; he is very bitter against Baabis, as you know; nothing that sahibs in Julfa may do will have any effect. Why, sahib, what would your Prince of Wales say if *he* were interviewed, and letters written to him about confessed criminals by obscure Persians? The missionary, the missionary, he only troubles me to make himself notorious.'

I explained that these Syuds were really personal friends of the missionary as well as my own.

'All disaffected people are friends of missionaries, as you very well know.'

I again asked him if they would be spared or not?

'I can tell you nothing more,' he said; 'one has cursed Baab, he will not die. As for the others the king will decide; for me, I wish personally to kill no one; you have known me long enough to know I dislike blood. I am not the Hissam-u-Sultaneh' (the king's uncle, a very severe Governor). He changed the subject and declined to return to it. I cannot tell if the two elder brothers had been offered their lives or not. I went back to Julfa hoping that they would all be spared. The

* i.e. Rev. Bruce
† i.e. Mr Hoeltzer (q.v.)

town was in great excitement. Next morning at dawn their throats were cut in the prison, and their bodies flung into the square. The prince had not dared to execute them publicly for fear of a tumult.

Their houses were looted, and part of their estates; the Imám-i-Juma's share of the plunder was large, and he never repaid the eighteen thousand tomans. Such was Persia in 1880. The youngest brother, who had cursed Baab,* was spared, and afterwards reinstated in part of his family property.[9]

There is a further account of the fate of the two brothers in a book entitled *Six Months in Persia*, by Edward Stack of the Bengal Civil Service:

. . . but the execution, or rather murder, of the two Bâbi merchants three years ago has left a stain on the Prince's character which not even the consideration of his comparative youth and inexperience can wholly remove. They were two respectable merchants, against whom the Imam-i-Juma, or chief ecclesiastical authority of Isfahan, for pecuniary reasons, had conceived a grudge. That they were in secret Bâbis, does not seem to be denied; but there are thousands of Bâbis in the Shah's dominions, and nobody had ever alleged that these two men were not quiet and loyal subjects. The Imam-i-Juma, however, raised the fanatic spirit among the mullas and their adherents, while respectable Isfahan looked on helplessly. The two unfortunate men were brought bound before the Prince, in the presence of the chief merchants convoked for that purpose. M. Collignon† was himself a witness of this scene. He rose at once and grasped the captives by the hand, addressing them as he had been accustomed to do in the days of their liberty. They wept, and asked the other merchants what dishonourable thing they had done that their old friends and brother-traders should sit thus aloof. One by one the merchants, moved to shame, imitated M. Collignon's example, and before the meeting broke up the Prince had promised that no harm should happen to the men. But the mullas returned, talked the Prince over, and their victims were put to death. It is but fair to the Zill-us-Sultan to add that he was then young in his government, that threats had been used of setting Isfahan in rebellion, and that he yielded much against his will. Nobody believes that such a crime could be perpetrated now. The Imam-i-Juma fell out of favour. He and his victims have been judged by this time. In Gulpaigan I heard the news of his death.[10]

Unfortunately, the British Embassy and Consular Archives for Persia for the year 1879 that would have contained the reports from Iṣfahán are missing from the Public Record Office. There has survived, however, a register of communications between Ṭihrán and Iṣfahán during this year. The relevant entries read:

Telegram: Messrs Bruce, Aganoor, Hoeltzer

12th March: *Baby* [Bábí] *persecution* being carried on at Isfahan

Telegram: Mr Aganoor

13th March: *Persecution by Prince etc*: continued

* I<u>sh</u>ráq-<u>Kh</u>ávarí in *Núrayn-i-Nayyirayn* (pp. 85–7) states that this third brother, Mírzá Ismá'íl, did not in fact recant, but that his father-in-law, a Muslim, forged a letter to this effect in his name to the Imám-Jum'ih and thus secured his release.

† M. Collignon was the agent in <u>Sh</u>íráz of Hotz & Co., a Dutch commercial firm with dealings throughout Persia.

Telegram: Mr Bruce
13th March: *Persecution by Prince etc:* further details
Dispatch: Major Smith*
13th March: *Persecution by Prince etc*: further details
Telegram: Mr Aganoor
17th March: *Persecution by Prince etc*: Two Syeds killed and bodies exposed in Meidan
Dispatch: Mr Aganoor
16th March: *Baby Persecutions by Prince etc.*
Dispatch: Mr Aganoor
20th March: *Baby Persecution*: two prisoners released[11]

In the Diplomatic Correspondence, moreover, the following passage occurs in a dispatch from the British Ambassador, Ronald F. Thomson (q.v.), to the Marquess of Salisbury (q.v.), dated 5 June 1879:

Several serious disturbances have lately occurred in Isfahan and unfortunately the governor of that province, being the Zil-i-Sultan a son of the Shah, instead of being censured or withdrawn was supported by the Government.

The Imam-i-Joomeh, or Chief Priest, owed sum of Eighteen thousand Tomans (Ts. 18,000) to two respectable and wealthy Seyeds, and to avoid payment of the debt he accused them of being Bábis and Socialists; they were accordingly seized, their property made away with by the authorities, and they themselves put to death. This gave rise to great excitement in Isfahan and news of the occurrence having been telegraphed to me, I immediately made representations through the Minister for Foreign Affairs to the Shah, and orders were sent down to Isfahan which resulted in putting a stop to further atrocities which were in contemplation.[12]

Nicolas writes:

Ẓillu's-Sulṭán was not happy about their execution, because he thought, 'If I kill them, I will be held responsible for it.' But the Imám-Jum'ih and Shaykh [Muḥammad-] Báqir intervened saying: 'We will reply to the Government.' They wrote a paper [*fatvá*] which they and all the Mullás signed.

When the Prince had thus had his conscience put at ease, the Imám-Jum'ih and Shaykh Báqir proceeded to the Talár Tavílih [dungeon]. At the prison they were happy and joyful. They summoned the executioner and, without further interrogation of the accused men, turned their attention to the execution.

I was not in Iṣfahán at this time. When I arrived, I called on Mírzá Muḥammad-Ḥasan-i-Najafí, who was one of the great Shí'ih 'ulamá. He said that to have killed Mírzá Ḥusayn in the conditions in which it was done did not conform to the laws of the Sharí'at . . .

Shaykh Muḥammad-Báqir began to read the khuṭbih [address] and made a sign to the executioner.[13]

Mírzá Ashraf of Ábádih, 1888

After the martyrdoms of the King and Beloved of Martyrs, almost a decade passed before the next episode of persecution. The victim on this

* Head of Indo-European Telegraph Department in Persia.

occasion was the elderly Mírzá Ashraf, a native of Najafábád, who had lived in Ábádih for many years and was thus generally known as being from Ábádih. Nicolas, who gives an account of this martyrdom, writes: 'I was, myself, in Iṣfahán at this time and I write this account from reliable sources.'

Nicolas gives an account of Mírzá Ashraf's life. He states that he went to India intending to proceed to 'Akká. But being unable to make this journey, he returned to Persia, firstly to Ábádih, then Najafábád, and finally to Iṣfahán, where he had been living for some two years prior to his martyrdom. Nicolas then recounts, on Siyyid Zaynu'l-'Ábidín's authority, a dream that Mírzá Ashraf had had two nights before his arrest.

Nicolas continues:

Siyyid Zaynu'l-'Ábidín said, '... The following day ... Mírzá Ashraf, together with a native of Ábádih, came to my house; they took tea and then wished to depart; I asked them to remain for lunch but they replied that they had arranged a rendezvous with someone and had to go. And so they left.' Ḥájí Mírzá Qannád (the confectioner) recounted: 'I saw them in the bazaar and said to them: "I must go with you to such and such a place."' In short, three or four people wished to detain him, but he did not accept, saying, 'I must go where I have promised.' Áqá Ḥusayn-Qulí, Vakíl-Báshí of the Cossacks, recounts: 'I met him in the Maydán-i-Sháh; I said to him, "We are gathered today to go to such and such a place"; he said, "I have arranged to see someone at the Madrisiy-i-Chahár-Bágh." But he did not say with whom, and I did not insist. "When you have seen him", I said, "we will meet again." "So be it!" he said, and we went into the college. In the corridor I saw Náyib 'Abdu'r-Raḥím with an old Bábí who was very faithful but inexperienced, although he was 80 years of age. He was named Áqá 'Alí. Both were seated.' Áqá Ḥusayn-'Alí recounts: 'When I saw him, I said, "you have probably arranged to meet the Náyib?" "Yes!" he said. I replied, "It is not a good thing for you to talk with him." We wanted to retrace our steps but Áqá 'Alí and the Náyib realized my intentions. They rose and came towards us. We conversed a little and left the college. He was arrested by the Náyib; I wanted to make him release him, but was not successful in my efforts.'

Then he was taken before Ẓillu's-Sulṭán with the papers that he possessed. He was guarded for several days in the prison, until at last the 'ulamá came together. They made him appear before the assembly. One of the officers present at the session recounted: 'He discussed very calmly with the 'ulamá, and engaged in arguing from the verses of the Qur'án and the Ḥadíth. He talked in such a manner that his voice rose to a high pitch. He did not deny any of his doctrines.' Several of the 'ulamá gave testimony against him on that day. In 1306, in the month of Ṣafar, he was taken to the scaffold in the Maydán-i-Sháh.[14]

[Nicolas continues:]

At this very hour, I arrived at the Maydán. I saw him hanging in a corner, then they burnt his body. His remains were buried in the street named Kuchiy-i-Siyyid 'Alí Khán.[15]

On 18 October 1888, Mr Aganoor, the British Agent in Iṣfahán, telegrammed to the British Legation in Ṭihrán: 'A Persian has been imprisoned on the accusation of being a Bawbe by the ulemas here. It is said that the Prince might be compelled to comply with the request of the Ulemas and execute him in a day or two unless something be done from Tehran.'[16]

On receipt of this telegram, Sir Henry Drummond Wolff (q.v., see fig. 28) went to see the Prime Minister, Amínu's-Sulṭán*. His report to the Marquess of Salisbury about the proceedings of that interview is in a dispatch dated 1 November 1888:

My Lord,

Some days ago the Agent at Ispahan informed me that a man was about to be executed on the charge of Babism.

In the evening I saw the Ameen-es-Sultan and speaking non officially I said that I regretted to hear this circumstance as capital punishment for religious opinions were very much against the ideas and feelings of civilization.

His Excellency replied that the Shah had sanctioned the execution on the representation of the Zil that the man was the cause of dangerous disturbance and I found it impossible to push the subject further. In fact it was evident that the execution had been decided on and it is more than probable that it had already taken place.[17]

Mr Aganoor wrote on 24 October 1888: 'With reference to my telegram of 18th Instant I respectfully beg leave to report that the man accused of being a Bawbe was executed yesterday morning in the Maidan-e-Shah of Ispahan and his body remained there till late in the evening in a most disgraceful state.'[18]

Browne first learnt of this martyrdom from General Houtum-Schindler (q.v.) on 15 April 1889 at the meeting of the Royal Asiatic Society at which he presented the first of his papers on the Bábís. He made enquiries about this episode and received a reply from one of the Afnán, Mírzá 'Alí Áqá,† giving details of the episode.[19]

On receiving Mírzá 'Alí Áqá's letter, Browne wrote to Rev. Dr Bruce of the Church Missionary Society in Iṣfahán to obtain further information. The reply, dated 6 September 1889, stated: 'Yes, it is quite true that Aga Mirza Ashraf of Ábâdé was put to death for his religion in the most barbarous manner in Ispahan about October last. The hatred of the Mullas was not satisfied with his murder, but they mutilated the poor body publicly in the *maidan* in the most savage manner, and then burnt what was left of it.'‡[20]

In his Annual Letter dated 22 November 1889, Bruce also refers to this episode. He writes: '*Persecutions* – last autumn, a short time before our

* 'Alí-Asghar Khán, Amínu's-Sulṭán (q.v.)

† Mírzá 'Alí Áqá, later Muvaqqaru'd-Dawlih. The full text of Mírzá 'Alí Áqá's letter, which gives very different details from those reported in these accounts, may be found in Browne *A Traveller's Narrative* pp. 404–6. The translation may be found in Browne 'The Bábís of Persia' pp. 998–9. The original letter is among Browne's papers at Cambridge University Library (Folder 2, item 1).

‡ The reason for the brevity of Bruce's reply is that he was not in Iṣfahán at the time. He had been on leave in England, and at the time of this episode was on his way back. He would of course have heard much about it on his return.

return from England, a very respectable man, a native of Abadeh, was put to death by the Mohammedan priests in Ispahan in a most cruel manner for being a Babi, and the poor body was most barbarously mutilated and burnt. A fanatical priesthood, like a man-eating tiger, having once tasted human blood, thirsts for more.'[21]

The Najafábád Upheaval of 1889

When Shaykh Muḥammad-Báqir died in about 1881, it was far from being a relief to the Bahá'í community of Iṣfahán. For this man's son, Shaykh Muḥammad-Taqí (q.v., see fig. 44), known as Áqá Najafí (and to Bahá'ís as Ibn-i-Dhi'b – the Son of the Wolf), was ready to fill his father's plaçe as the leading divine of Iṣfahán and the scourge of the Bahá'í community. He was already notorious for having signed along with his father the order for the deaths of the King and Beloved of Martyrs. Soon he demonstrated that he was eager to resume where his father had left off.*

On 5 July 1889, Mr Preece (q.v.), the Assistant Superintendent of the Indo-European Telegraph Department, who was at this time acting for Aganoor, reported that Áqá Najafí had begun a campaign against the Jews and Bahá'ís. After enumerating a number of measures against the Jews, Preece continues: 'This same man Agha Nedjify is the one mainly concerned in the present crusade against the Babis. It is only a short time ago that he came to a village just at the back of Julfa and preached against Dr Bruce declaring he would have him killed for protecting the Babis.'[22]

Preece, having drawn Ẓillu's-Sulṭán's attention to Áqá Najafí's activities, reported the following reply from the Prince:

'He was very nice and pleasant over it all, told me that Agha Nedjify [was] but a bit better than a fool, but that he was most inconvenient with his Jew and Babi questions.'[23]

On the same day, Bruce wrote to the Church Missionary Society:

Since the Shah punished his oldest son the Zel-us Sultan by stripping him of a great part of his authority as Governor of Ispahan etc. etc. the Mulas have greatly risen in power – one of these the Mujtehid Aqa Nejify is doing all he can to oppress and persecute all non-Moslem religions. A great number of poor villagers accused of being Bábis were lately driven from their homes in a village near this [i.e. Najafábád] and their

* In *Livre de Sept Preuves* (pp. 57–8n), Nicolas relates the following story which demonstrates well the degree of Áqá Najafí's hatred of the Bahá'ís – he was even willing to distort the religion of Islam rather than see any advantage to Bahá'ís. Concerning the Muslim dawn prayer for the Fast, Nicolas writes, 'The Imám Báqir [the Fifth Imám of the Shí'ihs] has said that this prayer is the loftiest of prayers because it contains the greatest name of God – Bahá! The Muslim world naturally remained in agreement with this until the day when someone drew the attention of Áqá Najafí, the mujtahid of Iṣfahán, to the fact that in it was precisely the name of the *Man-Yuẓhiruhu'lláh* [Him Whom God shall make manifest] promised by the Báb. Áqá Najafí prohibited the saying of this prayer from that time on.'

families have been reduced to the greatest misery and distress. Formerly if a man denied being a Bábi he was let off. Now even denial does no good – he is driven from his house and if caught put to death (as one was not long ago in the most brutal manner) if any Muslims say he is a Bábi.[24]

On 17 and 18 July, Preece sent telegrams to the British Legation in Ṭihrán concerning the arrival of a large crowd of Bahá'ís from Najafábád seeking sanctuary in the British Telegraph Office.[25] On 20 July, he sent the following dispatch giving details of the episode:

I have the honour to report on the events which happened in this place last Wednesday the 17th Inst. as follows:

On my arrival at the Telegraph office at 9 a.m. on Wednesday morning, I found the whole place full of people, men women and children, all in a very excited state. Some of them rushed at me and began asking me to telegraph to the Shah and to the Minister in Tehran their grievances. After some considerable trouble I was enabled to make them understand that I had no right to do one or the other and tried to induce them to leave the office, in this I failed, but having got them in a quieter frame of mind, I was enabled to get a clearer story out of them. From this it appeared that they were people from Nejefabad, a flourishing town some 20 miles to the west of this. For some time things have been going badly between them and their fellow townspeople who accuse them of being Babis; some four or five days before an order was received in Nejef-abad from the Prince to the Mollahs to let the people alone for the present while the Shah was away out of the country. The Mollahs, instigated as I am told by Agha Nejafi, who lately has been very active in oppressing both Babis and Jews about here, ignored the order or request of the Prince and immediately raised a row, in the midst of which a woman of these people was stoned and killed. Matters quieted down for a day, they buried the woman, this seems to have stirred up the Mollahs again, who caused her remains to be dug up and wished to have them burnt. This insult these supposed Babis resented and there was a sort of free fight, which ended in their discomfiture, they were stoned and their women and children were maltreated, their houses broken into, their goods stolen, crops destroyed and houses wrecked, three of their number were taken prisoners and sent into Ispahan.

About 1000 of them took refuge in flight, some 300 coming in here, and distributed themselves about the place, seeking refuge (bast) in such places as the stables of the Prince and Mushir ul Mulk and the Persian and English Telegraph offices; about 200 have gone up to Tehran and 500 have fled to the hills.

Upon hearing their story I wrote to the Prince telling him of it and asking him to do something to clear the people away from the office as they were a great nuisance to us.

H.R.H. replied that he was very sorry for them and would do his best to redress their wrongs. The three men who had been arrested and put in prison, were so treated to appease the Mollahs, that he had put the matter into the hands of the Mushir-ul-Mulk who would send a proper man up to see the people and hear what they had to say.

This man, Hassan Khan, Ferrash Bashi of the Mushir-ul-Mulk came up very shortly and in my presence spoke to the people, or rather their representatives, five in number, heard their complaints, and solemnly promised them, on the part of the Prince redress and that their wrongdoers should be punished. He required them all to come to the Prince and state their wrongs before him and hear what he had to say. Everything was going on all right and the people had agreed to go to the Prince when some one unfortunately asked who the man was; when they learnt that he was not a man of the

Princes but of the Mushir's they would have nothing more to do with him, believing that he had been sent by the Mushir alone and not by the orders of the Prince and that when he got them away from here he would ill-treat them with the idea of forcing the remainder to return. In a short time the Ferrash Bashi left having induced five of the men to go into town with him.

I informed the Prince of the above and in a reply he told me that the Ferash Bashi had been to him and had his definite orders that he would come again with the five men who had been to see him and whose complaints he had heard, upon which he had caused the three men who had been in prison to be released and that they would shortly be with me.

The Ferrash Bashi came with the eight men. He made them tell the people who had by this time augmented by another 30 or so, what had happened before the Prince. These eight reassured the people that the Prince had listened to their complaints with great kindness, that he had ordered the Ferrash Bashi to get to-morrow morning a written order to go out to Nejefabad, giving him full powers to act for the Prince to redress their wrongs, punish the evil doers, compensate them for their losses and recover all stolen property. Even this, although told them by their own people, they would not accept, they thought it was simply done to hoodwink them. They said that to live at Nejefabad was now quite impossible, they begged that the Prince would give them villages where they would work for him; all they asked was to be allowed to earn their living, pay their taxes and be at peace.

After a great deal more talk and prolonged discussion on their part and on that of the Ferrash Bashi and as they appeared as far off a settlement as ever, I thought it time to say a word. I pointed out to them that in the first place the Prince, a great Shahzadeh, a son of the King, had been kind and considerate to them beyond anything I had heard of in the country, and beyond my utmost hopes. He had pardoned them a grave offence, that of appealing to us Faringhis in a question which in no way concerned us, that if they now did not accept his clemency and good will for them, he would have a right to be angry and shut his ears to all their complaints, that it was absurd for them to ask him to depopulate some of his villages to enable them to go into them, and so on. I caused it to be pointed out to them, that the Prince had been so good to them and promised so much, that even if he wished he could not go back on his word, it would be too bad for his name, his word having been pledged before all of us Faringhis (there were two or three of the Staff in the office).

This influenced them and had the desired effect; after a little talking among themselves they came to the Ferrash Bashi and pledged themselves to return at once to their town. Upon this the Ferrash Bashi left and the matter ended; this was just 9 p.m.

During the night the majority of the people left and by midday the next day, the office was clear.

This morning I learn that the Ferrash Bashi had acted up to the Prince's orders, he had fined the other people 2000 krans, recovered what property he could and taken security that there should be no further disturbances, the people were quite satisfied.[26]

Kennedy (q.v.), the British Chargé d'Affaires, forwarded this dispatch of Preece to the Marquess of Salisbury together with the following:

For some time past, I have been receiving telegrams from Mr G. Preece, an employé of the Indo-European Telegraph Department, who resides at Ispahan where he is temporarily acting as British Agent, reporting the state of ferment in which that town and district are constantly thrown by the fanatical conduct of certain Mollahs who are conducting a crusade against Babism. The inhabitants of the village of Nedjefabad appear to be most infected with this heresy, and to have been in consequence the chief victims of the persecution of the Mollahs headed by a certain Aga Nedjefy. From the enclosed report by Mr Preece Your Lordship will see that His Royal Highness the Zil-es-Sultan heartily sympathises with the unfortunate victims, hundreds of whom took refuge in His Royal Highness' stables and in the Telegraph Office and were with difficulty calmed, reassured and induced to return to their homes.

It would appear that the Zil-es-Sultan lacks the power effectually to restrain the zeal of Aga Nedjefy and his brother Mollahs, and can scarcely protect even his own soldiers and servants against their persecution.

I have, on one or two occasions, both personally, and through the Nawab Hassan Ali Khan,* called the attention of the Ameen-ul-Mulk† to these disturbances pointing out that although questions of internal administration do not directly concern this Legation yet anything which affects the peace and tranquillity of Persia is an object of interest to Her Majesty's Government in view of the friendly relations existing between Persia and Great Britain.

I also warned the Ameen-ul-Mulk that the fanaticism of the Mollahs, if not checked, might be turned against the European inhabitants of Ispahan, some of whom were already beginning to feel nervous about their position, and I suggested to His Excellency that it would be a wise step to give a word of serious warning to Aga Nedjefy.

The Ameen-ul-Mulk replied that he believed the Zil-es-Sultan had sufficient power and authority to maintain order in his district, that His Royal Highness had not applied for any assistance, which, however, was probably due to his reluctance to admit openly the weakness of his position, but the Ameen added that he would act upon any suggestion and warn the Mollah Aga Nedjefy that he should moderate his religious zeal and ardour.

It is possible that these disturbances have been instigated by the enemies of the Zil-es-Sultan in order to discredit His Royal Highness in the eyes of the Shah, and if this be the case the support of the Ameen-ul-Mulk, brother of the Ameen-es-Sultan, His Royal Highness' bitter enemy, is not likely to be very cordial or effective.[27]

In a letter to Browne, dated 6 September, Bruce relates the outcome of the Najafábád upheaval and also refers to a small episode in Sidih, another village near Iṣfahán.

. . . we have had two other persecutions of Bábís, one in Si-dih and the other in Najafábád. In Si-dih, where the Bábí community is small, their houses were burned and their wives and children ill-treated. The men saved themselves by flight to Ṭihrán, and I am told that about 25 of them have just returned to Iṣfahán and are in the Prince's stables in *bast*. In Najafábád there are about 2000 Bábís. They tried the same game with them, but some hundreds of them took refuge in the English Telegraph Office in Julfá, and the Prince took their part and banished from Najafábád to Karbalá the *Mujtahid* who persecuted them, so the result is that they are freer now than they have ever been. I took very great interest in the poor people not only for their own sakes, but for the sake of Persia also; as, if liberty is gained for them, it will be a great step towards breaking the power of the *Mullás* and getting liberty for all.[28]

* Ḥasan-'Alí Khán-i-Navváb (q.v.)

† Mírzá Ismá'íl Khán, Amínu'l-Mulk (d. Apr. 1899), was the brother of Amínu's-Sulṭán and was Minister of Finance. Amínu's-Sulṭán was absent at this time, accompanying the Sháh on his third European tour, and Amínu'l-Mulk was acting as his brother's deputy.

This small affair in Sidih was to have important repercussions in the following year.

The Sidih Upheaval, 1890

As related by Bruce in the above letter, a number of villagers from Sidih had been driven from their homes in the summer of 1889, following which some 20 or 30 of them had been to Ṭihrán to plead their case. In another letter of Bruce, dated 12 July 1890, the following further details are given:

> Just thirteen months ago forty men mostly heads of families were driven out of their houses in the village of Sehdeh – at the instigation of this man [Áqá Najafí] and the mujtahid of the place, leaving wives, children and property behind. The houses of many were broken into, their families ill-treated, and much of their property destroyed. The only crime laid to the charge of these unfortunates was Babiism, and they were thus treated without even the form of a trial. Since that time about thirty of them have made their journeys on foot to and from Tehran, about 1100 miles in all, and each time returned with a promise that justice should be done to them.[29]

Thus the Sidihís were successful in Ṭihrán, and returned with assurances for the safety of their lives and the security of their property. At this time Ẓillu's-Sulṭán was absent from Iṣfahán and his deputy Ruknu'l-Mulk* was in charge. Much to everyone's amazement, the 'ulamá, headed by Áqá Najafí, refused to let them return to their homes despite clear instructions sent by the Sháh himself, as the following documents show. On 13 February 1890, Preece telegrammed to Sir Henry Drummond Wolff at the British Legation:

> This morning about 30 villagers from Sihdeh came into office compound and have taken refuge there. They tell me that they have been to Tehran and have received letters from H.R.H. [presumably Ẓillu's-Sulṭán] by command of the Shah and also Mushir ud Dowleh to Rukhul Mulk [*sic*] to allow them to go to their home and remain there quietly that Rukhul Mulk wants to carry out his orders but is prevented by Mollahs headed by Agha Nedjefy and Agha Mohd. Hassim. I wrote to Rukhul Mulk who replies substantiating above that the Mollahs object to these people being allowed to return to their village as they are Babis, that he is in communication with Mollahs and hopes to overcome their opposition. Agha Nedjefy is the man who has created all the rows here during the last nine months. He has comparatively speaking been quiet since H.R.H. left but is again beginning to move. If he can be thoroughly sat on it will benefit Ispahan immensely . . .[30]

On the following day, Churchill was sent to have interviews with Ẓillu's-Sulṭán and Amínu's-Sulṭán, the Prime Minister. The former stated that 'he was powerless to act against Aka Nejefi, who had been the instigator of attacks on the Jews and the Babis during the last summer.'[31] Amínu's-

* Mírzá Sulaymán Khán, Ruknu'l-Mulk (Pillar of the Kingdom), a native of Shíráz in the service of Ẓillu's-Sulṭán. He often served as Acting Governor when Ẓillu's-Sulṭán was absent from Iṣfahán.

Sulṭán professed ignorance of all that had occurred and promised to 'immediately report the matter to the Shah.'[32] On the 16 February, in response to an enquiry from Churchill, Amínu's-Sulṭán wrote, 'strict orders were issued and telegraphed to Isfahan. The Ulema were also telegraphed to.'[33]

Yet despite this, Aganoor (now returned to Iṣfahán) reported on 17 February: 'Telegraphic orders have been sent by the Shah and the Zil-e-Sultan to the Rukn-ul-Mulk to allow the Sedehis in the English telegraph office who are accused of Babyism to go to their homes. These orders were sent by him to Agah Nedjefy who, backed by other mollas, refuses to obey the orders and allow the men to go. They are all still in the Telegraph office.'[34]

Ẓillu's-Sulṭán also telegrammed to Iṣfahán. In a telegram to Shaykh Muḥammad-'Alí, a brother of Áqá Najafí, he urges Áqá Najafí to obey the Sháh's orders. Referring to the Sháh, Ẓillu's-Sulṭán states:

By the Justice of the Almighty! he is more strenuous and persevering in the preservation of the glory of Islam than I or you even. By the Imperial Command of this very Shahinshah, Asylum of the Faith, may our souls be sacrificed to him . . . , thousands of Babis have been blown away from guns and by means of myself, several others have had their stomachs ripped up and have been rewarded with Hell. Now his policy is that a number of people whose Babism is not yet determined should go to their homes and occupations and remain there . . . [35]

At an interview between Amínu's-Sulṭán and Churchill on 18 February, the former is stated to have 'expressed astonishment at the attitude assumed by the ulema of Isfahan headed by Aka Nejefi towards the Shah's commands.'[36]

Nevertheless, Wolff continued to exert pressure on the Persian authorities, and on 21 February 1890 telegrammed to Aganoor: 'I have taken steps with the Govt. . . . I have been promised that the people shall be taken to their village under military escort.'[37]

The villagers were, eventually, taken to Sidih under escort but all was not yet well. On 26 February, Aganoor telegrammed: 'Yesterday seven of Sedehis were killed and their bodies burned with naptha. Others threatened with death. Deputy Governor helpless having but few soldiers.'[38]

Rev. Henry Carless (q.v.) of the Church Missionary Society, resident in Iṣfahán, gave further details in a letter to his society dated 8 March 1890:

They [the Sidihís who had been to Ṭihrán] returned to Ispahan with the Shah's protection and favour – another delay of three weeks occurred, and on the morning of Feby. 25 at dawn they returned to Seddie, accompanied by some servants from the deputy Governor. How gleefully did the poor men bid us farewell in Julfa, but how now was their glee to turn to deeper sorrow. Nearing their village, containing their homes and dear ones, the Mahommedans turned out to meet them, and in cold blood murdered six of them, seriously wounding another. Some of the corpses of the murdered men were afterwards burnt. Twenty-one of them managed to escape, and were back in Julfa by noon the same day. From us they went to the house of the deputy Governor in Ispahan. On Wednesday Feb 26, some 400 fanatics from Seddie invaded Julfa, wanting the blood of the remaining 21 – had they been here, there would doubtless have been a great commotion. The mob passed over the river to Ispahan, and the poor fugitives were with great difficulty protected by the deputy Governor, who in the absence of the Prince in Teheran has scarcely any soldiers in the city. Since then the Babis have been hidden in Julfa in the house of Mr Norollah, the honored representative of the London Jews' Society in Persia – the wounded man is in our Hospital progressing favourably.[39]

This was, of course, an affront to the British authorities, under whose promise of protection the Sidihís had agreed to leave the telegraph office. De Balloy (q.v.), the French Minister, wrote on 17 March 1890:

The inhabitants of a small locality around [Iṣfahán], Sidih, suspected of Bábism have been molested for a long time by Priests . . . they delegated some people from among them to come to Ṭihrán, and, according to the traditional formula, offer their lives to the King and ask for his protection. They were dismissed with friendly words ['bonnes paroles'] and took the road back to their usual places of residence. But when they arrived in Iṣfahán . . . [De Balloy here goes on to give details of the attack on the villagers on the road to Sidih.]

The English Legation was very annoyed at this event which is, in truth, a great disgrace for them . . .[40]

Wolff on hearing the news wrote immediately to the Sháh[41] and Amínu's-Sulṭán[42] informing them of what had occurred. The Sháh replied that he was appointing a special representative to look into this episode.*[43] In Iṣfahán, the survivors of the episode at Sidih had dispersed and were in hiding. Initially they went to the Deputy Governor's house but later, as mentioned by Carless, transferred to the house of Mírzá Núru'lláh, a Jew who had been converted to Christianity and was acting as agent for the London Society for Promoting Christianity Among the Jews (London Jews' Society). Bruce wrote to the Church Missionary Society a letter that was printed in *Jewish Intelligence*, the magazine of the London Jews' Society. After recounting the facts as described above, Bruce wrote: 'The presence of Mr Norollah of the Society for the Propagation of Christianity among the Jews was most providential. During the persecutions of both Jews and Babis he acted in the noblest way. During that of the latter, during my absence he took 25 Babis into his house and kept them for days. This was a brave act as it really endangered his own life especially as he is a Persian subject.'[44]

The same letter of Bruce mentions that 'Sir D. Wolff took their case most energetically, both interceding for them with the Shah and sending money

* The original letter in the handwriting of Náṣiru'd-Dín Sháh exists in the Public Record Office files.

to Mr Carless and Mr Norollah to help them.'[45]

On 2 March 1890, Churchill had an interview with Ẓillu's-Sulṭán, one of the results of which was that 'Hearing that the Sedehis had taken refuge in Julfa and that they were in difficulties for means of subsistence he offered to send 200 tomans to assist them, but he was afraid that if it were known he wd. have the whole of the Mollas against him and that the Shah himself might be angry with him – so he asked if it might not be possible to distribute it amongst them secretly through the British agent.'[46]

As it happened, Mr Bax Ironside (q.v.) of the British Legation was proceeding to Iṣfahán on a short visit, and Wolff was able to entrust the money provided by the Ẓillu's-Sulṭán to him, as well as giving him instructions to look into the whole matter on his arrival in Iṣfahán. Ironside's report dated 4 March was as follows:

I have the honour to inform you that, on my arrival here, I, at once, took steps to enquire into the truth of the news you had received just prior to my departure respecting the massacre of some supposed Babis of Sehdé. Sehdé or Three villages (consisting of Parishorn, Benispahan and Khorzan) is situated about twelve miles distant from Ispahan, and a section of the villagers have, for some time past, been noted for their leaning towards Babism, whereas the remainder displayed an unusual amount of Musulman fanaticism . . . [Ironside then relates the events leading up to the murders much as recorded by Preece and Aganoor.]

About two miles from their home they were met by a party of some two thousand people; they themselves numbering about thirty. The attacking party was armed with spades, clubs and knives and was headed by Seyed Ali, the religious chief of the Sehdé community. He loudly proclaimed a 'Jahad' or religious war and shouted out – 'We have no king but Agha Nedjefy; he is our king and representative of the Imam and I am his lieutenant: kill these infidels and blot out their names.'

The people at once attacked, killing six and badly wounding several, one of whom soon afterwards died of his wounds. Three were burnt when half dead. The few soldiers who were in charge of them were threatened and informed that, if they interfered, they also would be killed; so they fled. The corpses were eventually buried after three days exposure by the order of the Rukn-ul-Mulk, the Deputy Governor.

The survivors of the massacre fled and took refuge in the Deputy Governor's house, but, as they could obtain no food and were insulted by his servants they came to the Telegraph Office and afterwards proceeded to the house of Mirza Nuroollah, a converted Jew, in Julfa, where they now remain utterly penniless and supported by Dr Eustace and the Jew in question. This latter leaves Ispahan shortly for Bushire and it is important that the supposed Babis should be protected and sent to their homes or that the Persian Government should make some arrangements for their future. The action taken by you at Tehran, by means of which Agha Nedjefy left last night for the capital, at the Shah's orders, has created a most beneficial effect, but I hear on good authority that five hundred Mollahs have interceded with His Majesty in favour of the Agha.[47]

Wolff forwarded Ironside's report to the Marquess of Salisbury, together with the information he had received on 8 March to the effect that the Deputy Govenor, Ruknu'l-Mulk, had 'received the villagers into his house and has agreed to feed them and look after them for the present.'[48]

Wolff's pressure on the Sháh in Ṭihrán had produced two effects. Firstly, Áqá Najafí was summoned to Ṭihrán, leaving on 3 March 1890. Secondly, a special Commissioner was sent from Ṭihrán. On 15 March, Aganoor telegrammed:

Ezedullah Khan Sertip who came from Tehran lately for Sedehy Affairs paid me a visit yesterday. It appears he is collecting information to report to Tehran and is waiting for orders.

I saw the Sedehis in Rukn ul-Mulk's house, they were comfortable, and thankful, but very anxious to go to their homes.[49]

This special Commissioner returned to Ṭihrán on 22 March, and no great result seems to have been forthcoming from his efforts.

Consequently, on the advice of Ruknu'l-Mulk, the Sidihís left for Ṭihrán once more to plead their case.[50] On 10 July 1890, Aganoor telegrammed: 'Sedehis returned are in Prince's stable neglected. Nothing done for them.'[51]

Bruce, in a letter to the Church Missionary Society dated 12 July 1890, wrote: 'People in England cannot imagine the indescribable sufferings which these poor men and their families have endured for these many months.'[52]

News was, moreover, reaching Iṣfahán that Áqá Najafí had been well received in Ṭihrán (see p. 399) and was about to be sent back to Iṣfahán. This information was confirmed in an interview that Aganoor had with Ẓillu's-Sulṭán (now returned to Iṣfahán) on 11 July 1890.[53]

Wolff immediately wrote to Amínu's-Sulṭán urging him not to allow Áqá Najafí to return to Iṣfahán.[54] But in a reply received on 14 July 1890, Amínu's-Sulṭán merely stated: 'During his stay in Tehran he has been admonished and censured sufficiently so that he will never have the courage to take any steps beyond his functions or to do that kind of action.'[55]

And so Áqá Najafí was allowed to return to continue his mischief-making in Iṣfahán (see chapter 29).

Addendum

During the course of the Sidih upheaval one of the minor 'ulamá of Iṣfahán sent a letter about the Bahá'ís to Sir Henry Drummond Wolff. This letter is of interest since it is typical of the accusations which the 'ulamá levelled at the Bahá'ís and which they used to incite the rabble.

After compliments.

Y.E. is well aware that prophets and sovereigns are for the purpose of regulating the existence future and present of the world whether Mussulman or otherwise; and their followers are always endeavouring to secure order amongst the people. Y.E.'s presence in Tehran is for this purpose. Therefore if a party should arise who are a source of trouble to the religion and worldliness of the people; who defile the purity of the people and their minds, it is incumbent on all to endeavour to cast them out. It is evident that the Bábis depend not on either religion or religious laws. They even indeed deny all religious laws and prophets. All illegality and shame is pleasing to them. They are at strife with all people and Govts. and their existence is the source of troubles and difficulties. They are perhaps more devoid of sense than animals. Animals each have their special pair and have honour, but these people according to what I have heard, look upon the community of wives among several husbands even unto nineteen husbands as lawful. They look upon property as being the property of God, that is to say that the property of each is the property of all. If they increase in power they will be a source of trouble to the Christians. Enquire of the Nasaras [Christians] and you will find that they have found their way amongst them and are working mischief wherever they go. It is not possible to temporize with these people as it is possible with other creeds. They are the evildoers of all creeds. It is not uselessly that Islam is at strife with these people. They are in Islam like the Mormons amongst the English and other Europeans by whom they have been expelled and extinguished.

I have heard that certain Nasaras (Christians) have let it reach your noble hearing that what has been done to these people may befall them also, that which they say is slander and false. It is a thousand years that we have dealings with the Christians, why have they never been oppressed! On the contrary the Ulema always protect them, whereas these Babis on the other hand cannot be supported. If you are the well wisher of the Christian and Mussulman you should do your utmost to root out this sect. This is written for your information by Haji Sayyid Jevád, the servant of the Ulema of Ispahan, in order that Y.E. be not under a misapprehension and if Y.E. wishes give me information in order that I may supply you with proofs from the books of the prophets and the new and old Testament of the evildoings of the Babis.

If you send your answer to Haji Sd. Jevad at the Masjid Shah of Ispahan it will reach me. [Ḥájí Siyyid Javád of Iṣfahán to Sir Henry Drummond Wolff, 29 March 1890: FO 248 489]

References

1. Rochechouart to Drouyn de Lhuys, Direction Polit. No. 10, 5 May 1864: MAE Corr. Polit., Perse 33 (1864), pp. 65–6 (trans. from French)
2. Rochechouart to Drouyn de Lhuys, Direction Polit. No. 12, 1 June 1864: MAE Corr. Polit., Perse 33, pp. 70–71 (trans. from French)
3. Aganoor to Alison 13 Sept. 1864: FO 248 221
4. Bruce to Thomson 22 May 1874: FO 248 303
5. Bruce to Gen. Lake 22 May 1874. File CI 1/0 61/1–86, No. 154: CMS Archives
6. ibid.
7. Telegram quoted in Aganoor to Thomson 23 May 1874: FO 248 303
8. Nicolas *Massacres de Babis en Perse* p. 17 (trans. from French)
9. Wills *In the Land of the Lion and Sun* pp. 153–6
10. Stack *Six Months in Persia* pp. 29–31
11. Entries in Register of Correspondence, FO 250 11
12. Thomson to Salisbury No. 130, 5 June 1879: FO 60 421

13. Nicolas *Massacres de Babis en Perse* pp. 19–20 (trans. from French)
14. ibid. pp. 20–22 (trans. from French)
15. ibid. p. 22 (trans. from French)
16. Telegram quoted in Aganoor to Wolff 19 Oct. 1888: FO 248 475
17. Wolff to Salisbury No. 240, 1 Nov. 1888: FO 60 493
18. Aganoor to Wolff 24 Oct. 1888: FO 248 475
19. Browne *A Traveller's Narrative* p. 404
20. ibid. p. 406
21. *Annual Letters*: Bruce, dated 22 Nov. 1889: CMS Library
22. Preece to Kennedy 5 July 1889: FO 248 493
23. ibid.
24. Bruce to CMS 5 July 1889, File G2/PË O/1889, No. 56: CMS Archives
25. Telegrams Preece to Kennedy 17, 18 July 1889: FO 248 493
26. Preece to Kennedy 20 July 1889, enclosed in 27 *infra*
27. Kennedy to Salisbury No. 144, 30 July 1889: FO 60 501
28. Browne *Materials* pp. 291–2
29. Bruce to CMS 12 July 1890, G2/PE O/1890, No. 80: CMS Archives
30. Preece to Wolff 13 Feb. 1890, enclosed in Wolff to Salisbury No. 53, 18 Feb. 1890: FO 60 570
31. Memo by Churchill 17 Feb. 1890: FO 248 489
32. ibid.
33. ibid.
34. Aganoor to Wolff, 17 Feb. 1890, enclosed in Wolff to Salisbury No. 53, 18 Feb. 1890: FO 60 510
35. Ẓillu's-Sulṭán to Shaykh Muḥammad-'Alí 20 Feb. 1890, communicated by Ẓillu's-Sulṭán 28 Feb. 1890: FO 248 489
36. Memo by Churchill 18 Feb. 1890: FO 248 489
37. Wolff to Aganoor 21 Feb. 1890: FO 248 513
38. Aganoor to Wolff 26 Feb. 1890: FO 248 512
39. Carless to CMS 8 Mar. 1890, G2/PE O/1890 No. 36: CMS Archives
40. De Balloy to Spuller, Direction Polit. No. 14, 17 Mar. 1890: MAE Corr. Polit., Perse 42 (1890), pp. 111–12 (trans. from French)
41. Wolff to Sháh 26 Feb. 1890: FO 248 511
42. Wolff to Amínu's-Sulṭán 27 Feb. 1890: FO 248 511
43. Sháh to Wolff 27 Feb. 1890: FO 251 86. This is the original letter in the Sháh's own handwriting
44. Bruce to CMS 17 Apr. 1890, G2/PE O/1890, No. 43: CMS Archives. Also quoted in *Jewish Intelligence* Vol. 6, 1890, p. 126.
45. ibid.
46. Memo by Churchill 2 Mar. 1890: FO 248 489
47. Bax Ironside to Wolff 4 Mar. 1890, enclosed in 48 *infra*
48. Wolff to Salisbury No. 76, 14 Mar. 1890: FO 60 510
49. Aganoor to Wolff 15 Mar. 1890: FO 248 512
50. Aganoor to Wolff 25 Apr. 1890: FO 248 514
51. Aganoor to Wolff 10 July 1890: FO 248 514
52. Bruce to CMS 12 July 1890, G2/PE O/1890, No. 80: CMS Archives. A copy of this letter is also to be found in FO 248 514.

53. Aganoor to Wolff 11 July 1890: FO 248 514
54. Wolff to Amínu's-Sulṭán 12 July 1890: FO 248 511
55. Amínu's-Sulṭán to Wolff, no date, enclosed in Wolff to Salisbury No. 238, 16 July 1890: FO 60 512

EIGHTEEN

The Ṭihrán Upheaval (1882–3)

Throughout the 1870s the strict confinement of Bahá'u'lláh was gradually relaxed, and it became possible for more of his followers to make the pilgrimage to 'Akká. With Bahá'u'lláh established in the mansion of Mazra'ih outside 'Akká in 1877, the flow of pilgrims became even greater. The return of these pilgrims to Persia was the cause of an upsurge in Bahá'í activities throughout the country. Nowhere was this more marked than in Ṭihrán, where there were concentrated such eminent Bahá'ís as Ḥájí Mullá 'Alí-Akbar-i-Shahmírzádí,* Mullá Muḥammad-Riḍáy-i-Yazdí, the learned Mírzá Abu'l-Faḍl and others. The clerical authorities viewed with alarm the resurgence of a movement that they had thought to have been crushed. The opportunity to attack once again the oppressed community came when two informers infiltrated the Bahá'í meetings and went to the mujtahid Siyyid Ṣádiq-i-Sanglají (q.v.) willing to provide a list of the names of the leading Bahá'ís and to identify them. In concert with the Governor of Ṭihrán, Kámrán Mírzá, the Náyibu's-Salṭanih (q.v.), all those leading Bahá'ís referred to above, together with a large number of others, were arrested and condemned to death.

Shortly after instigating this upheaval in the last months of 1882, Siyyid Ṣádiq was seized with an inflammation of his legs. Eventually this affected his mind as he became delirious. He died in February 1883. The Bahá'ís arrested by Kámrán Mírzá remained imprisoned in very severe circumstances. Ronald Thomson (q.v.), the British Minister in Ṭihrán, noted these arrests in a dispatch to the Earl Granville (q.v.) dated 17 March 1883:

> I have the honour to report that several persons were lately arrested and imprisoned here in consequence of its having been represented to the Shah by one of the Chief Priests of this city that they belonged to the sect of Báb. The arrest of these people was quickly followed by that of others, and in a few days nearly fifty suspected Bábis were in custody and confined in one of the worst prisons in the town with heavy chains round their necks. It is understood that some of these prisoners belong to the above sect, but most of them are said to have been arrested by the Police, with the sanction of the Shah's

* Known as Ḥájí Ákhúnd and designated by Bahá'u'lláh as one of the Hands of the Cause.

son, the Governor of Tehran, with a view to the exaction of fines and such sums as they can afford in order to obtain their release.

Rumours being current that it was intended to put these people to death, and it having been stated, on apparently good authority, that they were to be thrown into a large pit and buried alive, I thought it right to communicate with the Minister for Foreign Affairs on the subject.

I accordingly sent His Excellency a message requesting that he would represent to the Shah from me the ill effect that would be produced in Europe if any measures of an extreme character were taken with regard to these persons, or if they were subjected to cruel punishment or ill treatment in respect to a simple question of religious belief, and I suggested that it would be better to send them out of the country than to keep them in prison where their detention and reported ill-treatment would obtain for them notoriety and public sympathy. Mirza Saïd Khan was seemingly well pleased with the opportunity thus afforded him of addressing the Shah in my name on their behalf. I have no means of knowing exactly what effect my communication made, but a few days after it was conveyed to the Shah, His Majesty expressed when Dr Tholozan [q.v.] and a number of the Court officials were present, his determination not to allow any of the prisoners to be put to death.

Several have since been released, but twenty one are still detained in prison. Amongst these are a naturalized Turkish subject, and a Persian named Syed Ali Akber,* who holds a passport issued to him in India as a naturalized British Subject. Having returned to his native country, where he reverts to his original nationality, I have not made any official demand in respect to this person, but I have communicated unofficially with the Minister for Foreign Affairs, and the Prince Governor of Tehran, with a view to proper enquiry being instituted as to the charge of his being a Bábi. I have been informed in reply that he belongs unquestionably to this sect, and that he is moreover an emissary sent specially to this country by Mirza Hussein Ali, the 'Head Centre' of Babeism, who was some years ago expelled from Kerbella and incarcerated in Syria by the Ottoman authorities in compliance with a demand to that effect which was then made by the Shah's Government to the Porte.[1]

Granville replied to Thomson on 30 April 1883 that he approved of Thomson's actions in this matter. As the weeks passed, however, Thomson became uneasy about the fate of 'Syed Ali Akber' and made several verbal representations about the matter to the Persian authorities. Having received only vague replies, he eventually determined to address a private letter to Mírzá Sa'íd Khán (q.v.), the Persian Foreign Minister. On 12 May 1883 he wrote:

I have repeatedly both verbally and in writing called Y.E.'s [Your Excellency's] attention in an unofficial form to the case of Syed Ali Akber who has an English passport and being charged with Bábism has consequently been imprisoned and chained up for more than two months, and who has recently fallen so seriously ill that there is danger for his life. In my previous applications I begged Y.E. to bring this prisoner before a Mujtahed to be examined as to his religious persuasions in the presence

* 'Syed Ali Akber' was in fact Siyyid Mihdíy-i-Dihají. This man was considered one of the prominent Bahá'ís at this time but was later to turn against 'Abdu'l-Bahá. He was using the papers of his deceased nephew Siyyid 'Alí-Akbar-i-Dihají who had possessed a British passport.

of an official from the Foreign Office and a person deputed from this Legation so that the case should be decided according to law and custom. Y.E.'s replies to my communications have hitherto been of a vague and indefinite character leading me to infer, much to my regret, that you did not intend to comply with my request. The communication made to me this day by Mirza Nasrullah Khan on the part of the Naïb es Sultaneh is a further source of disappointment to me, as I feel convinced that His Majesty the Shah, under the circumstances already set forth, and in a case where doubt must exist as to the truth of the charge, would never permit that one of his subjects, whatever might be his religion, should be exposed to suffering and persecution. I beg, therefore, that Y.E. will lay this letter before the Shah and communicate to me His Majesty's pleasure on the subject, so that I may inform my Govt of the result.[2]

In a dispatch dated 15 May 1883, Thomson gives Granville an account of his actions and the response of the Persian authorities:

In my despatch No. 33 of the 17th of March last, I had the honour to inform Your Lordship that a Persian named Syed Ali Akber of Yezd, to whom a passport had been issued in India as a naturalized British subject, was amongst the persons suspected of Babism who had been seized and imprisoned in Tehran.

Feeling doubtful as to the grounds on which this person was detained in prison, and understanding that he was suffering from severe illness, I made several unofficial and verbal representations to the Minister for Foreign Affairs with a view to his being treated with fairness and humanity.

The replies which I received from his Excellency were evasive and unsatisfactory, and I was led to believe from them that the statements made by Ali Akber's relatives that he was in no way connected with Babism were correct, and that his imprisonment was owing to some mistake or to false accusations having been made against him. I accordingly pressed for some more definite explanation of the circumstances under which he was kept in prison and having failed to elicit anything but a repetition of the same vague statements, I addressed a private letter on the subject to Mirza Saeed Khan . . .

On the 13th Instant I saw the Minister for Foreign Affairs, and His Excellency by order of the Shah, furnished me with the following particulars as to Syed Ali Akber's case. His Excellency said that he had been desired to assure me that it was the Shah's wish that every attention should be paid to any friendly representations coming from Her Majesty's Legation. Syed Ali Akber had, however, been imprisoned under the Shah's own order and His Majesty was unable to sanction his release. A strong movement had lately been observed amongst the Babis in this country and measures had been taken to watch their proceedings. The Shah considered that it was not only the public security that was threatened by the evil designs of these people, but that the safety of his own dynasty was endangered by their machinations. Syed Ali Akber had lately paid two visits to Mirza Hussein Ali, the successor of Bab, who is detained under the surveillance of the Turkish Authorities at St Jean d'Acre, by arrangement with the Porte. Since his arrival in Tehran, he had been actively engaged in organizing a secret society of Babis, and it was known from information derived from some of these people that he was employed in this country as an emissary of Mirza Hussein Ali, the present chief of that sect.

The Shah sent me a photograph of Ali Akber which had been taken when he was arrested at Tehran, and at the same time one of His Majesty's Albums that I might compare it with a group of the principal Babis now residing in Syria amongst whom were several of the sons and other relatives of Mirza Hussein Ali.* One of the principal figures in this group appeared to be the same as the Tehran photograph of Syed Ali Akber.

I am informed that, when he was examined before the Naïb es Sultaneh, Syed Ali Akber admitted having passed some time with the Babi party in Syria, and that he refused to make a formal renunciation of the tenets professed by that sect.

Ali Akber is unquestionably a native of Yezd in Persia, and under the circumstances which I have just described, I have thought it advisable to abstain from making any further representations on his behalf, as, by doing so, I should have to enter into questions in which the religious prejudices of the Mahomedans and the personal susceptibilities of the Shah are both involved.[3]

Granville, in reply to this dispatch, stated: 'I approve your proposal to make no further representations on his behalf, under the circumstances reported in that despatch, unless you hear that he is being treated with unnecessary harshness.'[4]

Following the death of Siyyid Ṣádiq, Kámrán Mírzá eased the conditions of the imprisoned Bahá'ís and, removing them from the dungeon, confined them to a house. Their confinement lasted a total of nineteen months, during which time their families suffered much hardship. Eventually, however, they were all released. On this occasion none of the Bahá'ís suffered martyrdom.

References

1. Thomson to Earl Granville No. 33, 17 Mar. 1883: FO 60 453
2. Thomson to Mírzá Sa'íd Khán 12 May 1883, enclosed in 3 *infra*. Trans. by G. Jenner
3. Thomson to Earl Granville No. 62, 15 May 1883: FO 60 453
4. Earl Granville to Thomson No. 61, 2 July 1883: FO 248 398

* This is probably the photograph reproduced in fig. 20, which was taken in Adrianople.

NINETEEN

Events in 'Ishqábád (1889–90)

The vast territory to the north-east of Persia had, before this century, been a mysterious and unexplored region in which tribes of unruly Turkomans roamed, and the only elements of order were a handful of stockaded towns which nominally controlled vaguely-defined areas. The Russians gradually advanced into this region throughout the years 1840 to 1880. By 1844, they had reached the Aral Sea; Tashkent was captured in 1865; Samarkand was occupied in 1868, Khiva in 1873. The last stage of the Russian advance involved the lands immediately to the north of the Persian province of Khurásán. In former days this area had been part of Persia, and the Persian Government still regarded the territory as being under its suzerainty. Despite the protests of Persia, the Russians advanced into it. General Lomakin fought a campaign against the Geok Teppe Turkomans in 1879 but was repulsed. The following year General Skobeleff returned with a more powerful force, and after a lengthy campaign eventually crushed the tribes in 1881. The border with Persia was delineated by an agreement signed in 1881 and the Russian province of Transcaspia was created, which in March 1890 was separated from the Government of the Caucasus.

The Russian Government set about bringing order to this vast area and had soon built a long railway from Uzun Ada on the Caspian Sea to Samarkand, parallel to the northern border of Persia. This railway passed through 'Ishqábád (literally 'City of Love') which at the time of the Russian invasion consisted of a handful of tents, but which was made capital of Transcaspia and consequently grew to a considerable size.

Martyrdom of Ḥájí Muḥammad-Riḍá

The Russian Government encouraged trade and settlement in the new province and from about 1883 onwards many Bahá'ís, with Bahá'u'lláh's consent and encouragement, moved to 'Ishqábád, hopeful that under a Christian Government they would be less oppressed and persecuted. The number of Shí'ih Persians in 'Ishqábád also grew, and there arose tension between the two communities. During the Muslim month of Muḥarram (1889), when the Shí‘ihs mourn the sufferings of the Imám Ḥusayn, and the zeal of the more fanatical elements is usually at its height, a plot was formed to murder Ḥájí Muḥammad-Riḍáy-i-Iṣfahání (see fig. 37), a prominent member of the Bahá’í community. The murder took place in cold blood in the middle of the day and in the main bazaar of ‘Ishqábád. Such an affront to the authority of Russia could not be tolerated, and the culprits were arrested and brought to trial.

The most accurate Western account is that published by Victor Rosen and based on notes by Captain Tumanski. This was translated by Browne in *A Traveller's Narrative*:

At 7 a.m. on September 8th (August 27th, old style) 1889, two fanatical Persian Shí‘ites, Mash-hadí ‘Alí Akbar and Mash-hadí Ḥuseyn, threw themselves, dagger in hand, on a certain Hájí Muḥammad Riẓá of Isfahán, who was peaceably traversing one of the most frequented streets of ‘Ishḳábád, and inflicted on him 72 wounds, to which he succumbed. Hájí Muḥammad Riẓá was one of the most respected of the Bábís of ‘Ishḳábád. The crime was perpetrated with such audacity that neither the numerous witnesses of the occurrence, nor the constable who was on the spot could save the victim of this odious attack. The assassins yielded themselves up to the police without any resistance; they were placed in a cab and conveyed to the prison. During the transit they fell to licking up the blood which was dripping from their daggers. The examination, conducted with much energy by the military tribunal, gave as its result that Muḥammad Riẓá had fallen a victim to the religious bigotry of the Shi‘ites. Fearful of Muḥammad Riẓá's influence, the Shi‘ites of ‘Ishḳábád, acting in accordance with the orders of Mullás who had come expressly for this purpose from Khurásán, resolved to cut short the Bábí propaganda by killing Hájí Muḥammad Riẓá. Knowing well, however, that the crime would not remain unpunished, they left it to chance to determine what persons should sacrifice themselves for the Shi‘ite cause. Thus it was that the individuals named above became the assassins of Muḥammad Riẓá, who had never injured them in any way. The sentence of the tribunal was severe: ‘Alí Akbar and Ḥuseyn, as well as two of their confederates, were condemned to be hanged, but the penalty of death was commuted by His Majesty the Emperor to hard labour for life.

This sentence was hailed by the Bábís with an enthusiasm easy to understand. It was the first time since the existence of the sect, *i.e.* for nearly fifty years, that a crime committed on the person of an adherent of the new religion had been punished with all the rigour of the law.[1]

In this account there is no mention of the fact that the Bahá’ís astonished the Russian authorities by interceding for the murderers and asking that the death penalty not be imposed. Tumanski, however, in an article[2] published at about the same time as Rosen's work, refers to an account from ‘Ishqábád in the journal *Novoye Vremya* which confirms this fact. Tumanski himself arrived in ‘Ishqábád in June 1890, nine months after the event.

On 18 December, Drummond Wolff forwarded to London a memorandum by Mr Bax Ironside on this episode and its consequences. It must be remembered that Mr Bax Ironside had not been in 'Ishqábád when this event occurred and was relying on reports that reached him in Persia, almost certainly through Shí'ih Persians.

A Babi was murdered in the bazaar at Askabad during the month of Moharram (August last) by some Persians of the Shiah sect. He was stabbed in cold blood for scoffing at the Mohammadan religion and faith in Islam.*

The prisoners nine in number were tried in Ashkabad in the Russian Court of Justice and, after a trial lasting several days, two of the prisoners were sentenced to death, two were acquitted, one was sentenced to rigorous imprisonment for one year at Ashkabad, and the remaining four, all respectable Persian merchants to fifteen years penal servitude in Siberia.

These sentences were delivered in Ashkabad on the 21st November and when known created intense excitement at Mashad and other religious quarters. The Babis of Ashkabad gave cash presents amounting to 6,000 roubles† to the Russian officials and begged the latter to protect them: they stated that they could not live in Persia and purposed taking refuge in the Russian Empire.

General Komaroff‡ took their part and reported to the Russian Government that if the sentences were not carried out he would be unable to maintain order in Ashkabad and the Mohammadans would commit murders daily.

On the news reaching the Russian Consul General at Mashad he went at once to see Agha Sheikh Mohammad Taki, one of the most influential of the Ulama, and he assured the Sheikh that he would get the prisoners released and the sentences cancelled.

On December 1st M. de Velassow§ sent his translator to inform the Sheikh that all the sentences had been cancelled. This statement has, however, so far not been confirmed from any other quarters.

The Governor General of Khorassan, H.R.H. the Rukn-ud-Dowleh [q.v.], the Shah's brother, the entire Ulama and all the religious party at Mashad employed their united influence to obtain the remission of the sentences and the Russian Legation was appealed to to get them annulled, it being pointed out that should they be carried out the Persians would, in future, regard Russia as the foe of Islam and the friend of Babis, renegades and of the Shah's enemies in general.

On December 17th Mr Churchill had a conversation with the Amin-us-Sultan, who said that the matter had been repeatedly discussed with the Russian Legation, who asserted that they were powerless to revoke a judgement already given by a law court; but that the Emperor had the power of altering the death sentence to one of imprisonment for life, and that the Persian Government should make any representations they had to submit to His Imperial Majesty through the Persian Minister at St Petersburgh.

The Persian Government, accordingly, had instructed its representative at St Petersburgh to submit the matter to the Emperor with the result that the death sentences have been commuted to transpor-

* See p. 266n.

† This is denied in the letter from Mírzá Abu'l-Faḍl written from 'Ishqábád (see p. 299).

‡ Governor-General of Transcaspia until early 1890, when he was replaced by Kuropatkin. At this time the province of Transcaspia was still under the supervision of the Government of the Caucasus. Komaroff is described by Curzon as 'a quiet and unwarlike professor, who was happier when labelling his insects than when reviewing his men.' (*Persia and the Persian Question* Vol. 1, p. 83)

§ P. M. Vlassov (q.v.)

tation to Siberia, and the other sentences to imprisonment of lesser durations.

The Shah has directed his representative at St Petersburgh to inform the Imperial Government that His Majesty is dissatisfied with what has been done, as he considers transportation to Siberia is equal to death.[3]

In the archives of the British Legation in Ṭihrán, there also exists a letter from an unnamed Bahá'í to a friend at Iṣfahán.* The native secretary of the Legation, Mírzá Ḥasan-'Alí K͟hán-i-Navváb (q.v.) obtained a copy of it from a Bahá'í friend of his in Ṭihrán. This letter was translated by the Navváb in a memorandum dated 1 May 1890. The last part of the letter reads thus:

It is the first justice and is the first support in this world that has been shewn by this Great Sovereign who has removed the atrocities of the powerful enemy from this oppressed sect . . . It is an astonishing contrast between the justice of the great Russian Govt. and the Persian Govt. as for instance if such a murder had taken place in Persia and great merchants, as were in this case, were concerned in it, it is evident to every one that how much both parties would lose in bribing the officials; but in this case the Russian officials did not take a penny from any one, even, on account of excess of justice and equity. No one dared to speak to any one of bribe or to intercede for the culprits. The Shia sect has given bribes to their Ulamas and officials in Persia, in order that they might intercede for them but it was a failure.[4]

Later Developments

The S͟háh, already uneasy at the events following the martyrdom of Ḥájí Muḥammad-Riḍá, was further alarmed by the evidences of the favour which General Alexsei Kuropatkin (q.v.), the new Governor-General of Transcaspia, showed towards the Bahá'ís on his arrival in 'Is͟hqábád.

The Russian Minister, de Butzov, was summoned to an interview with the Persian Prime Minister, Amínu's-Sulṭán, on 30 August 1890. At a later interview on 3 September with Sidney Churchill, Oriental Second Secretary at the British Legation, Amínu's-Sulṭán gave an account of what had been discussed. The following is from Churchill's memorandum:

The Amin us Sultan then made a complaint on the part of the Shah regarding a paragraph which has appeared in the 'Kavkaz' newspaper in which it is reported that on Genl. Kouroupatkine's arrival at Ashkabad he was met by a deputation of the Persian Babis who have taken up their residence in Transcaspia with an address. In this address the Babis tender the submission to Russia on the part of those residing in Transcaspia and all Babis in Persia and asking for protection and recognition of them and their coreligionists by the Russian Govt. Genl. Kouroupatkine replied that

* The letter is in fact from Mírzá Abu'l-Faḍl-i-Gulpáygání, the erudite Bahá'í scholar who played a leading role in the proceedings in 'Is͟hqábád after the martyrdom of Ḥájí Muḥammad-Riḍá, and was written to Mírzá Asadu'lláh K͟hán-i-Vazír in Iṣfahán. The whole letter is quoted in Mihrábk͟hání *S͟harḥ-i-Aḥvál* pp. 159–94.

he wd. be glad to receive their address if addressed to the Emperor and to recommend it to H.I.M.'s favourable consideration.

This paragraph the Amin us Sultan told M. de Butzow had very considerably excited the Shah, who wd. be exceedingly angry if the Russians in anyway countenanced Persian Babis. If, indeed, the address was recd. by the Russian Govt. and favourably considered the Shah wd. take most energetic steps to openly protest against any such interference with his independence by the Russian Govt.

To-day M. de Butzow replied that the Russian Government would not protect the Babis; but begged that the Shah would not insist on their being forced to return to Persia.[5]

According to a further memorandum from Churchill dated 3 October, further reassurances were later given by the Russian Government: 'The Russian Govt. has now reassured the Shah's Govt. on the subject and state that they do not intend to show the Babis any favour.'[6]

On 7 October 1890, Robert Kennedy, acting on behalf of Sir Henry Drummond Wolff, addressed a dispatch to the Marquess of Salisbury on this matter:

Among other topics the conduct of General Kouroupatkine in giving a favourable reception to a deputation of Persian Babis residing in Transcaspia, formed the subject of a strong remonstrance on the part of the Amin in the name of the Shah, who had expressed great annoyance at the occurrence.

The Russian Minister has, since then, acting apparently under instructions, assured the Amin-es-Sultan that His Majesty need feel no alarm on the subject as the Russian Government do not intend showing the Babis any favour.[7]

References

1. Browne *A Traveller's Narrative* pp. 411–12
2. Tumanski 'Dva poslednikh' p. 315
3. Memo by Bax Ironside 17 Dec. 1889, enclosed in Wolff to Salisbury No. 235, 18 Dec. 1889: FO 60 502
4. Memo of Ḥasan-'Alí Khán-i-Navváb 1 May 1890: FO 248 509
5. Churchill's memo of 3 Sept. 1890: FO 248 501
6. Churchill's memo of 3 Oct. 1890: FO 248 510
7. Kennedy to Salisbury No. 296, 7 Oct. 1890: FO 60 512

TWENTY

The Seven Martyrs of Yazd (1891)

The last major persecution to erupt in Persia within Bahá'u'lláh's lifetime occurred in Yazd. It was to be, however, despite its gruesome details, merely the portent of the much more serious and savage persecution that erupted in 1903 in that city. Concerning the causes of this 1891 upheaval see pp. 357–8.

Captain Vaughan (q.v.), of the 7th Bengal Infantry, chanced to be passing through Yazd a few days after the event. He refers to the martyrdoms in an account of his travels:

> . . . and two days more brought me to Yezd, where I heard that there was a movement against the Babis, three of whom were executed by having their throats cut by the public executioner, and were then stoned to death by the populace, after which their mangled remains were cut in pieces and exhibited to the victims' wives and children. I heard that the men who suffered showed great fortitude, and, though told that they had only to say that they believed in the true Mohammedan religion, that their prophet was false, and their lives would be spared, scorned to do so. I was also told that these persecutions would give a great impetus to the movement, and that each death caused numerous converts.[1]

He sent the following telegram direct to the British Legation at Ṭihrán through the Persian Telegraph Service, on 21 May 1891:

'Three days ago seven people of the Babi sect were killed at Yezd.'[2]

But, believing his telegram to Ṭihrán may have been interfered with, he sent a second via Iṣfahán where there was an office of the British-controlled Indo-European Telegraph Department:

> Following dated 22nd just received from Captn. Vaughan at Yezd requesting me forward you. Begins: wired from Yezd on twenty first to Legation that seven Babis had been executed on the nineteenth May, but believe Persian wire stopped message. Executions were ordered by Governor.* Victims throats cut then stoned to death at intervals in the bazaar. More arrests made yesterday and further executions anticipated. Great uneasiness prevails. Firm Hotz and Co. done no business for last week. Haji Mirza Muhammed Taki,† Russian Agent, is unsafe, and other leading merchants

* Sulṭán-Ḥusayn Mírzá, Jalálu'd-Dawlih (q.v.)

† Ḥájí Mírzá Muḥammad-Taqí, the Afnán (q.v., see fig. 45)

threatened. Moolah Shaikh Hussan and his son Shaikh Taki* are chief instigators of persecution. Supposed here executions sanctioned by Shah. Rumours executions at Teheran and other places prevail. Please inform Minister. Ends. He adds: here we are quite in the dark as to what is going on elsewhere, but the opinion prevails that the Babis are to be hunted down everywhere owing to one of them having threatened the Shah's life. I shall probably stay here until things are quieter.[3] [Punctuation added.]

This telegram arrived in Ṭihrán on 27 May 1891 and was forwarded to the British Legation, at once, by Col. H. Wells, the Superintendent of the Telegraph Department. The British Chargé d'Affaires, Mr R. J. Kennedy, wrote on the back of the second telegram '*Nawab*,† read this to Amin‡ and see what he has to say about it. R.J.K.'

In the meantime, Kennedy received an account of the upheaval from a Dutch merchant, via the Dutch Chargé d'Affaires. This report is of great interest as it is an eyewitness account:

On Monday last, 18th inst., 7 Bábis were executed quite unexpectedly. One was hung in the presence of the Prince and six others were killed in different quarters of the town. This is the first time that Bábis have been killed here and their execution occasioned some tumult. The bodies were buried at once by the mob under stones. The Prince gave orders that on Monday and Tuesday nights the Bazaars should be open and illuminated, and said that he intended to come himself on Tuesday evening. Tuesday morning he gave orders that the illuminations should not take place and that everyone who said a word upon the subject of Bábis should have his tongue cut out. Since Tuesday last the persecutions have continued. The priest of the Bábis, Mollah Ibrahim,§ has been arrested and escorted this morning from Taft to Yezd with music. A silk merchant of Yezd and four men from the environs have also been arrested. I think these six people will be killed this week. The principal merchants here are Bábis and several amongst them are decidedly more or less in danger; especially Haji Mirza Md. Takki, Shirazi,‖ and his son Haji Mirza Md., Haji Seyed Mirza, Shirazi,¶ Haji Md. Ibrahim, Haji Md. Jadegh, Afsjahi. The Prince is said to have ordered already some time ago that they had to provide themselves with passports signed by the first Mollahs. The situation is rather critical and as one is afraid of more serious occurrences there is no question of business.

The Mollahs who are the cause of the executions and persecutions are Shaikh Hassan and his son Shaikh Takki, Mirza Seyed Ali,⁂ Mollah Hassan and Mollah Husein.†† The names of the people killed are:

1. Mollah Mehti	from Getki
2. Mollah Ali	from Sabsevar
3. Ashghar	from Yezd
4. Muhammad Baker	from Yezd
5. Asghar	from Yezd
6. Hassan	from Yezd
7. Ali	from Yezd

all, except No. 5, are married and have children. Their property is taken from them and the Bábis are at the present moment too much afraid to assist them. The women and children of the victims have been insulted by

* Shaykh Ḥasan-i-Sabzivárí and his son Shaykh Muḥammad-Taqíy-i-Sabzivárí. The latter died in early 1897.

† i.e. Ḥasan-'Alí Khán-i-Navváb, (q.v.)

‡ i.e. 'Alí-Aṣghar Khán, the Amínu's-Sulṭán (q.v.), the Prime Minister

§ See p. 304n. ‖ i.e. Ḥájí Mírzá Muḥammad-Taqí, the Afnán.

¶ Also one of the Afnán. ⁂ Known as Mudarris. †† Both of Ardikán.

the mob. The Mollahs who have great influence with the Prince are Shaikh Hassan and his son Shaikh Takki. They send to several people known as Bábis threatening them that they will make a complaint against them if they do not give 25, 50 or 100 tomans. The Bábis have died like real martyrs without any fear and without saying anything but good about their religion. The Prince only desired that they would speak against the Bábi religion; seven refused; two men, however, sons of Mollah Mehti, did so and they were released.[4]

Not satisfied with Amínu's-Sulṭán's response to his verbal representations, and having received this disturbing Dutch account, Kennedy wrote a memorandum to Amínu's-Sulṭán on 2 June 1891.

I think it right to tell Y.H. [Your Highness] that I have received reports of great persecutions of Babis at Yezd. Similar reports have reached other Europeans at Tehran.

Several Babis have been put to death and their bodies mutilated. Others are in danger of their lives, unless they satisfy the Mollahs.

Y.H. knows of course how far these reports are true, and whether the Governor of Yezd is acting properly.

I mention the subject to you, as I am as Y.H. knows a sincere friend and well wisher of Persia, and I should deeply regret if, at any time, anything should be done which may injure the reputation of the Persian Government.[5]

On the following day, 3 June 1891, Ḥasan-'Alí Khán-i-Navváb was sent for an interview with Amínu's-Sulṭán. The following is his memorandum of that interview: 'H.H. the Amin-us-Sultan said that he represented the contents of your private note regarding the persecution of Babis at Yezd to H.M. [the Sháh] who at once sent two telegrams one to Zel-us-Sultan and the other to Jelal-u-Dawleh at Yezd commanding them to cease persecuting the Babis and not to listen to the Mulas, should further reports be heard of this sort H.M. would ask for explanations.'[6]

Mr Kennedy reported the matter to the Marquess of Salisbury (q.v.), the Foreign Minister, on 5 June 1891 in the following terms:

About a forthnight ago I received a telegram from Captain Vaughan, who is now at Yezd, saying that seven Bábis had been put to death by order of the Governor, and that other executions were impending. Although no details were given, I thought it advisable to mention the affair verbally to the Amin-us-Sultan, but as I saw by the manner and remarks of His Highness that the Governor of Yezd had acted, if not by the orders, at any rate with the knowledge of the Shah, I did not think it advisable to press the subject too much upon His Highness' notice.

Some days later the Dutch Chargé d'Affaires called on me to read a letter which he had received from a Dutch merchant residing at Yezd. I have the honour to enclose a copy of it.

Under these circumstances, seeing that there was every chance of the persecution of the Bábis leading to serious consequences, and being reported in the European Press, to the great injury of Persia, I wrote a confidential memorandum to the Amin-us-Sultan, which I requested His Highness to lay before the Shah.

The Amin-us-Sultan did so, and subsequently sent me a verbal message through the Nawab Hassan Ali Khan saying that His

Majesty, after reading my memorandum, at once sent two telegrams, one to the Zil-us-Sultan at Ispahan, the other to His Royal Highness' son, Jelal-ud-Dowleh, Governor of Yezd, ordering them to put a stop to the persecution of the Bábis and to pay no attention to the suggestions of the Mollahs. His Majesty added that if any further reports of this nature reached him he would at once call upon the local authorities for explanations.[7]

The telegrams that were enclosed with this dispatch were as follows:

[H.M. The Sh͟áh to the Jalálu'd-Dawlih, no date:]

With regard to the few Bábis whose infidelity was proved to the Shar' and who were put to death, hereafter other people must not be, by accusation of Bábism, interfered with and injured. Give strict orders to leave the people quiet and not to find fault with them.[8]

[The Jalálu'd-Dawlih to H.M. the Sh͟áh dated 26 Sh͟avvál 1308:*]

I have had the honour of receiving Y.M.'s tel.: The few Babis who were put to death by Y.M.'s orders were those whose infidelity was proved and who were condemned to death by the Ulamas. The verdicts of the Ulamas are kept by me. Although no one has the power to treat Y.M.'s subjects with oppression in any way, in order to be sure I showed the Royal tel.: to the Ulamas of Yezd and gave strict orders on the matter. In every respect Y.M. may rest assured. The life of this slave may be sacrificed to the dust under Y.M.'s feet. Husein Kájár[9]

[H.R.H. The Ẓillu's-Sulṭán to H.H. the Amínu's-Sulṭán dated 26 Sh͟avvál 1308:]

In such affairs the characters of the people are known and Your Highness can imagine what the Ulamas may be. I am always busy with such affairs in Ispahan and the repetition of them will make Y.H. sad. In compliance with your instructions I telegraphed to Yezd and this matter which is not serious will be settled soon.[10]

One further telegram, of 7 June 1891, from Vaughan, exists in the Public Record Office Archives: 'An execution supposed occurred privately in prison about 24th.† No further news since 27th when I left Yezd.'[11] [Punctuation added.]

Prof. Browne, receiving accounts of this episode from 'Akká, Alexandria and 'Is͟hqábád, prepared a report and submitted it to the editor of the *Daily News*. A much-shortened account appeared in the edition of that newspaper of 30 October 1891.‡[12] A detailed report from Browne appeared in the *Pall Mall Gazette* of 26 November 1891, however.

* 4 June 1891

† This was Ḥájí Mullá Muḥammad-Ibráhím-i-Masá'il-gú, who had left the city and proceeded some way when he was arrested, returned to Yazd and thrown into prison. His wife went to the Dutch merchants and begged them to intervene. These went to Jalálu'd-Dawlih but had no success. It was stated that Jalálu'd-Dawlih slew the man with his own hands and had the body thrown in a well (see Browne *Materials* p. 307).

‡ Prof. Browne published the four reports of this episode that he had received, including one from 'Abdu'l-Bahá (see p. 357), in *Materials* pp. 295–308. The most detailed of these is an account by one Ḥusayn written from Yazd to Ḥájí Siyyid 'Alíy-i-Afnán at 'Is͟hqábád and communicated by the latter to Browne. In this last-mentioned account it is stated that some Christian merchants of the Dutch nation (presumably the same ones who sent the report quoted above and intervened with Jalálu'd-Dawlih) sent food and water to the wives and children of the martyrs.

References

1. Vaughan 'Journeys in Persia (1890–1)' p. 171
2. Telegram Vaughan to 'The English Minister, Tehran' 21 May 1891: FO 248 530
3. Telegram Iṣfahán station of Indo-European Telegraph Dept. to Col. Wells, 27 May 1891, forwarding Vaughan's telegram, communicated to Mr Kennedy on the same day: FO 248 535
4. Enclosed in 7 *infra*
5. Kennedy to Amínu's-Sulṭán, private and confidential, 2 June 1891: FO 248 532
6. Memo of Ḥasan-'Alí Khán-i-Navváb 3 June 1891: FO 248 530
7. Kennedy to Salisbury No. 139, 5 June 1891: FO 60 523
8. Enclosed in 7 *supra*
9. ibid.
10. ibid.
11. Telegram Iṣfahán station of Indo-European Telegraph Dept. to Col. Wells, 7 June 1891, forwarding Vaughan's telegram, communicated by Wells to Kennedy. FO 248 535
12. No. 50, Folder 2, Browne Papers, Cambridge Univ. Library

TWENTY-ONE

The Cyprus Exiles

As previously noted in chapter 12, when Bahá'u'lláh was sent to 'Akká a number of Mírzá Yaḥyá's followers were sent with him. Conversely, four of Bahá'u'lláh's followers were exiled with Mírzá Yaḥyá to Famagusta in Cyprus, where they arrived 5 September 1868. These were Mishkín-Qalam, Mírzá 'Alíy-i-Sayyáḥ, Áqá 'Abdu'l-Ghaffár and Áqá Muḥammad-Báqir-i-Maḥallátí.

Of the Bahá'ís, Mírzá 'Abdu'l-Ghaffár succeeded in effecting an escape from Cyprus on 29 September 1870, and rejoined Bahá'u'lláh; Shaykh 'Alíy-i-Sayyáḥ died on 4 August 1871, and Muḥammad-Báqir-i-Maḥallátí died on 22 November 1872; Mishkín-Qalam alone was thus left. Mírzá Yaḥyá had arrived on the island with his entire family, but without a single disciple or even a servant. After a time, one or two followers arrived on the island and settled there.[1]

On 4 June 1878, Britain signed a defensive alliance with Turkey whereby, in exchange for Britain's undertaking to give military assistance to Turkey should Russia seize any Ottoman territories, Britain was granted the right to occupy and administer Cyprus (although it remained theoretically under Ottoman sovereignty). The British administration commenced on 12 July 1878. The first High Commissioner, Lt-Gen. Sir Garnet Wolsely, was succeeded on 23 June 1879 by Col. Robert Biddulph.

On 2 August 1878, shortly after the British took over the administration of the island, A. R. Greaves, the Chief Secretary of the Government of Cyprus, requested Leopold Swaine, the District Commissioner of Famagusta, to prepare a report on the prisoners held in the Fortress of that town. Five prisoners are named in this report:

1. Qáṭirjí Yání, a Greek sentenced for life for robbery.
2. Muṣṭafá, a Bosnian.
3. Yúsif, a Turk, sentenced for life for speaking against the Turkish religion.
4. Mírzá Yaḥyá Ṣubḥ-i-Azal.
5. Mishkín-Qalam.

The latter two are described thus: 'They wished to invent some new religion, and, when pressed, fled from Persia and settled in Turkey. After a time they again tried to carry out their madness, and were consequently condemned by the Turkish authorities to imprisonment for life.'[2]

In November 1878, further information was requested by the Chief Secretary in order to determine the amount of the pension to be allowed to the prisoners. In his reply of 5 November 1878, Jamas Inglis, the Commissioner of Famagusta, states that he cannot get any official information about them as the records are lost or destroyed. He then gives the following account of the two Persian prisoners, based on their own statements:

1st, *Subbe Ezel*. Handsome, well-bred looking man, apparently about 50. In receipt of Pias. 1193 per month (the *Ḳáẓí* only gets Pias. 1020). States that he was for a long time at the Persian Court, where his brother* was next officer in rank to the vizier. He afterwards went to Stamboul and then to Adrianople, where he was accused of plotting against the Porte and the religion of Islam. Sentence – for life. Been here 11 years.

2nd, *Maskin Kalam*. From Korassom [Khurásán]. Allowed Pias. 660 per month. Sentence – for life. Been here 11 years. Came here at same time as Subbe Ezel. Sentenced for religious offence against Porte. 53 years old. Has two families, one here, and one in Persia. In appearance is a dried-up, shrivelled old man, with long hair almost to the waist.[3]

On 20 June 1879, Mishkín-Qalam was accorded permission by the Chief Secretary to remove from Famagusta to Nicosia. Later that year, he addressed a petition, dated 15 August, to the High Commissioner of Cyprus begging to be released from his confinement in order that he could rejoin his family after 12 years of exile. The consequence of this petition was a request from F. M. Warren, the Chief Secretary, for further information about the prisoners. Consequently a further report was compiled from the statements of the former Turkish Qá'im-Maqám and the prisoners:

No. 3, Subbi Ezel of Iran. *Trade*? Nil. *Crime*? Falsely accused of preaching against the Turkish religion. *Where*? Adrianople. *Who was charge made by*? A man of Iran. *By whom tried*? Came from Bagdad and went to Adrianople where charge was made. Vali of Adrianople ordered him to Constantinople, where he was examined by Kamal Pasha (Prime Minister). *When*? Twelve years ago. *Previous imprisonment before coming here*? Five months in Constantinople, before coming here under arrest, five years at Adrianople. *Undergone here*? Twelve years. *Pension*? 38½ piastres a day current. *Do. before*? 38½ piastres a day Government exchange. Has family of 17. His father was Chief Secretary of State to the present Shah of Persia (Naṣaradin Shah).

No. 4. Muskin Kalem Efendi. *Trade*? Writer. *Crime*? Being in company with a preacher against Mahometanism who came from Persia and Akia ['Akká] in Syria. *Where*? Constantinople. *Punishment*? Transported for life, and to be imprisoned in Famagusta fortress. *By whom*? Authority of Sultan Aziz. *Date*? 1284 November (1876)†

* Probably this is a mistake for 'father', as Ṣubḥ-i-Ezel repeatedly described the position of his father Mírzá Buzurg in these very words. [EGB]

† Browne corrects this to 1868.

Previous Imprisonment? Six months in Constantinople. *Has undergone*? Twelve years. *Any lodging*? The *ferman* ordering banishment stated that he was to get free lodging, but he has not had any [free] lodging. This man has sent a petition to government about a week ago. 23/6/79.[4]

It was presumably as a result of this petition and subsequent enquiries that the High Commissioner, Robert Biddulph (q.v.), decided to refer the whole matter to the Foreign Office in a dispatch dated 5 September 1879:

I have the honor to transmit to Your Lordship the enclosed list copied from the register found at Famagusta of persons who, having been at various dates exiled to Cyprus by the Turkish Government, are now kept in this island as State Prisoners; they are in receipt of a monthly allowance but are not permitted to leave the island. I would urge Your Lordship to move the Sublime Porte to sanction the return of these persons to their native countries: without such permission they would be liable to apprehension on landing at any port in the Ottoman Empire. [See list opposite][5]

The Marquess of Salisbury, the Foreign Minister, forwarded the communication to Mr. E. B. Malet (q.v.), the British Minister at Istanbul, on 29 September 1879, asking him to bring it to the attention of the Ottoman authorities. On 10 October 1879, Malet addressed a note to the Sublime Porte:

Acting under instructions from H.M.'s P.S. of S. for F.A. [Her Majesty's Permanent Secretary of State for Foreign Affairs], H.M.'s Embassy has the honor to enclose a list of persons who, having at various times been exiled to Cyprus by the Ottoman Govt., are now detained there as State Prisoners, and to request either that permission may be granted to these persons to return to their homes or that they may be transferred to some other part of the Ottoman Empire, as their continuance in Cyprus is a source of inconvenience to the Administration of that Island.[6]

The Porte then instituted its own investigations of the matter. On 16 January 1880, a note from the Ministry of Justice was communicated to the British Legation for their information.

This note, appearing in French in the Public Record Office files, reads:

'Persian: Subhi Kémal.* Accused of Sodomism. Condemned to perpetual seclusion in a fortified enclosure in Cyprus.

– Ta<u>dh</u>kirih has been addressed to the Ministry of Police for the transfer of this man to the Fort of St Jean d'Acre.

Persian. Miskin Cassim Effendi†. Accused of heresy. Condemned to perpetual seclusion in a fortified enclosure in Cyprus.

– Idem.'[7]

('Hadidge' was to be freed and 'Katerdgi Yani' was also to be sent to 'Akká.

* i.e. Mírzá Yaḥyá, Ṣubḥ-i-Azal: presumably the offence with which he is charged is an unfortunate error of transcription at some point.

† i.e. Mi<u>sh</u>kín-Qalam

Name	Nationality	Offence	Sentence	Period under restraint in Cyprus	Remarks
Hadidge (woman)	Cypriote	Incendiarism	15 years Impt.	nearly 10 years	5 years were remitted
Katerdgi Yani	from Aideen, Asia Minor	Highway robbery	Transportation for life	20 years	Impd. previously for 7 years at Constantinople
Subbi Ezel [Mírzá Yaḥyá, Ṣubḥ-i-Azal]	Persian	Political	Transportation for life	12 years	5 years in arrest at Adrianople and 5 months impt. at Constantinople.
Muskin Kalem Effendi [Mishkín-Qalam]	Persian	Political	Transportation for life	12 years	6 months impt. in Constantinople
Youssouf Mehmet	Mersin, Asia Minor	(unknown)	Transportation for life. (Transportation for 15 years according to prisoner's statement)	nearly 20 years	(the offence and sentence are uncertain)
Mustapha Boshnak	Bosnian	Creating disturbances	Transportation for life. (Transportation for 15 years by prisoner's statement)	15 years	2 years impt. in Constantinople.
Hudaverdi	Ottoman subject	(doubtful)	(According to the register Transportation for life)	18 years	a blind man, formerly served in Turkish Artillery.[5]

No trace of the others was found, which is not entirely surprising since according to Browne, 'Hudaverdi' was not even a prisoner but a Turkish pensioner.)

A little later, 20 January 1880, the following note addressed by the Minister of Police to the Ministry of Foreign Affairs was communicated to Mr Marinitch (q.v.) of the British Embassy and was then sent on to Biddulph at Cyprus on 24 January 1880:

A letter was sent from the Ministry for Foreign Affairs to the Ministry of Justice containing a note from the British Embassy requesting either the liberation of the seven convicts who have been exiled to Cyprus and are there in prison, or their removal to another place. It appears from the correspondence exchanged with the Ministry of Justice that it has been decided that those whose names are on the enclosed paper, viz 'Katerji Yani', 'Subhi Kial', and his companion Meskin Cassum, sentenced to imprisonment in a fortress for life, should be removed to the fortress of St Jean d'Acre, and that proceedings are still going about the remaining four. As the Police Council has stated that in the Central Prison here there are no registrations regarding these latter, I have to request your Excellency to be pleased to consent that the necessary steps should be taken in accordance with the above statement. . . .

Katerji Yani.

For highway robbery in the beginning of Djemay al Akher 77, condemned to hard labour for life in Cyprus.

Persian Subhi Kiali.

Condemned for Sodomism, to detention in the fortress of Cyprus for life.

Persian Meskin Cassim.

Condemned for heresy, to detention in the fortress of Cyprus for life.[8]

The further developments of the case are summarized in a dispatch to the Foreign Office, dated 18 June 1889:

Sir R. Biddulph thereupon wrote a despatch (126/11 Mar. 80) giving the fullest information that could be procured respecting the prisoners. With regard to Subhi Ezzel, Sir R. Biddulph said that he could not discover any ground for the statement that his offence was [sodomy,]* his own statement being that he was falsely accused of preaching against the Turkish religion, and his bitter enemy – Muskin Kalem – also stating that the offence was heresy. Sir R. Biddulph went on to say that the original warrants under which the two Persians were confined were taken away at the occupation, but they had been previously noted in the Temyiz Court in whose register it is stated that they were condemned for '*Babieisme*' to seclusion for life in a fortress. This sentence was given by Imperial Firman and not by any judicial tribunal . . . The F.O. despatch which replied to this (5 Apr. 80) authorized the prisoners being left at large and not interfered with in respect of their alleged sentences and firmans, their stipends are to be paid to them as long as they remain in Cyprus.

This decision was communicated to the Turkish authorities, who however persisted in demanding the surrender of the prisoners. On this the Ambassador received instructions (F.O. 371 24 Sept. 80) not to answer the Sublime Porte's note and to let the matter drop, but, should the Ottoman Government continue to press for their surrender, the Ambassador was instructed to say that as one of them was at large when the Occupation took place and the other two confined to Famagusta on account of their

* Browne has left a blank at this point.

religious opinions, H.M. Govt. could not interfere with their personal liberty.

So far as I can find nothing further has been heard from Constantinople of the matter.[9]

On 24 March 1881, Mírzá Yaḥyá was informed that he might consider himself free to go where he pleased. In response to this, Mírzá Yaḥyá addressed a petition on 27 April 1881 to the High Commissioner, asking that he be made a British subject or taken under British protection, so that he could with safety return to his own country or to Turkey.* The Government did not see fit to accede to his request and consequently he remained in Cyprus for the rest of his life.

Mis͟hkín-Qalam's departure from the island is notified in a letter from Mr Cobham (q.v.),† who employed him to teach him Persian. The letter, dated 18 September 1886, states: 'The Persian heresiarch and calligraphist Mushkín Ḳalam left Cyprus for St Jean d'Acre on the night of Tuesday September 14–15, renouncing his pittances and the protection of the Island Government. He found an unwonted opportunity in a Syrian vessel going direct to Acre, the head quarters of the Báb [i.e. Bahá'u'lláh] . . . I am extremely sorry to lose him as a Persian *munshí*.'[10]

Thus, when in March 1890, Prof. Browne, on the journey that was to result in his famous interview with Bahá'u'lláh (see pp. 229ff), arrived in Cyprus, of the original exiles only Mírzá Yaḥyá, now a British pensioner, remained. Concerning his first interview with Mírzá Yaḥyá, Browne wrote:

. . . we ascended to an upper room, where a venerable and benevolent-looking old man of about sixty years of age, somewhat below the middle height, with ample forehead on which the traces of care and anxiety were apparent, clear searching blue eyes, and long grey beard, rose and advanced to meet us. Before that mild and dignified countenance I

* 'To the Commissioner [R. Biddulph],

I have received your kind letter of 24/4/81 and indeed I cannot express my feelings of gratitude to H.M. the Queen and to the Heads of the English Govt. in Cyprus. I thank you sincerely, sir, for the kind letter you had sent me releasing me from my exile here, and wish long life to H.M. the Queen. Another small favour I should like to ask, if it is possible that I might be in future under English protection, as I fear that going to my country my countrymen might again come on me. My case was simply heretic religious opinions, and as the English Govt. leaves free every man to express his own opinions and feelings on such matters, I dare hope that this favour of being protected by them, and which favour I most humbly ask, will not be refused to me. (signed) Subhi Ezzel.' (Cambridge Univ. Library, Browne Papers, Folder 6, Item 7, No. 21)

† Among Browne's notes on the Cyprus Archives (Cambridge Univ. Library, Browne Papers, Folder 6, Item 7), there is the following record of a note in Cobham's handwriting (No. 18): 'It appears that in 1867 Müskin Kalem Eff. came from Meshad in Khorassan to Constantinople. His fame as a scribe had preceded him, and Fuad and A'ali Pashas asked him to remain in Constantinople. He refused both pension and presents offered him by Abdul Aziz, for whom he executed some illuminations. Presently he was accused by one Subh-i-Ezel, a Persian then at Adrianople, himself a member of some schismatic sect, of heresy. He had lived six months at Constantinople, where [when] he was imprisoned, without question or trial, for another six months, and then sent to Famagusta.'

involuntarily bowed myself with unfeigned respect; for at length my long-cherished desire was fulfilled, and I stood face to face with Mírzá Yaḥyá *Ṣubḥ-i-Ezel* ('the Morning of Eternity'), the appointed successor of the Báb, the fourth 'Letter' of the 'First Unity.'[11]

For two weeks, Browne, according to his own testimony, went to Mírzá Yaḥyá every day, staying from two or three o'clock in the afternoon until sunset. Browne visited Mírzá Yaḥyá again in March 1896. The other great Bábí scholar of that period, A.-L.-M. Nicolas, while he was French Dragoman at Larnaca in 1894–5, also frequently visited Mírzá Yaḥyá in Famagusta.[12]

Mírzá Yaḥyá, deserted by the majority of his followers,* continued to live in Famagusta until his death on 29 April 1912. According to the testimony of his own son, in a letter communicated to Prof. Browne, there was no one even to recite any of the prayers of the Báb at his funeral, and he was buried according to Muslim customs: 'But none were to be found there of witnesses to the *Bayán*,† therefore the *Imám-Jum'a* of Famagusta and some others of the doctors of Islám, having uttered [the customary] invocations, placed the body in the coffin and buried it.'[13]

References

1. Information gathered by Browne from the official archives of Cyprus in 1890. Item 7, Folder 6, Browne Papers, Cambridge Univ. Library (*cf.* Browne *A Traveller's Narrative* pp. 376–89)
2. Swaine to Greaves 8 Aug. 1878: No. 2, Item 7, see 1 *supra*
3. Inglis to Greaves 5 Nov. 1878: No. 4, Item 7, see 1 *supra* (*cf.* Browne *A Traveller's Narrative* p. 378)
4. Packet attached to reply of Capt. Gordon, Acting Commsr Famagusta: No. 10, Item 7, see 1 *supra* (*cf.* Browne *A Traveller's Narrative* pp. 379–80)
5. Biddulph to Salisbury No. 115, 5 Sept. 1879: CO 67 5
6. Malet to Sublime Porte No. 272, 10 Oct. 1879: FO 195 1261
7. Note from Ottoman Ministry of Justice, communicated to the British Legation for their information on 16 Jan. 1880: FO 195 1325 (trans. from French)
8. Note from Ottoman Min. of Police to Ministry of For. Aff., communicated to the British Legation confidentially on 20 Jan. 1880: FO 195 1325
9. Confidential For. Off. dispatch 1394/89, 18 June 1889: No. 10, Item 7, see 1 *supra*
10. Cobham to Sweetenham 18 Sept. 1886: No. 9, Item 7, see 1 *supra* (*cf.* Browne *A Traveller's Narrative* p. 388)
11. Browne *A Traveller's Narrative* p. xxiv of Introduction
12. Nicolas *Qui est le successeur du Bab*? p. 15, and footnote on first page of Introduction to Vol. 1 of *Le Béyan Persan*
13. Browne *Materials* p. 312

* Even of his sons, several deserted him, and one, Riḍván-'Alí, took up the Christian religion under the name Constantine the Persian.

† *i.e.* Bábís [EGB]

Section D

The Ministry of 'Abdu'l-Bahá (1892–1921)

TWENTY-TWO

'Abdu'l-Bahá: Early Accounts

In the chapter 'Bahá'u'lláh in 'Akká', several early accounts of 'Abdu'l-Bahá have already been given. Almost without exception, all those who met him were immensely impressed by his personality and erudition. The latter was all the more remarkable since from the age of nine years he had been his father's companion-in-exile and had had no opportunity to undertake formal studies, nor had access to any libraries or institutions of learning. It was noted that at the age of 27, 'Abdu'l-Bahá was described by Dr Chaplin as having 'a remarkably earnest, almost solemn manner, spoke excellent Arabic fluently, and showed a minute and accurate knowledge of the Old and New Testaments, as well as an acquaintance with the history of religious thought in Europe.' One year later, Rev. Neil wrote of him: 'It was indeed strange to find an Eastern in Syria so well educated and to hear him speak so tolerantly and intelligibly of Christ and Christianity.' Two years later, when 'Abdu'l-Bahá was thirty years of age, Rev. Zeller wrote of him: 'he is a highly-gifted fascinating young man.' E. G. Browne's lengthy accolade includes such statements as: 'Seldom have I seen one whose appearance impressed me more . . . One more eloquent of speech, more ready of argument, more apt of illustration, more intimately acquainted with the sacred books of the Jews, the Christians, and the Muhammadans, could, I should think, scarcely be found . . .'[1]

Visitors to Haifa and 'Akká

Within the first few years of the ministry of 'Abdu'l-Bahá, an event occurred which was of resounding importance. Although up to this time there had been a few Europeans who had sympathized with the new religion (such persons as Prokesch-Osten, Nicolas, perhaps Eça de Queirós, and even E. G. Browne), no person from the West had publicly proclaimed his belief or actively worked for the furtherance of the Bahá'í religion. Then in the closing years of the nineteenth century this situation altered, through the conversion to the new faith of a small but rapidly growing number in

North America. Within a few years, the community in North America was several thousand strong and had spread to Europe. Now, for the first time, the people of the West could hear and read accounts of the new religion from their own countrymen. Some of these Western Bahá'ís came to Haifa and 'Akká as pilgrims and have left accounts of their visits. The subject of the rise of the Bahá'í religion in the West is, however, too large to be considered in this book, and in this and the following section mainly Western accounts of the Bahá'í Faith in the East will be considered. With regard to 'Abdu'l-Bahá, only those accounts by persons who were not Bahá'ís or who were later estranged from the religion will be considered here.

One of the most important and significant events of the ministry of 'Abdu'l-Bahá was the arrival of the first group of American Bahá'ís in 'Akká in December 1898. The pilgrimage was organized and financed by Mrs Phoebe A. Hearst (q.v.), the widow of the eminent Californian businessman and US Senator, George Hearst. Although at the time of this pilgrimage Mrs Hearst was considered a Bahá'í, because of the actions of some of the Bahá'ís on her return to America, she shut herself off from the Bahá'í community. Despite her estrangement, she was able to write very warmly of 'Abdu'l-Bahá. The following are two extracts from her letters:

> Although my stay in Acca was very short, as I was there only three days, yet I assure you those three days were the most memorable days of my life, still I feel incapable of describing them in the slightest degree.
>
> From a material standpoint everything was very simple and plain, but the spiritual atmosphere which pervaded the place, and was manifested in the lives and actions among the Believers, was truly wonderful, and something I had never before experienced. One needs but to see them to know that they are a Holy people.
>
> The Master I will not attempt to describe: I will only state that I believe with all my heart that He is the Master, and my greatest blessing in this world is that I have been privileged to be in His presence and look upon His sanctified face. His life is truly the Christ life and His whole being radiates purity and holiness!
>
> Without a doubt Abbas Effendi is the Messiah of this day and generation, and we need not look for another.[2]

and

> My stay in Acca was very short; if I remember correctly I was there but three days, though Mr and Mrs Getsinger were there three months. Acca is [now] a ruined fortification, its streets are narrow and dark and the houses are very primitive and rudely constructed, but when we were admitted to the Master's presence we lost sight of our surroundings entirely.
>
> It seems to me a real Truthseeker would know at a glance that He is the Master! Withal, I must say He is the Most Wonderful Being I have ever met or ever expect to meet in this world. Though He does not seek to impress one at all, strength, power, purity, love and holiness are radiated from His majestic, yet humble, personality, and the spiritual atmosphere which surrounds Him, and most powerfully affects all those who are blessed by being near Him, is indescribable. His ideas and sentiments are of the loftiest and most chaste character, while His great love and devotion for humanity surpasses anything I have ever before

encountered. I believe in Him with all my heart and soul, and I hope all who call themselves Believers will concede to Him all the greatness, all the glory, and all the praise, for surely He is the Son of God – and 'the Spirit of the Father abideth in Him.'

Regarding the Household, I found them all quiet, holy people, living only for the purpose of serving in the Cause of God. They dress very plainly, but with a grace that gives a sort of grandeur to their most humble abode. The purity of their morals is evident from the calm, benign and guileless faces, which characterize them as a people. To become spiritually more and more like them, and like the Blessed Master, is my daily supplication unto God.[3]

Over the ensuing years there were many persons from the West who visited 'Abdu'l-Bahá and have recorded their impressions. Some of these are extremely favourable while others are hostile. In the latter category is the account of Rev. H. H. Jessup who visited 'Akká in 1900. Together with a certain Capt. Wells, he called on 'Abdu'l-Bahá. Jessup writes: 'Abbas is an elderly and venerable man, very similar to a score of venerable Druse and Moslem Sheikhs I have met . . . The Lord deliver them (American Christians) from the delirious blasphemies . . . The claim that the Acca Sheikh is God is quite enough to condemn them.'[4]

At the other extreme was Myron H. Phelps of the New York Bar, who had come into contact with the Bahá'ís in London in the summer of 1902 and had been sufficiently impressed to make a journey to 'Akká to meet 'Abdu'l-Bahá. He spent the month of December 1902 in 'Akká, and he considered the new religion of sufficient importance to devote the ensuing two months to the preparation of a book on the subject (*Abbas Effendi: His Life and Teachings*). In the book, he writes thus about 'Abdu'l-Bahá in 'Akká:

He is of middle stature, strongly built. He wears flowing light-coloured robes. On his head is a light buff fez with a white cloth wound about it. He is perhaps sixty years of age. His long grey hair rests on his shoulders. His forehead is broad, full, and high, his nose slightly aquiline, his moustaches and beard, the latter full though not heavy, nearly white. His eyes are grey and blue, large, and both soft and penetrating. His bearing is simple, but there is a grace, dignity, and even majesty about his movement . . .

The Master has . . . a very tender, sensitive, and sympathetic nature.[5]

A certain G.H. writing in the French periodical *A Travers le Monde* in 1907 writes: 'M. Sébastien Voirol, who had the honour of being received by him ['Abdu'l-Bahá], described him as an old man at the same time both simple and with a majestic bearing. Of charming affability, he had gestures and mannerisms of rare distinction. His look is, like his words, profound and gentle. His beard is white and silky. He only wears clothes made of fine white wool. His hair and his turban are of the same colour. This is the man who dictates to all the followers of his sect their duty.'[6]

Ethel Stevens (q.v.), who later as Lady Drower became the foremost authority on the Mandeans of Iraq, stayed six months in Haifa and during this time had the opportunity to observe at close quarters both 'Abdu'l-Bahá and the Bahá'í community. In relation to her stay in Haifa, she wrote a novel, *The Mountain of God* (1911, see p. 50) and also the following statement in an article for the magazine *Fortnightly Review*:

> Any day in Haifa you may meet an old man whose flowing white hair, gathered up beneath his snowy turban, proclaims his aristocratic birth, accompanied at the slight distance prescribed by respect by Persian followers with folded hands. His white beard, his blue eyes slightly flecked with brown, his commanding bearing, his dignified walk, his keen kindly face, all proclaim him to be someone of importance and distinction. He wears the simple robe of white linen and grey linsey customary in Persia. This man is Abbas Effendi, or Abdul Baha, the recognised head of the Bahai movement throughout the world.
>
> Bahais have been accused by their Persian enemies of working an enchantment on those who visit them, so that an intoxication, an exultation like that of the hashish smoker, seizes their intellect and enchains their senses, lifting them into a dream-world of illusion. And anyone who has come into close contact with them, as I have been permitted to do during the past six months, is inclined to endorse this, for it is impossible to be with them for long without feeling the infection of this strange enthusiasm, this spiritual hashish, which has sent men to martyrdom with smiles on their faces and joyous ecstasy in their hearts . . .
>
> Abbas Effendi . . . had been carefully trained by his father to assume the leadership of the Bahai community and to become the head of the movement . . . He has in the highest degree that great gift which we call personality. His readily-given sympathy, his understanding of human nature, his power of interesting himself in every human soul which asks his advice and help, have made him passionately beloved by his people. Above all, he has that subtler quality of spirituality which is felt rather than understood by those with whom he comes into contact . . .
>
> ['Abdu'l-Bahá's] house is simply built and simply furnished . . . the walls are bare and white, the woodwork is painted white, and the chairs and divans ranged around the room are covered with an unpretentious light-coloured cotton holland material.[7]

The Renewal of 'Abdu'l-Bahá's Imprisonment

Over the course of the years, since the arrival of Bahá'u'lláh and his companions at 'Akká, the strict terms of the Imperial decree that had ordered their banishment were gradually put into abeyance until by the turn of the century there was virtually no restriction on 'Abdu'l-Bahá at all, and indeed he transferred his residence from 'Akká to Haifa, where a house had been built for him near the German colony.

One of the schemes which Bahá'u'lláh himself had entrusted to the care of 'Abdu'l-Bahá was the erection of a suitable monument to serve as a resting-place for the remains of the Báb.* 'Abdu'l-Bahá had acquired a fitting site on Mount Carmel overlooking the German Colony and had begun the construction of this building.

* The remains of the Báb had been shifted from one place to another in Iran under the direction of Bahá'u'lláh and subsequently 'Abdu'l-Bahá for a total of forty-nine years before arriving in 'Akká in Jan. 1899.

Since the passing of Bahá'u'lláh, 'Abdu'l-Bahá's half-brother, Mírzá Muḥammad-'Alí, had on numerous occasions shown himself to be in open rebellion against the authority of 'Abdu'l-Bahá, despite the clear text of Bahá'u'lláh's Will and Testament. Among the means by which he demonstrated his hostility to 'Abdu'l-Bahá was the sending of false rumours and reports to the Ottoman authorities. Now, seizing the opportunity proffered him through the construction of this building on Mount Carmel, Mírzá Muḥammad-'Alí sent his lieutenant Mírzá Majdu'd-Dín to Damascus with large bribes and alarming stories that 'Abdu'l-Bahá was building a fort on Mount Carmel and was intending to launch a rebellion against the Ottoman Empire.*

The Válí of Beirut visited Haifa and 'Akká in November 1900, and shortly thereafter Monahan (q.v.), the British Vice-Consul at Haifa, reported:

> Abbas Effendi, the chief of the Babists, who seems to be now permanently living in Haifa instead of Acre, began last summer to build a large house on Mount Carmel for an unknown purpose. About the beginning of October the work of building was stopped when half-finished, and it seems probable that the Turkish government stopped it. However, it is said that it will now soon be resumed. The visit of the Vali may perhaps not have been unconnected with this matter.[8]

The machinations of Mírzá Muḥammad-'Alí were to have even more serious results, however. The freedoms that had gradually been allowed the exiles were suddenly taken away, and the original Imperial decree for banishment to 'Akká enforced with renewed vigour.

In his report for the quarter ending 30 September 1901, Monahan writes:

> The Persian Babist leaders Abbas Effendi and his two brothers are shut up within the walls of Acre by an Imperial Iradé [order or decree] which arrived in the middle of the quarter. It is supposed that the Ottoman Government took alarm at Abbas Effendi's increasing wealth and influence especially his influence over Americans and other foreigners. His disciples are however at large in and around Haifa and Acre, except the one or two surviving original exiles who accompanied his father here from Adrianople in 1868. These are kept in Acre with the three brothers.[9]

As can be seen from the above report, the intrigue of Mírzá Muḥammad-'Alí had recoiled upon him, resulting in his being detained in 'Akká along with 'Abdu'l-Bahá. In his report for the quarter ending 31 December 1901, Monahan writes:

> The Babist leaders . . . have not yet been allowed outside the walls of Acre. It is said that the Persian Government demands that they should be kept thus confined. The construction of the Babist house on Mount Carmel . . . which has been several times stopped by the Turkish Authorities and resumed, was again resumed and is being

* This is confirmed by Mírzá Muḥammad-'Alí's brother, Mírzá Badí'u'lláh, in *An Epistle to the Bahá'í World* p. 17.

carried on actively. Two young American gentlemen,* disciples of Babism, arrived in November and stayed two or three weeks in Acre. They presumably came to console Abbas Effendi and transact business with him. I have heard that a considerable amount of money was received during the quarter from America for the Babists.[10]

One person who visited 'Abdu'l-Bahá at this time was the American journalist William E. Curtis (q.v.) who journeyed through Syria in 1900–1901:

He ['Abdu'l-Bahá] is a clever, learned and respectable man, having a magnetic presence, attractive manners and a great deal of tact . . .

Abbas Effendi is a fascinating mystic, a man of most impressive presence and conversation, and his voice is musical and mesmerizing. He seems to have a mercenary tendency, however, for he never lets an American leave him without an appeal for funds for the propagation of the faith.

He has been quite successful in that, as in other directions. Every year numbers of Americans come to see him and have brought him gifts of money, the most of which has been used in the construction of a shrine and temple upon Mount Carmel, above the town of Haifa, where Abbas Effendi intended to bury the remains of his father† and establish the center of his church. As the movement is supposed to be secret the Turkish authorities became alarmed at the number of American visitors and their liberal contributions, so Abbas Effendi was prohibited from leaving Acre, and has not been able to complete the shrine. The walls are up, the roof is laid, and part of the interior finished.[11]

The criticism that Curtis makes concerning 'Abdu'l-Bahá – that he never allowed a visitor to leave without an appeal for funds – is contradicted by numerous others who met him.‡ There were some, however, of 'Abdu'l-Bahá's retinue, especially Dr Amínu'lláh Faríd, who were wont to ask for funds on 'Abdu'l-Bahá's behalf but without his knowledge or sanction. It was such actions that estranged Mrs Hearst from the Bahá'ís and this may also have been the foundation of Curtis's account.

The Turkish Commission of Inquiry

Mírzá Muḥammad-'Alí's implacable hostility towards 'Abdu'l-Bahá drove him to make still further efforts to injure his half-brother. Not content with the harm that he had already caused, Mírzá Muḥammad-'Alí now wrote directly to Istanbul, accusing 'Abdu'l-Bahá of raising a revolt. With rebellion confronting it on all sides, the Ottoman Government could not

* These two may have been Thomas Breakwell, who was English but had lived in America for a long time, and Herbert Hopper (see Balyuzi *'Abdu'l-Bahá* p. 76). There is a pamphlet published in the United States entitled *Utterances to Two Young Men visiting Acca in 1901* (no author indicated, however).

† This is incorrect. It was intended as a shrine for the remains of the Báb from the very start, and its location was designated by Bahá'u'lláh in his lifetime.

‡ See for example the testimony of 'Abdu'l-Bahá's host in London, Lady Blomfield *The Chosen Highway* p. 168, and also Balyuzi *'Abdu'l-Bahá* pp. 171, 184, 234, 261, 336–7 and 368.

afford to ignore such charges, and a Commission of Inquiry was sent to 'Akká.

Concerning this Commission, Drummond Hay (q.v.), the British Consul at Beirut, wrote on 5 August 1905:

In the annexed report from Haifa by Mr P. Abela he mentions that a Commission with an unknown object had arrived from Constantinople composed of Aref Bey, President of the Commercial Court at the Capital, the Farik Shukri Pasha, a Luwa* and two Colonels.

I have since learned that they left Acre to return to Constantinople probably by the mail of this week. Their inspection resulted in the suspension of the Mutessarif Ibrahim Sarim Pasha and the dismissal of Colonel Beddri Bey and of the Commandant of the fortress of Acre who is placed under arrest.[12]

At this time Monahan had left Haifa, and the Vice-Consulate was in charge of Pietro Abela (q.v.). His report, alluded to in the above dispatch, was that for the quarter ending 30 June 1905, in which he wrote:

At the close of the last quarter a commission arrived at Haifa from Constantinople composed of the following persons: The president of The Commercial Court at Constantinople; the Farik (General of division) Chucri Pasha; one Liwa and two Colonels. The last four persons are staff officers. An hour after their arrival here, they left for Acre. Until now their commission is still kept secret. They however are making enquiries about Abbas Effendi of Acre, the Chief Babist, who is accused of trying to make the Moslems of Acre babists. It is supposed that their enquiries about Abbas Effendi will result in extorting from him a large sum of money. The Caimacam [Qá'im-Maqám] of Haifa tells me that they have to enquire also about the conduct of the Farik of Acre as many complaints have been made against him. This Commission has also called many notables and enquired about general things. It is rumoured that the Sultan has sent this Commission in order to enquire about the sincerity of his people in this part of his Empire.[13]

In connection with the visit of the Commission of Inquiry, it appears that the Persian Embassy in Istanbul sent a secretary to Haifa. Drummond Hay reports on 20 September 1905:

I have the honour to report that a secretary of the Persian Embassy at Constantinople lately visited Acre in connection with the interests of the Persian Babists residing at that place. When the Imperial Ottoman Commission visited Acre last spring as reported to Your Excellency in my despatch No. 50 of August 5th which resulted in the dismissal of the Mutessarif of Acre and other officials they appear to have made enquiries about the Babists and a report became current after their departure that Abbas Effendi and all persons belonging to his sect would be exiled to Tripoli in Barbary.

I am now informed by the Acting British Vice Consul at Haifa that the Government has come to an understanding with Abbas Effendi and that neither he nor his followers will be molested for the present.

* Military rank approximating to Brigadier.

The chief object of the Persian secretary's visit was I believe to obtain a reliable list of true Persian subjects domiciled at Acre by eliminating from the registers those whose families were originally exiled from their country and therefore ceased to be Persian subjects, amongst whom are Abbas Effendi and other descendants or surviving members of his father's suite.[14]

There is a problem concerning the dates of this Commission, since Bahá'í accounts agree that there were two Commissions of Inquiry,* one arriving in about 1904 and another in 1907. The details given in these accounts from the British Consular authorities agree well with the details for the second of these two Commissions: the name of the Chairman, the dismissal of the Governor of 'Akká and other officials, the dispatch of a representative of the Persian Embassy in Istanbul. It is quite clear from these British Consular accounts, however, that this Commission arrived in 1905 and not 1907. It may be, of course, that the Commission came twice. The editor has not seen sufficient of the Bahá'í accounts of this episode to form a definite opinion. In the addendum to this chapter the details of some of the documents found in the Ottoman State Archives, relating to this Commission, may be found. It will be seen that these documents confirm the date 1905 for the arrival of this Commission.

The end of 'Abdu'l-Bahá's confinement came in 1908 when the Young Turks rebelled against Sulṭán 'Abdu'l-Ḥamíd's rule and compelled him to accept a renewal of Midḥat Pásh͟á's constitution, suspended many years previously. Along with this, all religious and political prisoners were set free and after a lifetime of being either actually or technically a prisoner or an exile, 'Abdu'l-Bahá was, at last, free. He now set about using his freedom to spread the message of his father to the West.

Addendum

The following documents exist in the Ottoman State Archives. The dates given are according to the Rúmí or Turkish Calendar. Equivalent Gregorian dates are given in parentheses:

1. Telegram, Muḥammad 'Árif Bey to the Sublime Porte, 30 June 1321 Rúmí (13 July 1905). States that it was an Albanian by the name of Ádam Za'ím who sent the reports to the Sublime Porte that initiated the Commission of Inquiry. Having reached 'Akká, they questioned Ádam Za'ím and asked him if he had anything more to say which he did not mention in his report. He then added some important points which it was not wise to mention in this telegram but 'Árif Bey would explain them personally to His Majesty on his return.

* See for example Balyuzi *'Abdu'l-Bahá* pp. 111–23, and Shoghi Effendi *God Passes By* pp. 269–71.

2. Telegram, 'Árif Bey to the Sublime Porte, 2 July 1321 Rúmí (15 July 1905). The task of the Commission has been completely accomplished.
3. Telegram: 'Árif Bey to the Sublime Porte, 6 July 1321 Rúmí (19 July 1905). It has been found necessary to investigate certain matters in Haifa, therefore the Commission will go to Haifa and then proceed to Beirut.
4. Telegram, 'Árif Bey to the Sublime Porte, 7 July 1321 Rúmí (20 July 1905). A certain citizen of 'Akká, Ḥalíl 'Abbás by name, has been arrested because when his house was searched some Bábí writings and a picture of Shaykh 'Abbás [i.e. 'Abdu'l-Bahá] were found.

References

1. For details of these quotations, see pp. 211, 213, 216 and 228.
2. Adams *Persia by a Persian* p. 489
3. ibid.
4. Jessup *Fifty–Three Years in Syria* pp. 638 and 687, quoted, slightly altered, in Wilson *Bahaism and its Claims* p. 264
5. Phelps *Abbas Effendi* pp. 3 and 105
6. G.H. 'L'Influence de Babisme' pp. 17–20 (trans. from French)
7. Stevens 'Abbas Effendi' pp. 1067 and 1070
8. Quarterly report of Haifa V.-Consulate for quarter ending 31 Dec. 1900, enclosed in Drummond Hay to O'Connor No. 16, 15 Feb. 1901: FO 195 2097
9. Quarterly report of Haifa V.-Consulate for quarter ending 30 Sept. 1901, enclosed in Drummond Hay to O'Connor No. 84, 7 Nov. 1901: FO 195 2097
10. Quarterly report of Haifa V.-Consulate for quarter ending 31 Dec. 1901, enclosed in Drummond Hay to O'Connor No. 13, 28 Jan. 1902: FO 195 2117
11. Curtis *Today in Syria and Palestine* pp. 221–2
12. Quarterly report of Beirut Consulate-General for quarter ending 30 June 1905, enclosed in Drummond Hay to O'Connor No. 50, 5 Aug. 1905: FO 195 2190
13. Quarterly report of Haifa V.-Consulate for quarter ending 30 June 1905, enclosed with report detailed in 12 *supra*
14. Drummond Hay to O'Connor No. 59, 20 Sept. 1905: FO 195 2190

TWENTY-THREE

'Abdu'l-Bahá: The Western Journeys

Although occupying but a very short period of 'Abdu'l-Bahá's ministry, his journeys to the West may be regarded as its most important and portentous episode. Throughout Europe and North America, 'Abdu'l-Bahá was received with enthusiasm and admiration by every stratum of society. His progress through these countries was marked by a series of talks given to packed audiences, meetings with eminent persons and extensive newspaper coverage.

It would be impossible in a book of this nature and size to give an adequate survey of this journey, and all that will be presented here are a few examples of the newspaper and magazine coverage of his tour and what some of the eminent persons who met him said of him.

'Abdu'l-Bahá's freedom came with the general amnesty for political and religious prisoners that was the result of the Young Turks' revolution in July 1909. In August 1910, 'Abdu'l-Bahá moved to Egypt. It was generally expected that he would accept an invitation to address the Universal Races Congress in London in July 1911, but in the end it was not until August 1911 that he set sail from Egypt.* After resting for a few days at Thonon-

* 'Abdu'l-Bahá's decision not to attend the Universal Races Congress, which would undoubtedly have been a very prestigious platform from which to deliver Bahá'u'lláh's message to the world, may have been due to the presence there of Mírzá Yaḥyáy-i-Dawlatábádí, a leading Azalí. In his letter to the Central Organization for a Durable Peace at the Hague (dated 17 Dec. 1919), 'Abdu'l-Bahá refers to this: 'It may be that some foolish person among the Persians will affix his name to the contents of the Tablets of His Holiness Bahá'u'lláh or to the explanations given in the letters [Tablets] of 'Abdu'l-Bahá and send it to that esteemed Assembly. Ye must be aware of this fact, for any Persian who seeks fame or has some other intention will take the entire contents of the Tablets of His Holiness Bahá'u'lláh and publish them in his own name or in that of his community, just as happened at the Universal Races Congress in London before the war. A Persian took the substance of the Epistles of His Holiness Bahá'u'lláh, entered that Congress, gave them forth in his own name and published them, whereas the wording was exactly that of His Holiness Bahá'u'lláh. Some such souls have gone to Europe and have caused confusion in the minds of the people of Europe and have disturbed the thoughts of some Orientalists. Ye must bear this fact in mind, for not a word of these teachings was heard in Persia before the appearance of Bahá'u'lláh. Investigate this matter so that it may become to you evident and manifest. Some souls are like parrots. They learn any note which they may hear, and sing it, but they themselves are unaware of what they utter. There is a sect in Persia at present made up of a few souls who

les-Bains on the shore of Lake Leman, 'Abdu'l-Bahá proceeded to London, which he reached on 4 September 1911. A few days later, on Sunday 10 September, at the invitation of Rev. R. J. Campbell (q.v.), 'Abdu'l-Bahá gave at the City Temple, Holborn, the first public address that he had ever given to an audience. His address was reported in full by the *Christian Commonwealth*:

Abdul Baha attended the evening service at the City Temple on Sunday. No announcement of the visit was made, and, although the sight of the Persians and other members of the suite in the congregation excited curiosity, very few people were aware that the Bahai leader was expected. The service proceeded as usual until the hymn immediately preceding the sermon. Whilst this was being sung a venerable figure, clad in Persian robes, was seen slowly ascending the stairs of the pulpit. When the hymn was finished Mr Campbell placed the distinguished visitor in his own chair, and then, addressing the crowded congregation, said:

'I propose to shorten my sermon this evening because we have a visitor in the pulpit whose presence is somewhat significant of the spiritual drawing-together of East and West, as well as of the material drawing-together which has long been going on, and I think you would like to hear his voice, if only for a few moments.'

Mr Campbell spoke on 'The Use of the Will in Prayer' (Luke xviii. 1) . . . He then said: This evening we have in the pulpit of the City Temple the leader of one of the most remarkable religious movements of this or any age, a movement which includes, I understand, at least three million souls. The Bahai movement, as it is called, in Hither Asia rose on that soil just as spontaneously as Christianity rose in the middle territories adjoining, and that faith – which, by the way, is very closely akin to, I think I might say identical with, the spiritual purpose of Christianity – that movement stands for the spiritual unity of mankind; it stands for universal peace among the nations. These are good things, and the man who teaches them and commends them to three millions of followers must be a good man as well as a great. Abdul Baha is on a visit to this country – a private visit – but he wished to see the City Temple; and I think I am right in saying for the first time in his life he has consented to lift up his voice in public. He does not address public meetings, he does not preach sermons; he is just a religious teacher. He spent forty years in prison for his faith, and from his prison directed the efforts of his followers. There is not much in the way of organisation, but simple trust in the Spirit of God. We, as followers of the Lord Jesus Christ, who is to us and always will be the Light of the World, view with sympathy and respect every movement of the Spirit of God in the experience of mankind, and therefore we give greeting to Abdul Baha – I do not know whether I could say in the name of the whole Christian community – that may be too much – but I think in the name of all who share the spirit of our Master, and are trying to live their lives in that spirit. Abdul Baha, I think, intends to say a word or two in response to this greeting that I address to him in your name.

Abdul Baha then advanced to the front of

---

are called Bábís, who claim to be followers of His Holiness the Báb, whereas they are utterly unaware of His Holiness. They have some secret teachings which are entirely opposed to the teachings of Bahá'u'lláh and in Persia people know this. But when these souls come to Europe, they conceal their own teachings and utter those of His Holiness Bahá'u'lláh, for they know that the teachings of His Holiness Bahá'u'lláh are powerful and they therefore declare publicly those teachings of Bahá'u'lláh in their own name.' (*Bahá'í World* Vol. 15, pp. 34–5)

the pulpit, and addressed the congregation. He spoke for eight minutes in Persian, with considerable animation, his voice rising and falling as in a rhythmic chant. Towards the close he placed the palms of his hands together as in prayer. The translation was afterwards read by Mr W. Tudor Pole . . .[1]

The following week at the invitation of Archdeacon Wilberforce, 'Abdu'l-Bahá addressed the Sunday congregation at St John's, Westminster. Once more, full details were given in the *Christian Commonwealth*:*

Eighteen months ago Archdeacon Wilberforce, who had been watching the Bahai movement for some time with interest, sent a message to Abdul Baha. 'We are all one,' he said, 'there, behind the veil.' And Abdul Baha replied from his home in Akka, 'Tell him the veil is very thin, and it will vanish quite.'

All who were present in St John's, Westminster, last Sunday evening, could not fail to realise that the veil was vanishing. Archdeacon Wilberforce's beautiful intercessory service was a means to that end. He asked that each one in the vast congregation should at that time put away all selfish thought and use all energy in prayer for those in trouble . . .

Then Dr Wilberforce told of the teacher – 'Master' he called him – who had come to London to emphasise unity, and who was present that evening at St John's to proclaim the meaning of it. 'Whatever our views,' the Archdeacon said, 'we shall, I am sure, unite in welcoming a man who has been for forty years a prisoner for the cause of brotherhood and love.'

Abdul Baha is not an orator or even a preacher, but, in view of all he stands for, we are keenly interested in everything he has to say.

Full of expectation, the congregation waited when the Archdeacon for a brief moment left the church. Divested of his white surplice, he returned with Abdul Baha. All eyes were fixed on the leader of the Bahai movement. In his customary Eastern robe and head-dress, walking hand in hand with a leader of the West, it did indeed seem that the veil was vanishing.

Down the aisle they passed to the bishop's chair, which had been placed in front of the altar for Abdul Baha. Standing at the lectern, Archdeacon Wilberforce introduced the 'wonderful' visitor. He told of his life in prison, of his sufferings and bravery, of his self-sacrifice, of his clear and shining faith. He voiced his own belief that religion is one, as God is love.

Then Abdul Baha rose. Speaking very clearly, with wonderful intonations in his voice and using his hands freely, it seemed to those who listened almost as if they grasped his meaning, though he spoke in Persian. When he had finished, Archdeacon Wilberforce read the translation of his address.[2]

This first visit of 'Abdu'l-Bahá to London lasted one month, and after this he proceeded to Paris where he stayed nine weeks before returning to Egypt for the winter.

The following year, on 25 March 1912, 'Abdu'l-Bahá sailed for America to commence an exhausting tour that was to last thirteen months and cover

* This periodical described itself as 'The Organ of the Progressive Movement in Religion and Social Ethics'. Its editor Albert Dawson 'covered' 'Abdu'l-Bahá's period in London personally. On its editorial board were several persons who were to no small extent responsible for the success of 'Abdu'l-Bahá's British tours; such persons as Rev. R. J. Campbell, Prof. T. K. Cheyne and Sir Richard Stapley.

seven countries in North America and Europe, with speaking engagements sometimes two or even three times per day and a continuous stream of personal interviews with Bahá'ís and non-Bahá'ís, high and low, friends and enemies.

'Abdu'l-Bahá's itinerary* was as follows (where a brief journey was made to one town while staying in another, this is indicated by parentheses):

Departed Alexandria 25 March 1912
New York, 11–20 April 1912
Washington, 20–28 April
Chicago, 29 April – 6 May
Cleveland, Ohio, 6–7 May
Pittsburgh, 7–8 May
Washington, 8–11 May
New York, 11–14 May
(Montclair, N.J., 12 May)
Conference on Peace and Arbitration, Lake Mohawk, 14–16 May
New York, 16–22 May
Boston, 22–26 May
(Worcester, Mass., 23 May)
New York, 26–31 May
Fanwood, N.J., 31 May – 1 June
New York, 1–3 June
Milford, Pa., 3 June
New York, 4–8 June
Philadelphia, 8–10 June
New York, 10–20 June
Montclair, N.J., 20–25 June
New York, 25–29 June
West Englewood, N.J., 29–30 June
Morristown, N.J., 30 June
New York, 30 June – 23 July
(West Englewood, 14 July)
Boston, 23–24 July
Dublin, N.H., 24 July – 16 August
Greenacre, near Eliot, Maine, 16–23 August
Malden, near Boston, 23–29 August
Montreal, Canada, 30 August – 9 September
Buffalo, 9–12 September
Chicago, 12–15 September
Kenosha, 15–16 September
Chicago, 16 September
Minneapolis, 16–21 September
Omaha, 21 September
Lincoln, Neb., 23 September
Denver, 24–27 September
Glenwood Springs, Colo., 28 September
Salt Lake City, Utah, 29–30 September
San Francisco, 1–13 October
Pleasanton, Cal., 13–16 October
San Francisco, 16–18 October
Los Angeles, 18–21 October
San Francisco, 21–25 October
Denver, 28–29 October
Chicago, 31 October – 3 November
Cincinnati, Ohio, 5–6 November
Washington, 6–11 November
Baltimore, 11 November
Philadelphia, 11 November
New York, 12 November – 5 December
Liverpool, England, 13–16 December
London, 16 December, 1912 – 6 January, 1913
(Oxford, 31 December, 1912)
Edinburgh, 6–11 January
London, 11–15 January
Bristol, 15–16 January
London, 16–21 January
(Woking, 18 January)
Paris, 22 January – 30 March
Stuttgart, 1–9 April
(Bad Mergentheim, 7–8 April)
Vienna, 8 April
Budapest, 9–19 April
Vienna, 19–24 April
Stuttgart, 25 April – 1 May
Paris, 2 May – 12 June
Marseilles, 12–13 June
Port Said, 17 June, 1913

Of all the places visited by 'Abdu'l-Bahá on this journey, Montreal was exceptional in the amount of newspaper coverage he was accorded. Hardly

* Taken principally from Balyuzi's *'Abdu'l-Bahá* pp. 171–396.

a day passed without a lengthy article in either the *Montreal Daily Star* or the *Gazette*.

On 2 September 1912, the *Montreal Daily Star* reported: '*Persian Preacher in Flowing Robes calls for Unity.* Clad in flowing robes, and with a turbaned head, the great Persian apostle of peace, Abdul Baha, made a majestic appearance in the Church of the Messiah Sunday morning when he preached his message urging the oneness of religion and the doing away with strife and hatred over imaginary things . . .'[3]

On the same day, the *Gazette* stated, under the headline '*Racialism Wrong, says Eastern Sage*':

Both in matter and in style the message which was delivered in the Church of the Messiah yesterday morning by Abdul Baha, the Oriental prophet, was unique, and it had a picturesque setting all its own. A venerable looking figure, with a long white beard, just streaked with a dark shade . . . The chief points brought out by the speaker were the equality of the human race and the unnaturalness of the division of nations and countries, the horror of religious or any warfare whatever, and the equality of the sexes.

In introducing Abdul Baha, Rev. F. R. Griffin said he came not to unfold a fresh mystery or to teach a new theology, and much less to establish a new church. 'The strangest part of all about him is that nothing is strange. He seeks to be the embodiment of that which is most natural. Is this not turning back to religion itself? Venerable in years, he is young as a child in the purity of his outlook on life; disciplined by long years in prison, his spirit has never yet been crucified by pain.'[4]

The editor of the *Montreal Daily Star*, John Lewis, visited 'Abdu'l-Bahá on the evening of his arrival in Montreal. On 6 September the following editorial concerning 'Abdu'l-Bahá appeared in that newspaper: 'It was out of the East that the Wise Men came who first did homage at the cradle of the Prince of Peace; still it seems strange that two thousand years later the East must send another wise man to remind us of the Western World who are nominally pledged to His service, what His gospel is.'[5]

In an editorial published after 'Abdu'l-Bahá's departure from Montreal, the same newspaper stated: 'In a word, Abdul Baha is the great protagonist of peace in the world today. To bring about its accomplishment is the practical corollary of the two tenets which are the foundation of his creed – the fatherhood of God and the brotherhood of man.'[6]

In America, the most notable newspaper report was that of the *Palo Altan*:

A crowded Assembly Hall, holding nearly two thousand people, awaited with eager expectancy the appearance last Tuesday morning of Abdul Baha, Abbas Effendi, the world leader of the Bahai movement. The venerable prophet, with his long gray beard and Persian cloak and turban, gave a true impression of the Far Eastern prophet of old . . .

Abdul Baha is revolutionizing the religion

of Asia, bringing Mohammedans, Jews and Christians together . . .

A pilgrimage through England and America undertaken by Abdul Baha has created great interest in the Bahai movement. The knowledge of this movement has been brought home to thousands of people who are willing and eager to spread its beneficent teachings. On this far western shore of America the seeds of peace and welfare find fertile ground and abundant fruitage.[7]

The same issue of the *Palo Altan* gave, moreover, an account of the words of Dr David Starr Jordan (q.v.), President of Stanford University, in introducing 'Abdu'l-Bahá at a talk that the latter gave at Stanford University.

It is our portion to have with us, through the courtesy of our Persian friends, one of the great religious teachers of the world, one of the natural successors of the old Hebrew prophets.

He is said sometimes to be the founder of a new religion. He has upward of three millions of people following along the lines in which he leads. It is not exactly a new religion, however. The religion of brotherhood, of goodwill, of friendship between men and nations – that is as old as good thinking and good living may be. It may be said in some sense to be the oldest of religions.[8]

There were, of course, a few persons here and there who were displeased at the attention being paid to 'Abdu'l-Bahá and at the fact that Christian churches were being made a platform for the propagation of a non-Christian movement. During 'Abdu'l-Bahá's first tour in 1911, a Christian missionary, Rev. P. Z. Easton, had written articles in the *English Churchman* and *Evangelical Christendom* attacking 'Abdu'l-Bahá.[9] Similarly, after 'Abdu'l-Bahá's departure from Edinburgh there was some hostile correspondence in the *Edinburgh Evening News*, signed 'Old Paths', attacking both 'Abdu'l-Bahá and those churchmen who gave him a platform.[10]

However, even some of those who set out to attack 'Abdu'l-Bahá were won over by his personality. Rev. James T. Bixby (q.v.) wrote a hostile and critical article entitled 'What is Behaism?' for the *North American Review* while 'Abdu'l-Bahá was touring North America in 1912. But despite the tone of the article, when Bixby comes to write of 'Abdu'l-Bahá himself,* he is forced to admit:

In the brief personal acquaintance with the head of the new faith, with which I have been honored, Abbas has impressed me as a man of great mental ability, tact, and persuasive power; friendly in disposition, affable in his manners, and amiable and progressive in his spirit. He is wisely putting the emphasis in the Behai community more and more on those great principles of international fellowship and friendly relations between diverse faiths and races that best realize the essence of the Christian spirit. Moreover, he has practically exemplified these principles in his own pacific conduct and charitable activities. The description that visitors to Akka have given of his daily personal benefactions is, indeed, beautiful and impressive.[11]

* Howard Colby Ives appears to have been present at the interview. His account appears in *Portals to Freedom* pp. 47–9. See also *Star of the West* Vol. 3, No. 8 1912, pp. 5–8 (Vol. 2 of reprint).

'Abdu'l-Bahá's return to England at the end of 1912 was noted by the *Christian Commonwealth*:

> Abdul Baha is again in England on his way back from America to the Orient. London, the city where representatives of all races may be encountered, and the centre of a Government whose influence is felt at the far ends of the earth, has rarely sheltered a more significant and impressive personality than the leader of the Bahai movement . . . Even the Western stranger coming into the Master's presence for the first time acknowledges an emotion akin to awe, and after a few minutes' speech with him feels the stirring of a deeper spirit of devotion than the ordinary amenities of social intercourse are calculated to arouse. For Abdul Baha . . . is much more than a picturesque Eastern figure in the unromantic setting of Western civilisation. He is a prophet. A venerable figure of rather less than medium stature, clothed in long, flowing Persian garments, his white beard lying upon his breast, silver-grey plaited hair falling over his shoulders, dark, brooding, pitiful eyes that yet light up when a smile of singular gentleness and sweetness passes across his face, and a low, mellow voice whose tones are charged with a strange solemnity – that is the Master as the stranger sees him.[12]

When 'Abdu'l-Bahá was in Scotland, an interviewer of the *Scots Pictorial* called on him:

> To be ushered into the presence of Abdul Baha, Abbas Effendi, 'the Servant of God,' is to have the curtains of time lifted back and to hold converse with a prophet of Israel. The artistic dignity of his quietly coloured Eastern gown, the white folds of his turban, and the patriarchal beard which hangs upon his bosom all contribute towards giving the immediate impression of an Eastern scholar and divine. But it is the finely moulded contour of his face, the gentle movements of his hands, and the deep expression in his eyes which make it manifest that here, indeed, is an embodiment of the prophets of old. In comparing Abdul Baha to the Biblical prophets, there is a distinction to be made. The early prophets descended upon mankind as the scourgers of iniquity and as the swords of the Lord. This messenger comes as the great reconciler of all faiths, as the forerunner of universal peace. In his eyes there is suffering and love. He is a man who has looked aghast and with pity upon the turmoil of life, and has heartfelt thoughts to utter.[13]

From London, 'Abdu'l-Bahá proceeded to Paris and thence to Stuttgart, Vienna and Budapest. At Budapest 'Abdu'l-Bahá met Ignaz Goldziher* (q.v.) and Arminius Vámbéry (q.v.), two of the greatest Orientalists of that period. After 'Abdu'l-Bahá returned to Egypt, Vámbéry forwarded the following letter as testimony of his high regard for 'Abdu'l-Bahá:

> I forward this humble petition to the sanctified and holy presence of Abdul Baha Abbas, who is the centre of knowledge, famous throughout the world, and loved by all mankind. O thou noble friend who art conferring guidance upon humanity, may my life be a ransom to thee!
>
> The loving epistle which you have condescended to write to this servant, and the rug which you have forwarded, came safely

* See Goldziher *Tagebuch*, pp. 275–9.

to hand. The time of the meeting with your Excellency, and the memory of the benediction of your presence, recurred to the memory of this servant, and I am longing for the time when I shall meet you again. Although I have travelled through many countries and cities of Islam, yet have I never met so lofty a character and so exalted a personage as your Excellency, and can bear witness that it is not possible to find such another. On this account I am hoping that the ideals and accomplishments of your Excellency may be crowned with success and yield results under all conditions; because behind these ideas and deeds I easily discern the eternal welfare and prosperity of the world of humanity.

This servant, in order to gain first-hand information and experience, entered into the ranks of various religions – that is, outwardly, I became a Jew, Christian, Mohammedan and Zoroastrian. I discovered that the devotees of these various religions do nothing else but hate and anathematise each other, that all their religions have become the instruments of tyranny and oppression in the hands of rulers and governors, and that they are the causes of the destruction of the world of humanity.

Considering those evil results, every person is forced by necessity to enlist himself on the side of your Excellency, and accept with joy the prospect of a basis of the religion of God, which is being founded through your efforts.

I have seen the father of your Excellency from afar. I have realised the self-sacrifice and noble courage of his son, and I am lost in admiration.

For the principles and aims of your Excellency, I express the utmost respect and devotion, and if God, the Most High, confers long life, I will be able to serve you under all conditions. I pray and supplicate this from the depths of my heart.[14]

References

1. *Christian Commonwealth* Vol. 31, 13 Sept. 1911, p. 850
2. *Christian Commonwealth* Vol. 31, 20 Sept. 1911, front page
3. *Montreal Daily Star* 2 Sept. 1912, p. 2
4. *Gazette* 2 Sept. 1912, p. 6
5. *Montreal Daily Star* 6 Sept. 1912, p. 12
6. *Montreal Daily Star* 11 Sept. 1912, p. 12
7. *Palo Altan* Vol. 10, No. 43, 1 Nov. 1912, p. 1
8. ibid. p. 2
9. See Balyuzi *'Abdu'l-Bahá* pp. 149–50
10. ibid. pp. 366–7. See also *'Abdu'l-Bahá in Edinburgh* pp. 16–17
11. *North American Review* Vol. 195, 1912, p. 834
12. *Christian Commonwealth* Vol. 33, 1 Jan. 1913, p. 261
13. *Scots Pictorial* 18 Jan. 1913, p. 335. Article by 'Ion'.
14. First published in *Egyptian Gazette* 24 Sept. 1913. Quoted in Holbach 'The Bahai Movement' pp. 465–6. Original letter in Arabic held at Bahá'í World Centre, Haifa.

TWENTY-FOUR

'Abdu'l-Bahá: The War Years

For the first few months of the World War, 'Abdu'l-Bahá and the Bahá'í community in Palestine retired to the Druze village of Abú-Sinán. Later, 'Abdu'l-Bahá returned to Haifa and busied himself organizing the provision of food and supplies for the famine-stricken local population.

On 31 October 1917, Allenby (q.v.) and the Egyptian Expeditionary Force commenced an offensive from their lines between Gaza and Beer-sheba that led eventually to the surrender of Jerusalem on 9 December, and Allenby's formal entry into Jerusalem on 11 December 1917. Having secured his position during the rest of December, Allenby insisted on a period of recuperation for his troops. In spring of 1918, the last great German offensive had begun in the French theatre of operations, and therefore Allenby's advance had to be held up while troops were transferred to Europe. During the spring and summer, Allenby's activities were confined to a number of raids and tactical manoeuvres as well as training the fresh forces arriving from India. But towards the end of summer 1918, Allenby was instructed to renew his advance despite the fact that the experienced troops that had been sent to France had not been returned.

Danger to 'Abdu'l-Bahá

Major Tudor-Pole, who was an admirer of 'Abdu'l-Bahá, was serving in the Egyptian Expeditionary Force. During the operations around Jerusalem he was wounded by a sniper, and was transferred to Military Intelligence, first at Cairo and later at Ludd, Jaffa and Jerusalem. At Military Intelligence, Tudor-Pole was concerned with processing and correlating information arriving from many different sources concerning what was happening behind the enemy lines. This information came from reconnaissance flights, captured enemy soldiers and papers, and intercepted wireless broadcasts. To Tudor-Pole's concern, information began to reach him about serious danger threatening 'Abdu'l-Bahá's life. This information must have reached Tudor-Pole in December 1917, for on 24 December 1917 he wrote to Sir

Mark Sykes (q.v.), Member of Parliament and negotiator of the famous Sykes-Picot Agreement:

On returning to Cairo from the hills round Jerusalem, having received the close attentions of a Sniper in a fig tree; I ran across my friend Mohi-el-Dine Sabri. He was anxious to send you his greeting and friendly remembrances and I promised to oblige. The Turkish Line will probably run through Haifa shortly . . . the Bahai leader and his family are in imminent danger and at the moment, of course, we are powerless. His position and prestige is not understood among the Authorities here. It is not even realized that he controls a remarkable religious movement, wholly devoid of political and military associations; which can number many millions of adherents throughout the Near and Middle East. Jews, Moslems of various Sects, Christians, Parsis, Hindoos, Kurds unite under the Bahai banner of Spiritual Fellowship. May not these people contribute much, later, to the harmonising of Sectarian and Oriental Religious feuds? Is it too much to ask the Authorities at home to request the Authorities here to afford Abdul Baha every protection and consideration? Anxious enquiries reach me from America, England, France, Russia, Persia, India. A word from Whitehall works wonders. I am your obedient servant, W. Tudor-Pole 2/Lt. 16th Royal Devons. (In hospital).

Mrs J. Stannard c/o Hys. King & Co. London SW can supply full historic and other details of the Movement from first hand experience.[1]

Tudor-Pole's letter to Sir Mark Sykes did not reach the Foreign Office until 6 February 1918. Meanwhile he had found other ways of alerting the Bahá'ís in England to 'Abdu'l-Bahá's danger. Lady Blomfield, one of those contacted, went at once to Lord Lamington (q.v.), who had met 'Abdu'l-Bahá in London in 1912. Lamington, a former Governor of Bombay and a frequent speaker at the House of Lords on questions affecting the East, had considerable influence in government circles. He wrote immediately to Balfour, the Secretary of State for Foreign Affairs. His letter dated 24 January reads thus:

'I have been asked to intervene in the interest of Abdul Behar.

'I enclose a Memo. about him and I should be grateful could the action indicated be taken.'

The memorandum attached to Lamington's letter:

Abdul Behar sometimes known as Abbas Effendi, leader of the Bahai movement, having for its object the true peace of the world is believed to be at his home in Haifa, or else on M. Carmel. In the past he has undergone much persecution at the hands of fanatics and anxiety is felt by his many friends in Gt. Britain and America lest he, his wife and family should not receive adequate protection during the British advance owing to his identity not being known to our authorities. His friends therefore would be grateful if instructions would be cabled to secure on his behalf the good offices of those in command.[2]

Mrs Whyte, at whose invitation 'Abdu'l-Bahá had travelled to Edinburgh in 1913, received an account of 'Abdu'l-Bahá's danger from a Mr Russell.* She wrote at once to her son Frederick Whyte (q.v.), a Member of Parliament, who in turn wrote to Sir Mark Sykes on 25 January 1918.

> I have just received a letter from my Mother saying that she understands that Abdul Baha is living in some risk of his life at Haifa. My Mother's correspondent, as you will see from the enclosed letter, seems to think that we could do something to save him. I presume I need not waste your time in giving an account of Abdul Baha himself, whose personality and work must be well known to you. But as you are aware, he has a good many followers, if one may so call them, in this country; and in general there is a number of people who, like myself, are much interested in his work and will be prepared to do something to make sure that the Military Authorities in Palestine are aware of his presence. I know that at one time Lord Curzon was very deeply impressed with the Bahai Movement in Persia itself and he may be willing to interest himself in the matter now.
>
> In any case I shall be glad to hear from you whether you think there is anything in the suggestion contained in Mr Russell's letter, which please return to me.[3]

The letters of Lamington and Frederick Whyte arrived at the Foreign Office on the same day, 26 January 1918. R. Graham (q.v.) wrote in a note appended to Whyte's letter: 'The Bahais are splendid people, but I do not see how we can help Abdul Baha unless and until we get to Haifa.'[4]

Graham went on in the same note to suggest that all that could be done then was to 'call the attention of the British Authorities in Egypt to Abdul Baha's presence at Haiffa.'[5]

Accordingly, a telegram was dispatched to Sir Reginald Wingate (q.v.), the British High Commissioner in Egypt, who was at that time responsible for the political affairs of the Egyptian Expeditionary Forces. The telegram dated 30 January 1918 read:

'My attention has been called to the presence at Haiffa of Abdul Baha, head of the Bahais.

'Please warn the General Officer Commanding that he and his family should be treated with special consideration in the event of our occupying Haiffa.'[6]

Lamington and Whyte were informed in almost identical letters dated 31 January 1918: 'I am directed by Mr. Secretary Balfour to acknowledge the receipt of your letter . . . and to state that he has requested His Majesty's High Commissioner for Egypt to call the attention of the British Military Authorities to the presence of Abdul Baha at Haiffa, and to request them to treat him and his family with all possible consideration in the event of a further advance by the British forces in Palestine.'[7]

On 5 February, a telegram was dispatched on the authority of Sir Mark Sykes to General Clayton (q.v.), the Chief Political Officer attached to the

* The editor is uncertain as to this man's identity.

Egyptian Expeditionary Force, the officer responsible for adminstering the occupied enemy territory: 'Enquiries are being made here as to the present whereabouts of Abdul Baha the leader of the Bahai movement. His usual dwelling is at Acre. Can you give any information, his influence in America is appreciable.'[8]

Clayton's reply, dated 12 February, was: 'Abdul Baha Abbas (Abdul Effendi) leader of Bahais is reported to be living at Haifa with his family and a small colony of Persian followers.'[9]

According to Tudor-Pole's account cited in Balyuzi's *'Abdu'l-Bahá*, 'Means were found for making it known within the enemy lines that stern retribution would follow any attempt to cause death or injury to' 'Abdu'l-Bahá or his household.'[10]

The Capture of Haifa and 'Akká

On 18 September 1918, Allenby began the last great offensive that was to result in the complete rout of the Turkish Army, the capture of Haifa and 'Akká, and eventually Amman, Damascus, Beirut and Aleppo, and the capitulation of Turkey on 31 October 1918. Due to skilful manoeuvring during the summer months, Allenby had deceived the Turks into thinking that the main advance was to be along the Jordan valley. Consequently, when, after some preliminary skirmishing, the main advance along the coastal plain began on 19 September, the Turkish army was outnumbered there four to one and fell back at all points. By midday on 19 September, the Turkish Eighth Army had broken into hopeless confusion and the Battle of Megiddo (or Armageddon as it is more popularly known) was all but won. By the end of 20 September, the coastal plain had been cleared of Turkish forces and the Turkish Seventh Army, together with the remnants of the Eighth, were being pushed back to a line just south of Haifa – Nazareth.[11]

On 21 September, Nazareth was occupied, and Nablus was captured as the right flank advanced. The following day, 22 September, reports were received that the enemy had already evacuated Haifa, but when a small detachment was dispatched to occupy the town it came under heavy fire on the Nazareth-Haifa road. The next day, 23 September 1918, the whole of the Fifth Cavalry Division under Maj.-Gen. MacAndrew was ordered to advance on Haifa and 'Akká from Nazareth at 5.00 am.[12]

The advance broke up into two columns, the right column marching on 'Akká and the left column on Haifa. The advanced guard of the left column was the fifteenth Cavalry Brigade composed of the Mysore and Jodhpur Lancers. As they advanced along the Nazareth-Haifa road they came under heavy fire from Turkish guns positioned on Mount Carmel to the south. The Carmel range and the marshy, impassable banks of the Kishon

(Nahru'l-Muqaṭṭa') one mile to its north created a defile down which it was necessary to pass.[13]

A squadron of the Mysore Lancers and one from the Sherwood Rangers (part of the Fourteenth Cavalry Brigade of the Main Body of the Fifth Cavalry Division) made a bold attack up the steep hillside to capture the Turkish artillery positions. The rest of the force drove on along the main road and entered Haifa.[14]

According to the War Diary of the Mysore Lancers: 'A few Turks are killed in the streets and the rest lay down their arms.'[15]

According to the War Diary of the Fifth Cavalry Division: 'The town was entered by the G.O.C. [General Officer Commanding] and the remainder of the Division at 1500. Steps were immediately taken to stop all looting by Bedouins.'[16]

The right column, which consisted of the Thirteenth Cavalry Brigade, advancing on 'Akká, had an easier task. According to the Brigade's War Diary:

'1300 ACRE Captured with 2 Guns and 2 M.G.'s [machine-guns] and 150 prisoners . . . In the afternoon G.O.C. accompanied by Brigade Major and Lieut. BRAYNE (appointed Officiating Governor) entered the City with a small escort. The Population very friendly. Guards were placed on all important Depôts etc.'[17]

During the whole operation some 18 guns, 11 machine-guns, 2 German officers, 35 Turkish officers and 1,314 other prisoners were taken.[18]

The information concerning 'Abdu'l-Bahá's safety and health was speedily transmitted through the British lines to General Clayton, the Chief Political Officer, who telegrammed London on 25 September 1918: 'Reference to your despatch No. 41 of February 1st to High Commissioner on subject of Abdul Behar the leader of Bahai movement. He is now at Haifa, he is in good health and being well cared for.'[19]

Whyte was informed of this news by Sir Mark Sykes in person,[20] while Lamington received the following letter dated 30 September 1918:

'You will remember that you wrote to me in January last, regarding the safety of Abdul Behar and the Bahais at Haifa.

'I have now received a telegram from the Chief Political Officer in Palestine, reporting that on the occupation of Haifa, Abdul Behar was found to be still in the town in good health, and that he is being well cared for.'[21]

Gaselee (q.v.) at the Foreign Office wrote to Prof. Browne on 7 October informing him of the news concerning 'Abdu'l-Bahá: 'I think you will be interested (although you may already have heard the news through other channels) to hear that our army, on entering Haifa, found Abdul Baha

Abbas living there with his family and a small colony of Persian followers. He is in good health and is being well cared for by our people.

'In view of the interest taken in him in the United States, and the number of his followers there, I propose to tell Geoffrey Butler [q.v.] in New York this piece of news for publication there.'[22]

To which Browne replied in a letter dated 9 October 1918: 'Many thanks for your kindness in informing me of the safety of 'Abdu'l-Bahá and his followers, of which I was very pleased to learn, as I am sure will be a large number of his friends both in the East and in the West.'[23]

Gaselee telegrammed to Mr Bayley (q.v.), British Consul-General in New York, on 16 October 1918: 'In view of large and growing following in United States of Bahai Movement, you may think it worth while to publish fact that Abdul Baha was found by our troops at Haifa with a small Persian following, and that he is in good health and being well looked after by our people.'[24]

An enquiry concerning 'Abdu'l-Bahá was also received by the French authorities, originating, no doubt, from 'Abdu'l-Bahá's friends in Paris. On 14 December 1918, the French Foreign Minister telegrammed to the French High Commissioner in Beirut: 'Could you inform me what has become of the Persian Bahá'ís formerly gathered at St Jean d'Acre around 'Abdu'l-Bahá?'[25]

The reply from Picot in Cairo, dated 17 December, stated: "Abdu'l-Bahá is in good health, he continues to reside [at] 'Akká with his followers, who were not disturbed during the War.'[26]

When the British troops arrived in the Haifa-'Akká area, 'Abdu'l-Bahá was in Haifa. Immediately after the occupation of Haifa, 'Abdu'l-Bahá proceeded to 'Akká to visit the shrine of Bahá'u'lláh. Tudor-Pole, the first of 'Abdu'l-Bahá's Western followers to reach him after the War, found him at 'Akká on his arrival on 19 November 1920.* General Clayton in his weekly summary, dated 29 November 1918, states: 'Abbas Effendi Abdul Baha left Acre November 24th to take up his residence at Haifa.'[27]

References

1. File 23353/W/44: FO 371 3396
2. File 16545/W/44: FO 371 3396
3. File 16762/W/44: FO 371 3396
4. Note by Graham 28 Jan. 1918, File 16762/W/44: FO 371 3396
5. ibid.

* Balyuzi in *'Abdu'l-Bahá* (p. 431) states this date to have been 20 November 1920, but the editor is of the opinion that the date was 19 November in view of a letter from Shoghi Effendi to Dr Esslemont, dated 19 November, quoted in Momen *Dr J. E. Esslemont* p. 10.

6. For. Off. to Wingate No. 136, 30 Jan. 1918, File 16762/W/44: FO 371 3396
7. File 16762/W/44: FO 371 3396
8. Sykes to Clayton No. 8, 5 Feb. 1918, File 16762/W/44: FO 371 3396
9. Clayton to Sykes No. 18507, 12 Feb. 1918, File 27258/W/44: FO 371 3396
10. Balyuzi *'Abdu'l-Bahá* p. 428
11. Wavell *The Palestine Campaigns* pp. 192–213
12. ibid. pp. 214–15
13. ibid. p. 215, and War Diary of 5th Cav. Div., Haifa-Acre Operations, WO 95 4515
14. Wavell *The Palestine Campaigns* p. 215
15. War Diary of Mysore Lancers, Vol. 44, p. 2: WO 95 4519
16. War Diary of 5th Cav. Div., Haifa-Acre Operations: WO 95 4515
17. War Diary of 13th Cav. Brigade, Sheet 12: WO 95 4518
18. War Diary of 5th Cav. Div., Haifa-Acre Operations: WO 95 4515
19. Clayton to Sykes No. 68, 25 Sept. 1918, File 162590/W/44: FO 371 3396
20. According to a note in File 162590/W/44: FO 371 3396
21. File 162590/W/44: FO 371 3396
22. ibid.
23. ibid.
24. Gaselee to Bayley No. 2166, 16 Oct. 1918, File 162590/W/44: FO 371 3396
25. French For. Off. to High Commssr Beirut No. 500, 14 Dec. 1918: MAE File E368. 1, Asie-Perse, E22 (1918–1929) (trans. from French)
26. Picot to French For. Off. No. 728, 17 Dec. 1918: MAE File E368. 1, Asie-Perse, E. 22 (1918–1929) (trans. from French)
27. General Clayton, Weekly Report, No. 206, File 198031/W/44: FO 371 3412

TWENTY-FIVE

'Abdu'l-Bahá: After the War

As a result of the First World War, Palestine passed out of Ottoman hands and became the responsibility of Britain. It was always 'Abdu'l-Bahá's policy, whenever possible, to remain on friendly terms and be of service to whatever government was in power. This applied no less to the new British authorities then it had to the Turkish páshás who preceded them. The records concerning 'Abdu'l-Bahá's relations with the Turkish government are outside the scope of this book but several accounts may be found of his dealings with the British authorities. These dealings were always very warm and friendly, and many of the most important British administrators turned to 'Abdu'l-Bahá for wise and unbiased advice. Nor did 'Abdu'l-Bahá hesitate to turn to the authorities when he wished to appeal against an injustice. Since the British were the rulers of Palestine, 'Abdu'l-Bahá would appeal to them in cases involving injustice against Bahá'ís in Persia and elsewhere. In this 'Abdu'l-Bahá was following Bahá'u'lláh's injunction to appeal for redress and protection to the legally-constituted authorities, if wronged or persecuted.*

'Abdu'l-Bahá and the British Administrators

Among the British Administrators of Palestine who thought very highly of 'Abdu'l-Bahá was Sir Ronald Storrs (q.v.), who was the first Military Governor of Jerusalem, then the First Military Governor of Northern Palestine (Haifa), and later Civil Governor of Jerusalem. He refers to his meetings with 'Abdu'l-Bahá in his book *Orientations*[1] and also in a letter to Lady Blomfield:

> I met 'Abdu'l-Bahá first in 1909, on my way out from England and Constantinople through Syria to succeed, in Cairo, Harry Boyle as Oriental Secretary to the British Agency. (The episode is fully treated in my *Orientations*, published by Ivor Nicholson & Watson.) I drove along the beach in a cab from Haifa to 'Akká and spent a very pleasant hour with the patient but unsubdued prisoner and exile. When, a few years

* See 'Abdu'l-Bahá, quoting Bahá'u'lláh, in Browne *A Traveller's Narrative*, p. 68.

later, he was released and visited Egypt, I had the honour of looking after him and of presenting him to Lord Kitchener, who was deeply impressed by his personality, as who could fail to be?

The war separated us again until Lord Allenby, after his triumphant drive through Syria, sent me to establish the Government at Haifa and throughout that district. I called upon 'Abbás Effendi on the day I arrived and was delighted to find him quite unchanged. When he came to Jerusalem he visited my house and I never failed to visit him whenever I went to Haifa. His conversation was indeed a remarkable planing, like that of an ancient prophet, far above the perplexities and pettinesses of Palestine politics, and elevating all problems into first principles.

He was kind enough to give me one or two beautiful specimens of his own handwriting, together with that of Mishkin Kalam, all of which, together with his large, signed photograph, were unfortunately burned in the Cyprus fire.

I rendered my last sad tribute of affectionate homage when, early in 1921,* I accompanied Sir Herbert Samuel to the funeral of 'Abbás Effendi. We walked at the head of a train of all the religions up the slope of Mount Carmel, and I have never known a more united expression of regret and respect than was called forth by the utter simplicity of the ceremony.

(Signed) *Ronald Storrs.*[2]

Sir Herbert Samuel (q.v.), the first British High Commissioner for Palestine, was another distinguished guest of 'Abdu'l-Bahá. He writes:

In 1920 I was appointed as the first High Commissioner for Palestine under the British Mandate, and took an early opportunity of paying a visit to 'Abdu'l-Bahá Effendi at his home in Haifa.

I had for some time been interested in the Bahá'í movement, and felt privileged by the opportunity of making the acquaintance of its Head. I had also an official reason as well as a personal one. 'Abdu'l-Bahá had been persecuted by the Turks. A British regime had now been substituted in Palestine for the Turkish. Toleration and respect for all religions had long been a principle of British rule wherever it extended, and the visit of the High Commissioner was intended to be a sign to the population that the adherents of every creed would be able to feel henceforth that they enjoyed the respect and could count upon the goodwill of the new Government of the land.

I was impressed, as was every visitor, by 'Abdu'l-Bahá's dignity, grace, and charm. Of moderate stature, his strong features and lofty expression lent to his personality an appearance of majesty. In our conversation he readily explained and discussed the principal tenets of Bahá'ísm, answered my inquiries and listened to my comments. I remember vividly that friendly interview of sixteen years ago, in the simple room of the villa, surrounded by gardens, on the sunny hillside of Mount Carmel.

I was glad I had paid my visit so soon, for in 1921 'Abdu'l-Bahá died. I was only able to express my respect for his creed, and my regard for his person, by coming from the capital to attend his funeral. A great throng had gathered together, sorrowing for his death, but rejoicing also for his life.[3]

Among Viscount Samuel's papers in the House of Lords Record Office, there is an exchange of correspondence between 'Abdu'l-Bahá and Samuel concerning the question of whether certain villages where Bahá'ís lived were

* This is evidently a slight lapse of memory by Sir Ronald Storrs, since the funeral of 'Abdu'l-Bahá took place in November, 1921. [Lady Blomfield]

to be included in the Palestine administration or not. These letters are couched in warm and friendly terms, despite their being official correspondence.

'Abdu'l-Bahá's letter begins:

'My dear Friend,

The receipt of your letter was conducive of untold joy and pleasure; it was the cause of deepening the already formed impressions of your noble character and refined sentiments. I beseech the Almighty to favour this Land with persons, like you, who try to administer justice and to establish peace. . . .'

The letter concludes:

'At the conclusion, let me repeat, that I ever pray for your success and hope that God will assist you in all your undertakings.'[4]

Samuel's reply begins:

'My dear friend,

I have received, with much pleasure, your letter of September 30th . . . .'[5]

Other important persons who called on 'Abdu'l-Bahá included Viscount Allenby (q.v.), the Commander-in-Chief of the Egyptian Expeditionary Force and the conqueror of Palestine; Major-General Sir Arthur Money (q.v.), the First Chief Administrator of the Southern Occupied Enemy Territory (Palestine); Major-General Sir Harry Watson, his successor (q.v.); and Colonel Stanton (q.v.), the Military Governor of Haifa.

In his book *A Palestine Notebook*, C. R. Ashbee (q.v.), who was the Civic Adviser to the City of Jerusalem, relates his meeting with 'Abdu'l-Bahá in March 1920, and remarks upon the great importance that the British administrators attached to 'Abdu'l-Bahá's opinions:

On the ramparts, among the old masonry to a background of crumbling golden stone, there was an impressive little figure, white bearded, with waving white hair. He wore a white *'emma* and an *'abaya* of tender brown over his gray *galabia*. It was Abbas the Bahai. Later on, thanks to the courtesy of one of our Syrian schoolmasters, we were invited into the house. Word came that he would be very glad to see Mr and Mrs Ashbee, and we spent a wonderful hour with him. He was quite willing to talk and our interpreter was clear and true in his English. Old Abbas curled himself up in the corner of his divan, looked at us with his wonderful illuminating eyes that radiate love, and set forth the cardinal points of Bahaism.

I have rarely come across a man who so completely sums up the saint, or let us say saint and philosopher combined, for the presence and image of the man are of the Middle Ages, their spirit of personal holiness, while what he says has the lucidity of the Greek, is disruptive of all religions and mediaeval systems, is philosophic, modern, and synthetic.

'First,' said he, 'we must get rid of all glosses, Talmuds, codes of divinity, and clerical law. Get back to the revealed word of God where we can. Christ had the revealed word, so had Mohammed, so had others before them, but – and here's the point – those revelations were for their own day and environment. You cannot always take the literal interpretation of first-century Syria or eighth-century Arabia and say that in its application it is true now.'

He gave the impression of being very modest about his own teaching, adding that the East was in a bad way, needed light, and had to be told these things. That was the reason for Bahaullah and the Bab.

'Then,' said he, 'all the nations must come together, there must be a league of nations for the government of the world.'

He sketched out a sort of council appointed by the presidents, the kings, and the democracies.

'And the existing League?' we asked.

He smiled and shook his head. 'That is only the merest beginning. It is not representative of all. It palliates the disease, the disease of discord. It is no remedy.'

But Bahaism went much further, and here it cuts itself free from the orientalism of Pauline Christianity and from Mohammad. There must be equality of the sexes. 'Humanity,' said old Abbas as he took a pinch of snuff from a little enamelled box, 'is as a creature with two wings – man and woman – you must not cripple either, or you impede flight. Humanity needs both for progress.'

'And the common tongue that is to make it possible for man to speak with man?'

'It will come,' said he.

Janet suggested that the tongue might be English. He accepted the suggestion with a look of warm-hearted love that seemed to imply: 'We all of us would like to have our own, but God has found a tongue before.'

Who knows but it may be English yet? Still the last language in which God revealed himself was not Aramaic, nor Greek, nor Hebrew, nor Egyptian, but Arabic. And don't you make any mistake about it! But the languages of God are many.

He tells somewhere in his teaching: Release comes by making of the will a door through which the confirmations of the spirit move.

And those confirmations of the spirit? They are the powers and gifts with which some are born, and which men sometimes call genius, but for which others have to strive with infinite pains. They come to that man or woman who accepts his or her life with 'radiant acquiescence.'

A good phrase, 'radiant acquiescence.' Let's remember it!

As we motored back across the sands, we saw Lord Milner's destroyer lying outside the harbour. 'War,' old Abbas had said, 'is not of God because it does not unify.'

But may it not at times serve as a besom to sweep up ere we begin afresh? That is what it did in South Africa, after which came the peace of Vereeniging and Smuts and Botha became our friends.

The wise men of all time, be it Ptahotep on his tomb, Diogenes from his tub, Plato when he parted from Dion, or Christ with the tribute to Caesar, have always been the passive protest against power. When they offered Abbas his title, with whatever bit of ribbon or strip of paper it was accompanied, he said:

'As it comes from the British Government I accept it, as a teacher of God's word it will make no difference to me.'

It is pleasant to think that English administrators go to this wise old man for help and counsel. We dined in the evening with Colonel Stanton, the Military Governor of Haifa, Lord Milner, and Herbert Samuel. The two last were rather envious of our afternoon with Abbas, and Colonel Stanton told us how he often went to get his advice. 'Of course,' he added in the characteristic manner of the British Administrator, 'I have to listen for half an hour or so first to the beauty of the flowers and the wings of the mind; after that we get to business.'

I thought of the destroyer lying outside Akka, and waiting to take Lord Milner [q.v.] back to England. Somehow I rather wished he could have put his journey off another day and come with us if we went again to Akka. He was a little melancholy and pessimistic, but he always takes a big sweep . . .

Yes, say his friends, but Lord Milner is getting old, Abbas is older, and his sweep is bigger; for his is – shall we say? – a less bounded, because more oriental, faith in the goodness of God and the destiny of man.[6]

In this same book, Ashbee calls 'Abdu'l-Bahá 'one of the wisest men, I should say, that ever lived.'[7]

Sir 'Abdu'l-Bahá 'Abbás:

'Abdu'l-Bahá was highly respected for his humanitarian activities. One of the results of the high regard in which he was held by both the people of Palestine and the British Administration was the conferment upon him of a knighthood. In his capacity as Chief Administrator of the Southern Occupied Enemy Territories, it was General Sir Arthur Money who put forward 'Abdu'l-Bahá's name. The form of recommendation is reproduced on the next page.[8]

This form was forwarded by General Allenby as Commander-in-Chief of the Egyptian Expeditionary Force in a dispatch dated 7 August 1919, to the War Office. The War Office passed the recommendation to Lord Curzon of Kedleston (q.v.), then Secretary of State for Foreign Affairs, on 3 September 1919. The receipt of this recommendation at the Foreign Office brought forth the following comment from E. W. Light (q.v.): 'Perhaps this paper might now be sent on to Sir Frederick [Ponsonby] with a view to obtaining H.M. sanction for the award of a K.B.E. to the Head of the Bahai religion – Abdul Baha . . . I suppose we may take it that Sir A. Money in recommending Abdul Baha for the K.B.E., does not think that any injury will be done to that gentleman's religious susceptibilities by giving him a cruciform decoration, but perhaps the War Dept. wd. advise on this point, which seems one of some special importance in this particular case.'[9]

G. P. Churchill (q.v.) however, was more worried about the political questions arising and suggested that Sir Percy Cox (q.v.), the British Ambassador in Ṭihrán, and Nuṣratu'd-Dawlih, the Persian Minister for Foreign Affairs, be consulted.[10]

According to Lancelot Oliphant's (q.v.) note of 13 October 1919,[11] Nuṣratu'd-Dawlih saw no objection, and on 21 October Sir Percy Cox telegrammed that he also saw no objection.[12] The recommendation was therefore forwarded to Sir Frederick Ponsonby (q.v.), 'with a view to ascertaining whether the King approves the K.B.E. being given to Abdul Baha.'[13] In a short note dated 29 October 1919, Ponsonby wrote 'The King Approves.'[14] and subsequently V. Wellesley (q.v.) on 31 October wrote to Brig.-Gen. Sir Douglas Dawson (q.v.), Registrar and Secretary of the Central Chancery of the Orders of Knighthood, asking for the relevant

FORM OF RECOMMENDATION FOR CIVILIANS

Form 137/4669 'B'

THE ORDER OF THE BRITISH EMPIRE

Form of recommendation for Award

Full name and official designation of Officer or Official submitting the recommendation

Major Gen: Sir A. W. Money, KCB, KBE, CSI, Chief Administrator, Occupied Enemy Territory (S)., EEF

Descriptive particulars of Candidate Recommended

Rank and title (if any)

Surname in full
Christian names in full ABDUL BAHA ABBAS
(in the case of ladies state whether Mrs or Miss)

Present or past Corps (if any)

Appointment and Departmental grading
Salary to be specified if not graded

Leader and Head of the BAHAI religion which numbers some millions of adherents in Persia, India, America and England.

Length of service in present appointment

Full present address Haifa, Palestine.

Distinctions already conferred during the present War

Grade of the O B E, for which recommended

KNIGHT COMMANDER

Statement of service during the War for which this distinction is recommended

Has given consistently loyal service to the British cause since the occupation. His advice has been most valuable to the Military Governor and officers of the Administration in Haifa, where all his influence has been for good.
He was for many years placed in captivity by the Turks in the Citadel at Acre.

Signature of Officer or Official submitting the recommendation
[signed] A. W. Money
Major-General.
Chief Administrator.
O.E.T.A.(S)

Date 18th JULY 1919

[Signature difficult to read but may be Lt-Col. R. N. Renshaw]

For General,
Cmdg.-in-Chief, Egyptian Expeditionary Force. [i.e. Allenby]
7.8.1919.[8]

insignia.[15] These were forwarded on 3 November 1919 to the Foreign Office.[16] In a letter dated 7 November 1919, V. Wellesley of the Foreign Office wrote to the War Office informing them of the King's approval and forwarding the insignia for 'presentation through military channels'.[17]

'Abdu'l-Bahá's investiture occurred on 27 April 1920 at Haifa. Colonel Stanton, the Governor of Haifa, officiated at the ceremony (see fig. 36). It should be noted in passing, that 'Abdu'l-Bahá almost never used his title.

Various Letters

Nor was the appreciation shown by the British authorities towards 'Abdu'l-Bahá unreciprocated. On many occasions 'Abdu'l-Bahá commended the British Administration, contrasting it with the inefficient and corrupt workings of the Ottoman Empire. 'Abdu'l-Bahá was not unwilling, moreover, to use his influence with the British authorities to alleviate the sufferings of the Bahá'ís in Persia. Lord Curzon, Secretary of State for Foreign Affairs, sent 'Abdu'l-Bahá a telegram on 30 May 1920, which has not been preserved in the Foreign Office Records.* In reply to this telegram, 'Abdu'l-Bahá wrote to Curzon of the martyrdom of Ḥájí 'Arab and the persecution of the Bahá'ís in Persia (see pp. 444–5).

The persecutions and agitation against the Bahá'ís increased over the period following Ḥájí 'Arab's martyrdom, and in late May 1920 the following telegram from the Central Spiritual Assembly of Persia to 'Abdu'l-Bahá was intercepted by the British Censor at Cairo: 'Many contrarities at the capital and the provinces against Bahaism. No protection besides holy threshold. Waiting answer.'[18]

'Abdu'l-Bahá must have asked Col. Stanton, Military Governor of Haifa, to make enquiries, for on 29 May 1920 the latter telegrammed to Sir Percy Cox (q.v.), the British Minister in Ṭihrán:

'Sir Abdul Baha Abbas begs for information regarding Bahis [sic] situation. Has received telegram stating that these are in danger. Hopes you will give them all protection possible. Military Governor.'[19]

On 5 June 1920, Sir Percy Cox, having made enquiries, replied by telegram: 'Bahais are in no danger here.'[20]

Col. Stanton must have sent a similar telegram to the Foreign Office in London, for on 5 June 1920 a telegram was sent from Lord Curzon to the British Legation in Ṭihrán: 'Abdul Bahha Abbas telegraphs from Caiiffa [*sic*] that on account of present situation in Persia owing to British Agreement Bahais are in danger and begs protection for them.

'We propose to reply that there is nothing whatever in agreement can result in any danger to Bahaís and that in any case H.M.G. cannot undertake their protection in Persia.'[21]

* This telegram was presumably congratulations on receiving his knighthood.

However, it must be noted that there was no question of 'Abdu'l-Bahá having asked the British Government to undertake the protection of the Bahá'ís in Persia. Indeed, the Bahá'ís of Persia were at no time taken under the protection of any foreign power in the same way as the Christian, Zoroastrian and other minority groups were. In 'Abdu'l-Bahá's letter to Lord Curzon relating to Ḥájí 'Arab's martyrdom (text quoted on pp. 444–5), there is the following sentence specifically disclaiming any such desire: 'Our object is not this that His Majesty's Government should undertake any formal protection but rather to incite the Persian Government to undertake the protection of the Bahais and to shield them from the evil of the oppressors. Such a measure would lead to the strength and grandeur of Persia itself.'[22]

Later in the year of 1920, 'Abdu'l-Bahá opened, for the first time, direct communications with Mr Norman (q.v.), the British Ambassador in Ṭihrán. 'Abdu'l-Bahá's first letter, undated, was delivered to Mr Norman on 8 November by Siyyid Naṣru'lláh Báqiroff.[23] In this letter[24] 'Abdu'l-Bahá assures Mr Norman of prayers for the success of his endeavours towards the betterment of Iran, and appoints Báqiroff as intermediary for any messages that Norman may wish to send to 'Abdu'l-Bahá.

Norman sent a suitable reply, through Báqiroff, dated 9 November 1920.[25]

'Abdu'l-Bahá's second letter to Mr Norman was dated 29 October 1920. On 5 February 1921, Báqiroff wrote to Norman asking for an appointment in order to deliver the letter personally.[26] Norman's comment on this was: 'It is ridiculous that the letter cannot be sent round by a servant like any other, but as this appears to be impossible, he can bring it at 10 a.m. next Tuesday, Feb 8, if that will suit him.'[27]

'Abdu'l-Bahá's letter was translated thus by Col. T. W. Haig (q.v.): 'I trust in Almighty that you will be successful in your services to the just govt of G.B. and in supporting the oppressed people who are the wellwishers of the human kind. Agha Seyed Nasrullah Bagheroff who enjoys my confidence is at Tehran. He will inform you of the circumstances of the murder of Haji Arab. You should believe what he tells you.

'I always pray for the just govt of G.B. and wish you success. Please accept the assurances of my highest respect.'[28]

Norman appended the following note to 'Abdu'l-Bahá's letter: 'I think we might send a polite reply, thanking him for his letter, wishing him health, success and prosperity and promising to do all that I can in an unofficial way and so far as the very limited means at my disposal allow, to help his adherents here. He will no doubt make his desires known to me through Seyyed Noosrullah. In any case I always act on information received through our Consuls.

'I will sign the letter, which should be sent open to Seyyed Nasrullah for transmission. H.C.N. Feb. 9, 1921.'[29]

Norman's letter was eventually dispatched dated 14 February 1921.[30]

'Abdu'l-Bahá's third letter to Norman is addressed to 'His Excellency, the Well-wisher of the Persians' and dated 17 January 1921. The following is Kamál Báqiroff's translation:

> The answer of the letter which was a brilliant proof as to your equitable affections was the cause of extreme thankfulness and gratitude, and this great resolution and high intention will ever be the cause of cheerfulness and gladness among the Bahais and will never be forgotten. This justice-dispensing is in fact the call of eternity and in the annals of these well-wishers will decorate an important page. Jenabe Bagheroff and his friends are so very very grateful to you that made me extremely happy too, and all have highly praised your efforts and I shall ever with earnestness, to [at] His threshold, ask His protection' succour and bounty. With highest respect [I] write you this letter and beg your approval.[31]

In a note appended to this letter and dated 15 May 1921, Norman writes: 'I should like to send a polite reply in Persian through Bagherov, saying how much pleasure it has given me to receive this letter and assuring Abdul Baha that I shall never relax my efforts on behalf of his followers and always give an attentive hearing to any representation that they may make to me.

'(I presume that I should also enquire after Abdul Baha's health).'[32]

Norman's letter was eventually dispatched dated 21 May 1921.[33]

The Passing of 'Abdu'l-Bahá

'Abdu'l-Bahá passed away on 28 November 1921. The funeral which took place on 29 November was attended by many of the most important people in Palestine: Sir Herbert Samuel, the High Commissioner; Sir Ronald Storrs, the Governor of Jerusalem; Col. Symes (q.v.), the Governor of Phoenicia; and many of the leading religious figures and notables of the city of Haifa as well as the Consuls of various countries.

The passing of 'Abdu'l-Bahá was recorded in the *Palestine Weekly* on 2 December 1921: '(November 28th) Abbas Effendi, the head of the Bahaist movement, died here to-day.

(November 29th) The funeral of Abbas Effendi took place to-day. The procession from his house to the special cemetery on the way to Mount Carmel began at nine this morning, and continued till twelve. Thousands of people joined in the procession, and among them the High Commissioner and Mr Storrs of Jerusalem. The funeral was carried out with marked simplicity. On the deceased's coffin there was nothing but a single wreath of flowers. At the graveside many men of many faiths joined in the mourning.'[34]

Lord Lamington, having heard of the passing of 'Abdu'l-Bahá, wrote from his home in Scotland to Winston Churchill, then Secretary of State for the Colonies: 'I have just heard of the death of Abdul Baha; as leader of the Bahais his influence was widespread and beneficent. I have been asked to obtain if possible British Official Representation at his funeral. This may not be in keeping with ordinary official etiquette, but I hope it may be permitted in this case.

'. . . in his death I lose a cherished friend.'[35]

On receipt of this letter, G. L. M. Clauson (q.v.) penned the following memorandum: 'It is true that Sir Abbas Abdul Baha K.B.E. was originally the F.O.'s child, but it is our funeral as he died at Haifa.

'I am quite sure that the H.Cr. [High Commissioner] took the necessary steps to be represented at it as Sir 'Abbas was very well-known and I think the only native inhabitant of Palestine with a K.B.E. (he got it under the military administration) but you might perhaps think it worth while to instruct the H.Cr. by code tel. to express H.M.G's [His Majesty's Government's] condolences to the community (the funeral will certainly have taken place by now. It has to take place the same day.) and tell Lord Lamington what we have done.'[36]

Winston Churchill wrote to Lord Lamington on 1 December 1921: 'Thank you for your letter about Sir Abbas Abdul Baha. I think there should be no doubt that the High Commissioner took the necessary steps to be represented at his funeral, which in all probability will have taken place by now. But in any case I am instructing the High Commissioner by telegram to express to the Bahar [*sic*] community the condolences of H.M.'s Government.'[37]

On the same day, this telegram was sent in code to the High Commissioner for Palestine, Sir Herbert Samuel:

'I have learnt with great regret of the death of Sir Abbas Abdul Baha. Please convey to Bahai community suitable expression of condolence of His Majesty's Government.

CHURCHILL'[38]

The leading newspapers of the world took note of the passing of 'Abdu'l-Bahá and published obituaries, lavish in their praise and approbation of a life spent in the service of humanity. It was as though *The Times* of London, *Le Temps* of Paris, the *New York World*, the *Times of India* and many other newspapers and periodicals were vying with one another to give expression to the loftiest sentiments with respect to 'Abdu'l-Bahá. Among the sentences which occur in these newspaper obituaries are: 'He was a man of great spiritual power and commanding presence, and his name was held in reverence throughout the Middle East. He claimed that the revelation given to his father, Baha'ullah, expressed the essential truth of all the religions of the world. He advocated universal peace and brotherhood, the independent investigation of the truth, and the equality of the sexes, and frequently made earnest appeals to the rulers of Europe for universal disarmament . . . The British authorities recognised his position of influence, and it was at Lord Allenby's suggestion that he was knighted last year.' (*The Times* 30 November 1921)

'It was some ten years ago that this magnificent and good-natured elderly gentleman was spreading the holy word amongst us. He was clothed in a simple olive-green robe and on his head a white turban . . . His speech was soft and melodious, like a litany. One listened to him with pleasurable concentration, even though one did not understand him, for he spoke in Persian . . . Under the white turban his eyes reflected intelligence and kindness. He was paternal, affectionate and simple.' (*Le Temps* 19 December 1921)

'As recently as June of this year a special correspondent of the *World* who visited this seer thus described him: "Having once looked upon 'Abdu'l Baha, his personality is indelibly impressed upon the mind: the majestic venerable figure clad in the flowing aba, his head crowned with a turban white as his head and hair; the piercing deep set eyes whose glances shake the heart; the smile that pours its sweetness over all." . . .

'Even in the twilight of his life 'Abdu'l Baha took the liveliest interest in world affairs. When General Allenby swept up the coast from Egypt he went for counsel first to 'Abdu'l Baha. . . .' (*New York World* 1 December 1921)

' . . . we would pay a tribute to the memory of a man who wielded a vast influence for good, and who, if he was destined to see many of his ideas seemingly shattered in the world war, remained true to his convictions and to his belief in the possibility of a reign of peace and love, and who, far more effectively than Tolstoi, showed the West that religion is a vital force that can never be disregarded.' (*Times of India* January 1922)[39]

References

1. Storrs *Orientations* pp. 72, 375–6. American edn. pp. 70, 337
2. Blomfield *The Chosen Highway* pp. 226–7
3. ibid. pp. 225–6
4. 'Abdu'l-Bahá to Lord Samuel 30 Sept. 1921: Samuel (Israel) Papers, House of Lords Record Off. These papers are photocopies, the originals being in the Israel State Archives.
5. Samuel to 'Abdu'l-Bahá 6 Oct. 1921: Samuel (Israel) Papers (see note 4)
6. Ashbee *A Palestine Notebook* pp. 116–19
7. ibid. p. 173

8. File 126335/350 D/1918: FO 372 1297
9. Memo dated 7 Oct. 1919, from 8 *supra*
10. Memo dated 8 Oct. 1914, from 8 *supra*
11. Note added to 10 *supra*
12. Telegram to Sir Percy Cox No. 543, 16 Oct. 1919, in 8 *supra*. Reply from Cox, telegram No. 692, 21 Oct. 1919, File 144519/350 D/1918: FO 372 1298
13. Memo by Light dated 23 Oct. 1914, in File 144519/350 D/1918: FO 372 1298
14. Note in file detailed in 13 *supra*
15. Letter in file detailed in 13 *supra*
16. ibid.
17. ibid.
18. Telegram picked up by Censor at Cairo on 28 May 1920 and reported to Brit. Legation in Ṭihrán 31 May 1920, No. 384M, No. 3 in File 'Bahais': FO 248 1279
19. Telegram No. 2786, No. 2 in File 'Bahais': FO 248 1279
20. Telegram No. 234M, No. 3 in File 'Bahais': FO 248 1279
21. Telegram No. 296A, No. 3/1 in File 'Bahais': FO 248 1279
22. File C3491/3491/34: FO 371 4924
23. No. 24a in File 'Bahais': FO 248 1279
24. FO 248 1321
25. FO 248 1320
26. No. 7 in File 'Bahais': FO 248 1323
27. Memo appended to letter detailed in 26 *supra*
28. FO 248 1360
29. ibid.
30. FO 248 1361
31. Was originally No. 17 in File 'Bahais', FO 248 1323, but was removed and placed in FO 248 1360
32. Was originally No. 18 in File 'Bahais', FO 248 1323, but was removed and placed in FO 248 1360
33. FO 248 1361
34. *Palestine Weekly* 2 Dec. 1921, p. 782
35. Lamington to Churchill, 30 Nov. 1921, File CO 60042: CO 733 17A
36. Memo dated 30 Nov. 1921 in File CO 60042: CO 733 17A.
37. File CO 60042: CO 733 17A
38. Telegram No. 365, File CO 60042: CO 733 17A
39. With the exception of *The Times*, all other obituaries taken from *The Passing of 'Abdu'l-Bahá* (pp. 15–17) by Shoghi Effendi and Lady Blomfield

TWENTY-SIX

The Bahá'ís and Political Upheavals in Persia

During the last half of the nineteenth century, Persia became increasingly penetrated by European diplomats, merchants, travellers and missionaries. The resultant influx of Western thoughts and ideals had far-reaching effects within Persia. People were revolted by the self-indulgence and corruption of the Qájár dynasty, the sale of concessions of monopolies over the nation's resources to foreign bidders, the threat of loss of national sovereignty to powerful European states, and the contempt and derision with which this once-proud country was regarded by foreigners. From within the people, a great desire for change welled up and this manifested itself in a general discontent and a series of incidents and episodes, as the inevitable clash with those forces committed to maintaining the existing order occurred.

To consider the extent to which the religion of the Báb and Bahá'u'lláh influenced the origins and course of this movement for reform is beyond the scope of this book. All that will be presented here is the way that the political events of this period affected the Bahá'í community.

As history has demonstrated on numerous occasions, the adverse effects of social convulsions fall particularly heavily on minority groups. The Bahá'ís were no exception. The vast majority of the community, following 'Abdu'l-Bahá's exhortations, refrained from taking sides in the struggle. They were thus caught between the two parties and became pawns for use and abuse according to the dictates of political expediency.

One point that must constantly be borne in mind when reading the following Western accounts of this period is the fact that the Bahá'ís were at this time known to both Persians and Europeans alike as Bábís, despite the fact that it was now some thirty years that the majority had been calling themselves Bahá'ís or followers of Bahá'u'lláh. The importance of this point arises from the fact that the followers of Mírzá Yaḥyá, the Azalís, were also known as Bábís – and these did not hesitate to promote political agitation against the Qájár dynasty. The dispatch from Longworth in 1896, which will be quoted presently, exemplifies the great confusion that arose from this failure to distinguish between the Bahá'ís and the Azalís.

The following letter from 'Abdu'l-Bahá to Ḥájí Mírzá 'Abdu'lláh, Ṣaḥíḥ-Furú<u>sh</u>, translated and published by Prof. Browne in his work *The Persian Revolution*, clearly states the Bahá'í position. This letter also indicates that another reason that confusion may have arisen in the minds of some concerning the attitude of the Bahá'ís, is the fact that the Azalís were spreading false rumours to the effect that the Bahá'ís supported the <u>Sh</u>áh. (All parentheses in this passage are Browne's.)

You wrote that it had been stated in the *Ḥablu'l-Matín* published at Rasht that the Bahá'ís were partisans of the Autocracy, and at Zanján had collected aid for the Royalist Cause. One of the 'Friends' must write to some other newspaper, or it must be spread abroad amongst the people, that this is a calumny concerning the Bahá'ís [emanating] from the Yaḥyá'í [*i.e.* Azalí] Bábís, for these men are the enemies of the Bahá'ís. The aim of the Bahá'ís is the reformation of the world, so that amongst all these nations and governments a reconciliation may be effected and strife and war may be abolished. Therefore they hasten onward with heart and soul and spend themselves that perchance the Court and the Nation, nay, [all] parties and peoples, may be united to one another, and that peace and reconciliation may enter in. Hence they have no part in such quarrels. And a clear proof and conclusive argument as to the falsity of the accuser, which leaves no opening for doubt, is the decree of the *mujtahid* Mullá Ḥasan of Tabríz* for the slaughter of the Bahá'ís, and also the slanderous proclamations of the *mujtahid* Mírzá Faẓlu'lláh of Núr and Sayyid 'Alí Akbar,† which were posted on the walls in all the streets and *bázárs* of Ṭihrán. But the Yaḥyá'í [*i.e.* Azalí] Bábís, who are the enemies of the Bahá'ís, and who keep themselves in concealment, tell the Nationalists that the Bahá'ís are the partisans of the Court, while telling the Royalists that they are ready to lay down their lives for the Nation, in order to stir up both sides against the Bahá'ís and make them their enemies, that perchance they may seduce certain souls on either side. This is the truth of the matter; therefore it behoves that some just men should investigate the question of the [alleged] help [given to the Royalists] at Zanján. If such a thing hath been done by the Bahá'ís we will believe and admit [the charge]. Glory be to God! This is an awful calumny! From the very beginning of the Revolution it was constantly enjoined that the Friends of God should stand aside from this strife and struggle and war and contest, and should seek to reconcile the Court and the Nation, and should spend themselves so that Court and Nation should mix with one another like milk and honey: for safety and success are unattainable and impossible without [such] reconciliation. Now when they who wish us ill utter calumnies, the 'Friends' are silent, wherefore these our foes each day boldly enunciate some [new] slander.

Upon thee be the Most Splendid Splendour (*al-Bahá'u'l-Abhá*). *'A.'A.* (*i.e.* 'Abbás 'Abdu'l-Bahá).[1]

The Political Upheavals (1890–1911)

For the sake of convenience, the events of this period may be divided into:

* a reactionary

† both prominent reactionaries

a) *The Agitation against the Tobacco Régie (1891–2)*. On 8 March 1890, Náṣiru'd-Dín Sháh signed an agreement with Mr G. F. Talbot whereby in return for certain payments, the latter was granted full control over the production, sale and export of all tobacco in Persia for fifty years. Wide-ranging concessions such as these were by no means unusual during the latter part of the reign of Náṣiru'd-Dín Sháh, but they were usually concerned with such monopolies as railways, mining, banks, etc. Never before had a monopoly over a commodity that was of such direct concern to the people been granted. The agitation against the Régie began almost as soon as it commenced to function in early 1891. Such persons as Siyyid Jamálu'd-Dín-i-Afghání and Mírzá Malkam Khán were prominent in opposing it, but undoubtedly the most important role was played by Ḥájí Mírzá Ḥasan, Mírzáy-i-Shírází, who was at this time the greatest of the Shí'ih mujtahids and lived at Samarra in Iraq. When in December 1891 he wrote forbidding the people to smoke, there was universal obedience to his decree, even in the immediate entourage and harem of the Sháh. There was now no hope of saving the Régie. Finally, in January 1892, the concession was cancelled, and by April of that year the indemnity to be paid to the concessionaires was agreed.

b) *The Assassination of Náṣiru'd-Dín Sháh (1896)*. (See pp. 158–9 for an account of this event.) This act, performed by Mírzá Muḥammad-Riḍá of Kirmán, a disciple of Siyyid Jamálu'd-Dín, represented the culmination of the latter's efforts, which were principally directed towards Pan-Islamism, and the expulsion of European influence and domination in all Muslim countries. The attempt to unite Sunní and Shí'ih Islam was a prodigious task and he spent a considerable amount of time at both Ṭihrán and Istanbul trying to bring it about. Although at first Náṣiru'd-Dín Sháh received him favourably, in the end he turned on him and expelled him from Persia. It was then that Siyyid Jamálu'd-Dín turned against Náṣiru'd-Dín Sháh. Prof. Browne, who met him in autumn 1891, shortly after his expulsion from Persia, records him in *The Persian Revolution* as saying that no reform was to be hoped for in Persia until six or seven heads had been cut off, and 'the first must be Náṣiru'd-Dín Sháh's'. Mírzá Muḥammad-Riḍá, angered by the ignominious treatment of his master and embittered by his own prolonged ill-treatment, imprisonment and harassment at the hands of the Persian authorities, decided to carry out the assassination. It is not clear to what extent he was acting under the instructions of Siyyid Jamálu'd-Dín. Siyyid Jamálu'd-Dín, however, only survived Náṣiru'd-Dín Sháh by nine months. He died on 9 March 1897, of cancer of the jaw.

c) *The Constitutional Upheavals (1905–9)*. After the assassination of Náṣiru'd-Dín Sháh there was a period of relative quiet, since it was widely expected that the gentle and timid Muẓaffaru'd-Dín Sháh would introduce reforms. As the years passed, however, it became clear that he was in danger of putting Persia even further under foreign domination by his incessant raising of foreign loans in order to indulge himself in tours of Europe.

During the course of 1903, the protests against new customs tariffs and the regime of the reactionary Prime Minister, Amínu's-Sulṭán, grew until at last he was forced to resign in September 1903. During 1904 and 1905, protests against Amínu's-Sulṭán's successor, 'Aynu'd-Dawlih, grew. In December 1905, as a result of a large crowd taking sanctuary in the shrine of Sháh 'Abdu'l-'Aẓím near Ṭihrán, the Shah agreed to dismiss 'Aynu'd-Dawlih and convene an 'Adálat-Khánih (House of Justice). Whatever was meant by the latter, the Sháh, after the dispersion of the crowd at Sháh 'Abdu'l-'Aẓím, showed no intention of fulfilling his promises. Eventually, after riots in Ṭihrán, several thousand people took sanctuary in the British Legation (July–August 1906) until the Sháh dismissed 'Aynu'd-Dawlih and agreed to the establishment of a National Assembly, elected by the people. This Assembly began its deliberations on 7 October 1906 and had soon drafted a Constitution, which was signed by the Sháh on 30 December 1906. A week later, Muẓaffaru'd-Dín Sháh was dead.

Muḥammad-'Alí Sháh, who succeeded to the throne, was a very different person from his father. From the very start of his reign he showed a determined opposition to the new Constitution and the National Assembly. In December 1907 he made an abortive attempt to close down the National Assembly, but was more successful in June 1908 when he dispersed the National Assembly, arrested many leading Constitutionalists, and suspended the Constitution. Initially only Tabríz responded by rebelling against the Sháh, and for this the city was put under siege by Royalist forces. Just when the Royalist forces seemed about to triumph in early 1909, there developed a series of other revolts against the Sháh in major Persian towns. The two most organized towns in Nationalist hands, Rasht and Iṣfahán, sent forces out in the direction of Ṭihrán. These forces arrived in Ṭihrán on 13 July 1909, forced Muḥammad-'Alí Sháh's abdication and resurrected the Constitution.

In 1911, Muḥammad-'Alí, the ex-Sháh, made a bid to regain the throne and landed near Astarábád. He was, however, repulsed and once again fled the country.

Although the establishment of the Constitution and the overthrow of the autocratic Muḥammad-'Alí Sháh was hailed with great joy throughout Persia – and among liberal circles in Europe – as the beginning of a new era in Persia, in practical terms it brought no amelioration in the country's condition. In the ensuing years, the state of Persia deteriorated, and in most parts, anarchy prevailed. With the advent of the First World War, Russia promptly invaded the northern provinces of Persia, and it was probably only the Bolshevik Revolution that prevented their complete annexation by Russia.

The Arrests of April 1891

As details of the conditions of the Tobacco Régie began to reach Persia, voices of protest were raised in every corner and the Régie became a focal point for various disaffected groups. Towards the end of 1890, growing alarmed at the increasing evidence of dissatisfaction among his people and the demand for reform voiced by such newspapers as Mírzá Malkam Khán's *Qánún*, Náṣiru'd-Dín Sháh decided to act with vigour and determination to stamp out this movement. Foremost among those agitating for reform was Siyyid Jamálu'd-Dín-i-Afghání who was then in Ṭihrán. The Sháh ordered his arrest, and in February 1891 he was expelled from Iran. The Sháh then turned his attention to *Qánún*. He forbade its entry and circulation in Iran, and tried unsuccessfully to get the British to suppress its publication in London. Despite all his efforts, the newspaper still succeeded in circulating within Iran, and this incensed the Sháh. He instructed that a list of those suspected of being Mírza Malkam Khán's followers and other liberal elements be drawn up, and on the night of 26 April 1891, many of those on that list were arrested.

Among those arrested were:

1. Mírzá Muḥammad-'Alí Khán, Farídu'l-Mulk, previously Secretary to the Persian Legation in Ṭihrán.
2. Iskandar Khán, Mírzá Malkam Khán's brother.
3. Ḥájí Muḥammad-'Alíy-i-Maḥallátí, known as Ḥájí Sayyáḥ, a noted disciple of Siyyid Jamálu'd-Dín.
4. Mírzá Aḥmad-i-Kirmání, an Azalí.
5. Mírzá Muḥammad-Riḍáy-i-Kirmání, a disciple of Siyyid Jamálu'd-Dín, and the future assassin of Náṣiru'd-Dín Sháh.
6. Mírzá Naṣru'lláh Khán, who was later Minister for Foreign Affairs with the title Mushíru'd-Dawlih.

Also arrested on that day, despite their having no connection with Mírzá Malkam Khán's activities, were two Bahá'ís, Ḥájí Mullá 'Alí-Akbar-i-Shahmírzádí,* known as Ḥájí Ákhúnd, and Ḥájí Abu'l-Ḥasan-i-Ardikání,† known as Ḥáji Amín. This is probably the basis for the reference to Bábís in a report appearing in *The Times* of London on 25 June 1891:

* He was one of four persons designated by Bahá'u'lláh as 'Hands of the Cause'.

† He was Bahá'u'lláh's courier between 'Akká and Iran, as well as being trustee for the monies remitted by the believers in Iran for Bahá'u'lláh.

PERSIA.

VIENNA. JUNE 25.

According to intelligence received here from Teheran, a movement has been set on foot in Persia aiming at the introduction of liberal reforms. The Shah has received an anonymous petition, in which he is called upon to carry out without delay the following programme:- First, the establishment of an efficient control over the finances of the country, so as to insure the employment of the public money for public purposes and the economic improvement of the kingdom; secondly, the suppression of polygamy, which, as the petitioners set forth, is the real cause of Persian depopulation; thirdly, the promulgation of a law guaranteeing absolute freedom to all creeds; and, fourthly, the creation of a representative system giving the people its due share in the management of public affairs.

The Shah, it is reported, is far from being favourably inclined to such innovations, which would deprive him of a great deal of his power, and the police of Teheran have made about 40 arrests in connexion with this petition, especially among the members of the Babiste party, a politico-religious sect,* which seems to be gaining ground in the country. The Persian Government hopes to be able to stifle the movement, which might eventually become a danger to the present *régime. – Our Own Correspondent.*[2]

From the following statement in a dispatch from the French Minister, M. de Balloy (q.v.), dated 14 May 1891 it would appear that there was, at first, an intention of putting the two Bahá'ís to death:

They had announced, for yesterday, the execution of two Bábís who would each be attached to the mouth of a cannon, but it did not take place.

The situation is certainly serious, but it is complex. Apart from this, there is no need to hide the fact that one aspect of the agitation is a sham and the result of different intrigues. Bábism, which is a scapegoat, is a philosophical and religious doctrine much superior to the sensualist dogmas of Islam. The Bábís, evidently, are dreaming of an ideal for their country other than that which they find in the bad Government of the S͟háh and the exactions of his Governors. But for thirty-eight years they have remained perfectly quiet. To consider them responsible would be unjust; to proceed against them with bloody or cruel repressions would only result in exasperating them and awakening the heroism of which they have given proof at other times. The Queen of England has, it appears, recommended to the S͟háh clemency and moderation in his own interest and in that of Persia.[3]

After a period in detention in Kámrán Mírzá's garden at Amíríyyih, those arrested were transferred to Qazvín and imprisoned there. At the end of eighteen months the prisoners were brought back to Ṭihrán, and after six months in a dungeon there a large sum of money was extorted from each of them and they were released – with the exception of Ḥájí Amín and Mírzá Muḥammad-Riḍá.† Ḥájí Amín remained imprisoned for a further year (making three years in all).

* See p. 351.

† In connection with this see Mírzá Muḥammad-Riḍá's interrogation in Browne *The Persian Revolution* pp. 88–9.

The Seven Martyrs of Yazd, May 1891

But the story of the arrests of April 1891 does not end there. In a letter written by 'Abdu'l-Bahá to Browne on 19 August 1891 the following passage occurs, relating the Ṭihrán arrests of April 1891 to the martyrdoms of seven Bahá'ís in Yazd one month later (see chapter 20 for a description of this episode):

> The partisans of Malkom Khán and Jamálu'd-Dín devised a plan to alarm, intimidate, and greatly disturb the government by involving the Bábís also in suspicion, and wrote pamphlets so worded that it might appear that there was an alliance between these and themselves. To be brief, they arrested Malkom Khán's brother with your friend the Mírzá of Hamadán* and several others, and also two Bábís, and the government officials, without any enquiry or investigation, began on every side to persecute this oppressed community, although these poor innocents, as I swear by God's Might, knew absolutely nothing of this agitation and disturbance, non-interference in political matters being required by their creed.
>
> No sooner did this news reach Iṣfahán than the Prince [*Ẓillu's-Sulṭán*], one of whose confidential advisers had been accused and arrested, considered it expedient, for the exculpation of himself from all suspicion of complicity in this plot and for the concealment of his own evil deeds, to inaugurate a violent and cruel persecution of the Bábís. So he entered into correspondence with [his son] Prince Jalálu'd-Dawla, and a persecution was set on foot in the city of Yazd and the surrounding villages, where such cruelties and injustices were perpetrated as are unparalleled in the history of the world.[4]

The 'confidential adviser' of Ẓillu's-Sulṭán here referred to was Ḥájí Sayyáḥ. This man, in the course of his travels, had come to the conclusion that the best means for the progress of Iran was to remove Náṣiru'd-Dín Sháh from the throne and replace him by Ẓillu's-Sulṭán, and to this end he was constantly plotting and intriguing.† When Ḥájí Sayyáḥ was arrested in Ṭihrán in April 1891, Ẓillu's-Sulṭán was undoubtedly terrified in the expectation that he too would soon be severely punished or put to death for his designs on the throne. Thus, as indicated in 'Abdu'l-Bahá's letter, he inaugurated a persecution of the Bahá'ís in Yazd in order to divert attention from himself. Further evidence for this comes from a dispatch that Robert Kennedy, the British Chargé d'Affaires in Ṭihrán, sent to the Marquess of Salisbury on 11 June 1891. Evidently Ẓillu's-Sulṭán, wishing to ensure that no-one else received the approbation of the Sháh for the persecution of the Bahá'ís in Yazd, wrote to the Sháh to boast about his deeds:

* Farídu'l-Mulk

† He had even travelled to 'Akká in the hope of persuading Bahá'u'lláh to support this scheme. Bahá'u'lláh declined to become involved in his schemes despite being promised freedom of religion for the Bahá'ís if Ẓillu's-Sulṭán became Sháh.

. . . at an interview which I had yesterday with the Amin-us-Sultan, His Highness informed me in great confidence that His Royal Highness the Zil-us-Sultan had written to the Shah and had taken great credit to himself . . . for the energetic manner in which the Bábis of Yezd had been suppressed and the true interests of Islam had been protected . . .

The Zil-us-Sultan further contrasted his own conduct favourably with that of the Amin-us-Sultan. The latter, His Royal Highness hinted, had betrayed his Sovereign by recommending the issue of the Proclamation of 1888, guaranteeing security to life and property in Persia, thus tampering with the Shah's power and authority.

The Shah appears to have been much startled by the contents of the Zil-us-Sultan's letter, which His Majesty destroyed . . .[5]

The Tobacco Régie

The Bahá'ís were but little involved in the events of the protest against the Tobacco Régie although, as usual, their name was dragged into the conflict when it suited the purposes of either party. Thus when Siyyid Jamálu'd-Dín was writing to Mírzá Ḥasan-i-S͟hírází (Mírzáy-i-S͟hírází), trying to persuade him to issue a fatvá against the Tobacco Régie, he writes of Amínu's-Sulṭán (q.v.): 'This man as it is said, is unquestionably a Babi. The weaknesses of Islam are all caused by this mean man who sells the Moslems, oppresses the Ulamas and contemns the Seyyeds.'[6]

Towards the close of this episode, the Bahá'ís of Bombay wrote to the Persian Prime Minister, Amínu's-Sulṭán, pointing out that involvement in the rioting and protests was confined to the Azalís and that the Bahá'ís refrained from involvement in political matters and remained loyal to the Government. Amínu's-Sulṭán, in an interview with Frank C. Lascelles, indicated that he, at least, fully appreciated the difference between the two parties:

In the different conversations which I have had with the Amin-es-Sultan, his Highness has frequently impressed upon me that all the enemies of the Persian Government had taken the opportunity of the opposition to the Tobacco Corporation to join together in an attempt to overthrow the Government of the Shah. Among these enemies of the Government the sect of the Babis is not the least influential element.

The Amin-es-Sultan has been careful to explain to me that the Babis are divided into two branches, one of which, the Bahais, are inoffensive, and abstain from any interference in the affairs of State; whereas the other branch, known as the Azelis, seek for the destruction of all existing institutions, and are similar to the Nihilists in Russia.[7]

In the accompanying memorandum, Churchill, too, demonstrates this point clearly. After dealing with the early history of the Bábís, he writes:

After the execution of the Bab, in July 1850, his followers rallied around Mirza Yahia, of Tehran, who was styled 'Hazret Azel,' or the 'Eternal,' and whose head-quarters were at Bagdad, and subsequently at Adrianople.

Whilst at the latter place, about the year 1866, Mirza Hussein Ali, elder brother by another mother of Mirza Yahia, claimed to be the one designated by the Bab as 'he whom God shall manifest,' and therefore the leader of the sect.

Mirza Yahia disputed his brother's supremacy, and the Babis became split up into two sections, the majority following Mirza Hussein Ali, and being known by his spiritual title of Baha, as 'Bahais,' whereas the followers of Mirza Yahia were known as 'Azelis.'

In 1868 the quarrels between the two factions were such as to attract the attention of the Turkish Government, by whom they were separated – the Bahais being sent to Acre, and the Azelis to Cyprus. Mirza Yahia and his followers in Cyprus receive pensions from His Majesty's Government.

A good many influential Babis live at Bombay, and a considerable number have migrated from Yezd to Askabad, in Russian Trans-Caspia.

According to the Amin-es-Sultan the followers of Baha in India repudiate any connection with the recent revolutionary events which occurred at Tehran; and his Highness states, from letters which he has received from them, that it appears that the Bahai Babis accuse the Azelis of Socialism in its most virulent forms.[8]

The Assassination of Náṣiru'd-Dín Sháh, May 1896

A description of the assassination of Náṣiru'd-Dín Sháh has already been given (see pp. 158–9). As news of this event spread through Persia and then to the Middle East and Europe, it was at first linked with the 'Babis'. It was assumed that the Bábís, having once attempted the life of the Sháh in 1852 and failed, had now succeeded. Thus in London, *The Times** of 2 May 1896 announced the assassination in the following terms:

ASSASSINATION OF THE SHAH

TEHERAN, MAY 1.

The Shah was shot at in the Mosque of Shah Abdul Azim, near Teheran, this afternoon, and is said to have died of his wound on his arrival in the town.

There is considerable alarm, and the Prince Naib-es-Sultanah has retired to his palace at the request of the Government.

Much discontent has existed for some time through the dearness of provisions, which has been caused partly by the excessive issue of copper coins.

The murderer has been arrested. His name is Mollah Reza, and he is supposed to be a Babi.'[9]

The newspaper followed this up with the statement: 'He [the Sháh] treated his adversaries with great severity, and to none did he show more pitiless cruelty than to the followers of El Bab, the greatest reformer who has perhaps ever arisen in the Mussulman world. That he should after 50 years have died by the hand of a Babee is a strange and striking nemesis.'[10]

In another edition, *The Times* stated:

. . . the statement that the murderer is supposed to be a Babi points to fanaticism or revenge as the motive of the crime. Nearly half a century ago, soon after the SHAH

* Other newspapers similarly attributed this act to the 'Babis'. Browne in *The Persian Revolution* (p. 60) cites *The Scotsman*, the *Manchester Guardian*, the *Graphic*, the *Spectator*, the *Morning Post*, the *Pioneer*, *St Paul's*, and others.

ascended the throne, the BAB – literally 'The Gate' – a sort of religious enthusiast or Messiah, led a crusade against the corruption of public and private manners. His doctrines spread with great rapidity, and his followers quickly aroused the apprehensions of the authorities. They were put to death by thousands, and NASR ED DIN probably congratulated himself on having exterminated a pestilent heresy. These things, however, are extremely tenacious of life, and even a second persecution failed to extirpate the obnoxious sect. It is interesting to recall the fact that it endeavoured to retaliate by attempting the life of the SHAH as far back as 1852. The successor of the BAB now resides in Syria, and Acre is a Babi Mecca to which Persian sectaries make surreptitious pilgrimages. It is easily conceivable that some fanatic among them, excited by the preparations already begun to celebrate the SHAH's jubilee, may have thought it a laudable thing to revenge, even at this late period, the wrongs inflicted upon his co-religionists. There has, indeed, been no lack of continuing provocation for any man capable of imagining a reasonably just form of government. The SHAH of PERSIA is an absolute autocrat unfettered by laws, and NASREDDIN was not very largely endowed with the personal virtues which alone can mitigate the evils of such a system.[11]

It was only several days later, on 6 May 1896, that *The Times* printed a letter from E. G. Browne in which he stated that it is most improbable that this deed was the act of the 'Bábís'.

Sir, – The news of the tragic death of his late Majesty Nasiru'd-Din Shah by the hand of an assassin within a few days of the celebration of his jubilee will be received with consternation in all Persian communities, and will cause profound disquietude to all who have at heart the interests of Persia.

The perils of the situation created by this unexpected catastrophe are sufficiently obvious and have already been discussed in the Press. My object in writing is to ask for a suspension of judgment as to the alleged complicity of the Bábí sect, which has been falsely described in at least one journal as 'a secret criminal association.'

As one who has been intimately acquainted with many members of the sect (both in Persia and elsewhere), including their present leaders, and who has enjoyed unusual opportunities of studying their aims, doctrines, and character, will you allow me to express through your columns my conviction that they are, as a body, entirely innocent of participation in this outrage, and to state my reasons for this belief?

It is perfectly true that in August, 1852, an attempt on the Shah's life was made by three Bábís, who, acting, as it would appear, entirely on their own responsibility, sought to avenge in this way the persecutions endured by their co-religionists, and especially the execution of their founder. This ill-advised act resulted in a fresh persecution of unparalleled ferocity, in which many innocent persons suffered death in its most terrible forms. Nor did the mischief end there, for though from that time to this the Bábís, notwithstanding all that they have had to endure, have meekly borne their sufferings, living lawfully and peaceably, and systematically repelling the overtures from time to time made to them by disaffected persons and parties, no sooner has an act of violence like this taken place than an attempt has been made to lay it to their charge.

Now I will not insist on the fact that the responsible leaders of the Bábís have not only always disclaimed all sympathy with the attempt on the Shah's life in 1852, but have, on the contrary, condemned it in the strongest terms; nor on the fact that the use of a form of prayer for the safety of the Shah and his preservation from danger was enjoined on members of the sect by their leaders. I will only inquire what conceivable motives could, at the present time, prompt the Bábís to the perpetration of this act. The fierce irritation and reckless despair which existed amongst them in 1852 have long passed away. Persecutions have for many years been sporadic, and have, in almost every recent instance, been due either to the fanaticism of the *mollahs* (Shi'ite clergy) or the enmity or greed of individual governors.

The late Shah himself seems latterly to have recognized the inoffensive character of the sect, and has more than once interposed to curb the fanaticism of the orthodox clergy. From his death the Bábís have nothing to hope and much to fear. For if it be true, as is generally believed, that the new Shah is under the influence of the *mollahs*, persecution of the unorthodox is likely to wax fiercer in the future. Should anarchy prevail, the Bábís, along with the native Christians, Jews, and Zoroastrians, would be equally certain to suffer. And of all possible contingencies the accession of the Zillu's-Sultán would be most dreaded by them, for at his hands they have suffered much.

These and other considerations convince me that the outrage of Friday last cannot be laid to the charge of the Bábís, though it is but too probable that attempts will be made, especially by the *mollahs*, to fix it upon them, and thus to find an excuse for renewing the horrors enacted in 1852.

Apologizing for trespassing at such length on your valuable space,

I am, Sir, your obedient servant,

EDWARD G. BROWNE.[12]

Cambridge, May 3.

It was thus only gradually that there came the realization that the Bahá'ís were not responsible for this deed.

The Martyrdom of Varqá and Rúḥu'lláh

Mírzá 'Alí-Muḥammad, surnamed Varqá (Dove), was one of the leading Bahá'ís of Iran. Shortly before the assassination of the Sháh, he had been arrested in Zanján and led in chains to the royal palace in Ṭihrán together with his son Rúḥu'lláh, aged about 12 years, and two other Bahá'ís.* Ja'far-Qulí Khán, Ḥájibu'd-Dawlih (q.v.), the Farrásh-Báshí of the Sháh, thinking the Bahá'ís to be responsible for the assassination of the Sháh, took it upon himself to exact retribution by killing the prisoners in the royal palace. He killed Varqá and Rúḥu'lláh cruelly but spared the other two.† M. de Balloy, the French Minister, wrote:

They are seeking to agitate against the Bábís, who are very numerous . . . It is unfortunate that from the first the assassin was incorrectly said to be from among the members of this sect. The Bábís absolutely repudiate violence as a means of action, depending entirely on persuasion and on the purity of their doctrines, which are, in fact, much superior to those of Islam. They are now beginning to be terrorized because the murder of the Sháh has been attributed to them, and this terror is sufficiently justified by the fact that Ḥájibu'd-Dawlih, the Farrásh-Báshí of the King, in a fury on returning from Sháh 'Abdu'l-'Aẓím,‡ has put to death, with his own hands and without

* Ḥájí Ímán and Mírzá Ḥusayn, both natives of Zanján.

† For an account of the life and martyrdom of Varqá and Rúḥu'lláh see K. Kazemzadeh 'Varqá and Rúḥu'lláh'.

‡ Where the Sháh was assassinated.

orders from anyone, two Bábís imprisoned in the Palace who had been arrested in Zanján. It is doubtful whether they denied their principles despite the agitation of which they were the object . . .[13]

For an account of the murder of other Bahá'ís as a consequence of the assassination of Náṣiru'd-Dín Sháh see p. 405.

The Azalí Prisoners at Trabizond

Some time before the assassination of Náṣiru'd-Dín Sháh, two of the leading followers of Ṣubḥ-i-Azal, Shaykh Aḥmad-i-Rúḥí and Mírzá Áqá Khán-i-Kirmání, were arrested together with Mírzá Ḥasan Khán, Khabíru'l-Mulk, in Constantinople on a charge of writing seditious letters to the 'ulamá of Persia urging them to cast off the authority of the Sháh and unite under the Sulṭán of Turkey as the Caliph of all Islam (i.e. they were promoting Siyyid Jamálu'd-Dín's Pan-Islamic ideas). Their extradition was requested by the Persian authorities, and they were taken as far as Trabizond on the Black Sea before the Sulṭán changed his mind and ordered them to be detained there. When news came of the assassination of Náṣiru'd-Dín Sháh by Mírzá Muḥammad-Riḍáy-i-Kirmání, a disciple of Siyyid Jamálu'd-Dín, the Persian authorities now insisted upon the extradition of these three of his disciples. They were taken to Tabríz and there put to death.

The following dispatch from Henry Longworth (q.v.), British Consul at Trabizond, is here given because it illustrates well the confusion that existed in the minds of many between the Bahá'ís and the Azalís. It would appear that Longworth obtained some idea of the teachings of Bahá'u'lláh from a Bahá'í source and grafted these onto the actions of the Azalís, finally making the whole picture grotesque by stating Siyyid Jamálu'd-Dín to be the leader of the Bábís.*

The following facts may be of some interest if viewed in connection with the murder of Nasr-eddin Shah.

About six months ago the Vali acting on orders from Constantinople retained at Trebizond three individuals who were being extradited to Persia, namely Mirza Hassan Khan, Sheikh Ahmet and Mirza Khan Kermani. The first held the position of Persian Consul at Jeddah, the other passed as a sage, and the third had some connection with the Constantinopolitan Persian news-

* A mistake made by several others including the writer of the leader in the *Morning Post* of 11 May 1896, Major Phillott, the editor of the Persian translation of *Ḥájí Bábá* (see Browne *The Persian Revolution* pp. 62 and 94), and Sir Henry Drummond Wolff. Even more confused was the Belgian Minister, Baron de Beyens, who wrote that 'Mullá Riḍá . . . had been urged on in this crime by Jamálu'd-Dín, an implacable enemy of the Qájárs, by Yaḥyá-Ṣubḥ-i-Azal, a Persian refugee and former leader of the Bábís, and by Mírzá Malkam Khán, former Minister of Persia at London. These three publish in Constantinople, the clandestine newspaper *Qánún* (Law), which is secretly brought into Iran in order to promote revolution there.' (Belgian For. Ministry Archives, Direction Politique Dossier No. 4744, No. 268/65, 12 Aug, 1896; translated from French.)

paper 'Ahter'.They were lodged in a hotel and treated with some consideration though watched by a police officer and a Cavass of the Persian Consulate General until the day before yesterday when they were rather suddenly hurried off to Tabriz via Erzeroum under a strong guard.

It has leaked out that these men belong to the Persian secret sect of Babi, who have of late from the Turkish Capital despatched a number of circulars to their countrymen advocating the union of the Shiites and the Sunnites, a project started by their chief Sheikh Djemal-eddin. Further, that Mirza Reza who as deputed, succeeded in assassinating Nasr-eddin passed through Trebizond and stopped with them three days early in March.

Elated at first at the news of the Shah's death, their spirits have now sadly fallen, expecting as they do no leniency whatever at the hands of their government.

As the doctrines of Babism are not very generally known, I would venture to give here briefly such information on the subject as has been derived by me from a sufficiently reliable source.

The sect is a schism of Mahometanism founded some fifty years ago by Mirza Ali Mahomet. He was a Persian of liberal ideas who embodied in two standard works his sentiments in Arabic, and who termed the new faith 'Bab' or gate, presumably as a sole opening to Paradise. The rapidity with which he made converts alarmed, it would seem, the executive and priesthood of Persia. Hence the massacres from which he himself escaped to die abroad.* His disciples however continued to work secretly, inside as well as outside the state. The principles which were originally progressive became revolutionary. The lamentable event at Tehran shows at least that the prohibition of taking away a man's life is a precept kept in abeyance. The chief aim of Babism is still however the unity of every religion. It advocates therefore toleration of all creeds, abolition of polygamy, emancipation of females, and other reforms in the Mussulman world.[14]

The Upheavals of 1903

During the course of 1903, political agitation against the Prime Minister, Amínu's-Sulṭán, was gathering momentum. He had by this time been in power almost continuously for twelve years,† and by this time had accumulated many enemies. The agitation against him in the north took the form of attacks on foreign institutions such as schools.

In the south of the country there was also much discontent, and it was clear that trouble would sooner or later erupt. Under the aegis of Áqá Najafí (q.v.), when it did erupt the agitation took an anti-Bahá'í direction and there ensued the violent upheavals in Iṣfahán and Yazd (see chapter 27). A more detailed examination of the factors that sparked off this conflagration involves a consideration of the controversial figure, Abu'l-Ḥasan Mírzá, Ḥájí S͟hayk͟hu'r-Ra'ís (q.v.).

Ḥájí S͟hayk͟hu'r-Ra'ís

Ḥájí S͟hayk͟hu'r-Ra'ís was a Qájár prince who, despite his parentage, was one of the leading intellectual figures in the struggle for liberal reform in

* Presumably referring to Bahá'u'lláh: the Báb, of course, was killed in Persia.

† Except for a period Nov. 1896 – July 1898, for part of which Amínu'd-Dawlih was Prime Minister.

Persia during this period. He was also a Bahá'í and had spent several months in the presence of 'Abdu'l-Bahá in 'Akká, although most Persian historians prefer either to ignore or deny this fact. Despite 'Abdu'l-Bahá's injunction that Bahá'ís should not become involved in the political controversies of the period, Ḥájí Shaykhu'r-Ra'ís was too well known as an advocate of liberal reform to be able to withdraw from the scene. 'Abdu'l-Bahá, moreover, urged the Bahá'ís of Persia not to advertise the fact of Ḥájí Shaykhu'r-Ra'ís's adherence to the Bahá'í Faith lest it should cause him trouble. And yet partly due to the actions of the Bahá'ís and partly to Ḥájí Shaykhu'r-Ra'ís's own actions, it soon became notorious that he was a Bahá'í. Thus in 1902 when Ḥájí Shaykhu'r-Ra'ís was living in Shíráz, the British Consular Agent for Shíráz, Ḥaydar-'Alí Khán-i-Navváb, reported (15 January 1902): 'The 'ulamá have decreed Ḥájí Shaykhu'r-Ra'ís to be an infidel [*hukm-i-takfír*] and pronounced his death to be imperative [*vájibu'l-qatl*] because it has been proved to them that he is a Bábí.'[15]

When the Governor of Shíráz was changed and his old enemy Áṣafu'd-Dawlih (q.v.) became the new Governor, it became clear that Ḥájí Shaykhu'r-Ra'ís could not stay in Shíráz. Eventually in August 1902, he set out for Iṣfahán. The 'ulamá of Iṣfahán had been warned of his coming by their colleagues in Shíráz and were opposed to his settling in Iṣfahán. Nevertheless, Ḥájí Shaykhu'r-Ra'ís managed to find a house and began preaching to the people. His eloquence in oratory and his powerful intellect soon drew large crowds to hear him speak,* and foremost at these meetings were the Bahá'ís and in particular two of them, Áqá Muḥammad-Javád-i-Ṣarráf and Mírzá 'Alí Khán-i-Ṣarráf. These proceedings infuriated Áqá Najafí who could brook no competition to his paramount position among the 'ulamá of Iṣfahán and certainly not from a man reputed to be a Bahá'í. Áqá Najafí exerted every effort to have Ḥájí Shaykhu'r-Ra'ís removed from Iṣfahán and eventually succeeded, the latter moving on to Ṭihrán. This was not enough for Áqá Najafí however, and he bided his time waiting for a favourable opportunity to strike back at the Bahá'ís. His chance came when the death occurred of Ḥájí Muḥammad-Ismá'íl, a Bahá'í. Knowing that both Áqá Muḥammad-Javád and Mírzá 'Alí Khán, the two Bahá'ís who had played a prominent role in conducting Ḥájí Shaykhu'r-Ra'ís's meetings, would be present at the funeral, Áqá Najafí instructed his religious students to raid the funeral and conduct the two Bahá'ís to him. The raid succeeded in capturing only one of them, Mírzá Muḥammad-Javád, who was severely beaten, and it was this that caused the Bahá'ís to flock to the Russian Consulate (see pp. 376ff) and thus precipitate the Iṣfahán and indirectly the Yazd upheavals.

* Nicolas states that audiences of 10,000 persons came to hear him preach (*Massacres de Babis* p. 13).

The Shí'ih Mujtahids of Iraq

The most powerful and influential Shí'ih mujtahids resided in the holy cities of Najaf and Karbilá in Iraq, and were thus outside of the direct control of the Persian Government. From this advantageous position they could interfere with the internal affairs of Persia with impunity, and it was they who concerted the general agitation against Amínu's-Sulṭán in 1903. That they were to some extent responsible for pointing it in an anti-Bahá'í direction is clear from the following evidence. When news of the Iṣfahán upheaval first reached the British Minister in Ṭihrán, Hardinge (q.v.), he went to see Amínu's-Sulṭán on 9 June 1903:

> . . . His Highness told me – and he seems to have held the same language to M. Vlassoff* – that these outbreaks were not ordinary or isolated incidents, but were the outcome of an organized movement, whose source was at Kerbela and Nejef, and which he plainly intimated, without saying it in so many words, was encouraged and supported by his political opponents at Tehran. He said that the Shah had lately received a remonstrance from the Chief Priests of the Holy Cities of Turkish Arabia, amongst whom the most influential man at present was one Haji Mirza Sharabiani,† demanding that he should pursue a more Mahommedan policy, protesting against the employment of Europeans (i.e. the Belgians) in the Persian service and against the alleged proposed reorganization of the national finances under European auspices, and declaiming against Babism, and infidelity and heresy in every form.[16]

As has been mentioned above, the 1903 disturbances that were directed against the Prime Minister Amínu's-Sulṭán were in the first instance at the expense of foreign institutions, since one of the main grievances against the Government was the feeling that Persia was being sold out to the foreigners in order that the Sháh and the Prime Minister could feather their own nests. However, attacks on foreigners proved to be too uncomfortable a course of action. Foreign Governments were strong, Persia was weak, and there was the ever-present threat that such disturbances might precipitate a Russian invasion from the north.

Thus on 9 July 1903, when Hardinge went to see Amínu's-Sulṭán, the latter, having stated that the instigation of the anti-Bahá'í disturbances had been traced conclusively to Áqá Najafí (see pp. 395–6), went on to speak of the role of the mujtahids in Iraq:

> He [Amínu's-Sulṭán] went on to inform me that telegrams had just been received by the Shah from the four chief Mujteheds of Kerbela and Nejef, disavowing the anti-Christian and anti-European agitation at Tabriz, but approving the executions of Babi heretics at Isfahan and Yezd and expressing a hope that the Persian Government would encourage their repetition in other cities. He regarded the repudiation by Kerbela of the

* P. M. Vlassov (q.v.), Russian Minister.

† Ḥájí Mírzá Muḥammad-i-Sharabíyání (*c.* 1834–1904), one of a group of powerful Shí'ih mujtahids at Najaf.

proceedings of the Tabriz Ulema as very satisfactory, since attacks upon Christian schools and officials might have graver results than a mere outcry against Babism.[17]

When moves were afoot to remove Áqá Najafí from Iṣfahán, moreover, (see p. 399) the mujtahids in Najaf and Karbilá intervened with the Persian Government on his behalf and expressed their approval of his action. When, in early July 1903, Mírzá Muḥammad-Ḥasan Muḥsin, Dragoman of the British Consulate in Baghdád, called on Ḥájí Mírzá Ḥusayn ibn-i-Mírzá Khalíl,* one of the leading mujtahids of Najaf, he heard a full account of the Iṣfahán upheaval after which Ḥájí Mírzá Ḥusayn said:

The Persian Government now tried to bring some punishment on Agha Nejefi, when he sent several telegrams to the Mujtahids of Nejef explaining to them all the particulars relating to the Babi question, and lastly requested them to help and protect his person.

Haji Mirza Husein told me that they sent a telegram yesterday to the Persian Prime Minister, telling him that Agha Nejefi's action in the matter of the Babis was greatly approved and that he is hereby informed of his obligation to carry out similar instances in all parts of Persia i.e. to turn out all the Babis: put them under certain restrictions and prevent the sale of wine and other unlawful trades. Agha Nejefi must not in any way be interfered with as his action was just and commendable. This is roughly the substance of the telegram which the Mujtahids recently sent to Persia.[18]

The Constitutional Upheaval, 1905–9

Although, as has been stated at the beginning of this chapter, the Bahá'ís' direct involvement in the affairs of the Constitutional Movement was slight, there were many in Europe who believed that the extent of their influence was great. In an article called 'Le Bâbysme, levain des Révolutions en Perse' in *A Travers le Monde* in 1905, Jules Brocherel put forward this view, his concluding paragraph being: 'Henceforth, in Persia, anyone who is cultured, independent, open to the innovations of modern times, can only be a Bábí. At the present time, the partisans of the Sháh are still the masters, because they can still despoil and massacre the feeble as they please. But the law of revenge is not a long way off, and when it comes, it will be a serious matter in Iran.'[19]

One who went even further than the above article was Bernard Temple, a journalist with the Indian Press. In a paper presented before the Royal Society of Arts in 1910 (with Prof. E. G. Browne in the chair), Mr Temple argued for the Bahá'í Faith being the source of the Constitutional Movement in Persia and of the awakening in the Near East in general:

'Can anyone suppose it to be a mere coincidence that in Persia and Turkey the beginnings of religious reformation, as represented by Bahaism,

* Ḥájí Mírzá Ḥusayn-i-Khalílí (*c.* 1821–1908), one of a group of powerful Shí'ih mujtahids at Najaf.

have been followed by the first steps in political reformation, and that the wafting of Bahai ideas to Egypt, India, Arabia, Morocco and Algeria is being accompanied by new forms of Oriental unrest? Or can anyone believe that the influence of this regenerative spirit will carry no further than that?'[20]

The correspondent of *The Times* writing from Rasht on 18 March 1909, at the beginning of the final assault that toppled Muḥammad-'Alí Sháh, evidently considered that the Bábís were a prominent force in the struggle.* He wrote:

> It may be that the real explanation of this Caucasian immigration is that given me from a source likely to have accurate information. Every one interested in Persia has heard of the religious movement known as 'Babism', which was started in the middle of the last century. As it preaches anti-despotism and anti-clericalism it was put down by the Shah Nasr-ed-Din. Since that date – although until recently illegal and practised in secret – Babism has spread and flourished. Those who are in a position to judge estimate the present proportion of Babis in the population of Persia at from 10 to 30 per cent. I have, indeed, heard Persians estimate it as high as 50 per cent. Should the present revolutionary movement be successful . . . and should it really have Babism at its back, its results may be more far-reaching than is at present realized. Should it be found to aim not only at a change in the whole system and machinery of government, but at the renunciation of Shiah Mohammedanism in favour of the mystical doctrines of the Babis, the struggle may become embittered by an outburst of orthodox fanaticism. It is true that many of the Ulema are said to be secretly inclined to Babism; but the majority, even among those who now support the Nationalist Movement, would be driven into the arms of the Shah if its ulterior aim should turn out to be heretical, and, what is worse, anti-clerical.†[21]

An alternative opinion was expressed by a writer identified as 'X' in *Revue du Monde Musulman*[22] in 1914, who pointed out that it was the followers of Mírzá Yaḥyá (Ṣubḥ-i-Azal) who were the leaders of the Revolutionary Movement and that the Bahá'ís had little to do with it.‡

In any case, the Bahá'ís derived little benefit from the Constitutional Movement. When the Constitution itself was drafted it did not safeguard their rights, and when the electoral laws were introduced in 1906 and 1909

* Possibly as a result of this article in *The Times*, the matter was raised in the House of Commons on 20 April 1909, when a Member of Parliament, Mr Rees, asked 'whether the Foreign Office has any information to the effect that the Parliamentarians in Persia are acting in concert with the Babis or that there is any connection between the two movements?' The reply from Mr McKinnon Wood, the Parliamentary Under-Secretary of State for Foreign Affairs, was as follows: 'I have received no information as to the attitude of the Babis in connection with the Nationalist movement in Persia.' (*Hansard* (House of Commons) 20 Apr. 1909, p. 1379)

† Interestingly, precisely the same point was made by 'Abdu'l-Bahá (and quoted in Browne, *The Persian Revolution*, pp. 424–5, divergent view No. 1).

‡ A person identified as 'G.H.' in an article entitled 'L'Influence de Babisme' (see Bibliography) points out that the majority of Bábís were now Bahá'ís and that one of the tenets of the Bahá'ís was obedience to the Government.

there were specific provisions that prevented them from even being able to vote. In Article 5 of the Electoral Law of 1 July 1909, for example, 'Persons whose apostasy from the orthodox religion of Islam has been established in the presence of a duly qualified representative of the Holy Law' are absolutely disqualified from electoral functions, being thus classed together with fraudulent bankrupts, murderers, thieves and women.

Not only did the Constitutional Movement fail to bring the Bahá'ís any benefit, but in the ensuing upheavals the Bahá'ís inevitably suffered. As referred to by 'Abdu'l-Bahá in the letter quoted at the beginning of this chapter, the Bahá'ís became the butt of all sorts of false accusations and abuses. Thus when in 1908–9 the Royalist forces attacked Tabríz, which was in the hands of the Constitutionalists, they informed their troops that the inhabitants of Tabríz had all become Bábís and so it was a religious duty to fight against them. A. C. Wratislaw (q.v.), then Consul in Tabríz, wrote:

> One prisoner was taken, and from him confirmation was received of the rumour that the Royalist officers had circulated amongst their men the disgusting calumny that the inhabitants of Tabriz had all turned Babis – *i.e.*, heretics to Islam, – so that fighting against them might be looked on as a religious duty. After the victory this unfortunate was hustled into the presence of Sattar Khan [the Constitutionalist leader], who sat majestically smoking a water-pipe, with his elated followers around him. The prisoner, in the centre of the circle, gyrated on his axis, salaaming abjectly to each of his captors and babbling, 'I too am a Babi, gentlemen; I too am a Babi.'[23]

In April 1907, shortly after the signing of the Constitution, Karbilá'í Ṣádiq, a Bahá'í of Tabríz, fell a victim to the intrigues of some of those who were opposed to the reforms. 'A.L.C.'* recorded in the *Revue du Monde Musulman*:

> One understands the lively interest with which the *Revue* has followed the progress of the Persian Revolution. One will understand its regrets at the actions by which the reactionary parties, the *ancien régime*, seek to hold back the liberation of the Persian people, by [fomenting] disorder.
>
> Here are some examples: An *'aṭṭár*, a perfumer, of the Charandáb quarter of Tabríz, Karbilá'í Ṣádiq, who passed for a Bábí, was insulted almost every day by his neighbour, the baker Mas͟hhadí Ḥasan. On 25 April last, the latter, having warned another neighbour, a grocer, to disappear, arrived at half past seven in the evening in front of the perfumer's shop. He was accompanied by his brother-in-law K͟halíl, his brother, a servant and a farrás͟h. All five set about insulting Karbilá'í Ṣádiq, who was serving a customer.
>
> When Ṣádiq pleaded with them to leave him in peace, they fell upon him, pulling him out of his shop, and, after having knocked him down and beaten him cruelly, crushed his head with a rock.
>
> The Anjuman and the Governor, when informed, declared themselves powerless to do anything.
>
> Such violence calls for more, which itself has many repercussions.
>
> So the Bábís are felled in the streets of Tabríz, the mujtahids have been expelled

* Probably denotes Alfred Le Chatelier (q.v.).

from the town. But the National Assembly of Ṭihrán, fearing that they would go to plot intrigues at Najaf and Karbilá, have written to the Anjuman to make every effort to make them return.[24]

The Nayríz Upheavals of 1909

Following Muḥammad-'Alí Sháh's *coup d'état* in June 1908 and his abolition of the Constitution, it looked for a time as though he would be completely successful in his aims. Only Tabríz defied the Sháh, and that city was soon besieged and in a desperate plight. During the first few months of 1909 however, the Constitutionalist forces began to counter-attack. The two most effective centres of resistance to the Sháh were Rasht and Iṣfahán, and it was from these two places that the forces set out which were eventually to enter Ṭihrán and depose the Sháh. In other places, riots and disturbances occurred which were more probably incited by town ruffians looking for an opportunity to plunder. As usual when there were disturbances, the Bahá'ís suffered.

In southern Persia, one of those who took up the cause of the Constitution was Siyyid 'Abdu'l-Ḥusayn-i-Lárí. One of his lieutenants, a renegade named Shaykh Zakaríyyá, advanced on Nayríz and took the town with but little resistance. He then turned on the Bahá'ís of the town and massacred 19 of them, many others being forced to flee while their homes were looted. Communications were so bad due to the anarchy prevelant throughout the country at this time, that little news of this atrocity arrived even at Shíráz. J. H. Bill, Acting British Consul, in the Consular Report for the week ending 31 March 1909, only stated: 'He [Shaykh Zakaríyyá] is said to have burnt two Babis alive at Niriz.'[25]

Disturbances at Kirmánsháh

At Kirmánsháh generalized rioting occurred, directed particularly at the Jews of the city. Captain Haworth (q.v.), British Consul at Kirmánsháh, reported on 11 April 1909: 'On the 7th instant, there was a further rumour that an attack was to be made on the Jews, this time, on their lives not their property. A large number of the more important Jews in Kermanshah, and in Hamadan also, are Babis. In returning the stolen goods, amongst other things, a picture of the Bab appeared, and it was this that appears to have excited some of the Hooligans in the bazaar.'[26]

The Pamphlet to the King

In April 1911, Sir George Barclay (q.v.), the British Minister in Ṭihrán, was asked by the Foreign Office for a report on the Bahá'í movement. The cause of this enquiry was the receipt by King George V of some pamphlets on the Bahá'í movement from the Bahá'ís of London. In view of the unsettled political state of Persia, the King's private secretary, Sir Frederick Ponsonby (q.v.), wrote to the India Office asking whether there would be any objection to the King acknowledging these pamphlets. 'Of course a mere acknowledgement would not commit His Majesty to anything but even such an acknowledgement may when published be misinterpreted.'[27] The India Office sent the letter on to the Foreign Office. From the Foreign Office, Louis Mallet (q.v.) wrote to Ponsonby on 21 April 1911:

The movement in question, which is a development of Babism, may be harmless enough in itself as a religious development but its history shows that neither under its religious nor under its political aspect has it ever been regarded with favour by the Turkish or the Persian Government. There is always, as you say, a possibility that an acknowledgment of receipt sent in such circumstances may be interpreted as an encouragement and so referred to in some speech or written publication and as in the present instance, any supposed encouragement might cause annoyance in Turkey and in Persia, it would appear preferable that none should be sent.[28]

But a request was also sent to Sir George Barclay and Sir Gerard Lowther (q.v.), Ministers in Ṭihrán and Constantinople respectively, to supply further information. Sir Gerard's reply was: 'The Bahais are of no political importance in Turkey, and there is no reason to suppose that they have any adherents in this country other than Persians.

'. . . Any recognition of them would probably attract more attention in English religious circles than in Turkish political ones.'[29]

Sir George Barclay's reply dated 9 June 1911 stated:

. . . I find myself in some difficulty owing to the great obscurity which enshrouds the activity of the followers of the Bahai sect in Persia at the present time . . .

Those who have studied the question and are competent to form an opinion, are not at one as to the measure of influence exercised by the Babis, in bringing about the Nationalist movement in Persia. Professor Browne at any rate is not prepared to admit that their influence in the matter was great (see Journal of the Royal Society of Arts No. 3001 Volume LVIII. May 27 1910 page 663).

On the other hand, Mr Bernard Temple, an earnest investigator of the religions and philosophic problems of the East, who, while in Persia a short time ago, devoted much time to the study of Bahaism, seems to consider that this development of Babism has raised in Islam, 'thanks to the fineness and freshness of Persian thought, a regenerative influence of almost incalculable energy' (see Journal above referred to).

It is, however, at present impossible to express any definite opinion as to the spread of Babism (or Bahaism) in Persia or of the measure of influence exercised by the teachings of Beha Ullah or his successor Abbas Effendi upon those, who, by their political agitation from 1906 onwards, brought about the present constitutional development of Persia, because, as I have already pointed out, the Behais (with very few exceptions) do not openly avow their apostasy for fear of persecution by the Moslem clergy.

Though the political enemies of the Constitutional regime are very fond of describing it as the work of Babis, and even declaring that the majority of the deputies are of that persuasion, there is probably very little foundation for this accusation, and, at any rate in outward form, the Persian Mejliss is eminently orthodox and every form of respect to the National religion i.e. – Islam of the Shiah sect – is observed with scrupulous care. According to the Constitution the Sovereign when taking the Oath has to use the following formula: 'I will strive zealously to propagate the sect of the 12 Imams of the Shiah religion'.

Bahaism therefore is still distinctly a heresy in Persia – a heresy observed secretly by its followers, whose numbers it is quite impossible even approximately to estimate. Though persecutions have not been resorted to during the last few years, there was a period not long ago when the Shiah Ulema caused the massacre of hundreds of them at Isfahan and at Yezd and a repetition of these atrocities may yet occur.[30]

In any event, these dispatches arrived too late for any acknowledgement of the pamphlets to be sent.*

References

1. Browne *The Persian Revolution* pp. 428–9
2. *The Times* 25 June 1891, p. 5, col. 4
3. Balloy to Ribot No. 20, 14 May 1891: MAE Sér. Corr. Polit (trans. from French)
4. Browne *Materials* pp. 295–6
5. Kennedy to Salisbury No. 147, 11 June 1891: FO 60 523
6. Lascelles to Salisbury No. 14, 19 Jan. 1892: FO 60 594. See also Keddie *Sayyid Jamál ad-Dín al-Afghání* pp. 424–4
7. Lascelles to Salisbury No. 35, 16 Feb. 1892: FO 539 56
8. Churchill's memo enclosed with 7 *supra*. The full text of the letter of the Bahá'ís of Bombay is in FO 248 553
9. *The Times* 2 May 1896, p. 9, col. 1
10. *The Times* 2 May 1896, p. 8, col. 1
11. *The Times* 2 May 1896, quoted in FO 60 578
12. *The Times* 6 May 1896, p. 4
13. Balloy to Hanotaux, exact date not clear, June 1896: MAE Sér. Corr. Polit. (trans. from French)
14. Longworth to Sir Philip Currie at Istanbul No. 24, 15 May 1896, copy sent to Sir Mortimer Durand at Ṭihrán: FO 248 641
15. Ḥaydar-'Alí Khán's report of 15 Jan. 1902: FO 248 773 (trans. from Persian)
16. Hardinge to Lansdowne No. 85, 10 June 1903: FO 60 665
17. Hardinge to Lansdowne No. 102, 9 July 1903: FO 60 666
18. Muḥammad-Ḥasan Muḥsin to Newmarch, 13 July 1903, enclosed in Newmarch to Hardinge, 14 July 1903: FO 248 802
19. Brocherel 'Le Bâbysme, levain des Révolutions en Perse' pp. 134–5 (trans. from French)
20. Temple 'Persia and the Regeneration of Islam' p. 656 (this paper was read at the 20th ordinary meeting of the Roy. Soc. of Arts, 25 May 1910)
21. *The Times* 30 Mar. 1909, p. 4, col. 6

* Another point of interest is that although both Sir George Barclay and Sir Gerard Lowther refer to Prof. Browne in their replies, relations between the Foreign Office and Prof. Browne were so bad at this time that Mr Louis Mallet refused to countenance any contact being made with Browne for the purposes of acquiring further information about the Bahá'ís, and instructed that the passage referring to Browne be deleted from Lowther's dispatch when it was forwarded to Sir Frederick Ponsonby.

22. X 'La Situation Politique de la Perse' p. 254
23. Wratislaw *A Consul in the East* p. 246
24. A.L.C. 'La Révolution Persane' pp. 310–11 (trans. from French)
25. Bill, Shíráz News for week ending 31 Mar. 1909: FO 248 972
26. Haworth to Barclay No. 8C, 11 Apr. 1909: FO 248 968
27. Ponsonby to India Office 2 Apr. 1911, forwarded to For. Off. 11 Apr. 1911, File 13640: FO 371 1189
28. Mallet to Ponsonby 21 Apr. 1911, File 13640: FO 371 1189
29. Lowther to Sir Edward Grey 13 May 1911, File 19378: FO 371 1189
30. Barclay to Sir Edward Grey 9 June 1911, File 25675: FO 371 1189

TWENTY-SEVEN

The Upheavals of 1903

By 1903, the reactionary Prime Minister, Amínu's-Sulṭán, had been in office for over a decade. Throughout the country many diverse elements were beginning to react militantly against his rule. Not for the first time, the Bahá'ís came into the cross-fire between the opposing political forces, and agitation against them was stirred up to further personal and political ends. This time, however, the persecutions in Yazd reached horrifying proportions which had not been seen since the aftermath of the attempt on the life of the Shāh in 1852.

For a consideration of the causes and political significance of these disturbances as well as the role of the Shí'ih clergy see p. 363ff. The present chapter will be confined to a narrative of the principal events.

Rasht

The first disturbances against the Bahá'ís in this year occurred in Rasht. The cause of this episode was a photograph that the Bahá'í community of Rasht had had taken at a meeting.

The British Consul at Rasht, Alfred Churchill,* reported the first phase of this episode in a dispatch dated 8 May 1903 to Sir Arthur Hardinge (q.v.), the British Minister at Ṭihrán.

> I have the honour to report that a disturbance took place on Sunday last, the 3rd instant, between a Babi jeweller and some Mussulmans.
>
> The indirect cause of this disturbance was a photograph of a section of the Rasht Babi community which through the bad faith of a photographer has been circulating throughout the town. Two individuals passing by the jeweller's shop in the Bazaar made some jocular remarks in regard to this photograph, whereupon the owner of the shop† is reported to have roared out that he was a Babi and would allow no one to insult his religion.
>
> This resulted in a dispute followed by a

* Alfred Churchill does not appear to have been officially recognized as Consul at Rasht, however, and his name does not appear in the Foreign Office lists.

† The shop belonged to two brothers, Mashhadí Taqí and Mashhadí Riḍá, who were goldsmiths.

general mêlée in which students from a neighbouring college took part. No great harm however appears to have been done, the combatants, Gileks* inordinately afflicted with cacoëthes loquendi,† having no doubt exhausted themselves during the preliminary clamour.

The Governor General‡ sent for the Babi and his brother and detained them until the next day in order to keep them out of harm's way. On Monday the jeweller opened his shop and has not been molested in any way since.

A copy of the photograph found its way into the hands of Haji Hummami,§ one of the principal and perhaps the most learned of the Resht Ulema, who was astounded to see that a Syed,‖ his trusted henchman and Mutevalli [custodian] of a Saint's tomb near Sangar, was one of the group of Babis. The Syed had timely warning and has prudently kept out of the way of the Mujtehed who threatens to beat him severely. I am told that the Haji and others of the Ulema have decreed that the Syed and other Babis must divorce their Mussulman wives but that the Nasres Saltaneh has intimated to them that no interference will be allowed as it is the desire of H.M. the Shah that religion should be free. I am also told that the Nasres Saltaneh has sent for a further detachment of one hundred soldiers who are to come from Kasvin [Qasvín] and I may mention that since last Sunday the small force stationed at Resht has been served with ball cartridges.

There has been some talk on the part of the Mollahs of boycotting the Babis, who it was proposed, should not be allowed to enter the public baths but I trust that the firm and sympathetic attitude of the Governor General will prevent the execution of any plans which the Mollahs may have formed with the object of creating disturbance at the expense of the community at Resht.

I am informed that the Babis here amount to about one thousand persons of both sexes including at least one Greek and some Armenians.[1]

Then, a few days later, on 10 May 1903, Churchill reported:

With reference to my despatch No. 22 of the 8th instant, I have the honour to report a further incident created by the demise of a Babi mason¶ yesterday.

The relatives proposed the customary obsequies according to Mussulman rites but the arrival of the usual paraphernalia in the shape of bier and wooden sweetmeat trays caused some excitement in the neighbourhood which speedily resulted in the gathering of a large mob from all parts of the town.

A disturbance being feared, the Governor General requested the Shariat Madar⁑ to arrange matters. The Mujtehed did so in a very commendable manner as, although the crowd remained in the vicinity of the house during the whole of the day, no breach of the peace occurred.

During the night the corpse was secretly taken in the direction of the Boosar Toll Station by some soldiers, farrashes and two servants of the Shariat Madar, who dug a

* peasants of Gílán

† a mania for speech

‡ Muḥammad-Valí Khán, the Naṣru's-Salṭanih (q.v.)

§ Mullá Muḥammad, known as Ḥájí Khummámí, the Shaykhu'l-Islám.

‖ This man's name was Siyyid Ḥusayn; he was from Mázindarán and was entrusted with the care of much of the waqf properties in the Rasht area. According to 'Amídu'l-Aṭibbá's history of the Bahá'í Faith in Rasht, Ḥájí Khummámí instructed one of his pupils to strike Siyyid Ḥusayn's turban from his head and to beat him severely. Thereafter, he was expelled from Rasht.

¶ His name was Ustád Háshim-i-Banná of Qazvín.

⁑ Shaykh Mihdí, the Sharí'at-Madár

grave and interred the body.

Nothing further of importance has occurred but there can be no doubt that the people are excited. My Russian colleague is of opinion that the rise of prices has to a great extent irritated the lower classes and points out the recent disturbances at Meshed due to the same cause.

It is certain that the dearness of the common necessities of life is much felt at Resht and, with your Excellency's permission, I will on a future occasion revert to the question.[2]

On 15 May 1903, Churchill reported:

With reference to my despatch No. 24 dated the 10th instant, I have the honour to further report that a number of malefactors exhumed and mutilated the body of the Babi mason, which they subsequently proceeded to burn with naptha.

For this outrage many arrests were made and two rogues lost an auricle apiece besides being sticked. The executioner was also bastinadoed for being implicated as were likewise the other persons who had been arrested.

A servant of the Mujtehed Haji Hummami was arrested in connection with this outrage and was, I understand, well sticked but he was released in consequence of the threatening proceedings of the Haji in his mosque. The Mujtehed stopped the 'Rozeh'* which was being held and sent for the religious students for the purpose, it is said, of releasing his servant by force.

The release of this man, however, smoothed matters over for the time being but I fear that at the present juncture it will require little to cause an explosion if the Mollahs do not keep quiet.

It is generally suspected that the Nasres Saltaneh is himself a Babi. Whether this is the case or not there can be no doubt that he is helping them in every way.[3]

On 16 May 1903, Churchill sent a dispatch in the care of Major Douglas† to Sir Arthur Hardinge.

I am taking advantage of the departure of Major Douglas to communicate to your Excellency the latest news respecting the Babi agitation, which is if anything more acute, owing to an obscure placard discovered this morning on the door of the Mujtehed Haji Hummami.

This placard, purporting to have been written by a Babi, heaped the foulest abuse on Haji Hummami and his female relatives. The Ulema were held up to contempt for being powerless and Syed Assadullah, the head of the Transport Company, the Ferrash Bashi and Haji Mirza Mohamed Arbabi were praised as being the high protectors of Babis and members of the glorious community.

It requires little perspicacity to recognise that the offending document was not composed by a Babi but by some evil-disposed person‡ anxious to cause trouble. The Mollahs however insist that it was the work of the Babis and a meeting took place in the house of Haji Hummami this morning.

The wildest rumours are current throughout the town. The latest information I have is that two of the principal Babis were called to Government House this afternoon and that a Jew who has in turn been Mussulman,

* Rawḍih

† Douglas, Maj. James Archibald, appointed Military Attaché to the Ṭihrán Legation, 1 Jan. 1903.

‡ Amidu'l-Aṭibbá in his narrative history of the Bahá'í Faith in Rasht also states that the placard was concocted by some evil-disposed Muslims, and made to look as though it was from the Bahá'ís. He adds that Ḥájí Khummámí was not aware of this, however.

Babi and then Mussulman again was sticked this afternoon by order of the Nasres Saltaneh in connection with the placard incident. This shows that the Nasres Saltaneh's hand has been forced to a certain extent but it is difficult to obtain reliable information.

Some days ago a dervish was arrested for reviling Babis in the Bazaars. The Governor General caused his head to be shaved and expelled him from the town. This gives rise to much talk to the effect that dervishes singing in praise of Ali and true-believers who dig up the corpse of a renegade Mussulman are sticked, shaved and have their ears cut off.

I am told that a telegraphic petition complaining of the conduct of the Governor General has been sent to Menjil for despatch to Tehran from the Telegraph office there.

I will not fail to communicate to your Excellency any further occurrences which may take place.[4]

On 19 May, Churchill reported:

In continuation of my despatch No. 28 of the 16th instant, I have the honour to report that the Vezir Nizam, who arrived from Europe last week, has not yet left for Tehran having been instructed to remain at Resht to cooperate with the Governor General so long as the agitation against the Babis continues.

Two prominent Babis, the Ebtehaj ol Mulk and the Mudabber el Memalek,* left Resht on the 17th instant and matters have since taken a more favourable aspect giving rise to the hope that the agitation will gradually subside before more harm results.

The best remedy would be a heavy fall of rain which would be of great benefit to the crops and would at the same time prevent people gathering at the numerous rozeh khanehs and taziehs† which are being held in all parts of the town as is customary here.[5]

And so the agitation died away gradually, but the courage and efficiency of Naṣru's-Salṭanih was not rewarded. Indeed a short while later he was removed from his Governorship and left Rasht on 1 June 1903.[6]

Iṣfahán

At Iṣfahán, the notorious Áqá Najafí (Shaykh Muḥammad-Taqí, q.v., see fig. 44) was once again fomenting trouble for the Bahá'ís. In the first place, as described on p. 364, he moved against two Bahá'ís who had shown themselves to be enthusiastic supporters of Ḥájí Shaykhu'r-Ra'ís. Even then, he did not, initially, attack these two for being Bahá'ís but on a trumped-up charge of imbibing alcoholic drinks. There were rumours, however, in the town that this was but the opening blast of a campaign against the Bahá'ís, and when a crowd of them took sanctuary at the Russian Consulate, a mob took to the streets, pillaging their houses. The Rasht episode was hardly over before Dr Aganoor (q.v.), the British Acting Consul, telegraphed from Iṣfahán on 29 May 1903:

* Mírzá Ibráhím Khán, Ibtiháju'l-Mulk and Mírzá Ghulám-'Alí Khán, Mudabbiru'l-Mamálik.
† Recitals and passion-plays in honour of the martyrdom of the Imám Ḥusayn.

Owing to Agha Nedjefi having caused a Saraf* supposed to be a Babi to be beaten severely some two hundred of the sect have been at the Russian Consulate the last few days for protection and as a protest. Prince has given a writing assuring their safety and they are now likely to go back to their houses.[7]

The following day, 30 May 1903, Aganoor telegraphed:

Yesterday afternoon a concocted telegram purporting to be from the Atabeg to Aga Nedjifi giving latter full power over Mussulmans in religious matters was promulgated. As result some 4 or 5 thousand people collected before Russian Consulate threatening to forcibly take away those who had taken refuge there. Aga Nedjifi had to go personally and send crowd away. One man is reported to have been killed. The refugees in the Consulate have gone to their homes to-day on the prince's written assurance. Aga Nedjifi this afternoon preached in Mosque against ill-treating the sect and demonstrating against foreign consuls.[8]

A few days later, on 4 June 1903, Aganoor reported that the mob had killed two brothers: 'Two brothers well known merchants were killed today as Babis by the mob and their corpses burned with petroleum in the public squares by order of a second rate Mollah.'[9]

As soon as this telegram reached him, Hardinge responded by telegraphing to Aganoor instructing him to deliver the following message to Ẓillu's-Sulṭán: 'I have heard with deep regret of the murder in Isfahan of two Babi merchants by a fanatical mob, and I feel sure that Your Imperial Highness has taken prompt measures for the punishment of an outrage which if unrepressed might lead to serious disturbances.[10]

Ẓillu's-Sulṭán's response was notified to Hardinge by telegram from Aganoor on 5 June. 'Prince has sent me following message: H.E. the Minister knows well that I have not got any power at all and from the Govt. in Tehran I do not get any assistance or influence. With twenty five Cossacks and 200 soldiers how can I take any measures against the doings of Aga Nedjifi who you know is so powerful and this affair is not a small affair. It is the duty of Govt. to take special measures against their doings. I am ready to do what they will order me to do.'[11]

Dr Aganoor described these events in more detail in a dispatch dated 6 June 1903:

I have the honour to report that for some time past the Ulema of Isfahan, it would appear, had in their inner Counsels, been planning a crusade against Babis. On Saturday the 23rd ult. the students of Aga Nedjifi, under instructions from the latter seized Mahomed Javad, a saraf – supposed to be a Babi – while attending a funeral.† They took him before the Aga where he was formally charged with having been drunk (a year previously, it is said!). He was not accused there of being a Babi which was

* banker or money-changer

† This was the funeral of Ḥájí Muḥammad-Ismá'il.

however the real cause of his arrest and punishment. For the ostensible charge of having taken strong drink, he was ordered to be beaten and it was with some difficulty he got clear of his persecutors, and escaping hid himself in a corner of the Musjid-i-Shah until the crowd dispersed. Another man of independent means (Mirza Ally Khan*) was also wanted by the Aga, but he escaped. Both these men then went to the Russian Consulate for protection. They were followed by some 200 of their sect, who at first went there from fear, but soon assumed an aggressive attitude, protesting against the treatment of the sect and demanding their recognition. Telegraphic petitions were sent to the Shah. The Russian Acting Consul, M. Baronowsky, through the Persian Moonshee of the Consulate encouraged them and the number of the refugees at the Consulate increased. It is not known what replies came from Tehran, but it would appear, they were not very strongly favourable to the Babis. The Prince gave a written assurance, to M. Baronowsky, of their safety, but this not satisfying the refugees they would not leave the Consulate. On the afternoon of the 28th ult. the false telegram reported in my telegram No. 23 of the 29th ult. being placarded all over the town, a large mob collected before the Russian Consulate, used abusive language, and threatened to enter and kill the refugees. M. Baronowsky was at the time in Julfa, and on his return to the town about sunset, finding he could not gain entrance into his Consulate went instead to the Prince at the palace. The latter sent to Aga Nedjify, who went out and got the mob to disperse. M. Baronowsky was at the palace for some three hours, and was, after the crowd dispersed, escorted to the Consulate, in the company of Prince Bahram Mirza and the Foreign Office agent. I am not aware of what exactly passed at the Palace, or what instructions M. Baronowsky had received from his Legation, but during the night and the following morning, he sent them all away telling them he could not do anything more for them. When the crowd was around the Consulate an old Seyyed Babi was caught and while being taken to the Musjid-i-Shah, so ill-used that he died.† Several others were badly knocked about.

Mahomed Javad and Mirza Ally Khan were taken to the Palace, for greater security, and from there they have since left for Tehran, I understand.

For the next few days the excitement continued more or less and several people whether Babis or otherwise, who happened to have personal enemies, were charged with being Babis and more or less ill-treated.

Then on the 3rd inst. Haji Mahomed Husein, Khayat and Haji Mahomed Hadi, Khayat, two brothers,‡ and well-to-do merchants were called before Seyyed Abool Khaussem, Zinjanee,§ a second rate mollah of no standing, and charged with being Babis, were practically handed over to the mob, who killed them in a brutal manner, mutilated them, dragged them along the bazaars and finally poured petroleum on them and set them on fire. The action of this Mollah had been previously sanctioned by Aga Nedjify, on whom the real responsi-

* These two men, Áqá Muḥammad-Javád-i-Ṣarráf and Mírzá 'Alí Khán, had been in constant attendance on Ḥájí Shaykhu'r-Ra'ís during his stay in Iṣfahán. See p. 364

† His name was Siyyid Abu'l-Qásim-i-Márnání. He was more than ninety years old at the time.

‡ According to a manuscript history of the Bahá'í Faith in Iṣfahán prepared for Fáḍil-i-Mázindarání, and also *Ḥayát-i-Ḥaḍrat-i-'Abdu'l-Bahá* by Muḥammad-'Alí Fayḍí (p. 120), these two brothers were Azalís who had never openly acknowledged their adherence to any religion other than Islam and had always carried out the religious ordinances of Islam most dutifully. This would tend to add weight to the idea put forward by Aganoor that the killing of these two was strongly motivated by financial considerations.

§ Siyyid Abu'l-Qásim-i-Zanjání

bility rests. It is also known that Seyyed Abool Khaussem owed the two merchants a sum of thirteen hundred tomans, which probably explains his religious zeal.

The excitement has subsided outwardly but I have reason to believe that the Mollahs while pleased with what they have done, feel that they have not done enough and are quietly planning to deal with some influential personages. They are at the same time watching to see the effect of what they have done, in Tehran, that is to say in what manner the Persian Government will look on the question and on their doings.[12]

There is also in the British Foreign Office records an unsigned letter from Iṣfahán dated 2 June 1903, which gives an account of this episode:

Last week there was considerable excitement amongst the Babis owing to the punishment of one by Aga Nejafi, ostensibly for being a wine bibber, but the true reason was the man's faith and the fact that he possessed unorthodox literature.

A rumour quickly spread that a massacre of Babis was imminent, which caused great consternation amongst the sect.

The Russian Consul, no doubt imbued with political ambitions, was illadvised enough to offer protection to all comers and soon had the consulate occupied by some 600 refugees. Having found so powerful a champion it seemed at first that both the sect and its protector had scored heavily especially in view of a telegram from the central government granting liberty of religious thought provided all Babis wore some distinguishing sign, but they had yet to reckon with the fanatical clergy.

The consulate was surrounded by an infuriated mob which threatened to wreck the place, ammunition was served out to the cossack and native guards but before any violence was attempted M. Baronowsky abandoned his post, and secretly fled to the Palace where he spent the night under the Zil's protection. In the meantime His Highness sent for Aga Nejafi from whom he obtained a writing holding himself responsible for all consequences. Bahram Mirza and some Palace officials then proceeded to the Russian Consulate with the object of extricating the Babis. This was eventually accomplished, but not without some damage to the refugees, four of whom are said to have been killed and many badly wounded. Since then the head of the sect was called by the Zill who handed him over to Aga Nejafi, and as the unfortunate man is now missing it is believed that he must have tasted the fatal cup of coffee.

Many who exercised their faith in secret have now disclosed their identity and what first promised to be a victory has thus been turned into an ignominious defeat, both for the cause and its champion. European prestige as a whole and Russian in particular has suffered a blow and H.R.H. the Zil es Sultan has not been long in making the fact known. In case of further disturbances a hundred soldiers have been held in readiness at the Palace for the last few days, but things are quiet again and promise to remain so.[13]

Rev. Charles Stileman (q.v.), the Secretary of the Church Missionary Society Mission in Persia and a resident of Julfá, Iṣfahán, sent the following report to his society on 30 May 1903:

There has this week been a religious outbreak against the Babis in Isfahan. Some two hundred of them took refuge at the Russian Consulate (the British Consul General is on his way to England). Some 5000 Muhammadans assembled outside the Russian Consulate and demanded that the Babis should be given up to them. It was believed that the Shah had telegraphed to the chief Mujtahid giving him a free hand to do what he liked with the Babis. This was of course false, but the mob believed it to be true till the Mujtahid went in person and told them to disperse, assuring them that he had no authority from the Shah to act in the matter. It is difficult to learn the exact truth, but I believe the above to be a true account of what happened. Several who are known to us took refuge at the Russian Consulate, and I fear some of the Babis have been very severely beaten. Some are reported to have been killed. We are praying that this outbreak may be over-ruled and may tend to a greater measure of Religious Liberty. I know you at home will join in this prayer.[14]

On 6 June, Stileman further reported:

I mentioned in para 6 of my letter last week that there has been an outbreak against the Babis in Isfahan. I am sorry to say that matters have grown worse this week. Two well known Bábi merchants, Háji Hádi and Háji Husain were brutally murdered by the mob, their bodies mutilated, naphtha was then poured over them and one was burnt in the principal Maidán of the city, and the other in the old Maidán. An old Sayyid, whom I knew well, was murdered in the street and his body treated in the same way, and I am afraid there is no doubt that *eight* Bábis have been killed and many others injured. Two of the Christian converts have also been severely beaten, and there is something like a reign of terror in Isfahan. Many have fled and many more are in hiding.

It is many years since there has been such a violent outbreak of fanaticism, and I think it was quite unexpected. The Zillu's Sultan has called all the leading Mullas together and has I believe, told them that he will hold them responsible for any further disorder. Threats have been directed against the mission and I am informed that an attempt may be made tomorrow (Sunday) morning to take all converts and inquirers who come to Church. I am informing the Acting Consul of these threats and we shall take every possible precaution.

Please ask for special prayer at the Thursday Prayer Meeting that religious liberty may be granted to the people of Persia. It has been a very trying week for those living in town. Rev. J. L. Garland of the Jews' Society wrote to me on Wednesday night: 'The horrors of the day you have doubtless heard, the mutilated body of Háji Hádi lies not fifty yards from my house on a dung heap . . .'[15]

A Medical Missionary, Dr Winifred Westlake (q.v.), who chanced to be in Iṣfahán, wrote an account of her experiences in a letter dated 6 August:

During May, I was extremely busy visiting in Isfahan, being called to many new homes where I had not previously been. Towards the end of the month there broke out a fierce persecution of the Babis, and for a fortnight or so we had an anxious time. I cannot tell you how many men were murdered, with every torture imaginable, the most fiendish cruelties were perpetrated, we heard, by the fanatical mob on their victims. In broad daylight, in the chief square of the city, close by the Palace of the Governor . . . , some of the Europeans who happened to be driving through actually witnessed horrible things being done to two poor, unfortunate men. Rank, position, wealth, did not in many cases save them, I believe, if only the suspicion were whispered, 'So-and-so are Babis'.[16]

On 3 June 1903, Ẓillu's-Sulṭán addressed a letter to Hardinge in which he refers to these disturbances:

> Through the telegraphic dispatches of Dr Aganoor ... you know full well of the episode that occurred here through the intrigue of the Russians, on account of the Bábís; I could not describe to you the great sorrow that these few days have given me ... but I hope that it will pass soon. It was not a small affair, as Dr Aganoor will write to you, but, by the will of God, I stopped it in such a manner that there was not a massacre, and meanwhile this young man Baronowsky has been well punished for his stupidity, and he has well understood that they could not do what they want, but in any case it is all over.[17]

On 13 June 1903, Aganoor telegrammed:

> A few Babis killed at Najafabad since my last telegram. Isfahan quiet.
>
> Private. Prince anxious to know if any steps being taken by the Russian Minister and hinted I might ask you.
>
> Prince does not consider situation grave but my private information points to serious danger for rich Babis until severe measures taken such as expulsion of one or two Mollahs who were ringleaders.[18]

On the same day, he sent the following dispatch:

> I have the honour to report that the action of the Russian Consulate with respect to the Babis has had a somewhat disastrous result. It has probably put back the Babi Cause for some years. The Babis went there encouraged, by the Acting Consul and mainly by the Persian Moonshee of the Consulate, to do so, with the full conviction of getting protection, and an authoritative acknowledgement of religious liberty. Monsieur Baronowsky took up their case at first very strongly. The incident of the mob surrounding the Consulate seemingly unnerved M. Baronowsky. (The recent incident of the murder of the Russian Consul by an Albanian may have had something to do with it.) He may also possibly have had instructions from his Legation not to go on with the matter. In any case his sending away the men who had come to him for protection at a moment when they needed protection most had the effect on the Mollah mind that their fear of foreign interference and protection was uncalled for. It has reduced their fear of Russia and of outsiders generally. It has encouraged their belief that they may do much more than they have done recently with impunity. No Persian of means, whether a Babi or not now feels quite safe. The murder of the two merchants in a summary manner and with impunity, has made every one else feel that his turn might be next.
>
> I am informed that private meetings are held daily at Aga Nedjifys and plans prepared to deal with men of means and position, some of whom are Babis and others are not, in order, as they put it, to strike at the root. Among the men of this class talked of are the Fathe-ul-Mulk (the F.O. Agent), the Sons of Haji Mirza Hadi Dowlatabadi; the Sheikh ul Arakhain (a Turkish subject), and one or two Court people.
>
> His Royal Highness the Prince has done much to repress the ardour of the Mollahs, and does not think the situation so serious.
>
> The Mollahs actively working in this matter are Aga Nedjify his brothers and son, Seyyed Abool Khaussem Zinjanee and Aga Munir. If one or two of these were expelled the situation would change, but this cannot be done by the Prince unless he is strongly supported from Tehran and gets definite instructions.[19]

In the monthly summary of events, dated 23 June 1903, compiled by Major Douglas and sent by Hardinge to the Marquess of Lansdowne, the

British Foreign Secretary, there was a lengthy account of the Iṣfahán episode.[20]

The most detailed account of this episode is from Nicolas. He states: 'I was in Iṣfahán. I have seen with my own eyes what I write.' And continues:

Mírzá ['Alí-] Muḥammad,* known by the name Talávih, had borrowed from someone the book entitled *Fará'id*† in order to have it bound. He gave it to a bookbinder named Mullá Muḥammad, who bound most of the books of the Bábís. This binder wished to learn about the ideas of the Bahá'ís. On 6 Ṣafar [4 May 1903], he said to his client: 'Come back in three days, the book will be bound, and you can take it.' At this precise moment, one of Áqá Najafí's men happened to be there. He thought to himself, 'This book must belong to the Bábís!' and after Mírzá 'Alí-Muḥammad's departure he said to Mullá Muḥammad: 'Give me the book for tonight, I will bring it back tomorrow.' He insisted so much that the book was lent to him. He took it at once to Áqá Najafí, and explained to him the circumstances under which he had procured it. Áqá Najafí told him to return it to the binder and advised him thus: 'When the owner comes to take it, come quickly and tell me.' He ordered his men and a group of theological students to arrest the man who would be pointed out to them and bring him to his [Áqá Najafí's] house.

On the day arranged, Mírzá 'Alí-Muḥammad came to retrieve the book that he had given to the binder . . . [Nicolas then relates how Mírzá 'Alí-Muḥammad was accosted but managed to flee to the house of Mírzá Mullá Khán-i-Vazír.‡] After discussion with his host, it was decided that they should send that night for all the writings that he had in his house. So they wrote to Mírzá 'Alí Khán-i-Ṣarráf and Áqá Muḥammad-Javád-i-Ṣarráf, because their houses were near that of 'Alí-Muḥammad, asking them to collect the writings and bring them over. This they did.

The next morning, Ḥájí Ḥaydar-'Alí of Najaf, the students and some Government men threw themselves upon the house of Muḥammad-'Alí. They found neither him nor his papers. Mírzá 'Alí Khán and Muḥammad-Javád came to the house of Mírzá 'Alí-Muḥammad and called on Áqá Najafí's people to explain why they had entered the house without the permission of its owner. The Muslims came empty-handed to report to Áqá Najafí on their fruitless expedition. They related that the two Ṣarráfs had violently insulted him, Áqá Najafí. The latter gave orders that Mírzá 'Alí-Muḥammad be brought to him. But on the night of the 20th [18 May], his victim surreptitiously left the house of the Vazír and departed from Iṣfahán to Ábádih.

To be brief, the population, excited by its leaders, had been seeking for a long time to persecute the Bábís. They were only waiting for the opportunity.

[Nicolas then relates that Mírzá Ḥasan-i-Adíb§ and his son Shaykh Muḥammad-'Alí arrived in Iṣfahán on 20 May and the Bahá'ís gathered to greet them.]

On 25 Ṣafar [23 May], Ḥájí Muḥammad-Ismá'íl, a banker, who was one of the notables of the town and who had been converted to Bábism, died. Many persons met under the pretext of attending the funeral, among others, Muḥammad-Javád-i-Ṣarráf. Áqá Najafí learnt of this. He sent a group of theological students and ruffians to arrest Javád and Mírzá 'Alí Khán. They succeeded in arresting Javád and, torturing and leading him in an undignified way, they

* Mírzá 'Alí-Muḥammad-i-Rawḍih-Khán, later known as Ḥájí Ṣadr.

† This is the most famous book of the Bahá'í scholar, Mírzá Abu'l-Faḍl-i-Gulpáygání.

‡ Probably Mírzá Asadu'lláh Khán-i-Vazír is intended.

§ One of the foremost Bahá'ís of that era, designated by Bahá'u'lláh a 'Hand of the Cause'.

made him enter the Mosque of the Sháh.

Najafí said: 'It has not been proven to me that this individual is a Bábí! But two years ago he drank wine. He must be punished! But with a moderate punishment.' They despoiled the poor devil of his clothes and gave him 80 lashes with the whip. Then they released him and he returned home.

Adíb and the Bábís had anticipated what had occurred. That same night, they were invited to the garden of the Vazír. They held counsel and decided that the best course was to seek refuge in the Russian Consulate. Adíb knew Baronovski, then the Acting Consul, and said that it would be better for him to go and see him first.

He therefore wrote an account of what had happened to Mírzá Asadu'lláh Khán, the Munshí of the Consulate, who related it to Baronovski and told him that Adíb and 'Alí Khán were asking to be allowed to take refuge in the Consulate. 'Do you permit it?' he asked. 'Yes,' replied the Russian Agent. That same day these two people with their families came to their Consular refuge.

On the 26th [24 May], Baronovski declared: 'You are too few in number. If you want me to concern myself in your affairs you must gather *en masse*; the more numerous you are, the better it will be for you!' Thus the numbers increased and the Bábís thronged in until the 28th and 29th [26–27 May]. They were about 4,000 persons. They telegraphed on several occasions to Ṭihrán. Baronovski corresponded about this matter with Ẓillu's-Sulṭán. The Prince wrote that henceforward no one had the right any longer to make observations about what [religion] one was and why! Several copies were made of this, and in the margin Baronovski wrote his guarantee. They distributed these papers among the Bábís and told them to leave. On the evening of the 29th [27 May], the Prince sent Mírzá Aḥmad Khán, Fatḥu'l-Mulk, Kárguzar,* to the Russian Consulate. He was taken to Mírzá 'Alí Khán in the garden and gave the latter all the assurances in the world. The Prince then ordered that, for certain reasons, Mírzá 'Alí Khán should be taken to the Ábdár-Khánih [pantry]. Mírzá Muḥammad-Javád was also brought there.

Najafí realized that the next day the Bábís would leave the prison free, and that he had lost a superb opportunity. He forged a telegram which he pretended had come from the Atábik,† in the following terms: 'O Ḥujjatu'l-Islám, Áqá Najafí! In the matter of the actions of these people you are all-powerful, according to the Laws of the Sharí'at, which it is necessary to obey! So follow your understanding of them.'

Copies of this forgery were spread in the bazaars and mosques, rousing the population into a violent state.

Thus they were saying: 'Áqá Najafí has given the order to go to the Russian Consulate and to destroy it and to kill the Bábís!' On Friday, the first of Rabí'u'l-Avval [28 May 1903], during the night, men came to surround the Consulate. Baronovski had gone for a walk. When he returned he saw that men were walking in small groups towards the Consulate. They insulted him as he passed, and the crowd grew constantly.

He wanted to go and find the Prince.

Fatḥu'l-Mulk related: 'After Mírzá 'Alí Khán and Muḥammad-Javád were conducted to the Ábdár-Khánih, I went home to rest. I saw a messenger [Jilawdár] who came in haste saying, "Come! the Prince is asking for you!" While I was dressing I saw a second courier come, and then a third. I mounted a horse and galloped to the Prince. I saw Baronovski, Bahrám Mírzá and the Prince, all extremely troubled. Baronovski said, "If I am to be killed, then it must be at the Consulate!"

'At this moment, the eunuch Ḥájí 'Abdu'lláh Khán arrived and said, "The crowd is so dense that I could not reach Áqá

* Persian Foreign Office Agent

† i.e. Amínu's-Sulṭán, Prime Minister

Najafí. But eventually, with terrible trouble, I reached him and forced him to mount a donkey and disperse the crowd."

'The Prince had written to Najafí: "If this fire has been lit by you, you yourself must extinguish it. If it is not you who has lit it, you must do all in your power to disperse these people and remove them from the Consulate."'

It was announced that the crowd had not ceased to grow around the Consulate. The Prince said to Fatḥu'l-Mulk, 'You and Bahrám Mírzá go with Baronovski in my carriage. Go to the Consulate.' Fatḥu'l-Mulk said, 'I think that if Áqá Najafí mounts a horse and goes to the door of the Consulate, it will be thought that he has come to destroy the furniture and kill the Bábís. Even if he said, I have come for something else, no one will hear him. That is why I advise that Baronovski remains until I have taken Najafí back, then I will come to take him.'

[Fatḥu'l-Mulk related:] 'To be brief, I took Najafí to near the baths of the Prince, which are near the Consulate. I kept him there and sent to inform the people that the Áqá is here, come and hear what he orders. Little by little they withdrew from the Consulate, and he told them gently, "Go about your own affairs!" While I said, "Tomorrow, O people! Come to the mosque." Little by little the crowd dispersed.' Fatḥu'l-Mulk with Akbar Mírzá took Baronovski and conducted him to the Consulate, with the Prince firmly enjoining the expulsion of the Bábís upon him. [Fatḥu'l-Mulk continues:] 'We arrived at the Consulate four hours after nightfall. It was impressed upon the Bábís that they should leave, but they resisted, saying: "They have not finished with us!" In spite of their wanting to remain, that was not possible. They were obliged to leave in groups of two or three. As the mob had not entirely dispersed and most of the enemy were hiding, the first time that Siyyid Abu'l-Qásim with his son and Mírzá Muḥammad Khán-i-Chapar left the Consulate, they were stopped and subjected to blows with sticks, knives and metal chains. They were taken to the house of Najafí. Siyyid Abu'l-Qásim perished under the blows. Someone said: "I reached him at the moment of his death. I gave him a kick in the belly and that killed him."'

The two others were led to the Ruknu'l-Mulk, the Náyibu'l-Ḥukúmih [Deputy Governor]. He dismissed them unhurt.

Following this, Shaykh Muḥammad-'Alí,* Siyyid Muṣṭafá and Mírzá 'Abdu'l-Ḥusayn with Siyyid Jalál-i-Dih-Kurdí and three Najafábádís left the Consulate. They were also captured. They were beaten as they were taken to the house of Shaykh Murtiḍáy-i-Rízí, and from there to the house of Mírzá Muḥammad-'Alíy-i-Kalbásí. Siyyid Muṣṭafá escaped along the way. Until Friday evening, the Bábís continued to leave thus in small groups. Many of them could be seen, who were so wounded that they seemed near to death.

The next evening, Mírzá Muḥammad-'Alí sent them to the Ruknu'l-Mulk. The latter kept them a few days to protect them against attack, then released them one by one.

The Najafábádís were also tormented. On the morning of the following day, a Friday, on the word of Áqá Najafí, the crowd gathered at the Mosque of the Sháh. Towards morning, the Najafábádís left the Consulate all together, and, as they were numerous, no one dared to touch them. When this news reached Najafábád, great disturbances broke out and the majority of the sectaries were expelled from the town.

In short, all the Bábís were turned out of the Russian Consulate either by ruse or by force. There remained only Prince Ghulám-Ḥusayn Mírzá, Mírzá Báqir Khán and Khán Bábá Khán of Ábádih. The following night, they with a number of Cossacks left safe and sound.

* Shaykh Muḥammad-'Alíy-i-Qá'iní, nephew of Nabíl-i-Akbar: one of the most eminent and learned of the Bahá'ís.

36. Knighting of 'Abdu'l-Bahá. 'Abdu'l-Bahá is seated in the centre; standing immediately behind him to the right is Shaykh Muḥammad-Murád, Muftí of Haifa; behind the table is Col. E. A. Stanton, Governor of Haifa, and on his left is Mr W. F. Boustani, local adviser to the Governor, and Mírzá Badí' Bushrú'í, District Officer for Haifa. Standing in the background behind Col. Stanton is the white-bearded Shaykh Muḥammad-Ṭaríf.

37. Muḥammad-Riḍáy-i-Iṣfahání, Bahá'í martyr in Ishqábád

38. Ḥájí Muḥammad-i-Turk, Bahá'í martyr

39. Sulṭán-Ḥusayn Mírzá, Jalálu'd-Dawlih, Governor of Yazd

40. Muḥammad-Taqí Mírzá, Ruknu'd-Dawlih, Governor of Khurásán

41. Mírzá Maḥmúd-i-Furúghí (Faḍil-i-Furúghí), prominent Bahá'í of Khurásán

42. Mírzá Ya'qúb Muttaḥidih, Bahá'í martyr

43. Shaykh 'Alí-Akbar-i-Qúchání, Bahá'í martyr

44. Shaykh Muḥammad-Taqí (Áqá Najafí), and his brother, Áqá Núru'lláh. (L. to R.): Siyyid Siráju'd-Dín Ṣadr, Ḥájí Áqá Núru'lláh, Shaykh Muḥammad-Táqí, Ḥájí Siyyid Ismá'íl Rízí, Shaykh Hádí Karbilá'í

45. Laying of the Foundation-Stone of the Mashriqu'l-Adhkár of 'Ishqábád. In the foreground, standing next to each other, are General Subotich, Governor of Transcaspia, and Ḥájí Mírzá Muḥammad-Taqí, the Afnán, Vakílu'd-Dawlih.

The incident of the Consulate being over, the people began to agitate around the houses of the Bábís. The women and children were greatly troubled and uneasy. At last, on 6 Rabí'u'l-Avval, Ḥájí Hádí and Ḥájí Ḥusayn, who were merchants of note, were arrested and taken to the house of Áqá Najafí. He sent them to Ḥájí Mírzá Abu'l-Qásim-i-Zanjání. The latter owed them 1,000 tumans which they were asking for the return of at precisely this time. Ḥájí Abu'l-Qásim, in order to profit from the occasion and under the pretext of religion, girded his loins for the service of Religious Law. The two brothers were set upon. Never has anyone been killed in such an ignominious manner.

Siyyid Báqir-i-Ṭálib, on the orders of Áqá Munír, son of Áqá Jamál-i-Burújirdí, pursued the [two] Bábís. Eventually, someone came to tell Áqá Najafí and the Government of the exactions of this Ṭálib. The Prince and the Ruknu'l-Mulk sent Mírzá Fatḥ-'Alí Khán to deliver them from the hands of their tormentors. Siyyid Ḥusayn and a group of barefoot ruffians extracted the two brothers from prison and martyred them in such a manner that even their enemies wept. They cut them to pieces with blows from sticks, rocks and knives in the caravanserai of the Yazdís.

They tied a rope to their feet and Ḥájí Hádí was taken to the Maydán-i-Sháh and burnt, Ḥájí Ḥusayn suffered the same fate in the Maydán-i-Kuhnih.

The town was profoundly troubled, the uneasiness that prevailed was wide-spread.[21]

Yazd

Not only did Áqá Najafí stir up trouble for the Bahá'ís in Iṣfahán, but, according to Amínu's-Sulṭán in a letter to be quoted presently, he also wrote to the 'ulamá of the principal towns of Persia exhorting them to follow his example. Nowhere did he have greater success than in Yazd where the newly-appointed Imám-Jum'ih, Siyyid Muḥammad-Ibráhím, a young man of 30, was anxious to consolidate his authority and demonstrate his religious zeal. Siyyid Muḥammad-Ibráhím had, moreover, only recently returned from the Holy Shrines in Iraq and had passed through Iṣfahán during the anti-Bahá'í disturbances there. As he approached Yazd, rumours spread through the town that he was coming with special instructions from the great mujtahids at the Holy Shrines commissioning a general massacre of the Bahá'ís. The populace flocked to greet him as he approached the town. The day after his arrival was 17 Rabí'u'l-Avval (13 June 1903), the day on which the Shí'ih celebrate the birth of the prophet Muḥammad. The crowds that came to Siyyid Muḥammad-Ibráhím's residence to attend the customary prayers for that day were particularly large, and he took the opportunity to preach against the Bahá'ís. The same afternoon, a blood-thirsty rabble took to the streets. The first man that they sought was Áqá Muḥammad-Ḥusayn-i-'Aṭṭár, who had been one of the leading Shaykhís of the town before his conversion, and was now a prominent teacher of the Bahá'í religion. Unable to find him at his shop, they sacked it and several other shops belonging to Bahá'ís. For two days they rampaged through the streets, until on 15 June the first martyrdom, that of

Ḥájí Mírzáy-i-Halabí-Sáz, occurred. The Governor, Sulṭán-Ḥusayn Mírzá, Jalálu'd-Dawlih (q.v., see fig. 39), was powerless against the rabble.

There was no permanent member of the British Consular Corps in Yazd, but Mr Ernest Montague Eldrid, the local manager of the British-run Imperial Bank of Persia acted on behalf of the British Government as Pro-Consul. He sent his reports to Aganoor in Iṣfahán and thence they would reach Ṭihrán. Thus on 18 June 1903 Aganoor telegrammed the British Legation in Ṭihrán announcing the start of what was to become one of the most savage episodes in Bahá'í history: 'The following is from Yezd. On arrival of Mirza Mohammed Ibrahim newly appointed Imaum Juma there were rumours of anti-Babi demonstrations culminating on Monday morning in attack of [on] Babis, mob killed one shopkeeper* seriously wounded others. Prince took immediate steps quell disturbance and order restored. Simultaneous disturbances at Ardekan and Taft but order is restored and it is doubtful if any lives lost.'[22]

Thus in the monthly summary of news sent to the Foreign Office, dated 23 June 1903, the contents of this telegram were also reported to London.

For almost one week the disturbances died down, until suddenly violence erupted in the villages surrounding Yazd. On 24 June, Aganoor reported by telegram: 'My telegram No. 28 two babis have been killed at Ardekan and on Sunday four were killed at Taft. Yazd is quieter but there is uneasiness and babis are in fear.[23]

By 27 June 1903, the situation had deteriorated so greatly that Eldrid, not wishing to waste time, telegrammed directly to Ṭihrán sending his message through Mr Rabino,† the Ṭihrán Manager of the Imperial Bank.

Again yesterday (Friday) there were serious anti-babi disturbances here, twelve babis killed and bodies maltreated many babi houses raided and plundered, gholams and soldiers joined in looting, Naib Shatir of Governor‡ killed by mob. Today again rabble have searched out and killed babis dragging mutilated bodies through streets. At one time this afternoon Palace was surrounded by angry mob. Governor is absolutely without authority up to the present. Europeans are safe but would propose Yezd mullahs being held responsible for their safety as at present town is at caprice of mullahs and mob. Situation constantly changing. I have strongly advised European colony to abstain from sheltering babis in their houses. Do you confirm my action.[24]

On hearing of the deteriorating situation in Yazd, Hardinge wrote to the Amínu's-Sulṭán on 27 June 1903:

* Ḥájí Mírzáy-i-Halabí-Sáz

† Joseph Rabino di Borgomale, a French Jew who after working for some time with Crédit Lyonnais in Cairo had acquired British naturalization. He was the first General Manager of the Imperial Bank when it opened in Ṭihrán in 1889.

‡ Ma<u>sh</u>hadí Ḥasan-i-<u>Sh</u>áṭir, a Bahá'í. (A Ná'ib-<u>Sh</u>áṭir was a deputy footman.)

I have received from the Indo-European Telegraph Department and from the Imperial Bank of Persia telegrams from Yezd from which it would appear that serious disturbances have again broken out there, that 12 Babis have been massacred today and the houses of others have been plundered, and that the troops have joined the populace. The last news dated 3 hours ago was that the English missionaries in Yazd and other Europeans were in some danger, and that the officers of the Central Persia Telegraph line (Yezd-Kerman), had come into Yezd from their camp outside the town to assist them. The Governor is said to be powerless, the mob getting hourly stronger and the soldiers being with the mollahs. I do not myself anticipate any attack on the Europeans, but I think it might be well that a telegram should be sent by the Persian Government to the Chief Mujtehids of Yezd impressing upon them the importance of preventing attacks on the subjects of foreign powers, and calling on them to use their influence in this direction with the people. Your Highness has perhaps already taken the necessary steps.[25]

Hardinge replied to Eldrid on 28 June: 'I entirely approve your warning to Europeans. On receiving from telegraph news of riot I requested Grand Vizier to wire respecting safety of Europeans to principal mujtehids.'[26]

On the same day, Hardinge informed both the Foreign Office and the Governor of India by telegram of the events in Yazd.[27] On 28 June 1903, Eldrid sent a full report to Hardinge on the events of the preceding week.

I have the honour to confirm my telegram of yesterday's date anent the anti Babi disturbances in Yezd.

Previously I have kept Dr Aganoor, H.B.M.'s Vice-Consul in Isfahan fully informed of events here and he has doubtless advised you of the same but the disturbances of yesterday were of so serious a character that I consider it necessary to communicate direct with Your Excellency thereby economizing time.

The disturbances which commenced last Sunday week, the 14th instant, and were coincident to the arrival in Yezd of the newly-appointed 'Imam-i-Juma' culminated on Friday last in the Governor's authority being defied and the 'Naib-Shatír' killed.

H.I.H. Jellal ed Dowleh had given orders for a certain man who had killed a relative of this servant's to be taken out of the 'Imam zadeh', where he had taken refuge, but one of the 'mujteheds' disallowed it.* The mob thereupon, feeling encouraged, found the 'Naib-Shatir' whom they killed and afterwards sought out all the Babis they could find killing twelve of them and dragging their mutilated forms exultantly through the streets and bazaars.

Many Babi houses were looted and the Governor's gholams and soldiers joined in the plunder.

On Saturday the Governor issued a proclamation ordering that any accused of being Babis should be brought to the Palace and he would look into the case and administer the punishment.

The first Babi taken there however he refused to kill and immediately all the Bazaars were closed and the Palace surrounded for a time, by an angry mob.

The rabble continued visiting the houses of known Babis and during the day several were killed.

Although up to the present there has been

* This is not entirely accurate. The relative of Mas͟hhadí Ḥasan referred to, his son-in-law, Áqá 'Alí, was at first only wounded. The mob repaired to Imámzádih Ja'far and refused to yield to the *farrás͟hes* of the Governor. Mas͟hhadí Ḥasan sent for Dr White to tend Áqá 'Alí, and Dr White was present when the mob returned to kill Mas͟hhadí Ḥasan and Áqá 'Alí. See the following account by Dr White.

no suspicion of any anti-European feeling one can never be certain of the course a fanatical mob may take and on Thursday evening I urged upon the English Colony the personal danger they would incur by giving shelter and protection to the Babis (especially as there was no local Government authority to rely upon) as no act of theirs would be more calculated to irritate the mullahs and incite the fury of the mob.

Personally I think the only danger to the Europeans lies here as the mob are determined to search out certain well-known Babis. The mullahs gave an order for the death of a certain Babi servant in the employ of the English mission but fortunately the mob failed to find him and although they were constantly in the vicinity of the Hospital no attempt was made to search the Mission Houses otherwise the result might have been different.

Had the Governor dealt firmly from the onset it is most improbable that events would have reached their present serious state.

At Taft last week several Babis were killed and a less number at Ardekan. The renewed disturbances in town will probably result in further persecutions at these villages and possibly at others in the province.

In my wire I ventured to suggest to Your Excellency that the mullahs of Yezd should be held responsible for the safety of the European Colony and I await the favour of your reply.

Haji Mirza Mahmoud Shirazi, acting Vakil-ed-Dowleh-i-Russe* and a leading Babi, left town secretly about 5 days ago.[28]

The death of the 'Naib-Shatir', Mas͟hhadí Ḥasan-i-S͟háṭir, which Eldrid mentions in this dispatch, occurred on 26 June and signalled the recommencement of the upheaval in Yazd. Dr White (q.v.) of the Church Missionary Society was in Yazd at this time, having been asked by Jalálu'd-Dawlih to defer his departure for Kirmán when the upheaval started. When Áqá 'Alí was attacked by the mob on 26 June, Dr White was asked by Mas͟hhadí Ḥasan (Áqá 'Alí's father-in-law) to tend his wounds. While he was in the house, the mob returned to finish off their work and Dr White was a witness to what occurred. In a letter, dated 28 June, he wrote:

We are just now in the thick of the biggest riot ever seen in Yezd. The riot began about a fortnight ago, when one Bábi was killed. As there were very serious rumours in the town and acting on the Governor's express wish, I decided not to go to Kerman, but to remain here and see the thing through.

Things got much quieter and we all hoped the worst was over. Last Friday however another Bábi was killed, and two men – the murderers – took refuge in a mosque. The Prince gave orders that they were to be taken out, but the mob resisted the order, and the Prince was not strong enough to insist on it.

I went to attend the Bábi who was then dangerously wounded, and afterwards died, and while I was in his house the mob surrounded it, burned down the door, and swarmed in. I could do nothing to protect them, and as the mob promised not to touch the women, I came away. Since then the town has been in the hands of the mob. The Governor, whom I saw yesterday, cannot control them.

I do not know how many Bábis have been murdered, but at least twenty, I think.

* Acting Consular Agent for Russia. This was Ḥájí Mírzá Maḥmúd, son of Ḥájí Mírzá Muḥammad-Taqí, Vakílu'd-Dawlih, the Afnán (q.v., see fig. 45). He was Acting Consular Agent for Russia in place of his father who had left Yazd the previous year to proceed to 'Is͟hqábád to build the Mas͟hriqu'l-Ad͟hkár there (see p. 442).

Europeans up till now have been perfectly safe, but we do not know of course, how long we shall remain so. However we are doing what we can, and know that GOD ruleth on high. It has been a very difficult question to decide as to harbouring Bábis. I have talked the matter over fully with Malcolm and Eldrid, and we all agree we have no right to do so, with the exception of our own servants and our immediate friends . . . The ladies I have asked to come and stay with me for a day or two. It seemed very hard to refuse Bábis admission, but we had to respect the Governor, and also think of the Europeans generally, and our Mission in particular.[29]

Later, on 4 July, Dr White wrote a longer account of his experiences in an article entitled 'How Babis died for their Faith' for *Mercy and Truth*, the Medical Magazine of the Church Missionary Society.

No doubt you will have read in your papers of the terrible massacres among the sect called Babis in Persia. We in Yezd have been in the midst of the worst of it.

For some time I have noticed symptoms of unrest in the town; there seemed to be a suppressed excitement, a general undercurrent of feeling at work. We were not therefore surprised when on Monday, June 15, a Babi was killed, several others wounded, and some houses looted. H.I.H. the Jilal-ud-Dowleh, the Governor, sent for me and asked me to defer my proposed journey to Kirman till a later period and to remain in Yezd in the general interests of the Mission and the European colony.

Contrary to all our expectation, the town remained quiet and we all felt that perhaps the danger was past.

However, on Friday, June 26, just as I had finished my morning work at the hospital, an urgent message came to me to go to see a man who had been assaulted by a mob. I went off at once and at the opposite end of Yezd found my patient. He was a young man, a small manufacturer, and had evidently been severely and savagely dealt with by a mob. He had several large wounds on head, neck, and body, caused by a knife or sword, and was very faint with loss of blood, almost unconscious in fact, and the prognosis was bad. I began to stitch up the wounds, and before I had finished the mob began to howl round the house. Soon a battering-ram was brought to break the door in, and finally naphtha oil was poured on it and it was fired. The shouts of the mob got louder and louder, like the roar of an angry wild animal. Then the door gave way and with a rush the house was stormed. It was an exciting moment; my patient died of shock and another man was killed in the house. No one touched me; one man shouted out, 'We have no work with foreigners,' and, much to my annoyance, one huge Sayyid came up and kissed me. I pleaded for the women and I think they were all uninjured; certainly none were wounded in any way. Seeing that I could do no more, I rode home.

All that day the killing went on and all Saturday too. On Saturday afternoon the mob got completely out of hand, neither listening to their own Mullahs, or to the Governor, whom they besieged in his palace.

All work was suspended, and the shouts of the mob could be heard in all directions. It was a saturnalia of evil.

The hospital on Saturday afternoon might have been a field hospital after a battle. I had a very busy time with gun-shot wounds and sword and knife cuts.

We all felt very much the need of God's protecting care on Saturday and Sunday, as, although nothing was said against Europeans, yet an uncontrolled mob is not a pleasant neighbour.

By Monday the fury of the mob had a little spent itself in the city, but the same scenes were being enacted in the district round. In all from seventy to 100 people have been killed and a large amount of property looted. We do not know yet the full extent of the havoc that has been made.

The most heartrending details are coming to light. One of my wife's friends, a young newly-married woman, has lost husband, father, and father-in-law. Others have lost sons, brothers, and fathers. Many are absolutely ruined, and we must render what assistance we can.

A friend of mine, a large landowner, who lived in a town forty miles from Yezd, with whom I have stayed, was killed with all his male relatives, eight persons in all.

We could do comparatively little to help the sufferers, as by international law we are bound not to interfere in matters of internal politics, and at Ispahan, where there was a small outbreak, the Russian Consul was ordered to turn out a number of Babis who had taken refuge with him. It was with difficulty that those of us who had Babi servants were able to protect them.

Of course we must not forget that many of the Mussulman persecutors believe that they are doing God service in this matter, and many of them look with horror on what has taken place.

I have pointed out to several of them that persecution simply means propagation of a faith,* and that we believe our plan to be the best, to work by love for what we believe to be the truth. Many of the Babis through fear have again become Mohammedans, cursing openly their late faith. Many, on the other hand, have stood firm. One old man when asked to repent and curse the Bab said, 'I have been a Babi for fifty years, and will not curse the faith now,' and was killed.

Some who were afraid to become Christians have died as Babis for a false faith. Will you pray for God's blessing upon Persia and that God will reveal the truth to its people?[30]

Another missionary of the Church Missionary Society, Napier Malcolm (q.v.), was also in Yazd at this time, and in his book *Five Years in a Persian Town* he indicates some of the motives that may have been inciting the mob:

The Behái sectaries were not at that time being executed before the *mujtahids*, but were being torn in pieces by the crowd. What had excited the people was not simply religious feeling, but it was very largely the statement by the clerical authorities that the goods of the Beháis were 'lawful', that is, that any one might plunder them who cared to do so. The attacks were often made by men who had lived for a long while in close

* Another missionary, M. E. Hume-Griffith, records the following story from the Yazd upheaval in her book *Behind the Veil in Persia and Turkish Arabia* (p. 119): 'During the persecution in Yezd, a young man went to scoff and jeer, but when he saw with what courage the martyrs endured torture, and met death, he called out, "I am a Babi, kill me too."' In a letter dated 11 July 1903 printed in the *Church Missionary Intelligencer* (Oct. 1903, p. 768), Napier Malcolm states: 'There is, of course, no doubt that the horrors of the past three weeks will make Behaiism a much greater force in Yazd than it has hitherto been. In the course of the next few years it is probable that it will become the religion of half the population of the town.' In a résumé of the development of the 'religion of the Báb', prepared by the dragoman of the Belgian Legation in Ṭihrán and sent to Brussels by M. de Villegas, the Belgian Vice-Consul, is the following statement: 'It is scarcely likely, according to the opinion of those who have close knowledge of this sect, that these persecutions can halt the propagation of the reformist doctrine of the Báb. The view of its adherents is not to fear death; they consider it similar to a Divine bounty to which they aspire. And on the other hand, the diffusion of the new religion has established it not only in Persia but also in Turkey, Egypt, Russia and even America.' (Belgian Foreign Ministry Archives, Direction Politique, Dossier No. 4144, enclosure dated 16 Aug. 1903 in Dispatch No. 190/84 of same date; translated from French.)

companionship with the Beháis, knowing them all the time to be members of the sect, and yet consorting and eating with them freely. Holes were bored in the heads of some of these poor wretches with awls, oil was then poured into the hole and lighted. Other forms of torture were used about which one cannot write. Women and children were very seldom actually killed, but were fearfully ill-treated, and sometimes left to die of starvation. It was reported that in one of the villages Babi children died within full sight of the villagers, after waiting for days under the trees where their murdered parents had left them. . . .

. . . a soldier found a Yezdi who was dragging about another man, and trying to make out whether he was really a Behái. 'You see,' he said, 'I have been a wicked man all my life, and have never said my prayers or done any other *savabs* [pious acts], so, unless I can do a big *savab*, I shall certainly go to Hell. If this man is a Babi, I mustn't let him go, for if I kill an infidel of course I shall go straight to Heaven.'[31]

The holocaust at Yazd continued, with many Bahá'ís being killed every day. On 29 June, Eldrid telegrammed:

Yesterday the disturbance continued and the Governor killed two Babis brought to him. The mob also killed two or three dragging their bodies through the town. Agha Mirza Seyed Ali Hiere* a leading Mujtehed enjoined the populace yesterday to desist from plundering and bring all Babis to Governor or Mujtehed for judgment. To-day Monday town is more orderly but search for Babis continues. I understand no telegram has reached Mollahs from Tehran but I do not apprehend Europeans are in any danger.[32]

On 1 and 3 July, Eldrid sent further telegrams to Hardinge,[33] the contents of which are more fully explained in the following report sent by post and dated 3 July:

I have the honour to confirm my letter of the 28th June also my telegrams of the 29th and 30th June, lst and 3rd July anent the Babi persecutions.

On Sunday the Governor appeased the mob by blowing one well-known Babi from the cannon's mouth† and cutting the throat of another‡ but the Prince owns himself unable to punish either those responsible for the disturbances or those chiefly concerned in the murders owing to the want of specific instructions.

The Prince called me to the palace on Wednesday and severely complained of his lack of definite instructions and power from the Central Government stating that his orders were of a very general character and urging that drastic and severe measures must immediately be taken to avoid a recrudescence of the trouble which might be attended by grave danger to the Europeans. His summary of the position and the gist of his remarks were that unless the position was forced either in Teheran by the British Legation or in Yezd by an attack upon the European houses he would be without the justification for taking necessary action.

The opinion of His Imperial Highness, which I have quoted, was expressed in private with a request that when communicated to Your Excellency it should not be accredited to him but I could not consent

* Áqá Mírzá Siyyid 'Alí Ḥáyirí
† Sh̲áṭir Ḥusayn
‡ Ustád Mihdí, a builder from Mihdí-ábád

to eliminate the Governor's name from my telegram.

I must add that I think H.I.H., seeing he has lost power and prestige, thinks he may retrieve his lost position and dignity by this means, but I considered it better to allow Your Excellency to be the judge.

It speaks well for the prestige and standing of Europeans in Yezd that although the mob were diligently searching for certain known Babis on Saturday afternoon, the 27th June, in the vicinity of the residences of the European Missionaries, no attempt was made to enter any house, although the Governor was being surrounded in his Palace and Babi houses were being plundered by the rabble assisted by Gholams and Soldiers.

Since the report has reached here that H.I.H. Zil-es-Sultan has left Isfahan for Yezd with troops and artillery and that cavalry are on their way from Teheran, the town has quieted down but with the Babis still hidden and the guilty unpunished, it is early days to predict that the persecutions are at an end.

Disturbances of varying magnitude are repeated at most of the surrounding villages and it is estimated that about forty Babis have lost their lives in Yezd and forty to fifty in the district since the commencement of these disturbances.[34]

On 4 July 1903, Miss Jessie Biggs (q.v.), CMS missionary at Yazd, wrote the following lengthy account of the events of the preceding three weeks to Mr Durrant, the Society's Honorary Secretary in London.

No doubt you will have heard by public telegrams and also private communication of the trouble that this town has been going thro' lately, on account of the persecution of the Bábis by the Mohammedans. Each of our mission houses has naturally seen a different side, and I felt it might interest you to have a few pages from my journal, giving a description of what we saw and went through.

It was about June 13 that we heard of disturbances in Isfahan, set on foot mainly by some of the leading Mullas there.

On Monday June 15 we heard a Bábi had been killed in Yezd and some of our Bábi friends came to us in distress for advice. Our work was not interfered with in any way and we went visiting freely as usual. The Prince Governor, however, requested that Dr White should not go to Kerman as had been arranged, as he feared troubles would increase in Yezd. *On June 17* we heard of 2 more men being killed – one living next door to one of our converts, who is a teacher in Mr Malcolm's school, and who is also teaching me Persian. The wife of the man killed was also badly hurt by women beating her and biting her about the hands and face. I assure you these people become like beasts of prey in their fanaticism.

On Tues. June 23 our head-servant (a Bábi) told us of more deaths in town, and for the first time, he himself seemed nervous, and asked, if necessary, would we shelter his wife and children – and other relations. This man's father-in-law* is a leader and teacher among the Bábis, and he was very frightened for him. Our servant-man's wife and sister are practically Christians – the latter has been under definite teaching for some time, previous to her being baptised. But in May she married a strong Bábi, and so her baptism for the time being has been put off. *On Wed. June 24*, our servant's father-in-law and brother-in-law (the husband of this girl) came and stayed in our servants' compound with our servants. At this time we ourselves were not at all apprehensive,

* This was Mullá 'Abdu'l-<u>Gh</u>aní. The reader may be interested in an account of what befell Mullá 'Abdu'l-<u>Gh</u>aní and his son, 'Abdu'l-<u>Kh</u>áliq, written from a Bahá'í point of view in Gloria Faizi *Fire on the Mountain-Top* pp. 31–6.

indeed we were going about our usual work in town and never dreamt of all that was going to happen. We saw and heard nothing of these 2 men and gave them very little thought. We had heard that a Sayid from Isfahan had come to town (Imam Jumeh) and it was he who was stirring up the people. He had just returned from Kerbela, where no doubt his fanaticism had been roused – for later we heard that he said he intended to exterminate the Bábis. The Prince Governor has little or no power over these religious leaders, and I think was afraid to lift his hand against him. Things all seemed fairly quiet to us till *Friday June 26*. That day, at the invitation of Mr Eldrid, the Vice-Consul here, most of us went out for the day to a Persian garden. We left town at 6 a.m. because of the heat. In the evening, as we neared Yezd, Dr White came to meet us bringing us news of great disturbances in town since noon. He told us of his own experiences that day, and how 8 at least whom we knew well were either killed or badly hurt. The news touched home very closely, for some of our converts were amongst the number and we feared for the others. Also we did not know where this might end if the Prince had lost so much power. He has been looked on as a very strong Governor till now. When we ladies got in, our man told us, his wife and 3 little children, his mother (aged 60) and her sister (80) and also a sister and another brother-in-law were all here taking refuge. It was a terrible realisation to see these poor things creeping up out of our cellar. First one and then another, the little children and the baby in arms and the poor old woman of 80. They all looked so scared and terrified, even the little children who are usually so merry with us, did not speak a word. The sight of us, and the joy it gave them, quite upset them. But we soon made them braver and then giving them food and bedding left them fairly happy for the night. It seems at midday they fled from their house in a panic of fear, leaving their food half-cooked and bringing the children half-dressed. Now it was that the 2 men in the other compound began to trouble us, for we knew the older man had many enemies, and had been through a great deal of persecution before tho' we were not really apprehensive of the immediate danger for any of them.

Sat. June 27. We took dispensary as usual. At the finish one of our 2 women converts was brought in badly hurt during yesterday's mob. One of her sons, a Bábi had gone as usual to a small weaving factory close by, and some one told her he was in danger. With this she hastened to him but got into the house only to see him killed before her eyes. In her efforts to protect him she got badly beaten on her head and arm and leg, one finger broken and dislocated and another nearly cut off. We dressed her wounds, and did all we could for her. She was so brave and patient but fainted with pain and exhaustion. One of her brothers was killed and also a small child only a few months old. These people do not know what they do in their frenzy and one realises more and more every day, that nothing can alter them, or the country but the spirit of God. . . . Come home from the dispensary, I heard that the mob thought that very 2 men we were sheltering, had taken refuge in the Castle. This was quite possible and probable to the people. The mob was collecting round the Castle demanding them to be brought out, that they might be killed. After lunch, one of our servants (a Moham.) verified this statement. He lives near the Castle and had seen the mob. We next heard the crowd was getting furious, and the Sayids were urging them not to care for the Prince or the Sháh, but to get the men. All this made us realise, that we were in some danger now, and *if* the crowd got scent of where the men were, we did not know what would happen. Mr Malcolm and Dr White both said if the mob came, there was nothing for it but to give the men up. Mr Malcolm kindly went and spoke to the men on this matter and they quite agreed that the mob, if irresistible, would have to be turned into the servants' compound and thus the women and children who were still sheltering in our cellar would be saved. It was wonderful to see the old man's composure, as he sat smoking a 'Qalian' and waiting for death. He seemed as tho' he glorified in the thought of martyrdom. Then the afternoon began to wear away. Our hospital door-keeper who had been with us all day in refuge said he would fly to the desert as he knew of holes he could hide in. Our other Bábi man implored us to let him go to Shiraz, at nightfall, as he had relations and friends there, and could send for his wife etc. later. Mr Eldrid wrote down to us saying that if he expressed a wish to go, he ought to do so and the other 2 men should be got off at nightfall also. We did what we could for our man giving him a letter of introduction to Mr Rice etc. We ladies were by ourselves again and it seemed a terrible time of suspense. The women and children afraid to be long away from us and the 2 men apparently awaiting death in the next compound. This latter seemed too awful and Dr Taylor finally went and fetched them over our side so they might be with their wives and friends a little longer. It was about 5.30 we thought we heard shouts and 3 of us running onto the roof were convinced the mob was coming. I rushed back and quickly got all the women and children into the farthest cellar and the men went back to their own compound. Miss Stirling wrote to Mr Malcolm who came to us like a shot, and the other 2 ladies kept watch on the roof. They saw part of the mob round the corner of our narrow, walled-in street, and turn into a house at the bottom. They were armed with sticks and poles as the weapons of death. Miss Stirling and I went to the poor women who thought their husbands would undoubtedly be killed, and had prayer with them. They were so brave, and so trustful to us and so grateful for prayer. Then we ladies with Mr Malcolm had prayer together and then there was nothing to do but wait. Strange as it seems, the mob went by, apparently entering into nearly every other house close by. Truly God blinded their eyes. After some time of suspense the immediate danger and noise seemed to pass away and then Mr M. left us. He had several people sheltering in his house and we all feared the mob might have gone there, but they did not. Gradually the sun went down and the evening 'call to prayer' went up all over the city. Never was I more grateful for the dark and never before did I appreciate these 'bear-pit'-like compounds of ours. Directly dark came on, we brought the men out, and bid them say goodbye. We gave them food and other necessaries for their flight, but it was with much reluctance that they went. They had asked us to pray with them and they all said they knew it was our prayer that had saved them. At last we had to fairly push them out. It was terribly sad for they did not know what they had to face. It was pathetic too, to us to have things left in our charge. One gave me 2 bags of money, and other things were given to the other ladies. What a day it had been and how we praised God for his marvellous deliverances. Truly 'if God be for us, who *can* be against us.'

Sunday June 28. We got all the women to the women's hospital as soon as possible as that seemed the better place. The children with their mother had gone last night. Today there was a report that all the European houses would be looted. However it was quite false and the Persians seem too frightened of England's power to dare to interfere with us. That is one of the hard things, we are so safe and these others so helpless. However, at Dr White's request we ladies spent the day at his house. Today the mob is reported to be after my teacher. He is in refuge with Mr Malcolm. Quite in the evening a note came from the Prince requesting we should get rid of all the Bábis, this meaning a great deal of work for Mr Malcolm as he had several with him. A command has also gone forth that searching of homes is to stop, and that any Bábi found is to be taken up to the Castle and there judged. The judgement seems simply to make the prisoner curse the Báb, which if he refuses to do, is punished by death, probably being blown from a cannon's mouth. Their modes of killing these poor hunted Bábis, have been dreadful. Some have been beaten and stoned to death, others shot over and over again, and others cut to pieces. How can anyone say this people's religion is good enough for them and the Gospel of Christ is not needed in this land. How little people realise the power of the Gospel of Christ when they talk so. I am glad to have been here and seen all I have seen – the horrors of a religion of man's making and the glorious power of God, ruling over all.

Dr White had one boy* in his house, a hospital student (the brother-in-law of our servant who until this morning we had been sheltering). He is about 17 yrs old and one of our enquirers, who is waiting for baptism – a splendid Christian at heart but known to the town as a Bábi, because of his father's notoriety. Dr White felt it necessary to get rid of him. It was pitiful to hear him implore to be allowed to stay, and saying he was afraid to go alone. However, Dr White did his best for him and at last he went.

Monday June 29. We admitted an old woman about 70, well known to Miss Stirling, into our hospital. She had a bad knife or sword cut to the elbow joint and other hurts. We heard further reports of deaths. Today our poor hospital door-keeper came back to us. He is in a pitiful plight, but we had to get rid of him at nightfall again.

Tuesday, June 30. When we came down to breakfast we found our servant man back again. His story is as follows: He with 2 companions got as far as Mayriz, a village about 30 miles off. There they were recognised as Bábis. A large mob surrounded them beating them. Our man was just going to have his throat cut when a Sayid came forward and forbade it. He said he had orders to send everyone back to town to be judged and put to death, and if they killed him he would shoot on them. He then told the people he would give our man an escort and send him back to town. Our man had had all his money, his shoes, and 'kamr-band' stolen from him, the 2 latter this Sayid replaced, and then got the escort together and muler and sent them off, with secret orders that when they got well into the desert, they were to set our man and his companions free and to watch a while that no harm came to them. The Sayid had known our man some years back but that could hardly account for his behaviour at such a time as this. Our man seems to think it was entirely God's intervention that saved him. He said, so pathetically, 'just as they were going to kill me, I prayed to God that He would take care of my little ones', and tears rolled down the poor man's face at the remembrance. I feel, and we all feel, I think, that all these men have been *sent* back to us, for strange to say everyone connected with us in anyway has come back safe.[35]

On 8 July, Aganoor telegrammed:

The following telegram dated Yezd 7 July has been received by Mr Stileman from Dr White begins: 'Governor sent for me today he says situation here is very critical, he is firmly convinced that unless strong measures are at once taken and he is at once supported by authority and troops and late offenders punished another outbreak will take place and then European colony will be in great danger. He especially asked me to wire today. Ends.'[36]

On receiving this telegram, Hardinge wrote on 8 July to the Prime Minister, Amínu's-Sulṭán, urging that the proposed reinforcements be sent to Yazd quickly and the ringleaders of the disturbances removed from the town.[37]

On the following day, 9 July 1903, Hardinge had an interview with Amínu's-Sulṭán at which the latter confirmed that the root cause of the disturbances had been Áqá Najafí. In a dispatch to the British Foreign

* 'Abdu'l-K͟háliq; see 392n.

Secretary, the Marquess of Lansdowne, Hardinge wrote:

His Highness said that these troubles had been conclusively traced to Agha Nejefi, who had attempted to provoke similar massacres in many other towns of Persia, and had sent emissaries for this purpose to Sultanabad, Kazvin, Shiraz, and Tehran. In the three former places the clergy had declined to become his accomplices: the attitude of the Tehran Mollahs was still uncertain, but the more enlightened of them disapproved of such savage methods, and the others would he hoped be overawed by the military measures which the Persian Government were taking for the maintenance of order.[38]

On 21 July, Hardinge sent a summary of the news from Yazd to the British Foreign Secretary, the Marquess of Lansdowne.[39]

The town had more or less returned to normal when a fresh episode threatened the peace once more. This was the arrival at Yazd of a caravan of pilgrims from Mas͟hhad. With this caravan was a party of Bahá'ís, foremost among them being 'Alavíyyih K͟hánum-i-Máhfurúzkí, the wife of a martyr of Mázindarán. On their way, the Bahá'ís had not hesitated to teach their religion openly to the pilgrims. But as the caravan approached Yazd, news of the anti-Bahá'í upheaval reached them, and some ill-disposed persons sent word to Yazd that they had a party of Bahá'ís in their midst. On their arrival at Yazd, the Bahá'ís, not wishing to place any of the Bahá'ís of Yazd in danger by going to their house, repaired to a caravanserai. Jalálu'd-Dawlih had left Yazd at this time, leaving responsibility for order in the town in the hands of the Náyibu'l-Ḥukúmih (Deputy Governor) and Káẓim K͟hán-i-Dárúg͟hih.* The latter took his responsibilities seriously, and when news reached him that a crowd had collected outside the caravanserai, he set out with a group of *farrás͟hes* to disperse the mob. Eldrid reported on 24 July 1903:

The town has remained superficially quiet since the Prince Governor's departure to his village of Abbasabad but contrary, I think, to his wishes. From his demeanour previous to his departure I have little doubt that he would have welcomed a disturbance, having other than an anti Babi origin, which would give him sufficient excuse for punishing the offenders in the recent riot. The Palace-concocted rumour of an organised run on the Imperial Bank which was to take the form of a rush and afterwards His Highness's somewhat hasty departure from town followed by the removal from the Palace to Abbasabad of an exceptional amount of baggage gave colour to this view and were parts of a scheme which His Highness's loss of power and prestige in the town have brought to nought.

Although no Babis have been killed in town during the past three weeks emissaries of the mullahs have twice left on hearing of the hiding place of a town Babi and have returned with his head.

An incident occurred on Friday last which at first gave signs of serious developments but which were averted by the arrival of the 'daroga'.† A party of pilgrims arriving from Meshed en route for Fars gave notice on their arrival that they had in their caravan a family of four Babis. A mob immediately assembled and commenced battering the doors of the caravanserai when the 'daroga' chanced to appear. Promising to take the

* Dárúg͟hih – Chief of Police

† Dárúg͟hih

accused to the palace he enticed the mob to disperse and I hear the travellers were hurried on their journey southward the following morning.

A proclamation has been issued this week chiding the populace for ignoring the advice of both Prince and Priest (Mirza Syed Ali Haere) and indulging in the wanton destruction of life and property and terminating with a threat to bind to the cannon's mouth all future disturbers of the peace without trial or enquiry.

It is rumoured that the Governor has ordered his followers to send their 'anderoons' from Yezd in order that his hands may not be hampered on his return.

With reference to Your Excellency's advice regarding the advisability of refusing protection to Babis I presume reservations be made in the cases of old servants in direct employ. I have replied in this strain to questions put to me by Europeans but have advised that the families and other connections of Babi servants should be left in their own houses.[40]

News of the events in Yazd was reported in newspapers throughout the world. *The Times* of London carried a brief reference to disturbances in Iṣfahán and Yazd in its issue of 13 July 1903, [41] with a much fuller report on 30 July:*

SERIOUS DISTURBANCES IN PERSIA

According to information received from trustworthy sources, the city and province of Yezd, in Southern Persia were the scenes of very serious disturbances during the latter part of June. Rioting, which lasted for more than a fortnight at Yezd, culminated towards the end of June in a popular outbreak directed against the Babis, religious reformers whose aspirations have always been viewed with great suspicion by the ruling classes. Rumours of a demonstration against them circulated in Yezd early in June on the arrival from Nedjef of a new Mujtehid, or high priest, Mirza Muhammad Ibrahim. On the 27th and 28th especially the position, even of foreign residents, became at times critical when the mob were searching for certain well-known Babis in the quarter of the town in which the houses of the English missionaries are situated. Throughout the whole of those two days every Babi who fell into the hands of the rabble was butchered in whatever manner was most pleasing to the mob at the moment, and mutilated bodies were drawn through the town in all directions, followed by an exultant crowd. Houses were searched and plundered, women beaten and in one or two cases killed, and the town was in the hands of a mob whose only programme was to kill. The houses of Babis were broken into and plundered by the mob, assisted by Gholams and soldiers. On Sunday, the 28th, the Mujtehids enjoined the populace to bring all Babis either before them or before the Governor for judgment. The Prince refused at first to give way to the threats of the mob. But his Palace was surrounded by a turbulent crowd, and on the next day he gave way and had one man taken before him blown from the mouth of a cannon and the throat of another one cut, the body being dragged afterwards through the town. Order is reported to have been finally restored in the city, but the province was very disturbed and no one could leave the town with safety. All Babis who attempted to fly were either killed or had to return and hide themselves in the ruins and ditches around the town, some to be captured, others to escape.[42]

* The *New York Times* of 30 July 1903 also carried the news of the Bahá'í massacre at Yazd. Its information was drawn from this article in *The Times* but it appeared on the front page of the *New York Times* under the headline 'Horrible Massacre in Southern Persia'.

On 3 August, *The Times* published the following account based on reports in the *Köln Gazette*:

The chief centres of anti-Babist agitation were Ispahan and Yezd. The governors of these towns were powerless against the mob, and were obliged to countenance the movement lest they should fall victims themselves. The Governor of Ispahan is an elder brother of the Shah. According to the Rhenish organ, Babism has a number of adherents in the United States, and Abbas Effendi, the chief Babist leader, frequently receives visits from Americans.

The same journal publishes a telegram from St Petersburg, which states that 3,200 Babis have been expelled from Ispahan because the Government feared they might be butchered by the mob. At Yezd 120 Babis were killed, of whom two were blown from the mouth of a cannon. The telegram further states that the priests have gone so far as to raise the question of the suzerainty of the Sultan (as Khalif). They hope to reconcile the Shiah and Sunni sects, of whom the former dispute and the latter admit the Sultan's claim to be regarded as the head of the Mahomedan religion.

As there is at the moment a brisk traffic in news from all parts of Asia between St Petersburg and Berlin, it is not impossible that the first as well as the second communication to the *Cologne Gazette* is derived from Russian sources.[43]

After the Upheavals

At Iṣfahán, although the open agitation against the Bahá'ís had ceased, all was not yet back to normal as the following letter from Dr Aganoor, dated 10 July 1903, indicated:

With reference to my despatches No. 20 of June 6 and No. 23 of June 13 last, I have the honour to report that this active persecution of the Babis has ceased, but there is reason to believe that all is not over.

The mollahs and their followers are continually taking counsel together, and continue corresponding with the mollahs of other towns. They are quite pleased with the news from Yezd, and ask each other why so much less was done here, although they express satisfaction that what was done in Yezd was, as they say, the result of their work here, and the effect of the advice contained in their letters to the Yezd mollahs.

At a meeting at Agha Nedjify's house it has been asserted that the authorities in Tehran meant to punish those who had caused the disturbances in Yezd. Agha Nedjify had declared that he would not allow even a common ryot to be punished or taken to Tehran for the part he had taken in this cause.

I understand they are quietly preparing evidence against some men of position whom they consider to be Babis. The two sons of Haji Mirza Hadi Dowlatabadi* are most frequently spoken of. The father is a known Babi who had to leave Ispahan several years ago and take up his residence in Tehran. The sons are not known to be Babis, but are known to be wealthy. One of them has already left Ispahan from fear. Agha Nedjify is reported to have written to Mujtaheds in Tehran to condemn the father to death, as also to start a general crusade against the sect in Tehran.

Should a suitable opportunity present itself, it is highly probable that the mollahs will not scruple to start the persecution afresh with vehemence.

* Ḥájí Mírzá Hádíy-i-Dawlatábádí was one of the leading Azalís of Persia.

> His Royal Highness the Prince has frequently expressed surprise at the central authorities taking no severe measures. As far as Ispahan is concerned, His Royal Highness says, he requires definite instructions to send away Agha Nedjify, which His Highness says he could easily do if he was provided with 200 sowars [mounted soldiers].[44]

The Russian Consul-General, Prince Dahija, returned from leave on 28 June and Baronovsky, the Acting Consul who had played such an important role in initiating the Iṣfahán upheaval, left for Ṭihrán the following day, a chastened man. The Ẓillu's-Sulṭán was a well-known sympathizer of the English and it was probably because of this and to cover up the Russian discomfiture that Prince Dahija made the accusations reported by Dr Aganoor on 10 July:

> I have the honour to report that H.R.H. the Zil-es-Sultan told me at an interview that when Prince Dahija, the Russian Consul-General called on His Royal Highness after his return he told His Highness that the Babi disturbances in Ispahan were due to the Prince, who had caused them at the instigation of the English. Prince Dahija added that there were 1000 Cossacks ready on the frontier, to which His Royal Highness says he replied that that was alright but there would probably be 5000 Sikhs from the South too.
>
> During a conversation with Prince Dahija the latter expressed to me the same belief as to the disturbances in Ispahan and Yezd being due to the Prince without however expressing his opinion as to the supposed instigators.[45]

In a dispatch dated 25 July, Dr Aganoor reported: 'I have the honour to report that the uneasy state of feeling continues, and one hears of blackmailing going on, on pretended charges of being Babis. . . .

'A few days ago, two supposed Babis of Najafabad were beaten by order of Agha Nedjify.'[46]

As indicated by Aganoor in the dispatch of 10 July, moves were afoot to have Áqá Najafí removed to Ṭihrán, but this was no easy matter; it was doubtful whether the people of Iṣfahán would allow him to be sent against his wishes. However, when news arrived that a force of some five or ten thousand under Naṣru's-Salṭanih* was gathering outside Ṭihrán to march south and enforce order, Áqá Najafí began to worry. While privately admitting his fear that he would be poisoned or strangled in Ṭihrán, in public he put on an attitude of defiance, stating: 'When I killed six Babis in Sehdeh a few years ago and was called up to Tehran, the Amin-i-Akhdas (one of Nasreddin Shah's wives) sent for the water in which I had washed my hands.'[47] And at another time: 'I have sacrificed myself to Mussulmans. Two parties will be very pleased at this viz (1) Christians and Europeans

* Previously Governor of Rasht, see pp. 373–6.

(2) Babis. But this pleasure shall be short lived. I shall convince the authorities by argument and force them to root out these dirty roots which cause disturbances (i.e. Christians and Babis). If the Government does not agree I shall myself give an order for the massacre of all ("Hokm-i-Khatl-i-om").'[48]

Over the next few months, various attempts were made to put pressure on Áqá Najafí to go to Ṭihrán. The latter, however, was determined to stay. Nor was the situation made any easier when, because of financial difficulties, the force that was to have been sent south under Naṣru's-Salṭanih was disbanded in early August. Áqá Najafí, moreover, had a few tricks up his sleeve. In late August, there was published in Iṣfahán a telegram purporting to be from Sulṭán 'Abdu'l-Ḥamíd, addressing Áqá Najafí. 'The chief of the Jaaferi* religion, His Highness (the pilgrimage of Moslems) Haji Sheikh Mohammad Taki Agha Nejefi – Isfahan.

'The telegram of Sharabiani† has been received and its contents understood. Telegram sent to Tehran. Continue your occupation where you are with the greatest honour and respect.

'I have given and will give every kind of support to the learned clergy. Hamid ibn Majid.'[49]

Later, Áqá Najafí denied the authenticity of this telegram and attributed its publication to his enemies, although it was generally believed to be the work of his supporters. Eventually, however, on 12 October, after further telegrams from the Prime Minister, Áqá Najafí left Iṣfahán for Ṭihrán.[50]

From Yazd, Eldrid reported the various feeble measures taken by Jalálu'd-Dawlih to punish the instigators of the disturbances. His letter is dated 29 August 1903:

I have the honour to confirm the information telegraphed to Dr. Aganoor of the banishment of the 'Imam-i-Juma' from this province during the last few days of July.

He was at the time residing in one of the mountain villages a few miles from Yezd and messengers were sent to bring him to Abbasabad, the Prince Governor's village about 11 farsachs distant from here. On his entering the Prince's presence he is said to have flung himself at his feet beseeching mercy. Although ostensibly banished to Kerbela via Shiraz I hear he is at present in the care of Isa Khan (local Governor) at Shahbabek.

Ahkund Mulla Hassan has also been banished to Mereez about 8 farsachs from town.

The Prince Governor commenced a tour of the mountain villages about the 12th instant and at Taft, a large village always famous for its 'lootis', he razed to the ground the houses of several of them who had fled but left after a few days without inflicting any severer punishment.

Masha, a mountain village which was the scene of the most ghastly and repulsive crimes perpetrated during the disturbances and where some 30 to 35 Babis were killed, was next visited by the Prince Governor who levied a fine upon the village which contains some 400 dwellings of Tomans 10 per house.

* i.e. Shí'ih

† Sharabíyání – see p. 365n.

I hear that a few days since a looti was executed at Taft and one or two have been killed at villages in the mountains. In town a certain Syed Haider Barnavees, who was a prominent tool of the mujteheds during the disturbances, received a severe sticking but with this single exception no punishment has been administered in town and it is said that this man would not have been so dealt with had he not offered personal insult [to] the Prince Governor at the commencement of the troubles.

One kran per toman has, I understand, been added to the Revenues on account of the increased military expenditure and in view of this and the large number of families without supporters I fear there will be great poverty in Yezd during the approaching winter.[51]

In the following year, Auguste Bricteux, a Belgian, visited Yazd. He has recorded something of the aftermath of the terror among the Bahá'ís:

Invited by some Bábís, I dined in a house whose proprietor was felled the previous year under the blows of the young Shí'ite executioners, leaving a widow and a young child. The poor little thing was presented to me; pale and sickly, shaken by the memory of terrible scenes, his big black eyes with a fixed stare still seeming to be filled with the dreadful vision.

In their zeal, the barbarians had even stopped up the water conduits of the house and killed the red-fish in the pond! They had taken good care to carry off everything that was movable as the reward for their courage.[52]

Addendum

In the P.R.O. records there is a letter from W. Winth, the Agent of Zeigler & Co. in Yazd, reporting the death of their broker, Áqá Muḥammad-Háshim, son of Muḥammad-Ḥaníf Big of Íraván. This account seems to indicate that Háshim was not a Bahá'í, but this differs from what Ḥájí Muḥammad-Ṭáhir-i-Málmírí writes in his *Táríkh-i-Shuhadáy-i-Yazd.* Of course, if Háshim was accused of being a Bábí, which is what the account seems to imply, then he could with justification have denied that, since he was a Bahá'í. The two accounts differ in other respects also. The letter is dated 29 July 1903:

We regret to have to bring to your notice that our broker Hashim fell a victim to the Babi persecutions, which took place here some while ago, assumed such an enormous extension and upset the whole town, business and market. We need hardly point out to you that the loss of our broker caused us great damage, as we were entirely unable to carry on business for some time and as the engagement of a new broker hampers us still a great deal, until the new man is fully acquainted with his duties and our business.

On the afternoon of June 13 Hashim did not come to the office, the following morning he gave us the following reasons for his absence: a certain Ali bin Haji Mehmed Sefer had some days before threatened Hashim to beat him accusing him to be a Babi and on the above mentioned afternoon Hashim, when returning home, noticed two individuals, known for their bad characters, roaming about his house. Hashim naturally suspected these men of having the intention to beat him, and he therefore preferred to stay at home that afternoon. As soon as Hashim had explained the reasons for his absence, [the] writer went to see H.I.H. Jellal ed dowleh, governor of Yezd and asked him to take measures to protect Hashim from further molestation. The governor promised to send for this Ali bin Haji Mehmed Sefer and to order him not to persecute Hashim any more. Ali hearing of the governor's intention and being afraid of a severe punishment concealed himself. The following morning (June 15th) the first outburst of the disturbances took place, a Babi was killed in the Bazaar and Hashim, being afraid, did not come to our office, we at once applied to the governor and requested him to grant Hashim his protection. The latter had left his house and taken refuge with Haji Mirza Mahmud, Vekil ed dowlih. We informed the governor of this, and asked him to let us know, whether he preferred that Hashim should remain at Haji Mirza Mahmud's home, or whether he ought to take shelter at the kala, (the governor's place). The governor advised Hashim to stay a few more days at the place where he was, until the excitement in town had subsided. Hashim therefore remained there until the following Monday, June 22nd. The town having been quiet the whole week Hashim was anxious to take up his duties again, but having requested the governor from the beginning to protect our broker, we decided to ask the former's opinion before allowing Hashim to put in his appearance again in the Bazaar. The governor however advised Hashim to remain a few more days at Haji Mirza Mahmud's house, until he (the governor) was able to guarantee the safety of the town, for which end he expected soldiers from Isfahan. Hashim however declared not to be able to follow Jellal ed dowleh's advice, Haji Mirza Mahmud being a well known Babi, it was only logical that people considered Hashim's staying at the former's house as a proof of Hashim being a Babi too. We then ordered Hashim to see the governor himself and put the matter before him and thereby succeeded in inducing Jellal ed Dowleh to declare that everybody, who molested or was going to molest Hashim, would have his tongue cut out. Seeing however that our customers, for fear of the mollahs, raised objections to Hashim's appearance in these offices, we instructed Hashim to take steps to plainly and openly establish that he was no Babi, all the more as he also always declared not to belong to this sect. On Friday morning the 26th inst. he went to see the chief mushtehid Aqa Mirza Seid Ali Hayeri, who however refused to hear his case on the pretext that it did not concern him. The day before a certain Seid Haider, notwithstanding this governor's order, openly declared in the Bazaar, he would not rest until Hashim was not [*sic*] killed and cut to pieces. The same Friday, June 26th, the disturbances broke out anew and assumed a very serious and disquieting character. Hashim who hid himself the whole day, i.e. soon after he had seen Aqa Mirza Seid Ali, escaped the same night and went to Mehris, a village near Yezd, where he stayed a few days, but his hiding place got to be known he was again persecuted and threatened and fled on June 30th, but at Teng e Djenar, 5 Farsakhs south of Mehris he was attacked and killed by three men. They first struck him down with stones and poles and afterwards shot him in the abdomen, they also poured petroleum over his corpse and burned him.

Hashim was married and leaves a widow and two sons, one five and the other seven years old, besides whom he also supported his old mother and his sister. He certainly must have had a little fortune of a few hundred tomans, but singularly no trace of it is to be found now, the accounts he kept have vanished. We only know that a certain Mirza Essedullah, a Babi who was also killed, owes him about £30.0.0 and that his relations find it at present impossible to collect this money. If Hashim's savings cannot be found his relations who were entirely dependent upon him will soon be destitute. [FO 248 802]

References

1. Churchill to Hardinge No. 22, 8 May 1903: FO 248 792
2. Churchill to Hardinge No. 24, 10 May 1903: FO 248 792
3. Churchill to Hardinge No. 26, 15 May 1903: FO 248 792
4. Churchill to Hardinge No. 28, 16 May 1903: FO 248 792
5. Churchill to Hardinge No. 29, 19 May 1903: FO 248 792
6. Churchill to Hardinge No. 31, 6 June 1903: FO 248 792
7. Telegram Aganoor to Hardinge 29 May 1903: FO 248 782
8. Telegram Aganoor to Hardinge 30 May 1903: FO 248 782
9. Telegram Aganoor to Hardinge 4 June 1903: FO 248 782
10. Telegram Hardinge to Aganoor 4 June 1903: FO 248 784
11. Telegram Aganoor to Hardinge 5 June 1903: FO 248 782
12. Aganoor to Hardinge No. 20, 6 June 1903: FO 248 788
13. Unsigned letter dated 2 June 1903: FO 248 788
14. Letter from Stileman 30 May 1903. No. 98, G2/PE/O/1903: CMS Archives
15. Letter from Stileman 6 June 1903. No. 102, G2/PE/O/1903: CMS Archives
16. Letter from Westlake 6 Aug. 1903. No. 140, G2/PE/O/1903: CMS Archives
17. Ẓillu's-Sulṭán to Hardinge 3 June 1903: FO 248 788 (trans. from French)
18. Telegram Aganoor to Hardinge 13 June 1903: FO 248 782
19. Aganoor to Hardinge No. 26, 13 June 1903: FO 248 788
20. Hardinge to Marquess of Lansdowne No. 95, 23 June 1903: FO 60 665
21. Nicolas *Massacres de Babis en Perse* pp. 22–8 (trans. from French)
22. Telegram Aganoor to Hardinge 18 June 1903: FO 248 782
23. Telegram Aganoor to Hardinge 24 June 1903: FO 248 782
24. Telegram Eldrid to Hardinge 27 June 1903: FO 248 782
25. Hardinge to Amínu's-Sulṭán 27 June 1903: FO 248 798
26. Telegram Hardinge to Eldrid 28 June 1903: FO 248 784
27. Telegrams Hardinge to For. Off. No. 86, and to Govt. of India No. 92, 28 June 1903: FO 248 784
28. Eldrid to Hardinge 28 June 1903: FO 248 802
29. White to Stileman 28 June 1903. No. 119, G2/PE O/1903: CMS Archives
30. White 'How Babis died for their Faith in Persia' pp. 275–6
31. Malcolm *Five Years in a Persian Town* pp. 88, 89, 104
32. Telegram Eldrid to Hardinge 29 June 1903: FO 248 782
33. Telegrams Eldrid to Hardinge 1 July 1903 and 3 July 1903: FO 248 783
34. Eldrid to Hardinge 3 July 1903: FO 248 802
35. Biggs to Durrant 4 July 1903. No. 120, G2/PE O/1903: CMS Archives
36. Telegram Aganoor to Hardinge 8 July 1903: FO 248 783
37. Hardinge to Amínu's-Sulṭán 8 July 1903: FO 248 798
38. Hardinge to the Marquess of Lansdowne No. 102, 9 July 1903: FO 60 666
39. Hardinge to Lansdowne No. 107. 21 July 1903: FO 60 666
40. Eldrid to Hardinge 24 July 1903: FO 248 802
41. *The Times* 13 July 1903, p. 5, col. 6
42. *The Times* 30 July 1903, p. 3, col. 6
43. *The Times* 3 Aug. 1903, p. 4, col. 1
44. Aganoor to Hardinge No. 30, 10 July 1903: FO 248 788
45. Aganoor to Hardinge No. 31, 10 July 1903: FO 248 788
46. Aganoor to Hardinge No. 34, 25 July 1903: FO 248 788

47. Aganoor to Hardinge No. 35, 26 July 1903: FO 248 788
48. Aganoor to Hardinge No. 44, 14 Aug. 1903: FO 248 788
49. Aganoor to Hardinge No. 45, 24 Aug. 1903: FO 248 788 (trans. by Aganoor)
50. Aganoor to Hardinge No. 74, 3 Dec. 1903: FO 248 788
51. Eldrid to Hardinge 29 Aug. 1903: FO 248 802
52. Bricteux *Au Pays du Lion et du Soleil* p. 227 (trans. from French)

TWENTY-EIGHT

Persecutions in Khurásán (1896–1915)

The Five Martyrs of Turbat-i-Ḥaydarí

When the news of the assassination of Náṣiru'd-Dín Sháh spread through Persia, it was assumed by many that the 'Bábís' were responsible because of their previous attempt in 1852. In most places the correct version of the event arrived, exculpating the Bahá'ís before any serious harm could result, but one exception was Turbat-i-Ḥaydarí in Khurásán. Here five unoffending Bahá'ís were seized, with the consent of the Governor, and put to death by a mob.

Ney Elias (q.v.), the eminent Central Asian explorer, was British Consul-General in Khurásán at this time. A network of agents (newswriters) sent him information from all parts of Khurásán, Transcaspia and Afghanistan. A letter from Turbat-i-Ḥaydarí dated 23 August 1896 contained the following report:

> Five natives* of the Tabas and Turbat-i-Haidari districts who were accused of being Bábis were recently imprisoned by the Governor of this place. Sheikh Ali Akbar, Mujtahid (Priest) of Turbat and another Yezdi Mujtahid of the same name, who was passing through here on his way back to Yezd from Meshad denounced them as infidels and declared that they deserved to be killed. Thereupon a mob collected, pulled the prisoners out of the jail, and stoned them to death. Two of the men were respectable and wealthy traders.
>
> It is said that the Asaf-ud-Dowleh [q.v.], at first intended to send sowars [*savvárs*] to arrest the perpetrators of the deed, but that he has given up the idea on the advice of a certain priest.[1]

At this time the affairs of Khurásán were in great disorder. A succession of corrupt and inefficient Governors, the recent assassination of the Sháh, and the intrigues of the Russian and British Governments had reduced the province to a state of near anarchy. On 2 September 1896, Elias telegrammed to the British Legation in Ṭihrán: 'Several leading priests in

* These five were: Ḥájí Ṣádiq who was killed in his home at the start of the episode, and four others who were first imprisoned and then killed: Áqá Mírzá Ghulám-Riḍá, Ustád Ghulám-'Alí, Ustád Muḥammad-'Alí, and Ustád Muḥammad-Ḥasan.

favour of order are urging Governor to expel chiefs of unruly mullahs and otherwise act with energy, but he will not move. Kárguzár during last few days has also abandoned his functions and virtually refuses duty. Impossible to settle anything. Five persons, accused of being Babis, been killed by priests, of which Governor takes no notice. Sole remedy for existing state of things is early despatch of new Governor with full powers.'[2]

In a note in the Mashhad Political Diary for 3 September 1896, Elias states: 'I learn today that the Russian Consul-General, at an interview yesterday, formally demanded of the Governor-General whether or not the Meshed authorities were capable of protecting Russian subjects. His action is based on the murder of the five Babis at Turbat-i-Haidari, a crime which he regards (and probably rightly) as having had its origin among the unruly priests of Meshed. Apparently Mr Vlassow [q.v.] obtained no satisfactory answer from the Governor-General.'[3]

In the Summary of News from Mashhad for 12–26 September 1896, prepared by Horace Rumbold (q.v.), there is the following entry: 'The Governor-General of Khorassan has not taken any steps to punish the perpetrators of this deed notwithstanding a peremptory order for their punishment sent by the Sadr Azam at the command of the Shah.'[4]

The Martyrdom of Ḥájí Muḥammad-i-Turk

On 9 February 1898, Ḥájí Muḥammad-i-Turk (also known as Tabrízí; see fig. 38), a Bahá'í, was dragged to the main street of Mashhad and there burnt to death. This episode was fully reported from Mashhad. The Consul-General, Lt-Col. Charles Yate (q.v.), wrote in the Political Diary for the week ending 11 February 1898: 'On the afternoon of the 9th February a man accused of being a Bábi was pulled out of his house by a mob of religious students, beaten with sticks, wounded by revolver shots, drenched with kerosine oil and publicly burnt to death in the main street of Meshed close to the Shrine gates, full details of which are given in the Newsletters.'[5]

One Newsletter, dated 9 February 1898, stated:

There was one Haji Muhammad, a Turk, who was accused of being a Babi and who had been expelled several times from Meshed on that account.

He had now-a-days instituted a plaint against his sons who had taken possession of his landed and other property and got the authorities to send out an official to dispossess his sons. The latter told the Governor-General and the Ulema that their father was a Babi and an unbeliever.

Today some religious students pulled him out of his house in the Khiaban (street) fired five pistol shots at him one of which missed him and struck one of [the] on-lookers in the leg. When he fell he was beaten with sticks and kicked until he was dead. They poured kerosine oil over him and burned him. All this took place without the knowledge of the Governor-General* who sent for Haji Mirza Mahmud Khan, the Beglar Begi, and having called him to account for not preventing the mischief, had him severely flogged, suspended him from the office of Beglar Begi and imprisoned him. It now remains to be seen what will be the consequences of this incident for the Rais-ut-Tullab.†[6]

A further Newsletter, dated 10 February, stated:

The students who have murdered the man who was accused of being a Babi had it is said no permission from the Rais-ut-Tullab or any of the Ulema to do so. It is said that they held an order from the late Haji Sheikh Muhammad Taki, Mujtahid, denouncing the man as a Babi and an apostate. It is also said that they held a similar order from Haji Ismail, Mujtahid, also.

A Turk merchant who is a native of Baku went to the Russian Consul-General today and complained to him that the Rais-us-Tullab had summoned him to appear before him to answer to a claim brought against him by somebody, but that as he did not obey his summons the priest had denounced him as a Babi and that now he was not assured of his safety as he might at any moment be murdered on that accusation.[7]

Further details were given in a Newsletter dated 11 February:

The following men were concerned in the murder of Haji Muhammad Babi:–

Agha Saiyid Muhammad Sadik, religious student.

Mulla Shir Ali, Sar Wilayati, religious student.

Agha Saiyid Abdul Karim, religious student.

Agha Saiyid Agha, religious student.

Mulla Shir Ali committed the murder. He held the revolver, which he had obtained from another person on the occasion, and fired five shots at the victim.

It was he who dragged the victim out of his house. Agha Saiyid Muhammad Sadik poured naphtha over the body of the victim.

Mulla Shir Ali is one of the followers of Haji Shaikh Ismail. Agha Saiyid Sadik, Yezdi, is one of the followers of Agha Haji Mirza Saiyid Ali, Yezdi, Mujtahid. It is said that the culprits hold a permission in writing from Haji Shaikh Ismail. They are said to hold a paper from the late Haji Shaikh Muhammad Taki also denouncing the man as an apostate.

Haji Muhammad had been recently getting a paper signed by certain Ulema certifying that he was a Musalman and not a Babi. The certificate had already been signed by the priests Haji Shaikh Abu Muhammad, the Imam Juma and the Shaikh-ul-Islam.

The murder had been committed at the instigation of the victim's own sons who were not on good terms with their father owing to his having transferred his property to his second wife who is not their mother. It is also said that the man had two wives who are sisters while according to the Muhammadan religious law a man cannot marry two sisters unless he divorces one and marries the other.

However, the public do not approve of the deed and blame the perpetrators.[8]

In another Newsletter, dated 11 February 1898, the following information was given:

* Muḥammad-Taqí Mírzá, the Ruknu'd-Dawlih (q.v., see fig. 40)

† lit. Head of the Religious Students, Mírzá Zaynu'l-'Ábidín

Haji Muhammad Turk, who was murdered in the main street of Meshed two days ago with great cruelty by the students of the Khairat Khan college and was burned while he was still alive, his body afterwards being thrown into a gutter, was accused some years ago of being a Babi. He had two wives and had sons by both of them. At one time he had transferred his property to the sons of his first wife and after some time he retransferred to his second wife and her children a part of the same property which he had already transferred to the sons of his first wife, and treated his second better than the first one. The sons of the first wife thereupon entered into litigation with their father and as he was accused of being a Babi they also brought the same accusation against him and denounced him before the Ulema. The accusations against him became so strong that three years ago the late Haji Shaikh Muhammad Taki, Mujtahid, ordered that it was proper to expel him from Meshed or to kill him. The Muaiyid-ud-Dowleh, the then Governor-General of Khorasan, caused him to be arrested and kept him in prison for a long time. He afterwards obtained a large sum of money from him as a present and released him. After his release the man proceeded to Teheran and thence he went to Ashkabad and Kelat and constantly kept moving from place to place. In order to do away with their father the sons of the first wife transferred a part of their property to Saiyid Sádik, a religious student, who began to persecute Haji Muhammad. The second wife being afraid of Saiyid Sádik transferred the property which she had received from her husband, to Haji Mirza Bákir, Shafti,* who, with the assistance of the Ain-ul-Mulk, took possession of the property.

A few days [ago] Haji Muhammad was preparing to take the management of his affairs into his own hands. The sons of the first wife who were supported by Saiyid Sádik and other religious students went to the Rais-ut-Tullab two days ago and brought accusations against the man. Whether they obtained an order from the Rais-ut-Tullab or not it is not known. They, however, forced their way into Haji Muhammad's house, dragged him out and murdered him with great cruelty.

The people of Meshed are greatly alarmed by this incident.

Haji Mirza Mahmud Khán, Beglar Begi of Meshed, has been flogged and imprisoned by the Governor-General for having taken no measure to prevent the occurrence. It is said that the Governor-General's object in taking this measure is not to restore order but to obtain money from the Beglar Begi.

Saiyid Sádik, Yezdi, was the chief instigator in the matter and caused the Turk to be murdered. One Mulla Shir, Kuchani, Saiyid Agha, Bujnurdi, and another Saiyid, whose name is not known as yet, committed the deed. The criminals when committing the hideous crime were saying that they had the sanction of the Rais-ut-Tullab and Shaikh Ismail in the matter.[9]

When apprised of the facts of the case, Hardinge (q.v.), the British Chargé d'Affaires, wrote to Ḥájí 'Alí Khán, the Amínu'd-Dawlih, Prime Minister of Persia, on 14 February.

I have the honour to bring to Y.H. [Your Highness]'s knowledge the following details which I have received from H.M. Consul General in Meshed respecting a most barbarous and inhuman murder which occurred in Meshed in the main street of the town at 4 o'clock in the afternoon of the 10th Feb. last.

A certain Hadji Mahmoud accused of being a Babi was dragged out of his house by

* One of the priests of Meshed [note in Newsletter].

a mob of religious students headed, it is said, by Seyid Sadik, Mollashir Kurdi and Seyid Agha Bujnurdi. He was beaten in the streets with cudgels and then wounded by revolver shots. The unfortunate victim of this outrage while still alive was then saturated with naphtha and burnt to death.

Without entering into the motives of this atrocious crime I wish to impress upon Y.H. that the possibility of such a barbarous act taking place in broad daylight in the main street of one of the largest towns in Persia is a striking proof of the disorder and insecurity which prevail in Meshed and for which the Governor should be strongly called to account. I trust also that Y.H. will take the most stringent and effective measures for the summary and condign punishment of those guilty of one of the most atrocious and inhuman murders in the history of modern times.[10]

Hardinge telegrammed on 17 February, giving details of the steps that he had taken in Ṭihrán: 'I have officially brought incident reported in your telegram No. 4 to the notice of the Persian Government and have urged punishment of the guilty. Sadr Azam has informed me that orders have been given for the punishment of the assassins and the expulsion of certain Mollahs. You should call on Governor and inquire of him what steps he is taking in the sense of the information given me by the Sadr Azam.'[11]

On 20 February, Yate reported by telegram the arrest of four of the murderers but stated that the Sháh's orders were awaited regarding the punishment to be inflicted on them. On receipt of this telegram, Hardinge sent a copy of it to the Persian Prime Minister together with the following note, dated 20 February 1898: 'I trust that Y.H. will impress upon H.I.M. the Shah the very urgent necessity of issuing promptly orders for the summary punishment of the murderers as a necessary and salutary measure against the repetition of scenes of such unusual barbarity and inhumanity.'[12]

In the Mashhad Political Diary for the week ending 18 February 1898, Yate reported:

. . . the Governor-General was summoned to the Telegraph Office on the 16th instant by the Shah and directed by His Majesty to deal with the murderers of the man accused of being a Babi very severely, full powers being given to him in the matter. The first thing the Governor-General did was to arm the soldiers in the Guard-houses with breech-loading rifles in place of the old muzzle-loading muskets they have hitherto possessed. He also posted guns in the main streets of the town and sent out patrols of Persian Cossacks and Police. Two of the murderers and about fifteen so-called religious students have already been arrested and imprisoned in the citadel and steps are being taken to arrest the others. Under orders from the Shah the shrine authorities are giving assistance by arresting criminals in the sanctuary and handing them over to the Police, but the ring-leader of the murderers, one Saiyid Sadik, is still at large and has not been arrested yet. The Priests Zainal Abidin and Sheikh Ismail, who are said to have sanctioned the murder, are in hiding and have not yet been arrested or deported, but guards have been posted round their houses.[13]

In the Newsletters attached to the Diary, the following additional information is given:

[*Newsletter dated 14 February:*] It is reported on good authority that Saiyid Sádik, Yezdi, and the other three religious students, who murdered Haji Muhammad Turk in a disgraceful manner, received four mans of clarified butter each from the sons of the victim.

The public in general disapprove of the hideous crime committed by these men.

It is rumoured among the people that the foreign consulates are strongly protesting against the commission of this disgraceful act.[14]

[*Newsletter dated 16 February:*] I am informed by a friend that the other day in a meeting presided over by Sheikh Ismail, the new Beglar Begi warned in a friendly manner, Saiyid Sadik, Yezdi, the religious student who was the ringleader of the murderers of Haji Muhammad Turk, not to come out of the sanctuary as he would be arrested if he came out.[15]

[*Newsletter dated 17 February:*] It is stated that last night Mulla Shir Ali and one of the other murderers of Haji Muhammad Turk were arrested in the Shrine and taken out of the Sanctuary where they were handed over to the Persian Cossacks who took them to the citadel.

Some guns with ammunition and artillerymen have been posted today in the various parts of the town and it was proclaimed by the beat of drum this morning that if any of the shopkeepers closed their shops by the order of the Mullas their shops and houses would be plundered.

The infantry soldiers and Persian Cossacks have all been armed and are patrolling the town.

It is said that guards have been posted at the house of some of the Ulema also.[16]

[*Newsletter dated 17 February:*] The town is in a perfect tranquil state. The students are quiet and dare not say a word. Ten or fifteen of the mischievous students were arrested today and taken to the citadel. Four men have been arrested from the Páinpá College. The students wanted to mutiny but as soon as they saw that the men who are making the arrests were going to use their arms they dispersed.

One man has been arrested from the Madrasa-i-Nawáb and several arrests have been made from the other colleges also. The Khairat Khan college was searched for Saiyid Sadik but he could not be found. The Ulema did not come to the mosque today.

It is stated that two Turk religious students, Russian subjects, asked some of the mischievous Razawi Saiyids to render assistance to the students but that the Razawi Saiyids declined to do so.

There is a talk among the people that Agha Shaikh Ismail, Turshizi, and the Rais-ut-Tullab will be arrested tonight.[17]

Also included with the Political Diary were translations of communications that passed between the Prime Minister, Amínu'd-Dawlih, and the authorities in Mas͟hhad over the issue.

On 12 February, Ruknu'd-Dawlih telegrammed to the Amínu'd-Dawlih:

I have repeatedly written to you clearly pointing out the obstacles experienced by me in the administration of state affairs and the enforcing of order in the country. I have also pointed out the defects but I have not yet received a decided answer from you.

Gradually the impudent and fearless conduct of the religious students has acquired such an aggravated form that yesterday [*sic*], it being the 9th of February, two hours before sunset, by the order of the Rais-ut-Tullab and certain other Ulema, some religious students forced their way into the house of Haji Muhammad Turk, an old man of eighty years, who was accused of being a Babi, pulled him out, dragged him through the principal street of Meshed and on arriving near the entrance to the precincts of the Shrine fired several revolver shots at him and afterwards burned him with kerosine oil. Haji Muhammad owned six thousand Tumans worth of landed property which, according to the judgement passed by the Ulema of Meshed and Teheran, had been taken possession of by his four sons. He himself did not agree to the transfer of the property and it had been arranged to hold, last night, a meeting in the court-house to enquire into the matter.

Haji Mirza Mahmud Khan, Beglar Begi, who for personal motives had a secret understanding with the Ulema and the religious students took no steps whatever to prevent the mischief and by the time information was received by me the deed had been committed. The students who committed the crime went with great courage into their colleges situated inside the sanctuary of the Shrine where it is out of my power to touch them. I at once sent for Haji Mirza Mahmud Khan and having punished him, dismissed him from his office and imprisoned him. The same night I conferred the office of the Beglar Begi upon Mir Panj Mehdi Khan son of the late Haji Abul Fath Khan, Bizaki, who is a faithful servant of the Government. I shall also arrest within the next few days the perpetrators of the hideous crime and punish them. But I beg to observe,

'The fountain head can be stopped with a spade.
But when it is filled it cannot be crossed on an elephant.'

I shall report the other particulars by post.[18]

The Prime Minister replied on 14 February:

Your Highness's telegram regarding the bold conduct of the students living inside the sanctuary caused great displeasure and astonishment to His Majesty. Now there is no further occasion for any consideration or to let any delay to take place. Haji Mirza Mahmud Khan deserved the punishment you awarded him and he is, in my opinion, liable to a severe punishment. According to His Majesty's order you should have all the students who were concerned in the murder and burning of the man, to be arrested, put in chains and punished one by one on the same spot where they murdered the old man, the late Haji Mulla Muhammad. Then they should be imprisoned. You should also cause Haji Mirza Zain-ul-Abidin to be handed over to some Ghulams to take him to some other place so that he may have a little rest from making mischief and the people from his mischievousness. Your Highness should exercise a little more diligence in the preservation of good order so that nobody should have the courage to create mischief in an independent manner.

In the matter of the preservation of order in the town His Majesty holds your Highness personally responsible in the matter. You may entrust the maintenance of good order in the town to whomsoever you deem advisable.[19]

On 14 February, the Guardian of the Shrine of the Imám Riḍá telegrammed to the Amínu'd-Dawlih, the Prime Minister:

With regard to the murder of Haji Muhammad Turk who was put to death in the middle of the Khiyaban outside the sanctuary of the Shrine on the accusation of being a Babi I beg to state that notwithstanding that some of the culprits remained outside the sanctuary for a day or two nobody arrested them. Now that they have gone into the colleges situated inside the sanctuary and have mingled with the students the Governor-General is demanding their surrender from the officials of the Shrine.

In view of the attitude which the students have at present adopted in Meshed and about which you are well aware, the Shrine officials beg to represent that they were never called upon to perform this kind of service, that they are not fighting men, that it requires an armed force to effect the arrest of the culprits and that it is the Governor-General of the province who has been furnished with such means by the Government. Should the culprits be taken away even from inside the sanctuary there will be no opposition on the part of the Shrine officials. The Governor-General's order can be enforced inside the sanctuary in the same manner as it is done outside it.[20]

To which the Amínu'd-Dawlih replied on the same day:

The conduct of the students living inside the sanctuary who have been guilty of this hideous crime shows the state of the management of the affairs of the Shrine. Your good management of the various establishments of the Shrine is indeed praiseworthy. A man should not be so mild and meek as to allow everybody to do what he likes. Properly speaking this matter concerns you. In order to make amends for this negligence you should cause all the students who have committed the crime to be turned out of the colleges situated inside the sanctuary and handed over to the officers of the Governor-General.

You should also take care that in future this kind of persons are not accommodated in the colleges otherwise you will be held responsible.[21]

On 23 February, Hardinge telegrammed to Yate: 'Sadr Azam has informed me that orders have been sent to Governor General to send murderers to Tehran. Please ascertain if these orders have been received.[22]

In his Political Diary for the week ending 25 February 1898, Yate reported:

I received a telegram from H.B.M's Chargé d'Affaires at Teheran requesting full details of the murder with barbarous cruelty of the man accused of being a Babi, reported in para 1 of my diary for last week and on the receipt of my report the incident was officially brought to the notice of the Persian Government by Mr Hardinge, who urged the punishment of the murderers.

The Sadr-i-Azam informed Mr Hardinge that orders had been given for the punishment of the assassins and the expulsion of certain Mullas and I was directed to call upon the Governor-General and enquire what steps he was taking in the matter.

I saw the Governor-General on the afternoon of the 19th February, when His Highness informed me that he had arrested four out of the six murderers, deported the two priests, Zain-ul-Abidin and Shaikh Ismail, and was awaiting the Shah's orders regarding the punishment to be inflicted on the murderers.

In reporting this to Mr Hardinge I was able to inform him that 14 other mischievous religious students had been arrested as well and that many others had doffed their student's white turbans and were leaving the town, which was perfectly quiet.

The Governor-General I found had taken excellent measures to secure this result. He first of all left the body of the murdered man as it lay for some days till he was strong enough to act and then had it taken to the Shrine and washed and buried with full mussalman rites. The Shrine officials by consenting to this did away once and for all with the allegation that the man was a Babi. As a matter of fact it is now known that the man was murdered at the instigation of his own sons who wished to deprive him of his property.

The Governor-General by next causing the arrest of men sheltered in the sanctuary of the Shrine has proved at last that the Persian Government, if it will only pluck up courage to deal with the priesthood with a firm hand, has the power to do so. The priesthood when once they see that the Government is acting in earnest give in. At least they have done so here and the Governor-General is to be congratulated upon the result.

H.B.M's Chargé d'Affaires telegraphed on the 23rd informing me that the Sadr-i-Azam had stated that orders had been issued for the despatch of the murderers to Teheran and directing me to ascertain whether these orders had been received. The Governor-General in reply to my enquiries informed me that no such orders had as yet reached him.

In acquainting Mr Hardinge with this I mentioned what a much better effect it would have if the murderers were executed on the spot; not to mention the danger of their escaping on the road as the last batch of prisoners that were sent from here did. M. Ponafidine [Russian Consul-General] in talking the matter over with me was greatly in favour of severe measures and naturally was much concerned in the matter as Russian subjects in Meshed might be subjected to similar treatment if the agitation was permitted to run on unchecked. I believe he personally urged the execution of the criminals at Meshed on the Governor-General.[23]

In the Newsletters attached to the Political Diary, the following reports occur:

[*Newsletter dated 19 February:*] The Governor-General caused a proclamation to be issued yesterday evening warning the people that whoever kept Haji Mirza Zain-ul-Abidin in his house and did not inform the authorities of his whereabouts would be liable to capital punishment and his property would be confiscated. Thereupon Haji Mirza Zain-ul-Abidin, who was in hiding in the house of Haji Mirza Abdul-Majid, one of the Shrine officials, sent a message at once to the Wazir informing him of his whereabouts and expressing his readiness to go over to his house. The Wazir thereupon sent his Farrash Báshi and had Haji Mirza Zain-ul-Abidin brought to his house. At night the Wazir took the priest with him to the Governor-General who informed the latter that as orders had been received from the Persian Government that he should not remain in Meshed he must leave the town the next day. His Highness then handed him over to the Wazir with instructions to send him off the next day to Káin under an escort of Persian sowars with an order to the address of the Governor of Káin directing him to keep the priest at Birjand under surveillance.

Háji Sheikh Ismail who is also in hiding has been allowed two days to make his preparations and then leave Meshed. He intends to go back to Turshiz, which place he is a native of.

Four of the murderers have been arrested but two of them have not yet been found. One of the latter is Saiyid Sadik Yezdi, who is in hiding in the town, and the other is Saiyid Abdul Karim who has taken flight from the town. Telegrams have, however, been despatched in all directions to arrest him wherever he is found.

Besides the above mentioned four men ten or twelve other students who are known as mischievous persons have also been arrested.

The Governor-General has telegraphed to Teheran asking for orders regarding the four murderers who have been arrested.[24]

[*Newsletter dated 20 February:*] Haji Mirza Zain-ul-Abidin has been deported to Káin.

Haji Sheikh Ismail, accompanied by three of his followers, has also left the town.

Saiyid Sadik Yezdi, the ringleader of the murderers, who was in hiding in the town, has also been arrested.

The Governor-General says that after the murder of Háji Muhammad, the students intended to murder the customs officer of Meshed, who is also accused of being a Bábi, but that he saved his life.[25]

[*Newsletter dated 24 February:*] Agha Mirza Saiyid Ali Mujtahid came to the mosque to-day to conduct prayers. Haji Sheikh Hasan Ali was also present. At present all is quiet and no disturbance is likely to take place.[26]

In a Newsletter dated 24 February, it was reported that the 'ulamá of Mashhad were interceding on behalf of the arrested students and disturbances were threatened.[27]

There is also a further set of telegrams between the Prime Minister and the Mashhad authorities. On 16 February the Prime Minister enquired of the Governor-General what measures had been taken and instructed him to demand from the Guardian of the Shrine the surrender of anyone taking refuge there. On 18 February, the Prime Minister instructed the Guardian of the Shrine to deliver up the culprits to the Governor-General.

The following telegrams are also given in full in the Newsletters:

17 Feb.: Governor-General of Khurásán to Governor of Qúchán, instructing him to intercept and arrest Siyyid 'Abdu'l-Karím.

17 Feb.: Guardian of the Shrine to the Prime Minister, reporting arrest of Mullá Shír-'Alí and his delivery to Governor-General.

17 Feb.: Guardian of the Shrine to the Prime Minister, reporting arrest of a further ten students.

17 Feb.: Governor-General of Khurásán to the Prime Minister, stating that 600 men of the Fírúzkúh Battalion and 100 artillerymen with breech-loading rifles, together with *savvárs*, policemen and two guns, were placed around the Shrine to effect the arrest of the murderers. Two of the murderers had been arrested.

20 Feb.: Governor-General of Khurásán to the Prime Minister, reporting arrest of Ḥájí Mírzá Zaynu'l-'Ábidín and his intention to exile him to Bírjand the following day. All the murderers except two had been arrested. 'I am awaiting His Majesty's orders as to what punishment should be inflicted on the culprits.'

20 Feb.: Governor-General of Khurásán to the Prime Minister, reporting exile of Ḥájí Mírzá Zaynu'l-'Ábidín to Bírjand and his intention to exile Shaykh Ismá'íl to Turshíz.

20 Feb.: Prime Minister to Governor-General, transmitting approval of the Sháh for the Governor's measures and agreeing that the Shrine officials and servants who had been slow in arresting the culprits

should be punished.

20 Feb.: Prime Minister to Guardian of the Shrine, transmitting the Sháh's approval of his co-operation in the arrest of the culprits and adding that those officials of the Shrine who had been slow in carrying out these orders should be severely punished.[28]

In a later Newsletter, the text of a telegram from Ruknu'd-Dawlih, the Governor-General, to the Prime Minister, dated 25 February 1898, is given:

As directed by you, I have deported Shaikh Ismáil to Sistán and Háji Mirza Zain-ul-Abidin to Káin.

Order now prevails in the town. You have not sent me any orders with regard to the murderers of Háji Muhammad Turk who are in confinement. For certain reasons, which I shall explain by letter, it is not advisable that they should be punished in Meshed. Their punishment here will lead to certain difficulties. I would suggest that permission may be given to me to send them to Teheran where they may be punished or imprisoned for life, but it is most essential that after their arrival in Teheran they should not be released in order to prevent their return to Meshed where they might make mischief again.

With regard to Mirza Abdur Reza, one of the Shrine officials, I shall take the necessary steps, as directed by you. I find it necessary here to give you some information about the man. He is one of the most mischievous persons in Khorásán. During the Asaf-ud-Dowleh's time when Haji Mirza Zain-ul-Abidin was expelled from Meshed and Shaikh Ismail created a disturbance which compelled the Asaf-ud-Dowleh to bring back Háji Mirza Zain-ul-Abidin, Mirza Abdur Reza took the leading part in this agitation. It is not advisable that he should be allowed to live even in Teherán, and I would suggest that he should be expelled from there also. As directed by you I wrote to the Guardian of the Shrine who has dismissed from the Shrine service, Mirza Abdur-Reza's brother together with two or three other persons who were mischief-makers and acted against the orders of the Government.[29]

Other telegrams reported in the Newsletters include:

27 Feb.: Governor-General of Khurásán to the Prime Minister, stating that '. . . Mulla Muhammad Ali, known as Fázil, son of the late Mulla Abbas Ali, Ranzakhán, who was the chief instigator in the murder of Háji Muhammad, was deported by him to Daragez without any difficulty.'[30]

1 Mar.: Prime Minister to Governor-General of Khurásán, stating that he had laid before the Sháh the Governor-General's telegram reporting the deportation of Shaykh Ismá'íl and Hájí Mírzá Zaynu'l-'Ábidín. The Sháh had ordered that Mírzá 'Abdu'r-Riḍá and his brother, who had been guilty of mischievous conduct, be punished, the former being sent to Shíráz and detained there and the latter being dismissed from the service of the Shrine.[31]

On 28 February, Capt. J. F. Whyte (q.v.) took over as Acting Consul-General of Khurásán in place of Lt-Col. Yate. In the Political Diary for the week ending 11 March 1898, he reports:

Mons. Ponafidine, the Russian Consul General, returned my call on the 5th March.

During the course of conversation he referred with much satisfaction to the success which had attended the vigorous action of the Governor General in the matter of the murder of Haji Muhammad.

He told me that he had much to complain of in the Rukn-ud-douleh, but the energy which he had displayed on this occasion had quite redeemed his character in his (M. Ponafidine's) eyes.

He was not pressing for the execution or indeed for any particular form of punishment of the murderers, as he was of opinion that this question could best be settled by the Persian authorities themselves. His chief points had been gained, as the Russian colony which had been much alarmed by what had occurred had been completely reassured by the vigour with which the Governor General had acted, and the priesthood had been shown that the Government was both able and determined to suppress all outbursts of fanaticism with a firm hand, and to punish even the most influential among them, if guilty of instigating them.

The Russian Consul General spoke with great frankness, and I have heard from other sources that his attitude has been throughout the affair most correct.

There can be no doubt as to the excellent effect which had been produced in Meshed by the manner in which the matter has been dealt with, and as to the increase of the power and prestige of the Government at the expense of that of the priests which has resulted. The latter have been for the moment certainly completely cowed, and it is to be hoped that they will never be allowed to regain the power which they have lost.

The whole affair has been a striking instance of the ease with which the Persian Government can cope with the priesthood if it will only act with courage . . .[32]

In a Newsletter attached to this Diary, a telegram from Ruknu'd-Dawlih to the Prime Minister, dated 2 March, is quoted:

Three of the late Haji Muhammad's sons, who paid fifty-eight Tumans to the students to murder their father fled towards Kelat, but I have caused them to be arrested and brought back to Meshed. I request that whatever orders are to be passed with regard to the murderers and these three men may be passed without delay. It is not at all advisable that they should be executed in Meshed. Kindly give me permission to send them to Teheran where they can either be executed or imprisoned for life.

You have ordered that the number of the Persian Cossacks, policemen and Ghulams in Meshed should be reduced. I beg to point out that it is not at all advisable to do so and I would request that I may be allowed to maintain them at their present strength. One hundred and thirty six policemen and their officers are hardly sufficient for guarding the town of Meshed. If their number is not increased it should in no case be reduced.[33]

At this stage, it appeared likely that for the first time on Persian soil the perpetrators of a violent act against the Bahá'ís would receive their just punishment. But it was not to be. The energy of the Governor-General, which had succeeded in wresting the murderers from the holy Shrine and exiling the instigators of this atrocity, flagged at this moment. Despite continuing pressure from the foreign Consuls, he failed to take any further steps and allowed the perpetrators of the crime to slip from his grasp.

In the Political Diary for the week ending 8 April, it is reported that one of the murderers, Siyyid Ṣádiq-i-Yazdí, 'who was confined in the citadel prison, pending the receipt of orders from Teherán, has been able, owing to the carelessness of the keepers of the prison, to escape.'[34]

In the Political Diary for the week ending 22 April, Lt-Col Temple (q.v.), acting Consul-General, reports:

'Saiyid Sádik Yezdi . . . surrendered himself on the night of the 14th April to the authorities of the Shrine where he is at present in nominal confinement.

'I understand that the Shrine authorities decline to give him up to the Governor-General and are determined to make a firm stand in the matter.'[35]

No further progress was made in persuading the Shrine authorities to hand over Siyyid Ṣádiq. The 'ulamá, moreover, were now agitating against any further punishment of the culprits. In an extract from local reports received during the week ending 20 May 1898, the following is to be found:

The Governor-General has received a letter from the Sadr-i-Azam saying that the Ulema in Teheran are agitating against the deportation of Shaikh Ismail on the grounds that he was not concerned in the least in the murder of the man accused of being a Bábi. The Sadr-i-Azam has asked the Governor-General to enquire into the matter and to inform him of the result of his enquiries before he gives an answer to the ulema in Teherán. The Governor-General has referred the matter for enquiry to the Principal of one of the colleges at Meshed.

It is stated that Agha Saiyid Ali Yezdi has sent a message to the Russian Consul-General asking him to intercede with the Persian Government for Shaikh Ismail.[36]

Furthermore, in a letter to Sir Mortimer Durand (q.v.) dated 7 June 1898, Temple reports: 'The Governor General who had acted with energy and promptitude in the affair [the murder of Ḥájí Muḥammad-i-Turk] appears to be now disposed to take a different course, as he has instructed the Governor of Deragez to allow Agha Muhammad Fazil* to return to Chanaran, a village near Meshed, where he is said to own property.'[37]

Later, on 30 September of that year, the new Prime Minister, Amínu's-Sulṭán, telegrammed to the Ruknu'd-Dawlih, reversing the earlier sentences of exile on two of the 'ulamá responsible for instigating the murder: 'In accordance with His Majesty's command please order that Haji Sheikh Ismail, Turshizi, Mujtahid, may return to Meshed and occupy himself in praying for His Majesty's long life. You may also order Haji Mirza Zain-ul-Abidin to proceed to Sabzawar and pray there for His Majesty.'[38]

The Dúghábád Episode

The first two decades of the twentieth century were a very unsettled period in Persian history, and the Bahá'ís were subjected to continuous

* One of the 'ulamá who instigated the murder.

harassment, particularly in the more remote parts of the country. Many of these episodes were of course not noted by the British Consuls, but since this period also marks the climax of British interest and involvement in the affairs of Persia, British Consular representation in Persia increased to a remarkable degree, with Consuls even in some rather small towns. Thus Turbat-i-Ḥaydarí could not be called a large town and yet for strategic reasons it was considered necessary to have a British Consul there.*

Near Turbat-i-Ḥaydarí there is a village named Dúghábád which the Bahá'ís know as Furúgh. The most prominent of the Bahá'ís of Dúghábád was Mírzá Maḥmúd-i-Furúghí, known as Fáḍil-i-Furúghí (see fig. 41). He was the son of one of the survivors of the Shaykh Ṭabarsí upheaval.

In the Mashhad Diary for 11 April 1907, the British Consul-General, Percy Sykes (q.v.), reported an attack by the villagers of Dúghábád on Mírzá Maḥmúd.

On the 11th Muharram at Dughabad, near Turbat-i-Haidari, Mirza Mahmud and his brother were attacked by a mob on the ground of being Babis. They fled to Nishapur and petitioned the acting Governor General, who sent twelve *mamurs* to Dughabad to enquire into the matter. The villagers appealed to the local Majlis and as a result the acting Governor General has been requested to remove the *mamurs* and to bring the two brothers for trial by a religious court. The Secretary of the Babi Anjuman appealed to me secretly to forward a long telegram to the Tehran Majlis. This I have declined to do: but have said that if matters look ugly, I will inform the Legation. The Secretary states that they have always been helped by the Russian Consulate but that, as they know that the Russians wish to upset the *majlis*, they appealed to me. I should not be surprized if the mullas tried an anti-Babi campaign in order to reassert their authority.[39]

On 16 April, Sykes reported: '*The anti-Babi movement.* With reference to entry No. 2 of 11th instant, it is reported that the mullas of Turbat-i-Haidari have sent men to Dughabad, one of the villages of the Muhavalat to the S.W. of Turbat, to bring in all the Babis. The Runk-u-Dola ['Alí-Naqí Mírzá, Ruknu'd-Dawlih (q.v.)] has telegrammed a strong order holding the Salar-ul-Mukarram responsible for any persecution of the Babis. The community in Meshed numbers 200.'[40]

On 21 April, Sykes reported: 'Mustafa Mirza, late Governor of Turbat

* In 1909, there occurred an agitation against the Bahá'ís in the village of Ḥiṣṣár resulting in the death of one of them, a Kad-Khudá [headman] named Ismá'íl. This episode is reported in the Turbat-i-Ḥaydarí Diary but the Consul at Turbat-i-Ḥaydarí, Capt. A. Grey, appears to have confused this episode with the deeds of some robbers who were operating in that area (perhaps a deliberate slander against the Bahá'ís by their enemies). On 8 October, Grey reported: 'A religious quarrel between Shias and Babis has taken place at a village named Hissar, at the foot of the Koh-i-Mazar Range. The disputants referred the matter to Meshed and the Anjuman there has ordered the Governor of Turbat to hold an enquiry.' On 14 October, Grey reported: 'The Governor, acting on orders received from Meshed sent some sowars to Hissar who captured six of the so-called Babis and killed another named Ismail.' On 15 October, Grey reported: 'The Governor has received telegraphic orders from Meshed to release the six prisoners captured at Hissar.' (FO 248 969)

and a friend of Captain Watson, called with the Etabar-u-Taulia. He owns Dughabad, the scene of the anti-Babi movement. In this connection, orders have been issued to prevent known Babis from frequenting the mosques and baths.'[41]

Lt Daukes (q.v.), acting Consul for Turbat-i-Ḥaydarí, reported in his Confidential Diary for 26 April:

Anti-Babi Movement. With reference to the entry in the Meshed Diary under date 16th April – the facts as far as can be ascertained locally are as follows:-

During the last Muharram a dispute arose between the Shiahs and Babis of Dughabad caused apparently by the tactless remarks of the latter who openly expressed the opinion that it would better befit the Shiahs to lament the death of the Babis martyred at Turbat-i-Haidari some five years ago rather than the death of Imam Hussein who was killed over a thousand years ago! It does not appear that any violence was perpetrated but both parties became excited and vented their feelings in the usual manner i.e. by telegraphing to Teheran. The Salar-ul-Mukarram was, it is said, instructed to make enquiries and accordingly sent an Agent who passed through Turbat on the 1st April. As a result of his investigations four Babis were arrested and brought into Turbat-i-Haidari. Their case has not yet been disposed of.[42]

On 9 May, Lt Daukes reported: 'A telegram has been received by the Local Majlis instructing them to punish the arrested Babis. The new Governor, Adal-u Sultana, has also telegraphed saying no steps should be taken pending his arrival in Turbat.'[43]

In the subsequent reports from Daukes, there are a series of statements to the effect that no action had been taken in the matter of the Bahá'ís, who were still under arrest, until on 3 June 1907 there occurs the following entry: 'The four Babis who were arrested at Dughabad have been released. They had each to pay a fine averaging about Ts. 20 each.'[44]

Attack on Fáḍil-i-Furúghí

In the preceding section, an account of an attack upon Mírzá Maḥmúd, Fáḍil-i-Furúghí, has been given. A few years later, Fáḍil was in Mashhad. The 'ulamá of Mashhad, and in particular Mullá Muḥammad, known as Áqázádih (see p. 420), were eager to terminate his activities. In the Mashhad Diary for the last week of October 1910, an attempt on his life is reported by Maj. W. F. O'Connor (q.v.), the Mashhad Acting Consul-General:

25th Oct. *Assault on a Behai.* A respectable elderly man, an inhabitant of the Turbat district, was assaulted today in his house at Meshad by three men armed with revolvers. He was severely wounded and was brought to our hospital for treatment.

26th Oct. I saw the wounded man and heard his story. He says that his assailants, who were previously strangers to him, came to call upon him and remained to converse upon religious subjects. At the close of the discussion, as they were about to leave the house, they drew their revolvers and shot at him, narrowly missing his head and wounding him in the chest. The wounded man is a well-known Behai, and he believes that the Aga-zada and other of the leading clericals here were at the bottom of the affair.[45]

The Martyrdom of Shaykh 'Alí-Akbar-i-Qúchání

Shaykh 'Alí-Akbar-i-Qúchání (see fig. 43) was one of the most eminent of Bahá'ís of Khurásán. As a young man, he had undertaken religious studies in both Mashhad and Iraq and had eventually reached the rank of Mujtahid with an *ijázih* from the most prominent of the 'ulamá of Iraq, Mullá Káẓim-i-Khurásání. The latter had been so pleased with his pupil that he had entrusted to his care the education of his son, Muḥammad. Later, on his return to Persia, Shaykh 'Alí-Akbar had come into contact with Bahá'ís and been converted. He became famous as a Bahá'í throughout Khurásán and was forced for a time to leave the province for his own safety. Later, however, he returned to Mashhad in the course of travelling through Persia. At this time, the most prominent of the 'ulamá of Mashhad was his former pupil, Mulla Muḥammad, known as Áqázádih or Áyatu'lláhzádih, the son of Mullá Káẓim-i-Khurásání, and it was he who signed Shaykh 'Alí-Akbar's death warrant (fatvá).

Col. Haig (q.v.), British Consul-General in Mashhad, reported the murder of Shaykh 'Alí-Akbar in the Mashhad Diary for the week ending 20 March 1915: 'Shaikh Ali Akbar, Kuchani, a Bahai who recently came to Meshed to preach the doctrines of his sect, was shot dead on March 14 in the Bazar-i-Kulahduzan near the courtyard of the Shrine. The people, suspecting an intention of burying the body in a Muhammadan burying ground and resenting the arrest of those suspected of the murder, raised a disturbance in the Shrine. The body was at last removed secretly by night from the place where it lay and carried off to Kuchan.'[46]

In each subsequent Diary there is some further word about this episode.

[*Mashhad Diary for week ending 27 March 1915*:] It is reported that the Bahais have the intention of avenging Shaikh Ali Akbar's death by killing Aghazada, but that the latter and his friends are on the alert. There is a movement among the people to protest against the punishment of Shaikh Ali Akbar's murderers.[47]

[*Mashhad Diary for week ending 3 April 1915*:] I hear that the Persian Government has ordered the Governor-General [Sulṭán-Ḥusayn Mírzá, Nayyiru'd-Dawlih, q.v.] to arrest and send to Tehran Aghazada, Agha Fazil, and three other *mullas* who issued a *fatwa* for the murder of Shaikh Ali Akbar, the Bahai. The Governor-General is refusing to obey this order, on the ground that he can neither arrest *mullas* nor punish the murderers locally without danger of disturbances, but he has offered to send the murderers to Tehran for trial and punishment.[48]

[*Mashhad Diary for week ending 10 April 1915*:] The agitation against Bahais continues. They are excluded from the Shrine and the authorities have not yet ventured to arrest the murderers of Shaikh Ali Akbar. Two Bahais have recently recanted.[49]

[*Mashhad Diary for week ending 17 April 1915*:] The agitation against the Bahais still continues. Haji Musa, Jadid, a banker, recently took sanctuary in the Russian Bank and has since moved to the Russian Consulate General. Ustad Muhammad, another leading Bahai, is in *bast* in the British Consulate General. The leader of the Bahais in Turbat-i-Haidari has asked me to extend my protection to his son, living in Turshiz, and I have replied that I cannot be responsible for the safety of anybody at such a distance, but if his son's life is really in danger and he cares to come to Meshed I will extend my hospitality to him.[50]

[*Mashhad diary for week ending 24 April 1915:*] The trouble in connection with the murder of Shaikh Ali Akbar, the Bahai, is not yet past. Husain, a cloth merchant and a democrat', was arrested on April 18 on suspicion, but the cloth merchants closed their shops in protest and Aghazada, a *mulla* who is said to have given a *fatwa* for the murder and is therefore anxious that no charge should be pressed against anybody, insisted on and obtained Husain's release. The Governor-General does not venture to take any strong measures and, by way of giving effect to the orders of the Persian Government that the murderers should be arrested and sent to Tehran, he has taken security from two suspected persons for their appearance in Tehran, but he does not believe that they will go there. The tradesmen and *mullas* of Meshed threaten to demonstrate against measures taken for the arrest or punishment of the murderers . . .

I hear that Caucasian Turks, Russian subjects, are agitating against the punishment of the murderers of the Bahai, Shaikh Ali Akbar.[51]

[*Mashhad Diary for the week ending 8 May 1915:*] Prince Nayyir-ud-Daulah is displaying lamentable weakness in the matter of the agitation against the Bahais. After promising my Colleague that he would report Ustad Ali Akbar and Meshedi Husain, the two men suspected of the murder, to Tehran, he is afraid to fulfil his promise. I have urged him to stand to it as I am no less interested in the matter than my Colleague, having a *basti* of whom I cannot get rid until some action is taken. I now hear that he proposes to deport Ali Akbar who is comparatively friendless, and to take no steps against Meshedi Husain, who is strongly supported by *mullas*.[52]

[*Mashhad Diary for the week ending 5 June 1915:*] Nayyir-ud-Daulah, on whom age is beginning to tell, is growing either extremely lazy or extremely nervous and invariably excuses himself from taking strong action against disturbers of the peace and other criminals on the ground that decided measures are likely to cause disturbances in the city. This was for a long time his excuse for not arresting the murderers of the Bahai, Shaikh Ali Akbar. He now says that he wishes to arrest both of them at once and that this is difficult to arrange; but this is merely another excuse.[53]

In the month following the martyrdom of Shaykh 'Alí-Akbar, as indicated in these diaries, the Bahá'ís of Khurásán were under constant threat of a general massacre. The Bahá'í Spiritual Assembly in Ṭihrán sent a telegram to the prominent British Bahá'í, Lady Blomfield. The telegram, dated 15 April, stated: 'Venerable Behai martyred Meshed. Preparing uprising against Behais. Help us, ask justice from Persian Government, parliament. Telegraph your Legation here. Advertise Paris others.'[54]

Lady Blomfield wrote to Mary, Countess of Wemyss (q.v.), on 25 April 1915, asking for her assistance: 'This telegram arrived this morning . . . One thing of great use which occurs to me, (*can* you do this?) to write to Mr J. Tennant. *Could* he have a telegram sent to the British Legation at Teheran, or to the British Consulate at Meshed, to stop the persecution of the

Bahaïs, the dear harmless people! Meshed is a sacred city of the Shia Mahommedans, and the people are very fanatical there, for this reason comes the danger to the Bahaïs. *Some way* of helping will, I know, occur to you, it is *very urgent*!'[55]

Mary Wemyss wrote to Jack Tennant (q.v.), a friend and distant relative who worked in the War Office:

Dear Mr Jack Tennant

You will I fear think me *quite mad*, and very bad too to trouble you when such a load of care and responsibility which already rests upon your shoulders. I feel I ought not to take the few seconds it may take you to read this letter but you will please believe me when I say that you certainly must not answer.

I received yesterday a rather mad letter from Lady Blomfield (Theosophist!!! of a sort). She used to put up the venerable Behaï from Persia (who is or was quite a genuine old saint, I believe and who with his followers are really harmless (preaching *peace*! and harmony! and *love*) and *non*-political). But I imagine these sort of people are particularly *maddening* to fanatics and are bound to fare badly in troublous times – still they are really I believe most innocent and really put their non-aggressive and non-political principles into practise – and the Engl. Gov. [English Government] is supposed to protect the weak – I gather that if harm (a rising) was really meant them it is all over by now, but I felt I must send on the telegram, with some sentences from Lady B's letter ommitting [*sic*] the Balderdash – as much as I can – if there is or has been trouble you will of course have heard of it – through the proper, recognized channels, which makes my writing seem doubly futile and intrusive. The *Christian Commonwealth* recognizes the Behaï and his followers and I visited him in London and used to talk about him to Lord Hugh Cecil. I am curious to know what has happened to him – it's an ill world for peaceful souls![56]

In a note appended to her letter, Mary Wemyss quoted the short extract from Lady Blomfield's letter given above and added:

. . . she says she has written to the wife of Col. Percy Sykes, formerly British Consul General at Meshed. Now please forgive me! for obeying this wild and worried lady's bequest [*sic*] – my sister Pamela knows the old Bahaï too as he came to her house – If the Behaïs are in danger – can *Sir E. Grey* reach out a paw of protection?

Of course I can't help feeling that if there is an innocent population in danger of persecution – that they have *some means* of communicating through the recognized channels to the *proper* source.[57]

Mr Tennant forwarded the letter to the Foreign Office, where on its arrival Lancelot Oliphant (q.v.) made the following memorandum, dated 29 April:

Lady Blomfield has written to various personages urging enquiry at Teheran regarding a reported massacre of that unorthodox sect in Meshed – the Bahaïs.

I submit, however, that our most able Consul General at Meshed – Col. Haig – and Mr Marling at Teheran are well able to take any action locally that may be necessary. Moreover, while numerous, the sect is *anathema* to the orthodox Persian and while there is still some faint sign of agitation for a *jehad* it would not be politic to champion the cause of the Behaï.[58]

To which George Clerk (q.v.) appended: 'I think we might enquire whether Colonel Haig has reported any violence against the Bahaïs. They are an inoffensive people, with sympathizers in this country, and we might find out what is happening to them.'[59] And Sir Arthur Nicolson (q.v.) added: 'I agree. A.N. 30/4/15.'[60]

As a result of this, the following telegram was sent to Mr Marling (q.v.), British Minister at Ṭihrán, on 2 May 1915:

'Reports have reached London of massacres of Bahai at Meshed.

'Have you any confirmation from Consul General.

'*Confidential.*

'I realize undesirability in any case of making official representations on subject at present.'[61]

To this enquiry, Marling replied: 'No truth in reports of massacres. One Bahai was murdered March 14th.'[62]

Following the receipt of this telegram, Oliphant, suspicious as to the motives behind these enquiries, wrote:

'I am by no means certain that the agitation got up on this subject – I had two visitors on the question yesterday – may not be an attempt to embroil H.M.G. [His Majesty's Government] with the Persian Govt., and to depict H.M.G. as championing an heretical sect in Persia.

'I submit that no action is necessary or desirable . . .'[63]

Another enquiry to reach the Foreign Office regarding this same matter originated from Lord Lamington (q.v.), an admirer of 'Abdu'l-Bahá. He wrote to Lord Lansdowne on 31 May 1915:

'I have various communications relating to the persecutions that members of the Bahai sect are subjected to in Persia, particularly in Khorassan.

'I understand that you are engaged in work at the Foreign Off. and therefore I ask whether representations could be made or other steps taken to secure some protection for these people, whose doctrines are those of peace and goodwill to all.'[64]

A reply was sent to Lord Lamington dated 5 June 1915:

In reply to your letter to Lord Lansdowne of 31st May, regarding the Bahai sect in Persia, Lord Crewe [q.v.] desires me to state that an enquiry was recently addressed to His Majesty's Minister at Teheran on the subject of various reports which had reached here.

Mr Marling replied that there was no truth in the reports that massacres had occurred, though one Bahai was murdered on the 14th of March.

You will thus see that the question has not been lost sight of though the present political situation entirely precludes any steps being taken on the subject at Teheran.[65]

A short while later on 5 June, Lord Lamington forwarded to the Foreign Office a letter that he had received from Muḥammad-'Alí Khán-i-Shaybání, a Bahá'í of Mashhad, reassuring him that there was no general massacre of the Bahá'ís. The letter is dated 8 May 1915:

Yesterday I had gone to see Colonel Haig, Consul-General of His Britannic Majesty, to see what was happening, and he showed me a dispatch from Ṭihrán from Mr Marling, the English Chargé d'Affaires, asking if it was true that there has been a massacre of all the Bahá'ís of Mas͟hhad, because this report had reached London. This was the reason that I was authorized to write to Your Honour and formally to contradict this news. A single assassination has occurred. It was Jináb Áqá S͟hayk͟h 'Alí-Akbar of Qúc͟hán. I wish to declare in this letter to Your Honour that the Bahá'ís of Mas͟hhad and myself know of the energetic approach and serious attitude of Lt-Col. T. W. Haig, Consul-General of His Brittannic Majesty at Mas͟hhad. We hope that the agitator, this S͟hayk͟h Muḥammad, son of Ák͟húnd Mullá Md. Káẓim K͟hurásání, and the two assassins of Jináb S͟hayk͟h 'Alí-Akbar of Qúchán will be punished as soon as possible.

I beg Your Honour to reassure all the Bahá'ís of London that this report of the massacre of all the Bahá'ís of Mas͟hhad is completely devoid of truth. In closing my letter I present my respectful greetings to Lady Lamington, Lady Blomfield, Miss Rosenberg, and Mrs Thornburg [Thornburgh-] Cropper.*[66]

References

1. Newswriter identified as 'Meshed B', Newsletter dated 1 Sept. 1896 containing information from Turbat-i-Ḥaydarí dated 23 Aug. 1896: FO 248 632
2. Telegram Elias to Durand No. 13, 2 Sept. 1896, quoted in Mas͟hhad Political Diary for week ending 4 Sept. 1896: FO 248 632
3. Entry in Mas͟hhad Political Diary for week ending 4 Sept. 1896: FO 248 632
4. Summary of News from Mas͟hhad 12–26 Sept. 1896 prepared by Horace Rumbold: FO 248 628
5. Yate, Mas͟hhad Political Diary No. 6 for week ending 11 Feb. 1898: FO 248 674
6. Newsletter 9 Feb. 1898 from 'Meshed B', enclosed with 5 *supra*
7. Newsletter 10 Feb. 1898 from 'Meshed B', enclosed with 5 *supra*
8. Newsletter 11 Feb. 1898 from 'Meshed B', enclosed with 5 *supra*
9. Newsletter 11 Feb. 1898 from 'Meshed D', enclosed with 5 *supra*
10. Hardinge to Amínu'd-Dawlih 14 Feb. 1898: FO 248 677
11. Telegram Hardinge to Yate No. 5, 17 Feb. 1898: FO 248 671
12. Hardinge to Amínu'd-Dawlih 20 Feb. 1898: FO 248 677
13. Yate, Mas͟hhad Political Diary No. 7 for the week ending 18 Feb. 1898: FO 248 674
14. Newsletter 14 Feb. 1898 from 'Meshed D', enclosed with 13 *supra*
15. Newsletter 16 Feb. 1898 from 'Meshed D', enclosed with 13 *supra*
16. Newsletter 17 Feb. 1898 from 'Meshed D', enclosed with 13 *supra*
17. Newsletter 17 Feb. 1898 from 'Meshed D', enclosed with 13 *supra*
18. Telegram Ruknu'd-Dawlih to Amínu'd-Dawlih 12 Feb. 1898, enclosed with 13 *supra*
19. Telegram Amínu'd-Dawlih to Ruknu'd-Dawlih 14 Feb. 1898, enclosed with 13 *supra*
20. Telegram Guardian of Shrine of Imám Riḍá to Amínu'd-Dawlih 14 Feb. 1898, enclosed with 13 *supra*
21. Telegram Amínu'd-Dawlih to the Guardian of the Shrine of Imám Riḍá 14 Feb. 1898, enclosed with 13 *supra*
22. Telegram Hardinge to Yate No. 6, 23 Feb. 1898. FO 248 671
23. Yate, Mas͟hhad Political Diary No. 8 for week ending 25 Feb. 1898: FO 248 674
24. Newsletter 19 Feb. 1898 from 'Meshed B', enclosed with 23 *supra*
25. Newsletter, 20 Feb. 1898 from 'Meshed B', enclosed with 23 *supra*
26. Newsletter 24 Feb. 1898, from 'Meshed B', enclosed with 23 *supra*

* The last three named were prominent English Bahá'ís.

27. Newsletter 24 Feb. 1898 from 'Meshed B', enclosed with 23 *supra*
28. All telegrams enclosed with 23 *supra*
29. Telegram Ruknu'd-Dawlih to Amínu'd-Dawlih 25 Feb. 1898, enclosed with Mashhad Political Diary No. 9 for week ending 4 Mar. 1898: FO 248 674
30. Telegram Ruknu'd-Dawlih to Amínu'd-Dawlih 27 Feb. 1898, enclosed with Diary detailed in 29 *supra*
31. Telegram Amínu'd-Dawlih to Ruknu'd-Dawlih 1 Mar. 1898, enclosed with Diary detailed in 29 *supra*
32. Whyte, Mashhad Political Diary No. 10 for week ending 11 Mar. 1898: FO 248 674
33. Telegram Ruknu'd-Dawlih to Amínu'd-Dawlih 2 Mar. 1898, enclosed with 32 *supra*
34. Whyte, Mashhad Political Diary No. 14 for week ending 8 Apr. 1898: FO 248 674
35. Temple, Mashhad Political Diary No. 16 for week ending 22 Apr. 1898: FO 248 674
36. Newsletter from 'Meshed M', enclosed in Mashhad Political Diary No. 20 for week ending 20 May 1898: FO 248 674
37. Temple to Durand 7 June 1898: FO 248 674
38. Amínu's-Sulṭán to Ruknu'd-Dawlih 30 Sept. 1898: FO 248 674
39. Sykes, Mashhad Diary No. 15 for week ending 12 Apr. 1907: FO 248 908
40. Sykes, Mashhad Diary No. 16 for week ending 19 Apr. 1907: FO 248 908
41. Sykes, Mashhad Diary No. 17 for week ending 26 Apr. 1907: FO 248 908
42. Daukes, Turbat-i-Ḥaydarí Confidential Diary No. 12 for week ending 28 Apr. 1907: FO 248 908
43. Daukes, Turbat-i-Ḥaydarí Confidential Diary No. 13 for week ending 9 May 1907: FO 248 908
44. Daukes, Turbat-i-Ḥaydarí Confidential Diary No. 17 for week ending 9 June 1907: FO 248 908
45. O'Connor, Mashhad Confidential Diary No. 43 for week ending 29 Oct. 1910: FO 248 1000
46. Haig, Mashhad Diary No. 12 for week ending 20 Mar. 1915: India Records Office, L/P & S/10/210
47. Haig, Mashhad Diary No. 13 for week ending 27 Mar. 1915: L/P & S/10/210
48. Haig, Mashhad Diary No. 14 for week ending 3 Apr. 1915: L/P & S/10/210
49. Haig, Mashhad Diary No. 15 for week ending 10 Apr. 1915: L/P & S/10/210
50. Haig, Mashhad Diary No. 16 for week ending 17 Apr. 1915: L/P & S/10/210
51. Haig, Mashhad Diary No. 17 for week ending 24 Apr. 1915: FO 371 2421
52. Haig, Mashhad Diary No. 19 for week ending 8 May. 1915: FO 371 2421
53. Haig, Mashhad Diary No. 23 for week ending 5 June 1915: L/P & S/10/210
54. Telegram Bahá'í Spiritual Assembly to Lady Blomfield 15 Apr. 1915, quoted in 56 *infra*
55. Lady Blomfield to Mary Wemyss 25 Apr. 1915, quoted in 56 *infra*
56. Mary Wemyss to H. J. Tennant 26 Apr. 1915, File No. 53440: FO 371 2425
57. ibid.
58. Memo by Oliphant 29 Apr. 1915, File 53440: FO 371 2425
59. Memo by Clerk 30 Apr. 1915, File 53440: FO 371 2425
60. Memo by Nicolson 30 Apr. 1915, File 53440: FO 371 2425
61. For. Off. to Marling 2 May 1915, File 53440: FO 371 2425
62. Marling to For. Off. No. 182, 6 May 1915, File 55735: FO 371 2425
63. Memo by Oliphant, 6 May 1915, File 55735: FO 371 2425
64. Lamington to Lord Lansdowne 31 May 1915, File 71726: FO 371 2425
65. Clerk to Lamington 5 June 1915, File 71726: FO 371 2425
66. Muḥammad-'Alí Khán-i-Shaybání to Lamington 8 May 1915, File 71726: FO 371 2425 (trans. from French)

TWENTY-NINE

Persecutions in the Iṣfahán Area (1899–1920)

Throughout the ministry of 'Abdu'l-Bahá, the persecutions in the towns around Iṣfahán, as well as in Iṣfahán itself, continued. The principal instigator of these episodes continued to be Áqá Najafí (Shaykh Muḥammad-Taqí, q.v., see fig. 44), and at Najafábád he found a willing assistant in Mírzá Fatḥ-'Alí Khán-i-Yávar.*

The Najafábád Upheaval of 1899

On 9 April 1899, a prominent Bahá'í of Najafábád, Mírzá Muḥammad-Báqir-i-Há'í (see fig. 15), who had been a Bahá'í from the earliest days of the Faith and was by this time about eighty years of age, was suddenly arrested in Najafábád on the orders of Áqá Najafí. Dr Aganoor (q.v.), Acting British Consul, on 18 April 1899 reported the circumstances of the arrest to Sir Mortimer Durand (q.v.):

I have the honour to report that on Sunday, the 9th Inst. Mahomed Hossein Khan, (Sartip-i-Sehdehi) who is in the service of the Zil-es-Sultan, went to Nejafabad, accompanied by Naib Abdool Rahim of Sehdeh and some Sarvazes,† all armed and seized Mollah Baukher in the street, put him on a horse and galloped off with him to Azizabad, a village belonging to the Prince some two farsakhs from Nejafabad. Mollah Baukher who is still in custody there, is an old man, reputed to be a Babi, and has been at times employed by the Church Missionary Society as Mirza and Persian teacher to Dr Carr and the Rev. Mr Blackett. His brother is the landlord of the house that has been in the lease of the CMS for some time past, at Nejafabad.

After taking him away, some of the party went into Mollah Baukher's house and looted everything. The party was assisted by the local governor or zabeth‡ (Mostafa Khan) and by Fathali Khan (Yavar), who is said to be the real instigator. No explanation was given for this arbitrary action, but it was understood that it had been reported to Aga Nedjify that Mollah Baukher was in possession of much Babi literature in his house and was spreading the tenets of this sect amongst the people, whereupon the Aga had told the Prince that the man was worthy of death and that the books should be seized – with the above result. The books are said to have been taken to Aga Nedjify.

* Yávar – Major
† Sarbáz
‡ Ḍábiṭ

The consequence has been a general lawlessness, and persecution of supposed Babis. Several houses have been looted, more or less, and many persons beaten, the Lutis making good use of their opportunity.

Some 300 men and women came to Ispahan and went to the Persian Telegraph office where the Telegraph Sartip refusing to take in their message for the Shah or Sadr Azam, the crowd went to the English Telegraph office, and begged that their telegram might be accepted for the Shah* or Sadr Azam, or their case represented in Tehran. Mr McIntyre, in charge of the Telegraph office, wrote to the Prince informing him of the presence of the people at the office. The Prince sent the Governor of Julfa to try and persuade them to go to their houses, but they refused to do anything of the sort until their grievance was put right. He however persuaded a few of the men to go with him to the Prince, who had spoken kindly to them, told them that he would order that everything that had been taken from them should be returned, but advised them to dissociate themselves from the case of Mollah Baukher, as he had been accused of being a Babi, and the case did not concern them. They however returned from the town without getting any satisfaction.

The chiefs of these people have been to me several times and begged that their position might be brought to the knowledge of the Shah. They felt sure that the Shah wanted nothing from them, but that they should be peaceful subjects and pay their taxes, and this they were most willing to do, if they were allowed to live in peace and security. There were, they said, 5000 of this sect at Nejafabad, and they were obliged to take up Mollah Baukher's case in self-interest, and to die with him or be expelled [from] the country. If one man was despoiled of his property and killed today – tomorrow there would be another, and so on, they never would have peace. They wanted the matter finished one way or another. They were willing that some of their number should be killed or sacrificed, provided they had peace and security thereafter. They were ready to emigrate, *en masse*, and become subjects of another country, if they could have no security in their own land. Did the Shah want religion from them? They were peasants, tillers of the soil and understood only to plough fields and pay their taxes. Religion, they did not understand; and so on much in the same strain.

The open and fearless way that they confess their belief and express their determination that their position must be made clear, once for all, is quite unusual for a body of a religious sect to do, in Persia, and is probably not without significance.

In my interview with the Prince on Saturday the 15th Inst. I drew His Royal Highness's attention to the fact that these people were still at the Telegraph office. The Prince replied that he had done all he could for them. He had not allowed Mollah Baukher to be brought into Ispahan, to prevent his being killed, but had had him taken to his own village to be secure there. (This fact was previously admitted to me by Mollah Baukher's brother and friends, who said they had no complaint against the

* The telegram that was eventually sent on 12 Apr. to the S͟háh, with a copy to the British Legation, is here translated: 'A petition to the dust of the feet of His Highness Muẓaffaru'd-Dín S͟háh, may we be his sacrifice. Several days ago, twelve *savvárs* came to Najafábád, carried off one *ra'yat* in chains, looted four houses and maltreated several other persons. This was a plan of Fatḥ-'Alí K͟hán carried out on the order of Áqá S͟hayk͟h Muḥammad-Taqí [Áqá Najafí] by the *farráshes* of Ẓillu's-Sulṭán and because of these *ra'yats* being called Bábís, they wanted to kill several of them. Of necessity, we who are six hundred persons have taken refuge in the English Telegraph Office and await the instructions of Your Highness.' (FO 248 703). The only indication of a response from the Persian Government is a note to Durand from Mus͟híru'l-Mulk stating that 'telegraphic orders have been sent to Ispahan about the people of Najafabad'.

Prince, but only against Aga Nedjify's action.) His Royal Highness said he could not openly protect them against Aga Nedjify's orders as he would himself be accused of being a Babi. Orders in this connection must come from Tehran. The Prince added that he had telegraphed the circumstances to Tehran five days previously, but had not received a word of reply. What could he do?

The men are still round about the Telegraph office.[1]

As can be seen from the above dispatch, Mírzá Báqir was a great friend of the English missionaries at Julfá, and Stileman (q.v.), the secretary of the Persia Mission of the Church Missionary Society, wrote the following report from Julfá on 15 April: 'A leading Bâbî (of the Behâî sect) in Najifâbâd, who has been a friend of mine for 6 years and is also very well known to other members of the mission, was condemned to death for his faith a few days ago, and it was likely that 3 others would also be put to death. But 200 or 300 people came from Najifâbâd to the English Telegraph office here and have now been waiting for several days, declining to go home until the Shah intervenes on behalf of their friends. I have just come up from the Telegraph office, and there seems a hope that their lives will be spared.'[2]

On 22 April, Stileman reported Mírzá Báqir's removal to Ṭihrán: 'The Behâî referred to in para. 7 of my letter to you of 15th inst. has now been taken off to Teheran and there is, we believe, no longer any danger of his being put to death.'[3]

The Najafábádí Bahá'ís, however, remained at the Telegraph Office and Aganoor reported further developments on 20 May 1899:

With reference to my Despatch No. 24 of the 18th Ult. I have the honour to report that the Nejafabadis are still at Julfa in the neighbourhood of the Telegraph office, where they have taken a house and are awaiting orders from Tehran for the redress of their grievances. They have sent several petitions to the Shah and Sadr Azam, and they have received orders from these on the Zil-es-Sultan to investigate into the case and report. These orders, the Prince says, are not sufficient. They are not explicit orders, allowing liberty of religion to the Babis. They are simply instructions to investigate. Such of the ones that the writer has seen are as described. With these orders, the Prince says, he cannot protect the Babis against the Mullahs, to any great extent. If it is true that the Shah allows religious freedom, why is there not a Farman issued in that sense? If His Royal Highness actively protects them without explicit and clear orders from Tehran, the Mullahs will accuse himself of being a Babi. If he is successful in protecting them the Government will get the credit. If he fails he will be blamed by the Government for going beyond his instructions in taking active steps against the Mullahs.

Under these circumstances, His Royal Highness says, vague instructions to investigate into grievances and report, are of no use. The grievances are well-known. These men are persecuted by the Mullahs and others because they are Babis – that is to say the fact of their being Babis is made an excuse for persecuting them and despoiling them of their belongings.

Petty persecutions are continued, and those who have come here dare not go back without getting redress, and before their position is made clear. It was reported that it had been arranged, by Aga Nedjify, for the

10th day of Mohurrum, that a crowd should organise a procession and under religious excitement make an attack on the Babis and kill some. The Prince heard of this and has put a stop to it.

The Babis are daily appealing to us for help. Being about our Telegraph office they consider that they have taken refuge with us, and seem to expect protection from us.

The Rev. Mr Tisdall tells me that these people do not care to go to the Russians, but that in despair of getting any assistance from us, they may appeal to the Russians. In such a case if the Russians take up their case and succeed in getting them redress, it would greatly increase their influence here.[4]

On 29 May, Aganoor transmitted to Ṭihrán an account of a conversation between Ẓillu's-Sulṭán and a 'Persian Gentleman', communicated to him by the latter, who is not identified.

Zil-es-Sultan asked what news he had about the Babis. The gentleman replied that he had none. H.R.H. then said that it was not his fault. He could do nothing without definite orders from Tehran giving the Babis religious liberty. H.R.H. then asked if the Babis were still in Julfa, and why they were not turned out from there. The gentleman replied that they were afraid to go back to Najafabad. H.R.H. said that he had nothing to do with them. The Government must write officially that the Babis are henceforth to be free. The orders sent from Tehran are simply instructions to investigate into their case 'according to law' – 'Sharan' – and according to the law Aqa Nedjify says that they ought to be killed. It is the policy of the Government to give vague and indefinite orders, which if they are acted upon and the result is successful the Government take to themselves all the credit; and if unsuccessful the Government would 'burn his (H.R.H's) father', as they did with the Mayed-ed-dowleh in Khonsar and Gulpaigan, so much so that the Mayed-ed-dowleh wished to commit suicide. The Zil-es-Sultan added that he could very well 'burn Aga Nedjify's father' even without troops – viz by diplomacy, but then the authorities in Tehran would blame him and act against him if something occurred and if he got into trouble the English would not protect him at all. H.R.H. said that he had told this repeatedly to Mr Preece* and asked him to give him assurances. H.R.H. then said that at Yezd ten persons had recently been killed, and no notice was taken by the Government of the representations of the British Legation.[5]

On 21 June 1899 Capt. C. Schneider, Acting British Consul in Iṣfahán, reported: 'Information was received that Aga Nejaffy, in the house of his brother Sheikh Noorulla, said with regard to the 'Babis', that he had given instructions that when Mulla Bhauker returned from Teheran, he was to be killed. He also made several disloyal remarks regarding H.I.M. the Shah – and said he was an infidel.

'Fatteh Khan Yawar, who is the real instigator of the persecution of the Babis, has been put in prison by the Prince.'[6]

Mírzá Báqir was in fact detained in Ṭihrán for over a year: a severe

* Mr Preece, British Consul in Iṣfahán, was absent at this time and Dr Aganoor was acting for him.

punishment for an elderly man. He then came to Iṣfahán and was allowed to return to Najafábád under certain restrictions. His books and manuscripts were never returned to him, however. He eventually died in Najafábád at an age in excess of 100.

Martyrdom of Ghulám-Riḍá, 1901

In a dispatch dated 16 June 1901, Preece reported the murder of a Bahá'í on the road between Najafábád and Iṣfahán. This man was Ghulám-Riḍá, who was taking a son of Ḥájí Ḥaydar (see p. 432) to Iṣfahán when he was attacked and killed by some of the more fanatical inhabitants of Najafábád:

'Just after my last report a Babi was killed on the road between this and Nejafabad by some ryots of that town, and it was stated that Aga Nejify was trying to get four men of Nejafabad killed as Babis. All this His Royal Highness has put a stop to. He also sent for a Seyed of Nejafabad and gave him such a scolding for agitating in these questions that the man left in great fear. The Prince complains that although he has telegraphed very strongly to Tehran he can get no strict orders to stop this agitation. The Shah fears to act in a proper way in the question.'[7]

Petition of the Bahá'ís of Najafábád

In about July 1901, shortly after the murder of Ghulám-Riḍá, the Bahá'ís of Najafábád decided to address another appeal to the Sháh for protection from persecution. Since the previous petition had not even been replied to, they decided to send this one through the British Legation. The British Minister, Sir Arthur Hardinge (q.v.), sent the appeal on to Amínu's-Sulṭán, the Prime Minister, with the following note dated 4 August 1901:

I enclose herewith a copy of a letter by certain inhabitants of Nejefabad forwarding a petition to H.M. the Shah, which I would beg Your Highness to lay before His Majesty.

The Petitioners as Your Highness will observe, state that they have already appealed to the Throne for protection and are only approaching the British Legation as a last resort. It is probable that their previous petition has not reached His Majesty, or has been overlooked amongst the great mass of business, embracing all the departments of the state, which a sovereign has to transact. I feel sure however that His Majesty will not take it amiss that I should through Your Highness, and in a purely unofficial and private manner (since it concerns his own subjects between whom, and himself, I have no right to interfere) bring the present appeal to his Royal notice.

His Majesty has in addition to his many other virtues, acquired in Europe a reputation for enlightened tolerance of all forms of religious belief. Before I had the honor of being accredited to his court, I had read in the newspapers of the impression produced in France and Germany by the marked respect shewn by him for Christian churches and religious processions, and he is, I think, the first Mahommedan sovereign who has shewn a desire to do honor to the Christian faith by despatching a special Embassy to announce his accession to His Holiness the

Pope. I feel convinced therefore that he would regard with the deepest disapproval the killing of harmless peasants, for holding the Babi heresy which, however foolish and superstitious in itself, is not dangerous to peace or public order. I am aware that the clergy maintain that apostacy from Islam to Babism is an offence punishable under Mahommedan Law with death, but the answer to them surely is, that the general interests of Islam must be considered and that it is not, in the present state of the world, in the interest of any Mahommedan State to weaken itself by turning, through persecution, large numbers of its subjects from loyal peaceable persons into discontented ones, and cause them to look to foreign powers for assistance and protection against their own native government. Persecution moreover shall not convert; it makes brave men martyrs, and timid men hypocrites. It can only succeed where a false opinion is in its infancy held only by a few persons. Once the opinion is wide spread, it cannot be rooted out, and the best way to make it as harmless as possible is to take from it, by toleration, the element of secrecy and enthusiasm, which has made all persecuted religions grow.

If the Mollahs were sensible they would see this, and abstain from disgracing this country by acts of cruelty such as those complained of. In our dependency of Cyprus where the Bab* himself lives in perfect freedom, I doubt if he has made a single disciple, but if once we began to persecute Babism, public attention would immediately be drawn to it, and the interest thus aroused would bring it many secret adherents. The most dangerous sects are always those, which for fear of persecution, are secret, and work in the dark.

I trust Your Highness will excuse my writing at this length on a purely internal matter which does not directly concern British interests. My apology must be that the prosperity and internal peace of Persia is really a British interest, and that, of late, I have repeatedly received reports of persecutions and executions for heresy, which the local authorities seem powerless owing to the influence of the clergy to prevent, and which must be harmful to the welfare of the country. I know how repugnant these things must be to the humane feelings of the Shah, which are shared by Your Highness, and I have therefore the less hesitation in bringing them to your notice, in case local governors should have hesitated to do so, being convinced that I have only to make them known in that exalted presence in order to ensure steps being taken to prevent their recurrence.[8]

Hardinge also wrote to Preece, the British Consul in Iṣfahán, telling him of the steps that he had taken and concluding with the following request: 'The petition is unsigned and I am therefore unable to send a reply to it, but I would request you to ascertain if possible who are the signatories and cause them to be informed that I have received their petition and have sent it on to the Shah.'[9]

Preece replied on 11 September 1901: 'The appeal made to you has been written, in all probability, by Hajji Haidar, the Babi Kadkhoda [Kad-Khudá] of Nejafabad and his associates who are now, I am told, in Tehran.

'I acquainted Bishop Stuart, who is at the present moment in Nejafabad, with the contents of your despatch and he promised me that he would,

* Hardinge is here referring to Mírzá Yaḥyá, Ṣubḥ-i-Azal, which is of course a mistake, since the petitioners were Bahá'ís.

should he find out there the writers of the petition, acquaint them with the fact that it has reached your hands and had been sent on to the Shah.'[10]

The Iṣfahán Upheaval of 1903

This episode is considered in detail in chapter 27, and also on pp. 363–6.

Martyrdom of Ḥájí Kalb-'Alí, 1905

The most prominent of the Bahá'ís of Najafábád at this time was Ḥájí Ḥaydar. In 1905 his son-in-law, Ḥájí Kalb-'Alí, was shot and killed.* Dr Aganoor reported on 2 April 1905:

'About four days ago at Nejafabad the son-in-law of Hajji Haidar late Kadkhuda of that place – a well known Babi – was shot by some mussulmans. Zil-es-Sultan sent men to take the murderers. The mollah of Nejafabad (a Seyyed) would not allow them to be taken. H.R.H. sent a sarteep with some cossacks who brought in the murderers. Aga Nejefi has sent to the Prince to say that these men, who have been taken, have done nothing wrong and should be released.'[11]

Martyrdom of Ḥájí Ḥaydar, 1909

The leading Bahá'í of Najafábád, Ḥájí Ḥaydar, had already suffered several spells in prison as well as previous attempts on his life. Through the hostility of Fatḥ-'Alí Khán-i-Yávar, Ḥájí Ḥaydar was eventually compelled to leave his native town and reside in Iṣfahán. But even this did not placate Fatḥ-'Alí Khán, who was determined to encompass his death, which he had failed to do on several previous occasions. Eventually, on 8 November 1909, Fatḥ-'Alí Khán's henchmen achieved their aim.

Thomas Grahame (q.v.), the British Consul-General in Iṣfahán, telegrammed on 8 November to Sir George Barclay (q.v.), the British Minister in Ṭihrán: 'Leading Babi of Najafabad who has often been threatened in previous persecutions shot dead about midday today by six armed men close to Consulate.'[12]

Two days later, Miss Annie Stuart (q.v.), Missionary of the Church Missionary Society, wrote to Grahame:

So many Persians have been speaking to me about that fearful murderer, who has again caused a man's life to be taken at our very doors within the last few days that I feel emboldened to write to you on the subject. As it seems almost impossible that the representatives of European Governments are powerless to use any influence with the Persian Govt. – now that it proposes to have a constitution. All who know Najafabad

* In Mírzá Fatḥu'lláh's narrative history of the Bahá'ís of Najafábád, Ḥájí Kalb-'Alí's death is stated to have occurred in March 1908. However, since the statement that he was Ḥájí Ḥaydar's son-in-law is common to both accounts, there would seem little doubt that Aganoor's report refers to Ḥájí Kalb-'Alí.

well know that if the life of this man, Yaver, is spared there will be still more murders committed in that place and in Isfahan. The murder of Hagi Hyder is the fifth one he has committed this year whose names are known to me – and I believe there are others besides – and many in former years. I know that the Bakhtiaris* only want to take money from the murderer, as they are in need of that; but surely if they desire to retain the support of Civilized powers they should be advised to use stronger methods of punishment for such outrageous crimes. Fining is evidently no deterrent to the Yavar – and it is a well known thing that no one's life is safe in Najafabad who opposes him in any matter. Being acquainted with the facts and the character of this man I have thought it only right to inform you in the matter that you may if possible see that justice is done.[13]

Grahame forwarded Miss Stuart's letter to Sir George Barclay and commented: 'The Stuarts frequently stay at Najafabad and I believe Miss Stuart knows what she is writing about.'[14]

In his weekly report for the week ending 13 November, Grahame gave further details of this episode:

About midday on 8th November opposite the 'Madresseh-i-Shamsabad' Haji Hayder of Najafabad (who is reputed to be the head of the large Babi community of that place) was fired on by five men on foot as he was riding, accompanied by a mounted servant, towards the CMS Hospital. Five shots entered his body and he fell dead. One bullet lodged in his horse. His servant was also fired on but escaped by hiding under a little bridge. The murderers at once made off and have not yet been found.

The body was taken to the Persian Telegraph Office.

Public opinion points to a certain Fath Ali Khan, generally known as 'Yavar' (Major) of Najafabad who has had a feud of long standing with the murdered man, as the author of this crime.

This murder is stated on good authority to be the fifth in the course of the last twelve months for which the Yavar is responsible.

Mr Grahame made unofficial representations both verbally and in writing to Samsam-ul-Sultaneh,† pointing out that a deplorable impression will be created if it become known through the European press that crimes of this nature can be committed with impunity under his Governorship in Isfahan.

Language of a similar nature was used by Mr Grahame to Sardar-i-Zafar.‡

Samsam stated that the actual perpetrators of the crime were being sheltered and shielded by Sardar-i-Zafar.[15]

Sir George Barclay wrote on the margin of this report a note addressed to 'Abbás-Qulí Khán-i-Navváb (q.v.), the Oriental Secretary of the Legation, for communication to Sardár-i-As'ad,§ the Minister of the Interior: 'Please rub in the deplorable impression that will be produced in Europe when it is known as it undoubtedly will be that Yavar, being protected by a

* The Bakhtíyárí under Ṣamṣámu's-Salṭanih were in control of Iṣfahán at this time.

† Najaf-Qulí Khán, Ṣamṣámu's-Salṭanih (q.v.)

‡ Ḥájí Khusraw Khán, Sardár-i-Zafar, brother of Ṣamṣámu's-Salṭanih.

§ Ḥájí 'Alí-Qulí Khán, Sardár-i-As'ad, the brother of Najaf-Qulí Khán, Ṣamṣámu's-Salṭanih (q.v.). He was the Bakhtíyárí Khán who led the Bakhtíyárí forces to Ṭihrán in the Constitutional Revolution in 1909 (see p. 354). He then became Minister of the Interior.

Bakhtiari Khan, goes unpunished for his atrocious crimes.'[16]

The Sardár-i-As'ad replied, according to a note by 'Abbás-Qulí Khán: 'The Sardar Asad says that the sons of the accused person are officers in a regiment under the command of Sardar Zafar and that is why he is interested in the case. H.E. promised to get the accused man tried in the Court of Justice at Ispahan as soon as the head of the department of justice, who will be nominated in a few days, gets there.'[17]

On 20 November, Grahame telegraphed: 'Samsam asks me to inform you that his efforts to punish culprit are being thwarted by misrepresentations made to Minister of the Interior by the Serdar Zafar, who protects him.'[18]

In his report for the week ending 20 November 1909, Grahame wrote:

> Fath Ali Khan Yavar, the reputed author of this crime, is lodged in the house of one of the dependents of Samsam-ul-Sultaneh but is allowed to go about freely. His sons are in the house of Sardar-i-Zafar. An attempt at an enquiry was made but, the actual assassins not having been apprehended, proved abortive.
>
> In the course of conversation with Samsam-ul-Sultaneh on 19th inst. Mr Grahame asked him how this matter now stood. In reply the Khan handed him a decypher of a long telegram just received from Sardar-i-Assad reproaching him for his lack of tact in pushing things to extremes against the Yavar at a time when that Officer's services were required and complaining of Samsam-ul-Sultaneh's delay in despatching troops to Tehran.
>
> Samsam said bitterly that while he was doing his best to get justice done in this matter, Haji Khosrou Khan was traducing him to the Sardar-i-Assad and doing all he could to protect the Yavar and his family. He requested that the British Minister might be informed of his good intentions and of the manner in which these had been misrepresented and thwarted.[19]

As was the usual pattern of events, matters were allowed to drift on and no result was forthcoming.

Persecutions at Ardistán

During the First World War, Persia became the scene of both intrigue and open warfare as both sides sought to control the country, and in particular the oil-producing areas in the south-west. For a brief period, Russia and Britain, the two powers that had been vying with each other for over a century in Persia, were united against a common foe.

In the midst of the intrigue and the breakdown of strong central government, it was again the Bahá'ís who suffered from certain unscrupulous individuals who saw in the situation an opportunity to benefit themselves.

It was just before the outbreak of the war, on 5 July 1914, that Áqá Najafí, who had terrorized the Bahá'ís in the Iṣfahán area for thirty years, died. His place, however, was taken by his younger brother, Áqá Núru'lláh (see fig. 44), who returned from Karbilá at about the time of his brother's death, and inherited his position at the head of the 'ulamá of Iṣfahán as well as his brother's zeal for persecuting the Bahá'ís.

On 14 February 1915, the signaller of the Indo-European Telegraph Department at Ardistán, a town to the north-east of Iṣfahán, reported the seizure of one of the most prominent Bahá'ís of that town, Mírzá 'Abdu'l-Ḥusayn-i-Rafí'á (or Rafí'í): 'Deputy Governor seized Mirza Abdul Hussein Ardestani who had just arrived from Isfahan accused of being Bahai leader also all his tenants and sealed all the rooms in his and his brother, Mirza Agha's houses also carried away some property from latter's house and demanding big fines from all.'[20]

On 21 February, the signaller reported: 'Deputy Governor has taken from Mirza Abdul Husseyn 1300 tomans cash besides valuable property carried off from his and his brother's and late Moad-ul-Sultan's houses and by Governor General's orders has handed over Mirza Abdul Husseyn to Mojahed Sultaneh who arrived from Isfahan for that purpose and probably will return with Mirza Abdul Husseyn.'[21]

Grahame telegrammed to Sir Walter Townley (q.v.), in Ṭihrán:

'Deputy-Governor of Ardestan, son of Zeigam-us-Sultaneh . . . is conducting an anti-Behái movement under orders from Isfahan clergy who are in close touch with Pugin.*

'British Indian Seyyid Assadullah resident at Ardestan telegraphed to me on Feb. 26th imploring the immediate release of his son-in-law Mirza Refai arrested by the Deputy-Governor under accusation of being a Behai.

'I have addressed local authorities of Isfahan unofficially. Would you consider it desirable to invite the attention of the P.G. [Persian Government] to the situation at Ardestan, and mischievous attitude of Isfahan clergy [?]'[22]

On receipt of this telegram, Sir Walter Townley asked 'Abbás-Qulí Khán to bring it to the attention of the Persian Minister for Foreign Affairs who replied promising to send 'peremptory orders'[23] to Ardistán and Iṣfahán.

In the meantime, Grahame himself had communicated with the Deputy Governor-General of Iṣfahán, Sardár-Fátiḥ, sending him a copy of Siyyid Asadu'lláh's telegram and asking: 'How does Y.E. [Your Excellency] view this matter? What fault has Mirza Rafia committed? I would request Y.E. to give orders that no one molest him.'[24] The Deputy Governor-General replied, sending a copy of the telegram that he had dispatched to Ardistán: 'To Solat ul Mulk Deputy Governor Ardistan. Release Mirza Rafia immediately whom you have arrested. Abstain from troubling him further let him be content and never do such things again without orders from Governor General Isfahan.'[25]

* German Consul in Iṣfahán

On 28 February 1915, Grahame wrote to Sir Walter Townley reporting on the mischief-making of the 'ulamá.

A reference to passages *passim* in the Isfahan News of the last seven or eight weeks will serve to show that since [the beginning of January] Haji Agha Nourullah and his followers have been actively engaged in endeavours to exalt the Pure Faith as by them understood and incidentally their own horns. My telegram No. 16 of yesterday's date will serve to show that the ardour of the Isfahan clergy has of late carried them beyond such local tyranny as the whipping of prostitutes, the intimidation of schoolboys attending the Church Missionary Society schools and attempts to impose a distinctive garb on the Jews to the nobler task of Behai baiting in Ardistan.

I have caused enquiries to be made here regarding the present situation in that place and, if even a quarter of the tales of spoliation reported to me be true, I think it is time that some measures be taken by the Persian Government to break up the unholy alliance between the Isfahan clergy and Chiragh Ali Khan Sardar-i-Soulat Deputy Governor of Ardistan (son of Ziegham us Saltaneh . . .).

I have no reason to believe the reign of terror now prevailing in Ardistan to be other than an ignoble attempt to make money. If the movement be really a fanatical one the Persian Government might perhaps be reminded of the deplorable massacre of the Babis in Yazd in July 1903 . . .

My Russian colleague who is perhaps better informed than I about the intrigues of the Clergy lays stress in his conversations with me on the participation of Dr Pugin in these. I incline to share Monsieur Hildebrandt's view but I am not at present in a position to submit any documentary proof in support thereof.[26]

On 28 February, the Ardistán signaller reported: 'Mujahed ul Sultaneh left for Isfahan on Friday leaving Mirza Abdul Husseyn with Deputy Governor. An agent of Isfahan Mullas arrived here on Thursday to investigate the Bahai affair. On Friday the Deputy Governor sent Mamoors and seized all suspected Bahais in Ardistan and Zavareh causing great commotion. Some were let off on paying fines, others still imprisoned.'[27]

And on 4 March, the signaller telegraphed: 'Mirza Rafia and his two brothers who were seized by Deputy Governor on excuse of being Bahais were set free on payment of 1500 tumans and they had to seal a telegram to Governor General, Isfahan, stating that they had no complaint against Deputy Governor.'[28]

On receiving this information, Grahame communicated it to the Deputy Governor-General stating: 'I should feel greatly obliged if Y.E. [Your Excellency] would be good enough to cause this matter to be examined by some impartial person and if the report above-mentioned be true, cause justice [to be] done. I may add that numerous reports of similar cases of extortion in Ardistan by the Deputy Governor have reached me in the course of the last few weeks.'[29]

The Deputy Governor-General's reply of 6 March stated: 'I much regret if such things have happened. It is not right that such occurrences be in men's ears. Urgent measures have been taken such as the sending of an inspector and maamur to investigate these matters.'[30]

In a dispatch to Sir Walter Townley dated 8 March, Grahame indicated that the former's intervention in Ṭihrán had also not been without effect: 'I may mention that I received a verbal message on the 6th instant from the Karguzar to the effect that he had received instructions from the Persian Foreign Office to enquire into this case and asking what action I wished taken.'[31]

At about this time, the signaller at Ardistán telegraphed: 'Some of the Bahais seized by the Deputy Governor were severely bastinadoed on Sunday last and all of them were fined then released. As a result several Ardistanis and Zavarehis have run away towards Tehran. Isfahan Mullas have ordered their Agent to take Mirza Abdul Hussein to Isfahan but Deputy Govenor is waiting for orders from Governor General.'[32]

On 14 March, the signaller reported: 'Deputy Governor has gone Mozdabad and taken Mirza Abdul Husseyn there. Mamoor from the Governor General arrived to take latter to Isfahan but former has not handed him over yet. Rumoured that a new Deputy been appointed, hence present Deputy is getting people to send telegrams to Governor General with recommendations to retain his post.'[33]

On 21 March, the signaller reported: 'New Deputy Governor Rashid-ul-Sultan arrived 15th March. Sardar-i-Soulat is still keeping Mirza Abdul Hussein at Muzdabad.'[34]

Eventually, in his report for the week ending 28 March, Grahame was able to report about Ardistán: 'The situation is said to have improved by the arrival of the new Deputy Governor Rashid-i-Sultan, Sardar-i-Soulat has released Mirza Abdul Hussein and special mamoors have arrived at Ardistan to recover the property of the latter. This however has not yet been effected. (Private information shows that Mirza Abdul Hussein has paid Ts.2500 to the Isfahan Authorities to obtain his release and their intervention for restitution of his property).'[35]

The Tombs of the King and Beloved of Martyrs, 1920

During 1920 there were several episodes concerning the Bahá'ís in the Iṣfahán area. In about June, the 'ulamá were trying to incite the populace against certain Bahá'ís who were teaching in the schools of Iṣfahán. Later there was a persecution of the Bahá'ís of Gaz. The main event, however, occurred in September when a mob broke into a cemetery and demolished the tombs of the two famous Bahá'í martyrs, the King and the Beloved of Martyrs (see pp. 274–7).

The Bahá'í Assembly of Ṭihrán brought this to the attention of the British Legation. Norman telegrammed to Crow (q.v.), the British Consul in Iṣfahán, who replied on 13 September 1920 by telegram: 'Governor* says Bahais erect large brick platform over tomb mentioned and other Bahais graves in Isfahan cemetery and included several Mussulman graves. At the request of Mullahs who agitated he had platform removed.

'Mullahs afterwards caused a door and window in Mausoleum over the tomb of Mirza As. . .llah† in the same cemetery to be destroyed. Governor imprisoned guardians of cemetery and is taking steps to punish offenders. He will restore door and window . . .

'It is clear that Governor is entirely in the hands of the Mullahs and follows their lead trying to save his face to us as best he can.'[36]

The contents of this telegram were communicated to the representatives of the Ṭihrán Bahá'í Assembly, Siyyid Naṣru'lláh Báqiroff and Mírzá Raḥím Khán Arjumand, by Smart. In a telegram to Crow dated 20 September, Smart recorded their response to the statements of Sardár-i-Jang: 'Bahai committee here states that the G.G.'s [Governor-General's] explanation as given in para. 1 of your telegram is false. They say that the platform, which has been in existence for the past thirty years covered the graves of two famous Bahai martyrs, Haji Mirza Hasan and Haji Mirza Husain, killed 35 years ago at the instigation of Zill-us-Sultan. Haji Mirza Sadiq, a son of Haji Mirza Husain was buried beside this platform six months ago, and it included no Musulman graves. It was destroyed in the presence of Sardar Jang . . .

'On a favourable opportunity you might explain to Sardar Jang that the days of religious persecution are past and that he will do himself harm by acting as the agent of the *mullas* in their anti-Bahai movement.'[37]

On 26 September, Crow forwarded the following report on the episode:

With reference to my telegram No. 132 of the 22nd inst. I have the honour to report that Sirdar Jang dined with me last night and I took the opportunity of speaking to His Excellency about the desecration of the Bahai tombs in the sense of your telegram No. 83.

I had myself visited the tombs a few days before with my head servant, who is a Bahai, in order to ascertain as far as possible the extent of the damage done. I was informed that two small separate brick platforms formerly existed covering the graves of Haji Mirza Hassan and Haji Mirza Hussein and that when Haji Mirza Sadiq died some six months ago, he was buried a few yards distant from these two graves. Sadiq left money for the construction of his tomb and his son-in-law, who is not a Bahai, carried out the work on August 6th last. He also connected all the three graves together by erecting a continuous platform about 9 yards wide by 11 yards long, raised some 2 feet about [*sic*] the ground which covered them all. Platforms of this kind are used as meeting places by the relatives and friends of the deceased who generally congregate there on Fridays, and the larger the platform is the

* Sardár-i-Jang, a Bakhtíyárí Khán

† Mírzá Asadu'lláh Khán-i-Vazír who was Vazír of Iṣfahán for about thirty years and well-known to be a Bahá'í. He had died two years before.

greater is the importance attached by the people of Isfahan to such gatherings. I understand that the Bahais were rather averse at the time to this extension, and that they were not consulted. They felt that unnecessary attention might be drawn to the site, which is situated in the middle of the Takht-i-Pulad cemetery, a Moslem burial ground.

Certain fanatics urged on by the Mollahs attempted to destroy the new platform but were restrained by the police. When, however, Sirdar Jang returned from Tehran he received complaints on the subject and, acting on the advice of the Mollahs, he visited the cemetery and had the platform destroyed.

I found the new brick paving broken up and several pieces of broken marble tombstones lying on the debris. The perimeter of the ruined platform was still clearly defined. Mirza Asadullah's tomb and three others are situated in a mud-wall enclosure near the above platform. The entrance is through a small brick and mud archway. I was told that the door disappeared long ago and that there was no window over it. The brickwork of the arch had been recently destroyed and the four tombs in the enclosure had been desecrated and the stones and brickwork over them broken up and scattered.

I told Sirdar Jang exactly what I had seen and pointed out the iniquitous folly of the desecration which could only serve to injure his reputation and savoured of the savagery of the middle ages, and I urged him to take steps, as soon as Moharrem was over, to restore the tombs to their former condition and to cover them with separate platforms, as before, as was the custom. His Excellency promised me that he would certainly do so at the first favourable moment and I hope to be able to keep him to his word when Moharrem is past. I also related the circumstances to Prince Arfa-ed-Dowleh [q.v.], who was prevented from dining with me by indisposition. His Highness said that he was glad I had mentioned the subject as he himself was much interested in the Bahais and had frequently protected them from persecution both in Persia and Turkey. He assured me that he would take an opportunity of letting Sirdar Jang know of the steps that he had himself taken on frequent occasions on behalf of the Bahais and would urge the Governor General in his own interest to exercise greater toleration in future.[38]

References

1. Aganoor to Durand No. 24, 18 Apr. 1899: FO 248 699
2. No. 63, File G2/PE O/1899: CMS Archives
3. No. 65, File G2/PE O/1899: CMS Archives
4. Aganoor to Durand No. 27, 20 May 1899: FO 248 699
5. Enclosed in Aganoor to Durand No. 30, 29 May 1899: FO 248 699
6. Schneider to Durand No. 32, 21 June 1899: FO 248 699
7. Preece to Hardinge 16 June 1901: FO 248 742
8. Hardinge to Amínu's-Sulṭán 4 Aug. 1901: FO 248 749
9. Hardinge to Preece No. 10, 7 Aug. 1901: FO 248 742
10. Preece to Hardinge No. 36, 11 Sept. 1901: FO 248 742
11. Aganoor to Hardinge 2 Apr. 1905: FO 248 845
12. Grahame to Barclay No. 159, 8 Nov. 1909: FO 248 967
13. Miss Stuart to Grahame 10 Nov. 1909: FO 248 967. Enclosed in 14 *infra*
14. Grahame to Barclay 11 Nov. 1909: FO 248 967
15. Iṣfahán News No. 45 for week ending 13 Nov. 1909: FO 248 967
16. ibid.
17. Memo dated 23 Nov. 1909 by 'Abbás-Qulí Khán at foot of telegram detailed in 18 *infra*

18. Grahame to Barclay No. 160, 20 Nov. 1909: FO 248 967
19. Iṣfahán News No. 46 for week ending 20 Nov. 1909: FO 248 967
20. Iṣfahán News No. 7 for week ending 15 Feb. 1915: FO 248 1107
21. Iṣfahán News No. 8 for week ending 22 Feb. 1915: FO 248 1107
22. Grahame to Townley No. 15, 27 Feb. 1915: FO 248 1107
23. Note by Townley at foot of dispatch detailed in 22 *supra*
24. Grahame to Sardár-Fátiḥ 20 Feb. 1915, enclosed in dispatch detailed in 31 *infra*
25. In letter Sardár-Fátiḥ to Grahame 27 Feb. 1915, enclosed in dispatch detailed in 31 *infra*
26. Grahame to Townley No. 17, 28 Feb. 1915: FO 248 1107
27. Iṣfahán News No. 9 for week ending 1 Mar. 1915: FO 248 1107
28. Signaller at Ardistán to Asst Superintendent IET Dept. 4 Mar. 1915, enclosed in 31 *infra*. This passage also occurs, worded slightly differently, in Iṣfahán News detailed in 32 *infra*.
29. Grahame to Sardár-Fátiḥ 5 Mar. 1915, enclosed in 31 *infra*
30. Sardár-Fátiḥ to Grahame 6 Mar. 1915, enclosed in 31 *infra*
31. Grahame to Townley No. 19, 8 Mar 1915: FO 248 1107
32. Iṣfahán News No. 10 for week ending 7 Mar. 1915: FO 248 1107
33. Iṣfahán News No. 11 for week ending 14 Mar. 1915: FO 248 1107
34. Iṣfahán News No. 12 for week ending 21 Mar. 1915: FO 248 1107
35. Iṣfahán News No. 13 for week ending 28 Mar. 1915: FO 248 1107
36. Crow to Norman No. 126, 13 Sept. 1920, File 'Bahais': FO 248 1279
37. Telegram to Crow drafted by Haig, No. 83, 20 Sept. 1920, but based on memo by Smart dated 18 Sept. 1920. File 'Bahais': FO 248 1279
38. Crow to Norman No. 42, 26 Sept. 1920, File 'Bahais': FO 248 1279

THIRTY

Miscellaneous Events

The Body of Mírzá Muḥammad-'Alí, the Afnán

Mírzá Muḥammad-'Alí* was a cousin of the Báb – an adventurous and successful merchant whose trading activities took him as far afield as China and India. He was also a well-known Bahá'í, and when he died in Bombay in 1896, at about the time of the assassination of Náṣiru'd-Dín Sháh, the Muslims of Bombay refused to allow him to be buried there. His body was therefore loaded aboard the S.S. *Henry Bolckow* bound for Búshihr. Its fate on arrival is recorded by a Búshihr correspondent of the *Times of India*:

> About a fortnight ago the s.s. Henry Bolckow arrived here from Bombay with a corpse of one Haji Mirza Mahomedally *en route* for interment near the shrines at Kerbella. The deceased was believed, whether rightly or falsely, to be a Babi. On the arrival of that steamer here two young Seyeds of notorious character, instigated by others, boarded her and asked the Captain for the surrender of the coffin. The Captain referred them to the Company's agent on shore, Haji Ally Akbar, who, much to his credit and prudence, refused to comply with the pressing demands of the Seyeds, whose object, it was made evident, was to burn the corpse publicly when landed. A mob for the purpose was got ready to seize the corpse, which they intended to drag through the streets before consigning it to the flames. Had they succeeded in carrying out their plans, there is no doubt that it would have been a signal for the indescriminate [*sic*] assasination [*sic*] of the Babis throughout the length and breadth of the country, and perhaps with an attempt of retaliation on their part. It is impossible to conceive the extent of the mischief which the projected cremation of the corpse would have led to, and yet no attempts have been made by the local authorities to punish the Seyeds nor their instigator, perhaps through fear of giving extra publicity to the matter.[1]

The subsequent adventures that befell the body of Mírzá Muḥammad-'Alí are recorded in the Diary of Samuel Butcher, Acting British Vice-Consul at Muḥammarih, for 1 July 1896: 'The Babi corpse already noted in my diary of 18 and 25 June 1896 as having been aboard 'Henry Bolckow' now unloading at Busrah, was sent back this evening by Gray Mackenzie's steam launch to this place to be landed here, but the Muez's representative

* See 'Abdu'l-Bahá's account of him and of this episode in *Memorials of the Faithful* pp. 16–21.

would not allow it. The launch then returned to Busrah with corpse aboard.'[2]

The body was eventually allowed to land at Baṣra. It was taken overland and, after further adventures, was eventually buried at the site of Ctesiphon, the ancient capital of the Persian Sassanian kings, south of Baghdád.

The Construction of the Mashriqu'l-Adhkár in 'Ishqábád

In a previous chapter (chapter 19), the foundation of the Bahá'í community in 'Ishqábád has been described. Under the protection and freedom given by the Russian authorities, the number of Bahá'ís there rose to over 1,000 and for the first time anywhere in the world a true Bahá'í community was established, with its own schools, medical facilities, cemetery, etc. Eventually, the Bahá'ís in 'Ishqábád decided to build the institution that Bahá'u'lláh has ordained as the spiritual and social heart of the Bahá'í community, the Mashriqu'l-Adhkár (Dawning Place of the Praises of God) (see fig. 45).

A Russian official who was in 'Ishqábád at this time, A. D. Kalmykov (q.v.), has recorded in his memoirs:

I also took part in the founding of the first mosque [i.e. the Mashriqu'l-Adhkár] of the Persian sect of the Babi.

This harmless, progressive, liberal sect was founded by the Bab, who was shot in Tabriz in 1850, close to the wall of the citadel at a place which I tried in vain to locate. The Babis were persecuted in Persia in my time and had to conceal their faith; I had never met them there. They came to Russia and even spread to America, where they were called Baha'i.

The Babis in Ashkhabad formed a closely knit community of honest, law-abiding people, somewhat reminiscent of the early Christian churches in the first century after Christ. The great event in the life of the Babi colony was the arrival of Hadji Mirza M.Taghi,* a Babi chief, and nephew of Bab, from Yezd, Persia in 1902. A rich, wise, kind old man of Biblical appearance and dressed in floating Oriental garments, he looked like one of the Magi who came to Bethlehem to adore the birth of Christ. Hadji Mirza M. Taghi had been consular agent for Russia, England, and France† in his native town for many years. Although widely respected, he was finally forced to leave by persecution which continuously increased in violence. I had been informed beforehand about his arrival, and he was warmly recommended to me by my friend and future brother-in-law, Dr D. M. Vinogradov, who had visited him in Yezd.

After being welcomed with due reverence by all the Babi community of Ashkhabad and meeting with a hospitable reception on the part of the Russian authorities, Hadji Mirza M. Taghi decided to settle in Ashkhabad and, as the crowning act of his long religious life, to build there a beautiful Babi temple, the first on the continent of Asia. He lived in a very simple manner but spared no money for the completion of the temple or the cause of his religion.

I presented Hadji Mirza M. Taghi to the military governor of Transcaspia, General D. I. Subotich, who agreed to lay the corner-

* Ḥájí Mírzá Muḥammad-Taqí, the Afnán (q.v., see fig. 45).
† in fact for Russia only

stone of the Babi temple. It was an impressive ceremony, this Russian recognition of Babism as an established religion at a moment when hundreds of Babis were being slaughtered in Persia. The Babi community presented General Subotich with a picture by the famous calligrapher, Meshkin Kalam, representing a bird on a tree. The picture was formed with the letters composing the verse, 'On the Tree of Eternity sits the Bird of Truth repeating: "He (God) is one, is one, is one." '

Although the Babis in Ashkhabad kept the outward appearance of old-fashioned Moslems, their conceptions were entirely different. Babi women visited European families and enjoyed a freedom unknown at that time in Moslem countries. The Babis had a small book called *Kitabi Siossieh* (*The Book of Behavior*). They considered that each man had a divine spark which must be kept pure during his lifetime in order to ascend to heaven. The Babis in Ashkhabad presented various stages of evolution, ranging from a purely Oriental to a European way of life. However, they retained their Persian attire, whereas in European Russia they wore western clothes.

I was glad to hear that after the revolution the persecution of Babis ceased in Persia, and I have no doubt that they will prove to be excellent Persian citizens. They are certainly good examples of what may become of a Persian liberated from the suffocating atmosphere of an old decaying past.[3]

Martyrdom of Mírzá Muḥammad-i-Bulúr-Furú<u>sh</u>

Throughout the whole of 'Abdu'l-Bahá's ministry, Yazd was a turbulent town: the great upheaval of 1903 has already been described. Besides those of the 1903, there were other martyrs in Yazd, and the last of these during 'Abdu'l-Bahá's ministry was Mírzá Muḥammad-i-Bulúr-Furú<u>sh</u> (Seller of glass and crystal goods).

Treadwell, Acting Vice-Consul at Yazd, reported in his Diary for 2 May 1917:

2nd [May] – Great excitement caused by the murder of a Bahai at hands of Tullabs and mob. From reports which have reached me and also the official report from the Governor-General, the following circumstances led up to the murder: –

Mohamad Boloor Foroosh who was known to be a Bahai was sitting in his shop (which is opposite the Madrasseh of Syed Yahya Mujtahid), taking his lunch, when a beggar came and asked for some bread, he refused to give him any, whereupon the beggar abused him, a sailor who was sitting by the shop took out his chain and gave the beggar a few lashes with it. Two days later, 2nd May, early in the morning some 'tollabs' of the Madrasseh came to Mohamad's shop and took him before Seyed Yahya who urged him to abandon Bahaism, apparently he refused, for while he was sitting by Seyed Yahya who was holding his hand the 'tullabs' and mob (about 2000) seized him and threw him down from the upper storey of the school, and there he was dispatched with sticks and spades.

It is said that Seyed Yahya endeavoured to save the man but the mob forcibly took him.

When the Governor heard that Mohamad had been taken to the Madrasseh he immediately sent men to bring him to the Kaleh for safety but when they arrived they found he had been killed. Great excitement prevailed but the presence of the deputy governor with other leading men who were soon on the spot restored order.

The Governor is taking steps to discover the ringleaders of this outbreak.[4]

The Martyrdom of Ḥájí 'Arab in Sulṭánábád

In February 1916, when Iran was in a state of turmoil during the World War and Russian troops were occupying the area around Sulṭánábád (now Irák), there occurred in that town the particularly brutal murders of Mírzá 'Alí-Akbar and his family, who were Bahá'ís. Ḥájí Isfandíyár, known as Ḥájí 'Arab, a poor and illiterate Bahá'í of Sulṭánábád, helped in the burial of the bodies and openly reproached the perpetrators of this abominable act, thus overtly labelling himself as a Bahá'í. In May 1920, certain of the 'ulamá of Sulṭánábád who were ill-disposed towards the Bahá'ís began to agitate the populace. They invented a story that Ḥájí 'Arab had burnt a Qur'án and thus excited the mob.

The British Vice-Consul at Sulṭánábád, E. P. Hutton (q.v.), reported in his news-sheet for the month of May 1920:

On the 8th of the month, a Babee entered a mosque and burnt a Khoran. Rumour then said that the man was captured almost in the act and taken before the Governor* who set him free on the payment of a bribe said to be T's 4000. The priests and populace then became very incensed and demanded that the man should be handed over to them; a demonstration was made two days after before the Governor's house. In fear, however, the Governor closed his gates which the crowd then burst open; he made his escape by the back entrance to the Nazmiah, not without having several missiles thrown at him. The rabble then proceeded to destroy his household possessions and did considerable damage, the Governor's estimate being T's 1000. Up to the 15th, the Bazaars were all closed and so remained until the arrival of the Gendarmerie company from Malayir. Ultimately the Babee was captured and brought into town by the Gendarmerie, found guilty and hanged in the Maidan on the 21st. At one time the situation was most serious, large numbers of people collecting in the Maidan and demonstrating against the Governor; on one occasion several blank shots had to be fired before they dispersed . . .[5]

This report produced no particular response at the British Legation in Ṭihrán, and would have been forgotten had not 'Abdu'l-Bahá raised the matter with Lord Curzon, the British Foreign Secretary, in a letter dated 29 June 1920:

Your Excellency's cablegram was received.† I am exceedingly grateful to your noble sentiments and pray to God day and night that you may succeed in rendering great service to this Just Government and that the present difficulties might be solved. In truth you are energetically striving to bring about that which is conducive to betterment and surely Divine Assistance shall follow.

With reference to the Bahais. A certain leading member of the Bahai Community at Irak, Persia, named Sheikh Arab, has been innocently crucified; he became the victim of

* Qásím Khán-i-Válí, Sardár Humáyún (q.v.)

† 'Abdu'l-Bahá was in all probability replying to a telegram of congratulations from Lord Curzon on his knighthood. The editor cannot, however, find a copy of this telegram.

this great calamity simply because he was a Bahai.

Our object is not this that His Majesty's Government should undertake any formal protection but rather to incite the Persian Government to undertake the protection of the Bahais and to shield them from the evil of the oppressors. Such a measure would lead to the strength and grandeur of Persia itself.[6]

Curzon instructed that a copy of 'Abdu'l-Bahá's letter be sent to Norman, the British Minister in Ṭihrán, for his observations. When the letter arrived in Ṭihrán, Norman wrote immediately to Hutton at Sulṭánábád, asking for details. It was only after the dispatch to Hutton had gone that 'Abdu'l-Bahá's letter came to the attention of Smart (q.v.), who wrote on 11 November 1920:

This is the case of *Haji* Arab, a poor Behai, who was accused of burning a Koran in Sultanabad about six months ago. The Ulema of Sultanabad made a great disturbance, but the Governor, Serdar Humayun, took him into his own house and tried to protect him. The crowd broke into Serdar Humayun's house and sacked it but were unable to find Hàji Arab. The Ulema then telegraphed furiously to Vosough-ud-Dowleh, who sent telegraphic instructions to the Gendarmerie to hang Haji Arab. The Gendarmerie carried out the instructions. The body was exposed on the gibbet for a couple of days. He was hanged *not* crucified.

It is to be noted that the local authorities tried to save the man, and Serdar Humayun, who was knocked about by the mob invading his house, himself told me how sorry he was that he had been unable to save the poor man, whom he described as a beggar and almost half-witted.* The outbreak was probably due to political factors. It was an anti-Government riot, and the unfortunate Behai was only a pretext for disturbances embarrassing to the Govt.

Vosough-ud-Dowleh† must bear the responsibility of this quite unjustifiable execution. The accusation of burning the Koran was of course trumped up. It is the regular accusation made in such cases.[7]

As was to be expected, Hutton's reply to Norman's query merely referred the latter to the Sulṭánábád news-sheet for May quoted above. The following is Hutton's letter, dated 23 November 1920, together with the memoranda appended by Haig and Norman:

'This case was duly reported in my News Sheet for May. The Bahai, named *Isphendiar*, was tried and found guilty for the burning of a Koran, and hanged in the Maidan on 21st May.

'He was not a leading member of the Bahai community here, but a poor begger [*sic*].'

(E. Hutton)[8]

'There seems to be some confusion here. The man has hitherto been called Shaikh Arab. His name is now said to have been Isfandiyar.

T.W.H. 29.11.20'[9]

* It seems strange that a man described as 'a beggar and almost half-witted' should, according to the previously-quoted dispatch, have been able to pay a bribe of Ts. 4,000.

† Ḥasan Vuthúq (1873–1951), Vuthúqu'd-Dawlih, Iranian statesman who was at this time Prime Minister.

'Yes, and, according to Mr Hutton, he really burnt the book whereas, according to Mr Smart, he did not.

'Still, whatever his name was and whether he was guilty or not, I think it clear that the case is the one referred to by Abdul-Baha and that we have done all that is required by addressing our desp. No. 162 to the F.O.

H.C.N. Nov. 29, 1920'[10]

However, Smart's note dated 30 November cleared up some of the riddles and added the important personal testimony of Sardár-i-Humáyún to the effect that Ḥájí 'Arab had been innocent of the charge made against him:

' "Isfandiar" was probably his original name, but the title he was generally known by was "Háji Arab".

'The Behais state that a Mussulman, who was an enemy of Haji Arab, burnt the Koran and fixed the guilt on the latter.

'Serdar Humayun, who was Governor at the time, expressed to me personally the opinion that Haji Arab was innocent.

'Anyhow, we can let the matter rest here.'[11]

The Times of London carried a report of this episode in its issue of 3 November 1920:

A REAL MARTYR

(FROM OUR SPECIAL CORRESPONDENT IN THE MIDDLE EAST)

The Bahais, or followers of Bahai'ullah, and his predecessor the Bab, who are a kind of Oriental Quakers, sprung from Islam, and profess a universal quietist religion, which has brought them converts in Western Europe, and especially in America, have added another to their long list of martyrs. On May 29 last one Hadji Arab, a humble citizen of the town, was publicly hanged at Sultanabad, Persia, for his faith.

The event was the sequel to the martyrdom of a whole family, which took place at Sultanabad on February 16.* The friends of the family were at first afraid to give them burial, but Hadji Arab had this done, and had himself photographed with the naked bodies of the murdered children. In his right hand he held the head, and in his left the body of an infant of 38 days, who had been thus dismembered. The photograph reached the outer world, and became a cause of offence.

This year the Mollahs trumped up against Hadji Arab the charge that he had burnt a copy of the Koran. The charge is the most convenient one, and the most frequently brought in such cases. It is especially pointless in the case of Bahais, who revere the Koran and teach it in their schools in Persia. Appeal was made to the Government in Teheran, but without effect, and the execution took place.[12]

The Martyrdom of Mírzá Ya'qúb-i-Muttaḥidih

The last martyrdom to occur during the ministry of 'Abdu'l-Bahá was that of Mírzá Ya'qúb-i-Muttaḥidih (see fig. 42). This 25-year-old merchant from Ká<u>sh</u>án and his four brothers had become Bahá'ís from a Jewish background. His elder brother, <u>Kh</u>ájih Rabí', had been the principal founder of

* Feb. 1916 is meant.

the Bahá'í Vaḥdat-i-Bas͟har school in Kás͟hán. Mírzá Ya'qúb moved to Kirmáns͟háh and started to trade there. He soon achieved prominence as a merchant in the town as well as becoming known as a Bahá'í.

In the Kirmáns͟háh report from Major Greenhouse (q.v.) for the period to 30 June 1920, the following paragraph occurs:

'June 17th the end of Ramadhan was marked by attempts to excite religious zeal by action against the Bahai sect. The Governor* sent the principal Bahai merchant out of town and had a Bahai preacher mildly beaten; these measures appeased popular clamour as represented by the mullahs.'[13]

The merchant who was expelled was Mírzá Ya'qúb-i-Muttaḥidih.

On 27 August 1920 a deputation of Bahá'ís called on the British Minister, Norman. They spoke of persecutions of the Bahá'ís in Kirmáns͟háh and S͟háhrúd. Norman telegrammed immediately to the British Consuls in Kirmáns͟háh and Mas͟hhad asking for further information. From Kirmáns͟háh, Major Greenhouse reported on 29 August: 'Governor General expelled one respectable Bahai and had one other beaten mildly during Ramazan. Permission given for his return if delayed till after Mohurram would be wiser. I do not think reasons for expulsion were sound but sign of great weakness.'[14]

On 18 September, Walter Smart recorded the proceedings of an interview with a Bahá'í delegation: 'Behai delegation (Bagherov and Mirza Rahim Khan Arjumandi) informed of this. They state that the expelled Behai has already returned to Kermanshah with the permission of Sarim-ud-Dowleh.[15]

Thus Mírzá Ya'qúb came back to Kirmáns͟háh, and it was on his return in January 1921 from a visit to his mother in Hamadán that he was attacked as he was walking in the streets near the bazaar in the middle of the day, and shot dead. His assassin was the son of the Mu'ínu'r-Ru'áyá and the *fatvá* for his death had already been given by the mujtahid Ḥájí Siyyid Ḥusayn-i-Karbilá'í.

Major Greenhouse telegrammed from Kirmáns͟háh on 24 January 1921: 'It is reported for your information Chief Bahai named Muttahida on his return here was assassinated in main street at midday January 23rd. Motive reported to be purely religious.'[16] In a note appended to his telegram Haig commented wryly: 'We shall hear more of this.'[17] While Norman instructed that the following telegram be sent to Greenhouse on 26 January: 'You should impress on Gov. Gen. my abhorrence of this wanton crime and urge him to arrest and punish murderer forthwith.'[18]

Two delegates from the Central Spiritual Assembly, Mírzá Raḥím K͟hán

* The Governor was Akbar Mírzá, Sárimu'd-Dawlih, a son of Ẓillu's-Sulṭán. He was one of the signatories of the Anglo-Persian Treaty of 1919 about which there was so much bitterness and agitation (see p. 472n).

Arjumand and Mírzá Isḥáq-i-Ḥaqíqí, called on Smart in the first few days of February, and as a result of this interview the following telegram, dated 4 February, was sent to Greenhouse in Kirmánsháh:

'Delegates of Behai Spiritual Assembly called at Legation and invoked our support to secure punishment of murderer.

'They think motive was not religious but personal and they are suspicious of Gov. Gen.

'You should point out to Gov. Gen. that there were no anti-Behai outbreaks during the reigns of his predecessors at Kermanshah, that last summer he distinguished himself by his persecution of Behais, that Muttehida returned with his sanction and that failure to punish the murderer, who must be well-known, would be a stain on H.H.'s reputation.

'Please report result of your representations.'[19]

On 14 February, Greenhouse replied: 'Matter represented. Governor promised to deport individual after short interval but puts blame on action on [*sic*] central Government which trying to shelve responsibility. He will not actually punish man for fear of unpopularity.'[20]

To which Haig appended: 'I thought we should not get much more than this.'[21] Smart wrote: 'From this answer it would appear that Sarim-ud-Dowleh not only is refraining from adequately punishing the murderer but is leaving him at large.

'I think the answer is too unsatisfactory for communication to the Behai Spiritual Assembly. I suggest we ask Sipahdar* to send instructions to Sarem-ud-Dowleh to punish the murderer. When the instructions have been sent, we can request Greenhouse to return to the charge.'[22]

Norman reluctantly agreed, and Smart wrote to the Prime Minister on 15 February. The Prime Minister's response was an emphatic denial of the assertions of Sárimu'd-Dawlih. Norman telegrammed to Greenhouse on 17 February:

Prime Minister emphatically denies Governor General's allegation and has sent me copies of correspondence.

Jan. 25th Prime Minister telegraphed ordering arrest of murderer and expressing regret that such an incident should have occurred during Governorship of Prince.

Feb. 3rd Governor General answered to the effect that he was afraid to take suitable action.

Prime Minister has again telegraphed in the sense of his first telegram.

It is clear that Prince is entirely responsible. You should point out to H.H. that if murderers are allowed to exercise their trade in broad daylight in main street of town without being molested, the authority of the Government will practically have ceased to exist. You should insist that he should obey his instructions and arrest the murderer. H.H. must know that he is only being kept in office by my efforts and, if

* Sardár-i-Sipah Fatḥu'lláh Gílání, the Prime Minister

spoken to firmly, will doubtless cease prevaricating.[23]

In a letter dated 15 February 1921,[24] Mírzá Ghulám-'Alí, chairman of the Central Spiritual Assembly, forwarded to Norman a copy of a telegram from the Bahá'ís of Hamadán, reporting that the Bahá'ís of Kirmánsháh were still being threatened; some had hidden while others dispersed. Norman noted: 'Yesterday Mr Smart and I talked to Sipahdar about the matter. He said that he had sent the necessary instructions.'[25] This was communicated to the Spiritual Assembly by Smart.

On 22 February, Greenhouse telegrammed: 'Governor General's sole object has been to avoid unpopularity and put responsibility on Tehran. He has promised to arrest the murderers immediately and send them to Tehran within the next few days. Police have absolute proofs of the deed and if made to will willingly give such proofs. Every obstacle will of course be put in the way of proper investigation and evidence has not yet been taken here.'[26]

At this time, however, the *coup d'état* occurred that brought to power Siyyid Ḍíyá'u'd-Dín and Riḍá Khán. An inevitable suspension of all government activity occurred, so that eventually Norman had to telegram to Greenhouse on 21 March 1921: 'When are we to expect the murderers at Tehran?'[27]

Greenhouse replied on 1 April:

'Delay caused by political changes and Nauruz celebrations.

'Governor General will do nothing in support of the matter without direct orders from Tehran or until he knows his position vis-a-vis new Government.

'He will probably wire resignation sooner than take any action likely to offend any party, and I expect resignation any day.'[28]

On reading this telegram, Smart penned the following stern rebuke: 'Sarim-ud-Dowleh's attitude is disgraceful and Greenhouse's uncritical attitude towards the Prince's enormities is peculiar.'[29]

Norman discussed this question with Qavámu's-Salṭanih (q.v.), the new Prime Minister who had replaced Siyyid Ḍíyá'u'd-Dín, and Smart suggested that Greenhouse be telegraphed in the following terms: 'Prime Minister has promised telegraph instructions to Gov. Gen. to despatch murderers to Tehran.

'Please inform Prince in diplomatic language that I am disgusted with him.'[30]

Norman, however, amended the last phrase to read 'much discouraged by his attitude.'[31]

Matters drifted on inconclusively, and on 1 July Norman again enquired of Greenhouse about the state of the affair. Greenhouse replied on 5 July

1921: 'Governor General promised to take necessary steps but it would encourage him if orders to this effect were sent from Tehran. Orders sent by Sipahdar's Cabinet cannot be traced.'[32]

Later, on 24 July, Greenhouse telegraphed: 'As I expected Governor-General is afraid to act without explicit orders from Tehran. Can you expedite please?'[33]

As a result of these telegrams, Norman wrote to the Prime Minister, Qavámu's-Salṭanih, on 30 July:

> I have the honour to draw Y.H.'s [Your Highness's] attention to the fact that the assassination of the Chief Bahai at Kermanshah, named Muttahida, which occurred on Jan. 23rd, has up till now remained unpunished, although the identity of the murderer is well-known to the local authorities.
>
> H.H. Sipahdar Aazam telegraphed on Jan. 25th to the Governor-General of Kermanshah ordering the arrest of the murderer. On Feb. 3rd the Governor-General replied that he was afraid to take action, whereupon Sipahdar Aazam repeated his instructions. Nevertheless, no action was taken.
>
> This matter has been represented anew to H.M. Legation and I therefore take the liberty to submit to Y.H. the necessity of action, lest the [Persian Government] be accused of conniving at a persecution of the Bahais by allowing a prominent member of the sect to be murdered in broad daylight in the main street of a town like Kermanshah, and letting the murderers go scot free.[34]

Months passed and no steps were taken. Norman, his position as Minister having become untenable owing to Curzon's hostility towards him, resigned and left Persia – the end of a promising diplomatic career. In October 1921, Reginald Bridgeman (q.v.), Chargé d'Affaires, decided to have one last attempt to stir the Persian Government into action over this matter. Taking advantage of the appointment of a new Governor-General to Kirmánsháh, he wrote to the Prime Minister, Qavámu's-Salṭanih on 28 October 1921:

'I have the honour to refer Y.H. to Mr Norman's note of July 30th concerning the murder of a notable member of the Bahai community at Kermanshah, named Muttahida, on Jan. 23rd of this year.

'No steps whatever have yet been taken to punish the murderers, and I have the honour to suggest to Y.H. that advantage should be taken of the appointment of a new Governor General to Kermanshah to give H.E. explicit instructions to attend to this case.'[35]

However, even this was no use, and Mírzá Ya'qúb's murderer was never apprehended.

Other Episodes

During the troubled period 1920–21, there were many outbursts of persecution against the Bahá'ís only a few of which have been described above.

The full list of incidents reported by the British consular officials, the Indo-European Telegraph staff and the South Persia Rifles (a British army unit based in Shíráz) is as follows:

1. February 1920: Káshán: Anti-Bahá'í agitation.
2. May 1920: Shíráz: Anti-Bahá'í disturbances.
3. May 1920: Sulṭánábád: Martyrdom of Ḥájí 'Arab (see above).
4. June 1920: Iṣfahán: Anti-Bahá'í agitation.
5. August 1920: Kirmánsháh: Anti-Bahá'í agitation and expulsion of Mírzá Ya'qúb-i-Muttaḥidih (see above).
6. August 1920: Sháhrúd: Expulsion of eight Bahá'ís.
7. August 1920: Ban on importation of Bahá'í literature.
8. September 1920: Iṣfahán: Desecration of Bahá'í graves (see pp. 437–9).
9. September 1920: Gaz, near Iṣfahán: Anti-Bahá'í agitation.
10. September 1920: Ábádih: Anti-Bahá'í agitation.
11. October 1920: Farúgh, Fárs: Martyrdom of Mírzá Muṣṭafá.
12. November 1920: Shíráz: Anti-Bahá'í agitation.
13. November 1920: Káshán: Desecration of a Bahá'í grave.
14. January 1921: Miss Stewart, American Bahá'í, stranded at Baghdád and requesting assistance of British authorities to enable her to return to Ṭihrán.
15. January 1921: Kirmánsháh: Martyrdom of Mírzá Ya'qúb-i-Muttaḥidih.
16. February 1921: Káshán: Agitation against Bahá'í school.
17. April 1921: Sulṭánábád: Anti-Bahá'í agitation.
18. June 1921: Shíráz: Attacks on Bahá'ís.
19. July 1921: Sháhrúd: Anti-Bahá'í agitation.
20. July 1921: Káshán: Anti-Bahá'í agitation.
21. July 1921: Sulṭánábád: Attack on Bahá'í shops and on Mírzá Ya'qúb, a Bahá'í of Jewish origin.
22. July 1921: Yazd: Harassment of Bahá'ís of Zoroastrian background by Zoroastrian agent.
23. August 1921: Qum: 'Union of 'Ulamá' agitating against Bahá'ís.
24. August 1921: Iṣfahán: Ḥájí Áqá Munír and other mujtahids agitating against Bahá'ís.
25. September 1921: Káshán: Agitation against Bahá'í school.
26. November 1921: News of passing of 'Abdu'l-Bahá confirmed through High Commissioner in Palestine.
27. November 1921: Yazd: Anti-Bahá'í boycott.[36]

References

1. *Times of India* (Overland Summary) 24 July 1896, p. 6, col. 6
2. Butcher, Consular Diary for period ending 2 July 1896: FO 248 630

3. Kalmykow *Memoirs of a Russian Diplomat* pp. 151–3
4. Treadwell, Yazd News No. 18 for week ending 6 May 1917: FO 248 1189
5. Hutton, Sulṭánábád News-sheet for May 1920: FO 248 1316
6. 'Abdu'l-Bahá to Lord Curzon 29 June 1920, No. 25 in File 'Bahais': FO 248 1279. Original letter of 'Abdu'l-Bahá in File C3491/3491/34: FO 371 4924. Forwarded by R. Storrs to Curzon 21 July 1920, and forwarded by For. Off. to Ṭihrán 20 Aug. 1920
7. Note by Smart 11 Nov. 1920, No. 26 in File 'Bahais': FO 248 1279
8. Hutton to Norman No. T7, 23 Nov. 1920, No. 28 in File 'Bahais': FO 248 1279
9. Note by Haig 29 Nov. 1920, No. 28 in File 'Bahais': FO 248 1279
10. Note by Norman 29 Nov. 1920, No. 28 in File 'Bahais': FO 248 1279
11. Note by Smart 30 Nov. 1920, No. 28 in File 'Bahais': FO 248 1279
12. *The Times* 3 Nov. 1920, p. 11, col. 4
13. Greenhouse, Kirmánsháh Report No. 6, period to 30 June 1920: FO 248 1293
14. Greenhouse to Norman No. 94, 29 Aug. 1920, No. 11 in File 'Bahais': FO 248 1279
15. Note by Smart 18 Sept. 1920, No. 11 in File 'Bahais': FO 248 1279
16. Greenhouse to Norman No. T/21, 24 Jan. 1921, No. 1 in File 428 'Bahais: Murder of Chief Bahai named Muttahida at Kermanshah': FO 248 1352
17. Note by Haig 24 Jan. 1921, No. 1 in file detailed in 16 *supra*
18. Note by Norman 26 Jan. 1921, No. 1 in file detailed in 16 *supra*
19. Norman to Greenhouse No. 25, 4 Feb. 1921, No. 3 in file detailed in 16 *supra*
20. Greenhouse to Norman No. T/32, 14 Feb. 1921, No. 4 in file detailed in 16 *supra*
21. Note by Haig 14 Feb. 1921, No. 4 in file detailed in 16 *supra*
22. Note by Smart 14 Feb. 1921, No. 4 in file detailed in 16 *supra*
23. Norman to Greenhouse No. 37, 17 Feb. 1921, No. 5 in file detailed in 16 *supra*
24. Ghulám-'Alí to Norman 15 Feb. 1921, No. 6 in file detailed in 16 *supra*
25. Note by Norman 20 Feb. 1921, No. 6 in file detailed in 16 *supra*
26. Greenhouse to Norman No. T/39, 22 Feb. 1921, No. 7 in file detailed in 16 *supra*
27. Norman to Greenhouse No. 52, 21 Mar. 1921, No. 8 in file detailed in 16 *supra*
28. Greenhouse to Norman No. T/56, 1 Apr. 1921, No. 9 in file detailed in 16 *supra*
29. Note by Smart no date, No. 9 in file detailed in 16 *supra*
30. Draft telegram drawn up by Smart, No. 9 in file detailed in 16 *supra*
31. Amendment by Norman, telegram to Greenhouse sent 3 Apr. 1921, No. 9 in file detailed in 16 *supra*
32. Greenhouse to Norman No. 136, 5 July 1921, No. 11 in file detailed in 16 *supra*
33. Greenhouse to Norman No. 149, 24 July 1921, No. 12 in file detailed in 16 *supra*
34. Norman to Qavámu's-Salṭanih 30 July 1921, No. 13 in file detailed in 16 *supra*
35. Bridgeman to Qavámu's-Salṭanih 28 Oct. 1921, No. 15 in file detailed in 16 *supra*
36. List compiled from File 'Bahais': FO 248 1279; File 'Bahais': FO 248 1323; File 414 'Bahais: Anti-Bahai Demonstrations threatened at Shahrud, Kashan, Iraq and Yazd': FO 248 1352; File 428 'Bahais: Murder of Chief Bahai named Muttahida at Kermanshah': FO 248 1352. Also Subdivisional Reports FO 248 1316 and FO 248 1338, and South Persia Rifles Diary FO 248 1315 and FO 248 1338

Section E

The Guardianship

(1921–44)

THIRTY-ONE

Accounts of Shoghi Effendi and Events in Palestine

The passing of 'Abdu'l-Bahá marked the beginning of a new era in Bahá'í history. In his Will and Testament, 'Abdu'l-Bahá appointed Shoghi Effendi as the Guardian of the Bahá'í Faith and enjoined all Bahá'ís to turn to him. In character, Shoghi Effendi's ministry was a complete change from that of 'Abdu'l-Bahá. Whereas 'Abdu'l-Bahá had been a public figure, Shoghi Effendi tended to avoid publicity. Consequently, there are very few accounts of Shoghi Effendi by persons who were not Bahá'ís.

In 1925, Lady Dorothy Mills (q.v.) came to Palestine as part of a tour of the Middle East. In her book, *Beyond the Bosphorus*, she describes a meeting with Shoghi Effendi:

> He is a most charming young man, looking about thirty, small, slight featured, Persian in his general appearance, dressed in sober black robes, with composed and courteous manner. He seems to talk every known language, and spoke to me with willing fluency and conviction of the aims of his movement . . .
>
> In the midst of the acrid, all-against-all atmosphere of Palestine, it was a rest to stroll leisurely round the little green garden, while its owner ran on in his smooth cultured voice, and pulled the thorns from a huge bunch of roses that a queer little wizened smiling Jap gardener* gathered for me . . .

Then after recording some of the Bahá'í teachings Lady Mills continues:

> Much of this Shoghi Effendi expounded to me as we strolled round his rose-walled garden, with the picturesque metaphor and simile of his Persian forebears . . .
>
> They are a lovable and fascinating people, the Bahais: idealists who have dreamed a dream of a peace that passes all understanding, who seek to bring relief to restless unhappy human hearts, who, by co-operation, would replace competition, and blend all races, religions, nations and classes into one harmonious whole. A beautiful dream, too good, it is feared, to come true in our present state of imperfection and atavistic crudity, but a dream that it is pleasant to come into contact with, as I did, for a couple of hours, on a blazing April afternoon.[1]

* Saichiro Fujita, became a Bahá'í in 1905, being only the second Japanese to become a Bahá'í. In 1919 he proceeded to Haifa, where he worked for 'Abdu'l-Bahá and later Shoghi Effendi. d. Haifa May 1976.

In 1938, Rom Landau (q.v.) visited the Near East and met Shoghi Effendi. He writes:

> Even before I left England I made arrangements to go to Haifa to visit Shoghi Effendi, the head of the Baha'i creed. It is one of the most important and most cosmopolitan of the various revivals which have emerged within the last hundred years from the womb of Islam. It is the least orthodox and most independent of them all.
>
> . . . I was anxious to ascertain Shoghi Effendi's views on several subjects and to meet the guardian of a faith which, in its Christian tolerance and its supernational and super-denominational appeal, contains some very attractive features.
>
> Rarely has my imagination deceived me more blatantly than it did in the case of Shoghi Effendi. I imagined him a rather impressive-looking man, attractive by reason of some quality of gentleness or of a mixture of humanity and force. I expected dignity and should not have been surprised if I had met with unctuousness.
>
> When Shoghi Effendi entered the room with a buoyant step I could hardly believe that the dapper little man, so sprightly and neat in his European clothes with a black tarboosh, was connected with a movement of the spiritual significance of the Baha'is. He greeted me with a very charming smile, repeating several times: 'You are welcome, you are welcome, I am so glad you came.' His eyes and mouth did not cease smiling. . .
>
> His answers were as brisk and self-assured as his gestures and smiles. He spoke quickly, not nervously, but with a youthful alacrity, as if apprehensive lest the time at his disposal might not be fully utilised for the spreading of Baha'i doctrine. His English was excellent – he had been up at Oxford – and only rarely did too florid a turn of phrase betray him.
>
> When I asked Shoghi Effendi about the future there was no hesitation about his answer. 'There is a wonderfully bright future in store for humanity'—his words overflowed in a torrent – 'but before it can come about terrible suffering will be inflicted by a world war. It will be far worse than the last war. Only through war and suffering can humanity learn the bitter lessons without which the new revival is impossible.'. . .
>
> When I asked Shoghi Effendi whom he considered to be of spiritual significance in the Near East, he replied: 'Such men do not exist. Most of the Near East and particularly Palestine are given up completely to politics. Islam, which in earlier days had the power to spiritualise its followers, is crumbling just as much as institutional Christianity. Do not expect to find here meditation or other forms of spiritual activity. Even Near-Eastern Nationalism usually has to serve as cloak for the personal ambitions of those who call themselves patriots.'. . .
>
> At the end of our conversation he presented me with several Baha'i books, and, thus encouraged, I asked him whether I might take his photograph. 'No,' he said, 'all the Baha'is would like my photograph, but I don't believe in the worship of personalities. It can easily overshadow the essential adherence to a principle.' His refusal was the most personal and attractive statement of the afternoon, and I was glad that he would not let me photograph him.[2]

The Keys of the Shrine of Bahá'u'lláh

Much of the material relating to the Bahá'í community in Haifa during Shoghi Effendi's ministry which exists in the Public Record Office in London and in the Israeli State Archives in Jerusalem is concerned with the various attempts of persons inimical to Shoghi Effendi to obstruct his activities and damage his reputation. One of the first of these was the seizure of the keys of the Shrine of Bahá'u'lláh by the half-brothers of 'Abdu'l-Bahá, Mírzá Muḥammad-'Alí and Mírzá Badí'u'lláh. These persons claimed that, according to Islamic law, with the passing of 'Abdu'l-Bahá custodianship of the Shrine should pass to them as the nearest surviving relatives of Bahá'u'lláh. Following up this claim they forcibly seized the keys of the Shrine on 30 January 1922. In the ensuing commotion, the British Mandatory Authorities were forced to move in, and the Governor of 'Akká ordered the keys to be handed over to him. The matter went before the High Commissioner in Jerusalem. Sir Wyndham Deedes (q.v.), the acting High Commissioner, reported thus to the Colonial Secretary, Winston Churchill, on 13 June 1922:

I have the honour to inform you that after the death of the late Sir Abbas Effendi Bahai a question arose amongst the Bahai community as to the custody of the Shrine of Baha'ullah at Acre.

The claimants to the right of custody are: Mohamed Ali, the brother of Sir Abbas, Shoghi Effendi, the grandson of Sir Abbas, and Hussein Afnan, the son of the youngest daughter of Baha Ullah.

Numerous telegrams and letters have been received from the various Bahai communities of the world, the majority in support of the claim of Shoghi Effendi.

In view of the widespread interest caused by this controversy the Palestine Administration considered it advisable to make their attitude known and the attached statement was sent to the press for publication. As communities of Bahais exist in various parts of the British Empire and of America you may consider it desirable to communicate the contents of this statement to all the British authorities and representatives especially to those in the United States.[3]

The statement enclosd with this dispatch was published in the official gazette the *Palestine Weekly* on 23 June 1922:

BAHAI SHRINE AT ACRE (PALESTINE).

After the death of Sir Abbas Effendi Abdel Baha, a claim was made by his eldest brother to be given custody of the Shrine of Baha 'Ullah at Acre. This claim was keenly opposed by members of the Bahai Community as being contrary to the testamentary dispositions of the late Sir Abbas Effendi and to the latter's interpretation of the will of Baha 'Ullah.

The Palestine Administration feel that such matters should be decided by the Bahai Communities or their accredited representatives. They understand that in the will of the late Sir Abbas Effendi provision is made for the convocation by his grandson, Shoghi Effendi, of representative Bahais from the various countries of the world. They hope that this assembly will express an authoritative opinion on all points of disagreement, including the question of the custody of the Shrine at Acre.

As a temporary measure, and in order to prevent the possibility of discord at the Shrine, the key of the latter has been put in charge of the Sub-Governor of Acre who holds it at the disposal of Bahais and other pilgrims and visitors.[4]

Eventually, in February of the following year, as a result of unceasing effort on the part of Shoghi Effendi, the keys were returned to him.

Accusations against the Bahá'ís

On 17 January 1928, the following telegram was sent by the Foreign Office to Sir Robert Clive (q.v.), the British Ambassador in Ṭihrán:

'Most secret.

'An absolutely reliable informant assures me that the Shah has been informed that through our help some Persian Bahais have been put in touch with Salar-ed-Dowleh and that he has been helped financially by us.

'There is not a vestige of truth in these allegations which may do us harm by poisoning the Shah's mind against us and by prompting further outrages against the Bahais in Persia.

'The source of this information is so confidential that there must be no risk whatever of it being compromised, but I think it well to telegraph it to you for your secret information.'[5]

Saláru'd-Dawlih was a younger brother of Muḥammad-'Alí Sháh, who had been deposed by the Revolution of 1909. He was a troublesome figure who in 1907 had made a bid for the throne against his brother, and then in 1911, after his brother's deposition, he appeared in the west of Persia with troops to assist his brother in his futile attempt to regain the throne. In 1924, Saláru'd-Dawlih had supported Shaykh Khaz'al, the semi-independent Shaykh of Muḥammarih, in his attempt to defy Riḍá Khán. Thus it was not surprising that Saláru'd-Dawlih was looked upon with the greatest distrust by the Persian Government. In response to the above telegram, Sir Robert Clive wrote from Tihrán:

I really don't know what to make of this report. The Persian engagement to pay Salar-ed-Dowleh ended in November. As I have reported the Persian Government have, without engaging to go on paying him for any fixed period, stumped up for December and I am expecting any day to receive the cheque for January. Teymour* explained to me that this money had for the present to come out of the Shah's privy purse. Of course His Majesty hates parting, so possibly his idiotic suspicions have been more easily aroused owing to his own pocket being affected.

As regards the Bahais, there have been no outrages for a long time. Six months ago one was murdered in Kerman, but the murderer was caught and now reposes in Tehran jail. About nine months ago a Bahai got killed in a brawl at Ardebil. Beyond these two isolated cases which can not possibly be said to constitute persecution, we know of no recent Bahai troubles. Of course there are a lot of them living in Palestine at Haifa and elsewhere. In fact I gather Palestine is nowadays the main centre of their activities. I suppose some of them have been visiting Salar and the Shah has heard about it.

As you may know, two of our three Munshis are Bahais, but I have never heard that that is cause of suspicion against us.[6]

Eventually, the puzzle was resolved. The British High Commissioner in

* Mírzá 'Abdu'l-Ḥusayn Khán, Taymúrtásh, the all-powerful Minister of Court for the first six years of Riḍá Sháh's rule. He was dismissed in December 1932 and died shortly afterwards.

Palestine, Lord Plumer (q.v.), made enquiries and wrote from Jerusalem:

I reply to your letter of the 17th ultimo referring to stories about the Bahai Community at Haifa which were related to the Persian Minister at Cairo by one 'Mirza Jamil'. The man in question is almost certainly a certain Jamil Irani, a Persian, formerly adherent to the Bahai sect and now turned Moslem and anti-Bahai. He is an excellent Railway Inspector, a clever man educated in America but nourishes a grievance against the Bahai sect to which his own father left all his money on his death. That Prince Salar-ed-Dowleh has conducted intrigue in Persia with or through the Bahai Community at Haifa is most improbable and Jamil Irani's allegations to the contrary are, I suspect, trumped up to do the Bahais an injury. I should mention that when the question of Salar-ed-Dowleh settling at Haifa was first mooted the Bahais there formally protested on the grounds that his presence at Haifa would expose Bahai adherents in Persia to malicious persecution. If, as I presume, a report on this matter has gone to our Minister at Teheran it would be as well categorically to deny the truth of these allegations. I have told the District Commissioner at Haifa to keep an eye on Jamil Irani and, if possible, to prevent him from pursuing his grievance against the Bahais by the spread of untrue stories of their political actions.[7]

This Jamíl Írání was the grandson of one of the companions of Bahá'u'lláh, who was now in league with the enemies of Shoghi Effendi; the above reports indicate the lengths to which these persons were prepared to go.

The Status of the Bahá'í Community in Palestine

When the British Mandate in Palestine had been set up, one of the earliest measures enacted was an Order-in-Council that allowed each of the recognized religious communities in the country to be administered in all affairs of personal status according to their own religious laws and courts. The Bahá'í community had not, however, been accorded this 'recognized' status and was thus compelled to submit to the Muslim courts.

In 1929, on Shoghi Effendi's instructions, Mountfort Mills, a prominent American Bahá'í lawyer, raised the matter with Mr Luke (q.v.), Chief Secretary at Jerusalem. Later that year, when in London Mills raised the matter with Mr Shuckburgh (q.v.) at the Colonial Office. Shuckburgh made enquiries and from Jerusalem, Luke replied:

'Proposals, in point of fact, are under consideration for providing a civil law of personal status to be administered by the civil Courts, parallel with the system of administration of religious law by religious Courts. The High Commissioner is to consider these points . . . on his return from England.'[8]

As a result of these representations, the Bahá'í community was eventually accorded the right to administer its affairs in matters relating to personal status, according to its own laws.[9]

Various Court Cases

In the files of the British Mandate Authorities now preserved in the

Israeli State Archives, there are details of several court actions relating to plots of land around the Bahá'í Holy Places in the Haifa–'Akká area. These may be summarized thus:

1. Case of 'Azíz Sulaymán Dumit (Domet) v. the Head of the Bahá'í Religious Community, 1933. This case concerned a plot of land on the terracing leading up to the Shrine of the Báb on Mount Carmel and came before the Haifa District Court. But Shoghi Effendi then claimed that since the case involved a Holy Place, it was outside the jurisdiction of that Court under the Palestine (Holy Places) Order-in-Council, 1924. The Court upheld this plea and the case was referred to the High Commissioner for a decision. The file contains letters from the Bahá'í National Spiritual Assemblies of Persia, Germany, India and Burma, France, and the British Isles in support of Shoghi Effendi's claim that this was indeed a Holy Place.[10] (This case was finally abandoned by the Dumit family in 1935.)[11]
2. Mu'ayyid-ibn-Akbar Yazdí v. Shoghi Effendi (1934). A similar case to the above but concerning property surrounding the Shrine of Bahá'u'lláh at Bahjí.[12]
3. Objections raised by various parties against the plans of the Haifa Town Planning Commission for an access road to the Shrine of the Báb on Mount Carmel (1935). This file also contains a letter from Amín Faríd and his sister objecting to their land being included with the Bahá'í lands since '*we are not* included in this organisation nor are we members thereof.'[13]

Removal of Remains of Mírzá Mihdí and Ásíyih Khánum

The remains of Mírzá Mihdí, brother of 'Abdu'l-Bahá, and Ásíyih Khánum, mother of 'Abdu'l-Bahá, had been buried in Muslim cemeteries in 'Akká. In 1939, Shoghi Effendi decided to remove their remains to a more fitting site on Mount Carmel. The following is an extract from the Haifa District Commissioner's fortnightly report for the period ending 15 December 1939:

> An application was made at the beginning of the month by the representatives of the Bahai community to remove the remains of Mirza Mihdi and of his mother, Assiyeh, from the cemetery at Acre, where they were interred, to the Bahai Garden at Haifa. The removal was opposed by a dissenting faction led by Badia'u'llah. The original request had been made over a year ago and authority given by the Health Department but exhumation had not, for some reason, been carried out. The dissenting faction claimed that, as he stood nearer than Shoghi Effendi in relationship to Mirza Mihdi, whose exhumation it was proposed, he, not Shoghi Effendi, was entitled under Moslem law to

decide as to the disposal of the remains. Badia'u'llah and his faction, it may be explained, have identified themselves with the Moslem religion.

As I was satisfied that the request was made by the recognised heads of the Bahai community and had the approval of the greater part of the community, I authorised the reinterment to take place, and informed Badia'u'llah that I could only recognise a request from the recognised head of the community and that he must obtain satisfaction of any legal rights he claimed in the Courts. The reinterment was carried out without incident and, so far as I am aware, no court proceedings have yet been taken.[14]

References

1. Mills *Beyond the Bosphorus* pp. 98–100
2. Landau *Search for Tomorrow* pp. 211–16
3. Deedes to Churchill No. 425, 13 June 1922: High Commissioner's Dispatches, Israeli State Archives
4. Enclosed in 3 *supra* and also published in *Palestine Weekly* 23 June 1922, p. 428
5. Lancelot Oliphant to Clive No. 12, 17 Jan. 1928, File E313/313/34: FO 371 13061
6. Clive to Oliphant 28 Jan. 1928 in File E750/313/34: FO 371 13061
7. Lord Plumer to Shuckburgh (Colonial Off.) No. 2533/28, 20 Feb. 1928; forwarded by Shuckburgh to Oliphant at For. Off. in No. 57096/1928, File E750/313/34: FO 371 13061
8. Luke to Shuckburgh No. 4719/29, 1 Aug. 1929, File 67347: CO 733 173
9. See Rabbani *The Priceless Pearl* p. 284
10. File B 52/33: Chief Sec.'s Off., Israeli State Archives
11. See Rabbani *The Priceless Pearl* pp. 284–5
12. File A.G. 26/8: Attorney Gen., Israeli State Archives
13. File 214/135: District Commissioner's Off., Haifa, Israeli State Archives
14. File B 34/39: Chief Sec.'s Off., Israeli State Archives

THIRTY-TWO

Events in Iran, Turkey, and Russia

As has been mentioned in the Introduction, after the *coup d'état* in 1921 and more particularly after Riḍá S͟háh's coronation in 1925, S͟hí'ih clerical influence in Iran declined, and with this decline the nature of the Bahá'í persecutions changed. It may be said that one of the last of the persecutions in the period under review, that occurred in the former violent manner, took place in Jahrum in 1926 (see ensuing pages), while from about this time onwards the moves against the Bahá'ís assumed a more subtle, pseudo-legal nature.

The Murder of Vice-Consul Imbrie, 1924

During the course of 'Abdu'l-Bahá's ministry, very close links were built up between the growing American Bahá'í community and their co-religionists in Iran. These links were strengthened by the dispatch of a number of Iranian Bahá'ís to study in America, and even more significantly by the arrival in Iran of a number of skilled Americans who assisted the Bahá'ís in the setting up of schools and hospitals. The expertise of the Americans helped to make these institutions among the finest in Iran, a source of great envy to the Muslims. Matters reached such a state that any American in Iran was automatically assumed by the populace to be a Bahá'í.*

During the first half of 1924, anti-Bahá'í agitation was increasing and the Government was slack in holding it in check. Matters were greatly worsened by reports of the occurrence of certain miracles, which stirred up the fanaticism of the populace. When the inevitable outburst occurred, the unfortunate victim of the fanaticism of the mob was a certain Major Robert Imbrie (q.v.). He was not a Bahá'í, but so closely were Americans identified with the Bahá'ís in the eyes of many Iranians that when, on 18 July 1924, Imbrie arrived at a wayside fountain near Ṭihrán, the site of a supposed miracle, the mob fell upon him as a Bahá'í and would not leave until they

* For example, Morgan Shuster, the American financier who was employed by the Iranian Government to sort out Iran's financial predicament, wrote in his book *The Strangling of Persia* (p. 61): 'It was not until several weeks afterwards that the rumour began to reach me that the Americans were believed to be *Bahais*, and that we had come to Teheran, not to reform but to proselytise.'

had encompassed his death. To make matters worse, Imbrie was the newly-appointed American Vice-Consul for Ṭihrán, and the anger of the American Government and indeed the American people was great.

The *New York Times* printed a report of the murder on its front page, and a few days later, on 20 July 1924, also on the front page, the following extract, released by the State Department from the report of Joseph S. Kornfeld, US Ambassador in Ṭihrán, was published:

A telegram from the American Minister at Teheran, Joseph S. Kornfeld, dated evening, July 18, states that Vice-Consul Imbrie succumbed at 3 o'clock in the afternoon to the shock following an assault by a mob which practically cut him and beat him to death.

The Minister reports that for some days through the city there had been denouncements of Bahaists, a religious sect, and many religious demonstrations. It appears that at 11 A.M. the Vice-Consul accompanied by Seymour, a prisoner in the Consulate,* stopped their carriage in front of one of these demonstrations and it was alleged that the Vice-Consul had taken pictures. The mob rushed upon him, crying that he was a Bahaist and though the servant of an American Missionary cried out he was the American Consul, the mob took no heed of the statement, dragged the Americans from their carriage and attacked them savagely.[1]

Sir Percy Loraine (q.v.), the British Minister, in his Annual Report for the year 1924 gives an account of this episode:

For some months after Serdar Sepah† resumed the direction of affairs in April, his general hold on the internal situation seemed less sure, and he was less decisive in his conduct of affairs. Some of his enemies dared to attack him openly, and his acts were severely and intemperately attacked in the Opposition press. The editor of one of these papers was murdered by some unknown persons in June, and this caused a considerable stir. The excitement continued unabated, but a so-called miracle enabled it to be turned into a religious channel. A Bahai was said to have been struck blind for having openly expressed his religious belief, and again a Moslem was said to have recovered his sight by the aid of the water of a wayside fountain. Nobody had ever seen the individuals concerned in either case, but the news of the miracle spread like wildfire, and the fountain acquired great fame and was daily visited by hundreds of people having different ailments and hoping for a cure. Agitation against the Bahais grew apace, and many Persians who were known or thought to be Bahais received rough treatment and were even beaten, whilst some Bahai shopkeepers had their shops looted. American missionaries who followed the Bahai cult were likewise threatened, and the Government were obliged to take steps for their protection. Meanwhile, the fountain continued to be the scene of daily pilgrimages by dense crowds of people. On the 18th July the American vice-consul, Major Imbrie, accompanied by another American, drove up to the neighbourhood of the fountain in order to photograph the scene. The crowd objected and hustled them and generally became so threatening that the Americans hurried back to their cab and started to drive away. A section of the crowd shouted out that they were Bahais, and the crowd then chased the cab, spreading the cry that they were Bahais who had poisoned the water in the fountain. The excitement grew apace, and as the cab drove away with the crowd surging after it, others took up the

* In custody following a brawl in south Persia.

† Riḍá Khán, became in the following year Riḍá Sháh.

cry and the cab was stopped, the occupants being dragged out and beaten senseless. They were finally rescued by a number of police, who conveyed them to the police hospital near by that they might have their injuries attended to. Whilst they were still receiving attention in the hospital, the crowd broke in and murdered Major Imbrie whilst he was lying on the operating table, his companion only escaping because he was covered with a shroud and the crowd thought he was already dead.

As the outcome of vigorous steps taken by the American Legation and the Diplomatic Corps, military law was at once put into force in the capital and many provincial centres. The American Government addressed a strong note to the Persian Government formulating certain demands, upon the satisfactory execution of which future relations between the two countries would depend.[2]

Describing relations between Iran and the USA in the same report, Loraine stated:

During the first half of the year American relations with Persia were much the same as in 1923. In July, however, a dark cloud fell over them owing to the assassination of Major Robert W. Imbrie, the recently appointed United States consul in Tehran by a fanatical crowd in the streets of Tehran. This deplorable incident was due to religious excitement, following on anti-Bahai demonstrations and a supposed anti-Bahai miracle; it aroused the greatest indignation, and caused great consternation to the Persian Government. The most lamentable fact that emerged was that the police on duty at the spot and some soldiers who happened to be there took no steps, or, at all events, none which could have the slightest effect, to stop this barbarous assault on the United States consul and his American companion. It even appeared almost certain that some uniformed Persians took part in the assault; it is certain that even after the two wounded and exhausted Americans had been removed to the police hospital, the crowd pursued them and, quite unchecked, renewed the battering of these unfortunate American citizens in the operating room, to which they had been brought with great difficulty. The only pretext for the onslaught was that Major Imbrie was attempting to take photographs of the fountain at which the alleged miracle had taken place.

The whole Diplomatic Body joined in a vigorous representation to the Persian Government, and drew attention to the danger to which all foreigners were exposed . . .

The United States Government demanded the arrest, trial and punishment of the culprits; the expenses of transporting the body of Major Imbrie from a Persian port, to which it was to be accompanied by a Persian military guard of honour, to the United States of America on board an American man-of-war; and suitable compensation for Major Imbrie's widow; it added that continuance of American diplomatic and consular representation would depend on the manner in which the Persian Government observed its treaty obligations and fulfilled its duty to guarantee the lives and safety of American officials and nationals. These demands were substantially accepted by the Persian Government, who expressed profound regret at the incident, and gave full assurances of their determination to protect American citizens.

Arrests were made of persons shown to have participated in the crime, trial took place by court-martial, and three of the ringleaders were sentenced to death. One of these was a soldier, and efforts of various kinds were made to whitewash the Persian army of participation in the brutal assault. The United States Chargé d'Affaires, Mr Murray, had the greatest difficulty in securing the execution of these sentences, the theory being put forward that it was contrary to Moslem law that three lives should be taken for one. The United States Government threatened a curtailment of their diplomatic relations with Persia failing the execution of the sentences, and the Persian Government capitulated to this threat. The two remaining criminals were shot on the 2nd November. The indemnity of 110,000 dollars was duly paid by the Persian Government out of Treasury funds and without reference to the Majlis.[3]

The Jahrum Martyrdoms, 1926

In April 1926 a particularly savage attack was made on the Bahá'ís of Jahrum, with the result that many of them were beaten severely and eight died. The instigator of this atrocity was Ismá'íl Khán, Sawlatu'd-Dawlih, a chief of the Qashqá'í tribe, who was seeking to gain political popularity and prevent his defeat in elections for the Majlis, where he was the Deputy for Jahrum. Also implicated, according to the reports of the British Consul in Shíráz, Herbert Chick (q.v.), was the Russian Consul-General, Walden.

On 12 April 1926, Chick reported to Loraine:

I have the honour to report that a sanguinary affair occurred in the town of Jahrum on the 7th instant.

The fanatical Mujtahid Sayyid Abdul Husain Lari, who, it will be remembered, in the year 1909, posed as a 'Constitutionalist' and anti-Kawami leader (acting with Soulet-ed-Dowleh), raised the standard of revolt in Eastern Fars and went so far as to issue his own postage stamps in Lar, where he had put to death in cold blood seventy-two members of the Girashi family, and shed much Bahai blood in Niriz and other places, died at the end of 1923 in Jahrum, whither he retired from Firuzabad after the defeat of Soulet-ed-Dowleh in 1918, and where he lived quietly though . . . he was still regarded with apprehension by the Bahais. His mantle, as a leader of prayers, fell on a son.

It seems that for several days previous to the 7th instant, this son,* who has apparently inherited his father's fanaticism, and certain other sayyids of the Soulet connection had hurled abuse and invective from the pulpits against the Bahais. To what extent, if any, the Bahais riposted or remonstrated my informants were silent. But this obviously inspired campaign culminated on the 7th in thirteen adult Bahais and one babe of fifteen months being bludgeoned and stabbed and hacked to death in their houses and the streets; a number of others were missing – in hiding it was hoped – according to the account given me by the president of the Bahai Spiritual Assembly in Shiraz, who had had letters from Jahrum, where his co-religionists are numerous. (Amir Lashkar gave the figures to me as eight killed, twelve wounded, missing all found.) There were only fifteen soldiers, under a lieutenant, as garrison, and though it is said that the latter remonstrated with the clericals for provoking a quarrel before the massacre occurred, it is alleged that the soldiers took no steps to stop the bloodshed. The Governor, Khan Baba Khan Kawami, a first cousin of the wife of Mirza Ibrahim Khan Kawam, had to send some 16 miles to Kutbabad for 'tufangchis' for his own protection.

On the news of this shocking savagery reaching him, the Amir Lashkar of the south sent off some thirty-five soldiers, under Lieutenant Saifullah Khan (himself a Bahai), in motor vehicles on the 9th April; the track made during the winter by local

* named Siyyid 'Alíy-i-Píshnamáz

effort to permit of motor communication between Jahrum and Shiraz made this rapid movement possible, and has thus come in useful in this emergency.

As you are aware, Ismail Khan Kashkai (Soulet-ed-Dowleh formerly) was the Deputy for Jahrum in the fifth Majlis. I have deliberately refrained from enquiring from anyone what persons are candidates for constituencies in Fars; but from a chance remark in conversation by Amir Lashkar some three weeks ago, I gathered that Ismail Khan's re-election would be thwarted. However, it is now stated that he had been spending money freely in Jahrum in order to retain the seat, and had sent two of his henchmen there to work on the excitable elements . . .

On the evening of the 10th instant, Ismail Khan Kashkai was arrested by the military provost-marshal, and has since been confined in the barracks. It is held that he is responsible for the outrage at Jahrum. Amir Lashkar declared that his arrest increased the chagrin of M. Walden at the failure of his plans for disturbances, for Ismail Khan had been in frequent communication with the Soviet consulate during the past month or so in connection with his election campaign.[4]

In this dispatch, Chick also dealt with various other intrigues of Sawlatu'd-Dawlih and Walden, and concluded it in the following terms:

The above report may appear disjointed and to deal with several distinct matters, but really the intrigues of the Soviet consul-general with the malcontents of the elections and the intrigues of Ismail Khan Kashkai in the same direction and the massacre of Bahais at Jahrum are connected.

Owing to the drain on Fars for the Luristan operations there are few troops left in Shiraz, and with the presence of Amir Lashkar and Kawam being required at the coronation, the situation is possibly somewhat disturbing for the Bahais. The Amir Lashkar stated that the situation in Jahrum was well in hand, and an enquiry would have to be held. Though the Governor-General went so far as to affirm that M. Walden would like to start a similar anti-Bahai demonstration in Shiraz, this is an improbable development. Certainly, unless the military command in Fars make a ruthless example of the ringleaders, whether clericals or not, by summary execution, there will be a serious check to the security of the province in public opinion. Ismail Khan Kashkai appears to have acted with incredible folly after the warnings he received at Tehran. As to M. Walden, he is a thorn in the side of the Fars authorities and, by a policy of pin-pricks, quarrels and intrigues, seemingly wishes to convey to the public that Soviet Russia has strong influence in this province. The worst of it is that the authorities seem to be afraid of tackling him, and it will be interesting to see whether, as the result of his complaints to Tehran, some official is made a scapegoat.[5]

In transmitting Chick's report to the British Foreign Secretary, Sir Austen Chamberlain (q.v.), Loraine added his own comments:

. . . I have the honour to transmit to you herewith copy of Shiraz consulate despatch No. 21 of the 12th April, which proves rather conclusively how little worthy of faith were the promises of dutiful obedience and service to the Shah and the Persian Government which Soulet-ed-Dowleh expressed to me last December.

Although Soulet himself was sufficiently wary and clever to keep in the background, the troubles which Mr Chick narrates were undoubtedly due to the acts of men serving his cause and paid by him for that purpose. Amin-es-Sherieh, a Deputy from Fars in the last Majlis, who was in Shiraz at the time that the massacres occurred in Jahrum, has related the whole affair to the oriental secretary, and his account tallies in every way with Mr Chick's report, not only as regards the regrettable massacres at Jahrum, but also as regards Soulet's more or less intimate relations with the Soviet consul in Shiraz.

Soulet has violated his word to me, and I intend to have no further friendly intercourse with him, should he at any future date come to Tehran as a free man. He has had his chance and failed miserably, and at my next meeting with Sheikh Khazal I shall recommend him to have as little to do with Soulet hereafter as possible.

I am informed that Soulet's son in Tehran has petitioned the Shah for permission for his father to be allowed to go abroad, but I am unaware of the answer or how the Persian Government intend to deal with Soulet in the future.

I trust that the action which I propose to take, as recorded above, meets with your approval.[6]

On the arrival of this dispatch in London, Lancelot Oliphant (q.v.) added the following comments:

Solet ed Dawleh has for the last 17 years run crooked to my personal knowledge, and it was only because of Sir P. Loraine's immense success with the Bakhtiari tribal troubles that I was hopeful that his meeting with Solet ed Dawleh might have a lasting effect.

We need never again entertain any false hopes about this ruffian . . .

Mr Chick's despatch is in truth rather disjointed and hard to follow . . .[7]

Sir Austen Chamberlain wrote to Loraine on 9 June, approving of his proposal to have no further friendly intercourse with Sawlatu'd-Dawlih.[8]

The matter did not rest there, however. Mountfort Mills, a prominent American Bahá'í lawyer, asked Sir John Shuckburgh (q.v.) for an introduction to the Foreign Office in order that he could discuss the situation in Iran. Shuckburgh wrote, on 14 June, a private note to Sir Lancelot Oliphant introducing Mills. The latter, on 28 June, wrote to Oliphant asking for an appointment. From this letter it appears that Mills, who was then in Paris, had succeeded in obtaining the co-operation and assistance of the French Foreign Minister, M. Briand (q.v.), and the American Ambassador in Paris, Myron T. Herrick (q.v.), both of whom had telegraphed to Ṭihrán and had done what they could.[9] Enclosed in Mills's letter to Oliphant was an account of the martyrdoms in Jahrum from Fu'ád Rawḥání, a Bahá'í of Ṭihrán:

Once more we have to relate to you the horrible persecutions inflicted upon a number of our dear co-workers in Jahrom, a southern city of Persia, by a mob of fanatic Mussulmans. To describe this recent event in all its ferocity and violence would be but a futile attempt, and therefore we shall only quote here a brief summary of the report we have received from the Spiritual Assembly of Jahrom concerning the matter. Before we begin the narrative, however, we wish to say that it is by no means our intention to repine of, or wail over our conditions; no, our purpose is, as usual, to let our brothers and sisters in other parts of the world know just what is going on here in Persia. Now, to commence the sorrowful story:–

Last month some Mussulmans in Shiraz

laid a plot against the Bahais of Jahrom for the achievement of certain evil objects of their own, and enticed a Seyed Mohammad to proceed to Jahrom and execute the malicious plan. Upon his arrival in Jahrom, this man employed three others to carry out his intentions, and by their assistance began to instigate the local fanatic Mussulmans to rise against the Bahais. The intrigues of the four accomplices took effect in a short time, scurrilous language was used against the Cause everywhere and even from the pulpit, and after a few days two Bahais were pursued and beaten badly. The Bahais complained to the local authorities, but unfortunately the scheme against the Bahais was too deep-laid to be thwarted by the interference of the Government officials. A number of soldiers were told off to arrest the persecutors, who fled away, at the same time enticing the women and children to abuse the soldiers, pelt stones at them, and shout for help. As soon as, therefore, the women shouted out, the belligerent assailants, headed by the accomplices already mentioned, broke ambush, and blatantly rushed into the market-place and shut up the shops. Then they attacked the house of Seyed Hossein Rouhani, and as he was [away] from home they set fire to his house and plundered his property. Returning from this scene of devastation they found the object of their search, whom they immediately seized. Dragging him along the streets of the town they beat him with stick, club, dagger, knife and sword; and more dead than alive they pulled him on to the house of Agha Mohammad Hassan, a Bahai whom they treated with the same cruelty. From there, dragging the two victims, the assailants made for the house of Mohammad Reza, another Bahai whom they captured in the same manner. At the same time a mob rushed into the house of Seyed Abbas, seized him, pillaged his house, broke the doors, and beat his three children so much that they fainted away. Then they took hold of Seyed Abbas and one of his sons, named Ziaullah, and carried them to where the three other victims lay. Beating the five victims with sticks, stones, etc. the assailants made for the house of Abdul Rahim, one of the ring-leaders, who issued the final order for killing off the captives. The mob gathered around the victims and beat them so much that their bones were crushed. Only Ziaullah, horribly lacerated but not quite dead, was rescued by a stranger from the hands of the relentless persecutors, while the remains of Mohammad Hassan were burnt before the public. The mob then spread throughout the city, and wherever a Bahai was found he would be beaten almost to death, if not actually killed. Some of the assailants rushed into the house of Ostad Hassan, captured him, and beat him so much that he fell unconscious. Thinking that he was dead, they left him in the street and proceeded in search of the other friends; and as he lay there half dead a Karbelai Mohammad came up and probably hoping to enter the Kingdom of God as a reward for this act, dealt a deadly blow with a huge log upon the head of the insentient victim. Two of the sons of this martyr were seized and beaten badly, and the eldest, who was going to complain to the Governor, was attacked and captured, and would have shared his father's tragic fate had not some one interfered and released him. Three other Bahais were taken into a mosque to be put to death, but were rescued by some compassionate intercessors. The mob attacked the house of Mohammad Kazem and seized him as well as Shokrollah, his son-in-law. The former was beaten to death, but the latter was released. Agha Mohammad Shafi was then seized and though he was once released by a soldier, the persecutors pursued him again and eventually killed him. The next martyr was a Meshedi Abbas, who was killed with a blow of an axe, and whose mother was beaten dangerously. The mob attacked several other houses with unabated fury; 20 houses of the Bahais were plundered and set fire to, and the remains of the martyrs were thrown into a ditch and covered with stones. It is quite impossible to describe the extent of the cruelty of the persecutors; for instance, the father of Mohammad Reza, one of the martyrs, was made to tie a rope to his son's feet and drag him on to the place of his martyrdom. Thus, on the 7th day of April 1926 the below-named Bahais were martyred in the city of Jahrom.

1. SEYED HOSSAIN ROUHANI
2. OSTAD ABBAS
3. MOHAMMAD KAZEM
4. MOHAMMAD HASSAN
5. MOHAMMAD SHAFI
6. MESHEDI ABBAS
7. OSTAD MOHAMMAD HASSAN
8. MOHAMMAD REZA

Besides, a number of other Bahais are badly wounded, and some have lost all they had, and are actually homeless. This sad incident reminds us of the words of Abdul-Baha written on the occasion of the martyrdom of a number of Bahais in Isfahan and Yazd. He said: '. . . The recent events of Isfahan and Yazd are very deplorable. Although experience has proved that the Bahais are unexcelled in courage and bravery, and each of them can vanquish many in battle-field, as they are the bearers of the Message of Universal Peace they do not resist their oppressors, nay rather they crave God's forgiveness for them . . .' The Central Spiritual Assembly has got in touch with the competent authorities to obtain redress, and is still prosecuting the demand. It is hoped that the Government will judge the matter equitably and will punish the oppressors, and restore the plundered property to their owners.[10]

Oliphant met Mills on 30 June, and according to a memorandum penned by the former, 'brief extracts' from Chick's report were read to Mills. He was told, however, that 'official representations from London were out of the question.'[11]

On 11 October, Shuckburgh wrote again to Oliphant to say that he had just seen Mills who was very worried about the situation in Iran, particularly as it appeared that the murderers had now been released. Oliphant therefore wrote to the British Chargé d'Affaires in Ṭihrán, Harold Nicolson (q.v.), asking him to make enquiries.[12]

In the meantime, an appeal had reached Nicolson in Ṭihrán from the Bahá'í Assembly of Auckland in New Zealand, containing an account of the persecutions in Jahrum and Marághih (see next section) and asking him to use his influence to alleviate the position of Bahá'ís in Iran.[13] A little while later, in November 1926, the British Foreign Office received the text of an appeal made by the National Spiritual Assembly of the United States and Canada to the Sháh, asking him for justice and protection for the Bahá'í community of Iran.[14]

In his dispatch of 6 October, Nicolson, while relating the Bahá'í persecutions in Marághih, had nothing further to say about the Jahrum episode. However, on 4 November he was able to report the disquieting news that the persecutors of the Bahá'ís were being set free:

In reply to your letter ... of the 13th October asking for news about the release of the ringleaders of the mob who maltreated the Bahais at Jahrum last spring, the information which I have been able to gather is as follows:

Chick reports in his June diary that 'According to the President of the Bahai community, His Majesty the Shah has had sent to all postal and telegraph offices orders not to accept petitions or complaints from Bahais. No one has been suitably punished for the massacre of Bahais at Jahrum on April 7th: the Seyyids arrested have been released'.

From other sources I have received the story that at the beginning of the affair (April 7th–10th) the General Officer Commanding, named Mahmoud Khan, started to pursue the matter energetically and had all the Seyyids suspected of responsibility in the massacre brought to Shiraz for examination. At about this time also, Ismail Khan Qashqai, formerly Saulat-ud-Douleh, was arrested on the grounds of having incited the outbreak in order to gain popularity with certain religious circles in order to secure his re-election from Jahrum.

On the feast of Ghadir, however, (June 29th last), His Imperial Majesty the Shah, at the personal intercession of the present Prime Minister, released Saulat: and quite possibly the lack of energy in trying the arrested Seyyids may have had something to do with this.

The Bahais of Tehran say that after this another attempt to massacre Bahais was made at Niriz: an attempt which was unsuccessful owing to measures of defence taken by the Bahais of Niriz themselves: but I cannot trace having received news of this from Chick.

I give the above with all reserve but it certainly seems undoubted that no real measures have been taken to punish those responsible.

As for the future of the Bahais in Persia, about which you also ask. I fear I cannot predict anything useful: latent religious opposition is certainly strong all over the country.

The American Minister and, curiously enough, the French Minister also sometimes receive similar requests to interest themselves on the Bahais behalf. So we are not alone.[15]

On 24 December, Mountfort Mills, writing from Haifa, addressed an enquiry to Shuckburgh asking whether any fresh news had been received in London from Iran:

With reference to the recent massacre of Baha'is at Jahrum, Persia, about which you kindly spoke to Mr Oliphant of the Foreign Office a short time ago, I am taking the liberty of bringing to your attention further information that has come to me here, which, if true, confirms the fear expressed to you that the guilty parties have been freed officially from punishment.

It appears that the real cause of the massacre was political, – the determination of Saulatu'd-Dauleh to overthrow an election by which he had been defeated as a candidate for Deputy from Jahrum to the Majliss. His plan was to stir up trouble against the Baha'is in Jahrum, – unfortunately, always an easy thing to do, – and in the resulting confusion to prevent the public announcement of the ballot. It does not appear that he actually intended to go so far as to kill; in fact, the leading body of Baha'is in Persia has exonerated him from that intent. But the result of the open incitement resorted to was inevitable where so much latent fanaticism existed, and the murders followed.

Through the influence of the Deputy for Fasah, Zu'l-qadr, Amir Lashkar and Qavamu'l Mulk, political opponents, Saulatu'd-Dauleh and some thirty or forty others were arrested and imprisoned. All but Saulatu'd-Dauleh were later brought to trial. From the first, however, strong pressure was brought to bear to stop the proceedings, but while these three influential men were able to remain nearby and press the matter the trial continued. Unfortunately, just at this time the coronation ceremonies began at Teheran and they were obliged to leave to take part in them. Immediately the course of the trial changed and the prisoners were acquitted and allowed to go free, on the amazing ground that the murders were the result of mob action for which no individuals could be held responsible. And in the meantime, through the personal intervention of the Prime Minister, Mustawfiu'l-Mamalik,* the Shah pardoned Saulatu'd-Dauleh, after an imprisonment of three and a half months. Later, we are informed, the Shah, in a private interview, admitted that he had received the appeals for justice and the protests of Baha'is from all parts of the world, but had felt obliged to grant the plea of his Prime Minister. Subsequently, an order was issued instructing telegraph officials not to accept any further despatches relating to the subject. Thus we seem to have before us the well nigh incredible fact of official condonation of this hideous atrocity, and, worse, the implied sanction of its repetition in the future.

Such is the story as it comes to us here, apparently well authenticated; yet it is so difficult to be sure in these matters I am hoping that, without too much trouble, you may be able to find out and let me know whether the further information that may have been received from Persia by the Foreign Office substantially agrees with what I have written. The Baha'is, – and we are confident the civilized world will be in sympathy with us, – cannot sit still in the face of such a situation. But, in fairness to all, we wish to be as sure as possible of our facts before acting. If you could help us in the way suggested, we would be most grateful.[16]

Shuckburgh wrote to the Foreign Office proposing that he reply to Mills 'that no official dispatches have been received at the Foreign Office on the subject of Bahai affairs in Persia; but that informal advices from Tehran give accounts that correspond pretty closely with the statements contained in [your] letter to me.'[17]

One last appeal for the British authorities to use their influence to alleviate the position of the Bahá'ís in Iran came from the National Spiritual Assembly of Iraq. A letter dated 13 December 1927 was sent from that body to Sir Henry Dobbs (q.v.), the British High Commissioner in Iraq, asking whether a telegraphic appeal to the Sháh could be sent through the offices of the High Commissioner. The reply of Sir Henry Dobbs, sent through his political secretary and dated 30 December 1927, stated:

I am directed to acknowledge receipt of your letter dated the 13th of December, 1927, enquiring whether it would be possible for a protest to be sent through his Excellency the High Commissioner to the Persian Government in respect of recent occurrences in Persia in which certain Bahais were involved.

* Mírzá Ḥasan Khán-i-Mustawfí, Mustawfíyu'l-Mamálik, son of Mírzá Yúsif, Náṣiru'd-Dín Sháh's Prime Minister. He was Prime Minister a total of eleven times including 1923 and 1926–7. He died in 1932.

While appreciating the desire of yourself and of your community to take steps to protect your co-religionists in Persia, His Excellency regrets that, as the Bahais in Persia are not British or 'Iraqi subjects, he cannot properly advise you to submit your protest through him as you suggest in your letter.

On the other hand His Excellency sees no objection to your addressing a protest direct to His Majesty the Shah, though, of course, he is unable to say how far His Majesty will be moved by such a protest to take action in the sense desired by your community.[18]

Possibly the most noteworthy feature of the above correspondence relating to the Jahrum massacres is the remarkable and abrupt alteration in the attitude of the British authorities towards the Bahá'ís; the help and support given by Norman in 1920–21, which had won the praises of 'Abdu'l-Bahá, had given way to a cold refusal to involve themselves in any way in the matter of the Jahrum martyrdoms only five years later, this despite the fact that the American and French authorities were giving every assistance.

This abrupt change in attitude probably reflects the decline of British influence in Iran. The fiasco over the proposed Anglo-Persian Treaty,* and the bad opinion of this treaty that had been formed in Iran, had brought about a situation in which all British help and advice was repudiated and every British action was looked upon with suspicion and distrust. No doubt in their new position the British felt that they could not come to the support of what was considered a heretical sect. Thus the stance adopted by the British in the first two decades of the twentieth century, as guardians of Iranian morals, upholders of civilization and defenders of the rights of minority groups, was abandoned in the 1920s, and henceforth priority was given to diplomatic and political expediency.

The Marághih Persecutions, 1926

In Marághih in Ádharbáyján a particularly severe persecution of the Bahá'ís erupted in 1926. Through a series of decrees, the Governor of the district effectively suspended all constitutional and civil rights for the Bahá'í community. In the appeals mentioned above that were addressed to the British authorities and to the Sháh by the Spiritual Assembly of Auckland and the National Spiritual Assembly of the Bahá'ís of the United States and Canada respectively, as well as in the communication from the Iraqi Bahá'í Assembly, specific mention was made of the Marághih persecution. In his dispatch of 6 October 1926, Nicolson related what he had been able to learn of the affair:

* This treaty was the brainchild of Lord Curzon. It was intended to be the means whereby Iran would be put back on its feet after the War through British aid and advisers. Although signed, the Treaty was never ratified, since a tremendous furore over it arose in Iran where it was represented as an organ of British imperialism whereby Iran would be virtually annexed by Britain.

I have made enquiries in regard to the alleged persecution of Bahais at Maraghah, and find that the charges of Miss Stevenson's* correspondent are substantially confirmed by local Bahais in Tehran. It is affirmed that this persecution has been now in progress for some fourteen months and has been instigated by a fanatical sub-Governor of Shishvan near Maraghah, by name Sardar Javanshiri. No one appears to have been killed, but the following methods of persecution are adopted:

a) Refusal to allow Bahais to go to the bath.

b) No transactions with Bahais are permitted to Moslem merchants.

c) Constant abuse.

d) The cutting down of all trees belonging to Bahais.

e) The withholding of water supplies from the lands of Bahais.

f) Refusal to allow Bahais to obtain proper drinking water.

I fear that there is little that I can do to prevent or moderate anti-Bahai outbreaks in this country unless there happen to be British subjects among the victims. I shall not fail however to mention the matter to the Prime Minister, who is personally broad-minded in religious matters and opposed to all forms of oppression.[19]

Persecutions in Russia

The Bahá'í community in the various Russian provinces adjoining Iran had been prospering and growing since the time of Bahá'u'lláh, as has been described in previous chapters. Schools, libraries and printing presses had been established, and the first Mashriqu'l-Adhkár of the Bahá'í world had been built in 'Ishqábád. When the Bolsheviks assumed power in Russia they at first allowed the Bahá'ís to continue their affairs without undue interference. Later, however, under Stalin's regime, the Bahá'ís came under increasing pressure and eventually open persecution. In 1928 the Mashriqu'l-Adhkár was expropriated but leased back to the Bahá'ís, and in 1938 it was finally taken over completely by the Russians and used as an art gallery. The culmination of the persecutions in 1938 resulted in the complete break-up of the Bahá'í communities, with many Bahá'ís being exiled to Siberia and others deported to Iran. But long before that date, as testified by the following report from the Mashhad Consulate in May 1930, Bahá'ís were returning to Iran to escape the persecutions: 'It is reliably reported that a large number of Persian Bahais who had settled in Askhabad, where they had hitherto been allowed to maintain their own mosque, are now returning to Persia as the Soviet authorities have threatened to destroy their place of worship and had extended their anti-religious campaign against their community. The Bahais who are now no longer subject to persecution in this country are, nevertheless, not permitted by the Persian Government to maintain mosques in Persian territory.'[20]

* Secretary of the Auckland Bahá'í Assembly.

Persecutions in Turkey

In the new republic of Turkey, under Mustafa Kemal, again toleration of the Bahá'ís later gave way to opposition. The first indication of this was a newspaper campaign in 1928. The Constantinople correspondent of *The Times* of London read something of this in the Turkish newspapers and sent to his newspaper on 9 October 1925 the following report, which clearly demonstrates the misleading and malevolent nature of the reports in the Turkish press: 'The Smyrna police have discovered a group of Turks, Americans and Persians who had formed a secret society with the object of continuing the religious practices in vogue in the days of the Sultans. This society is apparently only one branch of an organisation having its headquarters in Constantinople, which is definitely hostile to the present Government and is suspected of being in touch with Turkish refugees in Europe and America.'[21]

The British Consul in Smyrna, James Morgan (q.v.), reported on 19 November 1928:

I have the honour to report that there are indications that not all Turks in Smyrna find it easy to endure the present dictatorship, or to join in the hearty and too well drilled chorus of praise which greets every new enactment of the Government.

The local press find it easy to disguise under the name of 'foreign propaganda' all symptoms of discontent. Thus labour grievances are labelled 'Communism,' and religious grievances are called 'Bahaism.' The population are told that Turkey has not suppressed the dervishes, in the interests of progress, to make way for the foreign sect of the Bahais, and are warned of the danger of belonging to secret societies, with special reference to Freemasonry and the Order of Bektashis.

The press does not grow over-excited in its denunciation of Communism or Bahaism, and thus indicates that it considers the danger from these two theories as unreal or insignificant.[22]

It was these newspaper reports that caused the arrest of several Bahá'ís in Smyrna and a close investigation of Bahá'í affairs in Turkey by the police and judiciary. The Bahá'ís, however, emerged creditably, having taken the opportunity of this opposition to state publicly the tenets of their religion and demonstrate the non-political nature of their activities.

Four years later, however, the persecutions in Turkey re-started on a more serious level. In Adana in November 1932 a number of Bahá'ís were arrested. On 22 December 1932 W. D. W. Matthews (q.v.), British Consul at Mersin and Adana, reported: '. . . another adherent of that sect, named Ferhat Naci, was recently arrested and lodged in the Adana gaol, bringing up the number of Bahaists imprisoned at Adana to fifteen.'[23] The arrests continued over the next few months, and on 6 February 1933, Matthews reported: 'I have the honour to report . . . respecting the imprisonment of adherents of the *Bahai* sect, that two more adherents of that sect, Ali Ekber oğlu Izzettin and his brother, Kemal, are stated to have been recently transported from Gazi Antep to Adana, where they were interrogated and lodged in prison. The Bahaists now imprisoned in Adana number fifty persons, and their trial is expected to begin within the next few days.'[24] On receipt of this report at the Foreign Office, G. W. Rendel (q.v.) commented: 'It is a great thing to know that under the Turkish Constitution there is complete freedom of conscience in Turkey and that all religions are equal before the law.'[25]

On 9 March 1933 Matthews wrote:

> I have the honour to report, with reference to my despatch No. 11 of the 6th February last, that the Adana newspaper 'Türk Sözü' of the 8th instant states that the trial of fifty-three Bahais of Adana, Mersin, Gaziantep and Birecik began before the Adana Criminal Tribunal on the 7th instant.
>
> These persons are charged with forming a secret society, having seals made, collecting money illegally, having books and documents relating to Bahaism, being in communication with one Şevki,* 'who is the Head of the Bahais at Hayfa and has been awarded a decoration by the British Government', paying the school-fees of Bahai children at the American School in Beirut, and performing divorces and marriages.
>
> Abdul Vahap Naci Efendi, the Head of the Adana Bahais, stated in examination that he was seventy-five years of age, and that he and all his relatives were Bahais. Most of the other accused admitted that they were Bahais, but a few denied being so.[26]

The trial continued until the end of March, at which time all imprisoned Bahá'ís were released.

The Closure of the Bahá'í Schools in Iran

Mention has already been made of the pre-eminent position achieved by the Bahá'í community in Iran in the field of education. The two Tarbíyat schools in Ṭihrán, one for boys and one for girls, had achieved such fame that many of the notables of Ṭihrán, Ministers, civil servants, army officers, etc., although not Bahá'ís, preferred to send their children to these two schools. For an assessment of the Bahá'í schools in the other parts of the country, there are the reports of O. A. Merritt-Hawkes, who visited Iran in the mid-1930s. She wrote:

> At Yezd I visited two girls schools run by the Bahais because the government would not provide enough. The head of the first school was an unmarried woman who had a married assistant. I sat talking to them in the small, neat, clean and charming courtyard while we had cold sherbet in bright yellow glasses that stood on glass plates and cucumbers which were dipped into iced vinegar. When a Bahais man appeared the children over eight raced away to get their *chadars*, which were neatly folded up on shelves. The teachers said that Bahallullah [*sic*] had wished the veil to be abolished, but they thought that neither men nor women were yet ready and that it would be ten to

* Shoghi Effendi

twenty years before either could look at the other without lascivious and passionate thoughts.

The students in one class were sitting round an octagonal pool in which goldfish were carrying on an anti-mosquito crusade. The pupils belonged to all the local sects, but most of them had a leather case with a charm round their necks, some of the cases green to make them yet more effective.

The other Bahais school, equally neat and tidy, was run by a remarkable woman, Hadji Bibi Sorghra,* whose face was thin, refined, full of eager enthusiasm. She very early became a widow and, having no children, went, in spite of her relations, to Tehran, where she lived with a Bahais family and attended school. That was fifteen years ago when the caravan took twelve days to do the journey. When she returned she realized how badly a school was needed in her own town and started one herself. Now she can do more because helped by Bahais funds, but she said pathetically:

'I am sorry we are doing so little. I learnt too long ago to be modern or to know much.

'Bahallullah said mankind had two wings, one was man, and one was woman, and it could not fly without both. I know by my life that that is true, but in Persia to-day few know that, so that my country goes slowly.'

I was sorry that I had to go on to Kerman without seeing her again, for she was like a flower that had never had an opportunity to open.[27]

In Kirmán, she visited another Bahá'í school and reported:

It was very difficult to get about Kerman as there was only one *droscha* in the town, the few cars were appallingly bad and to walk between 9 a.m. and 5 p.m. in June was to court disaster. Because the chauffeur made a mistake, I had to walk a mile to the school run by the Bahais. I arrived dusty and tired out, but everything unpleasant was forgotten when I looked at the charming Persian woman, immaculately clean and tidy, and her thirty happy, clean pupils. She was a widow with three children, who had studied modern methods in Turkestan and had come to Persia after the Russian revolution.

The children were from two to six years of age, paying only two *rials* a month, the local community of Bahais subscribing the remainder of the expenses. Each child had its own towel and on arrival washed its hands and nails and had its head examined. That doesn't sound much in Europe, but in Kerman it took your breath away. No corporal punishment was allowed; if a child did not behave, after being given several chances, it was sent away. That attitude of kindness to one another, of kindness to animals, the teaching that blows are not the only way to manage, was really startling in a land where corporal punishment, although theoretically abolished in the schools, was still considered the only practical discipline.

The children danced as they sang:

We are children of the twentieth century,
We go to school every day,
We learn Persian,
We are the children of the future,
We must be clean and honest for our country's sake.

Those children were gay and jolly, they all had shoes, most of them had stockings and they were learning to use a handkerchief. They would not, like their parents, feel it necessary to wipe their noses on every post. That would make a pleasanter Persia! I suddenly realized that the inventor of handkerchiefs had been one of the world's

* Ḥájíyyih Bíbí Sughrá. The details given here about this remarkable woman are essentially correct. She died in 1946.

greatest benefactors. Again the children walked in a circle, singing:

We are the children of the school,
We are like flowers in a garden.
We go out into the garden
To play and to run,
To use our watering cans and dig with spades.
We must be brothers and sisters,
Learning together in a class,
Wearing the same brown uniform.

I did not want to leave this place of happiness and hope, to go into the streets where the children's eyes were covered with flies, where their habits were cruel or disgusting.

Persia needs schools like this but has not the teachers and will not have foreigners. An excellent school of this type, with a clever Russian teacher, was shut up at Shiraz because, according to the new law, only a Persian can teach young children. They told me a Persian woman would take his place.

'Is she trained?' I asked.

'Oh, no; that is not necessary. She is very bright and will know what to do.'[28]

Thus, undoubtedly, envy was at least a factor in the Government's decision to close the Bahá'í schools. The pretext chosen for the closures was trivial. The following dispatch, dated 15 December 1934, from the British Ambassador, H. M. Knatchbull-Hugessen (q.v.), tells the whole story:

The Persian press announced on the 9th December last that the Ministry of Education had closed on that day the 'Tarbiat' schools at Tehran, owing to 'failure to comply with the instructions of the Ministry of Education.' The 'Tarbiat' schools belong to the Bahai community and are two in number, one for boys and the other for girls. The former, which has been in existence for thirty-six years, has about 700 boy pupils and the latter 800 girls. The closure has therefore affected about 1,500 students, whose ages range up to 20 years, and a number of teachers. Similar steps were taken by the local authorities in Hamadan, Kazvin, Sultanabad, Kashan and Yezd, and, I believe, some other towns which possess Bahai schools.

The head munshi of this Legation, Mirza Abdul Hussein Khan Naimi, is himself a Bahai. I have obtained from him a report on the whole circumstances of this somewhat remarkable action by the Persian Government, and the following facts are taken from his report.

The Bahais, as a matter of religion, hold nine days of each year sacred, and abstain from any work on those days. The present head of the Bahai religion, Shoughi Effendi, who lives, I believe, at Haifa, has enjoined the most strict observance of these days on his followers in every country. The Bahai schools in Tehran were therefore closed last year on the 28th Shaban, 1352 (the 17th December, 1933), the anniversary of the martyrdom of the Bab, one of the most important of the nine Bahai days. A few days later the Ministry of Education asked in writing the reason for the closure of the schools. The board of directors of the schools, who are appointed by the Bahai National Spiritual Assembly every year, explained the reason in writing. The principal of the boys' school was then summoned to the Ministry and told that the letter was not acceptable and must be taken back. He refused to do so, saying that it was not his letter; but a few days later the Minister sent back the letter in an envelope.

About last May the Ministry addressed to the schools a further letter, referring to the fact that the schools had been 'closed without reason' last year, and warning them that if the same thing were to happen this year the schools would be definitely closed down. The matter was referred to Shoughi Effendi, who, in reply, said that, although Bahais should subject themselves completely to the Government's orders in all matters connected with the programme of instruction and the general administration of the schools, they should nevertheless not fail to observe Bahai religious rules and not work on the specified days. The Bahai community were therefore determined not to give in, and declared themselves ready for death or martyrdom rather than obey the order not to close the schools. They therefore closed the schools on the anniversary of the death of the Bab.

Stories of further oppression in some of the provincial towns have also reached the head munshi. In Sultanabad, for instance, the archives of the Bahai community have been seized and sent to the Tehran Police Administration. In some places all meetings by Bahais have been prohibited. In Tehran, however, nothing of that sort has been reported, and the Government do not seem disposed to take further steps at present.

The Bahais argue that they have had to support their schools, beginning from about thirty-six years ago, by a large subvention, without the least encouragement from the Government; and they state that their schools have always been well managed and have attracted the children of the best families of Tehran. Naimi considers that only about one-half of the children attending the schools were Bahais, though all the staff were, as a rule, of the Bahai faith. Religious propaganda was forbidden in the schools, as in all other schools in Tehran. As for the ban against closing the schools, the Bahais point out that all other schools of Tehran close occasionally in similar circumstances; it often happens, for instance, that a school is closed as a mark of respect on the death of a prominent dignitary.

I hear that an American lady named Miss Sharpe,* a prominent Bahai, approached the American consulate with a request to transmit certain letters for her to the Bahais in America, as she was convinced that a strict censorship was being maintained against all communications from and to the Bahais of Tehran. The National Spiritual Assembly of the Bahais also endeavoured to telegraph to the Shah, but a few days later the secretary of the assembly was summoned to the office of the Director of Telegraphs, and the telegram was returned to him with the statement that he had orders from higher authorities not to send off the telegram. Naimi also informs me that the Government are now endeavouring to induce the teachers who formerly taught at the Tarbiat schools to transfer to other schools in Tehran, and to secure places for the pupils in other schools; even though the latter were previously said to be full.

The American College of Tehran is following these developments with great interest. It remains to be seen whether the Government will insist on that college keeping its schools open, for the first time in its history, on Christmas Day. I have heard no reports of interference from any of the British schools in the south.

I shall not fail to report any further developments which may follow. One member of the staff of the American College advances the theory that his Highness Feroughi† is really the cause of the opposition to the Bahais. I am inclined to wonder whether this curious assertion of governmental authority is connected with His Majesty's visit to Turkey; if so, we must, I suppose, expect a general attack on all forms of foreign instruction on the lines of the Turkish model.[29]

On receiving this report at the Foreign Office, A. E. Lambert (q.v.)

* Miss Adelaide Sharp (1896–1976) came to Iran in 1926 in order to teach in the Tarbíyat school. She remained in Iran until her death and became the first woman to be elected onto the Iranian National Spiritual Assembly.

† Mírzá Muḥammad-'Alí Khán-i-Furúghí, the first Prime Minister of Riḍa Sháh in December 1925. He was later Iranian delegate to the League of Nations, and Prime Minister in 1941–2.

wrote: 'The Persians did not choose a very good excuse for the closing of the schools, but perhaps they could find no other. We can only await further developments or possible attacks on English-speaking educational authorities.'[30]

While G. W. Rendel commented wryly: 'Typically Persian I am afraid.'[31]

Persecutions at Ábádih, 1944

In the province of Fárs in 1944 there was a brief flare-up of hostility and persecution of the Bahá'ís at Ábádih. On 12 May, a mob of about 4,000 stormed the local Bahá'í Centre. They broke up the furniture, carried away the library and set fire to the building. The mob attacked three persons who happened to be in the building and, having beaten and gouged them severely, left them for dead. H. G. Jakins (q.v.), British Consul in Shíráz, reported in his diary for the latter half of May 1944:

> On May 12 considerable pre-election activity took place in Abadeh where a mob incited by the preaching of Sheikh Ali Akbar attacked a Bahai house, burning it with its contents. The Embassy courier who arrived in Abadeh a few hours after the assault was told that two Bahais had been killed while the Gendarmerie made no attempt to interfere and the officers in fact continued to play cards in the shade of the hotel garden. They were certainly reclining in the garden when the courier arrived. Sheikh Ali is reported to be acting on the instance of Umid Salar. General Jehanbani despatched Colonel Amanpour to take charge of the situation and when it flared up again on May 22 he made a number of arrests on both sides. The arrested men were subsequently released and did not in any case include the ringleaders.[32]

In his report for the first half of June, Jakins stated: 'The Embassy courier stayed the night at Abadeh on June 12. Apparently fresh disturbances had occurred as a result of which guards had been posted at all Bahai houses.'[33]

Capt. Henry, who was passing near Ábádih in August 1944, was asked to go to the town to report on the situation. His report deals mainly with the political aspects of the disturbances. In relation to the Bahá'ís, he wrote:

> The present political situation of Abadeh is still very obscure. Two days were spent in making discreet enquiries from sources normally held to be reliable but in spite of this the amount and accuracy of the information obtained is still far from satisfactory. The various stories related by the different camps do not agree but it appears from all accounts that the present trouble in Abadeh started about one month before the 'NU RUZ' holidays. In February a certain SAYID QAYUMI, a resident of the village of SUQAT, was asked to come to ABADEH to read 'Rowzeh Khaneh' for one of the residents in mourning there. This he did, and while he was in ABADEH, whether by accident or design, another Sayid or Mullah happened to make a slighting reference to the BAHAIS in a public address in one of the mosques. The BAHAI section of the community took offence to this reference and started, very mildly it is understood, to demonstrate against the Moslems. The village of SUQAT is supposed to be noted for its anti-BAHAI

leaning and when the people of SUQAT heard of the anti-Moslem demonstration which had taken place in ABADEH they asked SAYID QAYUMI to return to SUQAT to preach a sermon against the BAHAIS behaviour. On his return to SUQAT it is understood that the Sayid preached a really fiery and thundering peroration against the Bahais and their religion.[34]

In his Intelligence Summary for the period 29 May – 4 June 1944, the Military Attaché of the British Embassy at Ṭihrán reported:

For some time past tension has been evident between Moslems and Bahais, and this resulted in demonstrations hostile to the Bahais at Senandaj, Hamadan and Abadeh, as reported in Summary No. 21, paragraph 8. This tension may be used, as it was at Abadeh, to provoke disturbances for political reasons. There has, in fact, been some increased missionary activity on the part of Bahais of late to celebrate the opening of the second century of the Bahai faith, and, although no evidence is as yet available that there has been any notable increase in converts, the greater freedom enjoyed by the Bahais to speak of their faith has probably frightened the Mullahs .... Bahaism, with its vague but kindly philosophy, is agreeable to Persian mentality, and the community has a tradition, resulting perhaps from years of oppression, of solidarity and co-operation among themselves, which contrasts with usual Persian characteristics.[35]

References

1. *New York Times* 20 July 1924, p. 1, col. 3
2. Annual Report on Persia, Loraine to Chamberlain No. 278, 22 May 1925, p. 3, File E3401/3401/34: FO 371 10848
3. ibid. pp. 7–8
4. Chick to Loraine No. 21, 12 Apr. 1926, enclosed in 6 *infra*
5. ibid.
6. Loraine to Chamberlain No. 206, 3 May 1926, File E3183/399/34: FO 371 11492
7. File E3183/399/34: FO 371 11492
8. ibid.
9. File E3979/3979/34: FO 371 11501
10. ibid.
11. ibid.
12. Shuckburgh to Oliphant, File E5836/3979/34; Oliphant to Nicolson, File E3979/3979/34: FO 371 11501
13. File E6013/3979/34: FO 371 11501
14. File E6552/3979/34: FO 371 11501. The text of this petition may be found in *Bahá'í World* Vol. 2, pp. 287–300
15. Nicolson to Oliphant 4 Nov. 1926, File E6516/3979/34: FO 371 11501
16. File E160/160/34: FO 371 12288
17. In letter Shuckburgh to Oliphant 8 Jan. 1927 in 16 *supra*
18. Sturges, Polit. Sec. to High Commssr, to Qassáb<u>ch</u>í 30 Dec. 1927, File E313/313/34: FO 371 13061
19. Nicolson to Chamberlain No. 485, 6 Oct. 1926, File E6013/3979/34: FO 371 11501
20. Ma<u>sh</u>had Intelligence Summary No. 14 for Week ending 3 May 1930: FO 371 14540
21. *The Times* 10 Oct. 1928, p. 15, col. 2
22. Morgan to Clerk No. 80, 19 Nov. 1928, File E5621/128/44: FO 371 13089

23. Matthews to Morgan No. 36, 22 Dec. 1932, File E260/260/44: FO 371 16918
24. Matthews to Morgan No. 11, 6 Feb. 1933, File E1050/260/44: FO 371 16918
25. Memo by Rendel 9 Mar. 1933, File E1050/260/44: FO 371 16918
26. Matthews to Morgan No. 26, 9 Mar. 1933, File E1568/260/44: FO 361 16918
27. Merritt-Hawkes *Persia: Romance and Reality* pp. 144–5
28. ibid. pp. 152–3
29. Knatchbull-Hugessen to Sir John Simon No. 554, 15 Dec. 1934, File E7789/7789/34: FO 371 17917
30. Memo by Lambert 2 Jan. 1935, File E7789/7789/34: FO 371 17917
31. Memo by Rendel 9 Jan. 1935, File E7789/7789/34: FO 371 17917
32. Shíráz Diary No. 91, 15–31 May 1944: FO 371 40162
33. Shíráz Diary No. 11, 1–15 June 1944: FO 371 40162
34. Captain Henry's Report, no date: FO 248 1437
35. Mil. Attaché's Intelligence Summary No. 22. for 29 May–4 June 1944, File E3463/422/34: FO 371 40205

APPENDIX I

Miscellaneous Tables

In tables of European diplomatic and consular officials, dates given are, except when stated otherwise, dates of appointment. These would often be 2 or 3 months before the date when that individual would take up his post. Further biographical material can be found about those persons marked with an asterisk in Appendix II.

IRAN

Sháhs of Iran

9 Sept. 1834	Accession of Muḥammad Sháh at Tabríz
4 Sept. 1848	Death of Muḥammad Sháh
12 Sept. 1848	Accession of Náṣiru'd-Dín Sháh at Tabríz
19 Oct. 1848	Entry of Náṣiru'd-Dín Sháh into Ṭihrán
1 May 1896	Assassination of Náṣiru'd-Dín Sháh
8 June 1896	Accession of Muẓaffaru'd-Dín Sháh
8 Jan. 1907	Death of Muẓaffaru'd-Dín Sháh
19 Jan. 1907	Accession of Muḥammad-'Alí Sháh
16 July 1909	Abdication of Muḥammad-'Alí Sháh
18 July 1909	Accession of Aḥmad Sháh
31 Oct. 1925	Aḥmad Sháh deposed
	Qájár dynasty terminated
13 Dec. 1925	Accession of Riḍá Sháh
	Commencement of Pahlaví dynasty
16 Sept. 1941	Abdication of Riḍá Sháh
	Accession of Muḥammad-Riḍá Sháh

Prime Ministers of Iran

Oct. 1834	Mírzá Abu'l-Qásim, Qá'im Maqám (executed 26 June 1835)
Late 1835	Ḥájí Mírzá Áqásí*
19 Oct. 1848	Mírzá Taqí Khán, Amír-Niẓám
13 Nov. 1851	Mírzá Áqá Khán-i-Núrí, I'timádu'd-Dawlih – dismissed 30 Aug. 1858

Between 1858 and 1871, Náṣiru'd-Dín Sháh ruled through a council of ministers, except for a short period, 1864–6, when Mírzá Muḥammad Khán, Sipahsalár-i-A'ẓam was Prime Minister.

13 Nov. 1871	Mírzá Ḥusayn Khán, Sipahsalár-i-A'ẓam* – dismissed Sept. 1873.

Between 1873 and 1884, there was no person formally named Prime Minister.

23 June 1884	Mírzá Yúsif, Mustawfíyu'l-Mamálik
1886	Mírzá 'Alí-Aṣghar Khán, Amínu's-Sulṭán* (Vazír-i-A'ẓam)
1888	Mírzá 'Alí-Aṣghar Khán, Amínu's-Sulṭán* (Ṣadr-i-A'ẓam)
June 1897	Ḥájí 'Alí Khán, Amínu'd-Dawlih*
3 July 1898	Mírzá 'Alí-Aṣghar Khán, Amínu's-Sulṭán
24 Jan. 1904	Sulṭán-Majíd Mírzá, 'Aynu'd-Dawlih
30 July 1906	Mírzá Naṣru'lláh Khán, Mushíru'd-Dawlih
26 Apr. 1907	Mírzá 'Alí-Aṣghar Khán, Amínu's-Sulṭán, Atábik-i-A'ẓam (assassinated 31 Aug. 1907)
Oct. 1907	Abu'l-Qásim Khán, Náṣiru'l-Mulk
20 Dec. 1907	Ḥusayn-Qulí Khán, Niẓámu's-Salṭanih

There were then several rapid changes in the Premiership until the abdication of Muḥammad-'Alí Sháh

17 Aug. 1909	Muḥammad-Valí Khán, Sipahdár-i-A'ẓam*

Foreign Diplomatic Representatives at Ṭihrán

British Ministers

17 Sept. 1844	Lt-Col. Justin Sheil*
(21 Oct. 1847 – 28 Nov. 1849	Lt-Col. Francis Farrant,* Chargé d'Affaires)
3 Sept. 1854	Hon. Charles A. Murray
16 Apr. 1859	Sir Henry Rawlinson*
7 Apr. 1860	Charles Alison*
15 July 1872	William T. Thomson*
14 June 1879	Ronald F. Thomson*
3 Dec. 1887	Sir Henry Drummond Wolff*
24 July 1891	Sir Frank Lascelles
1 May 1894	Sir Mortimer Durand*
21 Oct. 1900	Sir Arthur Hardinge*
1 July 1906	Sir Cecil Spring-Rice
1 Sept. 1908	Sir George Barclay*
24 Mar. 1912	Sir Walter Townley*
9 Mar. 1915	Charles M. Marling*
17 Sept. 1918	Sir Percy Cox*
1 Feb. 1920	Herman C. Norman*
1 Oct. 1921	Sir Percy Loraine*
7 Oct. 1926	Robert H. Clive*
12 Oct. 1931	Reginald H. Hoare
7 Nov. 1934	Hughe Knatchbull-Hugessen*
2 Oct. 1936	James S. Horace
6 Dec. 1939	Sir Reader Bullard
17 Feb. 1944	Sir Reader Bullard (Ambassador)

Russian Ministers

1839	Count Meden
June 1845	Prince Dimitri I. Dolgorukov*
May 1854	A. H. Anitchkov
(June 1857 – Aug. 1858	M. Lagowski, Chargé d'Affaires)
Aug. 1863	Nicolas de Giers
1869	A. de Beger
1877	Zinoviev
1883	Melnikov
1886	Prince Nicolai S. Dolgorukov
1890	De Butzov
1898	Argiropoulo
1902	P. Vlassov*
1905	A. de Speyer
1907	N. de Hartwig
1909	S. Poklerski-Koziel
1914	Korostowetz
1916	N. S. d'Etter

French Ministers

8 Sept. 1839	Comte de Sercey
16 Nov. 1847	Comte de Sartiges
9 May 1855	Nicolas Bourée*

(15 Oct. 1856 – 20 Jan. 1858, J. A. de Gobineau, Chargé d'Affaires)

16 Aug. 1857	Baron Pichon
28 Aug. 1861	J. A. de Gobineau*
5 Oct. 1864	Comte de Massignac
23 Mar. 1867	De Bonnières de Wierre
(17 July 1871	Belle, Chargé d'Affaires)

French Ministers (cont.)

28 Oct. 1872	Mellinot
24 Sept. 1879	Tricou
3 Oct. 1881	De Balloy*
9 Oct. 1898	Souhart
16 Oct. 1900	Bourgarel
5 July 1903	J. A. de France
2 Nov. 1905	Leon Descos
23 Apr. 1907	H. de La Martinière
13 June 1908	R. Lecomte
16 May 1919	Charles-Eudes Bonin

Iṣfahán

Governors

1838	Manúchihr Khán, Mu'tamadu'd-Dawlih (d. 21 Feb. 1847)

Between 1848 and 1874, the following were Governors in turn, each for 1–3 years:

Mírzá Nabí Khán, Amír-Díván
Sulaymán Khán, Khán-Khánán
Ghulám-Ḥusayn Khán, Sipahdár
Chiráq-'Alí Khán, Siráju'l-Mulk
Ḥamzih Mírzá, Ḥishmatu'd-Dawlih*
'Ísá Khán-i-Qájár, I'timádu'd-Dawlih
Khánlar Mírzá, Iḥtishámu'd-Dawlih
Sulṭán-Ḥusayn Mírzá, Jalálu'd-Dawlih
Sulṭán-Ma'súd Mírzá, Ẓillu's-Sulṭán*
Fatḥ-'Alí Khán, Ṣáḥib-Díván
Sulṭán-Murád Mírzá, Ḥisámu's-Salṭanih*

May 1874	Sulṭán-Ma'súd Mírzá, Ẓillu's-Sulṭán*
1907	Sulṭán-Ḥusayn Mírzá, Nayyiru'd-Dawlih*
1908	Muḥammad Khán, Iqbálu'd-Dawlih
1909	Najaf-Qulí Khán, Ṣamṣámu's-Salṭanih*

British Representatives

c. 1848	Peter Stephen (Consular Agent)
21 May 1858	Stephen P. Aganoor* (Consular Agent)
1 Aug. 1891	John Richard Preece* (Consul) (Consul-Gen. from 21 Nov. 1900)
1 Mar. 1906	Henry D. Barnham (Con.-Gen.)
1 Feb. 1908	Thomas G. Grahame* (Con.-Gen.)
1 June 1916	Lt-Col. Thomas W. Haig* (Con.-Gen.)
6 Nov. 1919	Francis E. Crow* (Con.-Gen.)
22 May 1923	Ernest Bristow (Con.-Gen.)

Post closed 1934

Fárs

Governors

Apr. 1843	Mírzá Nabí Khán-i-Qazvíní, Amír-Díván
Oct. 1844	Ḥusayn Khán, Niẓámu'd-Dawlih
Nov. 1848	Bahrám Mírzá, Mu'izzu'd-Dawlih
Mar. 1850	Fírúz Mírzá, Nuṣratu'd-Dawlih
May 1853	Ṭahmásb Míŕza, Mu'ayyidu'd-Dawlih

British Consular Agents at Shíráz

c. 1840	Mírzá Muḥammad-Riḍá
c. 1846	Mírzá Maḥmúd
Nov. 1850	Mírzá Faḍlu'lláh Khán-i-Qazvíní
Mar. 1854	Muḥammad-Ḥasan Khán-i-Navváb

Ádharbáyján

Governors

1839	Bahman Mírzá
Jan. 1848	Náṣiru'd-Dín Mirzá
Oct. 1848	Malik-Qásim Mírzá*
June 1849	Ḥamzih Mírzá*

British Consuls at Tabríz

2 Mar. 1846	Richard W. Stevens*
22 Apr. 1852	Keith E. Abbott* (until 1 July 1868)

Khurásán

Governors

1896	Ghulám-Riḍá Khán, Áṣafu'd-Dawlih*
1897	Muḥammad-Taqí Mírzá, Ruknu'd-Dawlih*
1901	Sulṭán-Ḥusayn Mírzá, Nayyiru'd-Dawlih*
1903	'Alí-Naqí Mírzá, Ruknu'd-Dawlih*
1904	Áṣafu'd-Dawlih
1907	Ruknu'd-Dawlih
1908	Nayyiru'd-Dawlih
1909	Ruknu'd-Dawlih
1912	Nayyiru'd-Dawlih

British Consuls-General at Mashhad

1 Feb. 1889	Maj.-Gen. Charles S. Maclean
14 Dec. 1891	Ney Elias*
11 Sept. 1896	Lt-Col. Charles E. Yate*
11 Feb. 1898	Lt-Col. Henry M. Temple*
23 Mar. 1901	Lt-Col. George F. Chevenix-Trench
1 Oct. 1903	Lt-Col. Charles F. Minchin
5 Feb. 1906	Maj. Percy M. Sykes*
1 Jan. 1914	Lt-Col. Thomas W. Haig*
24 Aug. 1916	Lt-Col. William G. Grey

OTTOMAN EMPIRE

Sulṭáns of Turkey

2 July 1839	Accession of 'Abdu'l-Majíd
25 June 1861	Accession of 'Abdu'l-'Azíz
30 May 1876	Deposition of 'Abdu'l-'Azíz (committed suicide or assassinated 4 June 1876) Accession of (Muḥammad-)Murád V
31 Aug. 1876	Deposition of Murád V Accession of 'Abdu'l-Ḥamíd

27 Apr. 1909	Deposition of 'Abdu'l-Ḥamíd
	Accession of Muḥammad (-Ris͟hád) V
3 July 1918	Death of Muḥammad V
	Accession of Muḥammad (Vaḥíyu'd-Dín) VI
2 Nov. 1922	Abolition of the Sultanate; Turkey becomes a Republic
17 Nov. 1922	Muḥammad VI leaves Turkey
19 Nov. 1922	Accession of 'Abdu'l-Majíd II as Caliph only
3 Mar. 1924	Abolition of the Caliphate
4 Mar. 1924	All members of House of 'Ut͟hmán leave Turkey

Ministers

Grand Vazírs (Prime Ministers)

27 May 1860	Kibrisli Mehmed Emin Paşa (Muḥammad Pás͟háy-i-Qibrisí)
6 Aug. 1861	'Álí Pás͟há*
22 Nov. 1861	Fu'ád Pás͟há*
5 Jan. 1863	Yúsif Kámil Pás͟há
1 June 1863	Fu'ád Pás͟há
5 June 1866	Muḥammad Rus͟hdí Pás͟há
11 Feb. 1867	'Álí Pás͟há (d. 7 Sept. 1871)
6 Sept. 1871	Maḥmúd Pás͟há

Foreign Ministers

6 Aug. 1861	Fu'ád Pás͟há*
22 Nov. 1861	'Álí Pás͟há*
11 Feb. 1867	Fu'ád Pás͟há (d. 12 Feb. 1869 at Nice)
12 Feb. 1869	'Álí Pás͟há (in addition to being Grand Vazír)

Foreign Diplomatic Representatives at Istanbul

British

16 Oct. 1841	Sir Stratford Canning*
10 May 1858	Henry L. Bulwer*
10 Aug. 1865	Lord Lyons
6 July 1867	Henry G. Elliot*
31 Dec. 1877	Austen H. Layard*
6 May 1880	George J. Goschen (Special Ambassador)
26 May 1881	Earl of Dufferin
1 Dec. 1884	Sir Edward Thornton
18 Apr. 1885	Sir William White (until 12 Jan. 1892)

French

10 Feb. 1851	Marquis de la Valette
17 Feb. 1853	De La Cour
30 Oct. 1853	Gen. Baraguey d'Hilliers
3 May 1855	Thouvenel
11 Feb. 1860	Marquis de La Valette
28 Aug. 1861	Marquis de Moustier
28 Oct. 1866	Nicolas Bourée* (until 9 July 1870)

Bag͟hdád

Governors (Dates of arrival at Bag͟hdád)

2 Dec. 1851	Námiq Pás͟há (Mehmed Namik Paşa)*
9 Sept. 1852	Muḥammad-Ras͟híd Pás͟há
18 Feb. 1858	'Umar Pás͟há
5 Mar. 1860	Muṣṭafá Núrí Pás͟há
13 Feb. 1861	Aḥmad Tawfíq Pás͟há
2 Feb. 1862	Námiq Pás͟há (Mehmed Namik Paşa)*

British Representatives

1822	Capt. R. Taylor (Con.)
16 Dec. 1843	Lt-Col. H. Rawlinson* (Con., Con.-Gen. from 1 Dec. 1851)
13 Apr. 1855	Capt A. Burrowes Kemball* (Con.-Gen.)
1 Sept. 1868	Col. Charles Herbert* (Con.-Gen.) (until 20 Dec. 1874)

French Representatives

1850	Favernier (V.-Con.)
1853	J. B. Nicolas* (Con.)
1854–5	Vacant – British Consul acting
1856	Eugène Tastu (Con.-Gen.)
1862	Delaporte (Con.)
1864	Pellissier de Reynaud* (Con.)

Persian Consuls-General (Dates of arrival at Baghdád)

Dec. 1846	Mírzá Ibráhím Khán
8 June 1859	Ḥájí Muḥammad Khán, Dabíru'l-Mulk
July 1860	Mírzá Buzurg Khán
11 Feb. 1863	Mírzá Muḥammad-Zamán Khán

Adrianople

Governors

Sept. 1861	Kibrisli Mehmed Emin Paşa(Muḥammad Pásháy-i-Qibrisí)
Apr. 1864	Sulaymán Páshá
Dec. 1864	'Árif Páshá
Mar. 1866	Khurshíd Páshá

Foreign Consular Representatives in Adrianople/Philippopolis area

Great Britain (J. E. Blunt*); France (Albert de Courtois, F. F. Ronzevalle*, acting); Austria (Camerloher); Russia; Belgium; Greece

Syria

Governors of Syria (Damascus) (dates of arrival at post)

1867	Rashíd Páshá
Oct. 1871	Ṣubḥí Páshá
Feb. 1873	Ḥalit Páshá
Sept. 1874	As'ad Páshá
Feb. 1875	Aḥmad Ḥamdí Páshá
June 1876	Nashíd Páshá
Feb. 1877	Ḍíyá Páshá
June 1877	'Umar Fivzí Páshá
Feb. 1878	Jivdit Páshá
Nov. 1878	Midḥat Páshá
Aug. 1880	Ḥamdí Páshá
Aug. 1885	Nashíd Páshá

In March 1888 a general reorganization of the provinces occurred, and a new Viláyat at Beirut was formed which included the Sanjak of 'Akká.

Governors of Beirut

Mar. 1888	'Alí Páshá
May 1889	Ra'úf Páshá
July 1889	'Azíz Páshá
Jan. 1892	Ismá'íl Kamál Bey
July 1892	Khálid Bey
Aug. 1894	Nasúhí Bey
Apr. 1897	Náẓim Páshá
Aug. 1897	Rashíd Bey
Sept. 1903	Ibráhím Khalíl Páshá

Governors of Beirut (cont.)

Aug. 1908	Muḥammad 'Alí Bey
Sept. 1908	Náẓim Páshá
Dec. 1908	Idhim Bey
Sept. 1909	Náẓim Páshá

Mutaṣarrifs of 'Akká

This listing is not complete. The dates in this list should be taken only as approximate.

1868	Hádí Páshá
1869	Muḥammad Bey
1871	Húlú Páshá
1872	Ṣáliḥ Páshá
1873	Aḥmad Bey
1874	'Abdu'r-Raḥmán Páshá
1875	As'ad Effendi
1876	Muṣṭafá Ḍíyá Effendi
1881	Aḥmad Aṣ-Ṣáliḥ Effendi
1886	Aḥmad Ḥamdí Páshá
1888	Ibráhím Páshá
1889	'Árif Bey
1891	Ṣádiq Páshá
1895	Ḥusayn Effendi
1899	Muḥarram Bey
1900	Jamíl Páshá
1901	Aḥmad Adíb Bey
1902	Ḥusní Bey
1905	Ibráhím Ṣárim Bey
1906	Aḥmad 'Árifí' Bey

(cont. overpage)

Mutaṣarrifs of 'Akká (cont.)

1907 Muḥammad Faríd Páshá
1908 Ismá'íl Raḥmí Bey
1909 Muḥammad Bihjat Bey

British Consuls-General at Beirut

29 Apr. 1863 George J. Eldridge*
5 Mar. 1890 Lt-Col. Henry Trotter
4 Oct. 1894 Robert Drummond-Hay*
22 Jan. 1908 Henry A. Cumberbatch

War declared 5 Nov. 1914

British Representatives in Haifa-'Akká Area

18 May 1839 Moses d'Abraham Finzi (Consular Agent, 'Akká)
July 1879 Dr J. Schmidt (Hon V.-Con. Haifa)
22 Sept. 1898 James H. Monahan* (V.-Con. Haifa)
12 Jan. 1904 Pietro Abela* (Acting V.-Con., Haifa. V.-Con. from 1 Apr. 1909)

War declared 5 Nov. 1914

Foreign Consular Representatives in Haifa-'Akká Area, 1882

Austria: Consular Agent, 'Akká and Haifa, M. A. Scoponich
Belgium: Consular Agent, 'Akká, H. Mazzinghi
France: Con. Haifa and 'Akká, J. Monge
Germany: V.-Con., Haifa, F. Keller
Gt Britain: V.-Con., Haifa, Dr J. Schmidt
Holland: V.-Con., Haifa, A. Leon
Italy: Consular Agent, 'Akká and Haifa, N. Datody
USA.: Consular Agent, Haifa, J. Schumacher*

PALESTINE

British Military Administration

Chief Administrators

Mar. 1918 Maj.-Gen. Arthur W. Money*
July 1919 Gen. Sir Harry Watson*
Nov. 1919 Gen. Sir Louis Bols

Military Governor of Phoenicia (Haifa)

1918–20 Col. Edward A. Stanton*

British Mandate

High Commissioners

30 June 1920 Sir Herbert Samuel*
Sept. 1925 Lord Herbert Plumer*
Dec. 1928 Sir John Chancellor
Jan. 1932 Sir Arthur Wauchope
June 1938 Sir Harold MacMichael

District Commissioners/Governors of Northern District (Haifa)

1920 Lt-Col. G. S. Symes*
1925 Lt-Col. A. Abramson
1928 Ernest F. Colvile
1931 E. Keith-Roach
1937 Morris Bailey

Chief Secretaries

1920 Sir Wyndham Deedes*
1922 Sir Gilbert Clayton*
1925 Lt-Col. G. S. Symes*
1928 H. C. Luke*
1930 M. A. Young
1933 J. Hathorn Hall
1937 W. D. Battershill
1939 J. S. McPherson

APPENDIX II

Biographical Notes

'Abbás-Qulí Khán a member of the Navváb family, b. 1864. Interpreter at British Legation 1885–1901. Asst Oriental Sec. 1 Apr. 1901. Head of Oriental Chancery 1908. ret. 1929. d. 21 Oct. 1938.

Abbott, Keith Edward British consular official. Appointed Con. Ṭihrán 22 July 1841. Con. Tabríz 24 Apr. 1842 – 23 Oct. 1845, and 10 May 1845 – 5 Apr. 1847. Then returned to Ṭihrán as Con. Made tour of Caspian Sea coast 1 Nov. 1847 – 17 Feb. 1848. Tour of southern Persia 1 Oct. 1849 – 27 June 1850. Left Ṭihrán for Tabríz 22 Aug. 1850, where he was to complete the report on his tour of southern Persia. On the way he visited the siege of Zanján (see p. 118). On leave in England 22 Aug. 1850 – 16 Nov. 1853. Con. Tabríz 22 Apr. 1854 until outbreak of war with Persia. Reappointed Con.-Gen. Tabríz 10 July 1857. Con.-Gen. Odessa 1 July 1868. d. 28 Apr. 1873. Disliked Persia, of which he wrote, 'A country I would fain have avoided' and 'this wretched country'.

Abela, Pietro Dragoman of the V.-Consulate in Haifa and also Lloyd's Agent. Was in charge of V.-Consulate on a number of occasions from 1900 to 1903 and from 12 Jan. 1904 – 1 Apr. 1909. On 1 Apr. 1909 he was appointed V.-Con. Haifa. d. 29 Mar. 1911.

Abu'l-Ḥasan Mírzá, Ḥájí Shaykhu'r-Ra'ís was the son of Muḥammad-Taqí Mírzá, Ḥisámu's-Salṭanih, uncle of Muḥammad Sháh, and was born in Tabríz in 1848. He studied in Ṭihrán under Mullá 'Alíy-i-Núrí. At the age of 14 his father died and his relatives coerced him to attend the Military College in Ṭihrán, but after two years he left for Mashhad where he discarded his princely clothes and donned the garb of the 'ulamá. Here he studied theology and religious jurisprudence as well as philosophy under the learned mujtahids gathered there. He then travelled to the Holy Shrines in Iraq and after further studies received from the leading mujtahid of that era, Ḥájí Mírzá Muḥammad-Ḥasan-i-Shírází (Mírzáy-i-Shírází), the rank of Mujtahid. He went on pilgrimage to Mecca and after a further period in Iraq, he returned to Mashhad. It was at about this time that he began to study the Bahá'í writings and became a believer, although it is said that his first introduction to the Faith was through his mother who had come to believe in the Báb many years previously. It was not until years later when he met 'Abdu'l-Bahá however, that his belief was confirmed. He incurred the enmity of the Governor of Khurásán, Áṣafu'd-Dawlih, and in about the year 1885 had to leave Khurásán whence he proceeded to 'Ishqábád and Istanbul. Through the intervention of Mu'ínu'l-Mulk, the Persian Ambassador in Istanbul, Ḥájí Shaykhu'r-Ra'ís was enabled to return to Ṭihrán, and with an order from the Prime Minister, Amínu's-Sulṭán, he proceeded to Mashhad. The 'ulamá of Mashhad arose against him once more, however, despite the orders of Amínu's-Sulṭán, and he was imprisoned and in 1892 left for 'Ishqábád and Istanbul once more. Here in Istanbul, he came into the circle of Siyyid Jamálu'd-Dín, and it was to promote the latter's ideas of Pan-Islamic unity that Ḥájí

Shaykhu'r-Ra'ís wrote one of his most famous works, *Ittiḥádu'l-Islám*. From Istanbul he proceeded to 'Akká, where he stayed for some time, meeting regularly with 'Abdu'l-Bahá. In 1894 he arrived in Bombay, and the following year proceeded to Persia where he settled in Shíráz. In 1902, he was forced to leave Shíráz following the riots there against Shu'á'u's-Salṭanih whom Ḥájí Shaykhu'r-Ra'ís supported. He then came to Iṣfahán where after a few months he was again forced to leave and went to Ṭihrán. Here he settled down for the remainder of his life, barring one journey to Khurásán and 'Ishqábád. When he died in 1918, he had arranged for his body to be taken to Mashhad for burial but Mullá Muḥammad Áqázádih refused to permit the desecration of Mashhad by the burial there of a known Bahá'í and threatened to burn the body if it was brought. It was therefore buried at Sháh 'Abdu'l-'Aẓím near the grave of Náṣiru'd-Dín Sháh. Ḥájí Shaykhu'r-Ra'ís was also an accomplished poet, using the pen-name Ḥayrat.

Adams, Rev. Isaac, MD b. Sangar, near Urúmíyyih, 1872, ed. at schools of the American missionaries in and around Urúmíyyih. In 1889 travelled to America where he lectured on Persia and raised money. Returned to Persia, having become an American citizen, 1894.

Aganoor, Dr Minas Stephen Peter physician and consular officer, b. 13 Feb. 1862. Son of Stephen Aganoor (q.v.). Qualified in medicine, MB, CM (Edinburgh 1884). Had a thriving medical practice in Iṣfahán as well as being physician to Ẓillu's-Sulṭán. Employed at Consulate-Gen. in Iṣfahán from 14 Dec. 1896 (i.e. from death of his father). Pro-Con. 1897–1907. On numerous occasions was Acting Con.: 1899–1901, 1903, 1905, 1906 and 1908. Con. Iṣfahán 1907. d. 1 Oct. 1930.

Aganoor, Stephen P. an Armenian merchant who, having been educated in Calcutta, spoke and wrote English well. Appointed British Agent in Iṣfahán 21 May 1858, and continued in this capacity until his death, although from 1891 there was also a British Consul in Iṣfahán. d. 14 Dec. 1896.

Ájúdán-Báshí *see* pp. 169–71.

'Alí-Akbar, Ḥájí Mírzá, Qavámu'l-Mulk (Strength of the Kingdom), b. 1789, younger son of Ḥájí Ibráhím Khán, the first Prime Min. of Fatḥ-'Alí Sháh. Became Kalántar of Shíráz 1811. Biglár-Bigí of Fárs 1840. Vazír of Fárs 1853. Appointed Guardian of the Shrine of Imám Riḍá at Mashhad 1862. d. Mashhad 1865. One of the most powerful magnates of Fárs.

'Alí-Aṣghar Khán, Mírzá, Amínu's-Sulṭán (Trusted of the King), Atábik-i-A'ẓam (Supreme Minister). Born *c.* 1859. Son of Áqá Ibráhím, Amínu's-Sulṭán, one of Náṣiru'd-Dín Shah's most trusted ministers. When his father died in 1883, Mírzá 'Alí-Aṣghar Khán inherited both his title and his posts: Minister of the Court – in charge of the Mint, the Customs and the Central Granary. He was aged 24 at this time. Within a few years, after the death of Mustawfíyu'l-Mamálik, Amínu's-Sulṭán became virtually Prime Minister, although he did not in fact acquire the title until 1888. He continued to be Prime Minister until 1903 with only a short break, 1897–8. Amínu's-Sulṭán is particularly remembered for sinking Persia deeper into debt with foreign powers, for the granting of the disastrous Tobacco Concession and his opposition to all pressure for reform. In 1903, after a violent campaign by his enemies, he was dislodged from his position and exiled abroad. On his accession in 1907, Muḥammad-'Alí Sháh asked Amínu's-Sulṭán to return as Prime Minister but this ministry lasted only a few months before he was assassinated, as a result of his opposition to reform, by 'Abbás Áqá on 31 Aug. 1907. He was aged 49 at the time of his death.

'Alí Khán, Ḥájí, Amínu'd-Dawlih (Trusted of the State), b. 1844. Served Náṣiru'd-Dín Sháh as Priv. Sec. and head of Council of Ministers. Shortly after Muẓaffaru'd-Dín Sháh came to the throne, Amínu'd-Dawlih was made Prime Min. (June 1897). He had a sincere desire to initiate reforms but failed to obtain a loan from the British for the Sháh's European journey and was dismissed in July 1898. Retired to Rasht where he died in May 1904.

'Alí Khán, Ḥájí, Ḥájibu'd-Dawlih of Marághih, a cruel and unprincipled man. Entered Muḥammad Sháh's service when the latter was Governor of Marághih and rose to become Chief Steward of the royal household. Was at one time disgraced and fell from favour but later regained his position through the influence of Muḥammad Sháh's wife, Malik-Jáhán Khánum. Appointed Farrásh-Báshí in 1265/1848–9 at suggestion of Mírzá Taqí Khán, whom he repaid in 1852 by supervising his execution when he had fallen from power. For this latter act he was given title of Ḥájibu'd-Dawlih. Was put in charge, together with Maḥmúd Khán, the Kalántar, of arresting, torturing and executing the Bábís following the attempt on the life of the Sháh. Is perhaps best known by Bahá'ís as the man responsible for the execution of Ṭáhirih. d. *c.* 1867. Dr Polak refers to him as 'a man without heart and, on command, ready for any cruelty.' (*Persien* Vol. 1, p. 352)

'Alí-Naqí Mírzá, Ruknu'd-Dawlih (Pillar of the State), son of Muḥammad-Taqí Mírzá, Ruknu'd-Dawlih (q.v.). Held the title 'Aynu'l-Mulk until his father's death in 1901 when he became Ruknu'd-Dawlih. Gov. of Khurásán 1903–4, Kirmán 1904–5, Khurásán 1907–8 and 1909–12.

'Álí Páshá, Muḥammad Amín (Mehmed Emin) Turkish statesman, b. Istanbul Feb. 1815, the son of a shopkeeper. Obtained knowledge of French and was appointed to translation dept. of the Imp. Díván 1833. Was sent on several foreign missions. Counsellor at London 1838. Ambass. London 1841. Counsellor in For. Ministry 1845. For. Min. 1846. Grand Vazír 1852 (for two months). For. Min. 1854, 1857–8, 1861–7. Grand Vazír 1855–6, 1858–9, 1861, 1867–71. He was regarded as authoritarian and overbearing, but was one of the pillars of the Tanẓímát (Reform) Movt. d. Bebek 7 Sept. 1871.

William Howard Russell who accompanied the Prince of Wales in his tour of the Eastern Mediterranean in 1869 has written (*A Diary in the East* p. 475): 'Aali Pasha is a very small, slight, sallow-faced man, with two very penetrating honest-looking eyes. He has a delicate air, and looks timorous and nervous; and his standing attitude is one of rather imbecile deference to everybody, but in the presence of the Sultan this becomes almost prostration. Yet, he is courageous, bold, enlightened, honest and just; full of zeal for the interests of his country, and unceasing in his efforts for its improvement.'

Alison, Charles British diplomat. Employed for some years at Consulate-General in Albania and at Istanbul. Oriental Sec. Istanbul 13 Dec. 1844. Sec. of Embassy 20 Feb. 1857. Min. Ṭihrán 7 Apr. 1860. d. Ṭihrán 27 Apr. 1872.

Allenby, Gen. (later Field Marshal) Sir Edmund Henry Hynman (1861–1936), 1st Viscount Allenby, British soldier, C.-in-C. Egyptian Exped. Force 1917. High Commsr Egypt 1919–25.

Amín Arslan, Amír son of Majíd Arslan. Lebanese Druze journalist and Con. for Turkish Empire. Studied at the Jesuit school in Beirut and later in Paris, where he founded and edited several Arabic newspapers. Ottoman Con.-Gen. Brussels and Buenos Aires. d. Buenos Aires 1943.

Amínu'd-Dawlih *see* 'Alí Khán, Ḥájí

Amínu's-Sulṭán *see* 'Alí-Aṣghar Khán

Amír-Niẓám *see* pp. 160–65.

Andreas, Friedrich Carl (1846–1930), oriental scholar. Contributed principally to early Iranian philology. Became Professor of Oriental Philology at Göttingen. His wife, Lou Andreas-Salomé, was famous as a close friend of Nietzche.

Áqá Khán, Mírzá, *see* pp. 165–7.

Áqásí, Ḥájí Mírzá *see* pp. 154–6.

Arbuthnot, Rev. Robert Keith British clergyman. ed. Trin. Coll. Dublin, BA 1861, ordained deacon 1861, priest 1862. Curate of Kempton, Herts., 1864–9, Vicar of Semperington with Pointon, Lincs., 1869–74, Holbeach, 1874–80. Vicar of St James, Ratcliff, London, 1880. Died *c.* 1894.

Arfa'u'd-Dawlih *see* Riḍá Khán, Mírzá

Arnold (later Sir) Arthur British politician, b. 28 May 1833. ed. privately. MP Salford (Lib.) 1880–83. Chairman of London County Council 1895–7. Kt. 1895. d. 20 May 1902.

Asadu'lláh-i-Rashtí, Siyyid *see* p. 271n.

Áṣafu'd-Dawlih *see* Ghulám-Riḍá Khán

Ashbee, Charles Robert British architect, b. Isleworth 17 May 1863. ed. Wellington Sch. and King's Coll. Cambridge. Architect, designer and town-planner. Civic Adviser to Palestine Admin. (Military, later Civil) 1918–22. Master of Art Workers' Guild 1929. Founder of Essex House Press. Many publications particularly on architecture. d. 23 May 1942.

Atherton, Gertrude Franklin (née Horn) American author, b. San Francisco 30 Oct. 1857. ed. Sayre Institute, Lexington, Ky. Wrote many novels from 1892–1940, the most popular being *The Conqueror*. d. 14 June 1948.

'Azíz Khán a Sunní Kurd of the Mukrí tribe, born *c.* 1792. He entered the army of Muḥammad Sháh as Major. He was present at the siege of Herat. Later he came under the influence of a darvísh, Mírzá Naẓar-'Alí. He was sent to Shíráz several times to quell disturbances there. Under Mírzá Taqí Khán, 'Azíz Khán rose to Ájúdán-Báshíy-i-Kull and was directly responsible to Mírzá Taqí Khán for all matters relating to the army. In 1850, he was sent on a mission to greet Grand Duke Alexander in the Caucasus and was given responsibility to deal with the Bábí upheaval at Zanján. When the fall of Mírzá Taqí Khán occurred, 'Azíz Khán was unaffected because of the Sháh's approval of him. In 1852 he became Sardár-i-Kull and was made director of the Dáru'l-Funún (Military College) in Ṭihrán. Because of Mírzá Áqá Khán's enmity, 'Azíz Khán eventually fell from power, but on the former's dismissal he was reinstated. In about 1859, he was made Minister (*píshkár*) to Bahrám Mírzá, Governor of Ádharbáyján, and in 1861 fulfilled the same role for the new Governor, Muẓaffaru'd-Dín Mírzá. A little later, he was brought to Ṭihrán as Minister of War and Commander of the Army, leaving Mírzá Qahramán as his deputy in Ádharbáyján. 'Azíz Khán was held responsible for the latter's embezzlement of army funds, stripped of his office and exiled in 1868. Although reinstated as Minister of Ádharbáyján in 1870, he was not able to exert his previous authority. He died in Jan. 1871. Eastwick describes him thus: 'He is a large brawny man, with blood-shot eyes, and inflamed features, and did not strike me as one who would err on the side of leniency.' (*Three Years' Residence in Persia* Vol. 1, p. 186.) Ferrier, who spent four months with 'Azíz Khán besieged by rioters in the citadel of Shíráz in 1848, writes of him: 'He is an ignorant Kurd, . . . not possessing even the simplest and first elements of the military art; a great embezzler, perfidious to excess, a gambler, debauched, and having the talent to make for himself a reputation for bravery although he always arrives at the end of the battle.' (Ferrier 'Situation de la Perse' p. 153)

Balloy, Marie-René-Davy de Chavigne de French diplomat and lawyer, b. 7 Apr. 1845. 3rd Sec. Peking 1871. Acting 2nd Sec. Ṭihrán 17 Oct. 1873. 2nd Sec. Ṭihrán 2 June 1874. Chevalier de la Légion d'honneur 1875. Chargé d'Affaires 28 Sept. 1875 – 30 Oct. 1876. 1st Sec. Tokyo 5 Dec. 1877. Min. Plen. (2nd Class) in charge of the Legation at Ṭihrán 3 Oct. 1881. Min. Ṭihrán 2 Mar. 1882. Officier de la Légion d'honneur 7 July 1885. Min. Plen. (1st Class) 1 Nov. 1886. At Ṭihrán until 9 Aug. 1898.

Barbier de Meynard, Charles-Adrien-Casimir (1826–1908), French orientalist. Went to Jerusalem as Dragoman to the French Consulate 1850–51. Paid Attaché Persia 1854–6. Taught Turkish at École des langues orientales vivantes 1863. Prof. of Persian, Collège de France 1876. Pres. of Société Asiatique 1892. Director of École des langues orientales vivantes 1898. Officer of Légion d'honneur 1884.

Barclay, Sir George Head (1862–1921), British diplomat. Entered Diplomatic Service 1886. 2nd Sec. Istanbul 1898. 1st Sec. Tokyo 1902. Counsellor 1905. Istanbul 1906. Min. Ṭihrán 1 Sept. 1908, Bucharest 24 Mar. 1912. KCMG 1908. KCSI 1913. ret. 1919.

Barker, S. Louie British missionary. Was Deaconess at Mildmay. Accepted as missionary by CMS 1889. Departed for Palestine 4 Dec. 1890. Hon. Missionary 'Akká 1890–91, Haifa 1891. Resigned 1899. Married Rev. R. B. Miller 1900. d. Woking 25 July 1931.

Bax Ironside see Ironside, H. G. O. Bax

Bayley, Charles Clive (1864–1923). ed. Harrow and Trinity Coll. Cambridge. Worked for Colonial Off. in Nigeria 1894–9. Con. New York 1899, Warsaw 1908, Moscow 1913. Returned to New York 29 Sept. 1915. ret. on pension 31 July 1919.

Benjamin, Samuel Greene Wheeler American author, artist and diplomat, b. Argos, Greece, 13 Feb. 1837 of missionary parents. ed. English Coll. Smyrna. Later studied Art. Asst Librarian, New York State Library, Albany, 1861–4. Opened studio in Boston as a marine painter and wrote extensively on Art. 1st American Min. to Persia 1883–5. d. 19 July 1914.

Bethune, Major-General Sir Henry Lindesay- Scottish artillery officer of Kilconquhar, Fifeshire, b. 1787. Came to Persia in 1810 with Sir John Malcolm's Mission. Remained in Persia to help train 'Abbás Mírzá's Army. Returned to Persia as Major in 1834 to help Muḥammad Sháh secure his throne. Played a major part in the defeat of the two pretenders, Ẓillu's-Sulṭán and the Farmán-Farmá. Less happy was Bethune's participation in the campaign against Herat in 1836, when he was eventually asked by the Sháh to leave the Persian Army. Bethune returned to Persia in 1850 and died at Ṭihrán on 19 Feb. 1851. His rank in the Persian Army was that of General, in command of Artillery (Amír-i-Túpkhánih).

Biddulph, Maj.-Gen. (later Gen. Sir) Robert British soldier and colonial administrator, b. London 26 Aug. 1835. ed. Roy. Mil. Acad. Woolwich. Served in Crimean War and Indian Mutiny. Priv. Sec. to Cardwell at War Off. 1871. Col. 1872. On special service to Cyprus 1878. Proceeded to Istanbul to settle financial terms of Anglo-Turkish Convention. High Commsr of Cyprus 23 June 1879 – 9 Mar. 1886. Gen. 1892. QMG 1893. Gov. and C.-in-C. Gibraltar 1893–1900. KCMG 1880, GCMG 1886, GCB 1899. d. London 18 Nov. 1918.

Biggs, Jessie English missionary, b. Brentwood 13 Dec. 1865. Accepted as CMS missionary 17 June 1902, proceeded to Yazd 3 Oct. 1902. Moved to Iṣfahán 1908. ret. due to ill health 28 Jan. 1931. d. Berlin 17 July 1931.

Binning, Robert Blair Munro Indian civil servant. Entered Madras Civil Service 1833, and occupied various posts. At the time of his journey through Persia, he was Sub-Collector and Joint Magistrate of the Northern Division of Arcot, and this appears to be the highest post he achieved, for in 1856 he proceeded on furlough to England, and in 1861, while still in England, he resigned the service. He died in England shortly thereafter.

Bixby, Rev. James Thompson American Unitarian clergyman and author, b. Barre, Mass., 30 July 1843, ed. Harvard and Leipzig. Prof. of Religious History, Meadville Theol. Sch. 1879–83. Pastor Yonkers, NY 1887. d. 26 Dec. 1921.

Bliss, Rev. Edwin Elisha missionary of the American Board of Commsrs for For. Missions, b. Putney, Vt. 12 Apr. 1817. ed. Amherst Coll. Missionary at Trabizond 1843, Istanbul 1856–92. d. Istanbul 20 Dec. 1892.

Blunt, (later Sir) John Elijah British consular official, b. 14 Oct. 1832. ed. Kensington Grammar Sch. Joined Consular Service 1850. Served in Crimean War as chief interpreter to the Cav. Div. 1854–5. V.-Con. Volo 1855, Uscup 1857, Philippopolis 1860–62, Adrianople 1 Nov. 1862. Con. Monastir 13 Feb. 1872. Con. Salonika and Monastir 1872. Con.-Gen. 1878. Con. (with rank of Con.-Gen.) Boston 1899. ret. 1902. Kt. 1902. d. 19 June 1916.

Blunt, Wilfred Scawen (1840–1922), English poet and traveller. After extensive travels in the Near East and India, he wrote several books in support of liberal and nationalist movements in Islamic countries, and in particular the revolt of 'Urábí Pá<u>sh</u>á. Also the author of several volumes of poems.

Bois, Jules French literary critic, b. Marseilles 1871. Achieved distinction as a literary critic, contributing to such periodicals as *Annales Politiques et Littéraires*, *Revue Blanche*, *Revue de Revues*, *Le Temps*, etc. Was noted as popularizer of various movements such as feminism, and also psychic and spiritual matters. Abandoned literary activities to pursue religious and spiritualist thought in 1913.

Borg, Raphael British consular official. Supernumerary Clerk to Consular Court at Alexandria, 1863. Chancellery Clerk Cairo 1865. Acting Con. Cairo 19 June – 12 Nov. 1868 and on several other occasions. V.-Con. Cairo 1880. Con. 1884. CMG 1895. Acting Con. Alexandria 1895. Con. Cairo 1900. d. 23 Jan. 1903.

Bourée, Nicolas-Prosper French diplomat, b. Boulogne 26 Mar. 1811. Entered service of French For. Off. 1836. Con. Beirut 1840–50. Chargé Morocco 1851. Min. China 1852. Chargé Turkey 1853–4. Min. Plen. Persia 9 May 1855 – 15 Oct. 1856. Mission to Germany. Min. Greece, Portugal. Ambass. Istanbul 28 Oct. 1866 – 9 July 1870. Nominated Sen. 20 June 1870. ret. 21 Jan. 1872. d. 9 July 1886.

Briand, Aristide (1862–1932) French statesman. Was several times Prime Min. of France: 1909–11, 1913, 1921–2, 1925–6, 1929. Head of Coalition Govt. 1915–17. Min. of For. Aff. 1925–32. Awarded Nobel Peace Prize 1926.

Bridgeman, Reginald Francis Orlando British diplomat, b. 14 Oct. 1888. ed. Harrow Sch. Attaché Madrid 1903. Clerk For. Off. 1904. Held various diplomatic positions including posts at the Paris and Athens Embassies. Was sent to Ṭihrán as Counsellor Nov. 1920. Chargé d'Affaires 1 Oct. 1921. Returned to London Mar. 1922, having incurred Curzon's displeasure. In much the same way as Norman, he was forced to give up his diplomatic career. Was several times prospective Lab. MP. Sec. of League against Imperialism 1933–7. d. 11 Dec. 1968.

Browne, Edward Granville British oriental scholar, b. Uley, Gloucestershire, 7 Feb. 1862. ed. Eton and Pembroke Coll. Cambridge. Graduated in Medicine after attending St Bartholomew's Hosp. London. He had acquired an intense interest in oriental languages and in 1887, when he was elected a Fellow of Pembroke Coll., he gave up Medicine in favour of

Oriental Studies. Visited Persia 1887–8, about which he wrote *A Year Amongst the Persians*. His first work in the field of Oriental Studies was on the Bábí and Bahá'í religions, and in 1890 he visited both Ṣubḥ-i-Azal in Cyprus and Bahá'u'lláh in 'Akká. He was appointed Univ. Lecturer in Persian, and in 1902 became the Sir Thomas Adams's Professor of Arabic. Apart from his writings on the Bábí and Bahá'í religions, he published important work on Persian literature and politics. He was actively and enthusiastically involved in the Persian Constitutional Movt, and his home was a refuge for many fleeing Persian liberals. d. Cambridge 5 Jan. 1926. (See fig. 4.)

Bruce, Rev. Robert British missionary, b. Charleville, Co. Cork, 1833. ed. Trin. Coll. Dublin, BA 1857, MA 1868, DD 1882. Ordained Deacon 1858, Priest 1858. Went to India as CMS missionary, Amritsar and Deejerat. In 1868, he returned to England and was given permission to go to Persia with a view to studying Persian and translating the New Testament. Arrived Julfá, Iṣfahán, 1869. Remained in Persia and in 1875 the CMS formally recognized him as missionary in Julfá, Iṣfahán. ret. 1893. Lecturer in Persian at University Coll. London 1896. Vicar of St Nicholas, Durham, 1896, Little Dean, Gloucester, 1903. d. Little Dean 28 Sept. 1912. (See fig. 31.)

Bulwer, William Henry Lytton Earle Baron Dalling and Bulwer. British diplomat, b. London 13 Feb 1801. ed. Harrow, Trinity and Downing Coll. Cambridge. Published poems 1822. In Army 1825–9. Entered Diplomatic Service 1829. MP for Wilton 1830, Coventry 1831, Marylebone 1835. Sec. of Legation Brussels 1835, Chargé 1835–9. Sec. of Embassy Istanbul 14 Aug. 1837. Ambass. Madrid 1843. Ambass. Washington 1849. Min. Florence 1852. Ambass. Istanbul 10 May 1858 – Aug. 1865. ret. 1865. MP Tamworth 1868. KCB 1848. GCB 1851. Created Baron Dalling and Bulwer 1871. d. Naples 23 May 1872.

Butler, (later Sir) Geoffrey G. entered For. Off. as Temp. Clerk 1915. Accompanied Balfour on Special Mission to USA (May–June 1916) and then became Director of British Bureau of Information in New York. Resigned 15 Apr. 1919. CBE Jan. 1918, KBE Jan. 1919.

Campbell, Rev. Reginald John (1867–1956), English clergyman (originally Congregational, then Church of England). Min. of City Temple London 1903–15; Chancellor of Chichester Cathedral 1930. Author of many books.

Canning, Sir Stratford later Viscount Stratford de Redcliffe, (1786–1880), eminent British diplomat. First visit to Istanbul 1808, with Adair's Mission. Appointed Min. at Istanbul 1809–12, Switzerland 1814, Washington 1820. Special Envoy to St Petersburg 1824, Istanbul 1826–7. MP 1828–41. Ambass. to Istanbul 1841–58. Became known as the 'Great Elchi' because of the manner in which he dominated the Ottoman Govt.

Carless, Rev. Henry British missionary, b. Richmond 1860. ed. King's Coll. Sch. and Corpus Christi Coll. Cambridge. Ordained Priest 1887. Curate of Deane, Lancs. 1886–8. Accepted by CMS as a missionary 5 Oct. 1888. Left for Julfá, Persia, 22 Oct. 1888. Kirmán 1896. d. Kirmán, 25 May 1898.

Carpenter, John Estlin eminent Unitarian Biblical scholar, b. Ripley, Surrey, 5 Oct. 1844. ed. University Coll. Sch. and University Coll. London. Served as a minister in Bristol and Leeds for 9 years. Prof. of Ecclesiastical History, Comparative Religion and Hebrew at Manchester New Coll., London 1875. V.-Principal of this institution 1889, and involved in its transfer to Oxford as Manchester Coll. Principal of Manchester Coll. 1906–15. Wilde Lecturer in Comparative Religion at Univ. of Oxford 1914–24. Author of numerous works on Biblical scholarship and comparative religion. d. Oxford 2 June 1927.

Chamberlain, Sir (Joseph) Austen (1863–1937), British statesman. Son of Joseph Chamberlain and half-brother of Neville Chamberlain. Held several Ministerial posts. Sec. of State for Foreign Affairs 1924–9. Nobel Peace Prize 1925.

Chaplin, Dr Thomas British medical missionary, born *c.* 1830. Graduated from Guy's Hosp. Med. Sch. MRCS, LSA 1853. MD (St Andrew's) 1858. Until 1860 he was Resident Med. Officer at the Bloomsbury Dispensary, London. In 1860 he proceeded to Jerusalem as chief medical missionary at the Jerusalem Hosp. of the London Jews' Soc. where he remained until his retirement in 1885. In addition to his medical duties, he was closely connected with the setting up and administration of the Palestine Exploration Fund and was one of the principal antiquarian and archaeological authorities in the Holy Land, After his return from Palestine, he was appointed Inspector of Missions of the London Jews' Society 1886–92, and also served on both the General and Executive Committee of the Palestine Exploration Fund. ret. from all his activities in 1902. d. St Leonards-on-Sea 20 Sept. 1904. (See fig. 24.)

Cheyne, Prof. Thomas Kelly eminent British Biblical scholar, b. London 18 Sept. 1841. ed. Merchant Taylor's Sch., Göttingen Univ. and Worcester Coll. Oxford. Ordained priest 1864. Elected Fellow of Balliol Coll. Oxford 1868–82. Oriel Prof. of the Interpretation of Scripture at Oxford 1885–1908. Initiated in England the critical movement in the study of the Old Testament. His *Encyclopaedia Biblica* (edited in collaboration with Dr Sutherland Black) remains to this day a standard work. His first wife, Frances Godfrey, died 1907, and he married in 1911 Elizabeth Gibson, a poet and mystic. d. Oxford 16 Feb. 1915. (See fig. 11.)

Chick, Herbert George British consular official, b. 19 Nov. 1882. Exhibitioner at Gonville and Caius Coll. Cambridge 1900. Student Interpreter in the Levant 1 Oct. 1903. Asst 1905. Acting V.-Con. Búshihr 8 Dec. 1906. V.-Con. Búshihr 1 Jan. 1909. Served in the 1st World War 1914–18. Employed at For. Off. 1918–19 and Morocco 1919–20. Con. Shíráz 24 Mar. 1921. Con.-Gen. Salonika 5 Apr. 1930. ret. 1933. Author of *A Chronicle of the Carmelites in Persia* (1939), published anonymously. d. 21 May 1951.

Chirol, Sir (Ignatius) Valentine British journalist, b. 23 May 1852. ed. Sorbonne. Clerk in For. Off. 1872–6. Travelled through Middle East as correspondent of the *Morning Standard*, journeying through Persia in 1884 and visiting Haifa in 1885. Joined staff of *The Times* as correspondent in Berlin 1892. Head of Foreign Dept. of *The Times* 1899–1912. ret. and Kt. 1912. On the outbreak of the 1st World War, he served as adviser to the For. Off. d. 23 Oct. 1929.

Christensen, Prof. Arthur (1875–1945), Prof. of Iranian Philology at Univ. of Copenhagen 1916.

Churchill, George Percy British diplomatic and consular official, b. 14 Aug. 1877. Acting Or. Sec. Ṭihrán 7 Apr. 1903. 2nd Sec. 7 Apr. 1916. Employed at For. Off. 11 Mar. 1919. Con.-Gen. Algiers 20 Oct. 1926. CBE 1924. ret. 30 Sept. 1937. d. 15 Mar. 1973. Brother of S. J. A. Churchill (q.v.).

Churchill, Sidney John Alexander British diplomatic and consular official, b. 1 Mar. 1862. ed. privately. Entered service of Govt. of India 1880, in Persian Telegraph Dept. Oriental 2nd Sec. Ṭihrán 9 July 1886. In attendance on the Sháh during visit to England 1889. Con. Dutch and French Guiana 1894, Palermo 1898, Naples 1900. Con.-Gen. Naples 1912 until his death 11 Jan. 1921. While in Persia 1880–94, he collected for the British Museum a fine selection of Persian, Arabic and Turkish manuscripts. Included amongst these are several important Bahá'í manuscripts. Brother of G. P. Churchill (q.v.).

Clarendon, 4th Earl of, George William Frederick Villiers (1800–1870), British statesman, For. Sec. 1853–8, 1865–6 and 1868–70.

Clauson, (later Sir) Gerard Leslie Makins British civil servant, b. 28 April 1891. ed. Eton and Corpus Christi Coll. Oxford. During War served in War Off., Gallipoli, Egypt and Mesopotamia. Capt. 1915. Entered Colonial Off. as Clerk 2nd Class 1919. Principal 1920. Asst Sec. 1934. Asst Under-Sec. of State 1940. Accredited rep. to Permanent Mandates Commission of League of Nations from 1926. KCMG 1945, ret. 1951. d. 1 May 1974.

Clayton, Gen. (later Sir) Gilbert Falkingham British soldier and colonial administrator, b. Ryde, Isle of Wight, 6 July 1875. ed. Isle of Wight Coll. Ryde and Roy. Mil. Acad. Woolwich. Served in Nile Exped. 1898. Joined Egyptian Army 1900. Capt. 1901. Priv. Sec. to Gov.-Gen. of Sudan 1908. ret. from Army 1910. Entered Sudan Govt. service. Director of Mil. Intelligence Cairo 1914. Brig.-Gen. and Chief Polit. Officer of Egyptian Exped. Force 1917. Was responsible for administration of occupied Turkish territories. Adviser to Egyptian Ministry of Interior 1919. Chief Sec. Palestine Govt. 1922–5. High Commsr Iraq 1929. KBE 1919, KCMG 1926. d. Baghdád 11 Sept. 1929.

Clerk, (later Sir) George Russell (1874–1951), British diplomat. Entered For. Off. 1898. Senior Clerk 1913. Ambass. Prague 1919, Ankara 1926, Brussels 1933, Paris 1934. ret. 1937.

Clive, Sir Robert British diplomat, b. 27 Dec. 1877. ed. Haileybury and Magdalen Coll. Oxford. Entered Diplomatic Service 1902. Min. Ṭihrán 1926–31, Holy See 1933–4, Japan 1934–7, Belgium 1937–9. KCMG 1927, GCMG 1936, PC 1934. d. 13 May 1948.

Cloquet, Dr Ernest French physician. Arrived in Persia May 1846 to act as the Sháh's personal physician. On Muḥammad Sháh's death, he continued to act in this capacity for Náṣiru'd-Dín Sháh. He died of accidental poisoning in Ṭihrán in 1855 and was buried at Akbarábád.

Cobham, Claude Delaval British colonial administrator, b. 1842. ed. Rugby and Univ. Coll. Oxford. BA 1866. BCL and MA 1869. Asst Commsr Larnaca 1 Oct. 1878. Commsr Larnaca 18 Mar. 1879. Acting Chief Sec. on 3 occasions. Acting Chief Collector of Taxes 1886. Author of several books on Cyprus.

Coote, Catherine C. British missionary, born *c.* 1867. Resident of Tunbridge Wells, Kent. Proceeded to Palestine as independent missionary 1891. Arrived to assist in 'Akká Nov. 1891. Accepted by CMS as Hon. Missionary. Appointed to Ramleh 7 Feb. 1893. Resigned 1894.

Cormick, Dr William British physician. The son of Dr John Cormick of County Tipperary, Ireland, a physician who had come to Persia in the suite of Sir John Malcolm and then became attached to 'Abbás Mírzá (Muḥammad Sháh's father) at Tabríz. William Cormick was born in Tabríz in 1820. He was sent by his father to England to study Medicine at University Coll. London, where he qualified MRCS in July 1840, LSA 1841 and MD (St Andrew's) 1841. He returned to Persia in 1844, and was appointed physician to the British Mission. When Náṣiru'd-Dín Mírzá was appointed Gov. of Ádharbáyján, Cormick accompanied him to Tabríz as his personal physician. On Muḥammad Sháh's death and Náṣiru'd-Dín's accession to the throne, Cormick came with him to Ṭihrán. This was, however, against Mírzá Taqí Khán's policy of not becoming dependent on either Britain or Russia, and Dr Cormick was replaced by Dr Cloquet, a Frenchman. Cormick returned to

Tabríz where he practised for many years. FRCS Oct. 1876. d. Tabríz 30 Dec. 1877.

Concerning him, Charles Burgess wrote in 1851: 'Dr Cormick is at Tabreez married to one of the most beautiful girls in the country; he has an income of about a thousand a year English money, besides the interest of his money in the funds. He is talking of asking for leave for England, to see the Great Exhibition and also pursue his medical studies in Europe. I ought to tell you that he has already passed his examinations as an apothecary surgeon and MD but medical study is his passion and he is actually thinking of getting leave for England for one or two years, by doing which he will have to give up his income all but two hundred pounds a year.' (Burgess *Letters from Persia* p. 112)

Cox, Sir Percy Zachariah British soldier and diplomat, b. Herongate, Essex, 20 Nov. 1864. ed. Harrow and Roy. Mil. Coll. Sandhurst. Commissioned to 2nd Cameronians in India 1884. Joined Indian Staff Corps 1889 and entered Polit. Dept. After several minor posts became Asst Polit. Resident in British Somaliland 1893. Polit. Agent and Con. at Muscat 1899–1904. Acting Polit. Res. and Con.-Gen. in Persian Gulf 1904–9. Res. 1909–14. Established ties with 'Abdu'l-'Azíz ibn Saud. Lt-Col. 1910. Chief Polit. Officer of Indian Exped. Force 'D' 1914–18. Acting Min. Ṭihrán 1918–20. High Commsr Iraq 1920–23. KCIE 1911, GCIE 1917, GCMG 1922. ret. Apr. 1923. d. Bedford 20 Feb. 1937.

Crewe-Milnes, Robert Offley Ashburton Marquess of Crewe, (1858–1945). Lord President of the Council 1905–8, 1915–16. Lord Privy Seal 1908–10, 1912–15.

Crow, Francis Edward (1863–1939), British consular official. Student Interpreter in the Levant 1885. Con. Baṣra 1903–17. Con.-Gen. Iṣfahán 1920–23, Salonika 1923–7. ret. 1927.

Curtis, William Eleroy American journalist, b. Akron, Ohio, 5 Nov. 1850. ed. Western Reserve Coll. Worked with several newspapers including *Chicago Record-Herald*. He specialized in S. American affairs. Wrote numerous books about his travels. d. 1911.

Curzon, George Nathaniel British statesman, b. Kedleston Hall, Derbyshire, 11 Jan. 1859. ed. Eton and Balliol Coll. Oxford. Travelled in Greece, Egypt, Turkey, 1882. Elected Fellow, All Souls Coll. Oxford. MP Southport 1886. Travelled in Persia 1889. Under-Sec. of State for India 1891–2. Under-Sec. of State for For. Aff. 1895–8. PC 1895. Viceroy of India 1898–1905. Lord Privy Seal 1915. Member of War Cabinet 1916–18. Min. for For. Aff. 1919–24. His bitterest disappointment came in 1923, when he was not asked to become Prime Minister. Created Earl Curzon of Kedleston, Viscount Scarsdale, 1911. Marquess 1921. d. London 20 Mar. 1925. Buried Westminster Abbey. He is remembered as one of the greatest of British statesmen.

Daukes, Lt (later Capt.) Clendon Turberville b. 24 Dec. 1879. Entered Army 1899. Lt 1900. Joined Indian Army 1901. Entered Polit. Dept. 1904. Acting Con. at Turbat-i-Ḥaydarí 1906–7. V.-Con. for Sístán and Qá'in 1907–9. Asst Polit. Agent, Chilas 1911–14, Fort Sandeman 1916–18. Special Mission to Persia 1918–19. Polit. Agent, Loralai 1921–7. Envoy to Nepal 1929–34. d. 1947.

Dawson, Brig.-Gen. Sir Douglas Frederick Rawdon (1854–1933), British soldier. Joined Coldstream Guards 1874. Master of Ceremonies to H.M. 1903–7. Registrar and Sec. of Order of Bath and Garter, later Registrar and Sec. of Central Chancery of Orders of Knighthood.

Decazes, Lois-Charles-Elié-Amadieu, Duc de Glücksberg (1819–86), French statesman. Min. of For. Aff. 1873–7.

Deedes, Brig.-Gen. Sir Wyndham Henry British soldier and administrator, b. 10 Mar. 1883. Mil. Attaché Istanbul 1918–19. Director-General of Public Security in Egypt 1919–20. Chief

Sec. of Palestine Admin. 1920–22. Created Kt. 1921. d. 2 Sept. 1956.

Dickson, Dr (later Sir) Joseph British physician, b. Tripoli, Libya. Was physician to the British Legation in Ṭihrán 1848–87. Accompanied Náṣiru'd-Dín Sháh in his first tour of Europe 1873.

Dieulafoy, Jane-Henriette-Paule-Rachel (née Magre), b. Toulouse 20 June 1851. Married the archaeologist Marcel Dieulafoy (1844–1920) in 1870. Accompanied husband on mission to Persia and Iraq 1880–87. She travelled dressed as a man in order to facilitate their journey. The Chaldean room at the Louvre was created as a result of the treasures brought back by these two. d. Château de Langlade (Hte.-Garonne) May 1916. (See fig. 2.)

Dobbs, Sir Henry Robert Conway (1871–1934), British colonial administrator. Entered Indian Civil Service 1890. Travelled across Persia 1902–3. Polit. Officer with Mesopotamian Exped. Force 1914–16. High Commssr for Iraq 1923–9. KCIE and KCSI 1921, KCMG 1925, GBE 1929.

Dolgorukov, Prince Dimitri Ivanovich Russian diplomat. He was a member of the famous Dolgorukov family who in the previous generation had almost succeeded in taking over the monarchy. Entered service of Moscow Provincial Govt. 1816. Later transferred to Diplomatic Service and was Secretary of Russian Legation in Madrid 1829–30, The Hague 1832–7, Naples 1838–42, Istanbul 1843–5. He was Chargé for a period at The Hague and Naples. He was appointed Russian Minister in Ṭihrán in June 1845, but did not arrive at his post until Jan. 1846. He remained at this post until May 1854, when he received an Imperial order to attend the Senate. Member of the Council of the Soc. of Arts. d. Moscow 31 Oct. 1867.

Dorn, Jean-Albert-Bernard German orientalist, b. Scheuerfeld, Coburg, 11 May 1805. ed. Univs. of Halle and Leipzig. Appointed Prof. at Charkow 1826, but did not take up appointment until 1829 after travelling through France and England. Appointed Prof. of the Hist. and Geog. of Asia at the Oriental Institute at St Petersburg 1835. Appointed Conservator of the Imp. Russian Library and Director of the Asiatic Museum 1843. Member of the Acad. of Sciences of St Petersburg. d. St Petersburg 31 May 1881.

Drouyn de Lhuys, Édouard (1805–81), French statesman. Min. for For. Aff. 1848–9, 1851, 1852–5, 1862–6.

Duff, Sir Mountstuart Elphinstone Grant (1829–1906), British statesman. Under-Sec. of State for India 1868–74, for Colonies 1880. Gov. of Madras 1881–6. His *Notes from a Diary* were published in 14 vols. and cover half a century.

Dumont, Charles-Albert-Auguste-Eugéne French scholar of Greek civilization, and archaeologist, b. Scey-sur-Saône 21 Jan. 1842. ed. La Roche-sur-Yon, Strasburg, and École normale supérieure, Paris. Worked at École d'Athènes, 1864–70. Mission to Thrace 1868. Participated in Franco-German War of 1870–71. Returned to Greece 1871. Founded École archéologique d'Athènes 1873, and was Director of it from 1875. Rector of Acadèmie de Grenoble 1878, and of Montpellier 1878. Director of Higher Education at Ministry of Education 1879. d. La Queue-les-Yvelines 11 Aug. 1884. The account of his journey to Adrianople is also recorded in his book *Le Balkan et l'Adriatique*.

Durand, Sir Henry Mortimer British diplomat, b. Sehore, Bhopal, India 14 Feb. 1850. Entered Bengal Civil Service 1870. Under-Sec. Indian For. Off. 1880. Indian For. Sec. 1885. Various Missions 1886–93. Min. Ṭihrán 1894. Ambass. Madrid 1900, Washington 1903. KCIE 1889, KCSI 1894, GCMG 1899. d. 8 Jan. 1924.

Eastwick, Edward Backhouse British oriental scholar, diplomat and MP, b. Warfield, Bucks. 13 Mar. 1814. ed. Charterhouse and Merton Coll. Oxford. Joined Indian Army 1836. Accompanied Pottinger to China 1842. Prof. of Urdu at the East India Company's College at Haileybury 1845. Sec. of Ṭihrán Legation 4 May 1860. Chargé d'Affaires 9 Dec. 1862 – 23 Jan. 1863. He had made charges against the British Minister at Ṭihrán, Alison, which were dismissed, and he himself was disgraced. Returned to England 20 May 1863. Priv. Sec. to Sec. of State for India 1866–7. MP Penryn and Falmouth 1868–74. d. 16 July 1883.

Eça de Queirós, José Maria Portuguese novelist, b. Póvoa de Varzim 25 Nov. 1845, the illegitimate son of an eminent magistrate. ed. Colégio de Lapa at Oporto and Univ. of Coimbra. Graduated in Law 1866. Journey through Near East (Egypt and Palestine) Oct. 1869 – Jan. 1870, with Count Resende. Associated with a group of intellectuals pressing for social reform. Portuguese Con., Havana 1872, Newcastle-upon-Tyne 1874, Bristol 1879, Paris 1888. Wrote many of his most famous novels while out of Portugal. d. Paris 16 Aug. 1900.

Eldridge, George Jackson Served in Crimean War 1855–6. Con. Kerch 1856. Con.-Gen. Beirut Apr. 1863 until death 23 Jan. 1890.

Elias, Ney British explorer and consular official, b. Bristol 1844 of a Jewish family. ed. in London, Dresden and Paris. Went to China to work in the family business but gained fame by exploring the new course of the Yellow River 1867–9. For his journey across Mongolia 1872–3 he received the Gold Medal of the Roy. Geog. Soc. Appointed Extra Attaché to For. Dept. of Govt. of India 1874. Member of expedition from Burma to western China 1874–5. Appointed Officiating Joint Commssr for Ladakh 1877. Two journeys into Turkestan 1879–80. Mission across the Pamirs to Afghanistan 1885–6. Boundary Settlement Officer in State of Jaipur 1888. Commssr of Anglo-Siamese Boundary Commission 1889. Con.-Gen. for Khurásán Dec. 1891. Absent on leave from his post because of illness March 1893 – May 1895. ret. due to ill health Nov. 1896. d. London 31 May 1897.

Elliot, (later Sir) Henry George British diplomat, b. Geneva 30 June 1817. 2nd son of the Earl of Minto. ed. Eton and Trinity Coll. Cambridge. Entered Diplomatic Service 1841. Envoy at Copenhagen 1858, Envoy to Italy 1863. Ambass. at Istanbul July 1867 – Feb. 1877. Left there because of ill health. Was British representative at the opening of the Suez Canal 1869. Ambass. Vienna 1877. ret. 1884. d. Ardington House, Wantage, 30 Mar. 1907.

Evans, Edward Payson American scholar, b. Remsen, Oneida Co., New York 8 Dec. 1831 (his parents were natives of North Wales). Graduated 1854 from Univ. of Michigan, studied in Germany for 3 years. Instructor in Modern Languages Univ. of Michigan 1862. Promoted in 1863 to Professorship. Resigned Professorship in 1870 and moved to Munich where he settled as a private scholar and journalist. Studied Persian. Wrote regularly for various magazines and also wrote a number of books. Returned to USA at outbreak of the 1st World War. d. New York City 6 Mar. 1917.

Eyres, (later Sir) Harry Charles Augustus (1856–1944). V.-Con. Beirut 1885–90. Later Con.-Gen. Istanbul 1905–14, and Albania 1922–6.

Farrant, Lt-Col. (later Col.) Francis British soldier and diplomat. Lt in 3rd Reg. Light Cav. in East India Company Army (Bombay Establishment). Selected by Lord Bentinck to proceed to Persia in 1833 to train a cavalry force for Fatḥ-'Alí Sháh. Helped Muḥammad Sháh to secure his throne on Fatḥ-'Alí Shah's death. Priv. Sec. to Sir John McNeill's Mission 1837. Attached to Mission in Persia Oct. 1842, and on arrival sent by Sheil to the Turko-Persian Commission at Erzerum. In early 1843 he was instructed by Canning, British

Ambass. at Istanbul, to investigate the Turkish massacre of Persians at Karbilá. This task brought him into close contact with Siyyid Káẓim-i-Rashtí, the Shaykhí leader who had figured prominently in this event. Sec. of Legation 13 Dec. 1844. Chargé d'Affaires during Sheil's leave of absence 21 Oct. 1847 – 20 Oct. 1849. Resigned his appointment in Ṭihrán on 15 Mar. 1852 after some friction between himself and Sheil. Promoted Col. 1855. d. Aug. 1865.

Ferrier, Joseph Philippe French soldier. After a period in the French Army (1st Reg. of Carabineers and 2nd Reg. of Chausseurs d'Afrique), he served in Africa attaining the rank 'Marachal de Logis'. He was selected in 1839, along with a number of other French officers, to proceed to Persia to train Muḥammad Sháh's Army (following the break in relations with Britain and the departure of British officers). He was employed in the Persian Army with the rank of Adj.-Gen. until 1842. Following his dismissal there were lengthy negotiations over money owed him in pay by the Persian Govt. (Ḥájí Mírzá Áqásí had conceived a dislike for Ferrier and was being uncooperative in paying him his dues.) In 1845, he made a daring journey in disguise into central Asia, an account of which he published (*Caravan Journeys and Wanderings* 1856). Ferrier eventually entered the service of Ḥusayn Khán, Gov. of Shíráz, and remained there until Ḥusayn Khán's dismissal and expulsion from Shíráz in 1849. During 1849–51, Ferrier was in Ṭihrán acting as a French Agent and writing reports which he sent direct to the French For. Ministry. He later proceeded to Pondicherry in India where he obtained a government position.

Feuvrier, Dr Jean-Baptiste (1842–1921), French military physician. Studied at École du service santé militaire, Strasburg 1861–5. Served as physician with French Army in France, Algeria and Tunisia. Special mission to Montenegro 1873–80, 1887; to Persia Sept. 1889 – Mar. 1893. ret. 1895.

Forel, Auguste Swiss scientist, b. Vaud 1 Sept. 1848. Prof. of Psychiatry at Univ. of Zurich and Director of l'Asile du Burghölzli 1879–98. Author of many works on natural science and sociology.

Franck, Adolphe (1809–93), French Jewish scholar. Having failed to obtain a rabbinical scholarship, Franck devoted his life to the study of philosophy. From 1840 he taught at Collège Charlemagne, Paris, and gave public lectures at the Sorbonne. He is famous for his *Dictionnaire des Sciences Philosophiques* and his works on the cabbala. He published over 22 works in all. Was elected member of L'Institut de France 1844. Chair of Natural and Civil Law, Collège de France 1856–86. Commdr of the Légion d'honneur 1869. One of the founders and presidents of the League of Peace; an active defender of Judaism and Pres. of Anti-Atheist League.

Fu'ád Páshá, Muḥammad (Mehmed Keçedji-Záde) Turkish statesman, b. Istanbul 1815. Son of 'Izzat Mullá, a famous poet. Studied Medicine, entered Army Med. Corps, and was sent to Tripoli. His knowledge of French secured him an appointment to the translation dept. of the Imp. Díván in 1837. Thereafter he saw service in diplomatic posts in various European capitals (London 1840–44, Madrid 1844) as well as in increasingly important positions at Istanbul (Dragoman of the Porte 1839, Member of Commission on Education 1845). For. Min. 1852–3, 1855–6, 1858–60, 1861 and 1867–9. Special Mission to Lebanon 1860. Grand Vazír 1861–3, 1863–6. He was a close associate of 'Álí Páshá and his name is linked with the Tanẓímát (Reform) Movt. Travelled to France 1868 because of deteriorating heart condition. d. Nice 12 Feb. 1869.

Gaselee (later Sir) Stephen British scholar b. London 9 Nov. 1882. ed. Eton and King's Coll. Cambridge. Tutor to Prince Leopold of Battenberg (later Lord Leopold

Mountbatten). Pepysian Librarianship at Magdalene Coll. Cambridge 1907. Fellow of Magdalene Coll. 1909. Entered For. Off. 1916. Returned to Cambridge 1919. Librarian and Keeper of Papers of the For. Off. 1920. KCMG 1935. d. London 16 June 1943.

Ghulám-Riḍá Khán, Áṣafu'd-Dawlih Gov. Gen. of Khurásán (1895 – Apr. 1897). He had previously been Gov. of Kirmán, Kirmánsháh, Mázindarán and Khúzistán and was later Gov. of Fárs. He was again Gov. of Khurásán in 1907 at which time the people rebelled against his rule. Head of Sháhsavan tribe of Khurásán and artillery commander.

Gobineau, Joseph Arthur, Comte de French diplomat and writer, b. Ville d'Array, nr Paris, 14 July 1816. ed. Coll. of Bienne, Switzerland. Came to Paris 1835. After various clerical positions he took up journalism. Priv. Sec. to Alexis de Tocqueville (For. Min.) 1849. Sec. to French Legation, Berne, Hanover, Frankfurt, 1849–54. Published his famous *Essai sur l'inégalité des races humaines* 1854. Appointed 1st Sec. to French Legation in Persia 1854. Arrived in Persia 1855. Chargé d'Affaires 15 Oct. 1856 – 31 Jan. 1858. Sent on mission to Newfoundland 1859. Member of International Commission on Savoy 1860. Min. Ṭihrán 3 Mar. 1862 – 16 Sept. 1863. Min. Greece 1864–8, Brazil 1868, Stockholm 1872–7. After the fall of the Empire in 1870 he was never again happy with the state of France. Among the papers of 'Álí Páshá in the British Museum (Add. 46697, fos. 31–2), is a letter from Count Prokesch-Osten to 'Álí Páshá, suggesting that the Turkish Government offer Gobineau some suitable employment. Towards the end of his life, Gobineau left France in self-imposed exile and wandered in Germany and Italy. d. Turin 13 Oct. 1882. (See fig. 3.)

Goldziher, Prof. Ignaz (1850–1921), distinguished Jewish Hungarian orientalist. Professor of Arabic at Univ. of Budapest 1894, being the first person of the Jewish religion to occupy a professorial chair in Hungary. He wrote several works that contain references to the Bahá'í Faith (see p. 536) but his most important contribution to oriental studies was his critical analysis of the Ḥadíth and also his study of the influence of other religions and philosophies on Islam.

Gollmer, Rev. Charles Henry Vidal British missionary. Ordained priest 1879. CMS missionary Lagos 1878–87, Jaffa 1889–94, Nazareth and 'Akká 1890–93. Curate of St Aidan's, Liverpool, 1910–15, and of Penrith, Cornwall, 1915. Died. *c.* 1918.

Gordon, Gen. Sir Thomas Edward (1832–1914), British soldier. Entered Army 1849 and served in India. Oriental and Mil. Sec. Ṭihrán 1889. Mil. Attaché 1891–3. Maj.-Gen. 1886. Lt-Gen. 1890. Gen. 1894. KCIE 1893. KCB 1900.

Graham, (later Rt. Hon. Sir) Ronald William British diplomat, b. London 24 July 1870. ed. Eton. Entered diplomatic service 1892. 2nd Sec. Ṭihrán 1897. St Petersburg 1899. 1st Sec. 1904. Acting Agent and Con.-Gen. Egypt 1907–9. Seconded as adviser to Min. of Interior of Egypt 1910, to General Officer Commanding troops in Egypt 1914. Asst Under-Sec. at For. Off. 1916. Min. to the Hague 1919. Ambass. to Italy 1921. ret. 1933. British Govt. Director of Suez Canal Co. 1939–45. PC 1921, GCVO 1923, GCMG 1926, GCB 1932. d. 26 Jan. 1949.

Grahame, Thomas George British consular official, b. 10 Jan. 1861. ed. Harrow. Resided in Paris for many years. Nominated V.-Con. Ṭihrán 30 June 1898. Passed examination 2 May 1900. Con. Shíráz 8 July 1903. Con.-Gen. Iṣfahán 1 Feb. 1908 – 1 June 1916. Con. Canea, Crete, 1917. d. 22 Oct. 1922.

Granville, 2nd Earl Granville George Leveson-Gower (1815–91), British statesman. For. Sec. 1851–2, 1870–74, 1880–85.

Greenhouse, Maj. Frank Stewart British soldier, b. 24 Dec. 1885. Entered Army as 2nd Lt Jan. 1905. Lt India Army 1907. Capt. 1914. Maj. 18 Jan. 1920. Con. Kirmánsháh 17 June 1920 – 1921.

Grinevskaya, Isabel (Izabella) Arkadyevna Russian poetess, born in Russian Poland, of German and Jewish parents. Mother languages German and Polish, but she learnt Russian and moved to St Petersburg. Became interested in philosophy but later began to write poetry. d. 1944.

Gumoens, Alfred von Austrian Capt. of the 43rd Reg. of Infantry, who was head of an Austrian Mission that arrived at Ṭihrán 24 Nov. 1851. The Amír-Niẓám, not wanting to obtain assistance from either Britain or Russia with regard to training Persia's Army, had, through the Persian Ambass. in Constantinople, negotiated for the recruitment of a group of Austrians to teach in the newly-established Dáru'l-Funún (Military College) of Ṭihrán. Von Gumoens, disgusted at the massacre of the Bábís, resigned his commission in 1852 and left Persia, receiving prior to his departure the Order of the Lion and Sun, 2nd Class. He returned however in 1857 on a mission to buy horses for the Austrian Army.

Haig, Col. (later Sir) Thomas Wolsely British soldier and consular official, b. 7 Aug. 1865. ed. Wellington Coll. and Sandhurst. Joined Seaforth Highlanders 1884, Indian Army 1887. Served in Upper Burma 1887–9. Asst Commssr and other civil posts in India 1897–9. Entered Polit. Dept 1901. Asst Sec. to Govt of India, For. Dept., 1907. Polit. Agent at Alwar 1907–8. Officiating ADC to Sec. of State for India 1909–10. Con. Kirmán 1910, Mashhad 1914, Iṣfahán 1916, Ṭihrán 1919. ret. 1920. Albany Herald 1927–35. Lect. in Persian at Sch. of Oriental Studies, London. Prof. of Arabic, Persian and Hindustani, Trinity Coll. Dublin. KCIE 1922. d. 28 Apr. 1938.

Ḥájibu'd-Dawlih (Chamberlain of the State) *see* 'Alí Khán, Hájí and Ja'far-Qulí Khán.

Hammond, Rt Hon. (later Lord) Edmund British statesman. Clerk For. Off. 1824. Under-Sec. of State for For. Aff. 1854. ret. 1873. d. 1890.

Ḥamzih Mírzá, Ḥishmatu'd-Dawlih (Splendour of the State) 21st son of 'Abbás Mírzá and uncle of Náṣiru'd-Dín Sháh. Gov. of Khurásán 1847–9. Was involved in the suppression of the revolt of the Salár and met Mullá Ḥusayn-i-Bushrú'í. Gov. of Ádharbáyján, June 1849–53. Later Gov. of Iṣfahán 1854. Khurásán 1858. Yazd 1861, Khúzistán 1863. Min. of War 1868. Gov. of Khúzistán 1872 until death in 1880.

Hardegg, Georg David German religious leader, b. near Ludwigsberg, Württemberg, 1812, son of an innkeeper. As a young man he lived for a time in Belgium where he was deeply affected by the revolutionary movement there. He returned to Germany and spent a period in prison for his political activities. However, he underwent a religious conversion in prison, and on his release in 1844 he took up Christoph Hoffmann's teachings with enthusiasm. Hoffmann and Hardegg met in 1849 and from that time on, while Hoffmann attended to the theoretical side, Hardegg threw himself into the practical organizational aspect of the Society of Templars. Had it not been for Hardegg, it is improbable that the Templars would ever have got to Palestine. There were, however, deep personal and ideological differences between Hardegg and Hoffmann and these came to a head in 1868, just before the departure for Palestine. Once in Palestine, Hardegg went ahead with ambitious plans for the development of the Haifa colony, virtually cutting himself off from Hoffmann and the Jaffa colony. The Central Council in Germany responded by cutting off funds to Haifa, and by 1874 the colony was almost bankrupt. In addition, the newer immigrants resented Hardegg's autocratic leadership. Circumstances forced the Haifa colony to approach Hoffmann in Jaffa in

Mar. 1874, and attempt a reconciliation. Hoffmann would accept nothing short of Hardegg's resignation and Hardegg withdrew from the Society taking about one-third of the Haifa colony with him. Jakob Schumacher took over control of the Haifa colony. d. Haifa 1879. (See fig. 23.)

Hardinge, Sir Arthur Henry British diplomat, b. 12 Oct. 1859. ed. Eton and Balliol Coll. Oxford. Fellow of All Souls Oxford 1881. Page of Honour to H.M. The Queen. Entered For. Off. 1880. 3rd Sec. Madrid 1883. 2nd Sec. and précis-writer to Marquess of Salisbury 1885. Then posted to Bucharest, Cairo and Zanzibar. Commsr and Con.-Gen. British E. African Protectorate 1896–1900. Min. Ṭihrán 1900–1905, then to Belgium, Portugal and Spain. ret. 1920. KCMG 1897. GCMG 1910. PC 1913. d. 27 Dec. 1933.

Ḥasan-'Alí Khán-i-Garrúsí Colonel of the Garrúsí Regiment. Was promoted to Adj.-Gen. as a result of the Zanján Campaign (1850). Minister at Paris and subsequently at Istanbul Jun. 1871. Given title of Amír-Niẓám (Commander of the Army) and held several important government posts. d. Kirmán *c.* 1899.

Ḥasan-'Alí Khán-i-Navváb, Mírzá was a member of the Navváb family which came from India and served in Persia for several generations as British agents and officials in various capacities. Ḥasan-'Alí Khán was native Sec. to the Indo-European Telegraph Dept., then for several years British Consular Agent at Shíráz, before becoming native Sec. to the Legation in Ṭihrán. It was at his house in Ṭihrán that E. G. Browne stayed in 1888. d. 1901. Col. Charles Metcalfe MacGregor of the Bengal Staff Corps met Ḥasan-'Alí Khán in Shíráz in 1875 and wrote of him: '. . . the British Agent, Nawab Mirza Hoosen Alee Khan, who had already a better knowledge of our language than most foreigners I have met. This gentleman, the descendant of an Indian Nawab and a Persian lady of blue blood, was the most English Asiatic it has ever been my good fortune to meet. His present was taken up in studying – regardless of trouble, or his own convenience – how he could best serve not only the British Government, but also all British people, and his future, I think, was a dream of going to London, to see us in our own homes, to complete his knowledge of the people he liked so well, and perchance, pluck from our famed garden of beauty, one little rose to brighten his eastern home.' (*Narrative of a Journey* Vol. 1, p. 33)

Ḥasan Khán, Mírzá, Vazír-Niẓám, the brother of the Prime Minister Mírzá Taqí Khán. He rose to power under the shadow of his brother and when the latter became Prime Minister, Ḥasan Khán took over the post he had vacated, that of Vazír-Niẓám (in charge of the troops in Ádharbáyján). Apart from being involved in the martyrdom of the Báb, he also participated in the Zanján upheaval of 1850. He fell from power at the same time as his brother. Died *c.* 1860. Concerning him, Ferrier wrote in 1852: 'He is a monster of perversity, a hundred times worse than the Prime Minister, committing each day revolting cruelties, the most scandalous exactions and depredations, and living in the most dissolute debauchery; he is in the widest meaning of the word what the Persians call *Sharáb-Khur*, *Bangí*, *Taryákí*, *Bachihbáz* – which is equivalent to all the most foul vices. It is at times when he is intoxicated, unfortunately a frequent occurrence, that he has a mania for delivering justice; his judgements are usually those of a savage, the slightest fault cannot find grace in his eyes. To have money and not give it to him is a crime above all others [Ferrier then goes on to give details of some of the punishments inflicted by the Vazír-Niẓám – details too gruesome to commit to these pages]. As to the exactions of the Vazír-Niẓám, they have now become proverbial, and as the punishments that he inflicts are always accompanied by heavy fines for his pocket, he has thus procured in four months a sum greater than 100,000 tomans . . . This then is the man who fills one of the foremost positions in the empire and whose power is the greatest after that of his brother, Mírzá Taqí Khán.' ('Situation de la Perse' pp. 151–2)

Haworth, (later Lt-Col. Sir) Lionel Berkeley Holt b. 30 Sept. 1873. ed. Dulwich Coll. and Elizabeth Coll. Guernsey. Entered Army 1893, and Indian Army 1898. Entered For. and Polit. Dept. of Govt. of India 1901. Con. Kirmánsháh 1906–9, Muḥammarih 1910–14. Served in European War 1914–16. Con. and Polit. Agent Musqat 1916–19. Con. Kirmán 28 Nov. 1922. Con.-Gen. Mashhad 19 Mar. 1924, Con.-Gen. Fárs and Polit. Resident in Persian Gulf 1 Jan. 1927. ret. 1927. d. 11 Sept. 1951.

Hay, (later Sir) Robert Drummond- (1846–1926), British consular official. Con. Beirut 4 Oct. 1894 – 22 Jan. 1908. Also Post Office Agent.

Hearst, Phoebe Apperson b. Franklin, Missouri, 1842. Married George Hearst 1862 and settled in San Francisco. Moved to Washington 1886, when George Hearst became a Senator. Her husband died in 1891 leaving her an immense fortune. She returned to San Francisco frequently and it was on one of these visits that Lua Getsinger introduced her to the Bahá'í Faith. She visited 'Abdu'l-Bahá in 'Akká in 1898, and later when 'Abdu'l-Bahá visited America she invited him to her home. d. 13 Apr. 1919. Her son was William Randolph Hearst, the well-known publisher and politician.

Hennell, Lt-Col. Samuel British soldier of 14th Reg. Native Inf., East India Company Army (Bombay). Enlisted 1819. Promoted Lt-Col. 1849. Resident at Búshihr 1838–52. Played an important part in suppressing the slave trade in the Persian Gulf.

Herbert, Lt-Col. (Later Maj.-Gen.) Charles British soldier and consular official. Entered the East India Company Army as an Ensign in 1841. Lt-Col. 30 Jan. 1867. Col. 30 Jan. 1872. Maj.-Gen. (Hon.) 25 Sept. 1878. Acting Polit. Agent Baghdád 29 May 1868. Also Acting Con.-Gen. 1 Sept. 1868. Polit. Agent Baghdád 1 Sept. 1870, and Con.-Gen. 15 Feb. 1871. Continued in this post until 21 Dec. 1874. ret. from Army 1 Aug. 1878. d. 18 Nov. 1897.

Herrick, Myron Timothy (1854–1929) American politician. Gov. of Ohio 1903–5. Ambass. to France 1912–14 and 1921–9.

Ḥisámu's-Salṭanih *see* Sulṭán-Murád Mírzá

Hoeltzer, Ernst German engineer, b. Thuringia 1835. Came to Persia to work in the Persian Telegraph Dept. as Inspector 1863. Put in charge of Iṣfahán office as Asst Superintendent Gd. I 1871, Gd. II 1880. ret. 1890. d. Iṣfahán 3 July 1911. Approx. 1,000 photographs taken by him between 1873 and 1897 have recently come to light in Germany.

Hoffmann, Christoph German religious leader, b. Leonburg 1815. Grew up in the Pietist community at Korntal which his father had helped found. Studied Theology at Tübingen Univ. Together with the Paulus brothers, he set up an educational institute called the *salon* at Ludwigsberg near Stuttgart where he taught. He came into prominence through his opposition to the appointment of a liberal to a professorship at Tübingen. Later he ran against the liberals in the election for the German National Assembly at Frankfurt and won. In 1848 he took his seat there, but was not a great success, and his activities soon returned to the *salon* and the journal *Süddeutsche Warte* which acted as an organ of the *salon*. In the 1850s there gradually evolved, through the decisive influence of G. D. Hardegg, the Society of Templars, and simultaneously the Society drifted further away from the Church until eventually there was a complete break in 1859, and even a certain amount of persecution. It was during the Crimean War (1854–5) that it became the principal aim of the Templars to set up colonies in the Holy Land so that thereby they could restore the Holy Land to a condition fitting for the return of Christ. Obtaining no satisfying result from appeals for help to the German authorities, nor authorization from the Ottoman authorities, the Templars decided to press on with their plans nevertheless. A Commission of three went out to Palestine to survey the land in 1856, but it was not until 1868 that the Society was able to organize the first migration to Palestine. On 26 July 1868 there was a farewell meeting of the Templars, and on 6 Aug. 1868 Hoffmann and Hardegg set out, arriving in Haifa 30 Oct. 1868. There were, however, serious rifts between Hoffmann and Hardegg, and when these two proved irreconcilable it was decided that Hardegg would run the Haifa colony and Hoffmann the Jaffa colony. Eventually in Mar. 1874 the Haifa community was forced to renounce Hardegg and link up with Hoffmann again. d. 1885.

Huart, Clément Imbault- (1854–1926), eminent French orientalist. Served in French Consular Service in the Orient (1875–98), mainly in Istanbul. Chevalier de la Légion d'honneur 1900. Prof. at the École nationale des langues orientales vivantes. His book *Littérature Arabe* has been translated into English.

Huber, James Jacob German missionary, b. Neckartenzlingen, Württemberg, *c.* 1826. Studied Basle Seminary. Became CMS missionary and was sent to W. Africa 1850, Palestine 1853. Was at Nazareth until 1885 then transferred to Gaza. d. Gaza 18 July 1893. (See fig. 26.)

Ḥusayn Kh͟án, Ájúdán-Bas͟hí *see* pp. 169–71.

Ḥusayn Kh͟án, Mírzá, Mus͟híru'd-Dawlih Con.-Gen. Tiflis *c.* 1854. Min. Turkey July 1859, Ambass. Turkey June 1869. Minister of War with title Sipahsálár-i-A'ẓam Sept. 1871. Prime Minister Nov. 1871. Accompanied S͟háh on his first European tour 1873. Dismissed from position as Prime Minister Sept. 1873. Minister of Foreign Affairs 1873–80. Accompanied S͟háh on second European tour 1878. d. Mas͟hhad 14 Nov. 1881, possibly poisoned by order of the S͟háh.

Hutton, Edward Peter Acting V.-Con. at Sulṭánábád 21 Apr. 1918. V.-Con. 6 Jan. 1920 to 10 Sept. 1932, when the post was closed.

Imbrie, Maj. Robert W. American consular official. Aged 41 when he died on 18 July 1924, after a picturesque career including Law, big-game hunting in Africa, and French Army during the 1st World War. Had been V.-Con. in St Petersburg in 1918 and had personally received the Bolshevik declaration of war on USA. Then V.-Con. in Ankara before being appointed V.-Con. in Ṭihrán in 1924.

Ironside, (later Sir) Henry George Outram Bax British diplomat, b. 15 Nov. 1859. ed. Eton and Exeter Coll. Oxford. Attaché Istanbul 1884. 3rd Sec. Copenhagen 1887, Ṭihrán 27 Nov. 1888. 2nd Sec. Ṭihrán 1 Nov. 1889, Vienna 22 July 1891. Also served at Cairo, Washington, Peking and Stockholm. Min. at Caracas 1902. Envoy Santiago 1907, Berne 1909, Sofia 1911. ret. 1918. KCMG 1911. d. 16 Apr. 1929

Jablonowski, Aleksandr Walerian (1829–1913), Polish historian and ethnographer. Travelled to the Middle East 1870.

Ja'far-Qulí Kh͟án, Ḥájibu'd-Dawlih born *c.* 1863. Son of 'Ísá Kh͟án, Qájár Quyúnlú, brother of Mahd-i-'Ulyá, Náṣiru'd-Dín S͟háh's mother. Was Child-Servant (G͟hulám-Bac͟hih) of the S͟háh and accompanied him to Europe on two occasions. In *c.* 1892, he became Farrás͟h-Bás͟hí to the S͟háh with the title Ḥájibu'd-Dawlih. After the assassination of Náṣiru'd-Dín S͟háh, he was given the title Mu'ínu's-Sulṭán.

Jakins, Herbert George (1897–), joined Levant Consular Service 1924. V.-Con. Mas͟hhad

1930. In charge Shíráz Consulate 14 May 1944. Con. Shíráz May 1945 – Dec. 1947. Polit. Agent Bahrayn and Kuwait 1949. ret. 1952.

Jalálu'd-Dawlih *see* Sulṭán-Ḥusayn Mírzá

Jessup, Dr Henry Harris American Presbyterian missionary, b. Montrose, Pa. 19 Apr. 1832. ed. Yale Coll. and Union Theol. Seminary, NY. Ordained 1855. Missionary of American Board of Commssrs for For. Missions to Tripoli, 1856, Beirut 1860. Later Director of Presbyterian Missionary Operations in Northern Syria. DD 1865.

Jordon, Dr David Starr Distinguished American scientist (ichthyologist) and university administrator, b. Gainesville, NY 19 Jan. 1851. ed. Cornell Univ. Principal of Appleton Collegiate Institute, 1874. Prof. of Natural Hist., N.-Western Christian Coll. 1875. Chairman of Dept. of Sciences, Indiana Univ. 1879. Pres. of Indiana Univ. 1885. Instituted the concept of a major field of study for college students. Pres. of Stanford Univ. 1891. Chancellor of Stanford Univ. 1913. d. 19 Sept. 1931.

Jowett, Benjamin Leading Oxford academic figure, b. Camberwell, Surrey, 15 Apr. 1817. ed. St Paul's Sch. and Balliol Coll. Oxford. Elected Fellow of Balliol while still an undergraduate in 1838. Became Tutor there 1842. Ordained Priest 1845. Regius Prof. of Greek 1855. Was severely criticized for his liberal views in theological matters and even prosecuted in the Chancellor's Court of the University. Master of Balliol 1870. V.-Chancellor of Oxford Univ. 1882–6. Encouraged University and College reform as well as the admission of women to Oxford. d. Oxford 1 Oct. 1893.

Justi, Ferdinand (1837–1907). Studied ancient Iranian history and philology. Prof. at Univ. of Marburg.

Kalmykov, Andrew D. (1870–1941), graduated from Sch. of Oriental Langs. at St Petersburg and joined Russian For. Ministry. Served in several important positions in Persia and Central Asia until the Bolshevik Revolution.

Kámrán Mírzá, Náyibu's-Salṭanih 3rd son of Náṣiru'd-Dín Sháh, b. 1856. Given title Náyibu's-Salṭanih (*c.* 1858). In *c.* 1861, when aged 5, was made Gov. of Ṭihrán, and in *c.* 1868 was made Amír Kabír (C.-in-C. of all Persia's forces and later also Min. of War), two positions that he held throughout almost all of the rest of Náṣiru'd-Dín Sháh's reign. On several occasions (in 1865, 1870, 1878 and 1889) when the Sháh was absent from the capital, Kámrán Mírzá remained as his deputy. From 1878 until 1888 he was Gov. of Ṭihrán, Qazvín, Gílán, Mázindarán, Qum, Káshán and many other provinces, as well as Min. of War, thus making him extremely rich and powerful. In 1888, however, following the intrigues of Amínu's-Sulṭán, he was reduced to just Gov. of Ṭihrán. After the assassination of Náṣiru'd-Dín Sháh, he was relieved of all his posts, and apart from a few brief periods as Min. of War and Gov. of Khurásán, he held no further important posts. Curzon, who met Náyibu's-Salṭanih in 1889, wrote: 'He is now thirty-five years of age and is also unusually stout for his years. Though generally reputed to be the favourite son of the Shah and a young man of amiable disposition, he is deficient in capacity or political influence, and, except for the importance attaching to his military rank, fills no part on the public stage.' (Curzon *Persia and the Persian Question* Vol. 1, p. 421.) He died in 1928.

Kazem-Beg (Kazem-Bek), Mírzá Aleksandr orientalist, b. Rasht 22 July 1802, the son of a *qáḍí* of Darband. Named Mírzá Muḥammad-'Alí. Undertook formal Muslim religious training but in 1821 was converted to Christianity by missionaries of the Scottish Missionary Society at Astrakhán. In 1825 he proceeded to Omsk to teach the Tartar language. Lecturer in Oriental Langs., Kazan Univ. 1827–44. Dean of Historico-Philological Faculty,

Kazan Univ. 1844–9. Prof. of Persian Literature, Univ. of St Petersburg, 1849–60. Together with A. O. Muchlinski helped to form the School of Oriental Languages of which he became dean in 1860. Died *c.* 1870. The library there possesses his collection of manuscripts and writings. (See fig. 1.)

Kemball, Capt. (later Gen. Sir) Arnold Burrowes British soldier and consular official, b. Bombay 18 Nov. 1820. ed. Military Coll. Addiscombe. Entered Indian Army 11 Dec. 1837. Served in 1st Afghan War 1839. Asst Polit. Agent Búshihr 1842. Acting Polit. Agent and Con. Baghdád 1847 and 1851. Promoted Capt. 1851, Polit. Agent and Con.-Gen. Baghdád 3 Oct. 1855 – 20 Dec. 1874. Took part in Anglo-Persian War 1856–7. Promoted Lt-Col. 1860, Col. 1863. Accompanied Sháh to England 1873. British Delegate on Turko-Persian Frontier Commission 1875. Participated in Turko-Russian War 1877. Founder and 1st chairman of East African Company 1888. Promoted Gen. 1880. KCSI 1866, KCB 1877. d. London 21 Sept. 1908. (See fig. 19.)

In *Vanity Fair* (No. 180, Vol. 10, 1878) there is an article about Kemball in which it is stated: 'Sir Arnold is one of the best and best-known of the race of soldier-statesmen bred by service in the East. He has an intimate acquaintance with the Arabic, Persian, and Turkish languages, and he not only understands well the habits, customs, and modes of thought of Oriental peoples generally, but has also what is at least equally important, a thorough knowledge of Oriental manners. Withal he is genial and kindly, honest, straightforward, and manly – and so great confidence does he inspire that when he was Consul General at Bagdad, it was found that a word from him would procure the presence of shy Arab chiefs when all the efforts of Turkish authorities had failed.'

Kennedy, (later Sir) Robert John British diplomat, b. 24 Dec. 1851. ed. Harrow and Univ. Coll. Oxford. Entered Diplomatic Service 1874. Served in several posts in Near East 1877–88. Sec. of Legation Ṭihrán 1 Oct. 1888. Chargé 28 Apr. – 16 Nov. 1889 and 13 Nov. 1890 – 14 Nov. 1891. Min. to Montenegro 1897. Min. to Uruguay 1906. ret. 1912. KCMG 1913. d. 11 Nov. 1936.

Khán Bábá Khán *see* Muḥammad-Ḥasan Khán-i-Sardár

Khanykov, Nicolai Vladimirovich (1819–79), Russian orientalist and consular official. Was Consul in Tabríz for a number of years and headed several exploratory Missions to Persia.

Knatchbull-Hugessen, Hughe Montgomery British diplomat, b. 26 Mar. 1886. Entered For. Off. as clerk 1908. 2nd Sec. at Paris Peace Conf. 1919. 1st Sec. 1919. Counsellor Brussels 1926. Min. Baltic States 1930, Ṭihrán 7 Nov. 1934. KCMG 1 Jan. 1936. Ambass. Peking 23 Sept. 1936. Employed at For. Off. 1938. Ambass. Ankara 1939, Brussels 1944. ret. 24 Sept. 1947. d. 27 Mar. 1971.

Kremer, Alfred, Baron von Austrian orientalist and statesman, b. Vienna 13 May 1828. ed. Univ. of Vienna. Travelled in Syria and Egypt. Appointed teacher in Arabic at Polytechnikium. V.-Con. 1858. Con. Cairo 1859, Galatz 1862. Con.-Gen. Beirut 1870. Counsellor 1872. Member of the International Commission on the Egyptian Debt 1876. Min. of Commerce 1880–81. d. 27 Dec. 1889.

Kuropatkin, Alexsei Nicolaevich (1848–1921), Russian General who distinguished himself in Russo-Turkish War of 1877–8. Gov. of Transcaspia 1890–98. Min. of War 1898–1904. Commanded Russian forces against Japan in 1904–5, but was defeated and relieved of command. Curzon writes of him in 1892: '[He] now returns in the prime of life to the highest command in a country [Transcaspia] of which he knows more than any living Russian general. His strategical abilities and reputation for courage render his appointment one of extreme significance.' (*Persia and the Persian Question* Vol. 1, p. 83)

LaHitte, Jean-Ernest Ducos, Vicomte de (1789–1878), French general, senator, and government minister. Served in French Army in several campaigns including the Napoleonic Wars. Min. of For. Aff. 16 Nov. 1849 – 9 Jan. 1851. Then Rep. of Department du Nord in Legislative Assembly.

Lake, General Edward John (1823–77), Indian Army. After his retirement, Lake was Hon. Lay Sec. of CMS 1867–76.

Lambert, (later Sir) Anthony Edward (1911–). Entered Diplomatic Service as 3rd Sec. at For. Off. 1934. Envoy Sofia 1958. Ambass. Tunis 1960, Helsinki 1963, Lisbon 1966–70.

Lamington, 2nd Baron, Charles Wallace Alexander Napier Ross Cochrane-Baillie British statesman and colonial administrator, b. London 29 July 1860. ed. Eton and Christ Church Oxford. Asst Priv. Sec. to Lord Salisbury 1885. MP (Conservative) for North St Pancras 1886. Succeeded to title 1890. Journey to Siam and Tongking 1890–91. Gov. of Bombay 1903. Resigned due to wife's health 1907. Organized recruiting, especially to Territorial Army, 1914–18. Went to Syria as Commsr of British Relief Unit 1919. Spoke frequently in the House of Lords especially on topics related to the Middle East. On 13 Feb. 1940 was shot at while on the platform at a meeting of the Roy. Asiat. Soc. GCMG 1900, GCIE 1903. d. Lamington House, Lanarkshire, 16 Sept. 1940.

Landau, Rom (1899–1974), British artist, scholar and writer. Professional sculptor, 1919–34. Min. of Information, Middle Eastern Div. 1941–2. Prof. of Islamic and North African Studies, Univ. of the Pacific, Stockton, Calif. Member of executive committee of World Congress of Faiths.

Lawrence, Lord John Laird Mair (1811–79), Viceroy of India 1863–9. Created 1st Lord Lawrence 1869. He was a member of the Council of the CMS.

Layard, (later Sir) Austen Henry (1817–94), English archaeologist and diplomat. Travelled in Iraq and Persia 1839–42. Excavated Nineveh 1845–51. Ambassador at Madrid 1869, Istanbul 1877–80.

Le Chatelier, Alfred (1855–1929), French orientalist. Prof. of Muslim Sociology and Sociography at Collège de France 1903. Founder of the Mission Scientifique du Maroc and of the periodicals *Archives Marocaines* and *Revue du Monde Musulman*.

Lessona, Prof. Michele Italian physician, b. Turin 20 Sept. 1823. ed. Royal Univ. of Turin in Medicine. Worked in Egypt for a time before becoming Prof. of Mineralogy and Zoology at the Roy. Univ. of Genoa. Appointed physician to Diplomatic Mission to Persia 1862–4. Taught at Univ. of Bologna. Prof. of Zoology and Comparative Anatomy at Univ. of Turin 1865. Rector of Univ. of Turin 1877. Senator for life 1892. Wrote several books and translated many others from English into Italian. d. Turin 20 July 1894.

Light, (later Sir) Edgar William British civil servant, b. 8 May 1885. ed. London Univ. Entered For. Off. 1903. Acting Staff Officer 1 June 1918. Staff Officer 4 Feb. 1920. 2nd Technical Asst, Treaty Dept., 1 Jan. 1927. Asst 10 May 1935. ret. 1953. KCVO 1953. d. 8 Jan. 1969.

Longworth, Henry Zohrab British consular official (1855–1912). Began service as clerk at Salonika Consulate, 1877. Served in various posts in Turkey, but principally at Trabizond where he was Con. 1885–1906 and 1909–12.

Loraine, Sir Percy Lyham British diplomat, b. 5 Nov. 1880. ed. Eton and New Coll. Oxford.

Entered Army and served in S. African War 1901–2. Attaché Istanbul 1904. 3rd Sec. 1906, Ṭihrán 25 Feb. 1907. 2nd Sec. 5 May 1909, Rome 9 May 1909, Peking, Paris, Madrid, 1911–17. Succeeded as 12th Bt. 13 May 1917. Attended Paris Peace Conf. 1918–19. 1st Sec. Warsaw 1919. Counsellor 1920. Min. Ṭihrán 1 Oct. 1921, Athens 7 Dec. 1926. High Commssr Egypt/Sudan 1929. Ambass. Ankara 1933, Rome 1939. ret. 1941. KCMG 1925, GCMG 1937, Privy Councillor 1935. d. 23 May 1961.

Lovett, Maj. (later Maj.-Gen.) Beresford British soldier and telegraph engineer, b. 16 Feb. 1839. ed. Addiscombe Mil. Coll. Joined Roy. Engineers 1858. Served in Telegraph Dept. in Persia 1866–70. On special mission in Sístán 1870–72. Con. Astarábád 1880–83. FRGS, FRSA. ret. 1894. d. 12 Sept. 1926.

Lowther, Sir Gerard Augustus British diplomat, b. 16 Dec. 1858. ed. Harrow. Entered Diplomatic Service 1879. Min. Chile 1901, Tangier 1904. Ambass. Istanbul 1908–13. KCMG 1907, GCMG 1911, created 1st Bt. 1914. d. 5 Apr. 1916.

Luke, (later Sir) Harry Charles (1884–1969), British colonial administrator. Priv. Sec. to High Commssr of Cyprus 1911–12. Asst Sec. to Govt of Cyprus 1912. Commssr for Famagusta 1918. Asst Gov. Jerusalem 1920–24. Colonial Sec. Sierra Leone 1924–8. Chief Sec. Palestine 1928–30. Lt-Gov. of Malta 1930–38. Gov. Fiji 1938–42.

Mackenzie, Capt. Charles Francis British soldier. Entered East India Co. Service as Ensign in 1845. Served with 28th Bengal Native Inf. in Punjab campaigns 1848–9, Peshawar 1850. Asst Commsr Arracan 1852. Served with Turkish contingent in the Crimean War. Con. in Gílán, Mázindarán and Astarábád, resident at Rasht, 27 Jan. 1858 – 11 Jan. 1862. d. 1881.

Malcolm, Napier b. Henley Castle 1870. ed. Haileybury and New Coll. Oxford. Ordained Deacon 1894, Priest 1895. Curate of St Andrews, Eccles 1894–6, of St Johns, Higher Broughton, 1896–8. Accepted by CMS as missionary 1898 and sent to Yazd. Moved to Shíráz 1904. Resigned on family grounds 1908. d. Altrincham 19 Oct. 1921.

Malet, (later Sir) Edward Baldwin (1837–1908), British diplomat. Attaché 1854–62. 2nd Sec. 1862–71. Mediated between Bismarck and the French in 1870. Sec. Legation Peking 1871, Athens 1873. Min. Plen. at Istanbul 29 Apr. 1878. Con.-Gen. Egypt 10 Oct. 1879. Envoy Brussels 1883. Ambass. Berlin 1884. Privy Councillor 1885. ret. 1895. Aptd. Member International Court of Arbitration, The Hague 1899, GCMG 1885, GCB 1886.

Malik-Jáhán Khánum, Mahd-i-'Ulyá daughter of Muḥammad-Qásim Khán-i-Qájár-i-Quyúnlú, and a great-grand-daughter of Fatḥ-'Alí Sháh. Became wife of Muḥammad Sháh in *c.* 1820 and was mother of Náṣiru'd-Dín Sháh. On death of Muḥammad Sháh, she took control of the Government pending the arrival of her son from Tabríz. She had four special protégés: 'Alí-Qulí Mírzá, the I'tiḍádu'd-Salṭanih; Mírzá Áqá Khán-i-Núrí; Ḥájí 'Alí Khán, the Ḥájibu'd-Dawlih; and Firaydún Mírzá, the Farmán-Farmá. She was a bitter enemy of Mírzá Taqí Khán whose downfall and death she eventually encompassed. She continued to be a powerful influence throughout the early years of her son's reign. The statement that she urged the Sháh on in his persecution of the Bábís (see p. 144) is also made by Shoghi Effendi in *God Passes By* (p. 63). She died 3 June 1873, while her son was in Europe. The best European account of her has come from Lady Sheil in her book *Life and Manners in Persia* (pp. 130–34): 'I now prepared to pay my respects to the Serkar e Mader e Shah, her highness the Shah's mother. Instead of his Majesty's principal wife, as one would anticipate, it is this lady who holds the chief place at court – among the womankind, be it well understood . . . The Khanum, or Lady, that being the name the Shah applies to his mother, as Napoleon the Great did Madame to his, having fixed the day, a large retinue of servants with a gaudy takhterewán were sent by her to convey me to the palace, which, joined to my own servants, made an inconvenient procession through the narrow bazars . . . In a few minutes a negress entered the room, and informed us that the Khanum waited, and that I was to "take my brightness into her presence." We were then ushered into the adjoining chamber, and found her seated on a chair at a table which was covered with coarse white unhemmed calico. On each side of her, on a chair likewise, sat a pretty young lady covered with jewels. The Khanum said a great many amiable things to me, and went through all the usual Persian compliments, hoping my heart had not grown narrow, that my nose was fat, etc. etc. She then introduced the two young ladies as the Shah's two principal wives and cousins. Neither of them uttered a word, but sat like statues during my interview, which lasted two hours. The Shah's mother is handsome, and does not look more than thirty, yet her real age must be at least forty. She is very clever, and is supposed to take a large share in the affairs of the government. She has also the whole management of the Shah's anderoon; so that I should think she must have a good deal to occupy her mind, as the Shah has three principal wives, and eight or nine inferior ones. These ladies have each a separate little establishment, and some a separate court from the rest, but all the courts have a communication with one another . . . All the Kajars have naturally large arched eyebrows, but, not satisfied with this, the women enlarge them by doubling their real size with great streaks of antimony: her cheeks were well rouged, as is the invariable custom among Persian women of all classes. She asked me many questions about the Queen; how she dressed, how many sons she had, and said she could not imagine a happier person than her Majesty, with her fine family, her devoted husband, and the power she possessed. She made me describe the ceremonial of a drawing-room. I much regretted I had no picture of the Queen to show her. She was also curious to have an account of a theatre . . . When I had acquired a sufficient knowledge of their language to be able to form an opinion, I found the few Persian women I was acquainted with in general lively and clever; they are restless and intriguing, and may be said to manage their husband's and son's affairs. Persian men are made to yield to their wishes by force of incessant talking and teazing.'

Malik-Qásim Mírzá 24th son of Fatḥ-'Alí S͟háh, was appointed Gov. of Ád͟harbáyján in Sept. 1848 on the accession of Náṣiru'd-Dín S͟háh, but was replaced in June 1849 by Ḥamzih Mírzá. He became Gov. of Urúmíyyih and was in that position when the Báb passed through the town. d. 1857. Lt-Col. Stuart describes him thus: 'I went with Ellis and Sir H. Bethune to call on that half civilized barbarian, Malek Cossim Meerza. His Highness is a handsome but vulgar looking man; the only one of the royal family, I am told, who at all resembles Abbas Meerza. Having been a pupil of Madame Le Mariniere, he speaks and writes French with tolerable fluency; and, to be thoroughly European, he was dressed this morning in a new blue surtout, with a pair of English lieutenant's epaulettes, and tight trousers; I need not say that he looked the very beau ideal of a continental tiger. Malek Cossim's mother was an Afshâr of high rank, and he is a pretender to the chieftainship of that powerful tribe.' (*Journal of a Residence* p. 317)

Mallet, (later Sir) Victor Alexander Louis (1893–1969), British diplomat. 3rd Sec. Ṭihrán 1919, 2nd Sec. 1920. Transferred to For. Off. 19 Oct. 1921. Counsellor Ṭihrán 1933, Washington 1936. Min. Stockholm 1940, Madrid 1945, Rome 1947. KCMG 1944. ret. 1954.

Manúc͟hihr K͟hán *see* pp. 167–9.

Marie Alexandra Victoria, Queen of Romania was descended from two of the most important royal houses of Europe. Her father, Alfred, Duke of Edinburgh and Saxe-Coburg, was Queen Victoria's second son, while her mother, Marie Alexandrovna, was the only daughter of the Emperor Alexander II of Russia. b. Eastwell, Kent 29 Oct. 1875. Her childhood and youth were spent in England, Malta and Coburg in Germany, and she frequented the courts of Europe. In 1893 she married Prince Ferdinand of the House of Hohenzollern, heir-apparent to the throne of Romania. Her husband succeeded to the Romanian throne in 1914. One of the happiest moments of her life was 15 Oct. 1922 when her husband and she were crowned King and Queen of Greater Romania (Bessarabia and Transylvania having been added to Romania after the War), for it was her own personal intervention with the allied leaders in Paris that had secured Romania advantageous terms at a time when it seemed that the country would be completely denied them. However, from that time on, her life became increasingly difficult and sorrowful. Her eldest son Carol lost his position as heir to the throne as the result of a scandalous extramarital affair. Her grandson, Michael, was made heir-apparent, but after her husband's death on 18 July 1927, Marie was denied a place in the Regency, and, despite her great popularity with the Romanian people, was pushed aside politically. Then in 1930, Carol staged a *coup d'état* and restored himself to the Monarchy, but his behaviour showed no signs of improvement and over the ensuing years he slighted his mother time and again. Relief from the oppression of the last years of her life was obtained in a very successful tour of USA in 1926, and an equally triumphant if less publicized visit to England in 1934. d. Sinaia, Romania, 18 July 1938. (See fig. 7.)

Marinitch, Hugo b. 1 Apr. 1839. Dragoman to British Embassy at Constantinople 19 Apr. 1876. Placed at disposal of H. D. Wolff 1885 and 1887. CMG 1888. ret. 1 July 1906. d. 21 Dec. 1922.

Marling, (later Sir) Charles Murray (1862–1933), British diplomat. ed. Wellington and Trinity Coll. Cambridge. Entered diplomatic career 1888. Posted to Madrid, Bucharest, Sofia, Athens, Crete. Counsellor Ṭihrán 1906, Istanbul 1908–13. Envoy Extraord. Ṭihrán in Mr Townley's absence 17 Apr. 1915. Made Envoy in his own right 9 Mar. 1916. Copenhagen 1919, The Hague 1921. ret. 1926. KCMG 1916, GCMG 1926.

Maspéro, Gaston Camille Charles (1846–1916), eminent French archaeologist.

Matthews, William David Woodside British consular official, b. 6 June 1883. ed. Roy. Sch. Dungannon, Co. Tyrone, and Pembroke Coll. Cambridge. Student Interpreter in the Levant 1904. V.-Con. Baṣra 1911, Adana 1912, Zurich 1917. Con. Istanbul 1920, Trabizond 1927, also Mersin 6 June 1930. ret. 7 June 1943. d. 3 Feb. 1961.

Midḥat Pás͟há b. Istanbul 1822. Began working in secretariat of Grand Vazír 1836. After a succession of responsible positions with provincial Govs. became Gov. of Adrianople 1854. Distinguished himself as a provincial Gov., and in 1864 was responsible for carrying out the reforms of the new law on Viláyats in Bulgaria, which he did very successfully. Gov. of Bag͟hdád and Commdr of 6th Army Corps in 1869. Grand Vizier 1872, and again on accession of Sulṭán 'Abdu'l-Ḥamíd in 1876. Dismissed and exiled 5 Feb. 1877. Gov. of Syria 1878–80. In 1881, was put on trial for the assassination of Sulṭán 'Abdu'l-'Azíz, and after a show-trial was banished to Ṭá'if in Arabia. Strangled, almost certainly on the Sulṭán's orders, in Ṭá'if 10 Apr. 1883. He was one of the most notable and able administrators of Ottoman Turkey and an important figure in the Reform Movement.

Mihdí-Qulí Mírzá the 20th son of 'Abbás Mírzá (Fatḥ-'Alí S͟háh's son and heir). He had been Gov. of Burújird in the reign of Muḥammad S͟háh. He was appointed Gov. of Mázindarán in late Nov. 1848, but remained in Ṭihrán to attend the celebrations of the S͟háh's accession to the throne. He left Ṭihrán on 28 Dec. 1848, accompanied by some 3,000 troops. A *farmán* from the S͟háh instructing him to deal with the Bábís, dated 30 Dec. 1848, reached him shortly after he had left Ṭihrán. He remained Gov. of Mázindarán until 1851, when he was dismissed at the insistence of Dolgorukov after a Turkoman raid on the Russians at Astarábád.

Mihr-'Alí Khán-i-Núrí, Ḥájí Shujá'u'l-Mulk, b. 1816. Son of Ḥájí Shukru'lláh Khán-i-Núrí and nephew of Mírzá Áqá Khán, the Prime Min. After participating in the first Nayríz upheaval, he was appointed Gov. of Bihbihan in 1851. Was Commdr of the Persian forces in the Anglo-Persian War 1856–7. Promoted to rank of Amír-Tumán 1857. Upon the fall from power of his uncle, Mírzá Áqá Khán, in 1858, he was imprisoned and fined. He became Gov. of Búshihr in 1860. d. 1870. When Browne was in Persia, he met Mírzá 'Alí-Akbar Khán-i-Núrí, a relative of Ḥájí Mihr-'Alí, who gave an account of the latter's death in 1870 (Browne *A Year Amongst the Persians* p. 441 and *A Traveller's Narrative* pp. 259–60).

Mills, Lady Dorothy R. M. British explorer and writer. Eldest daughter of 5th Earl of Orford. d. 4 Dec. 1959.

Milner, Alfred, Viscount (1854–1925), statesman remembered chiefly for his services in S. Africa 1879. Sec. for War 1918, Sec. for Colonies 1919–21.

Monahan, James Henry British consular official, b. 22 May 1864. Student Interpreter in the Levant 10 Mar. 1888. V.-Con. Monastir 1895, Bitlis 1896, Haifa 22 Sept. 1898. Acting Con. Jerusalem 1902 and 1903, Baṣrah 1904 and 1905. Con. Monastir 1905, Jeddah 1907, Erzerum 1912. Employed at For. Off. 1915. Con. at Bari, Italy 1915. Employed at Tripoli 1916–20. Con. Tripoli 1920. ret. 7 Aug. 1924. d. 11 May 1950.

Money, Major-General Sir Arthur Wigram British Soldier, b. 23 Oct. 1866. ed. Charterhouse, joined Roy. Artillery 1885, numerous expeditions and actions in India and S. Africa. During 1st World War served in Europe, Mesopotamia, and with Egyptian Exped. Force. Appointed Chief Administrator of Occupied Enemy Terr. in Palestine Mar. 1918 – Aug. 1919. ret. Mar. 1920. d. 25 Oct. 1951.

Morgan, James British consular official, b. 18 Nov. 1882. Student Interpreter in the Levant 1905. V.-Con. Salonika 1910, Smyrna 1919. Con. Aleppo 1920. Employed at For. Off. 1923. 2nd Dragoman Istanbul 1923. Con. Gen. Smyrna 1928, Istanbul 1930. Local rank of Counsellor 1930. Chargé on frequent occasions. Local rank of Min. Plen. 1940. ret. 29 Dec. 1943. d. 29 Mar. 1968.

Muḥammad, Mír Siyyid, Imám-Jum'ih *see* p. 271n.

Muḥammad-Báqir, Shaykh one of the leading mujtahids of Iṣfahán. Shortly after the 1874 episode (see pp. 269–73), he fell out with the Ẓillu's-Sulṭán, and after intriguing against the latter was forced to leave Iṣfahán in 1876 and proceed on pilgrimage to Mashhad. Even here, however, he pursued his relentless campaign against the Bahá'ís, and was responsible for the martyrdom of Ḥájí 'Abdu'l-Majíd, a prominent Bahá'í who was a survivor of Shaykh Ṭabarsí and the father of Badí', Bahá'u'lláh's messenger to Náṣiru'd-Dín Sháh. From Mashhad, the Shaykh proceeded to Ṭihrán where he was reconciled with Ẓillu's-Sulṭán, and arrived back in Iṣfahán on 16 Apr. 1878. He was deeply implicated in the martyrdoms of Mullá Káẓim of Ṭálkhunchih and of the 'King' and 'Beloved of Martyrs' (see pp. 274–7). Soon after these events, however, he was forced to retire to Iraq. While there, he was further humiliated by being forced to watch helplessly as his wife was seduced by Ẓillu's-Sulṭán. He died in Dec. 1883 at Najaf. At the time of his death he was extremely wealthy, most of his wealth having been obtained by hoarding grain in times of famine and selling it to the starving populace at exorbitant prices. (See fig. 32.)

Muḥammad-Ḥasan Khán-i-Sardár better known as Khán Bábá Khán. He was a Qájár from the town of Íráván who was prominent in the campaigns against the Russians in the years leading up to the treaty of Turkumancháy (1828). He was also prominent in campaigns against the Turks. After the accession to the throne of Náṣiru'd-Dín Sháh, Khán Bábá Khán was made Gov. of Yazd and sent Áqá Khán-i-Írvání as his deputy. The latter was involved in the Yazd upheaval in 1850 associated with Vaḥíd (see p. 106). Later, Khán Bábá Khán sent Shaykh-'Alí Khán, his nephew, as his deputy to Yazd, who captured and killed Muḥammad-'Abdu'lláh. Sheil seems to have considered Khán Bábá Khán as a Russian subject and protégé (although this seems strange in view of Khán Bábá Khán's campaigns against the Russians and the fact that he was dispossessed of all his property under the Treaty of Turkumancháy). Sheil, therefore, blocked his appointment as C.-in-C. of the Persian Inf. in early 1852. He was appointed Gov. of Kirmán in the middle of 1852 and moved to Kirmán, where after 3 years he died in the summer of 1855. He was married to a sister of Muḥammad Sháh.

Muḥammad Sháh *see* pp. 153–4.

Muḥammad-Taqí, Ḥájí Mírzá the Afnán, son of Ḥájí Siyyid Muḥammad, the maternal uncle of the Báb. He was converted through reading Bahá'u'lláh's *Kitáb-i-Íqán*, which was written in answer to questions that his father had put to Bahá'u'lláh. He settled in Yazd and became one of the most prominent merchants of that town. He was also made the Consular Agent for Russia and was hence known as Vakílu'd-Dawlih (Deputy of the Government). In 1892, T. E. Gordon visited Yazd with a view to appointing a British Consular Agent there; he wrote: 'I met many of the Yezd merchants, Mahomedan and Parsee, during my visit there in April last, and among them, Haji Mirza Mohamed Taqi-Shirazi (old Shiraz Family) the first Mahomedan merchant there. He is the Russian Agent in Yezd. He and all his family are of the Babi sect. He is an old man of over 70 with a fine presence and most agreeable manners. He married a daughter of Beha-i-Ullah, the Head of the Babi faith now at Acre, Syria [Vakílu'd-Dawlih in fact married his own cousin, named Bíbí-Zuhrá Bigum] . . . One of the brothers is very wealthy and the family altogether is the most influential in Yezd' (FO 60 539). In 1902, 'Abdu'l-Bahá instructed him to proceed to 'Ishqábád to superintend the construction of the Mashriqu'l-Adhkár. Vakílu'd-Dawlih spent unstintingly of his own resources for this project. Eventually, at an advanced age, he proceeded to 'Akká where he died in 1911. (See 'Abdu'l-Bahá *Memorials of the Faithful* pp. 126–9.) (See fig. 45.)

Muḥammad-Taqí, Shaykh, Áqá Najafí was born 19 Apr. 1846 in Iṣfahán. He studied at Najaf and then returned to Iṣfahán where after his father's death he took up his father's position as Imám of the Masjid-i-Sháh. By the time of his death in Iṣfahán on 5 July 1914, he had become the foremost mujtahid in Iran and one of the wealthiest men in Iṣfahán. (See fig. 44.)

Muḥammad-Taqí Mírzá, Ruknu'd-Dawlih (Pillar of the State) 4th son of Muḥammad Sháh and consanguineous brother of Náṣiru'd-Dín Sháh. Gov. of Khurásán from 1876 to 1891 with several short breaks (the longest being 1884–7). d. 1901. (See fig. 00.) Generally considered a very incompetent and corrupt Governor. (For many years his Vazír in Khurásán was Mírzá Muḥammad-Riḍá, Mu'taminu's-Salṭanih, a Bahá'í.) Described thus by Curzon in 1889: 'He had the reputation of being a mild but timid individual, who shared the family taste for saving, but temporises in politics . . . He is short and very fat, but wears an amiable expression, and, although unlike the Shah, has the distinctive Kajar features.' (*Persia and the Persian Question*, Vol. 1 pp. 168–9)

Muḥammad-Valí Khán, Naṣru's-Salṭanih (later the Sipahdár-i-A'ẓam and Sipahsálár-i-A'ẓam), was the grandson of one of Muḥammad Sháh's military commanders and a native of Tunukábun in Mázindarán. He was for many years Governor of Tunukábun and in *c.* 1885 became Sartíp (Brig.-Gen.) of the Tunukábun Reg. He was given the title Náṣru's-Salṭanih in *c.* 1887. After several other posts, he became Governor of Rasht in 1899, a post which he held for 4 years and 4 months until his dismissal (see pp. 373–6). He later achieved prominence as a leader of the Constitutional Movement. In 1908 he was sent to Tabríz to quell the Nationalist rioters, but he fell out with 'Aynu'd-Dawlih the Governor there and retired to Tunukábun, re-emerging in Feb. 1909 as the leader of the Nationalist forces, as they took the town of Rasht. He headed the march on Ṭihrán, entering it in July 1909 and thus forcing Muḥammad-'Alí Sháh's abdication. In the new regime, he served several times as Prime Minister until his death in Jan. 1926 in Ṭihrán. On 14 Sept. 1912, Muḥammad-Valí Khán, who was then Governor of Tabríz, called on Nicolas, who was then the French Consul in Tabríz. Nicolas reports: 'The conversation revolved entirely around the Báb, with whose doctrines my guest seemed to agree [dont mon hôte semblait partager les doctrines].' (Nicolas to French For. Ministry No. 71, 19 Sept. 1912. Sér. Corr. Polit., Consulat Tauris. Nouvelle Série, No. 9, 1913, p. 74. Also communicated to the Legation in Ṭihrán.) Muḥammad-Valí Khán met 'Abdu'l-Bahá in 1913 in Paris.

Muḥsin Khán, Ḥájí Mírzá Persian diplomat and statesman, b. 1820. Worked in St Petersburg and Paris Embassies. Chargé d'Affaires London 1866. Min. London 1869. Ambass. Istanbul 1872. Given title Mu'ínu'l-Mulk (Supporter of the Kingdom) *c.* 1873. Made Min. of Justice and given title Mushíru'd-Dawlih 1891–2. For. Min. 1896. Was Prime Min. in 1898, but having failed to obtain a loan from the English was dismissed after 2 months. Became ill in 1899 and travelled to Europe. d. 26 Aug. 1899.

Mu'tamadu'd-Dawlih *see* pp.167–9.

Na'ím-i-Núrí, Mírzá son of Muḥammad-Zakí Khán, Vazír of Fárs and cousin of Mírzá Áqá Khán, the Prime Minister. He became Lashkar-Nivís-Báshí (Registrar or Paymaster) of the forces of Fárs, and during the period when his cousin was Prime Minister he held great power and influence in Fárs. He became Gov. of Nayríz 1852 and of Daráb and Jahrum as well in 1856. When Mírzá Áqá Khán fell from power in 1858, Mírzá Na'ím was arrested, tortured and fined. Browne, when in Yazd in 1888, met Mírzá 'Alí-Akbar Khán-i-Núrí, a relative of Mírzá Na'ím, who gave a graphic account of the latter's punishments (see Browne *A Year Amongst the Persians* pp. 441–2, and *A Traveller's Narrative* pp. 259–61). Years later, Mírzá Na'ím fell foul of Ẓillu's-Sulṭán. Dr Wills (*In the Land of the Lion and Sun* pp. 272–3) records the tortures that led to Mírzá Na'ím's death in 1875: 'The Governor of Fars (at that time, 1870–5), the Zil-es-Sultan, wishing to wring a large fine, and a considerable sum of money supposed to have been appropriated by the paymaster-general, after numerous indignities placed Mirza Naim in a snow-chair – the man was seventy-five years of age – compelled him to drink water-melon juice, to produce the well-known diuretic effect, and while the sufferer was frozen to the snow-seat, caused a dog to be placed on his lap, thus insulting his aged co-religionist. Although the man had borne these horrible tortures for some hours, he now consented to pay the sum demanded. Of course the result to his aged frame was not long in doubt; he soon succumbed to the effects of the injuries he received.'

Najaf-Qulí Khán, Ṣamṣámu's-Salṭanih Bakhtíyárí leader (Ilkhání) who played a prominent role in the Constitutional Revolution. At the beginning of 1909 he had occupied Iṣfahán as leader of the constitutional forces; a move that initiated a process culminating in the overthrow of Muḥammad-'Alí Sháh and the re-establishment of the Constitution in July 1909 (see p. 354). He was made Governor of Iṣfahán and later, in 1911, became Prime Minister at the time of Muḥammad-Alí Sháh's abortive attempt to regain he throne.

Najafí, Áqá *see* Muḥammad-Taqí, Shaykh

Najmájer, Marie von Austro-Hungarian poetess, b. Ofen-pest 3 Feb. 1844, the daughter of a Hungarian *Hofrat*. Spent most of her life in Vienna becoming fully conversant with the German language. Writer of lyric and epic poetry, prose and drama. Was much involved in the promotion of women's education. d. Aussee, Steiermark, 25 Aug. 1904. (See fig. 10.)

Námiq Pásh͟á, Muḥammad (Mehmed Namik) Turkish provincial governor, b. 1804. Ambass. to London 1834. Commdr of Forces in Arabia 1843. Gov. of Bag͟hdád 1851–2. Mus͟hír of the Túpk͟h͟ánih 1852. Gov. of Bursa 1854. Gov. of Arabia 1857–8. Gov. of Bag͟hdád 1861–8. Went on to occupy several very important positions at Istanbul including a post in the Cabinet of 1876 which brought about many changes. d. 1892. Known as a liberal in his youth but later became reactionary. Fluent in French.

Náṣiru'd-Dín Sháh *see* pp. 156–60.

Naṣru's-Salṭanih *see* Muḥammad-Valí K͟h͟án

Náyibu's-Salṭanih *see* Kámrán Mírzá

Nayyiru'd-Dawlih *see* Sulṭán-Ḥusayn Mírzá

Nesselrode, Count Karl Robert (1780–1862) Russian diplomat. Dominated Russian foreign policy from 1812. For. Min. 1816. Also Chancellor 1844. ret. 1856.

Nicolas, Louise Alphonse Daniel (A.-L.-M.) French orientalist and consular official, b. Ras͟ht 27 Mar. 1864. ed. École des jeunes de langues and École des langues orientales vivantes. Entered service of French For. Off. 12 Aug. 1877. Student-Dragoman Ṭihrán 12 Aug. 1887. Dragoman 2nd class 9 Dec. 1893. Medaille d'honneur en argent 20 Jan. 1894. Dragoman-Chancelier Larnaca, Cyprus, 26 July 1894. Acting Con. Tangier 2 Dec. 1895. 1st Dragoman Smyrna 6 June 1896, Ṭihrán 10 Oct. 1898. Dragoman 1st class 19 Sept. 1899. 1st Interpreter Ṭihrán 1904–7. Acting Con. Tabríz 26 Nov. 1906. Con. 2nd Class 30 Jan. 1907. Con. Tabríz 7 June 1907. Chevalier de la Légion d'honneur 20 July 1909. Officier de l'Académie 16 May 1913. Con. 1st Class 6 Sept. 1913. Con. Tiflis 1916–20. Con.-Gen. Valence 1920–4. Served in French Admin. in Syria 1924–8. Was a regular contributor to several learned journals and especially *Revue du Monde Musulman*, occasionally writing under the pseudonyms *Ghilan* and *Rechti*. ret. to Paris. Died *c*. Feb. 1939. (See fig. 5.)

Nicolas, Louis Jean Baptiste (J. B.) French consular official, b. Hyères (Var) Mar. 1814. Studied oriental languages. Became Dragoman 25 Oct. 1846. Dragoman at Istanbul Embassy 1852. Dragoman-Chancelier Bag͟hdád 1854. In the same year, he was instructed to proceed to Ṭihrán to make preparation for the arrival of France's envoy to the Qájár court for a decade. M. Bourée. Sec.-Interpreter Ṭihrán 1 Nov. 1855. 1st Dragoman 1860. When in 1863 the French Govt. decided, for commercial reasons, to create a V.-Consulate at Ras͟ht, Nicolas was appointed to this post. In 1873 he was recalled to his former post at the Ṭihrán Legation. Chevalier de la Légion d'honneur 11 Oct. 1873. Rawlinson described him in 1855 as 'quite illiterate' but added that 'his natural shrewdness and knowledge of Persians, render of some value his report of facts and the inferences he draws from them.' (FO 78 1115) He was the author of a French – Persian dictionary. d. Ṭihrán 20 Oct. 1875.

Nicolas, Michel (1810–86), French theologian. ed. Geneva and Berlin. Doctorate, Strasburg 1838. Chair of Philosophy in Fac. of Protestant Theology, Montauban 1838.

Nicolson, Sir Arthur (1849–1928), British diplomat and statesman. Sec. Legation Ṭihrán 1885. Chargé 1885–6. Ambass. Morocco 1895, Madrid 1905, St Petersburg 1906. Permanent Under-Sec. of State for For. Aff. 1910. ret. 1916. Created 1st Baron Carnock 1916.

Nicolson, Hon. Harold George British diplomat, journalist and politician, b. Ṭihrán 21 Nov. 1886. Joined For. Off. 1909. Attaché Madrid 1911. 3rd Sec. Istanbul 1912. Paris Peace Conf. 1918–19. Seconded to League of Nations 1919–20. Counsellor Ṭihrán 19 Nov. 1925. Chargé 3 July – 5 Nov. 1926. 1st Sec. Berlin 1927. Resigned 20 Dec. 1929. Editorial staff, London *Evening Standard*, 1930. MP for W. Leicester (Nat. Lab.) 1935–45. Gov. of BBC 1941–6. KCVO 1953. Numerous publications. d. 1 May 1968.

Norman, Herman Cameron b. 8 June 1872. Son of Charles Lloyd Norman of Bromley Common, Kent, and Julia, daughter of Charles Hay Cameron. ed. Eton and Trinity Coll. Cambridge. Entered Diplomatic Service as Attaché 23 Oct. 1894. Cairo 15 Feb. 1896. 3rd Sec. 22 Dec. 1896. Istanbul 14 May 1897, Washington 22 Jan. 1900. 2nd Sec. 27 Oct. 1900. St Petersburg 1 Oct. 1903. 1st Sec. 27 Oct. 1907. Sec. of various International Conferences 1907–13. Counsellor Tokyo 14 Feb. 1914, Buenos Aires 6 Mar. 1914, Tokyo 28 May 1914. Sec. of British Delegation to Peace Conf. Paris 1919. Min. Plen. 1919. Withdrawn from the Delegation by Curzon and sent as Envoy to Ṭihrán 1 Feb. 1920. Forced to resign from this post after incurring Curzon's displeasure and left Diplomatic Service Sept. 1921. Privy Chamberlain of Sword and Cape to Pope Pius XI and Pius XII. CB 1920, CSI 1919, CBE 1917. d. 8 Sept. 1955.

O'Connor, Maj. (later Lt-Col) William Frederick Travers British soldier, b. 1870. Joined Roy. Artillery 1890, Indian Army 1905. Maj. 1908, Lt-Col 1916. Con. Sístán 1909. Acting Con.-Gen. Ma<u>sh</u>had, 1910. Acting Con. <u>Sh</u>íráz 1912, 1913, 1916. British Resident Nepal 1918.

Oliphant, (later Sir) Lancelot British diplomat and civil servant, b. 1881. Entered For. Off. 1903. 3rd Sec. Istanbul 1905, Ṭihrán 1909–11. Asst Sec. at For. Off. 1920. Counsellor 1923. Asst Under-Sec. of State 1927–36. Ambass. Belgium 1939. Captured by Germans and imprisoned June 1940 – Sept. 1941. ret. Nov. 1944. KCMG 1931. d. 2 Oct. 1965.

Oliphant, Laurence (christened Lowry), British mystic and author, b. Cape Town 1829. Was in Turkey during the Crimean War. Accompanied Lord Elgin's mission to China in 1857. 1st Sec. to Japanese Legation 1861, but was attacked and badly injured shortly after his arrival there. From about this time he became increasingly involved with Thomas Lake Harris, the American spiritualist. He was elected Liberal MP for Stirlingburgh in 1865 but after 2 years gave up everything and went to join Harris's community in America. In 1870, he returned to England and was *Times* war correspondent during the Franco-Prussian War. In 1872, he married Alice le Strange and in the following year returned to Harris in America. From 1878 onwards he took an increasing interest in a scheme for the return of the Jews to Palestine. In 1879, he visited Palestine and Syria looking for a place suitable for his proposed colony of Jews. This scheme failed and in 1882, after the final rupture with Harris, Oliphant settled in Haifa where he lived until his death. He died while in England on 23 Dec. 1888 at the house of Sir Mountstuart Grant Duff in Twickenham. He had married Rosamond Dale Owen (later Templeton) 4 months before his death.(See fig. 27.)

Pellissier de Reynaud, Pierre Hadjoute de French lawyer and consular official. Attaché (Archives and Chancellery Dept.) French For. Off. 1854. Dept. of Consular and Commercial Aff. 1854. Student Con. at Tangier 1858. Con. 2nd Class Jiddah 1862, Ba<u>gh</u>dád 18 Nov. 1864. Chevalier de la Légion d'honneur 31 Mar. 1867. Con. Port Said 27 Nov. 1869. Con. 1st Class 1869. Con. Cairo 1872, Malaga 1876, Smyrna 1878. Con.-Gen. 1879.

Pillon, François (1830–1914), French philosopher. Worked with Larousse at the École normale 1858–64. Worked on the *Grand Dictionnaire universel du XIXe siècle* 1865–71. Founded the publication *L'Année Philosophique* 1867, which, after a lapse, restarted publication in 1890.

Pisani, Étienne belonged to a Venetian family of Istanbul several of whom served in the British Embassy. Began working in the British Embassy as student interpreter 1823. Dragoman 1841. 1st Dragoman 1852 (ret. briefly 1857–8). ret. 1876. d. 7 May 1882

Plumer, Herbert Charles Onslow, Lord (1857–1932), British soldier and statesman. Field-Marshall 1919. Gov. of Malta 1919–20. High Commssr Palestine 1925–8. Created Bar. 1919, lst Viscount 1929.

Polak, Dr Jakob Eduard Austrian-Jewish doctor specializing in Opthalmology. Was recruited on the instruction of Mírzá Taqí Khán to teach at the Dáru'l-Funún. He was in von Gumoens's party and arrived in Ṭihrán on 24 Nov. 1851, shortly after Mírzá Taqí Khán's downfall. He taught Medicine and Surgery at the Dáru'l-Funún. After the death of Dr Cloquet (q.v.), was personal physician to the Sháh. Returned to Vienna 1861.

Ponsonby, Sir Frederick (later Lord Sysonby) (1867–1935), Asst Priv. Sec. to Queen Victoria, Edward VII and King George V. Served S. African War 1901–2, and World War 1914. Keeper of the Privy Purse 1914–35.

Preece, John Richard British consular official, b. 1843. ed. private School and Imp. Coll. Asst Traffic Manager, Indo-European Telegraph Dept. Ṭihrán 1868. Asst Supt. Gd. I 1876. Joined Consular Service 1891. Con. Iṣfahán 1891. Con.-Gen. 1900–1906. d. 25 Feb. 1917.

Prokesch, Anton, Baron (later Count) von Prokesch-Osten Austrian diplomat, b. Graz. 10 Dec. 1795. Entered Austrian Army and fought in battle of Leipzig and in the campaign against Napoleon, becoming ADC to the Austrian Gen. Schwartzenberg. He performed several military and diplomatic missions in Greece and Turkey (including a visit in 1829 to 'Akká, then under 'Abdu'lláh Páshá), and received in 1830 the title 'Ritter von Osten' (Knight of the Orient). Also in 1830, he met and became a strong supporter of Napoleon's son, the Duke of Reichstadt, until the latter's death in 1832. In 1831 Prokesch was put in charge of the army of occupation in Bologna and the following year sent on a mission to Rome. In 1833, he acted as mediator in the peace negotiations between the Sulṭán and Muḥammad-'Alí Páshá, the rebellious Viceroy of Egypt. From 1834 to 1849, he was Austrian Min. at Athens, and from 1849 to 1852 at Berlin. Created Bar. 1845 and Field-Marshal 1848. From 1853 to 1855, he was Austrian delegate and Pres. of the Assembly of German States at Frankfurt. In 1855 he was named as Internuncio (Min.) at Constantinople, and in 1861 was given the full rank of Ambass. He remained at this post until 1871. He was created Ct in 1871. d. Vienna 26 Oct. 1876. (See fig. 21.)

Qásim Khán-i-Válí, Sardár Humáyún born *c.* 1892. Son of 'Alí Khán-i-Válí. ed. in Paris. In 1913 received the title of Sardár Humáyún and occupied several important posts such as Gov. of Ṭihrán, Commdr of the Central Brigade, Gov. of Sulṭánábád. In 1920, was appointed head of the Cossack Brigade after the dismissal of its Russian officers.

Qavám, Aḥmad, Qavámu's-Salṭanih brother of Vuthúqu'd-Dawlih and cousin of Muṣṣadiq. He was secretary to 'Aynu'd-Dawlih when the latter was Prime Minister. He took a prominent role in the Constitutional Movement and afterwards held several important Cabinet positions. After the *coup d'état* occurred in 1921, he was arrested and charged with financial irregularities. When Siyyid Ḍíyá'u'd-Dín fell however, he was made Prime Minister. This ministry only lasted four months, but he was Prime Minister again on several further occasions until death in 1955.

Qavámu'l-Mulk *see* 'Alí-Akbar, Ḥájí Mírzá

Qavámu's-Salṭanih *see* Qavám, Aḥmad

Rawlinson, Maj. (later Sir) Henry Creswicke British statesman and archaeologist, b. Chadlington, Oxfordshire, 11 Apr. 1810. ed. Ealing Sch. Entered service of East India Co. as cadet. Sent to Persia to train troops under 'Abbás Mírzá 1833–9. Served Afghan War 1839–42. Con. Ba<u>gh</u>dád, arrived 6 Dec. 1843. Served there until 1855 with a break Oct. 1849 – Dec. 1851, achieving considerable renown as an archaeologist. MP Reigate 1858. Member of India Council 1858. Min. Ṭihrán 16 Apr. 1859 – May 1860. Resigned over issue of whether the Legation in Persia should be run by the India Off. or the For. Off. MP Frome 1865–8. Appointed India Council 1868. KCB 1856. d. 5 Mar. 1895.

Rees (later Sir) John David British colonial administrator and politician, b. 16 Dec. 1854. Entered India Civil Service 1875. Became Under-Sec. to Madras Govt and Priv. Sec. to several Governors of Madras. Government translator of several languages including Persian. Travelled widely throughout Asia. MP (Lib. Indep.) for Montgomery 1906–10. MP (Unionist) for E. Nottingham 1912–22. Chairman of British Central Africa Co. KCIE 1910. Created 1st Bt 1919. d. 2 June 1922.

Renan, Joseph Ernest (1823–92), French philosopher, philologist, historian, theologian and orientalist. Published numerous books on a wide variety of subjects. Travelled to Syria and Turkey 1860–61.

Rendel, (later Sir) George William British diplomat, b. 1889. ed. Downside and Queen's Coll. Oxford. Entered Diplomatic Service 1913. Served in Berlin, Athens, Rome, Lisbon, Madrid, and at For. Off. from 1919. 1st Sec. 1923. Counsellor 1930. Head of Eastern Dept. of For. Off. 1930–8. Min. Bulgaria 1938–41. Min. then Ambass. Yugoslav Govt-in-Exile in London 1941–3. Employed at For. Off. and UK Rep. on European Committee of UN Relief and Rehabilitation Admin. 1944–7. Ambass. Belgium 1947. ret. 1950.

Riḍá <u>Kh</u>án, Mírzá, Arfa'u'd-Dawlih Persian Con.-Gen. Tiflis 1889. Min. in Russia 1895, Norway and Sweden 1896. Persian delegate to the Hague Peace Conference 1899. Ambass. to Turkey 1900.

Rochechouart, Julien, Comte de French diplomat. Attaché Ṭihrán 5 Apr. 1860. 3rd Sec. 25 Oct. 1862. Chargé after Gobineau's departure from Persia 16 Sept. 1863. 2nd Sec. Peking 31 Dec. 1866. Chevalier de la Légion d'honneur 15 Aug. 1868. 1st Sec. Peking 1872. Con.-Gen. Belgrade 20 Apr. 1877. Min. Haiti 1877–9. Author of *Souvenirs d'un Voyage en Perse*, an extremely useful and detailed work on Persia that deserves to be more widely known. Rochechouart was very well thought of by Gobineau, who praises him in both his official dispatches and his letters to Prokesch-Osten.(See fig 3.)

Roemer, Hermann German cleric, b. Pfrondorf 8 July 1880. ed. Karlsgymnasium Stuttgart, and Univ. of Tübingen. Grad. 1902 in Theology. Studied at Basle Missionary Seminary 1903–6, and Evangelical Theol. Seminary at Tübingen 1907–10.

Rolland, Romain French writer, b. Clamecy, Burgundy, 1868. ed. Lycée Louis-le-Grand and École normale supérieure. Spent 2 years in Rome then returned to Paris 1895 to teach History at École normale and History of Music at Sorbonne (1900–1912). Began writing on the history of music but soon expanded into biography and novels. Awarded Nobel Prize for Literature 1916. d. 1944.

Ronchaud, Louis de (1816–87), French writer. At first wrote poetry but later turned to historical, archaeological and artistic research. Wrote for *Libre Recherche*, *Revue de Paris*, *Gazette des Beaux-Arts*, *Revue Nationale*. Became Inspecteur des beaux-arts 1872. Sec.-Gen. de l'administration des beaux-arts 1879; Directeur des musées nationaux 1881.

Ronzevalle, Ferdinand-Frederic French consular official, b. 4 May 1830. Auxiliary Dragoman to V.-Consulate of Philippopolis 1855. Transferred to Adrianople 25 Jan. 1868. Acting Con. 11 Apr. – 9 Nov. 1868. Dragoman without fixed base, 31 Aug. 1877. Dragoman-Chancellier Philippopolis 28 Dec. 1878, Adrianople 19 Apr. 1879. Dragoman 3rd Class 18 Sept. 1880, 2nd Class 1882. Dragoman-Chancellier Beirut 1885. Dragoman 1st Class 1887. 1st Dragoman Beirut 16 Dec. 1887. Chevalier de la Légion d'honneur 1892. Con. 2nd Class 1897. ret. 1901.

Rosen (Rozen), Baron Victor (Viktor) Romanovich Russian orientalist, b. Reval, Estonia, 5 Mar. 1849. ed. Univs. of St Petersburg, Leipzig and Greifswald. Lect. at Univ. of St Petersburg 1872. Prof. of Oriental Studies 1885. Pres. and Founder of the Oriental Section of the Imp. Russian Archaeological Soc. Editor of the *Zapiski* (Archives) of this Oriental Section from 1886 until his death. Member of the Academy of Sciences, St Petersburg, from 1879. Corresponding member of the Académie des inscriptions et belles lettres, Paris. d. St Petersburg 23 Jan. 1908. (See fig. 8.)

Rosenberg, Rev. Leon b. 5 Apr. 1828 of Austrian-Jewish parents. Visited Istanbul in 1841 and again in 1844 when he was converted to Christianity. Returned to Brussa and later spent 6 years at Malta Protestant Coll. He completed his preparation for the ministry in London and Edinburgh. For a time he was a missionary of the Jewish Committee of the Church of Scotland in Salonika and Smyrna. He then spent a period setting up British schools for boys in the towns around the Mediterranean. On 21 Aug. 1865 he was engaged by the British Soc. for the Propagation of the Gospel among the Jews and sent to Adrianople to work among the numerous Jews in that city. He remained at this post for 40 years until his death in Adrianople 6 May 1905. (See fig. 22.)

Ross, Sir Denison British orientalist, b. 6 Jan. 1871. Studied oriental languages at Paris and Strasburg. Principal of Calcutta Madrasah 1901. Curator of Oriental Art at British Museum 1914. First Director and chief creator of the Sch. of Oriental Studies, London, also Prof. of Persian, Univ. of London. ret. 1937. Represented Britain at Firdawsi Millenary, Ṭihrán. Went to Istanbul for British Information Off. d. Istanbul 20 Sept. 1940.

Ross, Col. (later Sir) Edward Charles British soldier and consular official, b. Rosstrevor, Co. Down, 23 Sept. 1836. ed. Edinburgh Mil. Acad. Entered service of East India Co. 1855. Entered polit. service 1863. Con. Musqát 1871. Resident Persian Gulf 1872–8. Con.-Gen. for S. Persia 28 Nov. 1878 – 26 Mar. 1891. Kt 1892. d. 2 Feb. 1913.

Ruknu'd-Dawlih *see* Muḥammad-Taqí Mírzá and 'Alí-Naqí Mírzá

Rumbold, (later Sir) Horace George Montague British diplomat, b. 1869. ed. Eton. Entered Diplomatic Service 1888. 3rd Sec. 1893, Ṭihrán 13 July 1895. 2nd Sec. 5 Feb. 1896, Vienna 26 July 1897, Cairo 1900. Counsellor at Tokyo 1909, Berlin 1913 until outbreak of War. Min. Berne 1916, Warsaw 1919. British High Commssr Istanbul 1920. Privy Councillor 1920. Ambass. Madrid 1924, Berlin 1928. ret. 1933. Chief Delegate and British Signatory to Lausanne Conf. 1922–3. V.-Chairman of Roy. Commission on Palestine 1936–7. Succeeded as 9th Bt 1913. GCB 1934, GCMG 1923. d. 24 May 1941.

Ṣádiq-i-Sanglají, Siyyid also known as Siyyid Ṣádiq-i-Ṭabáṭabá'í, b. *c.* 1812 in Iṣfahán. However, soon after his birth, his father, Siyyid Mihdí, moved to Hamadán where Siyyid Ṣádiq grew up. Siyyid Ṣádiq became one of the foremost 'ulamá of Ṭihrán, and was responsible for the denunciation of the liberal Mujtahid, Shaykh Hádíy-i-Najmábádí. Siyyid Ṣádiq was famous for the number of his children, amongst whom was the constitutionalist reformer, Siyyid Muḥammad-i-Ṭabáṭabá'í. Shoghi Effendi writes, 'the notorious Mujtahid

Siyyid Ṣádiq-i-Ṭabáṭabá'í, denounced by Bahá'u'lláh as "*the Liar of Ṭihrán*", the author of the monstrous decree condemning every male member of the Bahá'í community in Persia, young or old, high or low, to be put to death, and all its women to be deported, was suddenly taken ill, fell a prey to a disease that ravaged his heart, his brain and his limbs, and precipitated eventually his death.' (*God Passes By* p. 232.) He died 24 Feb. 1883.

Sa'íd Khán, Mírzá, Mu'taminu'l-Mulk b. 1816, the son of Mírzá Sulaymán, Shaykhu'l-Islám of Garmrúd. Would have become one of the 'ulamá had not Mírzá Taqí Khán persuaded him to become his private secretary. Foreign Minister, 1852. Mutavallí-Báshí of Shrine of Imám Riḍá, Mashhad 1873. Foreign Minister 1880. d. 5 Mar. 1884. Some three years after his death, his son delivered to the court about one thousand unopened letters, all official correspondence sent to his father, a sad commentary on the running of Iran's foreign affairs for over a quarter of a century.

Saint-Quentin, Ange-Pierre-Guillaume Ouvré de French consular official. Attaché Lisbon, Tunis 1852, Bucharest, Istanbul 1855. Sec. 3rd Class, Istanbul 13 Sept. 1856, Ṭihrán 17 Aug. 1857. At this time Saint-Quentin was a junior colleague of Gobineau, from whom he doubtless derived much of his enthusiasm for and knowledge of the Bábís. Delegated to Commission des Pyrenées 10 Dec. 1859. Sec. 2nd Class 1863, Stuttgart, Tangiers. Sec. 1st Class Lima 1872. Chargé 1872–3, Japan 1873. Agent and Con.-Gen. Belgrade 1877. Chargé at Montenegro 1878. Min. Plen. ret. 4 Jan. 1883.

Salisbury, 3rd Marquess of, Robert Arthur Talbot Gascoyne-Cecil (1830–1903), British statesman, For. Sec. 1878–81. Prim. Min. and For. Sec. 1885–6, 1886–92, 1895–1902. A Tory and Imperialist.

Ṣamṣámu's-Salṭanih *see* Najaf-Qulí Khán

Samuel, Herbert Louis, 1st Viscount Samuel of Mount Carmel and Toxteth (created 1937). British statesman, b. Liverpool 6 Nov. 1870. ed. Univ. Coll. Sch. and Balliol Coll. Oxford. MP for Cleveland, N. Riding, 1902–18, and Darwen, Lancs., 1929–35. Parl. Under-Sec. Home Dept. 1905–9. Chancellor of Duchy of Lancaster (with Cabinet rank) 1909–10 and 1915–16. Postmaster-Gen. 1910–14 and 1915–16. Sec. of State for Home Aff. 1916. British High Commsr to Belgium 1919. High Commsr Palestine 1920–25. Chairman of the Lib. Party 1927–29. Leader of Parl. Lib. Party 1931–5. Sec. of State for Home Aff. 1931–5. PC 1908, GCB 1926, OM 1958, GBE 1920. d. 5 Feb. 1963.

Sardár-Humáyún *see* Qásim Khán-i-Válí

Schindler, Gen. Sir Albert Houtum- (1846–1916), naturalized British subject of German origin. Joined Indo-European Telegraph Dept. 1868. Became telegraph adviser to Persian Govt. 1876. Served in Persian army with rank of General. Employed by Imperial Bank of Persia 1893. Worked for Persian Govt as adviser. ret. 1911. KCIE 1911. Author of many articles on Persia.

Schumacher, Jakob German-American Templar from Buffalo, NY, b. 1825. He was the architect who had drawn up the plans of the Haifa colony to Hardegg's specifications. Later when Hardegg was deposed as head of the colony in 1874, Schumacher assumed that role until his death in 1891. He was also American V.-Con.

Shaykhu'r-Ra'ís *see* Abu'l-Ḥasan Mírzá

Shedd, Rev. John H. American missionary. After 10 years as missionary at Urúmíyyih, returned to USA to become Prof. at Biddle Univ. Returned to Persia after a few years where he died 12 Apr. 1895.

Sheil, Lt-Col. (later Sir) Justin British soldier and diplomat, b. Bellevue House, nr Waterford, Ireland, 2 Dec. 1803. ed. Stonyhurst. Entered East India Co. Army (3rd Bengal Inf.) 1820. Capt. 1830. Commissioned to join a body of officers being sent to train the Persian Army 1833. Sec. British Legation Ṭihrán 16 Feb. 1836. Maj. 1841. Chargé 12 May 1842. Min. 17 Sept. 1844. Lt.-Col. 1847. ret. 3 Sept. 1854. Maj.-Gen. 1859. KCB 1855. d. London 18 Apr. 1871. He was a Roman Catholic. His wife Mary Leonora was the daughter of Stephen Woulfe, chief Baron of the Irish Exchequer. They were married in 1849 while Sheil was on leave of absence from Persia, and she returned with him to Persia. She died in 1869.

Shuckburgh, Sir John Evelyn British civil servant, b. 18 Mar. 1877. ed. Eton and King's Coll. Cambridge. Entered India Off. 1900. In 1921, was appointed by Winston Churchill to the post of Asst Under-Sec. of State in newly-formed Middle East Dept. of the Colonial Off. – charged with setting up civil administrations in the Mandate territories of Iraq, Palestine and Trans-Jordan. Deputy Under-Sec. of State 1931. ret. 1942 but removed to the Historical Section of the Cabinet Off. and wrote history of the Empire during the 1st World War. d. London 8 Feb. 1953.

Smart, (later Sir) Walter Alexander British consular official, b. 12 Nov. 1883. Student Interpreter in the Levant 1 Oct. 1903. Asst 18 Nov. 1905. V.-Con. Ṭihrán 1 Jan. 1909. Acting Con. in Persia various places 1909–13. Employed at Mazagan 1914, Tangier 1915, For. Off. 1916, New York 1917, Salonika 1919. Oriental Sec. Ṭihrán 9 May 1920. Acting Con. Aleppo, 31 Dec. 1920. Con. Aleppo 1923, Damascus 1924. Oriental Sec. to the Residency, Cairo 1926. Promoted to rank of Counsellor 1929. Rank of Min. Plen. 1945. ret. 1948. KCMG 1942. d. 11 May 1962. He had been a student of Prof. Browne at Cambridge.

Smith, Rev. Frederick British missionary. Association Sec. of London Jews' Soc. 1861. Arrived in Jerusalem 28 Feb. 1871 to take temporary charge of the Soc.'s mission there. Returned to London at end of 1871 and became Sec. of the Committee of the Society. Vicar of Woodchester, Glos., and Consulting Sec. to the Soc. 1879. Visitor of Associations 1891. d. Woodchester 12 Apr. 1913.

Stack, Edward MA LL.D., Bengal Civil Service. ed. Royal Academical Institution and Queen's Coll. Belfast. Entered Bengal Civil Service 1870, arrived in India 1872. Held various posts in India including Officiating Under-Sec. to Gov. of India; Home, Revenue and Agriculture Dept. Dec. 1879 – June 1880. Director of Agriculture (Assam), Sept. 1882. Officiating Sec. to Chief Commsr July–Oct. 1883.

Stanley, Lord Edward Henry Smith (1826–93), later 15th Earl of Derby. For. Sec. 1866–8 and 1874–8.

Stanton, Col. (later Gen. Sir) Edward British soldier and consular official. Entered Roy. Engineers as 2nd Lt 19 Dec. 1844. 1st Lt 1846. Capt. 1854. Lt-Col. 22 Jan. 1868. Served in S. Africa and Crimean War (battles of Alma and Inkerman). Con.-Gen. Warsaw 1860. Agent and Con.-Gen. Egypt 15 May 1865. Maj.-Gen. 1873. Chargé d'Affaires Munich 1876. Lt-Gen. 1877. ret. from Army with rank of Gen. 1881. KCMG 1882. d. 24 June 1907.

Stanton, Col. Edward Alexander b. York 15 Nov. 1867. ed. Marlborough and Sandhurst. Gazetted to Oxford Light Inf. 1887. Participated in several expeditions and actions in Sudan including Battle of Omdurman. Lt-Col. 1901. Gov. of K͟harṭúm 1900–1908. ret. 1908. Mil. Sec. to Duke of Connaught in Canada 1914–17. Mil. Gov. Phoenicia district, Palestine, 1918–20. Sec. of Roy. Patriotic Fund Corp. 1909–14 and 1939–42. d. 2 Dec. 1947.

Stern, Henry Aaron missionary, b. Unterreichenbach near Gelnhausen in the Duchy of

Hesse, 11 Apr. 1820, of Jewish parents. Converted to Christianity in London. Studied for missionary work at the Hebrew Coll. of the London Jews' Soc. Appointed to commence a mission to the Jews in Chaldea and Persia Jan. 1844. Ordained Deacon 14 July 1844 in Jerusalem. Based himself in Baghdád and undertook several missionary tours of Persia 1844–52. Then worked among Jews in Istanbul 1852–6, Crimea 1856, Yemen 1856–7, and among the Falasha (Jews) of Ethiopia 1857–61. Returned to Ethiopia 1863, where his maltreatment by the King of Ethiopia was one of the causes of Lord Napier's campaign against that country in 1867. d. London 13 May 1885.

Stevens, Ethel Stefana May later Lady Drower, b. London 1 Dec. 1879. ed. privately. Travelled extensively in Middle East. Initially wrote novels usually based in Middle East, including *The Mountain of God.* Married Sir Edwin Drower, legal adviser to Iraqi Ministry of Justice. Developed interest in, and became foremost authority on, Mandean culture. d. 27 Jan. 1972.

Stevens, George Alexander British consular official and merchant. born *c.* 1825 in Malta. Served as Consular Asst, Tabríz, to his brother, Richard (q.v.), and as Acting Con. during his brother's absences, 4 Mar. – 7 Apr. 1849, 9 June – 20 July 1850 and 20 Oct. 1852 – 3 Feb. 1853. Then left Tabríz, leaving behind considerable debts. Acting V.-Con. Trabizond 1855. V.-Con. Kherson 1858, Nicolaieff 1866. Acting Con.-Gen. Odessa 1866. Con. Nicolaieff 1870, St Thomas and St Croix, West Indies 1876, provinces of Bahia and Sergipe, Brazil 1881. d. 13 Dec. 1890.

Stevens, Richard White British consular official and merchant, b. Malta *c.* 1816. Appointed Con. in Tabríz 2 Mar. 1846, and also engaged in trading activities with his brother George (q.v.). Con. Ṭihrán 22 Apr. 1854. In 1856 retired with the rest of the British Mission to Baghdád. Took ratification of the Treaty following close of the Anglo-Persian War to England May 1857. Resumed duties as Con. in Ṭihrán July 1857. Resigned 8 Oct. 1860. d. 27 Jan. 1865.

Stileman, Rev. (later Bishop) Charles Harvey British missionary, b. Aden *c.* 1858. ed. Repton Sch., Trinity Coll. and Ridley Hall Cambridge. BA 1886. Ordained Deacon 1887, Priest 1888. Curate of St Peter's, Tynemouth, 1887–9. Proceeded as CMS missionary to Baghdád 24 Oct. 1889, Julfá 1891. In England 1893–5, then returned to Persia as Sec. of Persian Mission, resident at Julfá. ret. 1906 for family reasons. Consecrated as 1st Bishop of Persia 25 July 1912. DD 1912. Proceeded to Julfá 2 Nov. 1912. Returned to England 21 May 1914 because of ill-health. Resigned Bishopric 20 July 1915. d. Wimbledon 23 Feb. 1925.

Storrs, (later Sir) Ronald, British colonial administrator, b. 19 Nov. 1881. ed. Temple Grove, Charterhouse, Pembroke Coll. Cambridge. Entered Egyptian Govt., Ministry of Finance, 1904. Oriental Sec. to British Agency Egypt 1909. Asst Polit. Officer to Anglo-French Polit. Mission, Egyptian Exped. Force 1917. Secretariat of War Cabinet, autumn 1917. Mil. Gov. of Jerusalem 1917–20, with brief period as Mil. Gov. of N. Palestine in 1918. Civil Gov. of Jerusalem and Judea 1920–26. Gov. of Cyprus 1926–32. Gov. of N. Rhodesia 1932–34. Member of London County Council 1937–45. Numerous honorary and other positions. d. 1 Nov. 1955.

Stuart, Anne Isabella British/New Zealand missionary, born *c.* 1858. Went to Persia with her father, Bishop Stuart, in 1894. Accepted as CMS missionary 7 Oct. 1902. Remained at Iṣfahán until ret. 1926. d. 8 Mar. 1949.

Sulṭán-Ḥusayn Mírzá, Jalálu'd-Dawlih eldest son of Ẓillu's-Sulṭán, b. *c.* 1869. In 1881, when Ẓillu's-Sulṭán was made Gov. of Fárs, he sent Jalálu'd-Dawlih (then aged 12) as his deputy. Married daughter of Mírzá Yúsif, Mustawfíyu'l-Mamálik, *c.* 1882. In Feb. 1888, when Ẓillu's-Sulṭán was deprived of all his governorships except that of Iṣfahán, Jalálu'd-Dawlih was replaced as Gov. of Fárs. In 1890, Ẓillu's-Sulṭán was made Gov. of Yazd and sent Jalálu'd-Dawlih as his deputy. In 1892, a number of Yazdí notables went to Ṭihrán to ask for Jalálu'd-Dawlih's removal. In 1894 he was made Gov. of Burújird. Was again Gov. of Yazd in 1903 when there was a great upheaval against the Bahá'ís resulting in many martyrdoms (see ch. 27). In 1907 he was made Gov. of Zanján but became caught up in the Constitutional struggles. During these struggles, Jalálu'd-Dawlih tried to keep in with both sides and consequently was trusted by neither. When the Majlis was bombarded in 1908, the houses of Ẓillu's-Sulṭán and Jalálu'd-Dawlih were also bombed. After this he was again arrested and exiled to Europe. (See fig. 39.)

Sulṭán-Ḥusayn Mírzá, Nayyiru'd-Dawlih (Luminary of the Kingdom), son of Parvíz Mírzá, Nayyiru'd-Dawlih, 53rd son of Fatḥ-'Alí Sháh. Was a personal attendant of Náṣiru'd-Dín Sháh. On death of his father in 1888, received title Nayyiru'd-Dawlih and became Gov. of Níshápúr. Gov. of Ṭihrán 1897–8 and 1905. Gov. of Khurásán 1901–3 and 1912, until his death in 1916.

Sulṭán-Ma'súd Mírzá, Ẓillu's-Sulṭán (Shadow of the King) (1850–1918), 4th but eldest surviving son of Náṣiru'd-Dín Sháh. Since his mother was not of royal blood and only a temporary wife (*síghih*) of the Sháh, he was excluded from the succession to the throne in favour of Muẓaffaru'd-Dín. Became Gov. of Mázindarán at the age of 11 and Gov. of Fárs when aged 13. He married Hamdámu'l-Mulúk (the daughter of Mírzá Taqí Khán and Náṣiru'd-Dín Sháh's sister, 'Izzatu'd-Dawlih). In 1874, he became Gov. of Iṣfahán and continued in this post for 32 years. Over the years 1878 to 1882, various Governorships were added to his responsibility until at the end of this period he was Gov. of virtually all of southern Persia. He wanted to become Crown Prince, however. He was supported by England, and seemed to be on the verge of achieving his ends, when he suddenly fell from power in 1888 and was reduced to being just Gov. of Iṣfahán with much diminished prestige. On the assassination of Náṣiru'd-Dín Sháh, the English refused to support any pretension of his to the throne, and he submitted to Muẓaffaru'd-Dín Sháh. He remained Gov. of Iṣfahán until the accession of Muḥammad-'Alí Sháh. Following the Constitutional Revolution he was exiled to Europe, and only allowed to return towards the end of the First World War when he retired to Iṣfahán a broken man (see fig. 33). Curzon, who met him in 1890, wrote: The Shadow of the King is short of stature, unusually corpulent for one of his years, and is a chronic sufferer from gout. A defect in one of his eyes detracts from the smart appearance that he has commonly been made to present in photographs.' (*Persia and the Persian Question* Vol. I, p. 419)

Sulṭán-Murád Mírzá, Ḥisámu's-Salṭanih (Sword of the Kingdom) (1818–83), 13th son of 'Abbás Mírzá. Defeated the Sálár's rebellion in 1850 while Gov. of Khurásán. Captured Herat in 1856. Was several times Gov. of Khurásán and Fárs. He was noted for his severity and cruelty but as a result of this his provinces were usually settled.

Sykes, Sir Mark 6th Baronet of Sledmore, Yorks. British statesman, b. London 16 Mar. 1879 into a Roman Catholic family. ed. Jesus Coll. Cambridge 1897, but failed to graduate. Joined Yorkshire Militia and went to S. Africa 1902, then on a journey through Syria and Iraq. Priv. Sec. to George Wyndham at Dublin Castle 1904–5. Hon. Attaché at British Embassy, Istanbul 1905. MP (Conservative) for Central Hull 1911. During War: political duties in Serbia, Bulgaria, Egypt and India. In 1915 entered negotiations with Georges Picot, representing France, about the future of the Near East leading to Sykes-Picot Agreement, signed 16 May 1916 by Great Britain, France and Russia. Attached to For. Off. as chief adviser on Near East. Strong supporter of Zionism. Was of influence in determining the proclamations of Gens. Maude and Allenby on entering Baghdad and Jerusalem respectively. Died in Paris of influenza 16 Feb. 1919.

Sykes, Maj. (later Brig.-Gen. Sir) Percy Molesworth British soldier and consular official, b. 28 Feb. 1867. ed. Rugby and Sandhurst. Gazetted to 16th Lancers 1888, 2nd Dragoon Guards 1888. Capt. 1897. Maj. 1906. Lt-Col 1914. 1st British Con. for Kirmán and Persian Balúchistán 1894, Sístán 1899. Con.-Gen. Khurásán 5 Feb. 1905–Dec. 1913. Raised South Persian Rifles and GOC Southern Persia 1916–18. ret. Sept. 1920. KCIE 1915, CB 1919. Author of several books on Persia including a 2-vol. history. d. 11 June 1945.

Symes, Lt-Col. (Later Sir) George Stewart British soldier and colonial administrator, b. 29 July 1882. Entered Army 1900. Capt. 1907. Maj. 1915. Service in S. Africa 1902, Aden 1903–4, Sudan 1908, European War. Asst Director of Polit. Intelligence, Sudan Govt 1909–12. Priv. Sec. to Sirdar and Gov.-Gen. of Sudan 1913–16. Gov. of Northern District, Palestine (based in Haifa), 1921–5. Chief Sec., Govt of Palestine, 1925–8. Res. Aden 1929–31. Gov. Tanganyika 1931–3, Sudan 1934–40. Accredited Rep. to Permanent Mandates Commission of League of Nations, Geneva 1926, 1928 and 1933. d. 5 Dec. 1962.

Taqí Khán, Mírzá *see* pp. 160–65.

Temple, Lt-Col. Henry Martindale b. 1853. Entered Army as Lt 8 June 1872. Capt. 1884. Maj. 1892. Lt-Col. 8 June 1898. Con.-Gen. Khurásán and Sístán 11 Feb. 1898 – 31 Mar. 1901.

Tennant, Rt Hon. Harold John British politician, b. Innerleithen 18 Nov. 1865. ed. Eton and Trinity Coll. Cambridge. Priv. Sec. of Rt Hon. H. H. Asquith 1892–5. MP (Lib.) for Berwickshire 1894–1918. Served on various Govt committees 1893–9. Parl. Sec. of Board of Trade 1909–11. Financial Sec. to War Off. 1911–12. Under-Sec. of State for War 1912–16. Sec. for Scotland 1916. Deputy Lt of Aberdeenshire 1915. d. 9 Nov. 1935.

Tholozan, Dr (later Sir) Joseph-Désiré French physician, b. Mauritius 8 Jan. 1820. Obtained medical qualifications at Faculté de Medicine Militaire de Paris in 1843. Entered French Mil. Med. Service. Professeur Agrégé at Val-de-Grâce 1865. Took part in Algerian campaign and Crimean War. At the age of 38, he was offered and accepted the post of Personal Physician to Náṣiru'd-Dín Sháh. He spent the remainder of his life in Persia, being responsible for the introduction of much western Medicine to Persia. He wrote many books and articles. He was knighted by Queen Victoria in 1873 during the Sháh's first European tour. Commdr of the Légion d'honneur. d. 1905. (See fig. 30.)

Thomson, (later Sir) Ronald Fergusson British diplomat. 3rd Attaché Ṭihrán Legation 7 Sept. 1848. In charge of Mission 21 Nov. – 9 Dec. 1859. Oriental Sec. 19 July 1862. Chargé 1862, 1863, 1869–70, 1872–3. Sec. Legation 23 Jan. 1863. In attendance on the Sháh in Europe 1873. Min. Ṭihrán 14 June 1879. ret. 1 Nov. 1887. KCMG 1884. d. 15 Nov. 1888. He was the brother of William Taylour Thomson (q.v.).

Thomson, (later Sir) William Taylour British diplomat. Appointed paid Attaché to Persian Mission 12 June 1837. Sec. Legation 7 Apr. 1852. Chargé d'Affaires 7 Mar. 1853–17 Apr. 1855. Suspended diplomatic relations with Persia 4–26 Nov. 1853. Chargé Chile 24 Feb. 1858. Appointed Envoy to Persia 15 July 1872. ret. 1 Apr. 1879. KCMG 24 May 1879. d. 15 Sept. 1883. Brother of Ronald F. Thomson (q.v.).

Townley, Sir Walter Beaupré British diplomat, b. 1863. Joined For. Off. 1885. Numerous diplomatic posts including 3rd Sec. Ṭihrán 1889–92, Sec. of Embassy Istanbul 1903. Counsellor 1904. Washington 1905. Min. Paraguay 1906, Bucharest 1911, Ṭihrán 24 Mar. 1912. ret. 26 Aug. 1919. KCMG 1911. d. 5 Apr. 1945.

Tumanski, Capt. (later Maj.-Gen.) Alexander (Aleksandr) G. Russian soldier and orientalist. Spent several years in 'Ishqábád and the Transcaspia area from 1890. Also was sent on a number of missions into Persia. In the years immediately before the 1st World War he lived in Tiflis, where he taught Arabic and published several books. d. Istanbul 1 Dec. 1920.

Vámbéry, Prof. Arminius distinguished Jewish-Hungarian orientalist, b. Duna-Szerdahaly, Hungary *c.* 1832. Taught himself several languages and in 1852 proceeded to Istanbul, where he earned his living as a language teacher. In 1862–4 he undertook a perilous journey into Central Asia disguised as a darvísh, and as a result of his book describing these adventures, he achieved universal fame and acclamation. He was made Prof. of Oriental Languages in the Univ. of Budapest and was, until the end of his life, received in the highest social circles throughout Europe. d. 15 Sept. 1913.

Vaughan, Henry Bathurst British soldier, b. 27 Feb. 1858. Commissioned 2nd Lt 1880. Lt, Leinster Reg., 1881. Capt., Indian Staff Corps, 17 Apr. 1891. Maj. 1900. Lt-Col. 1904. Participated in Egyptian Expedition 1882, Burma 1891–2, Relief of Peking 1900.

Vazír-Niẓám *see* Ḥasan Khán, Mírzá

Vlassov (Velassow), P. M. Russian Con. at Rasht. Was appointed 1st Russian Con.-Gen. at Mashhad in Spring 1889. He is described by Curzon as 'a diplomatist widely known for his grasp of Persian politics.' (*Persia and the Persian Question* Vol. 1, p. 170.) Later Russian Minister, Ṭihrán 1902–3.

Wardlaw-Ramsay, Elizabeth Caroline British missionary, b. Edinburgh 1849. Accepted as CMS missionary 30 July 1889. Left for 'Akká Oct. 1889. Resigned for family and health reasons July 1907. Returned to Palestine Oct. 1912. d. Jaffa 18 Jan. 1913.

Watson, Maj.-Gen. Sir Harry Davis British soldier, b. 18 July 1866. Entered Dorset Reg. 1885. Capt. Indian Army 1896. Maj. 1903. Lt-Col. 1910. Extra Equerry to H.M. the King 1910. Col. 1914. Maj.-Gen. 17 Sept. 1918. Participated in numerous campaigns: Sikkim 1888, Chin Lushai 1899–1902, China 1900–1901. European War 1914–18. GOC Force in Egypt 7 Jan. 1918. GOC Cairo District 27 Mar. 1919. Chief Administrator, Occupied Enemy Terr. (South) 31 July–31 Dec. 1919. ret. 1924. KBE 1919, d. 7 May 1945.

Watson, Robert Grant British diplomat. Joined Indian Army in 1853. Attached to Persian Exped. Force, May 1857 and to Ṭihrán Legation, 1 June 1857. On active service in Indian Mutiny, Aug. 1857. Employed at Istanbul 1859, in the Caucasus 1862 and at Kirmánsháh and Hamadán 1865. Held various positions in S. America 1865–9. Sec. of Legation at Athens 1870, Washington 1874, Stockholm 1876. ret. 1 Jan. 1880, d. 28 Oct. 1892.

Wellesley, (later Sir) Victor Alexander Augustus Henry British civil servant, b. 1 Mar. 1876. God-son of Queen Victoria and Page of Honour 1887–92. Clerk to For. Off. 1899. Acting 2nd Sec. in Diplomatic Service 1905, Rome 1905–6. Commercial Attaché 1908. Asst Clerk For. Off. 1910. Senior Clerk 1913. Controller of Commercial and Consular Aff. 1916. Asst Sec. For. Off. 1 Apr. 1919. Deputy Under-Sec. For. Off. 1925–36. ret. 1936. KCMG 1926. d. 20 Feb. 1954.

Wemyss, Countess of, Anne daughter of the 1st Earl of Lichfield and first wife of Francis, 10th Earl of Wemyss. She was a close friend of Jowett. d. 1896.

Wemyss, Countess of, Mary née Wyndham (1864–1937). Married in 1883 Hugo Chateris, Lord Elcho, who in 1914 succeeded to the title Earl of Wemyss. Her daughter Cynthia married Herbert Asquith, second son of Lord Asquith, the Prime Minister. Lord Asquith's second wife, Margot, was the sister of Jack Tennant (See p. 422).

Wesselitsky, Gabriel de Russian journalist, b. Tsarkoe Selo near St Petersburg 1841. Entered Russian Army 1858. Worked in Russian For. Off. 1864. Travelled in Near East 1867–70. Much concerned in obtaining the independence of Bosno-Herzegovina. Began writing for newspapers 1867. Correspondent for *Novoe Vremya* in Vienna 1882, Berlin 1887, London from 1892 onwards. Pres. of For. Press Assoc. in London 1896–1911. After Russian Revolution became adviser to British For. Off. on Russian Affairs. d. 27 Aug. 1930.

Westlake, Dr Winifred Agneta British missionary, b. Chippenham, Wilts, *c.* 1871. London Sch. of Med. for Women 1889–93. LRCP, LRCS. Accepted as CMS Missionary 4 Feb. 1902. Departed for Julfá 3 Oct. 1902. Sent to Kirmán Sept. 1903. Continued to work in Kirmán until 1924 and in Iṣfahán until her retirement in 1933. d. 6 Mar. 1954.

White, Dr Henry British missionary, b. 1866. MRCS, LRCP (London Hosp.), 1896. Accepted as CMS Missionary 1895. Proceeded to Julfá 1896, and to Yazd 1898, where he remained until his resignation in 1922. d. Bromley 8 Jan. 1950.

Whyte, Sir (Alexander) Frederick (1883–1970), British statesman. Son of Rev. Alexander Whyte. MP Perth 1910–18. Travelled widely especially USA. Pres. of Legislative Assembly, India, 1920–25. Polit. Adviser to Govt. of China 1929–32. Director-Gen. of the English-Speaking Union of the British Empire, 1938. Head of American Div., Ministry of Information 1939–40.

Whyte, Capt. (later Maj.) John Frederick British soldier and consular official. Entered Roy. Marines as Lt 1889. Attaché For. Dept., Govt of India, 1893. 1st Asst to Resident at Bú<u>sh</u>ihr 1894–5. Acting Con.-Gen. Ma<u>sh</u>had May–Oct. 1895. Capt. 1895. Con. Baṣra 1895–7. Attached to Ṭihrán Legation June 1897 – Feb. 1898. Acting Con.-Gen. Ma<u>sh</u>had 28 Feb. – 14 Apr. 1898. Con. Ma<u>sh</u>had 10 Dec. 1899. Returned India Feb. 1900. Acting Con.-Gen. Ma<u>sh</u>had May 1902 – Oct. 1903.

Wilberforce, Ven. Albert Basil (1841–1916), British clergyman. Canon of Westminster 1894–1900. Rector of St John's, Westminster, and Chaplain to House of Commons 1896–1916. Archdeacon of Westminster 1900–1916.

Wills, Dr Charles James British physician, b. Chichester, Sussex, 13 Oct. 1842. Attended St Bartholomew's Hosp. Med. Sch. London, and Univs. of Aberdeen and Paris. Graduated MRCS and LM 1864; MB, CM 1866; MD 1867. Was Med. Officer with H.M. Indo-European Telegraph Dept. in Persia, then returned to England and practised in various towns: Croydon, S. Hampstead, Kew, Bexley and Hove. d. Hove *c.* 1910.

Wingate, Sir (Francis) Reginald (1861–1953), British soldier and colonial administrator. Served in Egyptian Army. Gov.-Gen. of Sudan 1899. High Commsr Egypt Jan. 1917 – 19. Bt 1920.

Wolff, Sir Henry Drummond Charles British diplomat, b. Malta 12 Oct. 1830, son of Rev. Joseph Wolff. ed. Rugby. Entered For. Off. as clerk 1846. Attached to British Legation Florence 1852. Asst Priv. Sec. to the For. Sec., the Earl of Malmesbury, 1858, and in the same year Priv. Sec. to Sec. for the Colonies, Sir Edward Lytton. Sec. to High Commssr of Ionian Islands 1859–64. Was observer and journalist of Franco-Prussian War of 1870. Conservative MP for Christchurch, Hants, 1874. Participated in several Commissions in Near East. MP for Portsmouth 1880. Proceeded in 1885 to negotiate with Turkey over Egypt's future. Appointed Min. in Persia Dec. 1887. Accompanied the <u>Sh</u>áh in England 1889. Fell ill in 1890 and was unable to return to Persia. Min. at Bucharest July 1891, Madrid

1892. ret. Oct. 1900. GCMG 1878, GCB 1889. d. Brighton 11 Oct. 1908. (See fig. 28.)

Wratislaw, Albert Charles British consular official, b. 17 Oct. 1862. ed. Rossall Sch. Entered Levant Consular Service 1883. V.-Con. Smyrna 1888, Philippopolis 1892. Con. Baṣra 1898. Con.-Gen. Tabríz 1903. Crete 1909. British Commsr on Turko-Persian Boundary Commission 1913. Con.-Gen. Salonika 1914, Beirut 1919. ret. 1920. d. 28 Apr. 1938.

Wright, Austin Henry American missionary, b. Hartford, Vt., 11 Nov. 1811. ed. Dartmouth Coll. and Union Theol. Seminary, New York. Became missionary of the interdenominational Protestant American Board of Commssrs. for For. Missions at Urúmíyyih, Persia, in 1840. Returned USA 1860 and began revision of the New Testament in Syriac. Returned to Persia 1864. d. Urúmíyyih 14 Jan. 1865.

Yate, Lt-Col. (later Col. Sir) Charles Edward British soldier. b. 28 Aug. 1849. Entered Army 1867. Lt 1871, Capt. 1879, Maj. 1887, Lt-Col. 1893, Col. 1901. Served in Afghan War of 1880 as Polit. Officer. Afghan Boundary Commission 1884–7. Con. Muscat 1890–91. Acting Con.-Gen. Mas͟hhad 1893–5 in Ney Elias's absence. Con.-Gen. 11 Sept 1896 – 10 Feb. 1898. Resident Jodhpur 1898, Udaipur 1899. Agent to Gov.-Gen. of Balúc͟histán 1900. ret. 1904. MP for Melton, Leics., 1910–24. Created 1st Bt 1921. d. 29 Feb. 1940.

Zeller, Rev. John German missionary, b. Bisigheim, Württemberg, *c.* 1830. Attended Basle Seminary. Ordained Deacon 1855, Priest 1858. In 1855 proceeded to Palestine as CMS missionary. Nazareth 1857–85, then Jerusalem. ret. to Saxony 1901. d. Wernigerode, Germany, 19 Feb. 1902. (See fig. 25.)

Zhukovski, Prof. Valentin Alekseyevich Russian orientalist, b. 23 Apr. 1858. Travelled in Persia 1883–5. Specialized in Persian language, literature, folklore and ethnography. Prof. at Univ. of St Petersburg. Member of Russian Acad. of Sciences 1899. d. 1918. (See fig. 9.)

Ẓillu's-Sulṭán *see* Sulṭán-Mas'úd Mírzá

Zotenberg, Hermann b. Breslau *c.* 1836. Librarian at Bibliothèque Nationale, Paris. Published several works on oriental subjects.

Abbreviations

The following is a list of abbreviations used particularly in the Biographical Notes in Appendix II. This list does not include standard abbreviations such as those used for decorations, e.g. CB, CSI, KCB, etc.

Acad. Academy
Admin. Administration
Aff. Affairs
Ambass. Ambassador
Aptd Appointed

b. born
Bar. Baron
Brig. Brigadier
Bt Baronet

Capt. Captain
Cav. Cavalry
ch. chapter
C.-in-C. Commander-in-Chief
CMS Church Missionary Society
CO British Colonial Office Archives
Co. Company
Col. Colonel
Coll. College
Commdr Commander
Commsr Commissioner
Con. Consul
Conf. Conference
Ct Count

d. died
Del. Delegate
Dept Department
Div. Division

Eccles. Ecclesiastical
ed. educated at
edn edition
Eng. English
Exped. Expedition, Expeditionary
Extraord. Extraordinary

Fac. Faculty
FO British Foreign Office Archives
For. Foreign

Gd. Grade
Gen. General
GOC General Officer Commanding

Hon. Honorary, Honourable
Hosp. Hospital

Imp. Imperial
Indep. Independent
Inf. Infantry
Insp. Inspector
Internat. International

Kt Knight(ed)

Lab. Labour
lang. language
Lect. Lecturer
Lib. Liberal
lit. literally
Lt Lieutenant

MAE Ministère des Affaires Etrangères, French Foreign Ministry Archives
Maj. Major
Med. Medicine
Mil. Military
Min. Minister
Movt Movement
Mt Mount

Nat. National
nr near
NS New Style, i.e. Gregorian calendar

Off. Office
Or. Oriental
OS Old Style, i.e. Julian calendar

Parl. Parliamentary
PC Privy Councillor
Philos. Philosophy
Plen. Plenipotentiary
PMG Paymaster General
Polit. Political

Pres. President
Priv. Private
Prof. Professor

QMG Quartermaster-General

Reg. Regiment(al)
Rep. Representative
Res. Resident
Roy. Royal

Sch. School
Sec. Secretary

Sen. Senator

Temp. Temporary
Terr. Territory
Theol. Theology
Trans. Translated

Univ. University

V.-Con. Vice-Consul
Vol. Volume

WO British War Office Archives

Glossary

Afnán lit. twigs, designation of members of family of the Báb descended from his three maternal uncles or the two brothers and sister of his wife.

Bast sanctuary.

Ḍábiṭ, Ḍábiṭíyyih (zapti), police, policeman, bailiff.

Farangí (faringhi) foreigner.

Farmán (firman) order, decree.

Farrá<u>sh</u> footman, attendant.

Farrá<u>sh</u>-Bá<u>sh</u>í chief footman.

Farsang (*farsa<u>kh</u>*) distance walked by a ladened mule in an hour: 3–5 miles.

Fatvá (*fatwá*, fitweh) the ruling of a mujtahid or other 'ulamá on a point of religious jurisprudence – usually in the passages quoted this would be the decree of death for a Bábí or Bahá'í for the religious crime of apostasy.

Firangi see *farangí*.

<u>Gh</u>ulám (golam) servant.

Ijázih (*ijáza*) written statement given by a mujtahid to one of his students certifying that the latter's knowledge and competence entitle him to the rank of mujtahid.

Imám-Jum'ih one of the 'ulamá designated to lead the congregational prayer and to deliver the *<u>kh</u>uṭbih*.

Kad-<u>Kh</u>udá the headman of a village or sector of a town.

Kalántar mayor, magistrate.

Kárguzar Persian Foreign Office Agent.

<u>Kh</u>uṭbih the Friday sermon.

Lúṭí (luttee) one of the town's riff-raff or ruffians.

Maḥallih one of the quarters of a town.

Majlis Parliament.

Ma'múr official, functionary.
Mashriqu'l-Adhkár Bahá'í House of Worship.
Maydán public square, piazza.
Mujtahid one who is considered able to deliver authoritative decisions on points of Islamic law, acting on his own judgement.
Munshí secretary.
Mutaṣarrif Turkish local governor (see p. 487).
Qáḍí religious judge.
Rawḍih, Rawḍih-Khání recital of the sufferings and martyrdom of the Imám Ḥusayn and his companions.
Ra'yat (ryot) peasant farmer.
Ṣadr-i-A'ẓam prime minister.
Sarbáz (sirbaz) soldier.
Sardár commander of an army.
Ṣarráf (Saraf) banker, money-changer.
Sartíp (Sartib) brigadier or colonel.
Savvár (sowar) horseman.
Sharí'at (*Sharí'ah, Sharí'a*) Islamic law.
Tufangchí rifleman.
Ṭulláb students of theology.
Túmán unit of Iranian currency. Its value dropped throughout the 19th century: in 1844, it was worth approx. 10 shillings; in 1852, 9*s*. 4*d*.; in 1863, 8*s*. 11*d*.; in 1880, 7*s*. 3*d*.; in 1891, 5*s*. 10*d*.; in 1900, 3*s*. 11*d*.; in 1914, 3*s*. 7*d*.
Túpkhánih artillery.
'Ulamá (Ulema) persons learned in Islamic law.
Vazír minister.
Zapti see *Ḍábiṭ*.

Bibliography

Unpublished Material – Western Languages

Belgium: Archives du Ministère des Affaires Étrangères, Bruxelles

British Museum, London; Papers of 'Álí Pá<u>sh</u>á, Add. 46697

—— Layard Papers, Add. 38994–5, Add. 39013–21, Add. 39105–13

Browne, E. G., diaries of his journey to Persia, Pembroke College Library, Cambridge

—— Browne Papers and Manuscripts, Cambridge University Library

Church Missionary Society Archives, London; files in series CM/O, CI/1, G2/PEO and G3/PO

Coupe, Alan, 'References to the Bahá'í Faith in Publications not published under Bahá'í Auspices' unpublished manuscript, Toronto 1975

France: Archives du Ministère des Affaires Étrangères, Paris; Série Correspondence Politique for Persia and Turkey, Correspondence Consulaire for Tabríz and Adrianople

Great Britain: House of Lords Record Office, London; Samuel Papers

—— Foreign and Commonwealth Office, India Office Records, London; series L/P&S/10

—— Public Record Office, London; principal series used are Foreign Office series FO 60, FO 78, FP 195, FO 248, FO 251, FO 371, FO 372, Colonial Office series CO 730, CO 733, and War Office series WO 95

Israel: State Archives, Jerusalem; files from High Commissioner's Dispatches, Chief Secretary's Office, Attorney General's Office and District Commissioner, Haifa

Jasion, Jan T., 'Articles on the Bahá'í Faith originating from Russia and Eastern Europe found in the Libraries of Helsinki University' unpublished manuscript, 1977

MacEoin, Denis, 'A Critical Survey of the Sources for Early Bábí Doctrine and History' unpublished manuscript, 1976

Unpublished Material – Persian

'Amídu'l-Aṭibbá, Mírzá Yaḥyá, manuscript history of the Bahá'ís of Ra<u>sh</u>t, 1345/1927

Fatḥu'lláh Mudarris-i-Jánumí, Mírzá, manuscript history of the Bahá'ís of Najafábád, n.d.

Ḥabíbu'lláh Afnán, Mírzá, manuscript history of the Bábí and Bahá'í religion in <u>Sh</u>íráz, n.d.

Ḥaydar-'Alíy-i-Uskú'í, Mírzá, manuscript history of the Bahá'ís of Á<u>dh</u>arbáyján, with notes by Muḥammad-Ḥusayn-i-Mílání, n.d.

Mihdíy-i-Dahají, Siyyid, untitled treatise sent to Prof. Browne, Manuscript F 57, Browne Collection, Cambridge University Library

Published Material

For books published in Iran, the date of publication is given as the year AH solar or lunar, or the year *badí'* (Bahá'í), followed by the approximately equivalent Christian year.

A. L. C. [Le Chatelier] 'La Révolution Persane' *Revue du Monde Musulman* Vol. 2, Paris 1907, pp. 310–12

Abbott, Evelyn, and Campbell, Lewis *The Life and Letters of Benjamin Jowett* 2 vols., London 1897

Abbott, Keith E. 'Geographical Notes taken during a journey in Persia in 1849 and 1850' *Journal of the Royal Geographical Society* Vol. 25, London 1855, pp. 1–78

'Abdu'l-Bahá ('Abbás Effendi) *Memorials of the Faithful* trans. Marzieh Gail, Wilmette 1971
—— 'The Bahai Movement' in G. Spiller (ed.) *Papers on Inter-Racial Problems* London 1911, pp. 154–7
'Abdu'l-Bahá in Edinburgh London 1963
Adamíyyat, Dr Firaydún *Andí<u>sh</u>ih-háy-i-Mírzá Áqá <u>Kh</u>án-i-Kirmání* Ṭihrán 1346/1967
Adams, Rev. Isaac *Persia by a Persian* London 1906
Algar, Hamid *Religion and State in Iran 1785–1906* Berkeley 1969
—— *Mírzá Malkum Khán* Berkeley 1973
Andreas, Friedrich C. *Die Babis in Persien* Leipzig 1896
Annual Letters, printed privately by CMS, London 1886–1912
Arnold, Arthur *Through Persia by Caravan* 2 vols., London 1877
Arnold, Matthew 'A Persian Passion Play' *The Cornhill Magazine* Vol. 24, London 1871, pp. 668–87. Also in Arnold *Essays in Criticism* London 1884, pp. 223–64
Arslan, Emin 'Une Visite au Chef du Babisme' *Revue Bleue: Revue Politique et Littéraire* 4th ser., Vol. 4, Paris 1896, pp. 314–16
Ashbee, Charles R. *A Palestine Notebook* London 1923
Atherton, Gertrude *Julia France and Her Times* London 1912
Atkins, J. B. 'Introductory Memoir' in E. D. Ross (ed.) *A Persian Anthology* trans. E. G. Browne, London 1927
Ávárih, 'Abdu'l-Ḥusayn *Al-Kavákibu'd-Durríyyih* 2 vols., Cairo 1342/1924
Avery, Peter *Modern Iran* London 1965
Báb, The (Siyyid 'Alí-Muḥammad-i-<u>Sh</u>írází) *Selections from the Writings of the Báb* Haifa 1976
'Babis in Persien, Die' *Allgemeine Zeitung* Vol. 1, 14 Mar. 1866, p. 1188
'Babys, The' *Church Missionary Intelligencer* London 1872
Badi ullah (Badí'u'lláh), Mírzá. *An Epistle to the Bahai World* Chicago 1907
Bahá'í World, The (published at irregular intervals) Vols. 2–7, New York 1928–40; Vols. 8–12, Wilmette 1942–56; Vols. 13–15, Haifa 1970–76
Bahá'u'lláh *Epistle to the Son of the Wolf* trans. Shoghi Effendi, Wilmette 1962
Balyuzi, Hasan M. *Edward Granville Browne and the Bahá'í Faith* Oxford 1970
—— *'Abdu'l-Bahá* Oxford 1971
—— *The Báb* Oxford 1973
—— *Bahá'u'lláh, The King of Glory* Oxford 1980
Banani, Amin *The Modernization of Iran 1921–48* Stanford 1961
Barbier de Meynard, Charles A. C., review of Browne *A Traveller's Narrative* in *Journal Asiatique* 8th ser., Vol. 20, Paris 1892, pp. 297–302
—— Review of Gobineau *Religions et Philosophies* in *Journal Asiatique* 9th ser. Vol. 14, Paris 1899, pp. 568–71
Barker, S. Louie 'A North Palestine Station' *Church Missionary Gleaner* London May 1892, p.74
—— 'Afternoon Calls in Palestine' *Children's World* London March 1892, pp. 40–42
Barrows, Rev. John H. *The World's Parliament of Religion* 2 vols., Chicago 1893
Bassett, James *Persia: Eastern Mission* Philadelphia 1890
—— *Persia, The Land of the Imams* London 1887
Batyushkov, Georgy 'Babidy: Persidskaya Sekta' *Vestnik Europy* Vol. 7, Moscow 1897, pp. 334–56
Bausani, Alessandro *The Persians* trans. J. B. Donne, London 1971
Bell, Archie *The Spell of the Holy Land* Boston 1916
Bellecombe, A. de 'Une Réformatrice Contemporaire: La Belle Kourret oul Ain, ou la

Lumière des Yeux' *L'Investigateur* 4th ser., Vol. 10, L'Institut Historique de France, Paris 1870, pp. 161–7

Benjamin, Samuel G. W. *Persia and the Persians* Boston 1886

Binning, Robert B. M. *Journal of Two Years' Travel in Persia, Ceylon, etc.* 2 vols., London 1857

Birukoff, Paul *Tolstoi und der Orient* Zurich 1925

Bixby, Rev. James T. 'Babism and the Bab' *The New World* Vol. 6, Boston 1897, pp. 722–50

—— 'What is Behaism?' *North American Review* Vol. 195, Boston 1912, pp. 833–46

Bliss, Rev. Edwin E. 'Bab and Babism' *Missionary Herald* Vol. 65, Cambridge, Mass., 1869, pp. 146–8

Blomfield, Lady *The Chosen Highway* Wilmette 1967

Blunt, Wilfred S. *The Future of Islam* London 1882

Bois, Jules 'The New Religions of America: III – Babism and Bahaism' *Forum* Vol. 74, Concord N. H. July 1925, pp. 1–10

Bricteux, Auguste *Au Pays du Lion et du Soleil: Voyage en Perse* Brussels 1908

Brocherel, Jules 'Le Bâbysme, levain des Révolutions en Perse' *A Travers le Monde* Paris 1905, pp. 134–5

Browne, Edward G., see pp. 29–32 for a complete list.

—— *A Traveller's Narrative* 2 vols., Cambridge 1891. All references in this book are to Vol. 2.

—— *The Tárikh-i-Jadíd* Cambridge 1893

—— *Materials for the Study of the Bábí Religion* Cambridge 1918

—— *A Year Amongst the Persians*, new edn, Cambridge 1926

—— *The Persian Revolution of 1905–1909* Cambridge 1910

Burgess, Charles *Letters from Persia* ed. Benjamin Schwartz, New York 1942

Cadwalader, R. 'Persia: An Early Mention of the Báb' *World Order* Vol. 11, No. 2, Wilmette 1976/7, pp. 30–34

Campbell, L., see Abbott, E.

Carmel, Alex *Die Siedlungen der württembergischen Templer in Palästina 1868–1918* Vol. 77 of Veröffentlichungen der Kommission für Geschichtliche Landeskunde in Baden-Württemberg Stuttgart 1973

—— *Palastina-Chronik (1853–1882)* Ulm 1978

Carpenter, John E. *Comparative Religion* London 1913

Chahárdihí, Murtiḍá Mudarrisí *Shaykhí-garí, Bábí-garí* 2nd edn., Ṭihrán 1351/1972

Chaplin, Dr Thomas 'The Babs of Persia' *The Times* London 5 Oct. 1871, p.8

Cheyne, Prof. Thomas K. *The Reconciliation of Races and Religions* London 1914

Chirol, Sir Valentine *The Middle Eastern Question* London 1903

Christensen, Prof. Arthur *Hinsides det Kaspiske Hav* Copenhagen 1918

—— 'Babismen in Persien' *Dansk Tidsskrift* Copenhagen Aug. 1903, pp. 526–39

—— 'En Moderne Orientalisk Religion' *Nordisk Tidskrift* Stockholm 1911, pp. 343–60

Church Missionary Society *Annual Letters*, published annually, London, and circulated privately

[Cloquet, Ernest] 'Perse' *Revue de l'Orient* 2nd ser., Vol. 5, Paris 1849, pp. 263–4

—— 'Perse' *Revue de l'Orient* 2nd ser., Vol. 8, Paris 1850, p. 124

Coleman, Henry R. *Light from the East* Chicago 1899

Cottrell, H. 'Babism' *The Academy* Vol. 47, London 9 Mar. 1895, p. 220

Curtis, William E. *Today in Syria and Palestine* Chicago 1903

Curzon, George N. *Persia and the Persian Question* 2 vols., London 1892

Dichter, B. *The Maps of Acre* 'Akká 1973

Dieulafoy, Jane 'La Perse, la Chaldée et la Susiane (1881–2)' *Tour du Monde* (Paris) Vol. 1, 1883, pp. 1–80; Vol. 2, 1883, pp. 81–160; Vol. 1, 1884, pp. 145–224; Vol. 2, 1884, pp. 47–144; Vol. 1, 1885, pp. 81–160. Also published separately as *La Perse, la Chaldée et la Susiane* Paris 1887

Dolgorukov, see 'Excerpts from Dispatches' *infra*

Dorn, Bernard 'Bericht über eine wissenschaftliche Reise in dem Kaukasus und den südlichen Kustenländern des Kapischen Meeres' *Bulletin de l'Académie Impériale des Sciences de St Pétersbourg* Vol. 4, 1862, pp. 344–93 and *Mélanges Asiatiques tirés du Bulletin de l'Académie Impériale des Sciences de St Pétersbourg* Vol. 4, St Petersburg 1860–62, pp. 429–500

—— 'Die vordem Chanykov'sche, jetzt der Kaiserl. öffentlichen Bibliothek zugehörige Sammlung von morgenlandischen Handschriften' *Bull. Acad. Imp. Sc. St Pet.* Vol. 8, 1865, pp. 245–91 and *Mél. Asiat.* Vol. 5, St Petersburg 1864–8, pp. 221–313. Also printed separately as *Die Sammlung von Morgenländischen Handschriften welche die Kaiserliche Öffentliche Bibliothek zu St Petersburg im Jahre 1864 von Hrn. V. Chanykov erworben hat* St Petersburg 1865

—— 'Nachträge zu dem Verzeichniss der von der Kaiserlichen öffentlichen Bibliothek erworbenen Chanykov'schen Handschriften und den da mitgetheilten Nachrichten über die Baby und deren Koran' *Bull. Acad. Imp. Sc. St Pet.* Vol. 9, 1865, pp. 202–31 and *Mél. Asiat.* Vol. 5, St Petersburg 1864–8, pp. 377–419. Also printed separately as *Morgenländische Handschriften der Kaiserlichen Öffentlichen Bibliothek zu St Petersburg: Nachträge zu dem Verzeichniss der im Jahre 1864 erworben Chanykov'schen Sammlung* St Petersburg 1865

—— 'Über drei dem Asiatischen Museum dargebrachte Persische Handschriften' *Bull. Acad. Imp. Sc. St Pet.* Vol. 19, 1874, pp. 540–44 and *Mél. Asiat.* Vol. 7, St Petersburg 1874, pp. 173–8

—— *Reise nach Masanderan im Jahre 1860* St Petersburg 1895

Dumont, Albert 'Souvenirs de la Roumélie. II: Adrinople. – L'Administration d'une Province Turque' *Revue des Deux Mondes* Vol. 94, 1871, pp. 811–38

Duval, Rubens, review of Browne *A Traveller's Narrative* in *Revue Critique* n.s. Vol. 34, Paris 1892, pp. 77–9

Eastwick, Edward B. *Journal of a Diplomate's Three Years' Residence in Persia* 2 vols., London 1864

Eça de Queirós, José M. *A Correspondencia de Fradique Mendes* Rio de Janiero 1889

Ethé, H. *Essays und Studien* Berlin 1872

—— Review of Browne *A Traveller's Narrative* in *Deutsche Literaturzeitung* Vol. 13, Berlin 30 Jul. 1892, pp. 1014–15

Evans, Prof. Edward P. 'Bab and Babism' *Hours at Home* Vol. 8, New York Jan. 1869, pp. 210–22

'Excerpts from Dispatches written during 1848–1852 by Prince Dolgorukov, Russian Minister to Persia' *World Order* Vol. 1, No. 1, Wilmette 1966, pp. 17–24

Fáḍil-i-Mázindaràní *Ẓuhúru'l-Ḥaqq* Vol. 3, Ṭihrán n.d.; Vol. 8, part 1, Ṭihrán 131/1974, part 2, Ṭihrán 132/1975

Fagergren, M., report on the S͟hiráz earthquake (from the magazine *Caucase*) in *Revue de l'Orient* 2nd Ser., Vol. 14, Paris 1853, pp. 215–16

Faizi, Gloria *Fire on the Mountain-Top* London 1973

Fasá'í, Ḥasan, *History of Persia under Qájár Rule* trans. H. Busse, New York 1972

Fayḍí, Muḥammad-'Alí *K͟hándán-i-Afnán* Ṭihrán 127/1970

—— *Ḥayát-i-Ḥaḍrat-i-'Abdu'l-Bahá* Ṭihrán 128/1971

Ferrier, Joseph P. 'Situation de la Perse en 1851' *Revue Orientale et Algérienne* Vol. 1, Paris 1852, pp. 141–59

—— *Caravan Journeys and Wanderings in Persia, Afghanistan, Turkistan and Baluchistan* trans. Capt. W. Jesse, ed. H. D. Seymour, London 1856

Feuvrier, Dr *Trois Ans à la Cour de Perse* Paris 1906

Fitzgerald, P. *Memories of Charles Dickens* London 1913

Flandin, Eugène 'Souvenirs de Voyage en Armenie et en Perse: II – Téhéran et Ispahan' *Revue de Deux Mondes* Vol. 11, Paris 1851, pp. 984–9

Forel, Auguste *Out of My Life and Work* trans Bernard Miall, London 1937

Franck, Adolphe, review of Gobineau *Religions et Philosophies* in *Journal des Savants* Paris Dec. 1865, pp. 767–87. Also published as a chapter, 'Une Nouvelle Religion en Perse', in Franck *Philosophie et Religion* Paris 1867, pp. 281–340

G.H. 'L'Influence de Babisme' *A Travers le Monde* 13th year n.s., Paris 1907, pp. 17–20

Gaulmier, J. 'Une mythe, la science orientaliste de Gobineau' *Australian Journal of French Studies* Vol. 1, Melbourne 1964, pp. 58–70

Giachery, Ugo R. 'An Italian Scientist Extols the Báb' *The Bahá'í World* Vol. 12, Wilmette 1956, pp. 900–904

Gobineau, Clément S. de *Correspondance entre le Comte de Gobineau et le Comte de Prokesch-Osten (1854–76)* Paris 1933

Gobineau, Joseph A. de *Les Religions et les Philosophies dans l'Asie Centrale* 10th edn., Paris 1957

Goldziher, Ignaz 'Verhältnis des Báb zu früheren Ṣúfí-Lehrern' *Der Islam* Vol. 11, Berlin 1921, pp. 252–4

—— 'Die Kultur der Gegenwart' in *Die Religionen des Orients* ed. Paul Hinneberg, Leipzig 1923

—— *Vorlesungen über den Islam* revised by F. Babinger, Heidelberg 1925

—— *Tagebuch* ed. Alexander Scheiber, Leiden 1978

Gordon, Sir Thomas *Persia Revisited* London 1896

Grant Duff, Sir Mountstuart *Notes from a Diary 1873–1881* 2 vols., London 1898

—— *Notes from a Diary 1886–1888* 2 vols., London 1900

Grinevskaya, Izabella *Bab, dramaticheskaya poema* St Petersburg 1903

—— *Beha-ulla, poema-tragedui v stikhakh* St Petersburg 1912

Gumoens, Alfred von 'Aus Persien' *Oesterreichischer Soldatenfreund* 5th Year, No. 123, Vienna 12 Oct. 1852, p. 513

Hamilton Charles *Oriental Zigzag* London 1875

Hitti, Philip K. *History of Syria* London 1957

—— *Lebanon in History* London 1962

Holbach, Maude 'The Bahai Movement: With some recollections of meetings with Abdul Baha' *Nineteenth Century* London Feb. 1915, pp. 452–66

Horn, Paul, review of Browne *A Traveller's Narrative* in *Literarisches Zentralblatt* Leipzig 23 July 1892, pp. 1043–4

Houghton, W. E. (ed.) *Wellesley Index to Victorian Periodicals (1824–1900)* 2 vols., London 1966

Huart, Clément *La Religion de Bab* Bibliothèque Orientale Elzévirienne, Paris 1889

—— 'Notes sur trois ouvrages Bâbis' *Journal Asiatique* 8th ser., Vol 10, Paris 1887, pp. 133–44

—— 'La Religion de Bab' *Revue de l'Histoire des Religions* Vol. 18, Paris 1888, pp. 279–96

—— review of Nicolas *Seyyèd Ali Mohammad* and *Le Béyan Arabe* in *Revue de l'Histoire des Religions* Vol. 53, Paris 1906, pp. 384–92

—— review of Dreyfus (trans.) *Les Préceptes du Béhaïsme* in *Revue de l'Histoire des Religions* Vol. 53, Paris 1906, pp. 392–6

—— review of Browne *Materials* in *Journal Asiatique* 11th ser., Vol. 12, Paris 1918, pp. 465–8

—— review of Browne *Materials* in *Journal des Savants* 16th year n.s., Paris 1918, pp. 312–20

—— review of Dreyfus (trans.) *L'Oeuvre de Bahâou'llah* in *Revue de l'Histoire des Religions* Vol. 88, Paris 1923, pp. 128–30

Hughes, Thomas P. *A Dictionary of Islam* London 1885

Hume-Griffith, M. E. *Behind the Veil in Persia and Turkish Arabia* London 1909

Hytier, Adrienne D. *Les Dépêches Diplomatiques du Comte de Gobineau en Perse* Études d'Histoire Économique, Politique et Sociale XXX, Geneva 1959

Isaacs, Rev. Albert A. *Biography of the Rev. Henry Aaron Stern D.D.* London 1886

Ishráq-Khávarí, 'Abdu'l-Ḥamíd *Núrayn-i-Nayyirayn* Ṭihran 123/1966

Issawi, Charles (ed.) *The Economic History of Iran 1800–1914* Chicago 1971

Ivanov, Mikhail S. *Babidskie vosstaniya v Irane (1848–1852)* Trudy Instituta Vostokvedeniya XXX, Moscow 1939

Ives, Howard C. *Portals to Freedom* London 1967

Jablonowski, Aleksandr W. 'Obecny postep w stanowisku kobiety na muzulmanskim wschodzie' [Present Progress in the Position of Women in the Muslim East] *Bluscz* Vol. 7, Nos. 12, 13 and 15, Warsaw 10, 17 and 31 Mar. 1871

—— 'Babyzm: Spoleczno – religijny ruch w Persyi. Nowe stanowisko kobiety'[Babism: Socio-Religious Movement in Persia. New Position of Women] *Gazeta Polska* Nos. 222, 223, 225 and 226, Warsaw 27, 28, 30 Sept. and 1 Oct. 1875

Jahángír Mírzá *Tárí<u>kh</u>-i-Naw* Ṭihrán 1327/1948

Jasion, Jan. T. ' "A. J." and the Introduction of the Bahá'í Faith into Poland' *Études Bahá'í Studies* Vol. 4, Thornhill, Ont. Dec. 1978, pp. 31–7

Jessup, Rev. Henry H. *Fifty-Three Years in Syria* 2 vols., New York 1910

—— 'The Babites' *The Outlook* New York 22 June 1901, pp. 451–6; condensed in *Missionary Review of the World* Vol. 25, New York Oct. 1902, pp. 771–5

Justi, Ferdinand review of Gobineau *Religions et Philosophies* in *Archiv für Religionswissenschaft Vol. 4, Tübingen 1901, pp. 75–8*

Kalmykow, Andrew D. *Memoirs of a Russian Diplomat* New Haven 1971

Kazem-Beg, Mírzá Aleksandr *Bab i Babidui: religiozno-politicheskiya smutui v Persy v 1844–1852 godakh* St Petersburg 1865

—— 'Bab et les Babis' *Journal Asiatique* (Paris, 6th ser.) Vol. 7, No. 26, April-May 1866, pp. 329–84; Vol. 7, No. 27, June 1866, pp. 457–522; Vol. 8, No. 29, Aug.-Sept. 1866, pp. 196–252; Vol. 8, No. 30, Oct.-Nov. 1866, pp. 357–400; Vol. 8, No. 31, Dec. 1866, pp. 473–507

Kazemzadeh, Firuz *Russia and Britain in Persia: a Study in Imperialism, 1864–94* New Haven 1968

—— 'Two Incidents in the Life of the Báb' *World Order* Vol. 5, No. 3, Wilmette 1971, pp. 21–4

Kazemzadeh, Kazem 'Varqá and Rúḥu'lláh: Deathless in Martyrdom' *World Order* Vol. 9, No. 2, Wilmette 1974–5, pp. 29–44

Keddie, Nikki R. *Sayyid Jamál ad-Dín al-Afghání* Berkeley 1972

Khanykov, Nicolai V. 'Compte rendu d'un voyage scientifique de M. Dorn dans le Mazandéran' *Journal Asiatique*, Vol. 19, 1862, pp. 214–25

Kojanen, R. 'Muhammedilainen babi-lakho' *Valvoja* Helsingfors 1897, pp. 416–23

Kremer, Alfred von *Geschichte der herrschenden Ideen des Islams* Leipzig 1868

al-Kurdí, Fáyiz *'Akká bayna'l-Máḍí wa'l-Ḥáḍir* 'Akká 1972

Lambton, Ann K. S. 'The Case of Hájjí 'Abd al-Karím' in C. E. Bosworth (ed.) *Iran and Islam* Edinburgh 1971

Landau, Rom *Search for Tomorrow* London 1938

Layard, Austin H. *Early Adventures in Persia, Susiana, and Babylonia* 2 vols., London 1887

Lessona, Michele *I Babi* Turin 1881

Longrigg, Stephen H. *Four Centuries of Modern 'Iraq* London 1925

—— *'Iraq 1900 to 1950* London 1953

Lorey, Eustache de, and Sladen, Douglas *Queer Things about Persia* London 1907

Lovett, Maj. Beresford 'Surveys on the Road from Shiraz to Bam' *Journal of the Royal Geographical Society* Vol. 42, London 1872, pp. 202 ff

Lukach, Harry C. *The Fringe of the East* London 1913

—— and Jardine, Douglas J. *The Handbook of Cyprus* 7th issue, London 1913

MacEoin, Denis 'Oriental Scholarship and the Bahá'í Faith' *World Order* Vol. 8, No. 4, Wilmette 1974, pp. 9–21

MacGregor, Charles M. *Narrative of a Journey through the Province of Khorassan and on the North-Western Frontier of Afghanistan in 1875* 2 vols., London 1879

Malcolm, Napier *Five Years in a Persian Town* London 1908

Malik-Khusraví Núrí, Muḥammad-'Alí *Kitáb-i-Aqlím-i-Núr* Ṭihrán 115/1958

—— *Táríkh-i-Shuhadáy-i-Amr* 3 vols., Ṭihrán 130/1973

Ma'oz, Moshe *Ottoman Reform in Syria and Palestine, 1840–61* Oxford 1968

Markham, Clements R. *A General Sketch of the History of Persia* London 1874

Maspero, Gaston C. C., review of Gobineau *Religions et Philosophies* in *Journal des Savants* Paris 1900, pp. 407–18

Maxwell, Sir Herbert *The Honourable Sir Charles Murray* Edinburgh 1898

Merritt-Hawkes, O. A. *Persia: Romance and Reality* London 1935

Mielk, R. 'Von Babismus in Deutschland' *Der Islam* Vol. 13, Berlin 1923, pp. 138–44

Mihrábkhání, Rúḥu'lláh *Sharḥ-i-Aḥvál-i-Jináb-i-Mírzá Abu'l-Faḍá'il-i-Gulpaygání* Ṭihrán 131/1974

Mills, Lady Dorothy *Beyond the Bosphorus* London 1926

Momen, Moojan *Dr J. E. Esslemont* London 1975

Muvaḥḥid, Muḥammad-'Alí 'Asnádí az Árshív-i-Dawlatíy-i-Istánbúl' *Ráhnámih-i-Kitáb* Vol. 6, Ṭihrán 1342/1963, pp. 102–10

Nabíl-i-A'ẓam (Mullá Muḥammad-i-Zarandí) *The Dawn-Breakers: Nabíl's Narrative of the Early Days of the Bahá'í Revelation* trans. and ed. Shoghi Effendi, London 1953 (signified in text by UK) and Wilmette 1962 (signified in text by USA)

Najmajer, Marie von *Gurret-ül-Eyn: Ein Bild aus Persiens Neuzeit* Vienna 1874

Neil, Rev. James 'Missionary Journey to Galilee' *Jewish Intelligence* London Dec. 1872, pp. 299–306

'New Religion, A' *All the Year Round* n.s., Vol. 2, London 17 July 1869, pp. 149–54

'New Religion, A' *The Nation* Vol. 2, New York 22 June 1866, pp. 793–5

Nicholson, Reynold A. (ed.) *A Descriptive Catalogue of the Oriental Manuscripts belonging to the Late E. G. Browne* Cambridge 1932

Nicolaides, Dr Cleanthes 'Leo Tolstois Stellung zu den Religionen' *Beilage zur Allgemeinen Zeitung* Vol. 3, Munich 1902, pp. 566–7

NICOLAS, A.-L.-M., see pp. 38–40 for complete list.

—— 'Le Club de la fraternité', *Revue du Monde Musulman* Vol. 13, Paris 1911, pp. 180–84

—— 'Le Dossier russo-anglais de Seyyed Ali Mohammed dit le Bâb', *Revue du Monde Musulman* Vol. 14, Paris 1911, pp. 357–63

—— *Massacres de Babis en Perse* Paris 1936

Nicolas, Michel 'Le Babysme' *Le Temps* Paris 14 Aug. 1868, p. 3, col. 2; 19 Aug. 1868, p. 3, col. 3; 20 Aug. 1868, p. 3, col. 2

Oliphant, Laurence *Haifa, or Life in Modern Palestine* Edinburgh 1887

'Perse' *Revue de l'Orient* 2nd ser., Vol. 14, Paris 1853, pp. 215–16

'Persische Gott in Akka, Der' *Aus Allen Weltteilen* Vol. 24, June 1893, p. 165–6
Petermann, H. *Reisen in Orient* 2 vols., Leipzig 1861
Pfeiffer, Ida *Visit to the Holy Land, Egypt and Italy* London 1852
Phelps, Myron H. *Abbas Effendi: His Life and Teachings* New York 1903
Piggot, John *Persia – Ancient and Modern* London 1874
Polak, Dr Jakob *Persien. Das Land und seine Bewohner* 2 vols., Leipzig 1865
Poole, W. F., and Fletcher, W. I. *An Index to Periodical Literature* 3rd edn., Boston 1882
Qazvíní, Muḥammad 'Yád-dáshtháy-i-Táríkhí: Vafiyát-i-Mu'ásirín' *Yádgár* 5th year, Nos. 6/7, Ṭihrán 1949, p. 127
Rabbani, Rúḥíyyih *The Priceless Pearl* London 1969
Reclus, Élisée *The Universal Geography* ed. A. H. Keane, Vols. 1 and 9, London n.d.
Rees, John D. 'Persia' *MacMillan's Magazine* Vol. 55, London 1887, pp. 442–53
—— 'The Bab and Babism' *Nineteenth Century* Vol. 40, London July 1896, pp. 56–66
Renan, Ernest *The Apostles* (no translator indicated) London 1869
—— *Études d'Histoire Religeuse*, Paris 1862
—— *Oeuvres Complètes de Ernest Renan* ed. Henriette Psichari, 10 vols., Paris n.d.
Ritter, H., review of Browne *Materials* in *Der Islam* Vol. 13, Berlin 1923, pp. 134–8
Rivadneyra, Adolfo *Viaje al interior de Persia* 3 vols., Madrid 1880–1
Rochechouart, Comte Julien de *Souvenirs d'un Voyage en Perse* Paris 1867
Roemer, Herrmann *Die Bábí-Behá'í* Potsdam 1911
Rolland, Romain *Clerambault* Paris 1920
Ronaldshay, Earl of *The Life of Lord Curzon* 3 vols., London 1928
Ronchaud, Louis de 'Une Religion nouvelle dans l'Asie Centrale' *Revue Moderne* Vol. 37, Paris 1 May 1866, pp. 337–60. Also in Ronchaud *Études d'Histoire Politique et Religieuse* Paris 1872
Root, Martha 'President Eduard Benes' *The Bahá'í World* Vol. 6, New York 1937, pp. 589–91
—— 'Denmark's Oriental Scholar' *The Bahá'í World* Vol. 6, New York 1937, pp. 665–7
—— 'Russia's Cultural Contribution to the Bahá'í Faith' *The Bahá'í World* Vol. 6, New York 1937, pp. 707–12
—— 'Queen Marie of Rumania' *The Bahá'í World* Vol. 8, Wilmette 1942, pp. 278–81
ROSEN, Baron Victor, see p. 42 for a complete list.
——*Collections Scientifiques de l'Institute des Langues Orientales du Ministère des Affaires Estrangères*: Vol. 1. *Manuscrits Arabes* St Petersburg 1877; Vol. 2. *Manuscrits Persans* St Petersburg 1886; Vol. 6. *Manuscrits Arabes* St Petersburg 1891
Ross, E. Denison 'Babism' *North American Review* Vol. 172, Boston 1901, pp. 827–36
—— *Both Ends of the Candle* London 1943
Rubin, Morton *The Walls of Acre* New York 1974
Russell, William H. *A Diary in the East* London 1869
Saint-Quentin, A.-P.-G. Ouvre de *Un Amour au Pays des Mages* Paris 1891
Sanderson, Edith 'An Interview with A. L. M. Nicolas of Paris' *The Bahá'í World* Vol. 8, Wilmette 1942, pp. 885–7
Sayyáḥ, Ḥájí *Khátirát-i-Ḥájí Sayyáḥ* ed. Hamíd Sayyáḥ, Ṭihrán 1346/1967
Serena, Carla *Hommes et Choses en Perse* Paris 1883
Shedd, Rev. John H. 'Babism – Its Doctrines and Relations to Mission Work' *Missionary Review of the World* Vol. 17, New York Dec. 1894, pp. 894–904
Sheil, Lady Mary E. *Glimpses of Life and Manners in Persia* London 1856
Shoghi Effendi *God Passes By* Wilmette 1965
—— and Lady Blomfield *The Passing of 'Abdu'l-Bahá* London n.d.
Shuster, W. Morgan *The Strangling of Persia* New York 1912

Sladen, Douglas, see Lorey, E. de
Stack, Edward *Six Months in Persia* London 1882
Stern, Rev. Henry A. *Dawnings of Light in the East* London 1854
Stevens, Ethel S. 'Abbas Effendi: His Personality, Work and Followers' *Fortnightly Review* Vol. 89, London 1911, pp. 1067–84
——*The Mountain of God* London 1911
Stewart, Col. Charles E. *Through Persia in Disguise* London 1911
Storrs, Sir Ronald *Orientations* London 1937 (1st edn.), New York 1937 (under the title *The Memoirs of Sir Ronald Storrs*)
Stuart, Lt-Col. Charles *Journal of a Residence in Northern Persia* London 1854
Sulaymání, 'Azízu'lláh *Maṣábíḥ-i-Hidáyat* 8 vols., Ṭihrán 104/1948 – 130/1973
Temple, Bernard 'Persia and the Regeneration of Islam' *Journal of the Royal Society of Arts* Vol. 58, London 27 May 1910, pp. 652–65
Tolstoy, Leo, see Birukoff, P. and Nicolaides, C.
Tumanski, Alexander, see pp. 42–3 for a complete list.
——'Dva Poslednikh Babidskikh Otkroveniya, *Zapiskie Vostochnago Otdeleniya Imperatorskagò Russkago Arkheologicheskago Obshestva* Vol. 6, 1891, pp. 314–21
Tweedy, Owen *Cairo to Persia and Back* London 1933
Ussher, J. *A Journey from London to Persepolis* London 1865
Vámbéry, Hermann *Meine Wanderungen und Erlebnisse in Persien* Budapest 1867
—— review of Browne *A Traveller's Narrative* in *The Academy* Vol. 40, London 12 Mar. 1892, pp. 245–6
Vaughan, Henry B. 'Journeys in Persia (1890–1)' *Geographical Journal* Vol. 7, London 1896, pp. 24–41, 163–75
Watson, Robert G. *A History of Persia* London 1866
Wavell, Col A. P. *The Palestine Campaigns* London 1936
Webb, F. C. *Up the Tigris to Bagdad* London 1870
Wesselitsky, Gabriel *A New Great Russian Poet* London 1907
White, Dr Henry 'How Babis died for their Faith in Persia' *Mercy and Truth* London 1903, pp. 275–6
Wills, Dr Charles J. *In the Land of the Lion and Sun or Modern Persia* new edn. London 1891
Wilson, Rev. Samuel G. *Bahaism and its Claims* New York 1915
Wilson, Mary F. 'The Story of the Bâb' *Contemporary Review* Vol. 48, London 1885, pp. 808–29. Also in *Littel's Living Age* Vol. 168, Boston 1885, pp. 151 ff. and *Eclectic Magazine* Vol. 106, New York 1885, pp. 264 ff.
Wratislaw, Albert C. *A Consul in the East* London 1924
Wright, Austin H. 'Bab und seine Secte in Persien' *Zeitschrift der Deutschen Morganländischen Gesellschaft* Vol. 5, Leipzig 1851, pp. 384–5
Wright, Denis *The English amongst the Persians* London 1977
X (Siyyid Ḥasan Taqízádih?), 'La Situation Politique de la Perse' *Revue du Monde Musulman* Vol. 27, Paris 1914, p. 254
Yaḥyáy-i-Dawlatábádí, Ḥájí Mírzá 'Persia' in G. Spiller (ed.) *Papers on Inter-Racial Problems* London 1911, pp. 143–54
Zarqání, Mírzá Maḥmúd, *Badá'i'u'l-Athár*, Vol. 2, Bombay 1921
Zhukovski, Valentin A. 'Nedavnya kazni babidov v gorode Ezde' [Recent Executions of Bábís in Yazd] *Zapiski Vostochnago Otdeleniya Imperatorskago Russkago Arkheologicheskago Obshestva* (hereafter *Zapiski*) Vol. 6, St Petersburg 1891, pp. 321–7
—— 'Razjasnenya k zametke Nedavnya kazni vogorde Ezde' *Zapiski* Vol. 7, St Petersburg 1892, p. 327
—— 'Rossiyskii Imperatorskii Konsul F. A. Bakulin v istorii izucheniya babizma' [The

Imperial Russian Consul F. A. Bakulin in the History of Bábí Studies] *Zapiski* Vol. 24, St Petersburg 1916, pp. 33–90
Zotenberg, Hermann, review of Gobineau *Religions et Philosophies* in *Revue Critique d'Histoire et de Literature* Vol. 1, Paris 2 June 1866, pp. 349–53

Newspapers and Magazines

Allen's Indian Mail (London)
Athenaeum (London)
Children's World (London)
Church Missionary Intelligencer (London)
Christian Commonwealth (London)
Constitutionnel, Le (Paris)
Daily News (London)
Eclectic Magazine of Foreign Literature, Science and Art (New York and Philadelphia)
Edinburgh Evening News
English Churchman (London)
Evangelical Christendom (London)
Gazette (Montreal)
Giornale di Roma (Rome)
Guardian (London)
Hamburger Nachrichten (Hamburg)
Hansard (House of Commons, London)
Jewish Intelligence (London)
Journal of the American Oriental Society (New York)
Kölnische Zeitung (Koln)
Literary Gazette and Journal of Belles Lettres, Arts, Sciences etc. (London)
Melbourne Argus
Mercy and Truth (London)
Monde, Le (Paris)
Montreal Daily Star
Morning Chronicle (London)
Morning Herald (London)
Morning Post (London)
New York Sun
New York Times
New York World
Oesterreichischer Soldatenfreund (Vienna)
Osservatore Trieste
Oxford Magazine
Palestine Weekly (Jerusalem)
Pall Mall Gazette (London)
Palo Altan (Palo Alto, California)
Port Phillip Herald (Melbourne)
Revue de l'Orient (Paris)
Rivista Orientale (Florence)
Scots Pictorial (Glasgow)
Semaphore (Marseilles)
Southern Cross (Auckland)
Spectator (London)
Star of the West (Chicago, reprinted Oxford 1978)

Süddeutsche Warte (Ludwigsburg)
Standard (London)
Sun (London)
Times, The (London)
Times of India (Bombay)
Union, L' (Paris)
World Order (Wilmette, Illinois)

Sources for Biographies (excluding works mentioned above)

Allgemeine Deutsche Biographie Vols. 1–56, Leipzig 1875–1912
Almanach de Gotha, published annually, Gotha 1800–1944
Annuaire diplomatique et consulaire, published annually, Paris 1879–1940
Bámdád, Mihdí *Taríkh-i-Rijál-i-Írán* 6 vols., Ṭihrán 1347/1968 – 1351/1970
Biographie Nationale de Belgique Vols. 1–39, Bruxelles 1866–1976
Brockhaus Enzyklopädie Vols. 1–23, Wiesbaden 1966–75
Churchill, George P. *Persian Statesmen and Notables* Calcutta 1905
Colonial Office List, published annually, London 1862–1925
Contemporary Authors (various editors) Vols. 1–72, Detroit 1962–78
Dictionnaire de Biographie Française (various editors) Vols. 1–12, Paris 1933–70
Dictionnaire Universal des Contemporains ed. G. Vapereau, Vols. 1–6, Paris 1858–93
Dictionary of American Biography ed. Duman Malone and Allen Johnson, Vols. 1–20, London 1928–36
Dictionary of National Biography ed. Leslie Stephen and Sidney Lee, Vols. 1–63, London 1885–1900, and supplements 1901–71
Dominions Office and Colonial Office List, published annually, London 1926–40
East India Register and Army List, published annually, London 1845–60
Elsberry, Terence *Marie of Romania* London 1972
Encyclopaedia Britannica 11th edn, Vols. 1–29, Cambridge 1910–11 and 15th edn, Micropaedia, Vols. 1–10, Chicago 1974
Encyclopaedia of Islam ed. B. Lewis et al., 2nd edn, Leiden 1960–
Encyclopedia of Missions ed. H. O. Dwight et al., 2nd edn, New York 1904
Foreign Office List, published annually, London 1852–1944
Grand Larousse encyclopédique Vols. 1–10, Paris 1960–64
Henderson, Philip *The Life of Laurence Oliphant* London 1956
Indian Army and Civil Service List, published annually, London 1861–76
Larousse du XXe Siecle ed. Paul Augé, Vols. 1–6, Paris 1928–33
Marie, Queen of Romania, *The Story of My Life* 3 vols., London 1934–5
Medical Directory, published annually, London 1845–
Morgan, Gerald *Ney Elias* London 1971
Nouvelle Biographie Generale ed. Dr Hoefer, Vols. 1–46, Paris 1852–66
Plarr, Victor G. *Plarr's Lives of the Fellows of the Royal Coll. of Surgeons of England*, revived by Sir D'Arcy Power, 2 vols., Bristol 1930
Rawlinson, George *Memoir of Sir Henry C. Rawlinson* London 1898
Register of Missionaries printed privately by CMS, London, Vol. 1, 1895; Vol. 2, 1905
Sykes, Sir Percy *Sir Mortimer Durand* London 1926
Waterfield, Gordon *Professional Diplomat* London 1973
Webster's Biographical Dictionary Springfield, Mass. 1957
Russkii Biograficheski Slovar, Vol. 6, St Petersburg 1905
Who was Who 6 vols, London 1920–72
Who was Who in America 6 vols., Chicago 1943–73

INDEX

Entries are alphabetized word by word; component parts of hyphenated names are treated as separate words, but the connective -i- is ignored. Thus, 'Alíy-i- is treated as if it were spelt 'Alí. Sub-entries are arranged in the order in which the subjects they deal with first appear in the book. Bold type is used for references to entries in the Biographical Notes.